Index of American Periodical Verse: 1982

Rafael Catalá
Editor

James D. Anderson
Managing Editor

James Romano
Consultant

The Scarecrow Press, Inc.
Metuchen, N.J., & London
1984

Library of Congress Catalog Card No. 73-3060
ISBN 0-8108-1731-4
Copyright © 1984 by Rafael Catalá
Manufactured in the United States of America

CONTENTS

PREFACE

This is the twelfth annual volume of the _Index of American Periodical Verse_. Last year saw the addition of major Spanish language literary journals published in the United States and Puerto Rico. This year, twelve Canadian journals were added to the _Index_, making its scope more truly "American." And, for the first time, the _Index_ was compiled, sorted, and formatted using a computer rather than the formerly ubiquitous 3x5 inch cards.

COMPILATION

Indexing was done on an Osborne 1 micro-computer using the Wordstar word-processing program. A three-line input format was used, with fields for author, title, note, journal citation, and page numbers. The entries for each journal issue were formatted and printed out on address labels for proof-reading. These labels also served as back-ups: if the computer-readable entries had been lost or destroyed, the labels could be put on cards and arranged in the old way. Once all indexing was complete, the entries were sorted using a suite of programs written especially for the index in CBasic. The Osborne 1 has a total memory capacity of 64K, not enough for sorting even 100 full index entries at one time, so sorting was done in a series of sort and merge steps, much as humans sort. After entries were sorted, title entries were extracted, and the author entries were formatted and entry numbers added.

The principal advantage in computer-based compilation was eliminating the repetitive entry of the same data. Within a single issue of a journal, for example, the journal citation will be the same for every poem, yet in the old card-based method, the citation had to be rewritten on every card. With the computer, it is simply copied, without re-keying, to each entry. Similarly, translations no longer call for a completely new entry for the translator. Instead, the original entry is simply modified, moving the name of the translator to the lead position, and the author to the note.

There has been no title index for several years due to the great amount of extra labor needed to create it in a card-based mode of operation. With the computer, no extra input was required. A computer program identified the title field and extracted it from the full author entry. Other programs sorted these title entries, formatted them, and added entry numbers which referred back to the author entries. Finally, the entire index was printed out on a NEC

3515 letter-quality printer in "camera-ready" form for printing.

Persons interested in the precise details of compilation, including the computer programs used, should write to the managing editor. The entire index is available from the editors on 5-1/4" Osborne format floppy disks.

CROSS REFERENCES

With the addition of many more poets with compound surnames and surnames containing various prefixes, we have recognized the need for systematic cross references from alternative forms of surname to the form chosen for entry in the index. In choosing the form of entry, we have followed the standards of the <u>Anglo-American Cataloguing Rules</u>, which are also used by every major library in the United States and Canada. We have included cross references from alternative forms of surname whenever the form used for entry did not fall under the last element.

FORMAT AND ARRANGEMENT OF ENTRIES

The basic format and style of the index remain unchanged. Poets are arranged alphabetically by surname and forenames. In creating this alphabetical sequence, we have adopted principles of the new filing rules issued in 1980 by the American Library Association and the Library of Congress. Names are filed as spelled, rather than as pronounced, so that, for example, names beginning with 'Mac' and 'Mc' are no longer interfiled. Similarly, the space consistently counts as a filing element, so that similar compound and prefixed surnames are often separated by some distance, as illustrated in the following examples. Note that "De BOLT" precedes "DeBEVOISE" by a considerable number of entries.

De ANGELIS	Van BRUNT
De BOLT	Van DUYN
De GRAVELLES	Van HALTEREN
De LOACH	Van TOORN
De PALCHI	Van TROYER
De RONSARD	Van WERT
De VAUL	Van WINCKEL
DEAL	VANCE
DeBEVOISE	Vander DOES
DeFOE	VANDERBEEK
DEGUY	VanDEVENTER
Del VECCHIO	
DeLISLE	
DeMOTT	
DENNISON	
Der HOVANESSIAN	
DESY	
DeYOUNG	

Abbreviations are also filed as spelled, rather than pronounced, so that "ST. JOHN" is <u>not</u> filed as "SAINT JOHN", but as "S+T+space+JOHN". Punctuation is not considered; a hyphen is filed as if it were a space. Finally, numerals are filed in numerical order preceding alphabetical letters rather than as if they were spelled out.

Under each poet's name, poems are filed alphabetically by title or, if there is no title, by first line. Poem titles and first lines are placed within quotation marks. All significant words of titles are capitalized, but in first lines, only the first word and proper nouns are capitalized. Incomplete excerpts from larger works are preceded with the word 'from', followed by the title of the larger work, but the 'from' is ignored in the arrangement of titles. The title or first line of the excerpt, within quotation marks, follows the title of the larger work. If excerpts are numbered, their numbers are placed within parentheses. For example:

from Lumb's Remains: "A primrose petal's edge."

from The Impossible: (85, 87, 93, 182).

If an excerpt is a complete "sub-work", it receives an independent entry, with reference to the larger work in a note. For example:

"Comunion" (from Bandera de Senales).

Notes about dedications, joint authors, translators, and sources follow the title, enclosed in parentheses. A poem with more than one author is entered under each author. Likewise, a translated poem is entered under each translator, as well as its author(s). Each entry includes the names of all authors and all translators. Multiple authors or translators are indicated by the abbreviation "w.", standing for "with". Translators are indicated by the abbreviation "tr. by", standing for "translated by", and original authors are indicated by the abbreviation "tr. of", standing for "translation of". For example:

CENDRARS, Blaise
  "Hotel Notre-Dame" (tr. by Perry Oldham and
    Arlen Gill). <u>WebR</u> (5:1) Wint 80,
    p. 32.

GILL, Arlen
  "Hotel Notre-Dame" (tr. of Blaise Cendrars
    w. Perry Oldham). <u>WebR</u> (5:1) Wint 80,
    p. 32.

OLDHAM, Perry
  "Hotel Notre-Dame" (tr. of Blaise Cendrars
    w. Arlen Gill). <u>WebR</u> (5:1) Wint 80,
    p. 32.

The journal citation includes an abbreviation standing for the journal title, volume and issue numbers, date, and pages. The journal abbreviation is underlined. An alphabetical list of these journal abbreviations is included at the front of the volume, along with the full journal title, name of editor(s), address, the numbers of the issues indexed in this volume of the Index, and subscription information. A separate list of indexed periodicals is arranged by full journal title, with a reference to the abbreviated title. Volume and issue numbers are included within parentheses, e.g., (16:5) stands for volume 16, number 5; (21) refers to issue 21 for a journal which does not use volume numbers. Dates are given using abbreviations for months and seasons. Please see the separate list of abbreviations.

Compiling this year's index has been an adventure into the wealth and variety of poetry published in United States, Puerto Rican and Canadian periodicals as well as the intricacies of bringing this wealth together and organizing it into a consistent index. The world of poetry publication is a dynamic one, with new journals appearing, older journals declining, dying, reviving and thriving. Keeping up with these changes is a big order, and we solicit our reader's suggestions as to journals which should be included in future volumes of the index, and also, journals which could be dropped.

Although indexing is indispensable for the organization of any literature so that particular works can be found when needed, it is a tedious business. I know that we have made mistakes. We solicit your corrections and suggestions, which you may send to me at the address listed below.

James D. Anderson, Managing Editor
Index of American Periodical Verse
P.O. Box 38
New Brunswick, NJ   08903-0038

ABBREVIATIONS

dir., dirs.	director, directors
ed., eds.	editor, editors
(for.)	price for foreign countries
(ind.)	price for individuals
(inst.)	price for institutions
(lib.)	price for libraries
p.	page, pages
po. ed.	poetry editor
pub.	publisher
mss.	manuscripts
(stud.)	price for students
tr. by	translated by
tr. of	translation of
U.	University
w.	with

Months

Ja	January	Jl	July
F	February	Ag	August
Mr	March	S	September
Ap	April	O	October
My	May	N	November
Je	June	D	December

Seasons

Aut	Autumn, Fall	Spr	Spring
Wint	Winter	Sum	Summer

PERIODICALS ADDED

Periodical titles are followed
by the acronym used in indexing.

Abraxas: <u>Abraxas</u>
Antigonish Review: <u>AntigR</u>
Black Warrior Review: <u>BlackWR</u>
Bogg: <u>Bogg</u>
Canadian Literature: <u>CanLit</u>
The Capilano Review: <u>CapilR</u>
Catalyst: <u>Catalyst</u>
Cross-Canada Writers' Quarterly: <u>CrossC</u>
Dandelion: <u>Dandel</u>
The DeKalb Literary Arts Journal: <u>DeKalbLAJ</u>
Gargoyle Magazine: <u>Gargoyle</u>
Germination: <u>Germ</u>
Grain: <u>Grain</u>
The Manhattan Review: <u>ManhatR</u>
Mendocino Review: <u>MendoR</u>
Poetry Canada Review: <u>PoetryCR</u>
Prismal/Cabral: <u>Prismal</u>
Quarry: <u>Quarry</u>
Revista Chicano-Riquena: <u>RevChic</u>
A Shout in the Street: <u>Shout</u>
Telescope: <u>Telescope</u>
Underground Rag Mag: <u>UnderRM</u>
Waves: <u>Waves</u>
West Coast Review: <u>WestCR</u>
The Writer's Lifeline: <u>WritersL</u>

PERIODICALS DELETED

No 1981 or 1982 issues have been received, after
repeated requests, from the following periodicals.

Ann Arbor Review
The Ark
Bachy
Black Forum
Chowder Review
Columbia
Dacotah Territory
Durak
Green River Review
The Greenfield Review

Hills
Journal of New Jersey Poets
Journal of Popular Culture
Negro History Bulletin
North Stone Review
Panache
Paunch
Russian Literature Triquarterly
Slow Loris Reader
Some
Urthkin

PERIODICALS INDEXED

Arranged by acronym, with names of editors, ad-
dresses, issues indexed, and subscription informa-
tion. New titles added to the Index in 1982 are
marked with an asterisk (*).

*Abraxas: ABRAXAS, Ingrid Swanberg, ed., 2518 Gregory St.,
    Madison, WI 53711.
    Issues indexed: (25/26); Subscriptions: $8/4 issues.

Academe: ACADEME, Bulletin of the American Association of
    University Professors, Donald Rackin, David S. Green,
    Sarah G. Womack, eds., Suite 500, One Dupont Circle,
    Washington, DC 20036.
    Issues indexed: (68:1-6); Subscriptions: $24/yr., $26/yr.
    (for.).

Agni: THE AGNI REVIEW, Sharon Dunn, ed., P.O. Box 229,
    Cambridge, MA 02138.
    Issues indexed: (16-17); Subscriptions: $13/2 yrs.,
    $7/yr.; Single issues: $3.50.

AmerPoR: THE AMERICAN POETRY REVIEW, David Bonanno, Stephen
    Berg, Arthur Vogelsang, et al., eds., World Poetry, Inc.,
    Temple U Center City, 1616 Walnut St., Room 405, Phila-
    delphia, PA 19103.
    Issues indexed: (11:1-6); Subscriptions: $19/3 yrs.,
    $23.70/3 yrs. (for.), $13/2 yrs., $16.15/2 yrs. (for.),
    $7.50/yr., $9.10/yr. (for.); Single issues: $1.50.

AmerS: THE AMERICAN SCHOLAR, Joseph Epstein, ed., United
    Chapters of Phi Beta Kappa, 1811 Q St. NW, Washington, DC
    20009.
    Issues indexed: (51:1-4); Subscriptions: $30/3 yrs.,
    $12/yr. plus $3/yr. (for.); Single issues: $4.

Annex: ANNEX 21, Patrick Worth Gray, ed., UNO-Community
    Writer's Workshop, University of Nebraska at Omaha, Oma-
    ha, NE 68182.
    Issues indexed: (3-4); Single issues: $4.95.

Antaeus: ANTAEUS, Daniel Halpern, ed., The Ecco Press, 18 W.
    30th St., New York, NY 1001.
    Issues indexed: (44-47); Subscriptions: $14/yr.; Single
    issues: $4.

*AntigR: THE ANTIGONISH REVIEW, George Sanderson, ed., St.
    Franics Xavier U., Antigonish, Nova Scotia B2G 1C0 Cana-
    da.

Issues indexed: (48-51); Subscriptions: $8/4 issues;
Single issues: $2.50.

AntR: THE ANTIOCH REVIEW, Robert S. Fogarty, ed., David St.
John, Po. ed., Antioch Coillege, P.O. Box 148, Yellow
Springs, OH 45387.
Issues indexed: (40:1-4); Subscriptions: $54/3 yrs.
(inst.), $39/3 yrs. (ind.), $38/2 yrs. (inst.), $28/2
yrs. (ind.), $20/yr. (inst.), $15/yr. (ind.) plus $5/yr.
(for.); Single issues: $3.50; P.O. Box 1308-R, Ft. Lee,
NJ 07024.

Areito: AREITO, Max Azicri, Emilio Bejel, et al., eds., GPO
Box 2174, New York, NY 10116.
Issues indexed: (8:30-32); Subscriptions: $18/yr.
(inst.), $8/yr. (ind)., $16/yr. (for.); Single issues:
$2; Back issues: $3.

ArizQ: ARIZONA QUARTERLY, Albert Frank Gegenheimer, ed., U.
of Arizona, Tucson, AZ 85721.
Issues indexed: (38:1-4); Subscriptions: $10/3 yrs.,
$5/yr.; Single issues: $1.50.

ArkRiv: THE ARK RIVER REVIEW, Jonathan Katz, Anthony Sobin,
et al., eds., Box 14, Wichita State U., Wichita, KS
67208.
Issues indexed: None received in 1982; Subscriptions:
$6/2 issues.

Ascent: ASCENT, Daniel Curley, et al., eds., English Dept.,
U. of Illinois, 608 South Wright St., Urbana, IL 61801.
Issues indexed: (7:2-3, 8:1); Subscriptions: $3/yr.,
$4.50/yr. (for.); Single issues: $1 (bookstore), $1.50
(mail).

Aspect: ASPECT, Ed Hogan, ed., 13 Robinson St., Somerville,
MA 02145.
Issues indexed: None received in 1982; Single issues:
$4.95.

AspenJ: ASPEN JOURNAL OF THE ARTS (continues ASPEN ANTHO-
LOGY), Encke M. King, ed., Don Child, Po. ed., Aspen
Leaves Literary Foundation, P. O. Box 3185, Aspen, CO
81612-3185.
Issues indexed: (1, 1:2) ; Subscriptions: $7/yr., $11/yr.
(Canada), $14/yr. (for.); Single issues: $4.50.

Atlantic: THE ATLANTIC, William Whitworth, ed., Peter Davi-
son, Po. ed., 8 Arlington St., Boston, MA 02116.
Issues indexed: (249:1-6, 250:1-6); Subscriptions: $45/3
yrs., $33/2 yrs., $18/yr., plus $2/yr. (for.); Single
issues: $2.

BallSUF: BALL STATE UNIVERSITY FORUM, Frances M. Rippy, Dick
Renner, eds., Ball State U., Muncie, IN 47306.
Issues indexed: (23:1-4); Subscriptions: $8/yr.; Single
issues: $2.50.

BaratR: THE BARAT REVIEW, Lauri S. Lee, ed., Barat College,
Lake Forest, IL 60045.

Issues indexed: (8:2); Subscriptions: $15/2 yrs., $8/yr.; Single issues: $4.50.

BelPoJ: THE BELOIT POETRY JOURNAL, Robert H. Glauber, David M. Stocking, Marion M. Stocking, eds., Box 2, Beloit, WI 53511.
Issues indexed: (32:3-4, 33:1-2); Subscriptions: $17/3 yrs., $6/yr.; Single issues: $1.50.

BerksR: BERKSHIRE REVIEW, Stephen Fix, et al., eds., Williams College, Box 633, Williamstown, MA 01267.
Issues indexed: None received in 1982.

BlackALF: BLACK AMERICAN LITERATURE FORUM, Joe Weixlmann, ed., PH 237, Indiana State U., Terre Haute, IN 47809.
Issues indexed: (16:1-4); Subscriptions: $8/yr. (ind.), $10/yr. (inst.), $12/yr. (for.); Statesman Towers West 1005, Indiana State U., Terre Haute, IN 47809.

*BlackWR: BLACK WARRIOR REVIEW, Michael Pettit, ed., Leslie Nail, Po. ed., U. of Alabama, P.O. Box 2936, University, AL 35486.
Issues indexed: (7:2); Subscriptions: $5/yr.; Single issues: $2.50.

*Bogg: BOGG, John Elsberg, ed., 422 N. Cleveland St., Arlington, VA 22201; George Cairncross, ed., 31 Belle Vue St., Filey, N. Yorks YO14 9HU, UK.
Issues indexed: (48-49); Subscriptions: $6/3 issues; Single issues: $2.50.

Bound: BOUNDARY 2, William V. Spanos, ed., Dept. of English, State U. of New York, Binghamton, NY 13901.
Issues indexed: (10:3); Subscriptions: $20/yr. (inst.), $13/yr. (ind.), $10/yr (stud.); Single issues: $8 (double), $5 (single).

Calib: CALIBAN, Roberto Marquez, ed., Box 797, Amherst, MA 01004.
Issues indexed: None received in 1982; Subscriptions: $10/yr. (inst.), $5/yr. (ind.); Single issues: $2.50.

CalQ: CALIFORNIA QUARTERLY, Elliot L. Gilbert, ed., Sandra M. Gilbert, Robert Swanson, Po. eds., 100 Sproul Hall, U. of California, Davis, CA 95616.
Issues indexed: (21); Subscriptions: $5/yr.; Single issues: $1.50.

*CanLit: CANADIAN LITERATURE, W. H. New, ed., U. of British Columbia, 2021 West Mall, Vancouver, B.C. V6T 1W5 Canada.
Issues indexed: (91-95); Subscriptions: $18/yr., $21/yr. (for.); Single issues: $7.50; Back issues: $2-5.

CapeR: THE CAPE ROCK, Ted Hirschfield, et al., eds., Southeast Missouri State U., Cape Girardeau, MO 63701.
Issues indexed: (17:2, 18:1); Subscriptions: $3/yr.; Single issues: $2.

*CapilR: THE CAPILANO REVIEW, Bill Schermbrucker, ed., Capilano College, 2055 Purcell Way, North Vancouver, B.C. V7J

3H5 Canada.
Issues indexed: (22-25); Subscriptions: $17.50/8 issues
(ind.), $9/4 issues (ind.), $10/4 issues (lib.), plus
$1/4 issues (for.); Single issues: $3.

Caribe: CARIBE, Miguel Santiago Santana, ed., Apartado 995,
San Juan, PR 00902.
Issues indexed: (3:4); Subscriptions: $5/yr. (ind.),
$6/yr (inst.), plus $1/yr. (USA), $2/yr. (for.); Single
issues: $4.

CarolQ: CAROLINA QUARTERLY, Marc Manganaro, ed., Daniel
Butterworth, Po. ed., Greenlaw Hall 066-A, U. of North
Carolina, Chapel Hill, NC 27514.
Issues indexed: (34:3, 35:1); Subscriptions: $12/yr.
(inst.), $9/yr. (ind.), $11/yr. (for.); Single issues:
$4; Back issues: $4.

*Catalyst: CATALYST, Kathleen McGann Kettern, Michael E.
Kettner, eds., McKettner Publishing, P.O. Box 12067,
Seattle, WA 98102.
Issues indexed: (2nd Annual Erotica Issue); Subscrip-
tions: $3/yr. (ind.), $5/yr. (inst., for.); Single is-
sues: $2.

CEACritic: THE CEA CRITIC, College English Association,
Elizabeth Cowan, ed., Dept. of English, Texas A&M U.,
College Station, TX 77843.
Issues indexed: (44:2-4, 45:1); Subscriptions: $18/yr.
(lib., inst.), $15/yr. (ind.).

CEAFor: THE CEA FORUM, College English Association, Eliza-
beth Cowan, ed., Dept. of English, Texas A&M U., College
Station, TX 77843.
Issues indexed: (12:3-4, 13:1); Subscriptions: $18/yr.
(lib., inst.), $15/yr. (ind.).

CentR: THE CENTENNIAL REVIEW, David Mead, ed., Linda Wagner,
Po. ed., 110 Morrill Hall, Michigan State U., East Lan-
sing, MI 48824.
Issues indexed: (26:1-4); Subscriptions: $5/2 yrs.,
$3/yr., plus $2/yr. (for.); Single issues: $1.

CharR: THE CHARITON REVIEW, Jim Barnes, ed., Division of
Language and Literature, Northeast Missouri State U.,
Kirksville, MO 63501.
Issues indexed: (8:1-2); Subscriptions: $7/4 issues;
Single issues: $2.

Chelsea: CHELSEA, Sonia Raiziss, ed., P.O. Box 5880, Grand
Central Station, New York, NY 10163.
Issues indexed: (41); Subscriptions: $8/2 issues or doub-
le issue, $9 (for.); Single issues: $4.50, $5 (for.).

ChiR: CHICAGO REVIEW, Molly McQuade, John L. Sutton, eds.,
Thomas Bonnell, Keith W. Tuma, Po. eds., U. of Chicago,
Faculty Exchange, Box C, Chicago, IL 60637.
Issues indexed: (33:2); Subscriptions: $33/3 yrs.,
$22.50/2 yrs., $12/yr., $9/yr. (ind.), plus $2/yr.
(for.); Single issues: $3.

ChrC: THE CHRISTIAN CENTURY, James M. Wall, ed., 407 S.
Dearborn St., Chicago, IL 60605.
Issues indexed: (99:1-41); Subscriptions: $54/3 yrs.,
$36/2 yrs., $21/yr., plus $2.50/yr. (for.); Single is-
sues: $.75.

CimR: CIMARRON RIVIEW, Neil J. Hackett, ed., Terry Hummer,
Po. ed., 208 Life Sciences East, Oklahoma State U.,
Stillwater, OK 74078.
Issues indexed: (58-61); Subscriptions: $10/yr.; Single
issues: $2.50.

Claridad: CLARIDAD, Juan Mari Bras, ed., EN ROJO, Literary
Supplement, Luis Fernando Coss, ed., Ave. Ponce de Leon
1866, Pda. 26-1/2, Santurce, PR 00911
Issues indexed: None received in 1982; Subscriptions:
$24/yr, $13/6 mo.; Box 318, Cooper Station, New York, NY
10276.

ColEng: COLLEGE ENGLISH, National Council of Teachers of
English, Donald Gray, ed., Brian O'Neill, Po. cons.,
Dept. of English, Indiana U., Bloomington, IN 47405.
Issues indexed: (44:1-8); Subscriptions: $35/yr. (inst.),
$30/yr. (ind.), plus $4/yr. (for.); Single issues: $4;
NCTE, 1111 Kenyon Rd., Urbana, IL 61801.

Comm: COMMONWEAL, James O'Gara, ed., Rosemary Deen, Marie
Ponsot, Po. eds., 232 Madison Avbe., New York, NY 10016.
Issues indexed: (109:1-22); Subscriptions: $43/2 yrs.,
$47/2 yrs. (Canada), $53/2 yrs. (for.), $24/yr., $26/yr.
(Canada), $29/yr. (for.); Single issues: $1.25.

ConcPo: CONCERNING POETRY, Ellwood Johnson, ed., Robert
Huff, Po. ed., Dept. of English, Western Washington U.,
Bellingham, WA 98225.
Issues Indexed: (15:1-2); Subscriptions: $5/yr. (USA,
Canada), $6/yr. (for.); Single issues: $3.

Cond: CONDITIONS, Elly Bulkin, Jan Clausen, Rima Shore,
eds., P.O. Box 56, Van Brunt Station, Brooklyn, NY 11215.
Issues indexed: (8); Subscriptions: $22/3 issues (inst.),
$11/3 issues (ind), $6/3 issues "hardship" rate, free to
women in prisons and mental institutions; Single issues:
$4.50 (ind.), $8 (inst.).

Confr: CONFRONTATION, Martin Tucker, ed., Dept. of English,
Brooklyn Center of Long Island U., Brooklyn, NY 11201.
Issues indexed: (23-24); Subscriptions: $15/3 yrs., $10/2
yrs., $5/yr.; Single issues: $3; Back issues: $2; Eleanor
Feleppa, Director of Public Relations, Southhampton Col-
lege, Southhampton, NY 11968.

CreamCR: CREAM CITY REVIEW, Tony Kubiak, ed., Ken Pobo, Po.
ed., English Dept., U. of Wisconsin-Milwaukee, Milwaukee,
WI 53201.
Issues indexed: None received in 1982; Subscriptions:
$5/yr.; Single issues: $2.50.

CropD: CROP DUST, Edward C. Lynskey & Heather Tervo Lynskey,
eds/pubs., Route 2, Box 389-1, Bealeton, VA 22712.

Issues Indexed: No issues received in 1982; Subscriptions: $5/2 issues (ind.), $8/2 issues (lib.); Single issues: $2.50.

*CrossC: CROSS-CANADA WRITERS' QUARTERLY, Ted Plantos, ed., Patricia Keeney Smith, Po. ed., Box 277, Station F, Toronto, Ontario M4Y 2L7 Canada.
Issues indexed: (4:1-4); Subscriptions: $10/yr. (ind.), $12/yr. (inst.); Single issues: $2.95.

CutB: CUTBANK, Carole DeMarinis, Bob Ross, eds., Dept. of English, U. of Montana, Missoula, MT 59812.
Issues indexed: (18-19); Subscriptions: $14/2 yrs., $7.50/yr.; Single issues: $3.

*Dandel: DANDELION, Robert Hilles, Beverly Harris, eds., John McDermid, Claire Harris, Po. eds., Alexandra Centre, 922 - 9th Ave., S.E., Calgary, Alberta T2G 0S4 Canada.
Issues indexed: (9:1-2); Subscriptions: $15/2 yrs., $8/yr., $12/yr. (inst.); Single issues: $4.

*DekalbLAJ: THE DEKALB LITERARY ARTS JOURNAL, William S. Newman, ed., DeKalb Community College, 555 N. Indian Creek Dr., Clarkston, GA 30021.
Issues indexed: (14:1/4); Single issues: $3.

DenQ: DENVER QUARTERLY, Leland H. Chambers, ed., U. of Denver, Denver, CO 80208.
Issues indexed: (16:4, 17:1-3); Subscriptions: $14/2 yrs., $8/yr., plus $1/yr. (for.); Single issues: $2.

EngJ: ENGLISH JOURNAL, National Council of Teachers of English, Ken Donelson, Alleen Pace Nilsen, eds., College of Education, Arizona State U., Tempe, AZ 85287.
Issues indexed: (71:1-8); Subscriptions: $35/yr. (inst.), $30/yr. (ind.), plus $4/yr. (for.); Single issues: $4; NCTE, 1111 Kenyon Rd., Urbana, IL 61801.

EnPas: EN PASSANT, James A. Costello, ed., 4612 Sylvanus Dr., Wilmington, DE 19803.
Issues indexed: (13); Subscriptions: $11/6 issues, $6/3 issues; Single issues: $2.25; Back issues: $1.75.

Epoch: EPOCH, James McConkey, Walter Slatoff, eds., 245 Goldwin Smith Hall, Cornell U., Ithaca, NY 14853.
Issues indexed: (31:1-3, 32:1); Subscriptions: $6.50/yr.; Single issues: $2.50.

Field: FIELD, Stuart Friebert, David Young, eds., Rice Hall, Oberlin College, Oberlin, OH 44074.
Issues indexed: (26-27); Subscriptions: $10/2 yrs., $6/yr.; Single issues: $3; Back issues: $10.

Focus: FOCUS/MIDWEST, Charles L. Klotzer, ed./pub., Dan Jaffe, Po. ed., 8606 Olive Blvd., St. Louis, MO 63132.
Issues indexed: (15:92-94); Subscriptions: $100/life, $29/30 issues, $19.50/18 issues, $14/12 issues, $8/6 issues, plus $4.50/6 issues (for.); Single issues: $1.25.

FourQt: FOUR QUARTERS, John Christopher Kleis, ed., Richard
  Lautz, Po. ed., La Salle College, 20th & Olney Aves.,
  Philadelphia, PA 19141.
  Issues indexed: (31:2-4, 32:1); Subscriptions: $7/2 yrs.,
  $4/yr.; Single issues: $1.

*Gargoyle: GARGOYLE MAGAZINE, Richard Peabody, Jr.,
  ed./pub., Paycock Press, P.O. Box 57206, Washington, DC
  20037.
  Issues indexed: (15-19); Subscriptions: $6/yr. (ind.),
  $7/yr. (inst.); Single issues: $3-4.

GeoR: GEORGIA REIVEW, Stanley W. Lindberg, ed., U. of Geor-
  gia, Athens, GA 30602.
  Issues indexed: (36:1-4); Subscriptions: $10/2 yrs.,
  $6/yr., plus $3/yr. (for.); Single issues: $3.

*Germ: GERMINATION, Allan Cooper, ed., General Delivery,
  Southampton, Nova Scotia B0M 1W0 Canada.
  Issues indexed: (6:1-2); Subscriptions: $6/2 issues
  (ind.), $8/2 issues (inst.); Single issues: $3.50.

*Grain: GRAIN, Saskatchewan Writers Guild, E. F. Dyck, ed.,
  Box 1885, Saskatoon, Saskatchewan S7K 3S2 Canada.
  Issues indexed: (10:1-4); Subscriptions: $10/2 yrs.,
  $6/yr.; Single issues: $2.

HangL: HANGLING LOOSE, Robert Hershon, et al., eds., 231
  Wyckoff St., Brooklyn, NY 11217.
  Issues indexed: (41-43); Subscriptions: $15/9 issues,
  $10/6 issues, $5.50/3 issues; Single issues: $2.50.

Harp: HARPER'S MAGAZINE, Michael Kinsley, ed., Two Park
  Ave., New York, NY 10016.
  Issues indexed: (264:1580-1585, 265:1586-1591); Subscrip-
  tions: $18/yr., plus $2/yr. (USA possessions, Canada),
  plus $3/yr. (for.); Single issues: $2; P.O. Box 2622,
  Boulder, CO 80322.

HiramPoR: HIRAM POETRY REVIEW, English Department, Hiram
  College, David Fratus, Carol Donley, eds., Box 162, Hi-
  ram, OH 44234.
  Issues indexed: (31-33); Subscriptions: $2/yr.; Single
  issues: $1.

Hol Crit: THE HOLLINS CRITIC, John Rees Moore, ed., Hollins
  College, VA 24020.
  Issues indexed: (19:1-5); Subscriptions: $5/yr.,
  $6.50/yr. (for.).

Hudson: THE HUDSON REVIEW, Paula Deitz, Frederick Morgan,
  eds., 684 Park Ave.,, New York, NY 10021.
  Issues indexed: (35:1-4); Subscriptions: $14/yr., $15/yr.
  (for.); Single issues: $4.

Humanist: THE HUMANIST, Lloyd L. Morain, ed., 7 Harwood Dr.,
  Amherst, NY 14226.
  Issues indexed: (42:1-6); Subscriptions: $35/3 yrs.,
  $25/2 yrs., $15/yr., plus $2.50/yr. (for.); Single is-
  sues: $2.50; Back issues: $3.

Images: IMAGES, Gary Pacernick, ed., Dept. of English, Wright State U., Dayton, OH 45435. Issues indexed: (8:1-2); Subscriptions: $3/yr.; Single issues: $1.

Inti: INTI, Revista de Literatura Hispanica, Roger B. Carmosino, ed., Dept. of Modern Languages, Providence College, Providence, RI 02918. Issues indexed: (12-14); Subscriptions: $16/yr. (inst.), $14/yr. (ind.).

Iowa: IOWA REVIEW, David Hamilton, ed., 308 EPB, U. of Iowa, Iowa City, IA 52242. Issues indexed: (12:2-4, 13:1); Subscriptions: $15/yr. (lib., inst.), $12/yr. (ind.), plus $3/yr. (for.); Single issues: $4.

KanQ: KANSAS QUARTERLY, Harold Schneider, et al., eds., Dept. of English, Kansas State U., Manhattan, KS 66506. Issues indexed: (14:1-4); Subscriptions: $18/2 yrs., $10/yr. (USA, Canada, Latin America), $20/2 yrs., $11/yr. (other countries); Single issues: $3.

Kayak: KAYAK, George Hitchcock, Marjorie Simon, Gary Fisher, eds., 325 Ocean View Ave., Santa Cruz, CA 95062. Issues indexed: (58-60); Subscriptions: $5/yr.; Single issues: $2.

LetFem: LETRAS FEMENINAS, Asociacion de Literatura Femenina Hispanica, Victoria E. Urbano, ed., Box 10023, Lamar U., Beaumont, TX 77710. Issues indexed: (8:1-2); Subscriptions: $15/yr.

LitR: THE LITERARY REVIEW, Martin Green, ed., Fairleigh Dickinson U., 285 Madison Ave., Madison, NJ 07940. Issues indexed: (25:2-4, 26:1); Subscriptions: $9/yr., $10/yr. (for.); Single issues: $3.50, $4/yr (for.)..

LittleBR: THE LITTLE BALKANS REVIEW, Gene DeGruson, Po. ed., The Little Balkans Press, Inc., 601 Grandview Heights Terr., Pittsburg, KS 66762. Issues indexed: (1:2-4, 2:1-4, 3:1-2); Subscriptions: $10/yr.; Single issues: $3.50.

LittleM: THE LITTLE MAGAZINE, David G. Hartwell, ed., Dragon Press, P.O. Box 78, Pleasantville, NY 10570. Issues Indexed: (13:3/4); Subscriptions: $13/4 issues (inst.), $12/4 issues (ind.), $15/4 issues (for.); Single issues: $3.

LittleR: THE LITTLE REVIEW, John McKernan, ed., Little Review Press, Box 205, Marshall U., Huntington, WV 25701. Issues indexed: None received in 1982; Subscriptions: $2.50/yr.; Single issues: $1.25.

Lugar: LUGAR SIN LIMITE, Ivan Silen, Myrna Nieves Colon, et al., eds., Boricua College, 2875 Broadway, New York, NY 10025. Issues indexed: None received in 1982; Single issues: $1.50.

Mairena: MAIRENA, Manuel de la Puebla, ed., Himalaya 257, Urbanizacion Monterrey, Rio Piedras, PR 00926.
Issues indexed: (4:9-12); Subscriptions: $10/yr. (inst.), $12/yr. (for. inst.), $6/yr. (ind.), $10/yr. (for. ind.).

Maize: MAIZE, Alurista et al., eds., Colorado College, Box 10, Colorado Springs, CO 80903.
Issues indexed: (5:1-4, 6:1/2); Subscriptions: $9/yr. (inst.), $8/yr. (ind.); Single issues: $5.

MalR: THE MALAHAT REVIEW, Robin Skelton, Constance Rooke, eds., P.O. Box 1700, Victoria, British Columbia, Canada V8W 2Y2.
Issues indexed: (61-63); Subscriptions: $40/3 yrs., $15/yr. (USA, Canada), $50/3 yrs., $20/yr. (other countries); Single issues: $6 (USA, Canada), $8 (other countries).

*****ManhatR**: THE MANHATTAN REVIEW, Philip Fried, ed., 304 Third Ave., Apt. 4A, New York, NY 10010.
Issues indexed: (2:1-2); Subscriptions: $8/yr. (ind.), $10/yr. (inst.), plus $2.50/yr. (outside USA & Canada); Back issues: $4.

MassR: THE MASSACHUSETTS REVIEW, John Hicks, Robert Tucker, eds., Memorial Hall, U. of Massachusetts, Amherst, MA 01003.
Issues indexed: (23:1-4); Subscriptions: $12/yr., $14/yr. (for.); Single issues: $4.

Meadows: THE MEADOWS, Mary Burrows, et al., eds, Art Dept., Truckee Meadows Community College, 7000 El Rancho Dr., Sparks, NV 89431.
Issues indexed: None received in 1982.

*****MendoR**: MENDOCINO REVIEW, Camille Ranker, ed., P.O. Box 888, Mendocino, CA 95460.
Issues indexed: (5-6); Single issues: $5.95.

Mester: MESTER, Librada Hernandez-Lagoa, ed., Dept. of Spanish and Portuguese, U. of California, Los Angeles, CA 90024.
Issues indexed: (11:1-2); Subscriptions: $14/yr. (inst.), $8/yr. (ind.), $5/yr. (stud.); Single issues: $7 (inst.), $4 (ind.)

Metam: METAMORFOSIS, Erasmo Gamboa, ed., Centro de Estudios Chicanos, GN-09, U. of Washington, Seattle, WA 98195.
Issues indexed: None received in 1982; Single issues: $5.

MichQR: MICHIGAN QUARTERLY REVIEW, Laurence Goldstein, ed., 3032 Rackham Bldg., U. of Michigan, Ann Arbor, MI 48109.
Issues indexed: (21:1-4); Subscriptions: $24/2 yr., $13/yr. (ind.), $15/yr. (inst.); Single issues: $3.50; Back issues: $2.

MidwQ: THE MIDWEST QUARTERLY, James B. Schick, ed., Michael Heffernan, Po. ed., Pittsburg State U., Pittsburg, KS 66762.
Issues indexed: (23:2-4, 24:1); Subscriptions: $4/yr.;

Single issues: $1.50.

MinnR: THE MINNESOTA REVIEW, Fred Pfeil, Laura Rice-Sayre, Michael Sprinker, eds, Anne E. Krosby, Henry Sayre, Po. eds., Dept. of English, Oregon State U., Corvallis, OR 97331.
Issues Indexed: (NS18-19); Subscriptions: $20/2 yrs. (inst. & for.), $12/2 yrs. (ind.), $12/yr. (inst. & for.), $7/yr. (ind.); Single issues: $4.

MissouriR: THE MISSOURI REVIEW, Speer Morgan, ed., Dept. of English, 231 Arts and Science, U. of Missouri, Columbia, MO 65211.
Issues indexed: (5:2-3, 6:1); Subscriptions: $18/2 yrs., $10/yr.

MissR: MISSISSIPPI REVIEW, Frederick Barthelme, ed., The Center for Writers, Southern Station, Box 5144, Hatties-burg, MS 39406-5144.
Issues indexed: (30); Subscriptions: $20/3 yrs., $14/2 yrs., $8/yr., plus $2/yr. (for.); Single issues: $3.

ModernPS: MODERN POETRY STUDIES, Jerry McGuire, Robert Mik-litsch, eds., 207 Delaware Ave., Buffalo, NY 14202.
Issues indexed: (11:1/2); Subscriptions: $9/3 issues (inst.), $7.50/3 issues (ind.).

Montra: MONTEMORA, Eliot Weinberger, ed., Box 336, Cooper Station, New York, NY 10276.
Issues indexed: None received in 1982; Single issues: $5.95.

Mund: MUNDUS ARTIUM, Rainer Schulte, ed., U. of Texas at Dallas, Box 688, Richardson, TX 75080.
Issues indexed: None received in 1982; Subscriptions: $10/2 issues (inst.), $8/2 issues (ind.); Single issues: $4.50.

Nat: THE NATION, Victor Navasky, ed., Grace Schulman, Po. ed., 72 Fifth Ave., New York, NY 10011.
Issues indexed: (234:1-25, 235:1-22); Subscriptions: $65/2 yrs., $35/yr., $17.50/half yr.; Single issues: $1.25; Nation Subscription Service, P.O. Box 1953, Mar-ion, OH 43305.

NewEngR: NEW ENGLAND REVIEW AND BREAD LOAF QUARTERLY, Sydney Lea, ed., Box 170, Hanover, NH 03755.
Issues indexed: (4:3-4, 5:1/2); Subscriptions: $12/yr.; Single issues: $4-7.

NewL: NEW LETTERS, David Ray, ed., U. of Missouri-Kansas City, 5346 Charlotte, Kansas City, MO 64110.
Issues indexed: (48:2-4, 49:1-2); Subscriptions: $50/5 yrs., $25/2 yrs., $15/yr. (ind.); $60/5 yrs., $30/2 yrs., $18/yr. (lib.); Single issues: $4.

NewOR: NEW ORLEANS REVIEW, John Mosier, ed., Box 195, Loyola U., New Orleans, LA 70118.
Issues indexed: (9:1-3); Subscriptions: $12/yr. (inst.), $10/yr. (ind.), $17/yr. (for.); Single issues: $5.

NewRena: THE NEW RENAISSANCE, Louise T. Reynolds, ed., Stan-
wood Bolton, Po. ed., 9 Heath Road, Arlington, MA 02174.
Issues indexed: (15); Subscriptions: $16/6 issues,
$8.50/3 issues; $20/6 issues, $10.50/3 issues (Canada,
Mexico, Europe); $22/6 issues, $11.50/3 issues (else-
where); Single issues: $4.25-5.

NewRep: THE NEW REPUBLIC, Martin Peretz, ed., Pobert Pinsky,
Po. ed., 1220 19th St., N.W., Washington, DC 20036.
Issues indexed: None received in 1982; Subscriptions:
$28/yr., $17/yr. (stud.); Single issues: $1.25.

NewWR: NEW WORLD REVIEW, Marilyn Bechtel, ed., 162 Madison
Ave., 3rd Floor, New York, NY 10016.
Issues indexed: (50:1-6); Subscriptions: $5/yr. $6/yr.
(for.); Single issues: $1.

NewYorker: THE NEW YORKER, Howard Moss, Po. ed., 25 W. 43rd
St., New York, NY 10036.
Issues indexed: (57:46-52, 58:1-45); Subscriptions: $46/2
yrs., $28/yr.; $34/yr. (Canada); $40/yr. (for.); Single
issues: $1.50.

NewYRB: THE NEW YORK REVIEW OF BOOKS, Robert B. Silvers,
Barbara Epstein, eds., 250 W. 57th St., New York, NY
10107.
Issues indexed: (28:21-22, 29:1-20); Subscriptions:
$25/yr. plus $5/yr. (Canada), plus $7/yr. (elsewhere);
Single issues: $1.50; Subscription Service Dept., P.O.
Box 940, Farmingdale, NY 11737.

Nimrod: NIMROD, Francine Ringold, ed., Joan Flint, et al.,
Po. eds., Arts and Humanities Countil of Tulsa, 2210 S.
Main, Tulsa, OK 74114.
Issues indexed: (25:2, 26:1); Subscriptions: $10/yr.,
$13/yr. (for.); Single issues: $5, $7 (for.).

NoAmR: THE NORTH AMERICAN REVIEW, Robley Wilson, Jr., ed.,
Peter Cooley, Po. ed., U. of Northern Iowa, 1222 West
27th St., Cedar Falls, IA 50614.
Issues indexed: (267:1-4); Subscriptions: $9/yr., $10/yr.
(Canada, Latin America), $11/yr. (elsewhere); Single
issues: 2.50.

Northeast: NORTHEAST, John Judson, ed., Juniper Press, 1310
Shorewood Dr., La Crosse, WI 54601.
Issues indexed: (3:12-14); Subscriptions: $25/yr.; Single
issues: $2.50.

Notarte: NOTICIAS DE ARTE, Frank C. Garcia, ed./pub., Flo-
rencio Garcia Cisneros, Director, 172 E. 89th St. #5-A,
New York, NY 10028.
Issues indexed: (7:1-3); Subscriptions: No information
given.

NowestR: NORTHWEST REVIEW, John Witte, ed., Maxine Scates,
Po. ed., 369 PLC, U. of Oregon, Eugene, OR 97403.
Issues indexed: (20:1-2/3); Subscriptions: $21/3 yrs.,
$14/2 yrs., $8/yr.; $13/2 yrs., $7/yr. (stud.); plus
$2/yr. (for.); Single issues: $3.

Obs: OBSIDIAN, Alvin Aubert, ed./pub., Wayne State U., Detroit, MI 48202.
Issues indexed: (7:2/3); Subscriptions: $8.50/yr., $9.50/yr. (Canada), $11.50/yr. (for.); Single issues: $3; Double issues: $6.

OhioR: THE OHIO REIVEW, Wayne Dodd, ed., Ellis Hall, Ohio U., Athens, OH 45701.
Issues indexed: (27-29); Subscriptions: $25/3 yrs., $10/yr.; Single issues: $4.25.

OntR: ONTARIO REVIEW, Raymond J. Smith, ed., 9 Honey Brook Dr., Princeton, NJ 08540.
Issues indexed: (16-17); Subscriptions: $21/3 yrs., $15/2 yrs., $8/yr., plus $1/yr. (for.); Single issues: $3.95.

OP: OPEN PLACES, Eleanor M. Bender, ed., Box 2085, Stephens College, Columbia, MO 65215.
Issues indexed: (33-34); Subscriptions: $11/2 yrs., $6/yr. (USA, Canada), plus $4/yr. (elsewhere); Single issue: $3.

Os: OSIRIS, Andrea Moorhead, ed., Box 297, Deerfield, MA 01342.
Issues indexed: (14-15); Subscriptions: $5/2 issues (USA, Canada, Mexico), $6/2 issues (elsewhere); Single issues: $2.50.

Outbr: OUTERBRIDGE, Charlotte Alexander, ed., English Dept. (A323), College of Staten Island, 715 Ocean Terrace, Staten Island, NY 10301.
Issues indexed: (8/9-10/11); Subscriptions: $4/yr.; Single issues: $2.

Paint: PAINTBRUSH, Ben Bennani, 1 Regis Rd., Medford, MA 02155.
Issues indexed: (7:13-9:18); Subscriptions: $20/3 yrs., $15/2 yrs., $8/yr.; Single issues: $5; Back issues: $3-5.

ParisR: THE PARIS REVIEW, George A. Plimpton, et al., eds., Jonathan Galassi, Po. ed., 541 East 72nd St., New York, NY 10021.
Issues indexed: (24:83); Subscriptions: $200/life, $20/8 issues, $11/4 issues, plus $4/4 issues (for.); Single issues: $3.50; 45-39 171 Place, Flushing, NY 11358.

PartR: PARTISAN REVIEW, William Phillips, ed., Boston U., 121 Bay State Rd., Boston, MA 02215; 1 Lincoln Plaza, New York, NY 10023.
Issues indexed: (49:1-4); Subscriptions: $32.50/3 yrs., $23/2 yrs., $12.50/yr.; $26.25/2 yrs., $14.25/yr. (for.); $18/yr. (inst.); Single issues: $3.50.

Peb: PEBBLE, Greg Kuzma, ed., The Best Cellar Press, Dept. of English, U. of Nebraska, Lincoln, NE 68588.
Issues indexed: (22); Subscriptions: $15/4 issues (lib.), $12/4 issues (ind.).

Pequod: PEQUOD, David Paradis, ed., 536 Hill St., San Fran-
cisco, CA 94114; Poetry Mss. to Mark Rudman, Po. ed., 817
West End Ave., New York, NY 10025.
Issues indexed: (14-15); Subscriptions: $21/3 yrs., $15/2
yrs., $8/yr., plus $1/yr. (for.); Single issues: $4.50.

Pig: PIG IRON, Rose Sayre, Jim Villani, eds., Pig Iron
Press, P.O. Box 237, Youngstown, OH 44501.
Issues indexed: (8-10); Subscriptions: $9/yr.; Single
issues: 5.95.

PikeF: THE PIKESTAFF FORUM, James R. Scrimgeour, Robert D.
Sutherland, eds./pubs., P.O. Box 127, Normal, IL 61761.
Issues indexed: (3-4); Subscriptions: $10/6 issues; Sing-
le issues: $2; Back issues: $2.

PikeR: THE PIKESTAFF REVIEW, James R. Scrimgeour, Robert D.
Sutherland, eds./pubs., P.O. Box 127, Normal, IL 61761.
Issues indexed: (3); No more published.

Playb: PLAYBOY, Hugh M. Hefner, ed./pub., 919 N. Michigan
Ave., Chicago, IL 60611.
Issues indexed: (29:1-2); Subscriptions: $18/yr.; Single
issues: varies.

Ploughs: PLOUGHSHARES, DeWitt Henry, Peter O'Malley, Direc-
tors, Box 529, Cambridge, MA 02139; Editorial offices:
Dept. of English, Emerson College, 100 Beacon St., Bos-
ton, MA 02116; 214A Waverly Ave., Watertown, MA 02172.
Issues indexed: (8:1-4); Subscriptions: $12/yr., $14/yr.
(for.); Single issues: $5.

Poem: POEM, Huntsville literary Association, Robert L. Wel-
ker, ed., U. of Alabama at Huntsville, English Dept.,
Huntsville, AL 35899.
Issues indexed: (44-46); Subscriptions: $5.50/yr.; P.O.
Box 919, Huntsville, AL 35804.

PoetC: POET AND CRITIC, Michael Martone, ed., 203 Ross Hall,
Iowa State U., Ames, IA 50011.
Issues indexed: (14:1-2); Subscriptions: $14/2 yrs.,
$7.50/yr., plus $1/yr. (for.); Single issues: $2.50; Iowa
State U. Press, South State St., Ames, IA 50010.

Poetry: POETRY, John Frederick Nims, ed., 601 S. Morgan St.,
P.O. Box 4348, Chicago, IL 60680.
Issues indexed: (139:4-6, 140:1-6, 141:1-3); Subscrip-
tions: $20/yr., $24/yr. (for.); Single issues: $2 plus
$.60 postage; Back issues: $2.25 plus $.60 postage.

*PoetryCR: POETRY CANADA REVIEW, Clifton Whiten, Ed./Pub.,
P.O. Box 1280, Stn. 'A', Tronot, Ontario M5W 1G7 Canada.
Issues indexes: (3:3-4, 4:1-2); Subscriptions: $6/yr.
(Canada), $7/yr. (USA), $8.50/yr. (elsewhere); $8/yr.
(inst., Canada); $9.50/yr. (inst., USA), $11/yr. (inst.,
elsewhere).

PoetryE: POETRY EAST, Richard Jones, Kate Daniels, eds.,
Star Route 1, Box 50, Earlysville, VA 22936.
Issues indexed: (7-8); Subscriptions: $10/yr.; Single
issues: $3.50.

PoetryNW: POETRY NORTHWEST, David Wagoner, ed., U. of Wash-
ington, 4045 Brooklyn Ave., NE, Seattle, WA 98105.
Issues indexed: (23:1-4); Subscriptions: $8/yr., $9/yr.
(for.); Single issues: $2, $2.25 (for.).

PoNow: POETRY NOW, E. V. Griffith, ed./pub., 3118 K Street,
Eureka, CA 95501.
Issues indexed: (6:4-6, 7:1; 34-37); Subscriptions:
$19/12 issues, $13/8 issues; $7.50/4 issues; Single is-
sues: $2.

PortR: PORTLAND REVIEW, Jhan Hochman, ed., Portland State
U., Box 751, Portland, OR 97207.
Issues indexed: (28:1-2); Back issues: $1.50-5.95, plus
$1.25 handling.

PottPort: THE POTTERSFIELD PORTFOLIO, Lesley Choyce, ed.,
Pottersfield Press, RR #2, Porters Lake, Nova Scotia B0J
2S0 Canada.
Issues indexed: (4); Subscriptions: $10/3 yrs.

PraS: PRAIRIE SCHOONER, Hugh Luke, ed., 201 Andrews Hall, U.
of Nebraska, Lincoln, NE 68588.
Issues indexed: (56:1-4); Subscriptions: $29/3 yrs.,
$20/2 yrs., $11/yr. (ind.); $15/yr. (lib.); Single is-
sues: $3.25.

Prima: PRIMAVERA, Julie Auburg, et al., eds., U. of Chicago,
1212 E. 59th St., Chicago, IL 60637.
Issues indexed: None received in 1982; Single issues: $5.

*Prismal: PRISMAL/CABRAL, Emma Buenaventura, et al., eds.,
Dept. of Spanish and Portuguese, U. of Maryland, College
Park, MD 20742.
Issues indexed: (7/8); Subscriptions: $5/yr. (ind.),
$10/yr. (inst.).

Puerto: PUERTO NORTE Y SUR, Jose M. Oxholm, ed., 19454
Woodbine, Detroit, MI 48219.
Issues indexed: None received in 1982;

*Quarry: QUARRY, David Schleich, ed., Box 1061, Kingston,
Ontario K7L 4Y5 Canada.
Issues indexed: (31:1-4); Subscriptions: $12/yr., plus
$2/yr. (for.); Single issues: $3.

QRL: QUARTERLY REVIEW OF LITERATURE, T. & R. Weiss, 26
Haslet Ave., Princeton, NJ 08540.
Issues indexed: (22-23, Poetry Series 3-4); Subscrip-
tions: $15/2 volumes (paper), $20/volume (cloth, inst.) ;
Single issues: $10 (paper).

QW: QUARTERLY WEST, David Baker, Robert Shapard, eds., Ed-
ward Byrne, Po. ed. 317 Olpin Union, U. of Utah, Salt
Lake City, UT 84112.

Issues indexed: (14-15); Subscriptions: $12/2 yrs.,
$6.50/yr.; Single issues: $3.50.

*RevChic: REVISTA CHICANO-RIQUENA, Nicholas Kanellos, ed.,
U. of Houston, Central Campus, Houston, TX 77004.
Issues indexed: (10:1/2-4); Subscriptions: $10/yr.,
$15/yr. (inst.); Single issues: $5-12.

RevIn: REVISTA/REVIEW INTERAMERICANA, John Zebrowski, ed.,
GPO Box 3255, San Juan, PR 00936.
Issues indexed: (10:4, 11:1-2); Subscriptions: $27/3
yrs., $20/2 yrs., $14/yr. (ind).; $45/3 yrs., $35/2 yrs.,
$20/yr. (inst.); $9/yr. (stud.); Single issues: $5 plus
$1.50 postage & handling.

Salm: SALMAGUNDI, Robert Boyers, ed., Peggy Boyers, Exec.
ed., Skidmore College, Saratoga Springs, NY 12866.
Issues indexed: (54-58/59); Subscriptions: $25/2 yrs.,
$16/yr. (inst.); $15/2 yrs., $9/yr. (ind.); plus
$1.50/yr. (for.); Single issues: $4.

Sam: SAMISDAT, Merritt Clifton, Robin Michelle Clifton,
eds., Box 129, Richford, VT 05476.
Issues indexed: (31:2-4, 32:2-4, 33:2-4, 34:1, releases
122-124, 126-128, 130-133; "#125, 129 contained no poet-
ry"); Subscriptions: $150/all future issues, $25/1000
pages, $15/500 pages; Single issues: varies.

SecC: SECOND COMING, A. D. Winans, ed./pub., Box 31249, San
Francisco, CA 94131.
Issues indexed: (8:2, 9:1/2, 10:1/2)); Subscriptions:
$7.50/yr. (lib.), $5/yr. (ind.), $9.50 (for.)..

SenR: SENECA REVIEW, James Crenner, ed., Hobart & William
Smith Colleges, Geneva, NY 14456.
Issues indexed: (31:1); Single issues: $3.50; Double
issues: $7.

SewanR: THE SEWANEE REVIEW, George Core, ed., U. of the
South, Sewanee, TN 37375.
Issues indexed: (90:1-4); Subscriptions: $37/3 yrs.,
$26/2 yrs., $15/yr. (inst.); $28/3 yrs., $20/2 yrs.,
$12/yr. (ind.); plus $2/yr. (for.);Single issues: $4;
Back issues: $5-10, plus $.50/copy postage & handling.

Shen: SHENANDOAH, James Boatwright, ed., Richard Howard, Po.
ed., Washington and Lee U., Box 722, Lexington, VA 24450.
Issues indexed: (33:1-4); Subscriptions: $18/3 yrs.,
$13/2 yrs., $8/yr. plus $2/yr. (for.); Single issues:
$2.50; Back issues: $4.

*Shout: A SHOUT IN THE STREET, Joe Cuomo, ed., Frederick
Buell, Marie Ponsot, Po. eds., c/o Editorial Services,
A1310, Queens College, Flushing, NY 11367.
Issues indexed: (2:3, 3:1); Subscriptions: $10/yr.; Sing-
le issues: $4.

SinN: SIN NOMBRE, Nilita Vientos Gaston, Dir., Box 4391, San
Juan, PR 00905-4391.
Issues indexed: (12:3-4, 13:1); Subscriptions: $20/yr.

(inst.), $15/yr. (ind.), $10/yr. (stud., Puerto Rico);
Single issues: $4.25.

Sky: SKYWRITING, Martin Grossman, ed., 511 Campbell Ave.,
Kalamazoo, MI 49007.
Issues indexed: (4:1/3, issues 10/12); Single issues:
$5.50.

SmPd: THE SMALL POND MAGAZINE OF LITERATURE, Napoleon St.
Cyr, ed./pub., Box 664, Stratford, CT 06497.
Issues indexed: (19:1-3, issues 54-56); Subscriptions:
$4.75/yr.; Single issues: $2.25.

SoCaR: SOUTH CAROLINA REVIEW, Richard J. Calhoun, Robert W.
Hill, eds., Dept. of English, Clemson U., Clemson, SC
29631.
Issues indexed: (14:2, 15:1); Subscriptions: $9/2 yrs.,
$5/yr. (USA, Canada, Mexico); $10/2 yrs., $5.50/yr.
(elsewhere); Single issues: $3.

SoDakR: SOUTH DAKOTA REVIEW, John R. Milton, ed., Dept. of
English, U. of South Dakota, Box 111, U. Exchange, Ver-
million, SD 57069.
Issues indexed: (19:4, 20:1-4); Subscriptions: $17/2
yrs., $10/yr. (USA, Canada); $20/2 yrs., $12/yr. (else-
where); Single issues: $3.

SouthernHR: SOUTHERN HUMANITIES REVIEW, Barbara A. Mowat,
David K. Jeffrey, eds., 9088 Haley Center, Auburn U.,
Auburn, AL 36849.
Issues indexed: (16:1-4); Subscriptions: $8/yr.; Single
issues: $2.50.

SouthernPR: SOUTHERN POETRY REVIEW, Robert Grey, ed., Eng-
lish Dept., U. of North Carolina, Charlotte, NC 28223.
Issues indexed: (22:1, 23, i.e. 22:2); Subscriptions:
$5/yr.; Single issues: $3.

SouthernR: SOUTHERN REVIEW, Donald E. Stanford, Lewis P.
Simpson, eds., Louisiana State U., Drawer D, U. Station,
Baton Rouge, LA 70893.
Issues indexed: (18:1-4); Subscriptions: $16/3 yrs.,
$12/2 yrs., $7/yr.; Single issues: $2.

SouthwR: SOUTHWEST REVIEW, Charlotte T. Whaley, ed., South-
ern Methodist U., Dallas, TX 75275.
Issues indexed: (67:1-4); Subscriptions: $10/2 yrs.,
$6/yr.; Single issues: $1.50.

Sparrow: SPARROW PRESS POVERTY PAMPHLETS, Felix Stefanile,
ed./Pub., Sparrow Press, 103 Waldron St., West Lafayette,
IN 47906.
Issues indexed: (42-43); Subscriptions: $6/3 issues;
Single issues: $2.

Spirit: THE SPIRIT THAT MOVES US, Morty Sklar, ed., P.O. Box
1585, Iowa City, IA 52244.
Issues indexed: (6:2/3); Subscriptions: $6/3 issues, $8/3
issues (lib.).

Stand: STAND, Jon Silkin, et al., eds., Jim Kates, USA ed., 45 Old Peterborough Rd., Jaffrey NH 03452; Howard Fink, Canadian ed., 4054 Melrose Ave., Montreal, Quebec H4A 2S4 Canada.
Issues indexed: (23:1-4); Subscriptions: $10/yr.; Single issues: $2.50.

StoneC: STONE COUNTRY, Judith Neeld, ed., The Nathan Mayhew Seminars of Martha's Vineyard, P.O. Box 132, Menemsha, MA 02552.
Issues indexed: (9:3/4, 10:1/2)); Subscriptions: $14/2 yrs., $7.50/yr.; Single issues: $4.50.

Sulfur: SULFUR, California Institute of Technology, Clayton Eshleman, ed., 852 South Bedford St., Los Angeles, CA 90035.
Issues indexed: (2:1-3, issues 4-6); Subscriptions: $22/yr. (inst.), $15/yr. (ind.); Single issues: $6; Box 228-77, California Institute of Technology, Pasadena, CA 91125.

SunM: SUN & MOON, Douglass Messerli, Literary ed., 4330 Hartwick Rd. #418, College Park, MD 20740.
Issues indexed: None received in 1982; Subscriptions: $15/3 issues (inst.), $10/3 issues (ind.); Single issues: $4.50.

Tele: TELEPHONE, Maureen Owen, ed., 109 Dunk Rock Rd., Guildord, CT 06437.
Issues indexed: None received in 1982; Subscriptions: $7/2 issues.

*Telescope: TELESCOPE, Jack Stephens, Julia Wendell, eds., The Galileo Press, P.O. Box 16129, Baltimore, MD 21218.
Issues indexed: (1-3); Subscriptions: $9/yr.; Single issues: $3.50.

Tendril: TENDRIL, George E. Murphy, Jr., ed., Box 512, Green Harbor, MA 02041.
Issues indexed: (12-13); Subscriptions: $15/6 issues, $8/3 issues (ind.); $10/3 issues (inst.); Single issues: $3.

13thM: 13TH MOON, Ellen Marie Bissert, ed., Drawer F, Inwood Station, Inwood, NY 10034.
Issues indexed: None received in 1982; Subscriptions: $17.85/3 issues, $11.90/2 issues; Single issues: $5.95.

ThRiPo: THREE RIVERS POETRY JOURNAL, Gerald Costanzo, ed., Three Rivers Press, Box 21, Carnegie-Mellon U., Pittsburgh, PA 15213.
Issues indexed: None received in 1982; Subscriptions: $5/4 issues; Single issues: $1.50.

Thrpny: THE THREEPENNY REVIEW, Wendy Lesser, ed./pub., P.O. Box 9131, Berkeley, CA 94709.
Issues indexed: (2:4, 3:1-3, issues 8-11); Subscriptions: $10/2 yrs., $6/yr. (ind.); $8/yr (inst.); $10/yr. (for.); Single issues: $2.

TriQ: TRIQUARTERLY, Reginald Gibbons, ed., Northwestern U.,
1735 Benson Ave., Evanston, IL 60201.
Issues indexed: (53-55); Subscriptions: $100/life, $35/3
yrs., $25/2 yrs., $14/yr., plus $3/yr. (for.); Single
issues: $5.95.

*UnderRM: UNDERGROUND RAG MAG, Andy Gunderson, ed., 931 3rd
Ave., S.E., Rochester, MN 55901.
Issues indexed: (1:1-2); Subscriptions: $12/2 yrs.,
$7/yr.; Single issues: $3.50; Sample copy: $1.50.

UnmOx: UNMUZZLED OX, Michael Andre, Erika Rothenberg, eds.,
105 Hudson St., New York, NY 10013.
Issues indexed: None received in 1982; Subscriptions:
$15/8 issues, $9/4 issues; Single issues: $4.95.

US1: US 1 WORKSHEETS, Deborah Boe, Dina Coe, Jack Wiler,
eds., US 1 Poets Cooperative, 21 Lake Dr., Roosevelt, NJ
08555.
Issues indexed: None received in 1982; Subscriptions:
$5/7 issues; Single issues: $1.50; Back issues: Prices on
request.

UTR: UT REVIEW, Duane Locke, ed., U. of Tampa, Tampa, FL
33606. Issues indexed: (7:1-2); To be replaced by ABATIS.

VirQR: VIRGINIA QUARTERLY REVIEW, Staige D. Blackford, ed.,
Gregory Orr, Po. consultant., One West Range, Charlotts-
ville, VA 22903.
Issues indexed: (58:1-4); Subscriptions: $24/3 yrs.,
$18/2 yrs., $10/yr., plus $.50/yr. (Canada), $1/yr.
(elsewhere); Single issues: $3.

Vis: VISIONS, Bradley R. Strahan, ed./pub., Black Buzzard
Press, 5620 South 7th Place, Arlington, VA 22204.
Issues indexed: (8-10); Subscriptions: $7/3 issues; Sing-
le issues: $2.50.

*Waves: WAVES, Bernice Lever, et al., eds., 79 Denham Drive,
Thornhill, Ontario L4J 1P2 Canada.
Issues indexed: (10:3-4, 11:1); Subscriptions: $8/yr.
(ind.), $12/yr. (lib.); Single issues: $3; Back issues:
$1.

WebR: WEBSTER REVIEW, Nancy Shapiro, ed., Webster College,
Webster Groves, MO 63119.
Issues indexed: (7:1-2); Subscriptions: $5/yr.; Single
issues: $2.50.

WestB: WEST BRANCH, Karl Patten, Robert Taylor, eds., Dept.
of English, Bucknell U., Lewisburg, PA 17837.
Issues indexed: (10-11); Subscriptions: $8/2 yrs.,
$5/yr.; Single issues: $2.50.

*WestCR: WEST COAST REVIEW, Fred Candelaria, ed., English
Dept., Simon Fraser U., Burnaby, B.C. V5A 1S6 Canada.
Issues indexed: (16:2/3-4, 17:1-2); Subscriptions:
$10/yr. (Canada), $12.50/yr. (USA, for.), $15/yr.
(inst.); Single issues: $3.50 (Canada), $4 (USA, for.).

WestHR: WESTERN HUMANITIES REVIEW, Jack Garlington, ed., U. of Utah, Salt Lake City, UT 84112.
Issues indexed: (36:1-4); Subscriptions: $20/yr. (inst.), $15/yr. (ind.); Single issues: $4.

Wind: WIND, Quentin R. Howard, ed., RFD Route 1, Box 809K, Pikeville, KY 41501.
Issues indexed: (12:44-46); Subscriptions: $6/3 issues (inst.), $5/3 issues (ind.), $7/3 issues (for.); Single issues: $1.50 (ind.), $1.75 (inst.), $2 (for.).

WindO: THE WINDLESS ORCHARD, Robert Novak, ed., English Dept., Indiana U.-Purdue U., Fort Wayne, IN 46805.
Issues indexed: (40-41); Subscriptions: $20/3 yrs., $7/yr., $4/yr. (stud.); Single issues: $2.

WorldO: WORLD ORDER, Firuz Kazemzadeh, et al., eds., William Stafford, Po. consultant, National Spiritual Assembly of the Baha'is of the United States, 415 Linden Ave., Wilmette, IL 60091.
Issues indexed: (16:2-4, 17:1); Subscriptions: $18/2 yrs., $10/yr.; $22/2 yrs., $12/yr. (for.); Single issues: $3.

WormR: THE WORMWOOD REVIEW, Marvin Malone, ed., P.O. Box 8840, Stockton, CA 95208-0840.
Issues indexed: (22:1-4, issues 85-88); Subscriptions: $15/4 issues (patrons), $6/4 issues (inst.), $5/4 issues (ind.), plus $1.75 (for.); Single issues: $2.

*WritersL: WRITER'S LIFELINE, Stephen Gill, ed., Box 1641, Cornwall, Ontario K6H 5V6 Canada.
Issues indexed: (F-Ap, Je-D '82); Subscriptions: $18/yr; Single issues: $1.50.

YaleR: THE YALE REVIEW, Kai Erikson, ed., William Meredith, Po. ed., 1902A Yale Station, New Haven, CT 06520.
Issues indexed: (71:2-4, 72:1); Subscriptions: $18/yr. (inst.), $12/yr. (ind.), plus $3/yr. (for.); Single issues: $4; Back issues: Prices on request; Yale U. Press, 92A Yale Station, New Haven, CT 06520.

Zahir: ZAHIR, Diane Krunchkow, ed., Weeks Mills, New Sharon, ME 04955.
Issues indexed: None received in 1982; Subscriptions: $4/2 issues (ind.), $6/2 issues (inst.); Single issues: $2.50; Back issues: $2.

ALPHABETICAL LIST OF JOURNALS INDEXED, WITH ACRONYMS

ABRAXAS: Abraxas
ACADEME: Academe
THE AGNI REVIEW: Agni
THE AMERICAN POETRY REVIEW: AmerPoR
THE AMERICAN SCHOLAR: AmerS
ANNEX 21: Annex
ANTAEUS: Antaeus
THE ANTIGONISH REVIEW: AntigR
THE ANTIOCH REVIEW: ANTR
AREITO: Areito
ARIZONA QUARTERLY: ArizQ
THE ARK RIVER REVIEW: ArkRiv
ASCENT: Ascent
ASPECT: Aspect
ASPEN ANTHOLOGY: See ASPEN JOURNAL OF THE ARTS
ASPEN JOURNAL OF THE ARTS: AspenJ
THE ATLANTIC: Atlantic

BALL STATE UNIVERSITY FORMUM: BallSUF
THE BARAT REVIEW: BaratR
THE BELOIT POETRY JOURNAL: BelPoJ
BERKSHIRE REVIEW: BerksR
BLACK AMERICAN LITERATURE FORUM: BlackALF
BLACK WARRIOR REVIEW: BlackWR
BOGG: Bogg
BOUNDARY 2: Bound

CALIBAN: Calib
CALIFORNIA QUARTERLY: CalQ
CANADIAN LITERATURE: CanLit
THE CAPE ROCK: CapeR
THE CAPILANO REVIEW: CapilR
CARIBE: Caribe
CAROLINA QUARTERLY: CarolQ
CATALYST: Catalyst
THE CEA CRITIC: CEACritic
THE CEA FORUM: CEAFor
THE CENTENNIAL REVIEW: CentR
THE CHARITON REVIEW: CharR
CHELSEA: Chelsea
CHICAGO REVIEW: ChiR
THE CHRISTIAN CENTURY: ChrC
CIMARRON RIVIEW: CimR
CLARIDAD: Claridad
COLLEGE ENGLISH: ColEng
COMMONWEAL: Comm
CONCERNING POETRY: ConcPo
CONDITIONS: Cond
CONFRONTATION: Confr

21

CREAM CITY REVIEW: CreamCR
CROP DUST: CropD
CROSS-CANADA WRITERS' QUARTERLY: CrossC
CUTBANK: CutB

DANDELION: Dandel
THE DEKALB LITERARY ARTS JOURNAL: DekalbLAJ
DENVER QUARTERLY: DenQ

EN PASSANT: EnPas
ENGLISH JOURNAL: EngJ
EPOCH: Epoch

FIELD: Field
FOCUS/MIDWEST: Focus
FOUR QUARTERS: FourQt

GARGOYLE MAGAZINE: Gargoyle
GEORGIA REIVEW: GeoR
GERMINATION: Germ
GRAIN: Grain

HANGLING LOOSE: HangL
HARPER'S MAGAZINE: Harp
HIRAM POETRY REVIEW: HiramPoR
THE HOLLINS CRITIC: Hol Crit
THE HUDSON REVIEW: Hudson
THE HUMANIST: Humanist

IMAGES: Images
INTI, REVISTA DE LITERATURA HISPANICA: Inti
IOWA REVIEW: Iowa

KANSAS QUARTERLY: KanQ
KAYAK: Kayak

LETRAS FEMENINAS: LetFem
THE LITERARY REVIEW: LitR
THE LITTLE BALKANS REVIEW: LittleBR
THE LITTLE MAGAZINE: LittleM
THE LITTLE REVIEW: LittleR
LUGAR SIN LIMITE: Lugar

MAIRENA: Mairena
MAIZE: Maize
THE MALAHAT REVIEW: MalR
THE MANHATTAN REVIEW: ManhatR
THE MASSACHUSETTS REVIEW: MassR
THE MEADOWS: Meadows
MENDOCINO REVIEW: MendoR
MESTER: Mester
METAMORFOSIS: Metam
MICHIGAN QUARTERLY REVIEW: MichQR
THE MIDWEST QUARTERLY: MidwQ
THE MINNESOTA REVIEW: MinnR
MISSISSIPPI REVIEW: MissR
THE MISSOURI REVIEW: MissouriR
MODERN POETRY STUDIES: ModernPS
MONTEMORA: Montra
MUNDUS ARTIUM: Mund

THE NATION: <u>Nat</u>
NEW ENGLAND REVIEW AND BREAD LOAF QUARTERLY: <u>NewEngR</u>
NEW LETTERS: <u>NewL</u>
NEW ORLEANS REVIEW: <u>NewOR</u>
THE NEW RENAISSANCE: <u>NewRena</u>
THE NEW REPUBLIC: <u>NewRep</u>
NEW WORLD REVIEW: <u>NewWR</u>
THE NEW YORK REVIEW OF BOOKS: <u>NewYRB</u>
THE NEW YORKER: <u>NewYorker</u>
NIMROD: <u>Nimrod</u>
THE NORTH AMERICAN REVIEW: <u>NoAmR</u>
NORTHEAST: <u>Northeast</u>
NORTHWEST REVIEW: <u>NowestR</u>
NOTICIAS DE ARTE: <u>Notarte</u>

OBSIDIAN: <u>Obs</u>
THE OHIO REIVEW: <u>OhioR</u>
ONTARIO REVIEW: <u>OntR</u>
OPEN PLACES: <u>OP</u>
OSIRIS: <u>Os</u>
OUTERBRIDGE: <u>Outbr</u>

PAINTBRUSH: <u>Paint</u>
THE PARIS REVIEW: <u>ParisR</u>
PARTISAN REVIEW: <u>PartR</u>
PEBBLE: <u>Peb</u>
PEQUOD: <u>Pequod</u>
PIG IRON: <u>Pig</u>
THE PIKESTAFF FORUM: <u>PikeF</u>
THE PIKESTAFF REVIEW: <u>PikeR</u>
PLAYBOY: <u>Playb</u>
PLOUGHSHARES: <u>Ploughs</u>
POEM: <u>Poem</u>
POET AND CRITIC: <u>PoetC</u>
POETRY: <u>Poetry</u>
POETRY CANADA REVIEW: <u>PoetryCR</u>
POETRY EAST: <u>PoetryE</u>
POETRY NORTHWEST: <u>PoetryNW</u>
POETRY NOW: <u>PoNow</u>
PORTLAND REVIEW: <u>PortR</u>
THE POTTERSFIELD PORTFOLIO: <u>PottPort</u>
PRAIRIE SCHOONER: <u>PraS</u>
PRIMAVERA: <u>Prima</u>
PRISMAL/CABRAL: <u>Prismal</u>
PUERTO NORTE Y SUR: <u>Puerto</u>

QUARRY: <u>Quarry</u>
QUARTERLY REVIEW OF LITERATURE: <u>QRL</u>
QUARTERLY WEST: <u>QW</u>

REVISTA CHICANO-RIQUENA: <u>RevChic</u>
REVISTA/REVIEW INTERAMERICANA: <u>RevIn</u>

SALMAGUNDI: <u>Salm</u>
SAMISDAT: <u>Sam</u>
SECOND COMING: <u>SecC</u>
SENECA REVIEW: <u>SenR</u>
THE SEWANEE REVIEW: <u>SewanR</u>
SHENANDOAH: <u>Shen</u>
A SHOUT IN THE STREET: <u>Shout</u>

SIN NOMBRE: <u>SinN</u>
SKYWRITING: <u>Sky</u>
THE SMALL POND MAGAZINE OF LITERATURE: <u>SmPd</u>
SOUTH CAROLINA REVIEW: <u>SoCaR</u>
SOUTH DAKOTA REVIEW: <u>SoDakR</u>
SOUTHERN HUMANITIES REVIEW: <u>SouthernHR</u>
SOUTHERN POETRY REVIEW: <u>SouthernPR</u>
SOUTHERN REVIEW: <u>SouthernR</u>
SOUTHWEST REVIEW: <u>SouthwR</u>
SPARROW: <u>Sparrow</u>
THE SPIRIT THAT MOVES US: <u>Spirit</u>
STAND: <u>Stand</u>
STONE COUNTRY: <u>StoneC</u>
SULFUR: <u>Sulfur</u>
SUN & MOON: <u>SunM</u>

TELEPHONE: <u>Tele</u>
TELESCOPE: <u>Telescope</u>
TENDRIL: <u>Tendril</u>
13TH MOON: <u>13thM</u>
THREE RIVERS POETRY JOURNAL: <u>ThRiPo</u>
THE THREEPENNY REVIEW: <u>Thrpny</u>
TRIQUARTERLY: <u>TriQ</u>

UNDERGROUND RAG MAG: <u>UnderRM</u>
UNMUZZLED OX: <u>UnmOx</u>
URTH-APL: <u>See</u> ASPEN JOURNAL OF THE ARTS
US 1 WORKSHEETS: <u>US1</u>
UT REVIEW: <u>UTR</u>

VIRGINIA QUARTERLY REVIEW: <u>VirQR</u>
VISIONS: <u>Vis</u>

WATER TABLE: <u>WatT</u>
WAVES: <u>Waves</u>
WEBSTER REVIEW: <u>WebR</u>
WEST BRANCH: <u>WestB</u>
WEST COAST REVIEW: <u>WestCR</u>
WESTERN HUMANITIES REVIEW: <u>WestHR</u>
WIND: <u>Wind</u>
THE WINDLESS ORCHARD: <u>WindO</u>
WORLD ORDER: <u>WorldO</u>
THE WORMWOOD REVIEW: <u>WormR</u>
WRITER'S LIFELINE: <u>WritersL</u>

THE YALE REVIEW: <u>YaleR</u>

ZAHIR: <u>Zahir</u>

THE INDEX

1. AAL, Katharyn Machan
   "Purple." _Vis_ (9) 82, p. 19.

2. AARNES, William
   "Going Down to Make Coffee." _SoCaR_ (15:1) Aut 82, p. 21.

3. ABBEY, Lloyd
   "The Fox." _MalR_ (62) Jl 82, p. 101-105.
   "Memory from a Past Life." _MalR_ (62) Jl 82, p. 96-100.

4. ABBOTT, Anthony S.
   "Up the Rabbit Hole." _SouthernPR_ (23, i.e. 22:2) Aut 82, p. 13-14.

5. ABBOTT, Mason
   "Chief." _Bogg_ (48) 82, p. 53.

6. ABERG, W. M.
   "Cymbeline." _Poetry_ (139:5) F 82, p. 285.

7. ABREU-VOLMAR, Cesar
   "Ciudad Sitiada" (A mi hijo, mas alla del llanto). _Mairena_ (4:9) Spr 82, p. 39.
   "Fugitiva Paloma." _Mairena_ (4:9) Spr 82, p. 39.

8. ABSE, Dannie
   "Apology." _GeoR_ (36:3) Aut 82, p. 589.
   "Bedtime Story." _GeoR_ (36:3) Aut 82, p. 588-589.
   "A Winter Visit." _GeoR_ (36:3) Aut 82, p. 590.

9. ACABA, Josefa E.
   "Con las Manos Vacias." _Mairena_ (4:10) Sum-Aut 82, p. 85.

10. ACHUGAR, Hugo
    "Apocaliptico Mortal" (from Soma, 22 textoscotidianos para ser leidos en voz alta). _Prismal_ (7/8) Spr 82, p. 88.
    "Poema de Amor." _Prismal_ (7/8) Spr 82, p. 87.

11. ACKER, A. M.
    "Gigi's Dream." _SouthwR_ (67:3) Sum 82, p. 299.
    "The Window." _SoDakR_ (20:4) Wint 82-83, p. 61-62.

12. ACKER, W. H.
    "Disco." _DekalbLAJ_ (14:1/4) Aut 80-Sum 81, p. 62.

13. ACKERMAN, Diane
    "Underworld." _MichQR_ (21:2) Spr 82, p. 345-346.

14. ACKERMAN, Stephen
    "Flag Days." PartR (49:3) 82, p. 439-440.

15. ACKERSON, Duane
    "A Repair Kit for Prose Poems." PoNow (6:6, issue 36)
    82, p. 12.

16. ACORN, Milton
    "The Conceit of a Raven." CanLit (94) Aut 82, p. 65.
    "The Grackle." CanLit (94) Aut 82, p. 64.
    "Parkdale." CanLit (94) Aut 82, p. 65-66.

17. ACUNA, Carlos
    "Alcon Moco's Ballet" (a border question). Maize
    (5:1/2) Aut-Wint 81-82, p. 33-37.

18. ADAMS, B. B.
    "At the 769th Writers' Workshop." SouthernPR (23,
    i.e. 22:2) Aut 82, p. 67.

19. ADAMS, Betsy
    from Child of Light: "The Beautiful Sister." NowestR
    (20:1) 82, p. 99. Reprinted (20:2/3) 82, p. 226.

20. ADAMS, David
    "Looking at a Map of the Midwest Interurban Lines."
    HiramPoR (32) Spr-Sum 82, p. 6.
    "The Shortest Day of the Year" (for Joan Meehan).
    StoneC (9:3/4) Spr-Sum 82, p. 12-13.

21. ADAMS, David A.
    "Choosing the Cornerstone." WormR (22:4, issue 88)
    82, p. 124-126.

22. ADAMS, Marianne
    "Breakfast" (For Margaret Atwood). KanQ (14:3) Sum 82,
    p. 42.

23. ADAMSON, Arthur
    "Bohemian Waxwings." PoetryCR (4:2) Wint 82, p. 6.

24. ADANG, Richard
    "Giving with One Hand." Outbr (10/11) Aut 82-Spr 83,
    p. 88.
    "In the Attic." HangL (41) 82, p. 3.
    "A Passing Reunion." Outbr (10/11) Aut 82-Spr 83, p.
    89.
    "The Underwater Route." UnderRM (1:2) Aut 82, p. 18.

25. ADCOCK, Fleur
    "A Friendly Warning" (tr. of Peter of Blois). MalR
    (61) F 82, p. 216-217.
    "A New Leaf" (tr. of Peter of Blois). MalR (61) F 82,
    p. 215.
    "A Touch of Impatience" (tr. of Peter of Blois). MalR
    (61) F 82, p. 214.

26. ADDIEGO, John
    "Bicycle Touring to Zydeko in Autumn" (for Cliftin
    Chenier). AspenJ (1) Wint 82, p. 28.

"Charles Ives." Epoch (31:2) Spr 82, p. 127.
"Fats Waller." AspenJ (1) Wint 82, p. 28.
"Rosary." AspenJ (1) Wint 82, p. 28.
"Snake Country." KanQ (14:3) Sum 82, p. 179.

27. ADKINS, Carl A.
    "The Man at Work in the Classroom" (for WRM) KanQ
    (14:2) Spr 82, p. 6.

28. ADKINS, JoAnn Yeager
    "An Introduction." DekalbLAJ (14:1/4) Aut 80-Sum 81,
    p. 101.
    "Sundog Man." DekalbLAJ (14:1/4) Aut 80-Sum 81, p.
    101-102.

29. ADLER, Hans
    "Old Man in October." ChrC (99:30) O 6, 82, p. 975.
    "Retired Farmer in the City Park." ChrC (99:27) S 1-
    8, 82, p. 885.

30. ADNAN, Etel
    "Pablo Neruda Is a Banana Tree." Maize (6:1/2) Aut-
    Wint 82-83, p. 44-47.

31. ADRIAN, Loretta
    "Over the Back Fence." CapeR (17:2) Sum 82, p. 39.

32. ADY, Endre
    "Hawk-Nuptials on Leafmold" (tr. by Bruce Berlind).
    PoNow (6:5, issue 35) 82, p. 44.

    AGHA SHAHID ALI
    See: ALI, Agha Shahid

33. AGOSIN, Margorie
    "Divagaciones." Mairena (4:10) Sum-Aut 82, p. 88.

34. AGRAIT, Gustavo
    "Greguerias sin Cuenta (IV)." Mairena (4:10) Sum-Aut
    82, p. 47-51.

35. AGRICOLA, Sandra
    "Armadillo." OhioR (29) 82, p. 69.
    "Backsliding." OhioR (29) 82, p. 67.
    "The Chore of Death." OhioR (29) 82, p. 77-79.
    "Fish Market." OhioR (29) 82, p. 73.
    "Gently Sinking." OhioR (29) 82, p. 68.
    "Long Shots." OhioR (29) 82, p. 71.
    "Of Grief." OhioR (29) 82, p. 72.
    "One Minute You're Dead to the World." OhioR (29) 82,
    p. 70.
    "Sweet Williams." OhioR (29) 82, p. 74.
    "Viscera." OhioR (29) 82, p. 76.
    "Wishbone." OhioR (29) 82, p. 75.

36. AGUERO, Kathleen
    "Elegy for St. Christopher." HangL (41) 82, p. 4.
    "Leaving the Medical Records Department." HangL (41)
    82, p. 6.
    "Winter Hill Apartment." HangL (41) 82, p. 5.

37. AGUILA, Pancho
    "Before the Aquarians." _Maize_ (6:1/2) Aut-Wint 82-83,
       p. 48.
    "The Ex-Marine." _Maize_ (6:1/2) Aut-Wint 82-83, p. 50.
    "Existential." _Maize_ (6:1/2) Aut-Wint 82-83, p. 49.
    "Folsom." _Maize_ (6:1/2) Aut-Wint 82-83, p. 51.

38. AGUILAR MORA, Jorge
    "Un Hermano Mas Sabio Que Mi Mano." _Prismal_ (7/8) Spr
       82, p. 86.

39. AGYEYA
    "Concerning Love" (tr. by the author). _NewL_ (48:3/4)
       Spr-Sum 82, p. 42.
    "The Dissenter" (tr. by the author). _NewL_ (48:3/4)
       Spr-Sum 82, p. 42.
    "Friendship" (tr. by the author). _NewL_ (48:3/4) Spr-
       Sum 82, p. 43.
    "Heroes" (tr. by the author). _NewL_ (48:3/4) Spr-Sum
       82, p. 43.
    "June Night" (tr. by the author). _NewL_ (48:3/4) Spr-
       Sum 82, p. 43.
    "Near and Far." _NewL_ (49:2) Wint 82-83, p. 48-49.

40. AHEARN, Catherine
    "Lone Hermit." _PoetryCR_ (4:1) Sum 82, p. 4.

41. AHMED, K. S. Nisar
    "A Lesson" (tr. by S. K. Desai). _NewL_ (48:3/4) Spr-Sum
       82, p. 235.

42. AI
    "The Priest's Confession." _Agni_ (17) 82, p. 53-56.

    AI, Qing
    See: QING, Ai

43. AICHINGER, Ilse
    "March" (tr. by Beth Bjorklund). _LitR_ (25:2) Wint 82,
       p. 208.

44. AIKEN, William
    "Is." _PoNow_ (7:1, issue 37) 82, p. 1.

45. AISENBERG, Nadya
    "Wreaths to the Temple." _Agni_ (17) 82, p. 24.

46. AJAY, Stephen
    "Coming to in Hawaii." _PoNow_ (6:4, issue 34) 82, p.
       29.
    "Daughter and Father." _Confr_ (24) Sum 82, p. 65.
    "The Easiest Magic" (For Anne). _HolCrit_ (19:3) Je 82,
       p. 19-20.
    "The Whales Are Burning" (for Barry Lopez). _Confr_ (23)
       Wint 82, p. 70-72.

47. AKERS, Ellery
    "The Case for Solace" (Port Townsend, Washington).
       Ploughs (8:2/3) 82, p. 171.

"Christmas Morning without Presents: The Depression,
Granite City, Illinois." Ploughs (8:2/3) 82, p.
170.
"The Dead." Ploughs (8:2/3) 82, p. 169.
"Sky." Ploughs (8:2/3) 82, p. 172-173.

48. AKHMADULINA, Bella
"Winter Day" (tr. by Mary Maddock). LitR (26:1) Aut
82, p. 102.
"Zhaleyka" (tr. by Mary Maddock). LitR (26:1) Aut 82,
p. 103-104.

49. AKHMATOVA, Anna
"I Possess" (tr. by Leonard Opalov). Spirit (6:2/3)
82, p. 187.
"In the High Stars" (tr. by Marija Maddock and Willis
Barnstone). NewL (48:2) Wint 81-82, p. 51.
"It's All Been Taken Away" (tr. by Mary Maddock). DenQ
(17:2) Sum 82, p. 122.

50. Al-MUTANABBI, Abu Tayyib
"On His Imprisonment" (tr. by Arthur Wormhoudt). Paint
(9:17/18) Spr-Aut 82, p. 30-31.

ALBA, Alice Gaspar de
See: GASPAR de ALBA, Alice

51. ALBERT, Samuel L.
"Hockey." PoNow (6:4, issue 34) 82, p. 45.
"Weight-Lifter." PoNow (6:4, issue 34) 82, p. 45.

52. ALDAN, Daisy
"Goodbye Lost City." Im (8:1) 82, p. 5.

53. ALEGRIA, Claribel
"Requiem." Maize (6:1/2) Aut-Wint 82-83, p. 92-93.

54. ALESHIRE, Joan
"Cloud Train." PoNow (7:1, issue 37) 82, p. 21.
"Learning Not to Love You." Tendril (12) Wint 82, p.
9.
"Marina Tsvetayeva." PoNow (7:1, issue 37) 82, p. 21.
"Museum of Natural History." Tendril (12) Wint 82, p.
10-11.

55. ALEXANDER, Charlotte
"Amaryllis in February." WestCR (16:4) Ap 82, p. 16.
"A Feeling of Nakedness." WestCR (16:4) Ap 82, p. 14.
"Necessities." WestCR (16:4) Ap 82, p. 15.
"Preparations." WestCR (16:4) Ap 82, p. 13.

56. ALEXANDER, Hannah
"An Interview with the Princess Cinderella." Vis (8)
82, p. 33-35.

57. ALEXANDER, Meena
"House of a Thousand Doors." NewL (48:3/4) Spr-Sum
82, p. 252.

58. ALEXIS, Austin
     "Broadcast." PoNow (7:1, issue 37) 82, p. 1.
     "Handicap." PoNow (7:1, issue 37) 82, p. 1.
     "I Bought a Black Dress." Shout (3:1) 82, p. 48.

59. ALGARIN, Miguel
     "Albuquerque." RevChic (10:1/2) Wint-Spr 82, p. 13-
       14.
     "El Jibarito Moderno." RevChic (10:1/2) Wint-Spr 82,
       p. 7.
     "Paris." RevChic (10:1/2) Wint-Spr 82, p. 15-19.
     "Paterson." RevChic (10:1/2) Wint-Spr 82, p. 8-9.
     "Taos Pueblo Indians: 700 Strong According to Bobby's
       Last Census." RevChic (10:1/2) Wint-Spr 82, p. 10-
       12.

60. ALI, Agha Shahid
     "Ghazal" (tr. of Faiz Ahmed Faiz). Kayak (60) O 82, p.
       25.
     "Ghazal #2" (tr. of Faiz Ahmed Faiz). DenQ (17:2) Sum
       82, p. 75.
     "Ghazal #3" (tr. of Faiz Ahmed Faiz). DenQ (17:2) Sum
       82, p. 76.
     "Ghazal #4" (tr. of Faiz Ahmed Faiz). DenQ (17:2) Sum
       82, p. 77.
     "Ghazal #6" (tr. of Faiz Ahmed Faiz). DenQ (17:2) Sum
       82, p. 78.
     "Ghazal: In the Sahara of longing" (tr. of Faiz Ahmad
       Faiz). Paint (9:17/18) Spr-Aut 82, p. 29.
     "Ghazal: Let me again assess my destiny" (tr. of Faiz
       Ahmad Faiz). Paint (9:17/18) Spr-Aut 82, p. 28.
     "Glass Bangles." BelPoJ (33:2) Wint 82-83, p. 2.
     "In the Mountains." BelPoJ (33:2) Wint 82-83, p. 3-4.
     "An Interview with Red Riding Hood, Now No Longer
       Little." MissouriR (6:1) Aut 82, p. 22-23.
     "Prayer Rug." BelPoJ (33:2) Wint 82-83, p. 4-5.
     "Refugee." SouthernPR (22:1) Spr 82, p. 50.
     "Survivor." BelPoJ (33:2) Wint 82-83, p. 2.
     "To Evanescence." SouthernPR (22:1) Spr 82, p. 51.
     "The Wolf's Postscript to 'Little Red Riding Hood'."
       MissouriR (6:1) Aut 82, p. 24.

61. ALKALAY, Karen
     "Deflections." WebR (7:1) Spr 82, p. 57-59.

62. ALLAN, Pat
     "Landscape." Dandel (9:1) 82, p. 74.

63. ALLDRED, Pauline
     "River Picture." HiramPoR (31) Aut-Wint 82, p. 5.

64. ALLEN, Dick
     "Dignity." Poetry (140:5) Ag 82, p. 286.
     "Grandfather's Jigsaw Puzzle." Poetry (140:5) Ag 82,
       p. 285.
     "Janes Avenue." Poetry (140:5) Ag 82, p. 284.
     "Young Poet's Lament." CutB (19) Aut-Wint 82, p. 35.

65. ALLEN, Elizabeth
     "Gerda." Grain (10:2) My 82, p. 32.

66. ALLEN, Gilbert
    "The Gifts." KanQ (14:3) Sum 82, p. 120.
    "The Man Who Buries Animals." SouthernHR (16:3) Sum
        82, p. 233.
    "Southern Fall." Wind (12:44) 82, p. 1-2.
    "This Day." PoNow (7:1, issue 37) 82, p. 1.

67. ALLEN, John
    "A Fleck of Salt." StoneC (9:3/4) Spr-Sum 82, p. 62.
    "Gloucester." StoneC (9:3/4) Spr-Sum 82, p. 62.
    "Reservoir." Os (14) 82, p. 26-28.
    "Suddenly." Os (14) 82, p. 9.

68. ALLEN, W. S.
    "Like a Cougar from Behind." SmPd (19:2, issue 55)
        Spr 82, p. 22.
    "Song of Sandpoiser." SmPd (19:2, issue 55) Spr 82,
        p. 29.

69. ALLGREN, Joe
    "Rose Predicts the Plague." Pig (8) 80, p. 90.

70. ALLMAN, John
    "Georgia O'Keefe Takes Over the Old Hacienda in
        Abiquiu, New Mexico" (1945). PoNow (6:6, issue 36)
        82, p. 44.
    "Marcus Garvey Arrested at the 125th Street Station."
        Agni (17) 82, p. 50-51.
    "Meeting You." PoetryNW (23:3) Aut 82, p. 45.
    "Turning to and from the Soul." PoetryNW (23:3) Aut
        82, p. 44.
    "The Wright Brothers at Kill Devil Hills." PoetryNW
        (23:3) Aut 82, p. 43-44.

    ALMASI SIDU JITU
    See: JITU, Almasi Sidu

71. ALMEDA, Lisa
    "Figures: The Language of Sight." Sam (33:3, issue
        131) 82, p. 30.

72. ALMON, Bert
    "Fog, Bridge, Flute Sonata." BelPoJ (32:3) Spr 82, p.
        1.

    ALONSO, Agustin Garcia
    See: GARCIA ALONSO, Agustin

73. ALONSO, Damaso
    "Search for Light: A Prayer" (tr. by Patrick Hugh
        Sheerin). LitR (25:3) Spr 82, p. 340-341.

74. ALTER, Michael
    "Sadie and God." HiramPoR (33) Aut-Wint 82, p. 6.

75. ALTIZER, Nell
    "Night Music." Tendril (13) Sum 82, p. 9.
    "Sea." Tendril (13) Sum 82, p. 10.

76. ALTMANN, Rene
    "Late Fall" (tr. by Beth Bjorklund). LitR (25:2) Wint
    82, p. 252.
    "When Will the Bird Cry Again?" (tr. by Beth
    Bjorklund). LitR (25:2) Wint 82, p. 252.

77. ALTSCHUL, Fernando
    "The Siren Rang." Maize (6:1/2) Aut-Wint 82-83, p.
    62.

78. ALURISTA
    "Cornfields Thaw Out." RevChic (10:1/2) Wint-Spr 82,
    p. 21.
    "Do U Remember." RevChic (10:1/2) Wint-Spr 82, p. 20.
    "En." Maize (6:1/2) Aut-Wint 82-83, p. 89.
    "Scratching Six, Plucking One." RevChic (10:1/2)
    Wint-Spr 82, p. 22-23.

79. ALVAREZ, Ernesto
    from Semiramis: (3). Mairena (4:9) Spr 82, p. 76.

80. ALVAREZ, Griselda
    "Ants" (tr. by Elizabeth Bartlett). WebR (7:1) Spr 82,
    p. 36.
    "Garden" (tr. by Elizabeth Bartlett). WebR (7:1) Spr
    82, p. 37.
    "Leaves" (tr. by Elizabeth Bartlett). WebR (7:1) Spr
    82, p. 37.
    "Worms" (tr. by Elizabeth Bartlett). WebR (7:1) Spr
    82, p. 36.

81. ALVAREZ, Julia
    "Heroics." Poetry (140:2) My 82, p. 87-88.
    "New Clothes." Poetry (140:2) My 82, p. 89-90.

82. ALVAREZ CALLE, Manuel
    "Oda a la Muerta" (Fragmentos). Mairena (4:10) Sum-Aut
    82, p. 89-90.

83. AMABILE, George
    "Anima (1)." PoetryCR (3:4) Sum 82, p. 8.
    "Anima (2)." PoetryCR (3:4) Sum 82, p. 8-9.
    "Anima (3)." PoetryCR (3:4) Sum 82, p. 9.
    "Deep Language." PoetryCR (3:4) Sum 82, p. 9.
    "Mystique." Quarry (31:1) Wint 82, p. 51-52.
    "Oil Rig." Quarry (31:1) Wint 82, p. 51.

84. AMICHAI, Yehuda
    "A Wild Peace." Nat (234:23) Je 12, 82, p. 727.

85. AMIS, George
    "Cremation Facility with Solar Energy" (found poem).
    Kayak (58) Ja 82, p. 14.

86. AMJAD, Majid
    "Urban Expansion" (tr. by S. R. Faruqi and F. W.
    Pritchett). NewL (48:3/4) Spr-Sum 82, p. 214.

87. AMMONS, A. R.
    "Meeting Place." Poetry (141:1) O 82, p. 3-4.

"Singling and Doubling Together." Poetry (141:1) O
82, p. 1-2.
"Yadkin Picnic" (For Jane and Pat Kelly). Poetry
(141:1) O 82, p. 4.

88. AMPRIMOZ, Alexandre L.
"Colonial Wars." CanLit (95) Wint 82, p. 101.
"Oily." KanO (14:1) Wint 82, p. 42.

89. ANAGNOSTAKIS, Manolis
"A Day Will Come" (tr. by Martin McKinsey). Chelsea
(41) 82, p. 126.
"The Great Decisions" (tr. by Martin McKinsey).
Chelsea (41) 82, p. 122.
"Not This Way" (tr. by Martin McKinsey). Chelsea (41)
82, p. 124.
"Now, I Speak Again" (tr. by Martin McKinsey). Chelsea
(41) 82, p. 123.
"There Is Not the Many" (tr. by Martin McKinsey).
Chelsea (41) 82, p. 125.

90. ANANTHAMURTHY, U. R.
"The Gipsy Girl" (tr. by S. K. Desai). NewL (48:3/4)
Spr-Sum 82, p. 149.

91. ANAPOLSLAY, Daisy
"Untitled: In the valley of time." MendoR (5) Sum 81,
p. 67.

92. ANASTAS, Charles Grace
"Always Stone." Hangl (43) Wint 82-83, p. 52.

93. ANAWROK, Edgar
"Silent Bird." NewL (49:1) Aut 82, p. 27.

94. ANDERSDATTER, Karla M.
"To Catch a Midnight Ferry." Shout (3:1) 82, p. 13.

95. ANDERSON, Barbara
"There and Here." Iowa (12:2/3) Spr-Sum 81, p. 1-2.

96. ANDERSON, Bruce B.
"Poem for the Governess at the Appleyard School."
Agni (17) 82, p. 10-11.

97. ANDERSON, David
"Glistening." Pig (8) 80, p. 31.
"In the Moonlight." Pig (10) 82, p. 47.

98. ANDERSON, Elizabeth M.
"What Matters It?" LittleBR (2:3) Spr 82, p. 29.

99. ANDERSON, Erland
"Against the Anniversary of Our Extinction" (closely
after W.S. Merwin and for Jonathan Schell). PortR
(28:2) 82, p. 1.
"Let's Never Try Love" (tr. of Luis Cernuda). PortR
(28:2) 82, p. 2.

100. ANDERSON, H. M.
        "Holiday." <u>PoetryCR</u> (4:1) Sum 82, p. 5.

101. ANDERSON, Harry M.
        "On Hearing the News." <u>PoetryCR</u> (3:4) Sum 82, p. 15.

102. ANDERSON, Jack
        "Conversation with Cats in It." <u>PoNow</u> (6:5, issue
        35) 82, p. 15.
        "The Demonstration." <u>PoNow</u> (6:5, issue 35) 82, p.
        15.
        "Good Morning." <u>HangL</u> (41) 82, p. 7.
        "Memorials." <u>Im</u> (8:2) 82, p. 8.
        "The Power of Healing." <u>PoNow</u> (6:5, issue 35) 82, p.
        15.
        "Sleepless Night." <u>PoNow</u> (6:5, issue 35) 82, p. 14.
        "Tar Bubbles." <u>Im</u> (8:2) 82, p. 8.
        "Time and Motion." <u>HangL</u> (41) 82, p. 8-9.
        "The Title of This Poem Comes at the End." <u>LittleM</u>
        (13:3/4) 82, p. 69.

103. ANDERSON, Jon
        "American Landscape with Clouds & a Zoo." <u>Antaeus</u>
        (47) Aut 82, p. 21-22.
        "Falling in Love" (Vivian). <u>Antaeus</u> (47) Aut 82, p.
        25-26.
        "A Globe of Snow" (for William Matthews). <u>Antaeus</u>
        (47) Aut 82, p. 23-24.
        "Sonnet / Thinking of Death / 1955." <u>Antaeus</u> (47)
        Aut 82, p. 27.

104. ANDERSON, Maggie
        "Far." <u>AmerPoR</u> (11:2) Mr-Ap 82, p. 7.
        "Palimpsest." <u>AmerPoR</u> (11:2) Mr-Ap 82, p. 7.

105. ANDERSON, Martin
        "Leaves in Late October." <u>Waves</u> (11:1) Aut 82, p.
        74.

106. ANDERSON, Michael (Michael P.)
        "The bell rings: I answer the door." <u>MendoR</u> (6) Sum
        81, p. 78.
        "Listening to songs long since played out." <u>MendoR</u>
        (6) Sum 81, p. 78.
        "The Salt Talks Come Home." <u>CapeR</u> (18:1) Wint 82, p.
        24-25.

107. ANDERSON, Nathalie
        "Mystery." <u>CimR</u> (60) Jl 82, p. 48.

108. ANDERSON, Nina Duval
        "The Alanna Rose Rose Case" (pending in the small
        claims court). <u>Annex</u> (3) 81, p. 40.
        "Apple!" <u>Annex</u> (3) 81, p. 16.
        "At the Village Dump." <u>Annex</u> (3) 81, p. 32-33.
        "The Auroscope Came, It Doesn't Work." <u>Annex</u> (3) 81,
        p. 30-31.
        "The Benson Branch." <u>Annex</u> (3) 81, p. 33.
        "Blending into the Beige Background." <u>Annex</u> (3) 81,
        p. 18.

"Cardinal! Cardinal!" Annex (3) 81, p. 17-18.
"Children's Art." Annex (3) 81, p. 20-21.
"Coming Down with the Flu." Annex (3) 81, p. 23-24.
"Conspiracy." Annex (3) 81, p. 31.
"Domiciles." Annex (3) 81, p. 32.
"A Double Separation." Annex (3) 81, p. 21.
"Drawing a Will." Annex (3) 81, p. 24-25.
"Elves." Annex (3) 81, p. 19-20.
"Empty Threats." Annex (3) 81, p. 26-27.
"Eurydice's New Cherry Preserves." Annex (3) 81, p.
    39.
"For Zora Cleatte." Annex (3) 81, p. 27.
"Haikus." Annex (3) 81, p. 38.
"The Heavy Stepper." Annex (3) 81, p. 21-22.
"Hymn to Both Hims." Annex (3) 81, p. 22-23.
"I Think Spasmodically of Those." Annex (3) 81, p.
    35-36.
"If I Were." Annex (3) 81, p. 37.
"In a Pine Forest." Annex (3) 81, p. 17.
"Knitting Lesson." Annex (3) 81, p. 36-37.
"Lest We Settle for Less." Annex (3) 81, p. 30.
"New Townhouse Complex Edging the Forest." Annex (3)
    81, p. 29.
"Old Superstitions for New." Annex (3) 81, p. 34.
"Peonies." Annex (3) 81, p. 19.
"Second Thoughts." Annex (3) 81, p. 26.
"Sunset Witnessed by a Cook." Annex (3) 81, p. 34-
    35.
"To the Last Offspring." Annex (3) 81, p. 38.
"Tracing Winter Animals." Annex (3) 81, p. 41.
"The Whistler." Annex (3) 81, p. 28.

109. ANDRADE, Carlos Drummond de
     "Busqueda de la Poesia" (tr. by Teodosio Munoz
        Molina). Mairena (4:10) Sum-Aut 82, p. 64-65.
     "In the Golden Age" (tr. by Mark Strand). NewYorker
        (58:38) N 8, 82, p. 40.
     "Looking for Poetry" (tr. by Mark Strand). Antaeus
        (44) Wint 82, p. 89-90.

110. ANDRADE, Eugenio de
     "Ariadne" (tr. by Alexis Levitin). PoNow (6:4, issue
        34) 82, p. 42.
     "Dissonances" (tr. by Alexis Levitin). NewOR (9:3)
        Wint 82, p. 62.
     "Litany" (tr. by Alexis Levitin). PoetryE (8) Aut 82,
        p. 76.
     "Metamorphosis of the House" (tr. by Alexis Levitin).
        PortR (28:1) 82, p. 63.
     "Penniless Lovers" (tr. by Alexis Levitin). MissR
        (10:3, issue 30) Wint-Spr 82, p. 44.
     "Three or Four Syllables" (tr. by Alexis Levitin).
        PoetryE (8) Aut 82, p. 77.
     "To My Mother" (tr. by Alexis Levitin). PoetryE (8)
        Aut 82, p. 78-79.

     ANDRADE, Jorge Carrera
     See: CARRERA ANDRADE, Jorge

111. ANDREA, Marianne
     "The Age" (tr. of Osip Mandelstam). DenQ (16:4) Wint
        82, p. 47.
     "History of a Meeting." Wind (12:45) 82, p. 2-3.
     "Night Walk" (for B.D.). Wind (12:45) 82, p. 1-2.

112. ANDRESEN, Sophia de Mello Breyner
     "Initial" (tr. by Alexis Levitin). PraS (56:1) Spr
        82, p. 38.
     "Lately" (tr. by Alexis Levitin). PraS (56:1) Spr 82,
        p. 39.
     "The Murder of Simonetta Vespucci" (tr. by Alexis
        Levitin). PraS (56:1) Spr 82, p. 38-39.
     "A Pale Winter" (tr. by Alexis Levitin). PortR (28:1)
        82, p. 34.
     "Summer Days" (tr. by Alexis Levitin). DenQ (17:1)
        Spr 82, p. 84.
     "The Tragic Poet" (tr. by Alexis Levitin). PortR
        (28:1) 82, p. 34.

113. ANDREWS, David
     "Old frog pond." WindO (40, Anti-Haiku issue) Sum
        82, p. 5.

114. ANDROLA, Ron
     "Country-Sketch." Gargoyle (15/16) 80, p. 49.
     "A Harrison Fisher Poem." Bogg (48) 82, p. 25.
     "In the Photograph" (for Gretchen). Bogg (49) 82, p.
        7.
     "Position." Bogg (48) 82, p. 31.

115. ANGEL, Ralph
     "Not to Reach Great Heights, But to Stay out of Great
        Valleys." PartR (49:3) 82, p. 432-433.

116. ANGELL, Barbara
     "Deer Season." Shout (3:1) 82, p. 77.
     "What Is." Shout (3:1) 82, p. 78.

117. ANGELL, Roger
     "Greetings, Friends!" NewYorker (58:45) D 27, 82, p.
        41.

118. ANGIOLIERI, Cecco
     "Advice to a Courtly Lover" (tr. by Felix Stefanile).
        Sparrow (43) 82, p. 26.
     "A Critique of Dante" (tr. by Felix Stefanile).
        Sparrow (43) 82, p. 27.
     "On Family Quarrels" (tr. by Felix Stefanile).
        Sparrow (43) 82, p. 18.

119. ANGLESEY, Zoe
     "Letter Sent from Guatemala Postmarked Panama
        December 7, 1981." StoneC (10:1/2) Aut-Wint 82-
        83,p. 82-83.
     "Presidents of Our World" (For Roque Dalton). MinnR
        (NS19) Aut 82, p. 21-22.
     "Swede Carlson's House." MinnR (NS19) Aut 82, p. 23.

120. ANGST, Bim
        "Banks" (from The Spirit of St. Louis). BaratR (8:2)
        Wint 81, p. 74.
        "Bobby Dalvet's Fighting Cocks." PoNow (7:1, issue
        37) 82, p. 1.
        "Le Bourget" (from The Spirit of St. Louis). BaratR
        (8:2) Wint 81, p. 75.
        "Land" (from The Spirit of St. Louis). BaratR (8:2)
        Wint 81, p. 75.
        "Sleep" (from The Spirit of St. Louis). BaratR (8:2)
        Wint 81, p. 74.
        "Visitors" (from The Spirit of St. Louis). BaratR
        (8:2) Wint 81, p. 74.

121. ANONYMOUS
        "All to myself I think of you." MendoR (5) Sum 81,
        p. 9.
        "Breakages" (tr. by Graeme Wilson). WestHR (36:1) Spr
        82, p. 24.
        "By the Han and the Yangtze" (tr. by Zuxin Ding and
        Burton Raffel). DenQ (17:2) Sum 82, p. 90.
        "Conversation among Five Frescoed Warrior Saints"
        (tr. by William McLaughlin). CapeR (17:2) Sum 82,
        p. 29.
        "The Drum Thunders" (tr. by Zuxin Ding and Burton
        Raffel). DenQ (17:2) Sum 82, p. 91.
        "In a Little Village" (folksong, collected by Patty
        Farris Kuhel). LittleBR (2:3) Spr 82, p. 18-20.
        "North Hill" (tr. by Zuxin Ding and Burton Raffel).
        DenQ (17:2) Sum 82, p. 92.
        "To Our Special Anonymous Patron of Issue #41."
        WindO (41) Aut-Wint 82-83, p. 3.

122. ANSON, John
        "The Broken Lamp." Thrpny (11) Aut 82, p. 8.
        "For My Son." Thrpny (8) Wint 82, p. 12.

123. APARICIO, Frances
        from Song of Madness: (Fragments) (tr. of Francisco
        Matos Paoli). Mairena (4:11/12) Wint 82, p. 39-51.

124. APPEL, Cathy
        "Enormous Appetites and Small Dinners Keep Us Awake
        Nights." Tendril (13) Sum 82, p. 11.

125. APPLEMAN, Philip
        "How My Light Is Spent." Nat (235:9) S 25, 82, p.
        282.
        "Reading Our Times." LitR (25:4) Sum 82, p. 502-504.

126. APPLETON, Sarah
        from Book of My Hunger, Book of the Earth: "I stand
        here." Iowa (12:2/3) Spr-Sum 81, p. 5-6.
        from Book of My Hunger, Book of the Earth: "It is
        this way the work builds." Iowa (12:2/3) Spr-Sum
        81, p. 3.
        from Book of My Hunger, Book of the Earth: "Knock,
        listen The harsh fly shines The beetle rubs." Iowa
        (12:2/3) Spr-Sum 81, p. 3.

from Book of My Hunger, Book of the Earth: "Now I see myself making the stars." Iowa (12:2/3) Spr-Sum 81, p. 4.
from Book of My Hunger, Book of the Earth: "The teachers of my child have forgotten memory." Iowa (12:2/3) Spr-Sum 81, p. 5.
from Book of My Hunger, Book of the Earth: "The thrust of life within into the world, gathering the world." Iowa (12:2/3) Spr-Sum 81, p. 4.
from Book of My Hunger, Book of the Earth: "Where is my body falling, quick, catch it!" Iowa (12:2/3) Spr-Sum 81, p. 4.
from Book of My Hunger, Book of the Earth: "Who has lifted the pen!" Iowa (12:2/3) Spr-Sum 81, p. 5.

127. APPLEWHITE, James
"Beyond the Romantic Destination." VirQR (58:1) Wint 82, p. 67-68.

128. APTER, Ronnie
"Poem: Then this will be forgotten." StoneC (10:1/2) Aut-Wint 82-83, p. 20.

AQUINO, Luis Hernandez
See: HERNANDEZ AQUINO, Luis

129. ARANA SOTO, Salvador
"Preferencias" (from Primeros Versos). Mairena (4:9) Spr 82, p. 77.

130. ARCHER, Anne
"Islam." Quarry (31:4) Aut 82, p. 44.
"Tell me the secret of your wedding band." Quarry (31:4) Aut 82, p. 43.

131. ARDINGER, Richard
"After a Long Journey." CapeR (18:1) Wint 82, p. 14.
"Woman of the Blue Cape Vs the Illustrated Man." Pig (9) 82, p. 70.

ARELLANO, Olga Ramirez de
See: RAMIREZ de ARELLANO, Olga

132. ARENAS, Bibi
"Poesia II" (from Motivos de Poeta). Mairena (4:10) Sum-Aut 82, p. 91.

133. ARENAS, Braulio
"Heart" (tr. by Mary Crow). DenQ (16:4) Wint 82, p. 42.

134. ARENAS, Rosa Maria
"Young Men/Her Brothers." LittleM (13:3/4) 82, p. 29-30.

AREVALO, Marta de
See: ISIS

135. ARGUELLES, Ivan
"Alexandria." Kayak (58) Ja 82, p. 23.

"Andre Breton Enters Heaven." Kayak (60) O 82, p. 7-
8.
"The Conquest of Mexico." RevChic (10:1/2) Wint-Spr
82, p. 26.
"The Cuban Decision." RevChic (10:1/2) Wint-Spr 82,
p. 27.
"El Dorado." Abraxas (25/26) 82, p. 15.
"Echoes of Life." Maize (5:1/2) Aut-Wint 81-82, p.
92.
"Ecstase du Jour." Abraxas (25/26) 82, p. 16.
"Election Day." Abraxas (25/26) 82, p. 16.
"Maquina de Coser." RevChic (10:1/2) Wint-Spr 82, p.
28.
"Modern Mexico." RevChic (10:1/2) Wint-Spr 82, p.
25.
"Mr Gonzalez Makes a Speech." RevChic (10:1/2) Wint-
Spr 82, p. 29.
"Republica Mexicana." RevChic (10:1/2) Wint-Spr 82,
p. 24.
"The Siege of Constantinople." Kayak (58) Ja 82, p.
27.
"Silhouette." Os (15) 82, p. 8.
"Summary." Os (15) 82, p. 7.

136. ARMAND, Octavio
"Blind Man's Dream" (tr. by Carol Maier). NewOR (9:2)
Aut 82, p. 56-57.
"Braille for Left Hand" (To My Translator, tr. by
Carol Maier). NewOR (9:1) Spr-Sum 82, p. 77.

137. ARMAS, Jose R. de
"The First Flower" (tr. of Carmen Conde, w. Alexis
Levitin). WebR (7:2) Aut 82, p. 23.
"First Night on Earth" (from Mujer sin Eden, tr. of
Carmen Conde, w. Alexis Levitin). PraS (56:1) Spr
82, p. 40-41.
"Fourth Canto" (tr. of Carmen Conde, w. Alexis
Levitin). Confr (24) Sum 82, p. 78.
"Prayer" (tr. of Carmen Conde, w. Alexis Levitin).
WebR (7:2) Aut 82, p. 24.
"Premonition" (tr. of Carmen Conde, w. Alexis
Levitin). Confr (24) Sum 82, p. 79.
"Voice of the Old Eve in Mary" (tr. of Carmen Conde,
w. Alexis Levitin). WebR (7:2) Aut 82, p. 22.

138. ARMSTRONG, James
"Rancher's Death." KanQ (14:3) Sum 82, p. 94-95.

139. ARNDT, Walter
"Before the Summer Rain" (tr. of Rainer Maria Rilke).
NewEngR (4:3) Spr 82, p. 346-347.
"The Courtesan" (tr. of Rainer Maria Rilke). NewEngR
(4:3) Spr 82, p. 348.
"Death of the Poet" (tr. of Rainer Maria Rilke).
NewEngR (4:3) Spr 82, p. 347-348.
"The Poet" (tr. of Rainer Maria Rilke). NewEngR (4:3)
Spr 82, p. 347.
"Spring Fragment (Paris)" (tr. of Rainer Maria
Rilke). NewEngR (4:3) Spr 82, p. 346.

140. ARNETT, Carroll
    "September." Telescope (2) Aut 81, p. 10.
    "Song of the Breed." Telescope (2) Aut 81, p. 76.
    "Travel Notes: Calumet to Mecosta." Telescope (2)
        Aut 81, p. 73-75.

141. ARNETT, Marie
    "Prerogative of Gender." SmPd (19:1, issue 54) Wint
        82, p. 31.
    "Sequoia." SmPd (19:2, issue 55) Spr 82, p. 29.

142. ARNOLD, Bob
    "December." Ploughs (8:2/3) 82, p. 258.
    "Ghosts." Ploughs (8:2/3) 82, p. 257.
    "Loss." Ploughs (8:2/3) 82, p. 258.
    "Passing." Ploughs (8:2/3) 82, p. 256.

143. ARNOLD, Les
    "Emigrant." Grain (10:3) Ag 82, p. 53.
    "The Hare." Grain (10:3) Ag 82, p. 52.

144. ARRILLAGA, Maria
    "Escuchando la Novena Sinfonia de Beethoven."
        Mairena (4:10) Sum-Aut 82, p. 86.
    "Melancolica camino cogiendo fresco, aire, calor"
        (from Frescura 1981). Mairena (4:9) Spr 82, p. 79.

145. ARROWSMITH, William
    "Buffalo" (tr. of Eugenio Montale). Pequod (15) 82,
        p. 108.
    "Keepsake" (tr. of Eugenio Montale). Pequod (15) 82,
        p. 109.

146. ARTMANN, H. C.
    "Now look here..!" (tr. by Beth Bjorklund). LitR
        (25:2) Wint 82, p. 209.

147. ARVEY, Michael
    "At the Creek." MendoR (6) Sum 81, p. 31.
    "Leaves are greener near the water." MendoR (6) Sum
        81, p. 57.

148. ARVIDSON, Ted
    "After the Magicians Picnic." StoneC (10:1/2) Aut-
        Wint 82-83, p. 46-47.

149. ARZOLA BARRIS, Miguel A.
    "A Ella." Mairena (4:10) Sum-Aut 82, p. 95-96.

150. ASBRIDGE, N. S.
    "Pas Devant les Enfants." Bogg (48) 82, p. 27.

151. ASHANTI, Asa Paschal
    "Grand Central Station." BlackALF (16:2) Sum 82, p.
        72.
    "Judith-Ester's Song." BlackALF (16:2) Sum 82, p.
        73.
    "Land of the Heart." BlackALF (16:2) Sum 82, p. 72.
    "The Live Lecturer" (for John Williams). BlackALF
        (16:2) Sum 82, p. 73.

"Madison Square Garden." BlackALF (16:2) Sum 82, p.
    73.
"The Perfect Poem." BlackALF (16:2) Sum 82, p. 73.
"Somehow." BlackALF (16:2) Sum 82, p. 72.

152. ASHBERY, John
    "37 Haiku." Sulfur (2:2, issue 5) 82, p. 100-101.
    "Landscape (after Baudelaire)." NewYRB (29:5) Ap 1,
        82, p. 4.
    "Never Seek to Tell Thy Love." NewYorker (58:23) Jl
        26, 82, p. 40.
    "Night Life." PoNow (6:4, issue 34) 82, p. 23.
    "Proust's Questionnaire." NewYorker (58:1) F 22, 82,
        p. 44.
    "Shadow Train." PoNow (6:4, issue 34) 82, p. 23.
    "So Many Lives." Sulfur (2:2, issue 5) 82, p. 102-
        103.

153. ASHE, Lynn
    "Goongapocks sloof their way." DekalbLAJ (14:1/4)
        Aut 80-Sum 81, p. 63.

154. ASKENASE, Alicia Daly
    "For Peter, Who May be Running." RevIn (10:4) Wint
        80-81, p. 551.
    "What Mother Knew." RevIn (10:4) Wint 80-81, p. 552.

155. ASKEW, Judy
    "The Glass Sculptor." PoNow (6:4, issue 34) 82, p.
        47.

156. ASPENSTROM, Werner
    "The Grasshopper" (tr. by Robin Fulton). Field (26)
        Spr 82, p. 16.
    "The House Sparrow" (tr. by Robin Fulton). Field (26)
        Spr 82, p. 19.
    "If There Were Only Two Words" (tr. by Robin Fulton).
        Field (26) Spr 82, p. 21.
    "Portrait" (tr. by Robin Fulton). Field (26) Spr 82,
        p. 17.
    "Shoes Long to be Out" (tr. by Robin Fulton). Field
        (26) Spr 82, p. 20.
    "The Snowflake" (tr. by Robin Fulton). Field (26) Spr
        82, p. 18.

157. ASPER, Doug
    "You Close Your Eyes for a Moment." DenQ (16:4) Wint
        82, p. 88.

158. ASPEY, Stacie
    "Untitled: Sublime blues." MendoR (5) Sum 81, p. 65.

159. ASTHANA, G.
    "Midnight" (tr. of Kedarnath Singh, w. R. K. Sharma).
        NewL (48:3/4) Spr-Sum 82, p. 185.

160. ASTOR, Susan
    "Housekeeper's Children." Confr (23) Wint 82, p.
        130.
    "In Loco Parentis." PoNow (6:4, issue 34) 82, p. 46.

"Stepsisters." PoNow (6:4, issue 34) 82, p. 46.

161. ASTRADA, Etelvina
    from Autobiografia: (16, 18, 22, 34, 38-39) (tr. by
        Timothy J. Rogers). Chelsea (41) 82, p. 127-129.
    from Autobiography at the Trigger: (8, 10, 31) (tr.
        by Timothy J. Rogers). CharR (8:2) Aut 82, p. 44-
        46.

162. ATKINS, Kathleen
    "Loon Hunting." Poetry (140:6) S 82, p. 336-337.
    "Middle of the Journey." Tendril (12) Wint 82, p.
        12.
    "A Physics Problem" (Einstein: e = mc2). Poetry
        (140:6) S 82, p. 338.

163. ATKINSON, Charles
    "Late Revelation on the Coast Road." BelPoJ (33:2)
        Wint 82-83, p. 29-30.
    "Learning to Float Again" (for my mother). BelPoJ
        (33:2) Wint 82-83, p. 30-31.

164. ATKINSON, Pamela Perkins
    "December Field." BelPoJ (33:1) Aut 82, p. 7.
    "If You Think It Is Hard to See the Shape of Water."
        BelPoJ (33:1) Aut 82, p. 9.
    "Our Late Garden." BelPoJ (33:1) Aut 82, p. 4-5.
    "Storm." BelPoJ (33:1) Aut 82, p. 6-7.
    "Summer Night Fog." BelPoJ (33:1) Aut 82, p. 8.

165. ATWOOD, Margaret
    "The Boom." CanLit (95) Wint 82, p. 15.
    "Bread." Iowa (12:2/3) Spr-Sum 81, p. 7-8.
    "The Healer." AmerPoR (11:6) N-D 82, p. 3.
    "The Light." AmerPoR (11:6) N-D 82, p. 4.
    "Small Poems for the Winter Solstice." MissouriR
        (5:2) Wint 81-82, p. 18-25.
    "The Words Continue Their Journey." AmerPoR (11:6)
        N-D 82, p. 3.

166. AUBERT, Alvin
    "How Do You Know." PoNow (6:6, issue 36) 82, p. 28.
    "Seven Year Old Man." PoNow (6:6, issue 36) 82, p.
        28.

167. AUBERT, Jimmy
    "Appointment." StoneC (9:3/4) Spr-Sum 82, p. 57.
    "For Father: Across Some Ocean." LittleBR (1:3) Spr
        81, p. 27.
    "M & M Speedway Blues." Sam (32:3, issue 127) 82, p.
        50-51.
    "Neosho Falls, KS (1859-1937)." LittleBR (3:1) Aut
        82, p. 67.
    "Protomartyr." PoetC (14:1) 82, p. 2-5.
    "This Pen." LittleBR (2:1) Aut 81, p. 70.

168. AUBERT, Rosemary
    "Ex-Wives." Waves (10:4) Spr 82, p. 60.
    "Things I Have Lost As Each by Each the Good Men Bade
        Farewell." Waves (10:4) Spr 82, p. 61.

"To Patricia Forest, Anne Page, Sara Lee, Especially
Betty Crocker and the Ghost of Laura Secord."
CrossC (4:4) 82, p. 12.

169. AUDEN, W. H.
"Pride." YaleR (71:2) Wint 82, p. 172.

170. AUDIBERTI, Jacques
"Vera-Cruz" (tr. by Jan Pallister). PoNow (6:5, issue
35) 82, p. 42.

171. AUER, Michael
"A Sixty Three Year Old White Male with Multiple
Sclerosis Watches Insects on the Window from His
Bed." Abraxas (25/26) 82, p. 100-101.

172. AUGUSTINE, Jane
"Aspen Stump and Willow" (a watercolor). Shout (3:1)
82, p. 47.

173. AUGUSTUS, Gemiann
"Fala-Me." Abraxas (25/26) 82, p. 64.
"Tell Me" (tr. by H. C. Tyson). Abraxas (25/26) 82,
p. 64.

174. AUMERLE, Jane
"Lucifer Descending." MendoR (6) Sum 81, p. 58.
"Siren." MendoR (6) Sum 81, p. 59.

175. AUSLANDER, Rose
"Cezanne" (tr. by Beth Bjorklund). LitR (25:2) Wint
82, p. 176.

176. AUSTIN, Bob
"Bear River Legend." Abraxas (25/26) 82, p. 60.

177. AUSTIN, Don
"It's the Same Old Story." Catalyst (Erotica Issue)
82, p. 23-26.

178. AUSTIN, F. A.
"Auto da Fe." PraS (56:4) Wint 82-83, p. 56-57.
"No Word, No Way." PraS (56:4) Wint 82-83, p. 55.

179. AVERILL, Tom
"On Grandma Layton's Refrigerator Excess Cat--A Sugar
Blues." KanQ (14:3) Sum 82, p. 41.

180. AVERY, Bob
"Rain." MendoR (6) Sum 81, p. 63.

181. AVILES CONCEPCION, Jorge Luis
from Desde Mi Arrabal -- Palabras, Tan Solo Palabras
al Viento: "Palabra III." Mairena (4:9) Spr 82, p.
77-78.

182. AWAD, Joseph
"Ocean View." Poem (46) N 82, p. 32-33.

183. AXEL, Claudia
"The Cold -- Your Voice." AntigR (49) Spr 82, p. 95.
"Whirl Dance." AntigR (49) Spr 82, p. 96.

184. AXELROD, David
"Bainbridge Dairy." PoNow (7:1, issue 37) 82, p. 2.
"In Our Sleep." PoNow (7:1, issue 37) 82, p. 2.
"Kaddish" (for my father). CutB (18) Spr-Sum 82, p.
95-96.

185. AXINN, Donald Everett
"The Fliers over Water Island." PoNow (6:5, issue
35) 82, p. 9.
"Homage to the Icons" (for Frances Whyatt). NewEngR
(4:3) Spr 82, p. 423.
"Into the Alpine Meadow." PoNow (6:5, issue 35) 82,
p. 9.

186. AYCOCK, Shirley
"Ada." UTR (7:2) 82?, p. 16.
"Cement." Wind (12:46) 82, p. 7.

187. AZRAEL, Judith Anne
"The Fisherman" (A portrait). Confr (24) Sum 82, p.
27-30.
"Miles." StoneC (10:1/2) Aut-Wint 82-83, p. 12.
"Song of Lost Numbers." StoneC (10:1/2) Aut-Wint 82-
83, p. 12.
"Song of Resolution." StoneC (10:1/2) Aut-Wint 82-
83, p. 12.

188. BABCOCK, Sherri Ann
"I Am Still Waiting." Pig (8) 80, p. 11.

189. BABENKO, Victoria
"Bol'shaia greshnitsa k ikone podoshla" (in Russian).
NewRena (5:1, 15) Aut 82, p. 78.
"Impromptu Thoughts at Midnight" (tr. by James E. A.
Woodbury). NewRena (5:1, 15) Aut 82, p. 75, 77.
"Nevol'nye Polunochnye Mysli" (in Russian). NewRena
(5:1, 15) Aut 82, p. 74, 76.
"A Sinner" (tr. by James E. A. Woodbury). NewRena
(5:1, 15) Aut 82, p. 79.

190. BABINKSI, Hubert F.
"Farewell to Ostend" (tr. of Bohdan Zadura). PartR
(49:2) 82, p. 238-245.

191. BABUN, Edward
"Eternity" (tr. of Arthur Rimbaud, w. Olga
Litowinsky). StoneC (9:3/4) Spr-Sum 82, p. 23.
"On a Letter Never Written" (tr. of Eugenio Montale).
StoneC (9:3/4) Spr-Sum 82, p. 25.

192. BABUTS, Nicolae
"Leaving the Car to Be Serviced." WindO (41) Aut-
Wint 82-83, p. 45.

193. BACA, Jimmy Santiago
"Destiny." Hangl (43) Wint 82-83, p. 68.

"For a Chicano Brother of Mine." RevChic (10:1/2)
    Wint-Spr 82, p. 33-34.
"I Pass La Iglesia." Hangl (43) Wint 82-83, p. 68.
"Let's compare our feelings of loving someone."
    Hangl (43) Wint 82-83, p. 69-71.
"On This Side of the Mountain." Hangl (43) Wint 82-
    83, p. 71-72.
"Sun Calendar." RevChic (10:1/2) Wint-Spr 82, p. 31.
"They're Used to Putting Things in the Ground."
    RevChic (10:1/2) Wint-Spr 82, p. 34-35.
"To the Face before This Face." Hangl (43) Wint 82-
    83, p. 69.
"We Knew It." RevChic (10:1/2) Wint-Spr 82, p. 32-
    33.
"The Word Love." RevChic (10:1/2) Wint-Spr 82, p.
    30-31.

194. BACHMANN, Ingeborg
    "Days in White" (tr. by Beth Bjorklund). LitR (25:2)
        Wint 82, p. 241.
    "A Kind of Loss" (tr. by Beth Bjorklund). LitR (25:2)
        Wint 82, p. 242.
    "Prague, January 1964" (tr. by Beth Bjorklund). LitR
        (25:2) Wint 82, p. 243.
    "Theme and Variations" (tr. by Beth Bjorklund). LitR
        (25:2) Wint 82, p. 244-245.

    BACHRI, Sutardji Calzoum
    See: SUTARDJI, Calzoum Bachri

195. BACON, Margaret H.
    "Rebirth." ChrC (99:13) Ap 14, 82, p. 448.

196. BAER, William
    "Speed-Skater, Dressed for Night in Black."
        SouthernHR (16:3) Sum 82, p. 212.

197. BAGRYANA, Elisaveta
    "River Run" (tr. by Jascha Kessler and Alexander
        Shurbanov). Kayak (59) Je 82, p. 68-69.

198. BAILEY, Alice Morrey
    "Flim-Flam Man." LittleBR (1:3) Spr 81, p. 47.

199. BAILEY, Don
    "Depression." Quarry (31:3) Sum 82, p. 47-48.
    "For a Friend Becoming Forty." Quarry (31:3) Sum 82,
        p. 48.
    "The Other Woman." Quarry (31:3) Sum 82, p. 45.
    "The Season" (for Anne Walshaw). CrossC (4:2/3) 82,
        p. 38.
    "Webs." Quarry (31:3) Sum 82, p. 45-46.
    "What Is This You Have Become?" Quarry (31:3) Sum
        82, p. 46-47.

200. BAILIN, George
    "Climber." KanQ (14:1) Wint 82, p. 42.

201. BAIZER, Eric
        "Around the House" (for Buster Keaton). _Gargoyle_ (19)
          82, p. 28.
        "Bent." _Gargoyle_ (19) 82, p. 26.
        "The Fourth World" (Adams Morgan, Washington, D.C.).
          Gargoyle (19) 82, p. 24.
        "Literature." _Gargoyle_ (19) 82, p. 23.
        "One Step Down" (for Rick Peabody). _Gargoyle_ (19) 82,
          p. 32.
        "A Shopping Mall in Delaware." _Gargoyle_ (19) 82, p.
          29.
        "Virginia." _Gargoyle_ (15/16) 80, p. 11.
        "Wonder Block" (for Susan Coleman). _Gargoyle_ (19) 82,
          p. 31.
        "You." _Gargoyle_ (19) 82, p. 34.

202. BAKER, David
        "A Banquet." _PortR_ (28:1) 82, p. 68.
        "Concurrent Memories: The Afternoon the Last Barge
          Left." _SouthernPR_ (22:1) Spr 82, p. 43-44.
        "Floor Exercise, or, The Breakfast of a Champion."
          PortR (28:1) 82, p. 68.
        "Hacking the Newly-Grown." _WebR_ (7:1) Spr 82, p. 62-
          63.
        "The Magpies." _KanQ_ (14:1) Wint 82, p. 32.
        "No Bait." _KanQ_ (14:1) Wint 82, p. 32.
        "Return to the Pond." _PoNow_ (7:1, issue 37) 82, p.
          21.
        "Utah: The Lava Caves." _PoNow_ (7:1, issue 37) 82, p.
          21.

203. BAKER, Donald W.
        "Essential Questions." _WindO_ (41) Aut-Wint 82-83, p.
          4-5.
        "Failure." _ColEng_ 44(4) Ap 82, p. 384.
        "Professor." _ColEng_ 44(4) Ap 82, p. 382-383.
        "Teaching." _ColEng_ 44(8) D 82, p. 808.
        "Unposted Letter." _ColEng_ 44(4) Ap 82, p. 383.

204. BAKER, Edward
        "Latinamerica" (tr. of Roque Dalton). _Maize_ (5:3/4)
          Spr-Sum 82, p. 40.
        "Love Poem" (tr. of Roque Dalton). _Maize_ (5:3/4) Spr-
          Sum 82, p. 41.
        "O.A.S." (tr. of Roque Dalton). _Maize_ (5:3/4) Spr-Sum
          82, p. 42.
        "Typist" (tr. of Roque Dalton). _Maize_ (5:3/4) Spr-Sum
          82, p. 39-40.
        "We all" (tr. of Roque Dalton). _Maize_ (5:3/4) Spr-Sum
          82, p. 38.

205. BAKER, Jean Morrison
        "Developing Your Own Solutions." _LittleBR_ (2:3) Spr
          82, p. 45.

206. BALABAN, John
        "Blue Mountain." _PoNow_ (6:6, issue 36) 82, p. 23.
        "Riding Westward." _NewEngR_ (5:1/2) Aut-Wint 82, p.
          52-53.
        "Tomato Pickers." _PoNow_ (6:6, issue 36) 82, p. 23.

207. BALAKIAN, Peter
     "Geese Flying Over Hamilton, NY." PoetryNW (23:2)
        Sum 82, p. 25.
     "I Wish Us Back to Mud." PoetryNW (23:2) Sum 82, p.
        24.

208. BALAZS, Mary
     "Caged Lion, Feeding." KanQ (14:3) Sum 82, p. 129.
     "For My Son, in a School Play." Wind (12:46) 82, p.
        3.
     "Great-Aunt, Dead." WebR (7:2) Aut 82, p. 57.
     "Night Grove." Wind (12:46) 82, p. 4.

209. BALDERSTON, Jean
     "After the Funeral" (In memory of my grandmother).
        PoNow (6:4, issue 34) 82, p. 20.
     "The Elderly Poet Reads." PoNow (6:6, issue 36) 82,
        p. 22.
     "Sweet Talk" (found poem). Kayak (60) O 82, back
        cover.

210. BALDWIN, Gary
     "13 Ways of Looking at a Baseball." Pig (9) 82, p.
        11.
     "City Game." Pig (9) 82, p. 55.
     "Vince Lloyd, Poet." Pig (9) 82, p. 62.

211. BALDWIN, Skip
     "Forgetting to Say Good-bye." Northeast (3:14) Wint
        82-83, p. 8.

212. BALDWIN, Sy Margaret
     "December 29, 1936, Saline Valley, Calif., 3000 Feet"
        (for Annie Montague Alexander). Cond (8) 82, p. 11-
        12.
     "The Desert Is Not the Enemy" (for the Salvadorans
        who died in Organ Pipe National Monument 7/80).
        Cond (8) 82, p. 13-15.
     "There Are No Rivers." Cond (8) 82, p. 16-17.
     "To an Ex-Lover." Cond (8) 82, p. 18.

213. BALDWIN, Tama
     "Storm Warning." GeoR (36:3) Aut 82, p. 555.

214. BALLANTYNE, Deirdre
     "Journey: A Sequence." MalR (61) F 82, p. 38-47.

215. BALLARD, Arthur H., IV
     "This is Real." MendoR (6) Sum 81, p. 152-153.

216. BALLARD, Richard
     "People Food." HiramPoR (31) Aut-Wint 82, p. 6.

217. BALLARD, Sandra
     "Seasonal." HiramPoR (31) Aut-Wint 82, p. 7.

     BALMACEDA, Margarita Sastre de
     See: SASTRE de BALMACEDA, Margarita

218. BALTENSPERGER, Peter
"Full Moon." Quarry (31:1) Wint 82, p. 20.
"Hidden Centre #6." Quarry (31:1) Wint 82, p. 21.

219. BANANI, Amin
"In an Eternity of Setting Sun: A Dialogue Between
Lovers" (tr. of Forugh Farrokhzad, w. Jascha
Kessler). MichQR (21:2) Spr 82, p. 246-248.

220. BANANI, Sheila
"We Are One." WorldO (17:1) Aut 82, p. 35.

221. BANCHS, Enrique
"Veterrima Laurus" (tr. by Michael L. Johnson). PortR
(28:1) 82, p. 23.

222. BANDHYOPADHYAY, Manohar
"Stormward" (tr. of Sati Kumar). NewL (48:3/4) Spr-
Sum 82, p. 209.

223. BANERJI, Dabashish
"Dance of the Twilight Junction" (tr. of Jibanananda
Das). Os (14) 82, p. 23.
"Pakhira/Birds" (tr. of Jibanananda Das). Os (14) 82,
p. 24-25.

BANUS, Jose Sanchis
See: SANCHIS-BANUS, Jose

224. BAPAT, Vasant
"If Return You Must" (tr. by Prabhakar Machwe). NewL
(48:3/4) Spr-Sum 82, p. 158-159.

225. BARAKA, Amina (Sylvia Jones)
"Sometimie Woman." BlackALF (16:3) Aut 82, p. 105.
"Sortin-Out." BlackALF (16:3) Aut 82, p. 106.

226. BARAKA, Amiri
"Sounding." BlackALF (16:3) Aut 82, p. 103-105.

227. BARANCZAK, Stanislaw
"Because Only this World of Pain" (tr. by Frank
Kujawinski). ManhatR (2:1) 81, p. 29.
"I'm Through with These" (tr. by Frank Kujawinski).
ManhatR (2:1) 81, p. 36.
"If Porcelain, Then Only the Kind" (tr. by Frank
Kujawinski). ManhatR (2:1) 81, p. 35.
"In Principle, It's Not Possible" (tr. by Frank
Kujawinski). ManhatR (2:1) 81, p. 32.
"It Was a Near Miss" (tr. by Valeria Wasilewski).
Abraxas (25/26) 82, p. 19.
"Lullaby" (tr. by Frank Kujawinski). ManhatR (2:1)
81, p. 33.
"These Words" (tr. by Frank Kujawinski). ManhatR
(2:1) 81, p. 28.
"Together with Dust" (tr. by Frank Kujawinski).
ManhatR (2:1) 81, p. 34.
"What's Being Played?" (tr. by Valeria Wasilewski).
Abraxas (25/26) 82, p. 20.

"Where Did I Wake Up?" (tr. by Frank Kujawinski).
ManhatR (2:1) 81, p. 27.
"Window" (tr. by Frank Kujawinski). ManhatR (2:1) 81,
p. 30-31.

228. BARBARITO, Carlos
"Diario de Abril, 6, 1979." Mairena (4:10) Sum-Aut
82, p. 61.

229. BARBAROTTA, Joseph
"Symbiosis." StoneC (9:3/4) Spr-Sum 82, p. 49.

230. BARBOUR, Douglas
"How it fluttered in my hand." AntigR (51) Aut 82,
p. 72.
"Oregon Coast." AntigR (51) Aut 82, p. 73.
"So it begins again." Quarry (31:3) Sum 82, p. 8.

231. BARCIA, Hugo
"Inmigrante." Mairena (4:10) Sum-Aut 82, p. 78-79.
"Llevame Siempre" (A Marcela). Mairena (4:9) Spr 82,
p. 34.

232. BARCLAY, Heather
"Gatherers." PottPort (4) 82-83, p. 13.
"Still Life." PottPort (4) 82-83, p. 29.

233. BARCOMB, Michael E.
"An American in London." Bogg (48) 82, p. 26.

234. BARDIS, Panos D.
"Julian's Despair" (For N.B.P.). BallSUF (23:2) Spr
82, p. 14.

235. BARGEN, Walter
"Bull in the Cereal." WebR (7:2) Aut 82, p. 63.
"Burning Brush." Abraxas (25/26) 82, p. 61.
"Just Today." WebR (7:2) Aut 82, p. 61.
"Ringmaster." WebR (7:2) Aut 82, p. 62.

236. BARKER, Vicki
"In Search of the Last Duchess." LittleM (13:3/4)
82, p. 52-53.

237. BARKER, Wendy
"January." Wind (12:45) 82, p. 4.

238. BARKS, Coleman
"Bedclothes." Agni (17) 82, p. 163-164.
"Fivepoints." GeoR (36:1) Spr 82, p. 164.

BARLETTA, Naomi Lockwood
See: LOCKWOOD BARLETTA, Naomi

239. BARNARD, Mary
"The Pleiades." NowestR (20:2/3) 82, p. 187.

240. BARNES, Elizabeth
"To Tony" (After the turtle dance at Taos Pueblo, New
Year's Day, 1981). OP (34) Aut-Wint 82, p. 30-32.

241. BARNES, G.
     "Kansas Is a Quilt." <u>PoNow</u> (7:1, issue 37) 82, p. 3.
     "Pedestrians/The Crows." <u>PoNow</u> (7:1, issue 37) 82,
        p. 2.

242. BARNES, Jane
     "Eating." <u>PoNow</u> (7:1, issue 37) 82, p. 3.
     "Eleanor Roosevelt" (for Marcie Hershman). <u>HangL</u> (41)
        82, p. 10-11.
     from Flagg, California: "Winifred." <u>Hangl</u> (43) Wint
        82-83, p. 2.
     from Flagg, California: "X." <u>Hangl</u> (43) Wint 82-83,
        p. 3.
     "The Hot Dog Poem." <u>HangL</u> (41) 82, p. 12.
     "Lessons of the Body." <u>PoNow</u> (7:1, issue 37) 82, p.
        3.

243. BARNES, Jim
     "Autobiography, Chapter III: Nearing El Paso." <u>Bound</u>
        (10:3) Spr 82, p. 184.
     "Dreams the Children Had" (for Bret and Blake). <u>Bound</u>
        (10:3) Spr 82, p. 183.
     "Memories of Oceanside." <u>NewL</u> (48:2) Wint 81-82, p.
        32-33.
     "Once in Winnemucca." <u>NewL</u> (48:2) Wint 81-82, p. 33.

244. BARNES, Katherine
     "Three Phases of Eve." <u>Poem</u> (45) Jl 82, p. 40-42.

245. BARNES, Katherine Russell
     "Graveyard at sundown" (Haiku). <u>LittleBR</u> (1:3) Spr
        81, p. 55.

246. BARNES, Katherine
     "Three Phases of Eve." <u>Poem</u> (45) Jl 82, p. 40-42.

247. BARNES, Mike
     "I Like You." <u>Grain</u> (10:3) Ag 82, p. 58.
     "The Paintings of Edward Hopper." <u>Grain</u> (10:3) Ag
        82, p. 56.
     "R." <u>Grain</u> (10:3) Ag 82, p. 57.

248. BARNES, W. J.
     "David Writing." <u>Quarry</u> (31:3) Sum 82, p. 9-10.
     "Hemerobios" (For Henry Vaughan). <u>Quarry</u> (31:3) Sum
        82, p. 10.

249. BARNIE, John
     "The Castle Meadows." <u>Kayak</u> (60) O 82, p. 31.
     "The Death of King Arthur." <u>YaleR</u> (71:3) Spr 82, p.
        390.
     "The Deri." <u>LitR</u> (25:3) Spr 82, p. 349.
     "Ilanfoist Bridge." <u>Kayak</u> (60) O 82, p. 31.
     "Knudshoved in April" (SW Sjaelland). <u>LitR</u> (25:3) Spr
        82, p. 350.
     "Lightning Country." <u>LitR</u> (25:3) Spr 82, p. 351.
     "Nothing to Report." <u>Kayak</u> (60) O 82, p. 32.
     "November Storm." <u>Kayak</u> (60) O 82, p. 32.

250. BARNSTEAD, John A.
      "127. Why am I again on the same circuit?" (tr. of
      Marina Glasov). Germ (6:1) Spr-Sum 82, p. 31.
      "In Time and the Public Garden" (In Memory of Luis
      Cernuda). PottPort (4) 82-83, p. 9.

251. BARNSTONE, Willis
      "Nothing." ArizQ (38:3) Aut 82, p. 234.
      "Dreamwords." Bound (10:3) Spr 82, p. 179.
      "Gospel of Imaginary Beings." SouthernPR (23, i.e.
      22:2) Aut 82, p. 12.
      "Gospel of the Mountain." CutB (18) Spr-Sum 82, p.
      8.
      "In the High Stars" (tr. of Anna Akhmatova, w. Marija
      Maddock). NewL (48:2) Wint 81-82, p. 51.
      "Letter to a Brother." Bound (10:3) Spr 82, p. 181.
      "Letter to a Dream." Bound (10:3) Spr 82, p. 178.
      "Letter to My Fingers." Bound (10:3) Spr 82, p. 177.
      "The Lilies." DenQ (17:1) Spr 82, p. 104.
      "Milk." Bound (10:3) Spr 82, p. 180.
      "One Depressing Evening, in the Mud Roots of the
      Night, I Ask, Who Am I Kidding?" Nimrod (25:2) Spr-
      Sum 82, p. 58.
      "A Rose in Hell." AntR (40:4) Aut 82, p. 441.
      "Strange River." Nimrod (25:2) Spr-Sum 82, p. 59.
      "Visions on the Way Down." Nimrod (25:2) Spr-Sum 82,
      p. 58.

      BARNSTORE, Willis
      See: BARNSTONE, Willis

252. BARON, Enid L.
      "Illinois." LitR (25:3) Spr 82, p. 430.
      "The Widow." LitR (25:3) Spr 82, p. 430.

253. BARON, Todd
      "A Sphere for Tristan Tzara." Sulfur (2:3, issue 6)
      82, p. 109-110.

254. BARONE, Patricia
      "Our Tenancy: A River Lien." Tendril (13) Sum 82, p.
      12-13.

255. BARR, Stan
      "Untitled: Hands that hold and roll a small jewel."
      MendoR (5) Sum 81, p. 25.

256. BARR, Tina
      "Moving to the Country." BelPoJ (32:3) Spr 82, p.
      30-31.

257. BARRACK, Jack
      "The Carpenter." Shout (3:1) 82, p. 34.
      "Two Sunfish." PoNow (7:1, issue 37) 82, p. 3.
      "Urn." PoNow (7:1, issue 37) 82, p. 3.

258. BARRAS-ABNEY, Jonetta
      "Identity." Obs (7:2/3) Sum-Wint 81, p. 192.
      "Secondline for Susan." Obs (7:2/3) Sum-Wint 81, p.
      192.

"Untitled: In quiet glowing saturday january
splendor." <u>Obs</u> (7:2/3) Sum-Wint 81, p. 193.

259. BARRETT, Edward
"Proem." <u>PartR</u> (49:2) 82, p. 248-250.

260. BARRIENTOS, Raul
"Amor Oscuro." <u>Inti</u>(12) Aut 80, p. 90.
"Colon Envia el Libro de las Profecias a Su Majestad"
(Para Pedro Lastra) <u>Inti</u>(12) Aut 80, p. 91.
"R.D. Lee Nomina de Fusilados y Escribe en un/Pedazo
de Periodico" <u>Inti</u>(12) Aut 80, p. 90.
"La Rabia, Caramba, y la Sordera." <u>Inti</u>(12) Aut 80,
p. 90-91.
"Varias Noches Despues Ante el Espejo." <u>Inti</u>(12) Aut
80, p. 91.

BARRIOS, Rolando Camozzi
<u>See</u>: CAMOZZI BARRIOS, Rolando

BARRIS, Miguel A. Arzola
<u>See</u>: ARZOLA BARRIS, Miguel A.

261. BARROWS, Sheila
"Hampshire Elegy." <u>HiramPoR</u> (32) Spr-Sum 82, p. 7.

262. BARRY, Jan
"Viet Nam." <u>StoneC</u> (10:1/2) Aut-Wint 82-83, p. 84.

263. BARTEL, Douglas
"Reasons for Postponing Suicide." <u>Sam</u> (32:3, issue
127) 82, p. 48-49.

264. BARTH, R. L.
"Arche: First Morning" (11 January 1970). <u>SouthernR</u>
(18:2) Spr 82, p. 386.
"The Brown Hills" (on arriving in Palo Alto, October
1978). <u>SouthernR</u> (18:2) Spr 82, p. 386-387.
"From the Forest of Suicides." <u>StoneC</u> (10:1/2) Aut-
Wint 82-83, p. 54.
"Just Another Love Letter." <u>SouthernR</u> (18:2) Spr 82,
p. 387.
"A Leave-Taking: To Susan." <u>SouthernR</u> (18:2) Spr
82, p. 388.
"An Old Soldier Reads The Iliad." <u>Iowa</u> (12:4) Aut
81, p. 60.

265. BARTKOWECH, R.
"I Keep Walking for Someone Else." <u>LittleBR</u> (3:2)
Wint 82-83, p. 40.
"Kick Me in the Head If You Love Me." <u>LittleM</u>
(13:3/4) 82, p. 60.
"My Pencil Has an Eraser at Both Ends." <u>LittleBR</u>
(2:4) Sum 82, p. 20.
"Paris Opera." <u>LittleBR</u> (3:2) Wint 82-83, p. 63.

266. BARTLETT, Elizabeth
"Ants" (tr. of Griselda Alvarez). <u>WebR</u> (7:1) Spr 82,
p. 36.
"April 14, 1912." <u>AntigR</u> (50) Sum 82, p. 96.

"Century, Ltd." <u>StoneC</u> (9:3/4) Spr-Sum 82, p. 18.
"Garden" (tr. of Griselda Alvarez). <u>WebR</u> (7:1) Spr
82, p. 37.
"Leaves" (tr. of Griselda Alvarez). <u>WebR</u> (7:1) Spr
82, p. 37.
"The Limit." <u>StoneC</u> (9:3/4) Spr-Sum 82, p. 19.
"Spring Miracle." <u>AntigR</u> (50) Sum 82, p. 97.
"The Voice Within." <u>ConcPo</u> (15:2) Aut 82, p. 70.
"Watchman, What of the Night?" <u>StoneC</u> (10:1/2) Aut-
Wint 82-83, p. 50-52.
"Worms" (tr. of Griselda Alvarez). <u>WebR</u> (7:1) Spr 82,
p. 36.

267. BARTON, David
"A Bestiary." <u>QRL</u> (22) 81, p. 36-38.
"Bird Skulls." <u>QRL</u> (22) 81, p. 26-27.
"Cattle." <u>QRL</u> (22) 81, p. 22.
"The Frog, the Serpent, the Rejected One." <u>QRL</u> (22)
81, p. 30-31.
"German Woodcuts." <u>QRL</u> (22) 81, p. 34-35.
"Homage to Agatha Christie." <u>QRL</u> (22) 81, p. 41-42.
"The Humboldt Trail, 1887." <u>QRL</u> (22) 81, p. 53-54.
"In the Heron's Sleep." <u>QRL</u> (22) 81, p. 58.
"Jasper Ridge." <u>QRL</u> (22) 81, p. 56-57.
"John Coniston." <u>QRL</u> (22) 81, p. 24-25.
"Journal Entry." <u>QRL</u> (22) 81, p. 12-13.
"July in North Georgia." <u>QRL</u> (22) 81, p. 23.
"Knight's Ferry." <u>QRL</u> (22) 81, p. 55.
"Late Autumn." <u>QRL</u> (22) 81, p. 10-11.
"Mendocino." <u>QRL</u> (22) 81, p. 50.
"Midsummer." <u>QRL</u> (22) 81, p. 14.
"Mushroom Hunting." <u>QRL</u> (22) 81, p. 49.
"New Hampshire." <u>QRL</u> (22) 81, p. 15-16.
"Northern California." <u>QRL</u> (22) 81, p. 44-46.
"Owls." <u>QRL</u> (22) 81, p. 28-29.
"Plum Island." <u>QRL</u> (22) 81, p. 19-20.
"Surviving the Cold." <u>QRL</u> (22) 81, p. 8-9.
"Theseus." <u>QRL</u> (22) 81, p. 39.
"Vermeer." <u>QRL</u> (22) 81, p. 33.
"The Wake." <u>QRL</u> (22) 81, p. 17-18.
"The Western Door." <u>QRL</u> (22) 81, p. 51-52.
"Wintering in the Sierras: a Letter." <u>QRL</u> (22) 81,
p. 47-48.
"Yorkshire." <u>QRL</u> (22) 81, p. 40.

268. BARTON, Fred
"The Poet after Reading." <u>EngJ</u> (71:1) Ja 82, p. 93.
"Terminal." <u>KanQ</u> (14:3) Sum 82, p. 180.

269. BARTON, John
"Above the Trees" (from West of Darkness). <u>MalR</u> (63)
O 82, p. 196-197.
"At the Back of Our Minds" (from West of Darkness).
<u>CanLit</u> (91) Wint 81, p. 47-48.
"Big Raven" (from West of Darkness). <u>MalR</u> (63) O 82,
p. 191.
"Blunden Harbour" (from West of Darkness). <u>MalR</u> (63)
O 82, p. 192-194.
"East Anglia Sanitorium, 1903: A Recurring Dream"
(from West of Darkness). <u>MalR</u> (63) O 82, p. 199.

"Haro Strait" (from West of Darkness). <u>MalR</u> (63) O
   82, p. 200-203.
"Indian Church" (from West of Darkness). <u>MalR</u> (63) O
   82, p. 189.
"Nirvana" (from West of Darkness). <u>MalR</u> (63) O 82, p.
   190.
"Quiet" (from West of Darkness). <u>MalR</u> (63) O 82, p.
   203-204.
"Sunshine and Tumult" (from West of Darkness). <u>MalR</u>
   (63) O 82, p. 197.
"Swirl" (from West of Darkness). <u>MalR</u> (63) O 82, p.
   198-199.
"Woo" (from West of Darkness). <u>MalR</u> (63) O 82, p.
   194-195.

270. BARTRAM, Phil
   "The Messenger." <u>StoneC</u> (10:1/2) Aut-Wint 82-83, p.
      56-57.

271. BARWELL, Jay
   "Mateus Bottle." <u>KanQ</u> (14:3) Sum 82, p. 96.
   "Persistence." <u>KanQ</u> (14:3) Sum 82, p. 97.

272. BASKFIELD, Jerry
   "Whip Out Your Bananas." <u>DekalbLAJ</u> (14:1/4) Aut 80-
      Sum 81, p. 64.

273. BASNEY, Lionel
   "Barn Waking." <u>CimR</u> (60) Jl 82, p. 18.

274. BASSANI, Giorgio
   "Waltz" (tr. by Ilaria Caputi and David St. John).
      <u>PoetryE</u> (8) Aut 82, p. 74.

275. BATALVI, Shiv Kumar
   "Loona" (A dramatic poem, tr. by Balwant Gargi). <u>NewL</u>
      (48:3/4) Spr-Sum 82, p. 164-165.

276. BATEMAN, David
   "Bear in the City at Night." <u>Bogg</u> (48) 82, p. 52-53.

277. BATES, Randolph
   "Meteors." <u>SouthernR</u> (18:4) Aut 82, p. 819-821.
   "Namesake." <u>SouthernR</u> (18:4) Aut 82, p. 818-819.

278. BATHANTI, Joseph
   "Easter, 1981." <u>CapeR</u> (18:1) Wint 82, p. 12.
   "Triad." <u>CapeR</u> (18:1) Wint 82, p. 13.

279. BATKI, John
   "Dumb Poet" (tr. of Attila Jozsef). <u>PoNow</u> (6:4, issue
      34) 82, p. 42.
   "Dusk" (tr. of Attila Jozsef). <u>Spirit</u> (6:2/3) 82, p.
      82.

280. BATTIN, Wendy
   "Billy Goat & the Tree of Life" (after a statue found
      at Ur). <u>Nat</u> (234:20) My 22, 82, p. 622.
   "Letters from Three Women." <u>Iowa</u> (12:2/3) Spr-Sum
      81, p. 9-10.

"The Lives We Invite to Flower among Us Flower beyond
Us." Iowa (12:2/3) Spr-Sum 81, p. 11-12.
"This World Begins on a Wharf." Nat (235:15) N 6,
82, p. 474.

281. BATTLO, Jean
"The Don and Dulcinea #84." WindO (41) Aut-Wint 82-
83, p. 31.
"A Note on the Kubler-Ross Studies." WindO (41) Aut-
Wint 82-83, p. 32.

282. BAUDELAIRE, Charles
"For a Creole Lady" (tr. by James McGowan).
SouthernHR (16:2) Spr 82, p. 116.
"A Former Life" (tr. by James McGowan). HiramPoR (32)
Spr-Sum 82, p. 33.
"Sorrows of the Moon" (tr. by James McGowan).
Northeast (3:12) Wint 81-82, p. 15.
"Spleen (I)" (tr. by James McGowan). HiramPoR (32)
Spr-Sum 82, p. 34.
"Spleen (II)" (tr. by James McGowan). HiramPoR (32)
Spr-Sum 82, p. 35.
"A une Dame Creole." SouthernHR (16:2) Spr 82, p.
116.

283. BAUER, Steven
"Daylight Savings." PraS (56:3) Aut 82, p. 13-14.
"Obsessive Reworkings of the Same Theme." CimR (58)
Ja 82, p. 62.
"This Silence." PraS (56:3) Aut 82, p. 14.

284. BAUER, Tricia
"Your Favorite Photographs." OhioR (27) 82, p. 118.

285. BAUMANN, Susan
"Separation." KanQ (14:1) Wint 82, p. 106.
"Snarls." Nat (235:1) Jl 3, 82, p. 24.

286. BAXTER, Charles
"Against the President." Kayak (59) Je 82, p. 32.
"Blind Boy Climbing a Watertower." PoetryNW (23:3)
Aut 82, p. 8-9.
"Imaginary Painting: Black Canvas." Iowa (13:1) Wint
82, p. 119.
"Imaginary Painting: Dr. Thomas Garvin and His Wife."
Iowa (13:1) Wint 82, p. 117-118.
"Imaginary Painting: the Convalescents." PoetryNW
(23:3) Aut 82, p. 9.

287. BAZHAN, Mykola
"Prince Igor's Campaign" (tr. by Mark Rudman and
Bohdan Boychuk). Pequod (14) 82, p. 40-41.

288. BEAM, Jeffery
"On the Horizon a Summer Storm." Catalyst (Erotica
Issue) 82, p. 32.
"The White Room: Ocracoke." Catalyst (Erotica Issue)
82, p. 31.

289. BEARDSLEY, Doug
     "Pacific Sands." PoetryCR (3:4) Sum 82, p. 13.
     "Penetanguishene." PoetryCR (4:1) Sum 82, p. 12.

290. BEARDSLEY, Sheila
     "Nature Inexorable." DekalbLAJ (14:1/4) Aut 80-Sum
     81, p. 106.

291. BEASLEY, Bruce
     "Elegy." SouthernPR (22:1) Spr 82, p. 32.

292. BEASLEY, Conger, Jr.
     "How Nuipaxikuri Was Cured of Boasting about His Big
     Penis" (A Huichol Indian Tale). Sky (10-12) Aut 82,
     p. 27-28.

293. BEATON, Andrea E.
     "Driftwood." PottPort (4) 82-83, p. 17.

294. BEAUDOIN, Kenneth Lawrence
     "Beyond" (tr. of Claude Vigee, w. J. R. LeMaster).
     WebR (7:2) Aut 82, p. 18-19.
     "King of Our Years" (tr. of Claude Vigee, w. J. R.
     LeMaster). WebR (7:2) Aut 82, p. 17.
     "Nothing Is Wholly Lost" (tr. of Claude Vigee, w. J.
     R. LeMaster). WebR (7:2) Aut 82, p. 19.

295. BEAUMONT, Alison
     "Migration." Quarry (31:4) Aut 82, p. 51-52.
     "Sundial." Quarry (31:4) Aut 82, p. 50-51.
     "When I Die." Quarry (31:4) Aut 82, p. 52-54.

296. BECHTEL, Lynn
     "Turning Thirty." Tendril (13) Sum 82, p. 14.

297. BECK, D. H.
     "Celluloid Logic." PottPort (4) 82-83, p. 48.

298. BECK, Marion
     "Art on Display." MalR (63) O 82, p. 160-161.

299. BECKER, Therese
     "The Eye of the Potato." BelPoJ (33:2) Wint 82-83,
     p. 27.
     "The Gift Shop." PoNow (7:1, issue 37) 82, p. 4.
     "My Grandfather's Arm." PoNow (7:1, issue 37) 82, p.
     4.

300. BEDOYA, Carlos
     "Capurgana." BelPoJ (32:4) Sum 82, p. 14.
     "Capurgana" (tr. by Ricardo Pau-Llosa). BelPoJ (32:4)
     Sum 82, p. 15.

301. BEDWELL, Carol
     "Primeval Forest" (tr. of Christoph Meckel). WebR
     (7:2) Aut 82, p. 21.
     "Song of Lademli Lolle" (tr. of Christoph Meckel).
     WebR (7:2) Aut 82, p. 20.

302. BEFFART, Mark
    "Street Scene." <u>DekalbLAJ</u> (14:1/4) Aut 80-Sum 81, p.
    65.

303. BEHLEN, Charles
    "Father Encountered Drunk under a Bridge in
    Yellowhouse Canyon." <u>PoNow</u> (7:1, issue 37) 82, p.
    4.

304. BEHM, Richard
    "Driving into Minnesota Dawn." <u>HiramPoR</u> (31) Aut-
    Wint 82, p. 8.
    "Simple Explanations." <u>Pig</u> (8) 80, p. 57.
    "Traveling Salesman's Soliloquy." <u>Abraxas</u> (25/26)
    82, p. 85.

305. BEHN, Bettina
    "From the Hospital" (tr. by Stuart Friebert). <u>Tendril</u>
    (12) Wint 82, p. 15.

306. BEIER, Ulli
    "Snail" (tr. of Jyotirmoy Datta, w. Prithvindra
    Chakravarti). <u>NewL</u> (48:3/4) Spr-Sum 82, p. 236.

307. BEILHARZ, Johannes
    "Since Today, But Forever" (tr. of Christine Lavant).
    <u>AspenJ</u> (1:2) Sum 82, p. 29.
    "Who Will Help Me Starve This Night?" (tr. of
    Christine Lavant). <u>AspenJ</u> (1:2) Sum 82, p. 29.

308. BEINING, Guy (Guy R.)
    "Stoma 144." <u>Abraxas</u> (25/26) 82, p. 34.
    from Stoma: "Intro: 4/4/79 now shivering." <u>Pig</u> (8)
    80, p. 45-47.

309. BELL, Charles G.
    "Lean to the Ponderosa." <u>Paint</u> (7/8:13/16) 80-81, p.
    37.
    "Rainbow." <u>Paint</u> (7/8:13/16) 80-81, p. 36.

310. BELL, John
    "Barsoom." <u>PottPort</u> (4) 82-83, p. 13.
    "Rear-View." <u>PottPort</u> (4) 82-83, p. 10.

311. BELL, Marvin
    "Against Stuff." <u>AmerPoR</u> (11:6) N-D 82, p. 5.
    "At the Airport." <u>MissouriR</u> (5:2) Wint 81-82, p. 13-
    15.
    "Banyan Tree before the Civic Center, Honolulu." <u>Atl</u>
    (249:3) Mr 82, p. 52.
    "Florence." <u>MissouriR</u> (5:2) Wint 81-82, p. 16-17.
    "How I Got the Words." <u>AmerPoR</u> (11:6) N-D 82, p. 5.
    "If by Poetry You Mean." <u>Agni</u> (17) 82, p. 45.
    "Jane Was with Me." <u>Atl</u> (250:6) D 82, p. 72.
    "Liverwort the Example." <u>MichQR</u> (21:3) Sum 82, p.
    442.
    "On the Illusion of Time in a Difficult Period."
    <u>Agni</u> (17) 82, p. 46.
    "Questions to Answers." <u>AmerPoR</u> (11:6) N-D 82, p. 5.
    "San Francisco." <u>MichQR</u> (21:3) Sum 82, p. 439-441.

"Some Shadows." <u>MissouriR</u> (5:2) Wint 81-82, p. 7.
"A True Story." <u>AmerPoR</u> (11:6) N-D 82, p. 4.
"What They Do to You in Distant Places." <u>MissouriR</u>
    (5:2) Wint 81-82, p. 8-9.
"Where Is Odysseus from and What Was He before He
    Left for the Trojan War?" <u>MissouriR</u> (5:2) Wint 81-
    82, p. 10-12.

312. BELLI, Gioconda
    "Dynamite Dresses." <u>Maize</u> (5:3/4) Spr-Sum 82, p. 22.
    "No Habra Perdon, Eden." <u>Maize</u> (5:3/4) Spr-Sum 82,
        p. 77.
    "Vestidos de Dinamita." <u>Maize</u> (5:3/4) Spr-Sum 82, p.
        22.

313. BELLINTANI, Umberto
    "Le Asine Passavano" (tr. by Jan Pallister). <u>PoNow</u>
        (6:5, issue 35) 82, p. 43.

314. BELOTE, Suzanne
    "Will We Survive to the Year 2000?" (for Lisa). <u>Vis</u>
        (8) 82, p. 26-27.

315. BELTRAN, Miguel Angel
    "Con Julia de Burgos" (from Julia Punto 40). <u>Mairena</u>
        (4:9) Spr 82, p. 78.

316. BELYEA, Barbara
    "La Fille des Bois" (tr. of Christine Dumitriu van
        Saanen). <u>Dandel</u> (9:1) 82, p. 53, 55.
    "J'irai Loin" (tr. of Christine Dumitriu van Saanen).
        <u>Dandel</u> (9:1) 82, p. 49.
    "The Lady and the Unicorn." <u>Dandel</u> (9:2) 82, p. 48.
    "Neiges/Snows" (tr. of Christine Dumitriu van
        Saanen). <u>Dandel</u> (9:1) 82, p. 51.
    "Our map is black." <u>Dandel</u> (9:2) 82, p. 49.
    "Un Point" (tr. of Christine Dumitriu van Saanen).
        <u>Dandel</u> (9:1) 82, p. 49.

317. BEN-TOV, S.
    "The Angel of Memory." <u>Agni</u> (17) 82, p. 21.
    "Fugue." <u>MissouriR</u> (5:2) Wint 81-82, p. 38.
    "Nocturne for Parvaneh." <u>Agni</u> (17) 82, p. 22-23.

318. BENBOW, Margaret
    "Bogeyman: 1950." <u>Poetry</u> (140:6) S 82, p. 319-320.
    "Out of Hand: Grant Park." <u>Poetry</u> (140:6) S 82, p.
        321.

319. BENDER, Sheila
    "In February." <u>PoetryCR</u> (3:3) Spr 82, p. 6.
    "Point Reyes" (for Maury Berman). <u>PoetryCR</u> (3:3) Spr
        82, p. 6.

320. BENEDIKT, Michael
    "Don Hall and Jane Kenyon of Eagle Pond Farm Invite a
        New York City Boy ... at Kate Fowler's 100th
        Birthday Party, July 16, 1978." <u>Agni</u> (16) 82, p.
        51-59.

"For Zekie as We Come and Go among the 20th Century
....." Agni (17) 82, p. 32-35.

321. BENEDITTI, Italo
from Island Suite: "The island, the veils of winter,
my heart" (tr. by Susan Thomas). PortR (28:1) 82,
p. 9.
"Prelude I" (tr. by Susan Thomas). PortR (28:1) 82,
p. 9.

322. BENGTSON, David
from The Man from Coal Lake: (1, 2). Northeast
(3:14) Wint 82-83, p. 34.

323. BENNANI, Ben
"Duned Marriage." Paint (7/8:13/16) 80-81, p. 38.
"Sorrow and Anger" (tr. of Mahmud Darwish). Paint
(7/8:13/16) 80-81, p. 44-46.

324. BENNET, Peter
"Redundant Steelmen Learning to Draw." Stand (23:1)
81-82, p. 27.

325. BENNETT, Bruce
"The Apprentice." PoNow (6:5, issue 35) 82, p. 13.
"Dusk." PoNow (6:5, issue 35) 82, p. 12.
"The Fanal Dance." PoNow (6:4, issue 34) 82, p. 13.
"The Fat Boy." PoNow (6:5, issue 35) 82, p. 13.
"The Hoard." PoNow (6:5, issue 35) 82, p. 12.
"Into the Light." PoNow (6:5, issue 35) 82, p. 13.
"Little Red Marks." PoNow (6:4, issue 34) 82, p. 13.
"Ones That Got Away." PoNow (6:5, issue 35) 82, p.
12.
"Saturday Afternoon." Wind (12:44) 82, p. 4.
"The Talk." Wind (12:44) 82, p. 3.
"The True Growth." PoNow (6:5, issue 35) 82, p. 12.
"The Wait." PoNow (6:5, issue 35) 82, p. 12.

326. BENNETT, John M.
"No Snakes." Abraxas (25/26) 82, p. 39.

327. BENTLEY, Beth
"Emily" (July 30, 1818--Dec. 19, 1848). PraS (56:2)
Sum 82, p. 38-44, Errata: (56:3) Aut 82, p. 79.

328. BENTLEY, Roy
"Christmas, Coffman's Farm." FourQt (32:1) Aut 82,
p. 2.

329. BENTZMAN, Bruce Harris
"Visiting a Class." HiramPoR (33) Aut-Wint 82, p. 7.

330. BERG, Sharon
"Absolutions" (for to err is human). PoetryCR (3:4)
Sum 82, p. 6.

331. BERG, Stephen
"Hearing Voices" (to Charlie). Iowa (13:1) Wint 82,
p. 101-103.
"The Rocks." Antaeus (47) Aut 82, p. 71-72.

332. BERGAMIN, Jose
"Every Morning" (tr. by David Garrison). DenQ (17:3)
Aut 82, p. 24.
"I Touch in My Heart" (tr. by David Garrison). DenQ
(17:3) Aut 82, p. 25.

333. BERGER, Suzanne E.
"In the Evening of Creatures." Agni (17) 82, p. 165-
166.
"The Inheritance." Tendril (12) Wint 82, p. 16.

334. BERGMAN, David
"The Madame Considers Her Future State." YaleR
(71:4) Sum 82, p. 583.

335. BERGMAN, Roger
"With My Daughter, Age 3, at the Fair." KanQ (14:3)
Sum 82, p. 42.

336. BERGSTROM, Vera
"Wild Houses." Bogg (48) 82, p. 14.
"Yorie." Bogg (49) 82, p. 12.

337. BERKE, Judith
"Children." SouthernPR (23, i.e. 22:2) Aut 82, p.
22.
"The Color TV." Sky (10-12) Aut 82, p. 35.
"Dance." Kayak (59) Je 82, p. 53.
"Ginger and Me." DenQ (17:2) Sum 82, p. 50-51.
"The House." Kayak (59) Je 82, p. 51.
"How Reading Lady Chatterly's Lover Ruined My Life."
LittleM (13:3/4) 82, p. 5.
"Note to Renoir & Company." KanQ (14:4) Aut 82, p.
34.
"Picasso's Women." KanQ (14:4) Aut 82, p. 4.
"Scenarios." Kayak (59) Je 82, p. 52-53.
"There." Kayak (59) Je 82, p. 52.

338. BERLIND, Bruce
"The Day Nobody Died." PoNow (6:4, issue 34) 82, p.
28.
"An Epistemology of Good Intentions." Paint
(7/8:13/16) 80-81, p. 16-17.
"Funeral Home" (tr. of Pierre Emmanuel). PoNow (6:6,
issue 36) 82, p. 42.
"Hawk-Nuptials on Leafmold" (tr. of Endre Ady). PoNow
(6:5, issue 35) 82, p. 44.
"Thomas" (tr. of Pierre Emmanuel). PoNow (6:6, issue
36) 82, p. 42.

339. BERNAL, Juan Manuel
"Happy Happy" (A Maria). Maize (5:3/4) Spr-Sum 82, p.
23.
"Mientras los salvadorenos estrellanse a morir."
Maize (5:3/4) Spr-Sum 82, p. 24.

340. BERRY, D. C.
"Ankle Bones." KanQ (14:1) Wint 82, p. 40.
"Olive Grove." NewOR (9:3) Wint 82, p. 15.
"Shins." KanQ (14:1) Wint 82, p. 40.

"Shoulder Blades." KanO (14:1) Wint 82, p. 41.
"Thighs." KanO (14:1) Wint 82, p. 41.

341. BERRY, Eleanor
"Meridian." Abraxas (25/26) 82, p. 105.

342. BERRY, Paul
"Cromer Seashore." Bogg (48) 82, p. 53-54.

343. BERRY, S. L.
"Fan Poems." WindO (40, Anti-Haiku issue) Sum 82, p. 17.

344. BERRY, Wendell
"For the Explainers." Ploughs (8:2/3) 82, p. 186.
"Geese." Ploughs (8:2/3) 82, p. 186.

345. BERRYMAN, Tony
"Untitled: The mist, placed on the lake." PottPort (4) 82-83, p. 29.
"Untitled: Thick books standing there." PottPort (4) 82-83, p. 33.

346. BERSSENBRUGGE, Mei-Mei
"The Beautiful Moth." Maize (5:1/2) Aut-Wint 81-82, p. 55.

347. BERTAGNOLLI, Olivia
"Bantry, 1965." NowestR (20:1) 82, p. 91.

348. BERTOLINO, James
"The Poem about Dust." Spirit (6:2/3) 82, p. 47.

349. BETHANCOURT, Marilyn
"Her Dusty Things Remain." Wind (12:46) 82, p. 5.

350. BETT, Stephen
"From 7th Avenue." CanLit (92) Spr 82, p. 70.
"Three Characters" (for Ho Hon). AntigR (51) Aut 82, p. 122-126.

351. BEVAN, Patricia
"Driver's License." Wind (12:44) 82, p. 32.

352. BEYER, Barbara Langham
"Summer Camp." PoNow (7:1, issue 37) 82, p. 5.

353. BEYER, William
"Moon for Grief." Wind (12:46) 82, p. 7.

354. BHAT, V. G.
"The Image" (tr. by K. Raghavendra Rao). NewL (48:3/4) Spr-Sum 82, p. 120.

355. BIAGIONE, Amelia
"Ant" (tr. by Melanie Bowman). DenO (16:4) Wint 82, p. 46.

356. BIBILONI, Rafael
"En Este Minuto." Mairena (4:10) Sum-Aut 82, p. 88.

BIEDMA, Jaime Gil de
See: GIL de BIEDMA, Jaime

357. BIELER, Steven Bryan
"Strike Out." Pig (9) 82, p. 47.

358. BIENVENU, Roberta
"Divorce." Poetry (140:6) S 82, p. 325.

359. BIERDS, Linda
"The Animals off Display." AspenJ (1) Wint 82, p. 32.
"Last Dance." Outbr (8/9) Aut 81-Spr 82, p. 83.
"Twins." AspenJ (1) Wint 82, p. 32.
"Understanding Flightless Birds." Outbr (8/9) Aut 81-Spr 82, p. 81.
"The Wish, at Dawn." Outbr (8/9) Aut 81-Spr 82, p. 82.

BIGAS, Guelcia M. Gonzalez
See: GONZALEZ BIGAS, Guelcia M.

360. BIGGS, Margaret Key
"Getting High." UnderRM (1:2) Aut 82, p. 35.
"Night Screams." UTR (7:2) 82?, p. 18.
"No More Nights of Fire." UnderRM (1:2) Aut 82, p. 35.
"A Thousand Purple Suns." UTR (7:2) 82?, p. 18.

361. BIGUENET, John
"On a Mutual Acquaintance." PoNow (6:5, issue 35) 82, p. 37.
"Scrimshaw." NoAmR (267:3) S 82,p. 24-25.

362. BILICKE, Tom
"Dragoness." Bogg (49) 82, p. 12.
"Holy Family." Bogg (48) 82, p. 18.

363. BILLINGS, Robert
"Blizzard in April." AntigR (48) Wint 82, p. 29-30.
from Cayuga: (vi). PoetryCR (4:1) Sum 82, p. 12.
"Dogs at Night, North Toronto." CrossC (4:2/3) 82, p. 26.
"September." CrossC (4:2/3) 82, p. 26.
"Three Deer." CrossC (4:2/3) 82, p. 26.

364. BILOTTA, John George
"The Old Musician." Humanist (42:5) S-O 82, p. 48-49.

365. BIRDSALL, Jane
"Metal Sculpture." Ascent (7:2) 82, p. 18.
"Soft Sculpture." Ascent (7:2) 82, p. 18.

366. BIRJE-PATIL, J.
"The Secunderabad Club." NewL (48:3/4) Spr-Sum 82, p. 175.

367. BIRKERTS, Sven
"Chekhov's Fancy." Agni (17) 82, p. 52.

368. BIRTHA, Becky
     "The Woman in Buffalo Is Given to Waiting." Iowa
     (12:2/3) Spr-Sum 81, p. 13-14.

369. BISHOP, Bonnie
     "How it was before it all went bad." Hangl (43) Wint
     82-83, p. 49.
     "Invitaion." Hangl (43) Wint 82-83, p. 48.
     "Looking for Water in New Hampshire." Hangl (43)
     Wint 82-83, p. 51.
     "Stepping Out." Hangl (43) Wint 82-83, p. 49-50.

370. BISHOP, George
     "Against Hunting."StoneC (10:1/2) Aut-Wint 82-83, p.
     32.

371. BISHOP, Rand
     "Postcard from Paris." KanQ (14:3) Sum 82, p. 41.

372. BISHOP, W.
     "Wrestling." Thrpny (8) Wint 82, p. 9.

373. BISSONETTE, David
     "The Mind." Comm (109:5) Mr 12, 82, p. 158.

374. BIZZARO, Patrick
     "Fog." KanQ (14:1) Wint 82, p. 114.

375. BJORKLUND, Beth
     "Afternoon" (tr. of Gerhard Fritsch). LitR (25:2)
     Wint 82, p. 221.
     "As a boy I sometimes lifted a chair with my teeth"
     (tr. of Peter Turrini). LitR (25:2) Wint 82, p.
     294.
     "At the stand where we ate fish" (tr. of Peter
     Rosei). LitR (25:2) Wint 82, p. 304.
     "The barn is full of mice"(tr. of Peter Rosei). LitR
     (25:2) Wint 82, p. 305.
     "The car goes slowly around the curve" (tr. of Peter
     Rosei). LitR (25:2) Wint 82, p. 304.
     "The Cats" (tr. of Kurt Klinger). LitR (25:2) Wint
     82, p. 251.
     "Cezanne" (tr. of Rose Auslander). LitR (25:2) Wint
     82, p. 176.
     "Cinema" (tr. of Kurt Klinger). LitR (25:2) Wint 82,
     p. 250.
     "Clouds" (tr. of Jutta Schutting). LitR (25:2) Wint
     82, p. 283.
     "Concerning Rainy Shadows" (tr. of Ernst Jandl). LitR
     (25:2) Wint 82, p. 239.
     "Confirmation Day" (tr. of Juliane Windhager). LitR
     (25:2) Wint 82, p. 179.
     "Continually" (tr. of Herbert Zand). LitR (25:2) Wint
     82, p. 213.
     "The Crazy Lady" (tr. of Kurt Klinger). LitR (25:2)
     Wint 82, p. 251.
     "The Days Count Again" (tr. of Alfred Gesswein). LitR
     (25:2) Wint 82, p. 178.
     "Days in White" (tr. of Ingeborg Bachmann). LitR
     (25:2) Wint 82, p. 241.

"Dead Poet in the Mountains" (tr. of Michael Guttenbrunner). LitR (25:2) Wint 82, p. 199.

"Deserted Room" (tr. of Erich Fried). LitR (25:2) Wint 82, p. 211.

"Dialogue" (tr. of Jeannie Ebner). LitR (25:2) Wint 82, p. 190.

"Do Not Lock Your House" (tr. of Doris Muhringer). LitR (25:2) Wint 82, p. 206.

"A Dove-late Afternoon" (tr. of Jutta Schutting). LitR (25:2) Wint 82, p. 283.

"During the Day He Held a Low-level Position" (tr. of Wilhelm Szabo). LitR (25:2) Wint 82, p. 174.

"Edith" (tr. of Andreas Okopenko). LitR (25:2) Wint 82, p. 261-262.

"Everything Has Its Reason" (tr. of Liesl Ujvary). LitR (25:2) Wint 82, p. 285-286.

"Everything is in order folks" (tr. of Peter Henisch). LitR (25:2) Wint 82, p. 292.

"Everything is only an image in a mirror" (tr. of Ernst Schonwiese). LitR (25:2) Wint 82, p. 175.

"Experiences" (tr. of Christine Busta). LitR (25:2) Wint 82, p. 183.

"Fear" (tr. of Gerhard Fritsch). LitR (25:2) Wint 82, p. 217.

"Figure of Speech" (tr. of Ernst Jandl). LitR (25:2) Wint 82, p. 236.

"Four Attempts at Definition" (tr. of Ernst Jandl). LitR (25:2) Wint 82, p. 236.

"Francis Bacon Paints Velazquez' Pope" (tr. of Wieland Schmied). LitR (25:2) Wint 82, p. 255.

"The Gardener" (tr. of Herbert Zand). LitR (25:2) Wint 82, p. 214.

"The Guardian Angel" (tr. of Michael Guttenbrunner). LitR (25:2) Wint 82, p. 199.

"He Let the House Be" (tr. of Max Holzer). LitR (25:2) Wint 82, p. 189.

"The house is closed" (tr. of Alfred Kolleritsch). LitR (25:2) Wint 82, p. 270.

"Hunger" (tr. of Jeannie Ebner). LitR (25:2) Wint 82, p. 190.

"I am not I"(tr. of Peter Turrini). LitR (25:2) Wint 82, p. 295.

"I can understand why you need so much time for everthing"(tr. of Peter Turrini). LitR (25:2) Wint 82, p. 295.

"I Thought Myself to Be Guest" (tr. of Gerhard Fritsch). LitR (25:2) Wint 82, p. 218.

"I would like to love my enemies" (tr. of Peter Turrini). LitR (25:2) Wint 82, p. 294.

"Important!" (tr. of Liesl Ujvary). LitR (25:2) Wint 82, p. 286.

"In protest against government policies" (tr. of Peter Henisch). LitR (25:2) Wint 82, p. 293.

"In the empty center of the cyclone" (tr. of Christine Lavant). LitR (25:2) Wint 82, p. 184.

"Innery" (tr. of Reinhard Priessnitz). LitR (25:2) Wint 82, p. 301.

"Interpretations" (tr. of Jutta Schutting). LitR (25:2) Wint 82, p. 281.

"Into the Rivers" (tr. of Paul Celan). LitR (25:2)

Wint 82, p. 200.
"Judas" (tr. of Gerhard Fritsch). LitR (25:2) Wint
   82, p. 221.
"Jupiter uninhabited" (tr. of Ernst Jandl). LitR
   (25:2) Wint 82, p. 234.
"A Kind of Loss" (tr. of Ingeborg Bachmann). LitR
   (25:2) Wint 82, p. 242.
"The Landing" (tr. of Michael Guttenbrunner). LitR
   (25:2) Wint 82, p. 198.
"Late Fall" (tr. of Rene Altmann). LitR (25:2) Wint
   82, p. 252.
"Litanies" (tr. of Hertha Kraftner). LitR (25:2) Wint
   82, p. 248-249.
"Lost Goldfish in Dream" (tr. of Doris Muhringer).
   LitR (25:2) Wint 82, p. 207.
"The man sits at the table" (tr. of Peter Rosei).
   LitR (25:2) Wint 82, p. 305.
"The marble the stone-cool the early-spring-gray
   magic" (tr. of Friederike Mayrocker). LitR (25:2)
   Wint 82, p. 231.
"March" (tr. of Ilse Aichinger). LitR (25:2) Wint 82,
   p. 208.
"Mark Tobey's Legacy" (tr. of Wieland Schmied). LitR
   (25:2) Wint 82, p. 256.
"Mattina" (tr. of Kurt Klinger). LitR (25:2) Wint 82,
   p. 251.
"Meeting with Giorgio de Chirico" (tr. of Wieland
   Schmied). LitR (25:2) Wint 82, p. 254.
"Morning Stillness" (tr. of Klaus Demus). LitR (25:2)
   Wint 82, p. 247.
"My Poor Exploited Language" (tr. of Herbert Zand).
   LitR (25:2) Wint 82, p. 216.
"Mysterious Geometry" (tr. of Max Holzer). LitR
   (25:2) Wint 82, p. 187.
"The night in which one re-reads the sentences" (tr.
   of Alfred Kolleritsch). LitR (25:2) Wint 82, p.
   271.
"None of the easy remedies has proved effective" (tr.
   of Christine Lavant). LitR (25:2) Wint 82, p. 185.
"Not Provable" (tr. of Ilse Tielsch). LitR (25:2)
   Wint 82, p. 259.
"Now look here..!" (tr. of H. C. Artmann). LitR
   (25:2) Wint 82, p. 209.
"An Olive Tree in Korfu" (tr. of Christine Busta).
   LitR (25:2) Wint 82, p. 180.
"On the Journey to Your Heart" (tr. of Heidi Pataki).
   LitR (25:2) Wint 82, p. 290-291.
"On the Life of Trees" (tr. of Ernst Jandl). LitR
   (25:2) Wint 82, p. 240.
"Pain" (tr. of Herbert Zand). LitR (25:2) Wint 82, p.
   215.
"Perfection" (tr. of Ernst Jandl). LitR (25:2) Wint
   82, p. 237.
"Poems: a poem is something in the midst of a white
   plane" (tr. of Jutta Schutting). LitR (25:2) Wint
   82, p. 282-283.
"Prague, January 1964" (tr. of Ingeborg Bachmann).
   LitR (25:2) Wint 82, p. 243.
"The Prodigal Son" (tr. of Christine Busta). LitR
   (25:2) Wint 82, p. 181.

"Psalm" (tr. of Paul Celan). LitR (25:2) Wint 82, p. 200.

"Raymondsville" (tr. of Christine Busta). LitR (25:2) Wint 82, p. 182.

"Reflection" (tr. of Michael Guttenbrunner). LitR (25:2) Wint 82, p. 197.

"Resignation" (tr. of Wilhelm Szabo). LitR (25:2) Wint 82, p. 173.

"Rural" (tr. of Erich Fried). LitR (25:2) Wint 82, p. 210.

"Saint Maria Maggiore" (tr. of Gerhard Fritsch). LitR (25:2) Wint 82, p. 220.

"The Snake Star" (tr. of Michael Guttenbrunner). LitR (25:2) Wint 82, p. 197.

"Snowsong" (tr. of Reinhard Priessnitz). LitR (25:2) Wint 82, p. 302-303.

"Some Things" (tr. of Gerhard Ruhm). LitR (25:2) Wint 82, p. 260.

"Sometimes in some chance motion" (tr. of Friederike Mayrocker). LitR (25:2) Wint 82, p. 229.

"Speechless" (tr. of Erich Fried). LitR (25:2) Wint 82, p. 212.

"The Squadron-blue the hemp-yellow drink of triumph" (tr. of Friederike Mayrocker). LitR (25:2) Wint 82, p. 230.

"Successful Attempt" (tr. of Hermann Jandl). LitR (25:2) Wint 82, p. 273.

"Summer Report" (tr. of Klaus Demus). LitR (25:2) Wint 82, p. 246.

"The Summer's Cold" (tr. of Max Holzer). LitR (25:2) Wint 82, p. 187-188.

"Theme and Variations" (tr. of Ingeborg Bachmann). LitR (25:2) Wint 82, p. 244-245.

"These poems were anticipations of actions" (tr. of Alfred Kolleritsch). LitR (25:2) Wint 82, p. 272-273.

"Thinking of Constantin Brancusi" (tr. of Wieland Schmied). LitR (25:2) Wint 82, p. 253.

"This time we have not returned from a trip" (tr. of Alfred Kolleritsch). LitR (25:2) Wint 82, p. 268.

"Thus pressed to the edge, everything is inflexible for the flight" (tr. of Alfred Kolleritsch). LitR (25:2) Wint 82, p. 269.

"Travelogue" (tr. of Ernst Jandl). LitR (25:2) Wint 82, p. 235.

"Trip" (tr. of Reinhard Priessnitz). LitR (25:2) Wint 82, p. 303.

"Tropic Circle" (tr. of Reinhard Priessnitz). LitR (25:2) Wint 82, p. 302.

"Under a Reading Lamp" (tr. of Christine Busta). LitR (25:2) Wint 82, p. 183.

"Untranslatable" (tr. of Wilhelm Szabo). LitR (25:2) Wint 82, p. 173.

"Up and down without a bridge" (tr. of Christine Lavant). LitR (25:2) Wint 82, p. 184.

"Verdict" (tr. of Ernst Jandl). LitR (25:2) Wint 82, p. 238.

"Vita with Postscript" (tr. of Ilse Tielsch). LitR (25:2) Wint 82, p. 259.

"Waiting" (tr. of Doris Muhringer). <u>LitR</u> (25:2) Wint
    82, p. 207.
"Watteau's Coloration" (tr. of Alfred Gesswein). <u>LitR</u>
    (25:2) Wint 82, p. 177.
"We Think Farewell" (tr. of Kurt Klinger). <u>LitR</u>
    (25:2) Wint 82, p. 250.
"We're Satisfied" (tr. of Ilse Tielsch). <u>LitR</u> (25:2)
    Wint 82, p. 258.
"What Belongs to Me" (tr. of Ilse Tielsch). <u>LitR</u>
    (25:2) Wint 82, p. 257.
"When Will the Bird Cry Again?" (tr. of Rene
    Altmann). <u>LitR</u> (25:2) Wint 82, p. 252.
"When your name is added" (tr. of Christine Lavant).
    <u>LitR</u> (25:2) Wint 82, p. 186.
"Why the Many Words?" (tr. of Gerhard Fritsch). <u>LitR</u>
    (25:2) Wint 82, p. 219.
"Will wither like grass" (tr. of Friederike
    Mayrocker). <u>LitR</u> (25:2) Wint 82, p. 230.
"Words Persistently" (tr. of Gerhard Fritsch). <u>LitR</u>
    (25:2) Wint 82, p. 219.
"You Can" (tr. of Jutta Schutting). <u>LitR</u> (25:2) Wint
    82, p. 284.
"You have taken me away from all joy" (tr. of
    Christine Lavant). <u>LitR</u> (25:2) Wint 82, p. 185.
"You Have Taken My Language Away" (tr. of Heidi
    Pataki). <u>LitR</u> (25:2) Wint 82, p. 289.
"Your cage (said the caretaker) only seems too small"
    (tr. of Peter Henisch). <u>LitR</u> (25:2) Wint 82, p.
    293.
"The yew trees in the ice" (tr. of Friederike
    Mayrocker). <u>LitR</u> (25:2) Wint 82, p. 229.

376. BLACK, Charles
    "The Clockwinder." <u>SouthernR</u> (18:3) Sum 82, p. 547.
    "A Disturbed Vision of Spain." <u>DenQ</u> (17:1) Spr 82,
        p. 103.
    "Elegy." <u>DenQ</u> (17:1) Spr 82, p. 102.
    "Remarks for Law Day." <u>LittleM</u> (13:3/4) 82, p. 61.
    "The Shouting of a Huge Belief." <u>SouthwR</u> (67:2) Spr
        82, p. 178.

377. BLACK, Gordon
    "Cutting Moonlight." <u>MendoR</u> (6) Sum 81, p. 49.
    "Early." <u>MendoR</u> (6) Sum 81, p. 125.
    "Love and Lose." <u>MendoR</u> (6) Sum 81, p. 51.
    "Osculation of a Lunar Eclipse." <u>MendoR</u> (6) Sum 81,
        p. 48.

378. BLACK, Harold
    "The Gates of Hell" (A Sestina Inspired by Rodin).
        <u>Vis</u> (8) 82, p. 17-18.

379. BLACKBURN, Michael
    "Invitation" (tr. of Tarjei Vesaas, w. Erik Strand
        and John Morrow). <u>Stand</u> (23:3) 82, p. 8.

380. BLACKBURN, Paul
    "Alley Oop Speaks." <u>Sulfur</u> (2:1, issue 4) 82, p. 82.
    "Annuals." <u>Sulfur</u> (2:1, issue 4) 82, p. 93.

"Close to Home: The Intimations." <u>Sulfur</u> (2:1, issue
    4) 82, p. 88--89.
"Dea, Dia: An Aubade around the Clock." <u>Sulfur</u> (2:1,
    issue 4) 82, p. 71-72.
"Discourse on Values." <u>Sulfur</u> (2:1, issue 4) 82, p.
    76-82.
"From the Parked Car." <u>Sulfur</u> (2:1, issue 4) 82, p.
    96.
"The Ghost." <u>Sulfur</u> (2:1, issue 4) 82, p. 94-95.
"Gipsies in Malaga, 1956." <u>Sulfur</u> (2:1, issue 4) 82,
    p. 69-71.
"Keeping It Up." <u>Sulfur</u> (2:1, issue 4) 82, p. 74-75.
"The Language Lesson." <u>Sulfur</u> (2:1, issue 4) 82, p.
    91-92.
"The Lonelies." <u>Sulfur</u> (2:1, issue 4) 82, p. 92.
"M S." <u>Sulfur</u> (2:1, issue 4) 82, p. 89-90.
"Marseille." <u>Sulfur</u> (2:1, issue 4) 82, p. 65.
"Mediterraneo: a Litoral." <u>Sulfur</u> (2:1, issue 4) 82,
    p. 66-69.
"The Melody Lingers On." <u>Sulfur</u> (2:1, issue 4) 82,
    p. 71.
"Mestiza." <u>Sulfur</u> (2:1, issue 4) 82, p. 75-76.
"O Miles." <u>Sulfur</u> (2:1, issue 4) 82, p. 94.
"The Parallel Voyages." <u>Sulfur</u> (2:1, issue 4) 82, p.
    72-74.
"Statement." <u>Sulfur</u> (2:1, issue 4) 82, p. 64-65.
"To a Friend." <u>Sulfur</u> (2:1, issue 4) 82, p. 82-84.
"Untitled: A grey day at Gangway 4." <u>Sulfur</u> (2:1,
    issue 4) 82, p. 86-88.
"Untitled: Birds chirp listlessly in the heat."
    <u>Sulfur</u> (2:1, issue 4) 82, p. 84-86.
"The Voices, It's Cheap." <u>Sulfur</u> (2:1, issue 4) 82,
    p. 90-91.

381. BLACKFORD, Anne
     "Family Script." <u>Iowa</u> (12:2/3) Spr-Sum 81, p. 21-24.

382. BLADES, Joe
     "Angels Are White." <u>PottPort</u> (4) 82-83, p. 43.

383. BLAINE, Julien
     "Dedicace" (Poeme Metaphysique Numero 15). <u>Os</u> (15)
     82, p. 31.

384. BLAIR, Bill
     "Twilight Zone." <u>LittleBR</u> (2:3) Spr 82, p. 42.

385. BLANKENBURG, Gary
     "How to be Buried." <u>EngJ</u> (71:2) F 82, p. 100.

386. BLASING, Randy
     "Indian Point Fourth." <u>ModernPS</u> (11:1/2) 82, p. 149.
     "Living in the Garden." <u>ModernPS</u> (11:1/2) 82, p.
     148-149.
     "Spree." <u>ModernPS</u> (11:1/2) 82, p. 150.

387. BLAUNER, Laurie
     "The Gem-Cutter's Wife." <u>PoetryNW</u> (23:2) Sum 82, p.
     16.

388. BLAZEK, Douglas
     "The Birth of Igor Stravinsky." Kayak (60) O 82, p.
        64.
     "Games that Burn like Mars in Our Fists." Abraxas
        (25/26) 82, p. 5.
     "Playing the Piano." Abraxas (25/26) 82, p. 7.
     "Time Poem." Abraxas (25/26) 82, p. 6.
     "The Tree Climber's Song." PoNow (6:4, issue 34) 82,
        p. 16.
     "Yellow Weather in a Brown Room." Kayak (60) O 82,
        p. 64.

389. BLENGIO, Jose Rafael
     "Navegaciones" (from Testimonios para el Dia de la
        Ira). Mairena (4:10) Sum-Aut 82, p. 31-32.

390. BLESSINGTON, Francis
     "Feininger in Houston." StoneC (10:1/2) Aut-Wint 82-
        83, p. 33.

391. BLEVINS, Steven
     "Family Graveyard." Hangl (43) Wint 82-83, p. 73.
     "A Man Builds a Castle." Hangl (43) Wint 82-83, p.
        72-73.

392. BLISS, S. W.
     "Linear Equation." HiramPoR (31) Aut-Wint 82, p. 9-
        10.
     "Yehoshua." StoneC (10:1/2) Aut-Wint 82-83, p. 13.

393. BLOCK, Ron
     "Love in the Mid-West." Epoch (31:3) Sum 82, p. 215.

     BLOIS, Peter of
     See: PETER of BLOIS

394. BLOSSOM, Laurel
     "Trap." Poetry (140:3) Je 82, p. 146.
     "Under the Covers." Poetry (140:3) Je 82, p. 147.

395. BLUMENTHAL, Marcia
     "Caveat Emptor." WindO (41) Aut-Wint 82-83, p. 38.

396. BLUMENTHAL, Michael
     "For My Father." Nat (235:20) D 11, 82, p. 632.
     "The Garden." VirQR (58:1) Wint 82, p. 62-64.
     "Learning by Doing." PraS (56:3) Aut 82, p. 16.
     "Over Ohio." PraS (56:3) Aut 82, p. 15.
     "Puer Aeternus" PraS (56:3) Aut 82, p. 15-16.
     "Some Nights at Thirty." AspenJ (1) Wint 82, p. 27.
     "Squid." AmerS (51:1) Wint 81-82, p. 54.
     "Today I am Envying the Glorious Mexicans." GeoR
        (36:2) Sum 82, p. 406.

397. BLY, Robert
     "The Black Hen of Egypt." AmerPoR (11:6) N-D 82, p.
        6.
     "The Boy in the Ditch." Ploughs (8:2/3) 82, p. 209.
     "A Glad Morning." AmerPoR (11:6) N-D 82, p. 6.

"Harvest Time" (tr. of Olav N. Hauge). Ploughs_
   (8:2/3) 82, p. 212.
"The Hummingbird Valley." AmerPoR (11:6) N-D 82, p.
   6.
"Kennedy's Inauguration." Thrpny (11) Aut 82, p. 25.
"Looking at an Old Mirror" (tr. of Olav N. Hauge).
   Ploughs (8:2/3) 82, p. 211.
"A Love That I Have in Secret." AmerPoR (11:3) My-Je
   82, p. 18.
"A Man and a Woman Sit Near Each Other." Ploughs_
   (8:2/3) 82, p. 208.
"Reading an Old Love Poem." AmerPoR (11:3) My-Je 82,
   p. 18.
"The Silence Afterwards" (tr. of Rolf Jacobsen).
   Stand (23:3) 82, p. 10.
"The Stump." Ploughs (8:2/3) 82, p. 210.
"There Are Fiery Days." Ploughs (8:2/3) 82, p. 207.
"There Is Nothing So Scary" (tr. of Olav N. Hauge).
   Ploughs (8:2/3) 82, p. 211.
"Up on Top" (tr. of Olav Hauge). Stand (23:3) 82, p.
   15.

398. BOATRIGHT, Philip
   "For Ariadne of the Isle of Naxos." LittleBR (1:3)
      Spr 81, p. 43.
   "Mendicant." LittleBR (1:3) Spr 81, p. 42-43.
   "Nebraskapoem." LittleBR (1:3) Spr 81, p. 42.
   "Om Mani Padme Hum." LittleBR (1:3) Spr 81, p. 42.
   "Plainsong (Rime)." LittleBR (1:3) Spr 81, p. 43.
   "Winter Abstract." LittleBR (1:2) Wint 80-81, p. 35.
   "The word." LittleBR (1:3) Spr 81, p. 43.

399. BODEEN, Jim
   "At the Grain Terminal Association." CimR (59) Ap
      82, p. 45-46.

400. BOEHRER, Bruce
   "Farmland after Rain." Poem (44) Mr 82, p. 13.
   "Some Versions of a Meteor-Hole." Poem (44) Mr 82,
      p. 14.

401. BOERST, William J.
   "Incommunicado." EngJ (71:3) Mr 82, p. 97.

402. BOETHEL, Martha
   "Falling South." Iowa (12:2/3) Spr-Sum 81, p. 25-26.

403. BOGEN, Don
   "After the Splendid Display." AmerPoR (11:5) S-O 82,
      p. 46.
   "At the Concert" (for Cathryn). Thrpny (8) Wint 82,
      p. 3.

404. BOGGS, William
   "Electric Storm." HiramPoR (32) Spr-Sum 82, p. 8.

405. BOGIN, George
   "47 Boulevard Lannes" (to Marcel Jouhandeau, tr. of
      Jules Supervielle). AmerPoR (11:3) My-Je 82, p. 9.
   "Birth." BelPoJ (32:3) Spr 82, p. 22.

"Father." BelPoJ (32:3) Spr 82, p. 22.
"Grandmother." BelPoJ (32:3) Spr 82, p. 22.
"Horses without Riders" (tr. of Jules Supervielle).
   AmerPoR (11:3) My-Je 82, p. 7.
"Longing for the Earth" (tr. of Jules Supervielle).
   AmerPoR (11:3) My-Je 82, p. 7.
"Memory." BelPoJ (32:3) Spr 82, p. 22.
"The Photographed Hands" (tr. of Jules Supervielle).
   AmerPoR (11:3) My-Je 82, p. 9.
"The Portrait" (tr. of Jules Supervielle). AmerPoR
   (11:3) My-Je 82, p. 8.
"Prophecy" (tr. of Jules Supervielle). NewL (48:2)
   Wint 81-82, p. 36.
"War and Peace on Earth" (tr. of Jules Supervielle).
   AmerPoR (11:3) My-Je 82, p. 7.
"Wisdom." BelPoJ (32:3) Spr 82, p. 22.
"Without Us" (tr. of Jules Supervielle). AmerPoR
   (11:3) My-Je 82, p. 6.
"Without Walls" (to Ramon Gomez de la Serna, tr. of
   Jules Supervielle). AmerPoR (11:3) My-Je 82, p. 8.

406. BOGRAND, Ricardo
    "Dentro de un Pozo." Maize (6:1/2) Aut-Wint 82-83,
       p. 98.

407. BOIES, Jack
    "The Squirrels." BallSUF (23:2) Spr 82, p. 44-45.
    "Up in My Neighbor's Attic." BallSUF (23:2) Spr 82,
       p. 42-43.
    "Up in My Own Attic." BallSUF (23:2) Spr 82, p. 43-
       44.

408. BOISSEAU, Michelle
    "Eavesdropping." GeoR (36:2) Sum 82, p. 334.

409. BOISVERT, P. W.
    "Some Old Songs." StoneC (10:1/2) Aut-Wint 82-83, p.
       16.

410. BOJANOWSKI, Ted
    "Stooped Baker in Kitchen." KanO (14:3) Sum 82, p.
       184.
    "Waves." WindO (41) Aut-Wint 82-83, p. 30.

411. BOLAND, Eavan
    "A Ballad of Beauty and Time." OntR (16) Spr-Sum 82,
       p. 17-19.

412. BOLDEN, Tony
    "Notes from an Optometrist" (for the sake of every
       red blooded American). Obs (7:2/3) Sum-Wint 81, p.
       155-156.
    "Peek a Boo, or: Are You Blind?" Obs (7:2/3) Sum-
       Wint 81, p. 157.
    "To Quote a Black Prince, or: Miles Davis V.S.O.P."
       Obs (7:2/3) Sum-Wint 81, p. 158.

413. BOLEY, Charles W.
    "Amorosamente" (For Mary). Poem (46) N 82, p. 57.

"Canticle" (Song of Songs 5:1). Poem (46) N 82, p.
    55.
"A Poem for Ginger Drawn upon an Old Theme." Poem
    (46) N 82, p. 54.
"Sharp-Shin." Poem (46) N 82, p. 56.

414. BOLLS, Imogene L.
"Deer Watchng in Frijoles Canyon." Im (8:1) 82, p.
    4.

BOLT, William Walter de
See: De BOLT, William Walter

BOLTON, Ahmos Zu
See: ZU-BOLTON, Ahmos

415. BOLTZ, Fred
"Dream of Snow." AntigR (49) Spr 82, p. 90.
"Flight of the Canadian Snow Geese." AntigR (49) Spr
    82, p. 89.
"Pike." AntigR (49) Spr 82, p. 88.

BONALD, Jose Manuel Caballero
See: CABALLERO BONALD, Jose Manuel

416. BONAZZI, Alfredo
"Don't Shut My Eyes" (tr. by Frank Judge). PoNow
    (6:5, issue 35) 82, p. 43.
"Woman of the South" (tr. by Frank Judge). PoNow
    (6:5, issue 35) 82, p. 43.

417. BOND, Harold
"The Hand Itself." PoNow (6:5, issue 35) 82, p. 30.
"Hard Times." PoNow (6:5, issue 35) 82, p. 30.
"Scars." LitR (25:3) Spr 82, p. 370.

418. BONENFANT, Joseph
"La Loi de l'Oiseau." Os (14) 82, p. 5.

419. BONIFAZ NUNO, Ruben
"17." Inti (12) Aut 80, p. 83.
"La Bestia." Inti (12) Aut 80, p. 83-85.

420. BONINA, Mary
"Interlude for Julius Caesar." EngJ (71:4) Ap 82, p.
    53.

421. BONNELL, Paula
"Plain Speech." SouthernPR (22:1) Spr 82, p. 7.

422. BOOK, M. K.
"Herbron Nebraska." WormR (22:1, issue 85) 82, p.
    10.
"A Soul." WormR (22:1, issue 85) 82, p. 10.
"White Hands." WormR (22:1, issue 85) 82, p. 10.

423. BOOKER, Betty
"1939: They Said Fresh Air Would Do Her Good." PoNow
    (7:1, issue 37) 82, p. 5.
"1959: First Communion." Wind (12:45) 82, p. 5.

"Letter to an Unknown Brother c/o General Delivery."
   Wind (12:45) 82, p. 5-6.
"Walking Wounded for 37 Years." ChrC (99:30) O 6,
   82, p. 986.

424. BOOKER, Stephen Todd
   "Pigfish." Grain (10:3) Ag 82, p. 55.
   "A Reflection: Of the Sky on Wheat and the River."
      NewRena (5:1, 15) Aut 82, p. 97.
   "To Kick an Epic Tail." Obs (7:2/3) Sum-Wint 81, p.
      201-203.

425. BOOTH, Philip
   "Dreamboat." Pequod (14) 82, p. 49.
   "Five Figures." OntR (16) Spr-Sum 82, p. 90-91.
   "North Haven." Ploughs (8:2/3) 82, p. 36.
   "Positions." OntR (16) Spr-Sum 82, p. 92.
   "Procession." Hudson (35:2) Sum 82, p. 256.
   "So." Pequod (14) 82, p. 48.
   "A Two Inch Wave." Hudson (35:2) Sum 82, p. 257-258.

426. BORCHERS, Elizabeth
   "I Can Do Nothing" (tr. by Steven Polgar and Nicholas
      Kolumban). AmerPoR (11:1) Ja-F 82, p. 31.

   BORDA, J. G. Cobo
   See: COBO BORDA, J. G.

427. BORENSTEIN, Emily
   "An End without End." Shout (3:1) 82, p. 66.
   "In This Demented Place." Shout (3:1) 82, p. 67.
   "There Shall Be Time No Longer." Shout (3:1) 82, p.
      68.
   "Women of Valor." Shout (3:1) 82, p. 65.

428. BORGES, Carole A.
   "My White Belly Rises." Bogg (49) 82, p. 4.

429. BORKAR, Madhav
   "The Wound" (tr. by Olivinho Gomes). NewL (48:3/4)
      Spr-Sum 82, p. 89.

430. BORLI, Hans
   "By Kroksjoen" (tr. by Anne Born). Stand (23:3) 82,
      p. 52.
   "Morning" (tr. by Anne Born). Stand (23:3) 82, p. 50.
   "The Ship" (tr. by Anne Born). Stand (23:3) 82, p.
      51.
   "Summer Night" (tr. by Anne Born). Stand (23:3) 82,
      p. 51.
   "The Urge to Sing" (tr. by Anne Born). Stand (23:3)
      82, p. 51.

431. BORN, Anne
   "The Builder" (tr. of Leiv Knibestol). Stand (23:3)
      82, p. 48.
   "By Kroksjoen" (tr. of Hans Borli). Stand (23:3) 82,
      p. 52.
   "Captive Wild Rose" (tr. of Cecilie Loveid). Stand
      (23:3) 82, p. 47.

"The Gulf Stream" (tr. of Harald Sverdrup). <u>Stand</u>
(23:3) 82, p. 25.
"Houses" (tr. of Bodil Dyb Wedeld). <u>Stand</u> (23:3) 82,
p. 49.
"Morning" (tr. of Hans Borli). <u>Stand</u> (23:3) 82, p.
50.
"Potatoes" (tr. of Harald Sverdrup). <u>Stand</u> (23:3) 82,
p. 24.
"The Ship" (tr. of Hans Borli). <u>Stand</u> (23:3) 82, p.
51.
"Shopping Precinct" (tr. of Rolf Jacobsen). <u>Stand</u>
(23:3) 82, p. 9.
"Song behind the House (Puberty)" (tr. of Cecilie
Loveid). <u>Stand</u> (23:3) 82, p. 47.
"Summer Night" (tr. of Hans Borli). <u>Stand</u> (23:3) 82,
p. 51.
"The Urge to Sing" (tr. of Hans Borli). <u>Stand</u> (23:3)
82, p. 51.

432. BORN, Nicholas
"Horror, Tuesday" (tr. by Agnes Stein). <u>NewL</u> (49:1)
Aut 82, p. 62.
"It Is Sunday" (tr. by Agnes Stein). <u>NewL</u> (49:1) Aut
82, p. 61-62.
"Time Machine" (tr. by Agnes Stein). <u>NewL</u> (49:1) Aut
82, p. 60-61.

433. BORSON, Roo
"Dove." <u>Waves</u> (10:4) Spr 82, p. 57.
"July." <u>Grain</u> (10:2) My 82, p. 16.
"Night Train." <u>Grain</u> (10:2) My 82, p. 15.
"The Transparence of November." <u>PoetryCR</u> (4:2) Wint
82, p. 10.
"Trust." <u>Grain</u> (10:2) My 82, p. 15.
"Wild Strawberries." <u>Waves</u> (10:4) Spr 82, p. 57.

434. BORUCH, Marianne
"The Blue-black Light." <u>PartR</u> (49:3) 82, p. 431-432.
"The Furniture of Light." <u>Field</u> (26) Spr 82, p. 52.
"Gazing at the Pigs." <u>AmerPoR</u> (11:2) Mr-Ap 82, p.
48.
"Going around His Head for Years" (For Berkeley
Brown). <u>LittleBR</u> (3:1) Aut 82, p. 29.
"The Hammer Falls, Is Falling." <u>Ploughs</u> (8:1) 82, p.
68.
"Harvest." <u>LittleM</u> (13:3/4) 82, p. 43.
"Her Early Darkness." <u>AmerPoR</u> (11:6) N-D 82, p. 6.
"I Put on My Jonathan Edwards This Apple Season."
<u>Field</u> (26) Spr 82, p. 51.
"In a New Place, Through Its Icing." <u>LittleBR</u> (3:2)
Wint 82-83, p. 27.
"Late Summer." <u>AmerPoR</u> (11:2) Mr-Ap 82, p. 48.
"A Line Is Just a Series of Dots." <u>LittleM</u> (13:3/4)
82, p. 41.
"The Old Man Says." <u>KanO</u> (14:3) Sum 82, p. 200 .
"Still Life." <u>LittleM</u> (13:3/4) 82, p. 42.

435. BOSLEY, Keith
"Double Glazing." <u>AntigR</u> (51) Aut 82, p. 67.

"Harrow Hill" (homage to David Jones). <u>AntigR</u> (49)
   Spr 82, p. 51-52.
"Horace 1:11" (for Herbert Lomas). <u>AntigR</u> (49) Spr
   82, p. 53.
"To Take Away." <u>AntigR</u> (51) Aut 82, p. 66.

436. BOSS, Laura
   "There Are No Shades in My Bedroom." <u>Abraxas</u> (25/26)
      82, p. 36-37.

437. BOTTOMS, David
   "The Boy Shepherds' Simile." <u>Poetry</u> (141:3) D 82, p.
      169.
   "Dream of the Christmas Rifle." <u>AmerPoR</u> (11:5) S-O
      82, p. 20.
   "The Drowned." <u>Poetry</u> (140:3) Je 82, p. 130.
   "Drunks in the Bass Boat." <u>MissouriR</u> (5:2) Wint 81-
      82, p. 48-49.
   "Gigging on Allatoona." <u>QW</u> (14) Spr-Sum 82, p. 15.
   "In the Black Camaro." <u>Poetry</u> (140:3) Je 82, p. 125-
      126.
   "Light of the Sacred Harp." <u>MissouriR</u> (5:2) Wint 81-
      82, p. 46-47.
   "Rendezvous: Belle Glade." <u>Poetry</u> (140:3) Je 82, p.
      127-128.
   "Straying from Revival" <u>QW</u> (14) Spr-Sum 82, p. 14.
   "Under the Boathouse." <u>NewYorker</u> (58:27) Ag 23, 82,
      p. 32.
   "Wakulla: Chasing the Gator's Eye." <u>Poetry</u> (140:3)
      Je 82, p. 129.

438. BOUCHER, Alan
   "The Car That Brakes by the Glade" (tr. of Stefan
      Hordur Grimsson). <u>Vis</u> (8) 82, p. 12.
   "Climacteric" (tr. of Johannes ur Kotlum). <u>Vis</u> (8)
      82, p. 22.
   "Dance at the Spring" (tr. of Olafur Johann
      Sigurdsson). <u>Vis</u> (10) 82, p. 4-5.
   "Question" (tr. of Olafur Johann Sigurdsson). <u>Vis</u> (8)
      82, p. 9.
   "Summer" (tr. of Olafur Johann Sigurdsson). <u>Vis</u> (9)
      82, p. 18.
   "Where Does It Lead, This Road?" (tr. of Olafur
      Johann Sigurdsson). <u>Vis</u> (8) 82, p. 8-9.
   "White Night" (tr. of Olafur Haukur Olafsson). <u>Vis</u>
      (10) 82, p. 9.

439. BOULTER, Mike
   "Harvest Moon." <u>CrossC</u> (4:2/3) 82, p. 37.

440. BOURNE, Stephen R.
   "Amazed." <u>Waves</u> (10:4) Spr 82, p. 56.

441. BOUVARD, Marguerite Guzman
   "An American Dejak Visits the Cemetery at
      Sennosechia." <u>QRL</u> (23) 82, p. 52.
   "Branches Moving towards Light." <u>QRL</u> (23) 82, p. 65-
      68.
   "A Circle of Hands" (from Beautyway song of the Kiowa
      Indians). <u>QRL</u> (23) 82, p. 46-48.

"Coming Home" (For a Breton sailor). QRL (23) 82, p.
   59.
"Day's End." QRL (23) 82, p. 22-23.
"Dimensions." QRL (23) 82, p. 39.
"Distances: A Letter to My Father." QRL (23) 82, p.
   14-16.
"Dreams." QRL (23) 82, p. 24.
"Hopi Ceremonial Sash." QRL (23) 82, p. 43-44.
"Horse Shoe Falls Canyon." QRL (23) 82, p. 40.
"Jose Mimo at 60." QRL (23) 82, p. 41.
"Journeys of an Old Woman" (For my Grandmother). QRL
   (23) 82, p. 8-9.
"Journeys over Water." QRL (23) 82, p. 30-32.
"Learning the Scales of Touch." QRL (23) 82, p. 12-
   13.
"Looking Back." QRL (23) 82, p. 28-29.
"Luftmensch." QRL (23) 82, p. 51.
"Magician." QRL (23) 82, p. 45.
"The Man Who Lived on an Island." QRL (23) 82, p.
   37.
"Movements from the Symphony." QRL (23) 82, p. 63-
   64.
"My Father: Coming Home." QRL (23) 82, p. 26.
"My Mother's Garden." QRL (23) 82, p. 10.
"Orpheus." QRL (23) 82, p. 19.
"Passage." QRL (23) 82, p. 17-18.
"Plumbing the Silence." QRL (23) 82, p. 34-35.
"The Road Back." BaratR (8:2) Wint 81, p. 86.
"The Room in Which I Live." QRL (23) 82, p. 20-21.
"Scenes from an Hourglass." QRL (23) 82, p. 57-58.
"Soundings." QRL (23) 82, p. 38.
"Testimonial." QRL (23) 82, p. 36.
"Transformations: A Letter to My Son." QRL (23) 82,
   p. 11.
"Transparencies." QRL (23) 82, p. 61-62.
"Trieste Whose Color and Taste I Am." QRL (23) 82,
   p. 50.
"Trilogy." QRL (23) 82, p. 42.
"Uncle Fritz Remembering." QRL (23) 82, p. 25.
"Valerie: An Elegy for My Mother." QRL (23) 82, p.
   53-56.
"Vasco de Gama Wakes Up in a Strange Land." QRL (23)
   82, p. 60.
"White Nights." QRL (23) 82, p. 27.
"White." QRL (23) 82, p. 69.

442. BOVOSO, Antonio
   "Poem: I like to run a lot." PikeF (4) Spr 82, p.
   20.

443. BOWER, Roger
   "A-One-Companion-Frontier-Settlement-Fabricator."
   Pig (10) 82, p. 25.
   "Prisons." Pig (10) 82, p. 25.

444. BOWERING, George
   "Last Lyrics: From the Mystery." Epoch (32:1) Aut
   82, p. 83.
   "Road Games." Pig (9) 82, p. 57.

"Untitled: If you are squeamish dont prod my rubble."
    Epoch (32:1) Aut 82, p. 82.

445. BOWERING, Marilyn
    "Big Red Train." _MalR_ (63) O 82, p. 79.
    "Borderlines." _MalR_ (63) O 82, p. 76-77.
    "Middle Estuary." _MalR_ (63) O 82, p. 75.
    "Problem Solving." _MalR_ (63) O 82, p. 77-78.
    "Three Swans and an Owl." _MalR_ (63) O 82, p. 74-75.

446. BOWERS, Neal
    "Beginning Winter." _PoNow_ (7:1, issue 37) 82, p. 5.
    "Caring for Succulents." _PoetryNW_ (23:1) Spr 82, p.
        9.
    "Hunter's Moon." _SouthernPR_ (22:1) Spr 82, p. 34.
    "Impasse after Arguing." _SouthwR_ (67:2) Spr 82, p.
        137.
    "Killing Weather." _SouthernHR_ (16:2) Spr 82, p. 104.
    "The Passenger." _CimR_ (58) Ja 82, p. 15.
    "Tracker." _CharR_ (8:1) Spr 82, p. 50.
    "The Warning." _PoetryNW_ (23:1) Spr 82, p. 9-10.

447. BOWIE, Robert
    "Afterwords." _LittleBR_ (3:2) Wint 82-83, p. 85.
    "Presence." _LittleBR_ (2:4) Sum 82, p. 76.

448. BOWMAN, Melanie
    "Ant" (tr. of Amelia Biagione). _DenQ_ (16:4) Wint 82,
        p. 46.
    "The Name is Small and Pale." _Wind_ (12:45) 82, p. 7-
        8.
    "Xerxes' Plane-tree" (tr. of Silvina Ocampo). _DenQ_
        (16:4) Wint 82, p. 45.

449. BOWMAN, P. C.
    "Letter from Crete." _LitR_ (26:1) Aut 82, p. 108-109.
    "Tut." _LitR_ (25:3) Spr 82, p. 338-339.

450. BOYCE, Robert C.
    "Facial Expression." _Bogg_ (48) 82, p. 73.
    "Flight." _Bogg_ (49) 82, p. 38.
    "Follow the Leader." _Bogg_ (48) 82, p. 74.
    "Point of Conception." _Bogg_ (49) 82, p. 50.

451. BOYCHUK, Bohdan
    "The Blind Bandura Players" (tr. by the author and
        Mark Rudman). _Pequod_ (15) 82, p. 82.
    "The End" (tr. of Boris Pasternak, w. Mark Rudman).
        Pequod (14) 82, p. 118-119.
    "The Mirror" (tr. of Boris Pasternak, w. Mark
        Rudman). _Pequod_ (15) 82, p. 70-71.
    "Prince Igor's Campaign" (tr. of Mykola Bazhan, w.
        Mark Rudman). _Pequod_ (14) 82, p. 40-41.
    "Taxco" (tr. by the author and Mark Rudman). _Pequod_
        (15) 82, p. 78.
    "Three-Dimensional Love" (tr. by the author and Mark
        Rudman). _Pequod_ (15) 82, p. 80-81.
    "You Came" (tr. by the author and Mark Rudman).
        Pequod (15) 82, p. 79.

452. BOYD, Greg
     "Biting Irony." WormR (22:4, issue 88) 82, p. 123.
     from Fantastic Incidents, under the listing for
     "Siamese Twins." WormR (22:3, issue 87) 82, p. 78.
     "I Like Critics." WormR (22:3, issue 87) 82, p. 80.
     "Party Favor." WormR (22:3, issue 87) 82, p. 79-80.
     "A Performing Seal." WormR (22:3, issue 87) 82, p.
     80-81.
     "Please Bargaining." WormR (22:3, issue 87) 82, p.
     79.
     "Postcard from the Field: Hot Coal Walking." WormR
     (22:3, issue 87) 82, p. 78.

453. BOYER, Charles M.
     "Night of the Assassin." Abraxas (25/26) 82, p. 96.

454. BOYER, Patsy
     "To Pass" (tr. of Idea Vilarino, w. Mary Crow). DenQ
     (16:4) Wint 82, p. 40-41.

455. BOYLE, William
     "Learning to be Grounded." KanQ (14:3) Sum 82, p.
     98.

456. BOZANIC, Nick
     "Walking Once More to the Barn in Winter."
     SouthernPR (23, i.e. 22:2) Aut 82, p. 56.

457. BOZHILOV, Bozhidar
     "Lilies" (tr. by Jascha Kessler and Alexander
     Shurbanov). Kayak (59) Je 82, p. 71.
     "Troubles" (tr. by Jascha Kessler and Alexander
     Shurbanov). Kayak (59) Je 82, p. 71.
     "The Wise Ones" (tr. by Jascha Kessler and Alexander
     Shurbanov). Kayak (59) Je 82, p. 70-71.

458. BRADBURY, Elspeth
     "Given Moments." Quarry (31:3) Sum 82, p. 67.
     "He's a Jester." Quarry (31:3) Sum 82, p. 68.
     "Starting from Scratch." Quarry (31:3) Sum 82, p.
     67.

459. BRADD, Bill
     "I Was Never Locked Out of the House." MendoR (5)
     Sum 81, p. 62.

460. BRADLEY, Ardyth
     "Hunter." Tendril (13) Sum 82, p. 15.
     "Leah, 16, Dinosaur National Park." Tendril (13) Sum
     82, p. 16.
     "The Testimony of Anne Hutchinson." CutB (19) Aut-
     Wint 82, p. 77-79.

461. BRADLEY, George
     "Aubade." PartR (49:1) 82, p. 135.
     "La Battaglia Di San Romano." SenR (13:1) 82-83, p.
     31-32.
     "M31 in Andromeda." SenR (13:1) 82-83, p. 33-35.
     "Monument Valley." PartR (49:1) 82, p. 136.
     "Terms to Be Met." SenR (13:1) 82-83, p. 29-30.

462. BRADY, Bruce G.
     "A poem is like a letter to yourself." MendoR (5)
     Sum 81, p. 40.
     "Wildflower Afternoon." MendoR (5) Sum 81, p. 30.

463. BRAHAM, Jeanne
     "June Sunday Morning." OhioR (27) 82, p. 100.

464. BRAMAN, Sandra
     "Recess." Sulfur (2:1, issue 4) 82, p. 57-59.

465. BRAND, Alice Glarden
     "On the Occasion of Winning, Losing, and Watching at
     the Same Time." Confr (24) Sum 82, p. 89.

466. BRANDEIS, Irma
     "Mottetti VII" (tr. of Eugenio Montale). Field (27)
     Aut 82, p. 27.

467. BRANHAM, Robert
     "Pure Brightness" (tr. of Kao Chu-Ch'ing, w. Daniel
     Stevenson). PraS (56:1) Spr 82, p. 30.

468. BRASCH, Charles
     "You Do Not Come" (tr. of Amrita Pritam). NewL
     (48:3/4) Spr-Sum 82, p. 118.

469. BRASCHI, Giannina
     from Asalto al Tiempo: (VI). Mairena (4:9) Spr 82,
     p. 79.

470. BRASH, Edward
     "The Argument." Poetry (141:3) D 82, p. 152.
     "Depression." Poetry (141:3) D 82, p. 153.
     "Father of Twins." Poetry (141:3) D 82, p. 153.
     "Forgotten Men 1." Poetry (141:3) D 82, p. 150.
     "Forgotten Men 2." Poetry (141:3) D 82, p. 150.
     "Forgotten Men 3: Geoffrey Graysbook." Poetry
     (141:3) D 82, p. 151.
     "Kate Brash as Divorced Midget." Poetry (141:3) D
     82, p. 151.
     "More Argument." Poetry (141:3) D 82, p. 152.
     "Rachel at Kitty Hawk." Poetry (141:3) D 82, p. 155.
     "Solo-Singing at Temple Knesseth Israel." AmerS
     (51:1) Wint 81-82, p. 103-104.
     "Vive E. E." Poetry (141:3) D 82, p. 154.
     "Wallace Stevens in Hartford." Poetry (141:3) D 82,
     p. 154.

471. BRASS, Lorne
     "Autumnal Acquisitions." AntigR (51) Aut 82, p. 49.
     "Celine." Grain (10:3) Ag 82, p. 52.
     "Night and Day." MalR (63) O 82, p. 72.
     "Public Amuser." MalR (63) O 82, p. 73.
     "Waiting for Spring." AntigR (51) Aut 82, p. 50.
     "Watersounds." Waves (10:3) Wint 82, p. 62.

472. BRAULT, Jacques
     "For a long time I believed for a long time I wanted
     for a long time" (from L'en dessous l'admirable,

tr. by Gertrude Sanderson). <u>AntigR</u> (48) Wint 82, p. 71.

"I have seen my tattered one I have seen her with her flower-eyes" (from L'en dessous l'admirable, tr. by Gertrude Sanderson). <u>AntigR</u> (48) Wint 82, p. 69.

"J'ai vu ma dechiree je l'ai vue de ses yeux-fleurs" (from L'en dessous l'admirable) <u>AntigR</u> (48) Wint 82, p. 68.

"Longtemps j'ai cru longtemps j'ai voulu longtemps" (from L'en dessous l'admirable) <u>AntigR</u> (48) Wint 82, p. 70.

"The old adventure" (from L'en dessous l'admirable, tr. by Gertrude Sanderson). <u>AntigR</u> (48) Wint 82, p. 67.

"Vieille aventure" (from L'en dessous l'admirable) <u>AntigR</u> (48) Wint 82, p. 66.

473. BRAVERMAN, Kate
     "Danielle." <u>Kayak</u> (60) O 82, p. 36-37.

474. BREAZEALE, Daniel
     "The Radar Watcher." <u>Poetry</u> (139:5) F 82, p. 278-280.

475. BREIT, Luke
     "Poem for John Fremont." <u>MendoR</u> (5) Sum 81, p. 26.
     "The Question." <u>MendoR</u> (6) Sum 81, p. 54.
     "Why We Listen." <u>MendoR</u> (5) Sum 81, p. 26.

476. BRENEMAN, Bret
     "Towards Harvest." <u>WorldO</u> (16:4) Sum 82, p. 14.

477. BRETT, Brian
     "The Man in the Snowskin Suit." <u>PoetryCR</u> (4:2) Wint 82, p. 12.

478. BRETT, Peter
     "Closing Riley's Bar." <u>Vis</u> (8) 82, p. 6.
     "Ice Chunks" (Gold Run, California). <u>Vis</u> (8) 82, p. 5.
     "Manzanilla Heat." <u>Wind</u> (12:46) 82, p. 6.

479. BREWER, Kenneth
     "Indiana Weather." <u>Wind</u> (12:45) 82, p. 9.

480. BREYFOGLE, Valorie
     "Jessie's Old Place, Cascade, Iowa." <u>Wind</u> (12:46) 82, p. 8.

     BREYNER ANDRESEN, Sophia de Mello
     <u>See</u>: ANDRESEN, Sophia de Mello Breyner

481. BRICUTH, John
     "Song: Vox." <u>VirQR</u> (58:4) Aut 82, p. 695-696.
     "Song: `Days Since You Have Gone.'" <u>VirQR</u> (58:4) Aut 82, p. 696-697.

482. BRIDGFORD, Kim
     "In Direct Light." <u>ConcPo</u> (15:2) Aut 82, p. 32.

483. BRIGHAM, Besmilr
     "I Dreamed of a Beauty, Love." PoNow (6:5, issue 35)
        82, p. 19.
     "The Muscadine Trellis." Hangl (43) Wint 82-83, p.
        8-10.
     "On a Disturbing Day How Calmly the Needle Moves: The
        Seamstress." Hangl (43) Wint 82-83, p. 6-7.
     "Out of Bluefields, the Ship Loaded with Mahogany."
        Hangl (43) Wint 82-83, p. 4-5.

484. BRIGNONI, Yanina
     "Alma de Antano" (from Rebeldia Abierta). Mairena
        (4:9) Spr 82, p. 80.

485. BRILLIANT, Alan
     "Oil." Paint (7/8:13/16) 80-81, p. 32-35.

486. BRINES, Francisco
     "Perpetual Confinement" (tr. by Anthony Kerrigan).
        DenQ (17:3) Aut 82, p. 47.

487. BRINGHURST, Robert
     "Poem without Voices." CanLit (93) Sum 82, p. 176.
     "The Song of Ptahhotep" (for George Payerle). MalR
        (63) O 82, p. 69-71.

488. BRINSON-PINEDA, Barbara
     "Fire." RevChic (10:1/2) Wint-Spr 82, p. 36-37.
     "Maria la O." RevChic (10:1/2) Wint-Spr 82, p. 38-
        41.

489. BRISSEY, Paul
     "August Nocturne." UnderRM 1(1) Spr 82, p. 31.
     "Spring forth first breath from sodden earth."
        UnderRM (1:2) Aut 82, p. 12.

490. BRITT, Alan
     "About Death." UTR (7:1) 81, p. 10.
     "The Afternoon of the Light." UTR (7:1) 81, p. 6.
     "The Baby Harp Seal." UTR (7:1) 81, p. 7.
     "Brother." UTR (7:1) 81, p. 10.
     "Brown Tipped Butterfly." UTR (7:1) 81, p. 26.
     "Butterfly Tango." UTR (7:1) 81, p. 11.
     "Cheyanne." UTR (7:1) 81, p. 22.
     "The Dancer." UTR (7:1) 81, p. 26.
     "Delightful Myth." UTR (7:1) 81, p. 6.
     "The Despair World." UTR (7:1) 81, p. 30-31.
     "Dining at Maria's" (for Ernie Kosmakos). UTR (7:1)
        81, p. 15.
     "A Dream along the Road." UTR (7:1) 81, p. 24.
     "First Winter Snow." UTR (7:1) 81, p. 29.
     "For the Unborn." UTR (7:1) 81, p. 8-9.
     "Gentle and the Dead." UTR (7:1) 81, p. 7.
     "In the Middle of Backgammon." UTR (7:1) 81, p. 23.
     "Incidentally." UTR (7:1) 81, p. 20.
     "Jewish School Teacher Tango." UTR (7:1) 81, p. 25.
     "Little Black Dog." UTR (7:1) 81, p. 23.
     "Men are carrying sacks of darkness." UTR (7:1) 81,
        p. 22.
     "Midnight." UTR (7:1) 81, p. 24.

"Moonhand." <u>UTR</u> (7:1) 81, p. 25.
"The Morning-Glory." <u>UTR</u> (7:1) 81, p. 29.
"No Doubt about It, This Is Senseless." <u>UTR</u> (7:1)
    81, p. 5.
"O." <u>UTR</u> (7:1) 81, p. 21.
"Orange." <u>UTR</u> (7:1) 81, p. 14.
"Our Nuclear Future and Jazz." <u>UTR</u> (7:1) 81, p. 16-
    17.
"Poem Washed in from a Fragment of Cold Moon (#9)."
    <u>UTR</u> (7:1) 81, p. 15.
"Prelude 2." <u>UTR</u> (7:1) 81, p. 12.
"Procession of the Sardar." <u>UTR</u> (7:1) 81, p. 21.
"The Silver Violin." <u>UTR</u> (7:1) 81, p. 12.
"Solitary." <u>UTR</u> (7:1) 81, p. 20.
"Solitude." <u>UTR</u> (7:1) 81, p. 20.
"Southern Evening." <u>UTR</u> (7:1) 81, p. 18.
"The Stranger" (after Charles Baudelaire). <u>UTR</u> (7:1)
    81, p. 18.
"There Is No Space Wider Than That of Grief, There Is
    No Universe Like That Which Bleeds." <u>UTR</u> (7:1) 81,
    p. 13-14.
"Today was sadder than usual." <u>UTR</u> (7:1) 81, p. 28.
"Together." <u>UTR</u> (7:1) 81, p. 27.
"La Valse." <u>UTR</u> (7:1) 81, p. 21.
"Visiting My Wife at the Hospital." <u>UTR</u> (7:1) 81, p.
    19.
"The Waltz." <u>UTR</u> (7:1) 81, p. 28.
"Young Man in March." <u>UTR</u> (7:1) 81, p. 27.

491. BROCK, Randall
    "Holding." <u>SmPd</u> (19:3, issue 56) Aut 82, p. 36.
    "In Me." <u>SmPd</u> (19:3, issue 56) Aut 82, p. 8.

492. BROCK, Van K.
    from The Nazi Poems: "Hitler." <u>NoAmR</u> (267:2) Je
        82,p. 51.
    "Novas." <u>SouthernR</u> (18:4) Aut 82, p. 808-809.
    "Snake." <u>SouthernR</u> (18:4) Aut 82, p. 806-808.
    "The Survivor" (To Viktor Frankl and Martin Buber:
        for the songs). <u>NoAmR</u> (267:4) D 82,p. 9.

493. BROCK-BROIDO, Lucie
    "The Wind in Search of the Heat." <u>SouthernR</u> (18:3)
        Sum 82, p. 536-537.

494. BROCKLEBANK, IAN
    "The Chair and What Is on It." <u>Bogg</u> (49) 82, p. 53.

495. BRODER, Dean
    "Afterimage: Tampa Warehouse." <u>UTR</u> (7:2) 82?, p. 21.
    "It Is 8 A.M. and I Am Dreaming of Chickens, Cows,
        Pigs, Fish, and Turkeys." <u>UTR</u> (7:2) 82?, p. 23.
    "Kettle Whistles." <u>UTR</u> (7:2) 82?, p. 22.
    "The Mailbox on Route 145." <u>UTR</u> (7:2) 82?, p. 22.
    "Private Life Trauma," <u>UTR</u> (7:2) 82?, p. 23.

496. BRODINE, Karen
    "We Are the Ones We Have Been Waiting for" (June
        Jordan). <u>HangL</u> (41) 82, p. 13-15.

497. BRODSKY, Joseph
    "Eclogue IV: Winter" (tr. by the author). NewYorker
        (58:6) Mr 29, 82, p. 46-47.
    "Epitaph for a Tyrant." NewYRB (29:20) D 16, 82, p.
        18.

498. BRODSKY, Louis Daniel
    "Between Connections." SouthernR (18:1) Wint 82, p.
        178.
    "Joseph K." SouthernR (18:1) Wint 82, p. 176-177.
    "Manager of Outlet Stores." SouthernR (18:1) Wint
        82, p. 175-176.
    "Plant Manager No. 3." KanQ (14:1) Wint 82, p. 73.
    "The Voyage of A. Gordon Pym." CapeR (18:1) Wint 82,
        p. 34.

499. BRODY, Harry
    "The End of the Good Months." FourQt (31:4) Sum 82,
        p. 22.
    "Iowa." PoNow (7:1, issue 37) 82, p. 5.

500. BRODY, Polly L.
    "February Eagle." BallSUF (23:4) Aut 82, p. 54.

501. BROMLEY, Anne
    "Birds in the Hand." PartR (49:3) 82, p. 433-434.
    "The New Lunch Poems: Graveyard Respite." PoetC
        (14:2) 82, p. 41.
    "The New Lunch Poems: Man beside Tree Trunk." PoetC
        (14:2) 82, p. 39.
    "The New Lunch Poems: Rain." PoetC (14:2) 82, p. 40.
    "The New Lunch Poems: Today's Special." PoetC (14:2)
        82, p. 40.
    "The New Lunch Poems: Woman beside Fountain." PoetC
        (14:2) 82, p. 39.
    "Teel St. Trailer Court." PoetC (14:2) 82, p. 38.

502. BROOK, Donna
    "The Eyes of Children as They Drown" (for Mira
        Rothenberg). HangL (42) 82, p. 8-9.
    "Fear." HangL (42) 82, p. 5.
    "It's So Simple It's Complex." HangL (42) 82, p. 7.
    "Pose." HangL (42) 82, p. 3.
    "The School of Pain." HangL (42) 82, p. 6.
    "Smell." HangL (42) 82, p. 4.

503. BROOKS, David
    "The Compost Quinces" (for Pier Giorgio Di Cicco)
        NewEngR (4:4) Sum 82, p. 505-506.
    "Domino Theory." WestB (10) 82, p. 41.
    "The Horsemen." NewEngR (4:4) Sum 82, p. 507-509.
    "The Magi." NewEngR (4:4) Sum 82, p. 502-504.
    "Red Wagon." WestB (11) 82, p. 62.
    "Visitation." WestB (10) 82, p. 41.

504. BROOKS, Jack
    "Birches on a Summer Hill." CrossC (4:2/3) 82, p.
        50.
    "D-Jay" (for Hal Stubbs). Bogg (49) 82, p. 45.

505. BROOKS, James
    "Arts: Hokudoso." <u>SoCaR</u> (14:2) Spr 82, p. 50.
    "Arts: Kuragash." <u>SoCaR</u> (14:2) Spr 82, p. 50.
    "Arts: Uekimi." <u>SoCaR</u> (14:2) Spr 82, p. 50.
    "Chinya." <u>BallSUF</u> (23:3) Sum 82, p. 58.

506. BROOKS, Thomas Earl
    "Prime Time." <u>Obs</u> (7:2/3) Sum-Wint 81, p. 195.

507. BROSMAN, Catharine Savage
    "Cleaning the Shed." <u>SewanR</u> (90:2) Spr 82, p. 218.
    "Clear Creek." <u>SouthernR</u> (18:3) Sum 82, p. 570-571.
    "Letter to Padre Island." <u>SouthwR</u> (67:1) Wint 82, p.
        31-32.
    "Reading Old Letters." <u>SewanR</u> (90:2) Spr 82, p. 217.
    "River Bend." <u>SouthernHR</u> (16:3) Sum 82, p. 256.
    "Windmills." <u>SouthernR</u> (18:3) Sum 82, p. 572-573.

508. BROSMER, Mary
    "In Poetry Class." <u>EngJ</u> (71:3) Mr 82, p. 46.

509. BROUGHTON, James
    "Elohim and Emmanuel were a supremely handsome
        couple." <u>PoNow</u> (6:6, issue 36) 82, p. 23.
    "Phallus wakes the morning Sun." <u>PoNow</u> (6:6, issue
        36) 82, p. 23.
    "Thanks to you running mate." <u>PoNow</u> (6:6, issue 36)
        82, p. 23.

510. BROUGHTON, T. Alan
    "Aria Da Capo." <u>MichQR</u> (21:2) Spr 82, p. 350.
    "A Dream Before Breakfast." <u>NewEngR</u> (4:4) Sum 82, p.
        537.
    "Invocations." <u>Northeast</u> (3:14) Wint 82-83, p. 3.
    "January Thaw." <u>VirQR</u> (58:1) Wint 82, p. 67.
    "Les Nympheas." <u>WestB</u> (10) 82, p. 54.
    "Refrain." <u>Northeast</u> (3:14) Wint 82-83, p. 5.
    "Slow Motion." <u>LitR</u> (25:4) Sum 82, p. 508-509.
    "Waking Older." <u>Northeast</u> (3:14) Wint 82-83, p. 4.

511. BROUMAS, Olga
    "Epithalamion." <u>Iowa</u> (12:2/3) Spr-Sum 81, p. 29-30.
    "Mornings Remembering Last Nights." <u>Iowa</u> (12:2/3)
        Spr-Sum 81, p. 27-28.

512. BROWN, Harriet
    "The Chronicle of Misgivings." <u>OP</u> (33) Spr 82, p.
        26.
    "In Our Dream World." <u>OP</u> (33) Spr 82, p. 27.
    "In Our Mothers' World." <u>Outbr</u> (10/11) Aut 82-Spr
        83, p. 90.
    "Man with Bird" (For Ellen Sherman). <u>OP</u> (33) Spr 82,
        p. 24-25.

513. BROWN, Jeffrey R.
    "Let's Stop Here." <u>KanQ</u> (14:3) Sum 82, p. 129.

514. BROWN, Laurie Lew
    "Always the Reluctant Sportsman." <u>PoetryNW</u> (23:2)
        Sum 82, p. 36.

"Consolation." PoetryNW (23:2) Sum 82, p. 35-36.
"Ice." PoetryNW (23:2) Sum 82, p. 37.

515. BROWN, Lloyd
    "Blue Mitchell (1930-1979)." Obs (7:2/3) Sum-Wint
        81, p. 198-199.
    "From an Anthropologist's Notebook." Obs (7:2/3)
        Sum-Wint 81, p. 199-200.
    "Over Texas." Obs (7:2/3) Sum-Wint 81, p. 198.
    "Summer Heat (Jamaica 1980)." Obs (7:2/3) Sum-Wint
        81, p. 196-197.

516. BROWN, Polly
    "I haven't travelled this far alone in months." SmPd
        (19:1, issue 54) Wint 82, p. 30.
    "Winter in Eastern Massachusetts." SmPd (19:1, issue
        54) Wint 82, p. 29.

517. BROWN, Ronald
    "Ice Storm." SmPd (19:1, issue 54) Wint 82, p. 9.

518. BROWN, Simon
    "Crystal Spears." Bogg (49) 82, p. 46.
    "Orbit." Bogg (48) 82, p. 72.

519. BROWN, Spencer
    "Rorschach Test." SewanR (90:4) Aut 82, p. 514-515.

520. BROWN, Steven Ford
    "Baudelaire." Kayak (60) O 82, p. 9.
    "Conversation 4." UnderRM (1:2) Aut 82, p. 32.
    "Disappearance." Bogg (48) 82, p. 8.
    "Eyework." UnderRM (1:2) Aut 82, p. 31.
    "Her Glance." UnderRM (1:2) Aut 82, p. 32.
    "A Nude Woman under the Eyelid." Gargoyle (15/16)
        80, p. 26.
    "The Sea Is Everything." UnderRM 1(1) Spr 82, p. 38.
    "Sunlight Collapses." UnderRM (1:2) Aut 82, p. 31.

521. BROWN, Thelma
    "You Are a Grandpa Named Seth." NowestR (20:2/3) 82,
        p. 264-265.

522. BROWN, W. L.
    "Mushrooms, the Dark Wood in Kingston." Thrpny (11)
        Aut 82, p. 8.

523. BROWNE, Michael Dennis
    "Child's Elm Song." Kayak (59) Je 82, p. 50.
    "Little Women." Kayak (60) O 82, p. 65.
    "Now." Kayak (58) Ja 82, p. 58.

    BROWNE, Nicholas Mason
    See: MASON-BROWNE, Nicholas

524. BRUCE, Debra
    "Elegy for Cliches." GeoR (36:4) Wint 82, p. 852-
        853.
    "Fortune Cookies." LitR (25:3) Spr 82, p. 368.
    "Native Language." LitR (25:3) Spr 82, p. 369.

525. BRUCE, Lennart
"The March of the Future" (tr. of Edith Sodergran).
PoNow (6:5, issue 35) 82, p. 42.
"The Road Moves Up to Me." Spirit (6:2/3) 82, p.
148-149.

526. BRUCHAC, Joseph
"A Biography." Telescope (2) Aut 81, p. 69-60.
"Cambodia 1973." Abraxas (25/26) 82, p. 26-27.
"Salt." Nimrod (26:1) Aut-Wint 82, p. 82.
"This Car Climbed Mt. Washington." PoNow (6:4, issue
34) 82, p. 21.
"Tonawanda." Spirit (6:2/3) 82, p. 46.
"Windigo." Telescope (2) Aut 81, p. 77-78.

527. BRUEY, Alfred J.
"The Fable of the Famous Poet." PoNow (7:1, issue
37) 82, p. 5.

528. BRUHAC, Joseph
"In Wilderness." Stand (23:1) 81-82, p. 70.

529. BRUMMELS, J. V.
"After a Night in Church." SoDakR (20:4) Wint 82-83,
p. 35.
"Canton" (for Grace). MidwQ (24:1) Aut 82, p. 54-55.
"A Dream of the Great Depression." CharR (8:2) Aut
82, p. 34-35.
"Host." HolCrit (19:3) Je 82, p. 18.
"The Man Who Owns the Restaurant." MidwQ (24:1) Aut
82, p. 56.
"A Question of Need." MidwQ (24:1) Aut 82, p. 52-53.

530. BRUMMET, John
"Keltner's Pond." ConcPo (15:2) Aut 82, p. 49.
"Song (Peter Ahlberg, May 21, 1981)." ConcPo (15:2)
Aut 82, p. 50.

531. BRUNN, Don
"Kitchen Song." PoNow (7:1, issue 37) 82, p. 6.

532. BRUNNQUELL, Don
"How I Learned Silence." Northeast (3:14) Wint 82-
83, p. 13.

533. BRUNO, Gustavo Luis
"Me Abandono al Cristal de la Ensenada." Mairena
(4:10) Sum-Aut 82, p. 62.

534. BRUNOSKI, Elizabeth
"Be Careful." Epoch (32:1) Aut 82, p. 63.
"Millenium." Epoch (32:1) Aut 82, p. 62.

535. BRUSH, Thomas
"Doors" (for my father). Tendril (13) Sum 82, p. 20.
"Dreams." PoetryNW (23:3) Aut 82, p. 41.
"July" (for Frank). Tendril (13) Sum 82, p. 18-19.
"Opening Night." PoNow (7:1, issue 37) 82, p. 22.
"The Owl." PoNow (7:1, issue 37) 82, p. 22.
"Reno." Tendril (13) Sum 82, p. 17.

BRUNT, H. L. van
  See: Van BRUNT, H. L.

536. BRUTUS, Dennis
  "Somehow We Survive." ChrC (99:5) F 17, 82, p. 164.

537. BRYSMAN, Anita
  "Harvest." PoNow (7:1, issue 37) 82, p. 6.
  "Screen Test." LittleBR (2:3) Spr 82, p. 47.

538. BUCHANAN, Carl
  "His Face." KanQ (14:3) Sum 82, p. 25.

539. BUCKAWAY, C. M.
  "Winter." WritersL S 82, p. 15.

540. BUCKELS, Elizabeth
  "The Measure." AntigR (50) Sum 82, p. 114.
  "Touring Cornwall -- Mawnan: A Truth." AntigR (50)
  Sum 82, p. 115-116.

541. BUCKHOLTS, Claudia
  "In the Gooseberry Garden" (Samois-sur-Seine).
  HiramPoR (31) Aut-Wint 82, p. 11.

542. BUCKLAND, Karen
  "After the Party." Bogg (49) 82, p. 46.
  "Leaving You." Bogg (48) 82, p. 48.

543. BUCKLEY, Christopher
  "59th Street Studio" (from Shells -- Monologues on
  the Paintings of Georgia O'Keeffe). OntR (16) Spr-
  Sum 82, p. 25.
  "Blue Hooks in Weather." Nat (235:18) N 27, 82, p.
  570.
  "Like Noah's Dove" (for my grandmother Nora Pearl
  Miller(1896-1980). NewEngR (5:1/2) Aut-Wint 82, p.
  164-166.
  "Munch's `Evening on Karl Johan Street'." SewanR
  (90:1) Wint 82, p. 21.
  "Munch's `Harvesting Women'." SewanR (90:1) Wint 82,
  p. 22.
  "The New York Paintings" (from Shells -- Monologues
  on the Paintings of Georgia O'Keeffe). OntR (16)
  Spr-Sum 82, p. 24.
  "O'Keeffe's `Shell I'." SewanR (90:1) Wint 82, p.
  20.
  "Palo Duro Canyon" (from Shells -- Monologues on the
  Paintings of Georgia O'Keeffe). OntR (16) Spr-Sum
  82, p. 23.

544. BUCKLEY, Vincent
  "Hunger-Strike." Quarry (31:3) Sum 82, p. 31-37.

545. BUCKNER, Gloria
  "Near the open grave" (Haiku). LittleBR (1:3) Spr
  81, p. 55.

546. BUDY, Andrea Hollander
  "Advice." GeoR (36:4) Wint 82, p. 891.

547. BUELL, Tom
    "The Moon at Spetsai in Eclipse." <u>PortR</u> (28:1) 82,
    p. 17.

548. BUETTNER, Shirley
    "The Swiss Chalet Barometer." <u>Abraxas</u> (25/26) 82, p.
    55.
    "The Visit." <u>Northeast</u> (3:14) Wint 82-83, p. 22.

549. BUFIS, Paul
    "God Save Us from the Helpers #6." <u>Vis</u> (9) 82, p.
    37.
    "Route." <u>Vis</u> (8) 82, p. 11.
    "The Things We Do Are Serious to Whom." <u>DekalbLAJ</u>
    (14:1/4) Aut 80-Sum 81, p. 66.

550. BUGEJA, Michael J.
    "The Only Morning My Mother Didn't Worship Her
    Husband." <u>CimR</u> (58) Ja 82, p. 52.

551. BUISSON, Justine
    "Collapstars." <u>Nimrod</u> (25:2) Spr-Sum 82, p. 43.
    "The Hidden Glimmering Within All Things." <u>Nimrod</u>
    (25:2) Spr-Sum 82, p. 42.
    "Incident at Pond Creek" (In memory of Bud Wilkens).
    <u>Nimrod</u> (25:2) Spr-Sum 82, p. 9.
    "Rainmaker." <u>KanQ</u> (14:1) Wint 82, p. 174.

552. BUKER, Russell
    "Flower." <u>AntigR</u> (49) Spr 82, p. 21.

553. BUKOWSKI, Charles
    "Another Horse Poem for All My Many Dear Friends."
    <u>Spirit</u> (6:2/3) 82, p. 167-170.
    "Bearclaw Morning." <u>Abraxas</u> (25/26) 82, p. 31-34.
    "Brown." <u>PoNow</u> (6:6, issue 36) 82, p. 32.
    "Dig Me a Ditch." <u>SeC</u> (9:1/2) 80, p. 36-37.
    "The Drunk with the Little Legs." <u>WormR</u> (22:3, issue
    87) 82, p. 107-108.
    "The Eternal Players." <u>PoNow</u> (6:6, issue 36) 82, p.
    33.
    "Fog." <u>Abraxas</u> (25/26) 82, p. 28-31.
    "Getting My Money's Worth." <u>WormR</u> (22:1, issue 85)
    82, p. 2-4.
    "I Can't Stop." <u>WormR</u> (22:4, issue 88) 82, p. 153.
    "Louis-Ferdinand Destouches." <u>WormR</u> (22:1, issue 85)
    82, p. 1.
    "My God." <u>PoNow</u> (6:5, issue 35) 82, p. 7.
    "The Night I Broke Away from Hemingway." <u>PoNow</u> (6:5,
    issue 35) 82, p. 6-7.
    "No Chance in Pomona." <u>WormR</u> (22:3, issue 87) 82, p.
    108.
    "One for the Dark." <u>Abraxas</u> (25/26) 82, p. 28.
    "Parked." <u>WormR</u> (22:3, issue 87) 82, p. 105-106.
    "Parts Dept." <u>WormR</u> (22:3, issue 87) 82, p. 106.
    "Pretty Boy." <u>WormR</u> (22:4, issue 88) 82, p. 151-153.
    "Slaughter." <u>WormR</u> (22:1, issue 85) 82, p. 4-5.
    "Those." <u>WormR</u> (22:1, issue 85) 82, p. 5-6.
    "Trouble." <u>WormR</u> (22:1, issue 85) 82, p. 2.
    "Water the Plants." <u>PoNow</u> (6:4, issue 34) 82, p. 8.

554. BULL, Arthur
    "River Snow" (tr. of Liu Tsung-yuan). Dandel (9:1)
        82, p. 22.
    "Spring Dawn" (tr. of Meng Hao-jan). Dandel (9:1) 82,
        p. 22.

555. BULLIS, Jerald
    "Approaching Dinner." Poetry (139:6) Mr 82, p. 330-
        331.
    "Carpe Diem." Poetry (139:6) Mr 82, p. 333.
    "February 14." NewEngR (4:3) Spr 82, p. 391-394.
    "Raleigh and Marlowe Were Right." Poetry (139:6) Mr
        82, p. 332.
    "Trumansburg Creek." Poetry (139:6) Mr 82, p. 328-
        329.

556. BULLOCK, Michael
    from Lines in the Dark Wood: "Belladonna." WestCR
        (16:4) Ap 82, p. 32.
    from Lines in the Dark Wood: "Lines in the Dark
        Wood." WestCR (16:4) Ap 82, p. 32.
    from Lines in the Dark Wood: "Needle of Light."
        WestCR (16:4) Ap 82, p. 31.
    from Lines in the Dark Wood: "Soul of the Dead."
        WestCR (16:4) Ap 82, p. 31.
    from Lines in the Dark Wood: "The Thieves of Light."
        WestCR (16:4) Ap 82, p. 33.
    "Quadriga for Judy" (for Judy Fletcher). WestCR
        (17:2) O 82, p. 20-21.

557. BURAK, Kathryn
    "The Bee-Keeper's Wife." WestB (11) 82, p. 78.
    "Why Buildings Stand Up." WestB (11) 82, p. 79.

558. BURCH, Eva
    "Wharves." Pequod (14) 82, p. 103.

559. BURCHARD, Rachael C.
    "Escapade." HolCrit (19:5) D 82, p. 17.

560. BURGIS, Allan
    "Bar Scene, Eureka, California." Bogg (48) 82, p. 6-
        7.

561. BURGOS, Julia de
    "Una Cancion a Albizu Campos." Areito (8:31) 82,
        inside back cover.
    "Oh Mar, No Esperes Mas!" (from El Mar y Tu). Mairena
        (4:9) Spr 82, p. 80.

562. BURKE, Lianne
    "Daphne." Bogg (48) 82, p. 11-12.

563. BURKE, Richard J.
    "Shagbark Hickory." Comm (109:3) F 12, 82, p. 88.

564. BURKHARDT, Marilyn
    "To Mary." NowestR (20:2/3) 82, p. 231.

565. BURKMAN, Kay
"Jade Whiskers." AntigR (51) Aut 82, p. 120.
"Postcard from Niagara: Maid of the Mist." AntigR
(51) Aut 82, p. 121.
"Weather Report." AntigR (51) Aut 82, p. 120.

566. BURLINGAME, Robert
"The Visit." OhioR (29) 82, p. 38.

567. BURNES, Carol
"Finger Painting." LittleM (13:3/4) 82, p. 89.

568. BURNHAM, Deborah
"Goose Girl." LitR (25:3) Spr 82, p. 374.
"Winter Apples." LitR (25:3) Spr 82, p. 375.

569. BURNS, H. L.
"The cold dairy barn." WindO (40, Anti-Haiku issue)
Sum 82, p. 44.
"A full harvest moon." WindO (40, Anti-Haiku issue)
Sum 82, p. 44.
"The sound of water." WindO (40, Anti-Haiku issue)
Sum 82, p. 44.

BURNS, Lee
See: BURNS, H. L.

570. BURNS, Michael
"Backhoe." PoNow (7:1, issue 37) 82, p. 6.
"Fathers." MidwQ (24:1) Aut 82, p. 58.
"On My Twenty-Eighth Brithday" (for Vicki). MidwQ
(24:1) Aut 82, p. 57.

571. BURNS, R. W.
"The Testimony of Jonquils." HiramPoR (31) Aut-Wint
82, p. 12.

572. BURNS, Ralph
"CEC Tours a School for the Retarded." Epoch (31:2)
Spr 82, p. 128.
"Fishing in Winter." Field (27) Aut 82, p. 62.
"Only One" (After a painting by Georgia O'Keeffe).
Field (27) Aut 82, p. 61.
"Suicide: Leaving the Blame" (for my father). AspenJ
(1) Wint 82, p. 30.

573. BURQUE, Darrell
"Getting the Tulips In." RevIn (11:1) Spr 81, p.
128.
"The Yellow Iris in Jackie Kenedy's Head." RevIn
(11:1) Spr 81, p. 129.

574. BURR, Gray
"The Day After." MassR (23:1) Spr 82, p. 115-116.

575. BURRIS, Sidney
"On Living with a Fat Woman in Heaven." Poetry
(139:4) Ja 82, p. 208-209.
"Still Life, But One." Atl (249:1) Ja 82, p. 77.

576. BURROWS, E. G.
      "Anthology." MichQR (21:1) Wint 82, p. 152.
      "The Cave-in." Ascent (7:3) 82, p. 46-47.
      "Livingston Street." Sky (10-12) Aut 82, p. 54.
      "Migrations through the Middle Country." Epoch
        (32:1) Aut 82, p. 27.
      "The Misnamed." PoNow (6:4, issue 34) 82, p. 36.
      "The Mothering." Ascent (8:1) 82, p. 18.
      "The Park." PoNow (6:5, issue 35) 82, p. 20.
      "Wild Men." Sky (10-12) Aut 82, p. 53.

577. BURSK, Chris
      "At naptime she spread out a book of bugs." Shout
        (3:1) 82, p. 54-55.
      "Cleaning House." Shout (3:1) 82, p. 56.
      "No New Developments." Shout (3:1) 82, p. 57.

578. BURSK, Christopher
      "After I Wake, I Want to Shape My Body Still to
        Sleep." ManhatR (2:1) 81, p. 43-44.
      "Allowance." QRL (23) 82, p. 23-24.
      "At Grandfather's Place of Work." QRL (23) 82, p.
        10.
      "The Belltower." QRL (23) 82, p. 48.
      "Biographies of Famous Americans." QRL (23) 82, p.
        15.
      "Branch Sounds." QRL (23) 82, p. 37.
      "Buying Your Father's House Back." QRL (23) 82, p.
        82.
      "Correspondence." QRL (23) 82, p. 40-41.
      "Coulter's Hill." QRL (23) 82, p. 76-77.
      "Diseases of the Blood." QRL (23) 82, p. 29-30.
      "Dressing Up." QRL (23) 82, p. 18-20.
      "Drowning the Dolls." QRL (23) 82, p. 58.
      "Egypt, Massachusetts." QRL (23) 82, p. 35-36.
      "Empire Stamps." QRL (23) 82, p. 64.
      "The Eye Doctor's." QRL (23) 82, p. 71-72.
      "Falling Dead." QRL (23) 82, p. 59.
      "The Family Boat" (for Edward Collins Bursk Junior).
        QRL (23) 82, p. 51-52.
      "Farewell." QRL (23) 82, p. 81.
      "Father and Son Rock Hopping." PoNow (6:4, issue 34)
        82, p. 6.
      "First Offense." LitR (25:3) Spr 82, p. 364-365.
      "Four Catherines." QRL (23) 82, p. 65-66.
      "Habitats." ManhatR (2:1) 81, p. 37-38.
      "Handpuppets." QRL (23) 82, p. 38-39.
      "The Harbor Woman's Mahogany Boat." QRL (23) 82, p.
        25-26.
      "The Heating System." QRL (23) 82, p. 12.
      "The House All Ours for the Month." PraS (56:1) Spr
        82, p. 80-81.
      "Instructions." ManhatR (2:1) 81, p. 48-49.
      "Jerusalem Road." QRL (23) 82, p. 55-56.
      "Little Harbor." PoNow (6:4, issue 34) 82, p. 6.
      "Little Harbor." QRL (23) 82, p. 33-34.
      "The Man at the Upstairs Window." QRL (23) 82, p.
        11.
      "Miss Jessie Bates." QRL (23) 82, p. 21-22.
      "Missing." ManhatR (2:1) 81, p. 45.

"My Children's Treaties." QRL (23) 82, p. 60-61.
"My Collection of Dance Masks." ManhatR (2:1) 81, p.
    40-41.
"My Father's Timepieces." QRL (23) 82, p. 16-17.
"Nectar." QRL (23) 82, p. 78.
"The Only Thing Worse Would Be the Silence
    Afterward." QRL (23) 82, p. 13-14.
"Playing Dead." AmerPoR (11:3) My-Je 82, p. 31.
"Plywood" (for Eric Hastings Senior and for his son).
    QRL (23) 82, p. 67-68.
"Powers of Concentration." QRL (23) 82, p. 27-28.
"Preen Glands." QRL (23) 82, p. 73.
"Questions at the Back of the Chapter." AmerPoR
    (11:3) My-Je 82, p. 31.
"Questions at the End of the Chapter." QRL (23) 82,
    p. 79-80.
"The Quick, Harsh German We Spoke to the Gulls." QRL
    (23) 82, p. 47.
"Quiz at Bedtime." Tendril (12) Wint 82, p. 14.
"Red Cross Bloodmobile." AmerPoR (11:3) My-Je 82, p.
    30.
"Restoring the Wood." LitR (25:3) Spr 82, p. 365-
    366.
"Salt." QRL (23) 82, p. 53-54.
"Saying Goodnight to the Letters." ManhatR (2:1) 81,
    p. 39.
"Saying Goodnight to the Letters." QRL (23) 82, p.
    57.
"Second String." QRL (23) 82, p. 49-50.
"Secondary Boycott." AntR (40:1) Wint 82, p. 44-45.
"The Secret Island of the Teachers." QRL (23) 82, p.
    31-32.
"Sidereal Time." Tendril (12) Wint 82, p. 13.
"Storm Warnings." QRL (23) 82, p. 8-9.
"Subversive." ManhatR (2:1) 81, p. 52.
"Taking a Bath." QRL (23) 82, p. 70.
"Taking Role." ManhatR (2:1) 81, p. 50-51.
"Taking Turns." QRL (23) 82, p. 74-75.
"Teargas." ManhatR (2:1) 81, p. 46.
"Tearing Up the Tracks." QRL (23) 82, p. 45-46.
"Too Late to Tell If It Is Hawk or Crow." ManhatR
    (2:1) 81, p. 42.
"Too Late to Tell Whether It Is Crow or Hawk." QRL
    (23) 82, p. 69.
"Town Names for Parts of My Body." QRL (23) 82, p.
    43-44.
"The Trees, Old Diplomats." ManhatR (2:1) 81, p. 47.
"Tying My Wrists." QRL (23) 82, p. 42.
"Unemployment." QRL (23) 82, p. 62-63.
"Youngest Son." AmerPoR (11:3) My-Je 82, p. 30.

579. BURSTOW, Candace Adamson
    "Creation." PoetryCR (4:2) Wint 82, p. 12.

580. BUSCH, Trent
    "Late September Air." KanQ (14:1) Wint 82, p. 22.

581. BUSCHEK, John
    "M_____'s." Dandel (9:2) 82, p. 61.
    "Simple Physics." Dandel (9:2) 82, p. 60.

582. BUSH, Duncan
        "Ancestors" (tr. of Cesare Pavese). Stand (23:2) 82,
            p. 5.
        "Revolt" (tr. of Cesare Pavese). Stand (23:2) 82, p.
            6.
        "Two Cigarettes" (tr. of Cesare Pavese). Stand (23:2)
            82, p. 4.

583. BUSHA, Gary C.
        "Everyone Needs a Bear Poem." Abraxas (25/26) 82, p.
            80.

584. BUSTA, Christine
        "Experiences" (tr. by Beth Bjorklund). LitR (25:2)
            Wint 82, p. 183.
        "An Olive Tree in Korfu" (tr. by Beth Bjorklund).
            LitR (25:2) Wint 82, p. 180.
        "The Prodigal Son" (tr. by Beth Bjorklund). LitR
            (25:2) Wint 82, p. 181.
        "Raymondsville" (tr. by Beth Bjorklund). LitR (25:2)
            Wint 82, p. 182.
        "Under a Reading Lamp" (tr. by Beth Bjorklund). LitR
            (25:2) Wint 82, p. 183.

585. BUTCHER, Grace
        "Each in Our Turn." CapeR (17:2) Sum 82, p. 18.
        "Even So, in This Day and Age." HiramPoR (32) Spr-
            Sum 82, p. 9.
        "The First." PoNow (6:5, issue 35) 82, p. 4.
        "Motorcyclist in Winter." HiramPoR (32) Spr-Sum 82,
            p. 10.
        "Three Grammatical Chicken Stories." HiramPoR (32)
            Spr-Sum 82, p. 11.

586. BUTKIE, Joseph D.
        "Bus Stop" (Honolulu, November 1979). PoNow (7:1,
            issue 37) 82, p. 6.
        "Parting" (For David, Honolulu, November 1979). PoNow
            (7:1, issue 37) 82, p. 6.
        "Springday." PoNow (7:1, issue 37) 82, p. 6.

587. BUTLER, Elvie L.
        "One of Mother's Recipes." AntigR (51) Aut 82, p.
            94.

588. BUTLER, Will
        "A Kind of Contentment." Bogg (49) 82, p. 44-45.

589. BYER, Kathryn Stripling
        "Like a Mother Who Never Sleeps, Rain." Poetry
            (141:2) N 82, p. 73.
        "Old Orchard Road Again." Poetry (141:2) N 82, p.
            71-72.
        "Wide Open, These Gates." Poetry (141:2) N 82, p.
            74.

590. BYRNE, Edward
        "Husband and Wife." CimR (60) Jl 82, p. 12.

591. CABALLERO BONALD, Jose Manuel
"Ante Diem" (tr. by Anthony Kerrigan). DenQ (17:3)
Aut 82, p. 61.
"Fear of Impotence" (tr. by Anthony Kerrigan). DenQ
(17:3) Aut 82, p. 62.

592. CABANISS, Alice
"Ice Tongs / Wide-Mouthed Jar." Shout (3:1) 82, p.
76.

593. CABRA, Alberto
"El Cuarto Honrar a Padre y Madre." Mester (11:2) 82
[i.e. My 83], p. 15.

CACHO, Manuel Joglar
See: JOGLAR CACHO, Manuel

594. CADDELL, Marsha
"The Trapping." Sam (33:3, issue 131) 82, p. 34.

595. CADER, Teresa
"I Am Not Afraid to Tell You." TriQ (54) Spr 82, p.
60-61.
"In a House of Strangers." TriQ (54) Spr 82, p. 66.
"Let the Dead Bury Their Dead" (Auschwitz, 1977).
TriQ (54) Spr 82, p. 63-65.
"Night Watch" (for Marieve Rugo). TriQ (54) Spr 82,
p. 67.
"Shame, Shame, and Girls, Too?" -- Principal, Parkway
School (for Peggy Brink Warner). TriQ (54) Spr 82,
p. 62.

596. CADGER, Neil
"On Hearing a Siren in Paris, 10/02/82." Dandel
(9:2) 82, p. 50-51.

597. CADNUM, Michael
"The Cape." Comm (109:12) Je 18, 82, p. 375.
"Dingman's Creek." Tendril (13) Sum 82, p. 21.
"Eight Spider Poems." HiramPoR (32) Spr-Sum 82, p.
12.
"The Emperor Rises from the Dead." PortR (28:1) 82,
p. 43.
"Flat Valley in Darkness." VirQR (58:2) Spr 82, p.
274-275.
"The Horse." Comm (109:5) Mr 12, 82, p. 158.
"Margaret's Husband." PortR (28:1) 82, p. 43.
"Noah." PortR (28:1) 82, p. 43.
"The Reckoning." Comm (109:12) Je 18, 82, p. 375.
"To T.C." VirQR (58:2) Spr 82, p. 275.
"What It Was." MissR (10:3, issue 30) Wint-Spr 82,
p. 28-30.

598. CADSBY, Heather
"Art and Artist." Waves (10:4) Spr 82, p. 65.
"The Still Tempo." Waves (10:4) Spr 82, p. 64.

599. CAHN, Cynthia
"Florida Warns Her Colonists." CentR (26:2) Spr 82,
p. 177-178.

"It Must Have Bounced Off." Poem (46) N 82, p. 62.
"Manic Phase." StoneC (9:3/4) Spr-Sum 82, p. 64.
"On the Same Page" (for Larry Rubin, Southern
Humanities Review, Summer, 1981). Poem (46) N 82,
p. 61.
"Tomorrow." CentR (26:2) Spr 82, p. 177.

600. CAIN, John
"Insomnia." DekalbLAJ (14:1/4) Aut 80-Sum 81, p. 67.
"Seeing Eye Dog." DekalbLAJ (14:1/4) Aut 80-Sum 81,
p. 67-68.

601. CAIRNCROSS, George
"The Art of Rowing" (w. John Elsberg). Bogg (48) 82,
p. 65.
"At the Other Side of the Bed" (for Trevor Greenley,
w. John Elsberg). Bogg (48) 82, p. 65.
"Item" (w. John Elsberg). Bogg (48) 82, p. 65.

602. CAIRNS, Scott
"Edging through the Ruin." ConcPo (15:1) Spr 82, p.
33.

603. CALBERT, C. M.
"Our Minds to Meet." Confr (23) Wint 82, p. 82.
"This Advantage." Confr (23) Wint 82, p. 82.

604. CALDWELL, Justin
"126, Avenue de Versailles." SouthernR (18:3) Sum
82, p. 558.
"Back into Rooms." SouthernR (18:3) Sum 82, p. 559.
"Savonarola" (for Robert L. Nikirk). SouthernR (18:3)
Sum 82, p. 556-557.

605. CALLANAN, Deidre G.
"Grace Whispers, Kneeling." AspenJ (1:2) Sum 82, p.
23.
"Grace Wore a Veil All the Days of Her Marriage."
AspenJ (1:2) Sum 82, p. 23.
"Your Sister, Grace, Sends Up Her Regrets from
Limbo." AspenJ (1:2) Sum 82, p. 23.

CALLE, Manuel Alvarez
See: ALVAREZ CALLE, Manuel

CALVELLO, Raquel Montenegro
See: MONTENEGRO-CALVELLO, Raquel

606. CALVERT, L. D. E.
"The Cat with Africa on Its Back." Bogg (48) 82, p.
42.

607. CAMERON, Bella
"Forever?" Bogg (48) 82, p. 39.

608. CAMERON, J. M.
"A Christmas Garland for C. L. D. 1832-1898." Poetry
(141:3) D 82, p. 129.
"Let Us Now Praise Famous Men." Poetry (141:3) D 82,
p. 130-131.

"The Wizards." Poetry (141:3) D 82, p. 131.

609. CAMERON, Peggy
"The Bridge." WestCR (17:1) Je 82, p. 5.
"My Cousins Lie There." WestCR (17:1) Je 82, p. 5.

610. CAMOZZI BARRIOS, Rolando
"Desde el Umbral de las Heridas." Mairena (4:10)
Sum-Aut 82, p. 33-35.

611. CAMPBELL, Mary B.
"Aubade Solo." LittleM (13:3/4) 82, p. 6.
"A Case of Mistaken Identity." LittleM (13:3/4) 82,
p. 8.
"Noise." LittleM (13:3/4) 82, p. 7.

612. CAMPBELL, O. B.
"The Dalton Boys Ride By." LittleBR (2:1) Aut 81, p.
66-67.

613. CAMPBELL, Rick
"Roaches." OhioR (27) 82, p. 104.

CAMPOS, Alvaro de
See: PESSOA, Fernando

614. CANDELARIA, Fred
"Transfer, Please." Outbr (10/11) Aut 82-Spr 83, p.
15.

CANIZARO, Vince
See: CANIZARO, Vincent, Jr.

615. CANIZARO, Vincent, Jr.
"Orleans Revisited." BallSUF (23:3) Sum 82, p. 80.
"Silver Horses." WebR (7:1) Spr 82, p. 64.
"White Moon." WebR (7:1) Spr 82, p. 64.

616. CANNINGS, Robert A.
"All Those Other Ways." MalR (63) O 82, p. 133.
"Certainty." MalR (63) O 82, p. 134.
"Espana." MalR (63) O 82, p. 132.
"The Hollow." MalR (63) O 82, p. 133.
"July, 1969." MalR (63) O 82, p. 134.
"Magpies." MalR (63) O 82, p. 135.

617. CANNSTATT, Christian
"On Sancta Maria-Ave Euroshima." Maize (5:3/4) Spr-
Sum 82, p. 31-32.

618. CANSDALE, Theresa H.
"Winter Harbour." AntigR (51) Aut 82, p. 52.

619. CAPUTI, Ilaria
from Erotopaegnia: "It slept inside you like a dry
tumor" (tr. of Edoardo Sanguineti, w. David St.
John). PoetryE (8) Aut 82, p. 75.
"Waltz" (tr. of Giorgio Bassani, w. David St. John).
PoetryE (8) Aut 82, p. 74.

620. CARDENAL, Ernesto
    "A Ernesto Castillo Mi Sobrino." _Maize_ (5:3/4) Spr-
        Sum 82, p. 65.
    "Las Loras." _Maize_ (5:3/4) Spr-Sum 82, p. 66.
    "Nuestros poemas no se pueden publicar todavia."
        Maize (5:3/4) Spr-Sum 82, p. 65.

621. CAREME, Maurice
    "L'Aimee" _SouthernR_ (18:3) Sum 82, p. 566.
    "Death" (tr. by Dennis Tool). _SouthernR_ (18:3) Sum
        82, p. 569.
    "The Loved One" (tr. by Dennis Tool). _SouthernR_
        (18:3) Sum 82, p. 567.
    "La Mort." _SouthernR_ (18:3) Sum 82, p. 568.

622. CAREY, Barbara
    "Canticle." _CrossC_ (4:4) 82, p. 28.

623. CAREY, Michael A.
    "After Bean Walking." _WindO_ (41) Aut-Wint 82-83, p.
        9.
    "Dialogue." _CapeR_ (17:2) Sum 82, p. 28.
    "Inheritance." _WindO_ (41) Aut-Wint 82-83, p. 8.
    "The Neighbor's Man." _PoetC_ (14:1) 82, p. 41.
    "No Answers." _KanQ_ (14:3) Sum 82, p. 204.
    "The Reading." _Bogg_ (48) 82, p. 31.
    "Spring of the Last Campaign." _PoetC_ (14:1) 82, p.
        40.

624. CARLISLE, S. E.
    "Some Facts about Angels." _LittleM_ (13:3/4) 82, p.
        58-59.

625. CARLISLE, Thomas John
    "Involuntary Angelus." _ChrC_ (99:16) My 5, 82, p.
        541.
    "Sleepy Santa." _ChrC_ (99:40) D 15, 82, p. 1285.

626. CARLOS, Susan V.
    "Siesta." _ArizQ_ (38:1) Spr 82, p. 18.

627. CARLSON, R. S.
    "On a San Andreas Secondary." _CapeR_ (18:1) Wint 82,
        p. 40.

628. CARMEN, Marilyn
    "Birthday Party." _Obs_ (7:2/3) Sum-Wint 81, p. 211.
    "Camp Rielly with Crystall." _Obs_ (7:2/3) Sum-Wint
        81, p. 213.
    "Campsite Memory." _Obs_ (7:2/3) Sum-Wint 81, p. 213.
    "For My Mother" (Geneva Scruggs Opened the First
        Black Nursey School, Harrisburg, 1946) _Obs_ (7:2/3)
        Sum-Wint 81, p. 210.
    "Geneva." _Obs_ (7:2/3) Sum-Wint 81, p. 209.
    "Kiss." _Obs_ (7:2/3) Sum-Wint 81, p. 211.
    "Melting Pot to America." _Obs_ (7:2/3) Sum-Wint 81,
        p. 212.
    "Signs." _Obs_ (7:2/3) Sum-Wint 81, p. 212.

629. CARMI, T.
         "Experiment" (tr. by Grace Schulman). OntR (17) Aut-
             Wint 82, p. 88.
         "In the Air" (tr. by Grace Schulman). OntR (17) Aut-
             Wint 82, p. 87.

630. CAROL, Luiza
         "A dandelion" (Haiku). LittleBR (2:3) Spr 82, p. 50.

631. CARPENTER, Anne Nicodemus
         "Ars Poetica." Poetry (140:2) My 82, p. 96.
         "Chagall Paints a Picture." OntR (16) Spr-Sum 82, p.
             89.
         "Depreciation." Poetry (140:2) My 82, p. 94.
         "Divorce." OntR (16) Spr-Sum 82, p. 86.
         "Evening at Home." OntR (16) Spr-Sum 82, p. 87.
         "Motel." Poetry (140:2) My 82, p. 95.
         "We Really Couldn't Handle Mother at Home." OntR
             (16) Spr-Sum 82, p. 88.

632. CARPENTER, William
         "The Ice House." Poetry (139:5) F 82, p. 261-262.

633. CARPINISAN, Mariana
         "The Keys" (tr. of Nichita Stanescue, w. Mark Irwin).
             Pequod (15) 82, p. 74.
         "Lesson on the Circle" (tr. of Nichita Stanescue, w.
             Mark Irwin). Pequod (15) 82, p. 73.

634. CARREGA, Gordon
         "In Unison." PoNow (6:6, issue 36) 82, p. 17.
         "Stubborn Me." PoNow (6:6, issue 36) 82, p. 17.

635. CARREL, Ann
         "Buck Fever" (for my brother, Dan). KanQ (14:1) Wint
             82, p. 8.
         "To My Brother's Child, Born Soon." KanQ (14:1) Wint
             82, p. 7-8.

636. CARRERA ANDRADE, Jorge
         "The Clock" (tr. by Michael L. Johnson). PortR (28:1)
             82, p. 22.

637. CARRIER, Constance
         "Two, Remembered." Iowa (12:2/3) Spr-Sum 81, p. 31.

638. CARRIER, Warren
         "All Day Through the Dry Cold." Abraxas (25/26) 82,
             p. 104.

639. CARRILLO, Ernesto
         "Donde los desconocidos derramaron su sangre." Maize
             (5:3/4) Spr-Sum 82, p. 70.

640. CARRUTH, Hayden
         "Failure Intrinsic." Kayak (59) Je 82, p. 5.
         "I Tell You for Several Years of My Madness I Heard
             Her Voice Singing in the Trees of Chicago." Kayak
             (59) Je 82, p. 3-4.
         "Marvin McCabe." Antaeus (47) Aut 82, p. 91-94.

"On the Short of Onondaga." GeoR (36:2) Sum 82, p. 384.
"Onondaga, Early December." Ploughs (8:2/3) 82, p. 126.
"Words in a Certain Appropriate Mode." Ploughs (8:2/3) 82, p. 127.

641. CARTANA, Luis
"Pequena Redondata de los Olivos" (from Sobre la Musica). Mairena (4:9) Spr 82, p. 81.

642. CARTER, Jared
"Calling the Sun." WebR (7:1) Spr 82, p. 7.
"Digging." GeoR (36:1) Spr 82, p. 22.
"On Giving His Daughter a Deck of Tarot Cards." WebR (7:1) Spr 82, p. 8.
"Summer Day near Pogue's Run." Im (8:2) 82, p. 3.

643. CARTER, Jefferson
"At Hemingway's Grave, Ketchum, Idaho." PoNow (7:1, issue 37) 82, p. 7.
"A Photograph of My Brother & Curro Romero, Valencia Bullring, 1979" PoNow (7:1, issue 37) 82, p. 7.

644. CARTER, Judith
"Euterpe." DenQ (16:4) Wint 82, p. 56.
"Head Lines." DenQ (16:4) Wint 82, p. 55.
"St. Paul's Before Dawn." DenQ (17:2) Sum 82, p. 105.

645. CARVER, Raymond
"Alcohol." NewEngR (4:4) Sum 82, p. 530.

646. CASE, Sandra
"Driving to Dubuque." PoNow (7:1, issue 37) 82, p. 7.
"Woman He Almost Loved." Vis (9) 82, p. 14.

647. CASEY, Deb
"Familiar Fable #1: Old Woman." Epoch (32:1) Aut 82, p. 57.

648. CASH, Nancy
"Ibsen Relearning the Alphabet after a Stroke." SmPd (19:2, issue 55) Spr 82, p. 3-4.

649. CASSIAN, Nina
"Death in the Well" (tr. by Eva Feiler). Chelsea (41) 82, p. 135.
"Impervious" (tr. by Eva Feiler). Chelsea (41) 82, p. 134.
"Music by Varese" (tr. by Eva Feiler). Chelsea (41) 82, p. 134.
"Tongue of Cold" (tr. by Eva Feiler). Chelsea (41) 82, p. 135.

650. CASSIDY, Simon
"Even the cigarette machines were empty." Bogg (48) 82, p. 58.

651. CASSITY, Turner
  "A Distant View of the Chinese Wall." SouthernR
    (18:1) Wint 82, p. 173.
  "Hurricane Lamp" (corrected version, to replace 33:1,
    p. 45). ChiR (33:2) 82, p. 128.
  "Number One Nob Hill" (Hotel Mark Hopkins). MichQR
    (21:4) Aut 82, p. 633.
  "Pausing in the Climb." SouthernR (18:1) Wint 82, p.
    174.
  "Seeking a Level." ChiR (33:2) 82, p. 127.
  "To the Lighthouse." ChiR (33:2) 82, p. 126.

652. CASTANEDA, Jorge
  "Incestual." Mairena (4:10) Sum-Aut 82, p. 93.

653. CASTILLO, Ana
  "1975." RevChic (10:1/2) Wint-Spr 82, p. 45-46.
  "Cartas." RevChic (10:1/2) Wint-Spr 82, p. 43.
  "Encuentros #1." RevChic (10:1/2) Wint-Spr 82, p.
    42.
  "Napa, California" (Dedicado al Sr. Chavez, Sept.
    1975). RevChic (10:1/2) Wint-Spr 82, p. 44.

654. CASTILLO, Horacio
  "Homenaje a la Palabra Alcanfor." Mairena (4:10)
    Sum-Aut 82, p. 59-60.

  CASTRO, Sara Martinez
  See: MARTINEZ CASTRO, Sara

655. CASTRO RIOS, Andres
  "Elogio de la Ternura." Areito (8:31) 82, p. 38.

656. CASULLO, Joanne
  "Auspice." SoDakR (20:2) Sum 82, p. 37.
  "On Death's Black Elastic Shoe-String." HiramPoR
    (31) Aut-Wint 82, p. 13.

657. CASWELL, Donald
  "Letting Go." Wind (12:46) 82, p. 9.

658. CATALA, Rafael
  "Accion de Gracias." Maize (5:3/4) Spr-Sum 82, p.
    86.
  "Danzon Peruano." Maize (5:3/4) Spr-Sum 82, p. 85.
  "December 21." Catalyst (Erotica Issue) 82, p. 31.
  "Solo un Instante" (desde Yuri Lotman). Mairena
    (4:10) Sum-Aut 82, p. 82.

659. CATES, Marian Ward
  "Bottled Notes." HolCrit (19:5) D 82, p. 16-17.

660. CATHERS, Ken
  "Give Away." CrossC (4:1) Wint 82, p. 7.
  "Journeyman." CrossC (4:1) Wint 82, p. 7.
  "Reeling." MalR (61) F 82, p. 189.
  "Surfacing." MalR (61) F 82, p. 188.

661. CATINA, Ray
  "Busted." UnderRM 1(1) Spr 82, p. 14.

"Cowboy." StoneC (10:1/2) Aut-Wint 82-83, p. 70.
"General Death." UnderRM 1(1) Spr 82, p. 15.
"The Letting Go." StoneC (10:1/2) Aut-Wint 82-83, p. 70.
"Surgeon Generaled." UnderRM 1(1) Spr 82, p. 14.

662. CAVAFY, Constantin
"Desires" (tr. by John G. Trehas). CrossC (4:2/3) 82, p. 16.
"On a Ship" (tr. by John G. Trehas). CrossC (4:2/3) 82, p. 16.
"San somata opaia nekron pou den egerasan" (in Greek). CrossC (4:2/3) 82, p. 16.
"Sophist Leaving Syria" (1926, tr. by Costas Melakopides). Quarry (31:4) Aut 82, p. 42.
"To Stay" (1918, tr. by Costas Melakopides). Quarry (31:4) Aut 82, p. 40-41.
"Ton moiazei bebaia e mikre aute" (in Greek). CrossC (4:2/3) 82, p. 16.
"When They Are Aroused" (1913, tr. by Costas Melakopides). Quarry (31:4) Aut 82, p. 41.

663. CAVALCANTI, Guido
"Guarda Ben Dico, Guarda, Ben Ti Guarda" (tr. by Ezra Pound). Antaeus (44) Wint 82, p. 31-33.
"On the Mightiness of Love (Sonnet I)" (tr. by Felix Stefanile). Sparrow (43) 82, p. 25.

664. CAVALLARO, Carol
"Dream of an Accidental Heaven and Hell." Wind (12:46) 82, p. 10.
"Tristan Mad." Wind (12:46) 82, p. 11.

665. CAVANAGH, Margery
"Disinterring the Dead: Three Poems for My Father." Northeast (3:12) Wint 81-82, p. 6-8.

666. CAVANAUGH, Sarah
"Alverda." SouthernPR (22:1) Spr 82, p. 56.

667. CAWLEY, Kevin
"Elected Silence." HiramPoR (31) Aut-Wint 82, p. 14.
"Habituation." SmPd (19:1, issue 54) Wint 82, p. 10.

668. CAWS, Ian
"Love." MalR (62) Jl 82, p. 212.
"Lowry's Clocks." MalR (62) Jl 82, p. 213.

669. CEA, Jose Roberto
"El Potrero" (Fragmento). Maize (6:1/2) Aut-Wint 82-83, p. 96-97.

670. CECIL, Richard
"Abstinence." AmerPoR (11:6) N-D 82, p. 9.
"Concerts." AmerPoR (11:6) N-D 82, p. 8.
"First Night." Telescope (1) Spr 81, p. 14-15.
"Fredericksburg." GeoR (36:3) Aut 82, p. 652-653.
"My Trophy." PoNow (6:6, issue 36) 82, p. 40.
"Reichsmuseum." VirQR (58:3) Sum 82, p. 440.
"Waking." Telescope (1) Spr 81, p. 16.

"Wrinkles." VirQR (58:3) Sum 82, p. 438-439.

671. CEDERSTROM, Eleanor
"Life Line." PoNow (6:5, issue 35) 82, p. 47.

672. CEDRINS, Inara
"Through Evening Twilight" (tr. of Imants Ziedonis).
QW (14) Spr-Sum 82, p. 46.
"When Cats with Black Stripes" (tr. of Imants
Ziedonis). QW (14) Spr-Sum 82, p. 47.

673. CEELY, John
"Let Us All Stand and Snort like Air Hammers Ha-Da-
Da-Da-Dat." Abraxas (25/26) 82, p. 106.

674. CELAN, Paul
"Into the Rivers" (tr. by Beth Bjorklund). LitR
(25:2) Wint 82, p. 200.
"Psalm" (tr. by Beth Bjorklund). LitR (25:2) Wint 82,
p. 200.

675. CELAYA, Gabriel
"The Boundaries" (tr. by David Garrison). DenQ (17:3)
Aut 82, p. 23.

676. CENTOLELLA, Tom
"Sun Sang." NewEngR (4:4) Sum 82, p. 531-534.

CERDA, Hernan Lavin
See: LAVIN CERDA, Hernan

677. CERNUDA, Luis
"Let's Never Try Love" (tr. by Erland Anderson).
PortR (28:2) 82, p. 2.

678. CERVANTES, James
"For Comfort." StoneC (10:1/2) Aut-Wint 82-83, p.
32.
from The Hero's Ceremony of Possibilities: "1. Cafe."
Telescope (1) Spr 81, p. 61.
from The Hero's Ceremony of Possibilities: "2.
Alexandria." Telescope (1) Spr 81, p. 62.
"The Long Dream of His Life." Telescope (3) Sum 82,
p. 62-66.
"Shallow Music." Telescope (1) Spr 81, p. 10-11.

679. CERVANTES, Lorna Dee
"Heritage." RevChic (10:1/2) Wint-Spr 82, p. 47.
"Refugee Ship." RevChic (10:1/2) Wint-Spr 82, p. 48.
"Shells." RevChic (10:1/2) Wint-Spr 82, p. 50-53.
"You Are Like a Weed." RevChic (10:1/2) Wint-Spr 82,
p. 49.

680. CERVO, Nathan
"The Arch." AntigR (50) Sum 82, p. 10.

681. CESAIRE, Aime
"Bucolic" (tr. by Dennis Finnell). AmerPoR (11:5) S-O
82, p. 8.

"But There Is This Hurt" (tr. by Clayton Eshleman and
    Annette Smith). Sulfur (2:2, issue 5) 82, p. 43-44.
"Corpse of a Frenzy" (tr. by Clayton Eshleman and
    Annette Smith). Sulfur (2:2, issue 5) 82, p. 44-45.
"Debris" (tr. by Clayton Eshleman and Annette Smith).
    Sulfur (2:2, issue 5) 82, p. 34-35.
"From My Weariness" (tr. by Dennis Finnell). AmerPoR
    (11:5) S-O 82, p. 8.
"Griffin" (tr. by A. E. Stringer). AmerPoR (11:5) S-O
    82, p. 7.
"I Perseus Centuplicating Myself" (tr. by Clayton
    Eshleman and Annette Smith). Sulfur (2:2, issue 5)
    82, p. 45.
"It Is the Courage of Men Which Is Disjointed" (tr.
    by Dennis Finnell). AmerPoR (11:5) S-O 82, p. 8.
"Knives of Noon" (tr. by A. E. Stringer). AmerPoR
    (11:5) S-O 82, p. 7.
"Lost Body" (from Lost Body, 1950, tr. by Clayton
    Eshleman and Annette Smith). Sulfur (2:2, issue 5)
    82, p. 41-43.
"Marine Intimacy" (tr. by Dennis Finnell). AmerPoR
    (11:5) S-O 82, p. 8.
"Mississippi" (tr. by A. E. Stringer). AmerPoR (11:5)
    S-O 82, p. 7.
"Myth" (tr. by Joan C. Dayan). Paint (7/8:13/16) 80-
    81, p. 41.
"Noon Knives" (from Solar Throat Slashed, 1948, tr.
    by Clayton Eshleman and Annette Smith). Sulfur
    (2:2, issue 5) 82, p. 39-41.
"Ode to Guinea" (tr. by A. E. Stringer). AmerPoR
    (11:5) S-O 82, p. 6.
"The Oubliettes of the Sea and the Deluge" (from The
    Miraculous Weapons, 1946, tr. by Clayton Eshleman
    and Annette Smith). Sulfur (2:2, issue 5) 82, p.
    36-37.
"Rains" (tr. by A. E. Stringer). AmerPoR (11:5) S-O
    82, p. 7.
"Redemption" (tr. by Clayton Eshleman and Annette
    Smith). Sulfur (2:2, issue 5) 82, p. 38.
"Tangible Disaster" (tr. by Clayton Eshleman and
    Annette Smith). Sulfur (2:2, issue 5) 82, p. 37.
"Tom-Tom II" (for Wifredo, tr. by Clayton Eshleman
    and Annette Smith). Sulfur (2:2, issue 5) 82, p.
    35.
"Tomb of Paul Eluard" (from Ferraments, 1960, tr. by
    Clayton Eshleman and Annette Smith). Sulfur (2:2,
    issue 5) 82, p. 46-49.
"Visitation" (tr. by Clayton Eshleman and Annette
    Smith). Sulfur (2:2, issue 5) 82, p. 33-34.
"Who Then, Who Then" (tr. by A. E. Stringer). AmerPoR
    (11:5) S-O 82, p. 6.
"Your Hair" (tr. by Clayton Eshleman and Annette
    Smith). Sulfur (2:2, issue 5) 82, p. 38-39.

682. CHADWICK, Jerah
    "Aleutian Stare." CutB (19) Aut-Wint 82, p. 41.

683. CHAFFIN, Lillie D.
    "The Appointment." Wind (12:44) 82, p. 6.
    "Investments" (for J D M). Wind (12:44) 82, p. 6-7.

"Killing Time." Wind (12:44) 82, p. 5.
"Seeing." Wind (12:44) 82, p. 5.

684. CHAFIN, Shirley R.
    "Cycles." EngJ (71:6) O 82, p. 79.

685. CHAKRAVARTI, Prithvindra
    "Snail" (tr. of Jyotirmoy Datta, w. Ulli Beier). NewL
    (48:3/4) Spr-Sum 82, p. 236.

686. CHALFI, Raquel
    "Traveling to Jerusalem under a Full Moon" (tr. by
    the author and Helen Tartar). ManhatR (2:1) 81, p.
    3.

687. CHAMBERLAIN, Marisha
    "Corazon Amurao." Shout (3:1) 82, p. 38.

688. CHAMBERLAIN, William
    "The Wife." PoetryNW (23:4) Wint 82-83, p. 24-25.

689. CHAMBERS, Leland H.
    "On Tiburon Island" (tr. of Eliana Rivero, w. the
    author). DenQ (17:1) Spr 82, p. 82.
    "Sometimes" (tr. of Eliana Rivero, w. the author).
    DenQ (17:1) Spr 82, p. 80-81.
    "Spectators: Free Territory of America" (26th of
    July) (tr. of Eliana Rivero, w. the author). DenQ
    (17:1) Spr 82, p. 83.
    "Words Are Words, Etc." (tr. of Eliana Rivero, w. the
    author). DenQ (17:1) Spr 82, p. 78-79.

690. CHANDONNET, Ann Fox
    "Masks." Maize (5:1/2) Aut-Wint 81-82, p. 38.
    "Massage" (for Alexandre, four). KanQ (14:3) Sum 82,
    p. 146.
    "The Second Study in Aesthetics." KanQ (14:3) Sum
    82, p. 145.

691. CHANDRA, G. S. Sharat
    "Aliens." NewL (49:2) Wint 82-83, p. 46-47.
    "At the India Association." NewL (48:3/4) Spr-Sum
    82, p. 44-45.
    "Facts of Life." NewL (48:3/4) Spr-Sum 82, p. 45.
    "I Watched You Go." NewL (49:2) Wint 82-83, p. 46.
    "The Last Predator." NewL (49:2) Wint 82-83, p. 47-
    48.
    "A Quick Glimpse of Buddha's Children on the American
    TV between Its Commercials." NewL (48:3/4) Spr-Sum
    82, p. 46.

692. CHANG, Diana
    "On a Poet Reading His Own work" Im (8:1) 82, p. 3.
    "On Gibson Lane, Sagaponack." Im (8:1) 82, p. 3.

693. CHAPPLE, C. E.
    "Bait." AntigR (50) Sum 82, p. 14.
    "Dance." AntigR (50) Sum 82, p. 14.

694. CHAR, Rene
    "The Absentee" (tr. by Edouard Roditi). Kayak (60) O
       82, p. 11.
    "The Basketweaver's Companion" (tr. by Edouard
       Roditi). Kayak (60) O 82, p. 10.
    "Calendar" (tr. by Edouard Roditi). Kayak (60) O 82,
       p. 11.
    "Dismissing the Wind" (tr. by Edouard Roditi). Kayak
       (60) O 82, p. 10.

695. CHARACH, Ron
    "A 0% Chance" (A Refuge in the crawlspace). CanLit
       (91) Wint 81, p. 56.
    "Analysis with a Swimmer." CanLit (92) Spr 82, p.
       33.
    "Gravedigging at Lourdes." CrossC (4:4) 82, p. 7.
    "Restaurant Austerity Poem." CanLit (91) Wint 81, p.
       56-57.
    "This Far Out." AntigR (48) Wint 82, p. 84.
    "The Torso Findings." CrossC (4:4) 82, p. 7.
    "Why Not Try an Iguana." AntigR (48) Wint 82, p. 85.

696. CHASE, Josiah
    "Blindfolded Ox." Wind (12:46) 82, p. 9.

697. CHASE, Karen
    "The Abandoned Briggs Marble Quarry." Wind (12:45)
       82, p. 10-11.
    "A Poem Rumbles Out." Wind (12:45) 82, p. 10.

698. CHATFIELD, Hale
    "Insomnia: June, 1982." HiramPoR (32) Spr-Sum 82, p.
       13.
    "An Omen." PoNow (6:5, issue 35) 82, p. 41.
    "There Are More of You." HiramPoR (32) Spr-Sum 82,
       p. 14.

699. CHATTOPADHYAY, Birendra
    "In Front of the Visa Office" (tr. by Ramendra
       Narayan Nag). NewL (48:3/4) Spr-Sum 82, p. 166.

700. CHERNOFF, Maxine
    "The Apology Store." PoNow (6:5, issue 35) 82, p.
       11.
    "How We Went." Tendril (12) Wint 82, p. 17.
    "Prophecy." LittleM (13:3/4) 82, p. 63.
    "Sotto Voce." LittleM (13:3/4) 82, p. 62.
    "Spring." NowestR (20:1) 82, p. 98.

701. CHERRY, Kelly
    "Bringing in the Night." ConcPo (15:1) Spr 82, p.
       34.
    "Pangaea" (Directions sketched on a paper napkin in a
       neighborhood bar). ConcPo (15:1) Spr 82, p. 36.
    "A Scientific Expedition in Siberia, 1913."
       SouthernR (18:1) Wint 82, p. 161-165.
    "Your Going out" (To my mother). ConcPo (15:1) Spr
       82, p. 35.

702. CHESSER, Lewis
    "Prospect Mountain Colorado." PoNow (7:1, issue 37)
    82, p. 7.

703. CHHOTRAY, Devdas
    "Birthday" (tr. by Jayanta Mahapatra). NewL (48:3/4)
    Spr-Sum 82, p. 115.
    "Fear" (tr. by Jayanta Mahapatra). NewL (48:3/4) Spr-
    Sum 82, p. 114-115.
    "Sunday" (tr. by Jayanta Mahapatra). NewL (48:3/4)
    Spr-Sum 82, p. 114.

704. CHIESURA, Giorgio
    "The Council" (tr. by Rina Ferrarelli). Chelsea (41)
    82, p. 74-81.
    "The Crooked Birch" (tr. by Rina Ferrarelli). DenQ
    (17:2) Sum 82, p. 128.
    "The Survivors" (tr. by Rina Ferrarelli). NewOR (9:3)
    Wint 82, p. 88.

705. CHILDERS, David C.
    "For a Woman Not Put Off." Gargoyle (15/16) 80, p.
    8.

706. CHILDERS, Joanne
    "Morning Time." UTR (7:2) 82?, p. 13.

707. CHILDRESS, William
    "The Brown House." PoNow (6:4, issue 34) 82, p. 5.
    "The Jogger." PoNow (6:5, issue 35) 82, p. 27.

708. CHIN, Donna C.
    "Yearbook Portrait." Obs (7:2/3) Sum-Wint 81, p.
    178.

709. CHIN, Marilyn
    "A 17 Line Love Poem about Poverty" (for Bob). Kayak
    (59) Je 82, p. 60.
    "Li Ching, Heart of Han." MassR (23:3) Aut 82, p.
    411.
    "We Are a Young Nation, Uncle." MassR (23:3) Aut 82,
    p. 410.

710. CHIN, Woon Ping
    "A Long Alley" (tr. of Sutardji Calzoum Bachri).
    Stand (23:4) 82, p. 72.
    "One" (tr. of Sutardji Calzoum Bachri). Stand (23:4)
    82, p. 72.

711. CHISHOLM, Jan
    "The Bookdealer's Daughter." PoNow (7:1, issue 37)
    82, p. 8.
    "Circe's Lover." SoCaR (15:1) Aut 82, p. 66.
    "In the Country." PoNow (7:1, issue 37) 82, p. 8.
    "My Mother Painting." Paint (9:17/18) Spr-Aut 82, p.
    12.
    "Nothing You Can Touch." SoDakR (20:1) Spr 82, p.
    43.

712. CHITRE, Dilip
     "Dhulia." NewL (48:3/4) Spr-Sum 82, p. 113.
     "Evenings in Iowa City, Iowa" (for Danny Weissbort).
        NewL (48:3/4) Spr-Sum 82, p. 111.
     "I Laugh. I Cry." NewL (48:3/4) Spr-Sum 82, p. 112.
     "Of Garlic and Such." NewL (48:3/4) Spr-Sum 82, p.
        102.
     "One Day You Wake Up." NewL (48:3/4) Spr-Sum 82, p.
        111-112.

     CHONGJU, So
     See: SO, Chongju

713. CHORLTON, David
     "Encyclopedia Maniac." WindO (41) Aut-Wint 82-83, p.
        44.
     "Pilgrimage." PoNow (7:1, issue 37) 82, p. 8.

714. CHOYCE, Lesley
     "Believing Is Not Seeing: The Sprit Loses Face
        against the Flesh." AntigR (48) Wint 82, p. 28.
     "Modern Translations." PottPort (4) 82-83, p. 52.

715. CHRISTENSEN, E. J.
     "Christmas Eve." LittleBR (2:2) Wint 81-82, inside
        front cover.
     "State of the Union." LittleBR (2:2) Wint 81-82, p.
        63.

716. CHRISTENSEN, Nadia
     from Anna: (3-7, 9) (tr. of Eldrid Lunden). Stand
        (23:3) 82, p. 35.
     from The Roof People: "They call themselves nothing"
        (tr. of Arne Ruste). Stand (23:3) 82, p. 36.

717. CHRISTIAN, Paula
     "At a Stone with My Last Name." HiramPoR (31) Aut-
        Wint 82, p. 15.
     "On a withered bough a man is perching." WindO (40,
        Anti-Haiku issue) Sum 82, p. 8.

718. CHRISTMAN, Rick
     "Dogs: A Fable of the Vietnam War." WormR (22:3,
        issue 87) 82, p. 77.

719. CHRISTOPHER, Nicholas
     "Charting the Eclipse." Nimrod (26:1) Aut-Wint 82,
        p. 85-87.
     "Musical Chairs." NewYorker (58:17) Je 14, 82, p.
        36.

720. CHRISTOPHERSEN, Bill
     "Wintering." SoDakR (20:4) Wint 82-83, p. 59.

721. CHRISTY, Jim
     "Call of the Wild." CrossC (4:1) Wint 82, p. 21.

722. CHRYSTOS
     "Acrylic for Lee." Cond (8) 82, p. 49-50.
     "For Sharol Graves." Cond (8) 82, p. 48.

723. CHUKWUDI, Obioma
      "Walking Down the Street Once Again." Obs (7:2/3)
         Sum-Wint 81, p. 194.

724. CHUTE, Robert M.
      "The Film Version." KanQ (14:4) Aut 82, p. 42.
      "First Failures." KanQ (14:3) Sum 82, p. 118.

725. CIARDI, John
      "Habitat." Poetry (141:2) N 82, p. 66.
      "Mutterings." Poetry (141:1) O 82, p. 5-6.
      "Obsolescence." Poetry (141:2) N 82, p. 63-64.
      "The Project." Poetry (141:2) N 82, p. 65.

      CICCO, Pier Giorgio di
      See: Di CICCO, Pier Giorgio

      CINTRON, Nemir Matos
      See: MATOS-CINTRON, Nemir

726. CIORDIA, Javier
      "Eros: 1. Yo" (A mi esposa). Mairena (4:10) Sum-Aut
         82, p. 71.
      "Eros: 2. Tu" (A Jorge Luis, mi hijo). Mairena (4:10)
         Sum-Aut 82, p. 71.
      "Eros: 3. Nosotros" (Al Profesor Alejandro
         Apesteguia). Mairena (4:10) Sum-Aut 82, p. 72.

727. CIRINO, Leonard
      "The Best Years." MendoR (6) Sum 81, p. 122.
      "Gold" (for R). MendoR (6) Sum 81, p. 122.

728. CISNEROS, Sandra
      "Arturo Burro." RevChic (10:1/2) Wint-Spr 82, p. 58.
      "North Avenue/1600 North." RevChic (10:1/2) Wint-Spr
         82, p. 54-55.
      "Stone Men." RevChic (10:1/2) Wint-Spr 82, p. 56-57.

729. CITINO, David
      "Autobiography of a Post-War Baby: Chapter One."
         SoDakR (20:3) Aut 82, p. 33.
      "Autobiography of the Shaman." AspenJ (1) Wint 82,
         p. 33.
      "Autumn, Winter, Hickory and Elm." SouthwR (67:4)
         Aut 82, p. 400.
      "Familiar as Home." LitR (25:3) Spr 82, p. 359.
      "Guadalcanal, Feldspar, Sleeping with My Wife."
         SoDakR (20:3) Aut 82, p. 34.
      "Judgment." SoCaR (14:2) Spr 82, p. 48.
      "July 19: Arsenius the Great, Who Had the Gift of
         Tears." ModernPS (11:1/2) 82, p. 59.
      "July 24: Christina the Astonishing, Virgin." LitR
         (26:1) Aut 82, p. 176.
      "Letter from the Shaman: How to Wonder, How to Love."
         HiramPoR (33) Aut-Wint 82, p. 8.
      "Marion, Ohio 43302." SoCaR (14:2) Spr 82, p. 49.
      "My Son's Violin." HiramPoR (32) Spr-Sum 82, p. 15.
      "One Hundred Miles South of Cleveland." CapeR (18:1)
         Wint 82, p. 4.
      "Poem for Cities." KanQ (14:1) Wint 82, p. 61.

"The Reading." PoetryNW (23:1) Spr 82, p. 14-15.
"The Retired Pastor On Comparative Religions."
   HolCrit (19:2) Ap 82, p. 11-12.
"The Retired Pastor Praises the Creator." Nimrod
   (25:2) Spr-Sum 82, p. 44.
"Sister Mary Appassionata Lectures the Eighth Grade
   Boys on the Nature of Eloquence."SouthernHR (16:4)
   Aut 82, p. 317.
"Sister Mary Appassionata Lectures the Creative
   Writing Class: The Life of the Poet, the Storm."
   SouthernPR (23, i.e. 22:2) Aut 82, p. 36.
"Sister Mary Appassionata's Lecture to the Eighth
   Grade Boys: 'The Second Day.'" SouthernHR (16:4)
   Aut 82, p. 316.
"Six Ways to Test the Efficacy of Prayer." KanQ
   (14:1) Wint 82, p. 60.
"Two Ways, According to the Tao, to Keep Your Soul
   Intact." KanQ (14:1) Wint 82, p. 60.
"Upon the Death of Albert Einstein, the Retired
   Pastor Telephones the Pope." Nimrod (25:2) Spr-Sum
   82, p. 44.
"Where Would You Like It to Be?" HiramPoR (31) Aut-
   Wint 82, p. 16.

730. CLAESSENS, Eric J.
   "If I Were a Poet." MendoR (5) Sum 81, p. 7.
   "One Day." MendoR (6) Sum 81, p. 40.
   "She." MendoR (6) Sum 81, p. 155.
   "Sometimes, in the Middle of the Night." MendoR (6)
      Sum 81, p. 160-161.
   "There's a Dusty Road." MendoR (6) Sum 81, p. 146.

731. CLAIR, Maxine
   "Reincarnation." Gargoyle (17/18) 81, p. 8.

732. CLAMPITT, Amy
   "Black Buttercups." NewYorker (58:42) D 6, 82, p.
      48-49.
   "Botanical Nomenclature." PraS (56:2) Sum 82, p. 76.
   "Exmoor." NewYorker (58:25) Ag 9, 82, p. 86.
   "From a Clinic Waiting Room." NewYorker (58:17) Je
      14, 82, p. 42.
   "The Kingfisher." NewYorker (57:47) Ja 11, 82, p.
      36.
   "The Outer Bar." Nat (234:25) Je 26, 82, p. 790.
   "Stacking the Straw." YaleR (71:4) Sum 82, p. 580.
   "What the Light Was Like." NewYorker (58:34) O 11,
      82, p. 42-43.
   "The Woodlot." PraS (56:2) Sum 82, p. 77-78.

733. CLANCY, Lynda
   "Doeskin Gloves." UnderRM (1:1) Spr 82, p. 44.
   "The Plants Nod and Agree." UnderRM (1:1) Spr 82,
      p. 44.

734. CLARK, Constance
   "At Home." Outbr (10/11) Aut 82-Spr 83, p. 83.
   "Back When: Chicago." Outbr (10/11) Aut 82-Spr 83,
      p. 81.
   "Eclipse." Outbr (10/11) Aut 82-Spr 83, p. 82.

735. CLARK, Jim
      "Return." SouthernPR (23, i.e. 22:2) Aut 82, p. 42.
      "The Stone." SouthernPR (23, i.e. 22:2) Aut 82, p.
      42-43.

736. CLARK, Kevin
      "Santa Cruz, 1976." SoDakR (20:4) Wint 82-83, p. 55-
      56.
      "Sonnet for the Son of the Red-Haired Woman." Paint
      (7/8:13/16) 80-81, p. 30.
      "Stock and Root" (Sacramento Valley). SoDakR (20:4)
      Wint 82-83, p. 54-55.

737. CLARK, Naomi
      "Turnip." PoNow (6:5, issue 35) 82, p. 14.

738. CLARK, Robin A.
      "Going Up." NoAmR (267:4) D 82,p. 8.

739. CLARK, Rod
      "Hamm's Beer Mobile." Abraxas (25/26) 82, p. 67.

740. CLARK, Ron
      "Poem on a Phrase by Robert Duncan." Grain (10:3) Ag
      82, p. 51.

741. CLARK, Tom
      "Dear Doctor." Ploughs (8:2/3) 82, p. 161.
      "Free Lance." Ploughs (8:2/3) 82, p. 161.
      "Free Lance." PoNow (6:5, issue 35) 82, p. 27.
      "In a Vacuum, a Single Emission Can Become Smog."
      Ploughs (8:2/3) 82, p. 162.
      "Lines Composed at Hope Ranch." Ploughs (8:2/3) 82,
      p. 160.
      "More Crooked Lines from Paradise" (For Dennis
      Cooper). PoNow (6:6, issue 36) 82, p. 11.
      "The Nelsons in SR." Ploughs (8:2/3) 82, p. 163.
      "The Nelsons in SR." PoNow (6:5, issue 35) 82, p.
      27.
      "Off Goleta." PoNow (6:6, issue 36) 82, p. 11.
      "Things to Do in California (1980)." Ploughs (8:2/3)
      82, p. 159.
      "Valley in Relief." PoNow (6:5, issue 35) 82, p. 27.

742. CLARKE, George Elliott
      "Campbell Road Church." Germ (6:2) Aut-Wint 82, p.
      18.
      "Guysborough Road Church." AntigR (50) Sum 82, p.
      61.
      "Hammonds Plains African Baptist Church." PottPort
      (4) 82-83, p. 7.
      "Musquodoboit Road Church." AntigR (50) Sum 82, p.
      60.
      "The Sermon on the Atlantic." Germ (6:2) Aut-Wint
      82, p. 17.
      "Sydney African Methodist Episcopal Church."
      PottPort (4) 82-83, p. 17.

743. CLARKE, John
      "Anarchverse." PoetryCR (4:2) Wint 82, p. 2.

"School Bus." <u>KanQ</u> (14:1) Wint 82, p. 113.

744. CLARKE, Terence
    "Seisures." <u>DenQ</u> (16:4) Wint 82, p. 23.

745. CLAUDEL, Alice Moser
    "Moments of Grace." <u>KanQ</u> (14:2) Spr 82, p. 52.
    "Wit among the Haviland Roses." <u>KanQ</u> (14:2) Spr 82,
        p. 64.

746. CLAUSEN, Jan
    "Credential." <u>Cond</u> (8) 82, p. 86.
    "Rhyme." <u>Cond</u> (8) 82, p. 89.
    "Solstice." <u>Cond</u> (8) 82, p. 87-88.

747. CLEARY, Brendan
    "Contagious." <u>Stand</u> (23:4) 82, p. 55.

748. CLEARY, Michael
    "Catholic Girls." <u>CapeR</u> (18:1) Wint 82, p. 41.

749. CLEARY, Victoria
    "Grading Papers, Holistically." <u>DekalbLAJ</u> (14:1/4)
        Aut 80-Sum 81, p. 69.

750. CLEEVE, Cathleen
    "TV Afterimage." <u>CapeR</u> (18:1) Wint 82, p. 42.

751. CLEMENTE, Vince
    "Deer Dreaming at Night." <u>Im</u> (8:1) 82, p. 8.

752. CLEMENTS, Arthur
    "Lost Child." <u>Poem</u> (45) Jl 82, p. 56.
    "The Play Is Over." <u>Poem</u> (45) Jl 82, p. 55.

753. CLENDENIN, Chris
    "On the Merits of Brief Life." <u>HiramPoR</u> (33) Aut-
        Wint 82, p. 9.

754. CLEVELAND, Pamela
    "The Bargain." <u>Catalyst</u> (Erotica Issue) 82, p. 8.
    "The Lighthouse." <u>Catalyst</u> (Erotica Issue) 82, p. 8.

755. CLIFF, Michelle
    "Travel Notes." <u>Iowa</u> (12:2/3) Spr-Sum 81, p. 32-35.

756. CLIFTON, Lucille
    "My Dream about the Cows." <u>VirQR</u> (58:4) Aut 82, p.
        687.
    "My Dream about the Inevitability of the Second
        Coming." <u>VirQR</u> (58:4) Aut 82, p. 688.
    "My Dream about Time." <u>VirQR</u> (58:4) Aut 82, p. 687.

757. CLIFTON, Merritt
    "And the Least Shall Save Us." <u>Sam</u> (33:4, issue 132)
        82 or 83, p. 3.
    "And the Least Shall Save Us." <u>UnderRM</u> (1:1) Spr 82,
        p. 49.
    "Baseball Men." <u>Sam</u> (32:4, issue 128) 82, p. 6.

"Bleeding Ulcer." Sam (33:4, issue 132) 82 or 83, p.
    7.
"Bobby Sands." Sam (33:4, issue 132) 82 or 83, p. 7.
"Deterrent." Sam (33:4, issue 132) 82 or 83, p. 3.
"Deterrent." UnderRM (1:1) Spr 82, p. 49.
"Foreign Aid." Sam (33:4, issue 132) 82 or 83, p. 5.
"From Oak Knoll Naval Hospital." Sam (33:4, issue
    132) 82 or 83, p. 4.
"Green Mountain Grade." Sam (33:4, issue 132) 82 or
    83, p. 5.
"Heritage." Sam (33:4, issue 132) 82 or 83, p. 2.
"Human Progress." Sam (33:4, issue 132) 82 or 83, p.
    16.
"Judgement." Sam (32:3, issue 127) 82, p. 39.
"Judgement." Sam (33:4, issue 132) 82 or 83, p. 15.
"Kampuchea, Land of Children." Sam (32:3, issue 127)
    82, p. 38-39.
"Kampuchea, Land of Children." Sam (33:4, issue 132)
    82 or 83, p. 14-15.
"The Last Warrior-Hero." Sam (33:4, issue 132) 82 or
    83, p. 9.
"The Least Grain." Sam (33:4, issue 132) 82 or 83,
    p. 8.
"The Man Said, 'Do unto Others'." Sam (33:3, issue
    131) 82, p. 16.
"Mavericks." Sam (33:4, issue 132) 82 or 83, p. 10-
    11.
"Nothing Deader." Sam (33:4, issue 132) 82 or 83, p.
    6.
"Revolution." Sam (33:4, issue 132) 82 or 83, p. 16.
"Scribbler sends haiku & card." WindO (40, Anti-
    Haiku issue) Sum 82, p. 46.
"Semanticist with an M-16." Sam (33:4, issue 132) 82
    or 83, p. 12.
"Serving Allah." Sam (33:4, issue 132) 82 or 83, p.
    12.
"Starlings & Starfighters." Sam (33:4, issue 132) 82
    or 83, p. 16.
"Ted Williams on the Art of Hitting." Sam (32:4,
    issue 128) 82, p. 16.
"Ted Williams, Age 63, Takes Batting Practice." Sam
    (32:4, issue 128) 82, p. 2.
"Three Sisters Raped & Shot." Sam (33:4, issue 132)
    82 or 83, p. 12.
"Wisdom of the Orient." Sam (33:4, issue 132) 82 or
    83, p. 13.
"Writer's Market." WindO (40, Anti-Haiku issue) Sum
    82, p. 46.

758. CLIMENHAGA, Joel
    "Coming back Home Again Blues." KanQ (14:3) Sum 82,
        p. 178.
    "Crying Need on a Rundown Street." Wind (12:45) 82,
        p. 12.
    "One for Kenneth Beaudoin." Wind (12:45) 82, p. 12.

759. CLINTON, D.
    "A Jupiter's Moon." Im (8:1) 82, p. 8.

760. CLOMPUS, Bradley
     "A Circle." <u>Outbr</u> (8/9) Aut 81-Spr 82, p. 20-23.
     "Its Fall." <u>Outbr</u> (8/9) Aut 81-Spr 82, p. 18.
     "Luring the Pronghorn." <u>Outbr</u> (8/9) Aut 81-Spr 82,
         p. 19.

761. CLORAN, Martin
     "Trotsky in Flowers." <u>PartR</u> (49:1) 82, p. 136-137.

762. CLOSSON, Kay L.
     "Cat's Cradle." <u>WebR</u> (7:2) Aut 82, p. 56.

763. CLOVES, Jeff
     "A Hymn of Hate to America." <u>Bogg</u> (49) 82, p. 54.

764. CLOYD, Beth
     "Turning Thirty." <u>Pig</u> (8) 80, p. 30.

765. CLUTTS, Oneda
     "Another layer unfolds." <u>MendoR</u> (6) Sum 81, p. 95.
     "To Little River and Mendocino." <u>MendoR</u> (6) Sum 81,
         p. 94.

766. COBIAN, Ricardo
     "He Descubierto a Muchos" (from Caminante Adjunto).
         <u>Mairena</u> (4:9) Spr 82, p. 82.
     "Hostia del Salario." <u>Maize</u> (6:1/2) Aut-Wint 82-83,
         p. 90-91.

767. COBIN, Susan
     "A Fat Lady." <u>WormR</u> (22:3, issue 87) 82, p. 89.
     "For Days You Haven't Heard." <u>MalR</u> (63) O 82, p.
         185.
     "In the Soap Opera an Unexpected Death." <u>MalR</u> (63) O
         82, p. 187.
     "Noise." <u>MalR</u> (63) O 82, p. 184.
     "Rain." <u>WormR</u> (22:3, issue 87) 82, p. 90.
     "What You Choose." <u>MalR</u> (63) O 82, p. 186.

768. COBO BORDA, J. G.
     "Roncando al Sol, Como una Foca en las Galapagos."
         <u>BelPoJ</u> (32:4) Sum 82, p. 14.
     "Snoring in the Sun, Like a Seal in the Galapagos"
         (tr. by Ricardo Pau-Llosa). <u>BelPoJ</u> (32:4) Sum 82,
         p. 15.

769. COCHRAN, William
     "Doing Chores." <u>Abraxas</u> (25/26) 82, p. 21.

770. COCHRANE, Shirley G.
     "Irish Sweaters." <u>Bogg</u> (48) 82, p. 26.
     "Wednesday 3 A.M." (For Peter). <u>HolCrit</u> (19:3) Je 82,
         p. 11.

771. CODAS, Ana Maria
     "A Esteban y Maria." <u>Prismal</u> (7/8) Spr 82, p. 91.

772. COFER, Judith Ortiz
     "About a Love Poem Written to Me." <u>Sam</u> (33:3, issue
         131) 82, p. 28.

"Moonlight Performance." SouthernHR (16:3) Sum 82,
p. 211.

773. COFFEY, Ann
"Storm Force 10." Bogg (48) 82, p. 42-43.

774. COFFIN, Lyn
"Amelia and John." HiramPoR (31) Aut-Wint 82, p. 17.
"Colors Like Spokane." SouthernHR (16:2) Spr 82, p.
127.
"The Duel." Wind (12:44) 82, p. 8.
"Escape from the Locker Room." PoNow (6:4, issue 34)
82, p. 27.
"Floating Women." Wind (12:44) 82, p. 8.
"Guess Who." WebR (7:1) Spr 82, p. 20.
"Lady Psychologist, Leaving Home" (for Ludmila).
AspenJ (1:2) Sum 82, p. 46.
"On His Deathbed." WebR (7:1) Spr 82, p. 18.
"Rhapsody on Terry." WebR (7:1) Spr 82, p. 19.
"Riverbeds in Times of Drought." LitR (25:3) Spr 82,
p. 376-377.
"Shadow-Children." WebR (7:1) Spr 82, p. 18.

775. COGGESHALL,Rosanne
"After Reading Blood, Hook, and Eye" (for Dara Wier).
SoCaR (14:2) Spr 82, p. 21.

776. COGSWELL, Fred
"How It Was." Germ (6:2) Aut-Wint 82, p. 21.
"Monition." Germ (6:2) Aut-Wint 82, p. 22.
"Myth." AntigR (51) Aut 82, p. 90.
"Where Once a Country Graveyard Used to Be." AntigR
(51) Aut 82, p. 91.

777. COHEN, Gerald
"Aerialist." Confr (24) Sum 82, p. 108.

778. COHEN, Helen Degen
"The Trains." Ascent (8:1) 82, p. 37.

779. COHEN, Keith
"Arabesque." Abraxas (25/26) 82, p. 97.

780. COHEN, Marc
"Lines Written in a Barbershop." MassR (23:1) Spr
82, p. 112-114.

COHEN, Maree Zukor
See: ZUKOR-COHEN, Maree

COHEN, Miriam
See: COHEN, Miriam A.

781. COHEN, Miriam A.
"From Observing the Effects on Females of Exposure to
the New York Borough of Queens." Sam (33:3, issue
131) 82, p. 29.
"So This Is Safe Space." HiramPoR (33) Aut-Wint 82,
p. 10.
"Troubled Sleep." Bogg (49) 82, p. 24.

782. COLBY, Joan
     "Conservation." Telescope (3) Sum 82, p. 71-72.
     "Emeralds." PortR (28:1) 82, p. 34.
     "The Evolution of Language." StoneC (9:3/4) Spr-Sum
        82, p. 32-33.
     "The Fat Man" (Jon Minnich, Age 37, 1400 lbs.). PoNow
        (6:4, issue 34) 82, p. 32.
     "Final Solutions." Poem (46) N 82, p. 63.
     "First Memory." HolCrit (19:2) Ap 82, p. 19-20.
     "How to Fall." BallSUF (23:2) Spr 82, p. 27.
     "Imposters." Poem (46) N 82, p. 64.
     "Instructions." BallSUF (23:2) Spr 82, p. 26.
     "The Quality of Light." Im (8:2) 82, p. 12.
     "Sestina." EnPas (13) 82, p. 17.

783. COLE, Henri
     "Patroclus: A Love Song." Shen (33:2) 82, p. 34-35.

784. COLE, James
     "The Cold Beach." PoNow (7:1, issue 37) 82, p. 8.
     "Postcard from Dick." KanQ (14:1) Wint 82, p. 39.
     "Regatta." PoNow (7:1, issue 37) 82, p. 9.

785. COLEMAN, Mary Ann
     "Strip Poker." PoNow (7:1, issue 37) 82, p. 9.

786. COLEMAN, Wanda
     "Growing Up Black." Epoch (32:1) Aut 82, p. 28-30.
     "High Time Lovers." PoNow (6:4, issue 34) 82, p. 39.
     "Tomboy." Tendril (13) Sum 82, p. 22.

787. COLES, Don
     "Ah! Qu'ils Sont Pittoresques, les Grands Jardins
        Manques!" Waves (10:3) Wint 82, p. 54-55.

788. COLINAS, Antonio
     "Dead City" (tr. by Anthony Kerrigan). DenQ (17:3)
        Aut 82, p. 74.

     COLLADO, Liliana Ramos
     See: RAMOS COLLADO, Liliana

789. COLLIER, Michael
     "Eye-piece." TriQ (54) Spr 82, p. 267-268.
     "The Lacquered Table." TriQ (54) Spr 82, p. 266.
     "Practicing Stalls." TriQ (54) Spr 82, p. 264-265.

790. COLLINS, Billy
     "Insomnia." Im (8:1) 82, p. 9.

791. COLLINS, Brewster
     "The Invasion of the People-Sized Superbugs." PoNow
        (7:1, issue 37) 82, p. 9.

792. COLLINS, Floyd
     "Drawing a Sea Horse." SouthernPR (23, i.e. 22:2)
        Aut 82, p. 23.
     "The Figure-Skater." Poem (46) N 82, p. 36.
     "Keys." Poem (46) N 82, p. 35.
     "Wine." Poem (46) N 82, p. 34.

793. COLLINS, Jeffrey
     "Hearing the Heartbeat of My First Child." CapeR
     (17:2) Sum 82, p. 1.
     "Perfect Fit." CapeR (17:2) Sum 82, p. 2.
     "The Prayer of a Man Who Hates Women." CapeR (17:2)
     Sum 82, p. 3.

794. COLLINS, Louis W.
     "Question." PottPort (4) 82-83, p. 24.
     "The Seafarers." PottPort (4) 82-83, p. 13.

795. COLLINS, Martha
     "373 East Park Street." Field (26) Spr 82, p. 24-25.
     "The Catastrophe of Rainbows." Agni (16) 82, p. 5-
     15.
     "Eclipse." Agni (17) 82, p. 167-168.
     "How It's Been." Field (26) Spr 82, p. 22-23.
     "Poem in the Fourth Dimension." Agni (17) 82, p.
     169.
     "The Purple Tree." DenQ (17:1) Spr 82, p. 99-101.
     "Waiting for Your Bus to Leave." WestB (10) 82, p.
     10.

796. COLLINS, Michael N.
     "1953 (I)." HangL (41) 82, p. 21.
     "1953 (II)." HangL (41) 82, p. 22.
     "1956." HangL (41) 82, p. 23.
     "1964." HangL (41) 82, p. 24.
     "Then, and Now." PoNow (6:6, issue 36) 82, p. 47.

797. COLLINS, Pat Lowery
     "MacDonald's, 34th and Broadway." Wind (12:45) 82,
     p. 33.

798. COLLINS, Robert
     "Those Who Have Vanished." HiramPoR (32) Spr-Sum 82,
     p. 16.

     COLON, Luis Rios
     See: RIOS COLON, Luis

799. COLON OLIVIERI, Rafael
     "Hoy, con la voz iluminada" (from Recurrencias).
     Mairena (4:9) Spr 82, p. 83.
     "Instantes" (Cinco momentos del yo). Mairena (4:10)
     Sum-Aut 82, p. 29-30.
     "Rompiendose en la busqueda" (from Rompiendose en la
     Busqueda). Mairena (4:9) Spr 82, p. 83.

800. COLON RUIZ, Jose O.
     "Juicio Final." Mairena (4:10) Sum-Aut 82, p. 91.

801. COLSON, Theodore
     "To Examine Synonyms: Search, Probe, Explore."
     PottPort (4) 82-83, p. 27.

802. COMAISH, Pete
     "At Dawn." Bogg (49) 82, p. 56-57.

803. COMANN, Brad
    "The Census Taker on the Navajo Reservation." Thrpny
        (10) Sum 82, p. 26.
    "Philosopher in the Midwest." Thrpny (11) Aut 82, p.
        19.

804. COMFORT, Daniel
    "A Child of the Back Porch." AmerPoR (11:2) Mr-Ap
        82, p. 27.
    "To a Southern Blackbird." AmerPoR (11:2) Mr-Ap 82,
        p. 27.
    "You." AmerPoR (11:2) Mr-Ap 82, p. 27.

    CONCEPCION, Jorge Luis Aviles
    See: AVILES CONCEPCION, Jorge Luis

805. CONDE, Carmen
    "The First Flower" (tr. by Jose R. de Armas and
        Alexis Levitin). WebR (7:2) Aut 82, p. 23.
    "First Night on Earth" (from Mujer sin Eden, tr. by
        Jose R. de Armas and Alexis Levitin). PraS (56:1)
        Spr 82, p. 40-41.
    "Fourth Canto" (tr. by Jose R. de Armas and Alexis
        Levitin). Confr (24) Sum 82, p. 78.
    "Prayer" (tr. by Jose R. de Armas and Alexis
        Levitin). WebR (7:2) Aut 82, p. 24.
    "Premonition" (tr. by Jose R. de Armas and Alexis
        Levitin). Confr (24) Sum 82, p. 79.
    "Voice of the Old Eve in Mary" (tr. by Jose R. de
        Armas and Alexis Levitin). WebR (7:2) Aut 82, p.
        22.

806. CONGDON, Kirby
    "Artist." PoNow (6:6, issue 36) 82, p. 15.
    "The Train." PoNow (6:4, issue 34) 82, p. 15.

807. CONKLIN, Joyce
    "1944." Gargoyle (15/16) 80, p. 14.

808. CONN, Jan
    "Red Branches of Trees." PoetryCR (3:3) Spr 82, p.
        7.
    "Snow Cranes in Rice Fields." PoetryCR (4:2) Wint
        82, p. 13.
    "Transition." Germ (6:1) Spr-Sum 82, p. 27.
    "White Lake." Germ (6:1) Spr-Sum 82, p. 28.

809. CONNOLLY, Geraldine
    "Our Parents Are Gone for the Day." PoNow (7:1,
        issue 37) 82, p. 9.

810. CONNOLLY, J. F.
    "Alchemist." PoetryNW (23:2) Sum 82, p. 21-23.
    "Love Poems in June." Tendril (12) Wint 82, p. 18-
        19.
    "Wild Hart." PoetryNW (23:2) Sum 82, p. 23.

811. CONNOR, Tony
    "And leave the voice of commerce blaring through an
        empty house." MassR (23:2) Sum 82, p. 368.

"A British Military Graveyard in the Himalayas."
NewL (48:3/4) Spr-Sum 82, p. 90-91.

812. CONOLEY, Gillian
"Maybe You Should Say Something." PoNow (7:1, issue
37) 82, p. 9.

813. CONRAD, Monique
"Driving through the Cape." PottPort (4) 82-83, p.
32.

814. CONRAN, Tony
"Lapwing" (for Joy when she suffered). Stand (23:4)
82, p. 65.

815. CONROW, M.
"After the Funeral." KanQ (14:2) Spr 82, p. 125.
"Lost and Found." KanQ (14:2) Spr 82, p. 124-125.

816. CONROY, James V.
"Late Night Caller." Vis (9) 82, p. 27.

817. CONTOSKI, Victor
"Flute Music." PoNow (6:4, issue 34) 82, p. 17.

818. CONTRAIRE, A. U.
"Callipygous Graffiti." WindO (40, Anti-Haiku issue)
Sum 82, p. 14.
"The Haiku Assassin." WindO (40, Anti-Haiku issue)
Sum 82, p. 12.
"The Haiku Machine." WindO (40, Anti-Haiku issue)
Sum 82, p. 1.
"Right Brain, Left Brain." WindO (40, Anti-Haiku
issue) Sum 82, p. 50.
"The Teacher Is to Blame." WindO (40, Anti-Haiku
issue) Sum 82, p. 13.
"The Tourist's Overconscious Description of Buddha."
WindO (40, Anti-Haiku issue) Sum 82, p. 14.

819. CONTRERAS, Armando
"Escaleras Reales" (from 20 1/2). Prismal (7/8) Spr
82, p. 83.

820. CONWAY, Rosalind
"The Night-Hawk." CrossC (4:4) 82, p. 11.

821. COOK, Albert
"Holding It Up." DenQ (17:1) Spr 82, p. 35.
"I Have Succumbed." DenQ (17:1) Spr 82, p. 36-37.
"The Veil Between." DenQ (17:1) Spr 82, p. 32-34.
"XII." DenQ (17:2) Sum 82, p. 118-121.
"XIII." DenQ (17:2) Sum 82, p. 121.

822. COOK, Gladys M.
"The City Dweller." ChrC (99:20) Je 2, 82, p. 662.

823. COOK, Gregory M.
"All That Is Left." PottPort (4) 82-83, p. 50.
"Antique Finish." PottPort (4) 82-83, p. 42.

"Come" (from Love in Flight). PoetryCR (4:2) Wint 82,
    p. 11.
"Driving Weather" (For Mary, from Love en Route).
    Germ (6:2) Aut-Wint 82, p. 26.
"Strangers in the Night." AntigR (48) Wint 82, p.
    47.
"The Unbroken Book." AntigR (48) Wint 82, p. 46.
"A Winning Self-Defense on a Speeding Summons."
    PottPort (4) 82-83, p. 45.

824. COOK, Jeanne
    "The Black Dress." MalR (61) F 82, p. 154-155.
    "Grass." MalR (61) F 82, p. 153.
    "To You." MalR (61) F 82, p. 153.
    "Tunnel Vision." MalR (61) F 82, p. 155.

825. COOK, Karmen
    "August in Florida." UTR (7:2) 82?, p. 14.
    "Speaking of Poets." Wind (12:46) 82, p. 20.

826. COOK, Paul H.
    "Casa de Luz" Outbr (8/9) Aut 81-Spr 82, p. 42-43.
    "Dream Wars of Spring." Outbr (8/9) Aut 81-Spr 82,
        p. 40-41.

827. COOK, Rhoby
    "Signs Your Wife Is Going Crazy." Maize (5:3/4) Spr-
        Sum 82, p. 28.
    "Subtle As Growth, the Process Has Begun." Maize
        (5:3/4) Spr-Sum 82, p. 29-30.

828. COOKSHAW, Marlene
    "The Blue Silk Shirt." Waves (10:4) Spr 82, p. 67.
    "Cinquefoil." CapilR (22) 82, p. 54-55.
    "Find the Inside Contour in a Ten-Minute Pose."
        CapilR (22) 82, p. 53.
    "Here, for Instance." CapilR (22) 82, p. 52.
    "Resolutions." CapilR (22) 82, p. 51.
    "Signatures." CapilR (22) 82, p. 49.
    "Waiting for the Light to Change." CapilR (22) 82,
        p. 50.

829. COOLEY, Dennis
    "Light Lingers." Dandel (9:1) 82, p. 88-89.
    "Running in the Street." Dandel (9:1) 82, p. 90-91.

830. COOLEY, Peter
    "After Men, After Women." PoNow (6:6, issue 36) 82,
        p. 33.
    "The Carp Pond." Northeast (3:14) Wint 82-83, p. 7.
    "The Heaven of the Vampires." NewYorker (58:37) N 1,
        82, p. 50.
    "The Lilies." SewanR (90:3) Sum 82, p. 402.
    "Necessities." SewanR (90:3) Sum 82, p. 400.
    "The Night Speaks to a Man." SewanR (90:3) Sum 82,
        p. 399.
    "Nightpiece." PoNow (6:6, issue 36) 82, p. 33.
    "Ode to the Statue." Northeast (3:14) Wint 82-83, p.
        6.
    "Psalm: The Roaring." PraS (56:2) Sum 82, p. 78-79.

"Such Comfort as the Night Can Bring." <u>SewanR</u> (90:3)
    Sum 82, p. 401.
"To a Child, a Spring Poem." <u>BaratR</u> (8:2) Wint 81,
    p. 69.
"To a Wasp Caught in the Storm Sash at the Advent of
    the Winter Solstice." <u>SouthernPR</u> (22:1) Spr 82, p.
    29.
"To the Statue of a Young Satyr." <u>PoNow</u> (6:6, issue
    36) 82, p. 33.
"Toward Morning." <u>BaratR</u> (8:2) Wint 81, p. 68.
"The Unasked for." <u>GeoR</u> (36:1) Spr 82, p. 165.

831. COOLIDGE, Clark
    "Peru Eye, the Heart of the Lamp." <u>Sulfur</u> (2:3,
        issue 6) 82, p. 39-45.

832. COOPER, Allan
    "After Rain." <u>StoneC</u> (9:3/4) Spr-Sum 82, p. 31.
    "Dream of My Grandfather." <u>StoneC</u> (9:3/4) Spr-Sum
        82, p. 31.
    "Horses." <u>PoetryCR</u> (3:4) Sum 82, p. 15.

833. COOPER, Dennis
    "Billy McCall's Summer." <u>Spirit</u> (6:2/3) 82, p. 48-
        49.
    "John Kennedy Jr. Faces the Future." <u>PoNow</u> (6:5,
        issue 35) 82, p. 23.
    "Touch Control." <u>PoNow</u> (6:5, issue 35) 82, p. 23.

834. COOPER, Dona Maddux
    "And It Came to Pass." <u>LittleBR</u> (3:2) Wint 82-83, p.
        18.
    "Time Is a Magician." <u>LittleBR</u> (3:2) Wint 82-83, p.
        18.

835. COOPER, James
    "Gabriel Rossetti: A Self-Portrait" (October, 1869).
        <u>MidwQ</u> (23:2) Wint 82, p. 182.

836. COOPER, James E.
    "Yardbird Yardstick for a Green Midget, or, Myth of
        the Eternal Emerald on Iscariot Street." <u>AntigR</u>
        (48) Wint 82, p. 36-38.

837. COOPER, Jane
    "Flute Song." <u>Ploughs</u> (8:1) 82, p. 29.

838. COOPER, Laura
    "Spring, 1981." <u>EngJ</u> (71:7) N 82, p. 78.

839. COOPER, Wyn
    "Song of the Observed." <u>CimR</u> (58) Ja 82, p. 4.

840. COOPERMAN, Robert
    "Odysseus Remembers His Adventure in the Cave of
        Cyclops." <u>Confr</u> (24) Sum 82, p. 80-81.

841. CORBETT, William
    "Washington's Birthday." <u>Sulfur</u> (2:3, issue 6) 82,
        p. 90-92.

842. CORDING, Robert
     "Fulton Fish Market." QW (14) Spr-Sum 82, p. 36-37.
     "Summer Town after Labor Day." SouthernHR (16:3) Sum
        82, p. 234.
     "There" (Jeane Henri Fabre: The Early Years). CarolQ
        (34:3) Spr 82, p. 8.
     "Work." QW (14) Spr-Sum 82, p. 38.

     CORDOVA, Antonio Ramirez
     See: RAMIREZ CORDOVA, Antonio

843. COREY, Chet
     "The Coming of His Age." UnderRM (1:1) Spr 82, p.
        39.
     "Journey through Rings of Light." UnderRM (1:1) Spr
        82, p. 40-41.
     "Self-Immolation by Fire before a Child." KanQ
        (14:1) Wint 82, p. 61.

844. COREY, Stephen
     "Fighting Death." GeoR (36:3) Aut 82, p. 636-637.
     "Museum of Her Leaving." GeoR (36:3) Aut 82, p. 637.
     "Third Love Poem." StoneC (9:3/4) Spr-Sum 82, p. 38.
     "Two Ways" (to J. G.) StoneC (9:3/4) Spr-Sum 82, p.
        38.
     "What We Did, What You Will Know." StoneC (9:3/4)
        Spr-Sum 82, p. 39.

845. CORKERY, Christopher Jane
     "February 14." Poetry (139:5) F 82, p. 267.
     "Spoken Spanish." Poetry (139:5) F 82, p. 265-266.

846. CORN, Alfred
     "Corneille's Le Cid, Act One." Hudson (35:3) Aut 82,
        p. 363-376.
     from Notes from a Child of Paradise: (I, II, VII, IX,
        X, XIV, XVI, XVIII). Poetry (140:6) S 82, p. 311-
        318.

847. CORNELL, Brian R.
     "The Historian." AntigR (49) Spr 82, p. 20.
     "Hope." PottPort (4) 82-83, p. 51.
     "The Verdict." PottPort (4) 82-83, p. 22.

848. CORONEL URTECHO, Jose
     "No Volvera el Pasado." Maize (5:3/4) Spr-Sum 82, p.
        71-74.

849. CORPI, Lucha
     "Denuncia." RevChic (10:1/2) Wint-Spr 82, p. 59.
     "Lamento" (a Maria Auxilio). RevChic (10:1/2) Wint-
        Spr 82, p. 60-61.

850. CORREA, Miguel
     "Ciudad" (para Maria Mujica). NotArte (7:3) Mr 82, p.
        12.
     "Poema Primero" (a H. Wempe). NotArte (7:3) Mr 82, p.
        12.

851. CORRETJER, Juan Antonio
     "Alabanza en la Torre de Ciales" (Fragmentos). Areito
     (8:31) 82, inside front cover.

852. CORT, John
     "Banaras, 1980" (for Robert Nichols). Abraxas (25/26)
     82, p. 83.

853. CORVAIA, Vince
     "Eugenio." Telescope (3) Sum 82, p. 67-68.
     "The Porch." Telescope (3) Sum 82, p. 44-45.

854. CORWIN, Phillip
     "The Harijans." KanQ (14:1) Wint 82, p. 82.

855. COS, Charles
     "In Spite of All" (tr. by Karl Patten). CharR (8:1)
     Spr 82, p. 53.
     "Sonnet" (tr. by Karl Patten). CharR (8:1) Spr 82, p.
     54.
     "Testament" (tr. by Karl Patten). CharR (8:1) Spr 82,
     p. 54.

856. COSIER, Tony
     "Sylvia Plath." Bogg (48) 82, p. 72.

857. COSTA, Marithelma
     "Roma se derretia bajo un sol insensato." Mairena
     (4:10) Sum-Aut 82, p. 69.

858. COSTANZO, Gerald
     "Introduction of the Shopping Cart" (Oklahoma City,
     1937). OhioR (29) 82, p. 127.
     "The Resurrection of Lake Erie" (for Bill Boggs).
     OhioR (29) 82, p. 126.
     "The Riot of Nickle Beer Night." PoNow (6:4, issue
     34) 82, p. 45.

859. COSTLEY, Bill
     "Letting Lowell Alone Officially" (for Emerson B.
     Griswold, BSME/MIT). Bogg (49) 82, p. 20.

860. COTE, J. Marc
     from Sustaining Mythologies: "He wanted to see
     higher." Quarry (31:1) Wint 82, p. 22.

861. COTTERILL, Sarah
     "After Long Solitude." WestB (10) 82, p. 52.
     "Hitchhiker in Winter." PoNow (6:4, issue 34) 82, p.
     47.
     "The Hive Burning." PoNow (7:1, issue 37) 82, p. 10.

862. COUCH, Larry
     "Gauguin, 1981." Vis (8) 82, p. 30.

863. COULETTE, Henri
     "The Art of Translation." Iowa (12:4) Aut 81, p.
     116.
     "Coming to Terms." Iowa (12:4) Aut 81, p. 115.
     "Confiteor." Iowa (12:4) Aut 81, p. 117.

123   COULETTE

"The Desire and Pursuit of the Part." Iowa (12:4)
     Aut 81, p. 112-114.

864. COUNTRYMAN, Bill
     "Planting in February". ChrC (99:6) F 24, 82, p.
     208.

865. COURSEN, H. R.
     "Maine: December." SmPd (19:1, issue 54) Wint 82, p.
     13.

866. COUTO, Nancy Lee
     "1958." PraS (56:3) Aut 82, p. 22-23.
     "Living in the La Brea Tar Pits." Iowa (12:4) Aut
     81, p. 46-47.

867. COVINO, Michael
     "Autumn Leaves." Poetry (140:4) Jl 82, p. 202.
     "Prescribed Form." Poetry (140:4) Jl 82, p. 203.
     "Sports Event." Pig (9) 82, p. 62.

868. COWELL, Allan
     "Incident." Bogg (49) 82, p. 60.
     "A Moment with Emily." Bogg (48) 82, p. 62.

869. COWEN, Sonia
     "Letting Go." Telescope (2) Aut 81, p. 8.

870. COWING, Sheila
     "Cat." Tendril (12) Wint 82, p. 20.
     "Sustenance" (for Ethel). GeoR (36:1) Spr 82, p. 150.

871. COX, Carol
     "The Calm." HangL (41) 82, p. 25.
     "An Hour in the Smokies." HangL (41) 82, p. 26.
     "The Last Year." HangL (41) 82, p. 27.

872. COX, Elizabeth
     "Across the Road." CarolQ (34:3) Spr 82, p. 34.
     "Departures and Arrivals." SouthernPR (22:1) Spr 82,
     p. 57-60.
     "Do Not Tap on the Glass." CarolQ (34:3) Spr 82, p.
     35.

873. COX, Terrance
     "Clear As Black & White." PoetryCR (3:3) Spr 82, p.
     7.

874. COXE, Louis
     "Forbidden City." Paint (7/8:13/16) 80-81, p. 20.
     "Halcyon Days." MassR (23:2) Sum 82, p. 244.

875. COXE, Louis, Jr.
     "The Visitor." PoNow (7:1, issue 37) 82, p. 10.

876. COZART, Shanna
     "What Is Green?" LittleBR (2:3) Spr 82, p. 76.

877. CRAIG, David
    "And to All Our Troops at Sea." StoneC (10:1/2) Aut-
    Wint 82-83, p. 55.

878. CRAIG, Liz
    "The Circle Almost Closes" (for Mother Maybelle
    Carter). Grain (10:3) Ag 82, p. 61.

879. CRAMER, Kevin
    "No Door, No Key." DekalbLAJ (14:1/4) Aut 80-Sum 81,
    p. 70.

880. CRAMER, Steven
    "The Narcissus" (for Leonard and Sarah). Agni (17)
    82, p. 15-16.
    "Uncle in Sunshine" (after Wallace Stevens). Nat
    (235:18) N 27, 82, p. 568.

881. CRASNO, Brian Lee
    "A Lyric in Process." MendoR (6) Sum 81, p. 126.

882. CRAVEN, Jerry
    "Golden Bird of Immortality." Paint (7/8:13/16) 80-
    81, p. 29.

883. CRAWFORD, Nicholas
    "Mechanics." StoneC (9:3/4) Spr-Sum 82, p. 59.

884. CREELEY, Robert
    "Age." Ploughs (8:2/3) 82, p. 83.
    "Death." Ploughs (8:2/3) 82, p. 84.
    "The Sound." NewYorker (58:15) My 31, 82, p. 40.
    "Versions" (after Hardy). Ploughs (8:2/3) 82, p. 81-
    82.
    "The Visit." Ploughs (8:2/3) 82, p. 84.

885. CREGAN, Patricia
    "Springturn." ModernPS (11:1/2) 82, p. 104-106.

886. CRESCIONI, Olga
    from Cuando Se Seque el Rocio: (II). Mairena (4:9)
    Spr 82, p. 82.

887. CREW, Louie
    "Separate & Unequal." Sam (33:3, issue 131) 82, p.
    28.

888. CREWE, Jennifer
    "One Ending." Nat (235:6) S 4, 82, p. 186.
    "Opening the Matrioshka Doll." Nat (234:20) My 22,
    82, p. 623.

889. CREWS, John
    "Caught Caught Caught." CarolQ (35:1) Aut 82, p. 17.
    "Lifeboat." PoNow (7:1, issue 37) 82, p. 10.

890. CREWS, Judson
    "All the Wild Dogs That Yap." PoNow (6:6, issue 36)
    82, p. 3.

"Blue Hyacinth, Pale Blue Hyacinth." PoNow (6:6, issue 36) 82, p. 38.
"The Cock." WormR (22:4, issue 88) 82, p. 146.
"Dear Empire Smelling Fair." PoNow (6:6, issue 36) 82, p. 38.
"Hemingway Said, I Wonder If." PoNow (6:6, issue 36) 82, p. 3.
"Her." PoNow (6:6, issue 36) 82, p. 2.
"I Am Still as Stone." PoNow (6:6, issue 36) 82, p. 3.
"I Came Back to That Same Desolate Place." PoNow (6:6, issue 36) 82, p. 3.
"It Is Not." WormR (22:4, issue 88) 82, p. 146.
"Memory." Pig (8) 80, p. 43.
"The More." WormR (22:4, issue 88) 82, p. 146.
"The Noose." PoNow (6:6, issue 36) 82, p. 38.
"Pieces." WormR (22:4, issue 88) 82, p. 146.
"A Procession." Abraxas (25/26) 82, p. 46.
"The River." PoNow (6:6, issue 36) 82, p. 38.
"She Hated Rattlers, Does It Matter." PoNow (6:6, issue 36) 82, p. 3.
"That Quaint." PoNow (6:6, issue 36) 82, p. 2.
"Was It Through All the San Joaquin Area." PoNow (6:6, issue 36) 82, p. 3.
"When I." WormR (22:4, issue 88) 82, p. 146.
"When We Were Young." PoNow (6:6, issue 36) 82, p. 38.
"Whit-." WormR (22:4, issue 88) 82, p. 146.
"The White Whale, the White Whale." PoNow (6:6, issue 36) 82, p. 38.

CRIADO, Yolanda Gracia de
    See: GRACIA de CRIADO, Yolanda

891. CRISS, Darlene
    "Education." EngJ (71:4) Ap 82, p. 83.

892. CRIST, Lyle
    "Shells." HiramPoR (31) Aut-Wint 82, p. 18.

893. CROBAUGH, Emma
    "The Mortal Disk." DekalbLAJ (14:1/4) Aut 80-Sum 81, p. 70.

894. CROFT, Greg
    "Between Us." PottPort (4) 82-83, p. 9.
    "Only." PottPort (4) 82-83, p. 24.

895. CROMARTIE, Susan T.
    "Friends in Christ." ChrC (99:7) Mr 3, 82, p. 239.

896. CROOKER, Barbara
    "Applewood." WestB (11) 82, p. 18-19.
    "Nothing Is Given, Everything Burns." WestB (11) 82, p. 17.
    "The Refugees." SoDakR (20:4) Wint 82-83, p. 63.

897. CROSBY, Heather Lee
    "The Crows." AntigR (50) Sum 82, p. 104.
    "Pinpoint." AntigR (50) Sum 82, p. 104.

898. CROW, MARY
        "Heart" (tr. of Braulio Arenas). DenQ (16:4) Wint 82,
        p. 42.
        "To Pass" (tr. of Idea Vilarino, w. Patsy Boyer).
        DenQ (16:4) Wint 82, p. 40-41.

899. CROW, Mary
        "To-Be-America" (tr. of Carlos Latorre). DenQ (16:4)
        Wint 82, p. 39.

900. CROWELL, Doug
        "Laughing with the Angels." HiramPoR (33) Aut-Wint
        82, p. 11.

901. CROWELL, Peter
        "The Drowning." Quarry (31:4) Aut 82, p. 58.
        "Justice for the Teacher." Quarry (31:4) Aut 82, p.
        57.
        "Mumps." Quarry (31:4) Aut 82, p. 59-60.

902. CRUM, Robert
        "The Forest." NowestR (20:2/3) 82, p. 246.

903. CRUSZ, Rienzi
        "Ritual at Dawn" (for the children of the village of
        Boralesgamuva, Sri Lanka). PoetryCR (3:4) Sum 82,
        p. 5.
        "Where Adam First Touched God." Quarry (31:4) Aut
        82, p. 55-56.

     CRUZ, Luis Gonzalez
     See: GONZALEZ CRUZ, Luis

904. CRUZ, Victor A.
        "Heaven's Eternal Cigarette." WindO (41) Aut-Wint
        82-83, p. 43.
        "Its Theme." WindO (41) Aut-Wint 82-83, p. 43.

905. CRUZ MILLER, Wilfredo
        "Esta noche voy a dormir como siempre." Mairena
        (4:10) Sum-Aut 82, p. 77.

906. CSOORI, Sandor
        "At Home, in the Night" (tr. by Nicholas Kolumban).
        MalR (63) O 82, p. 54.
        "Poem for Two Women at the Same Time" (tr. by
        Nicholas Kolumban). MalR (63) O 82, p. 52-53.
        "September Confessions" (tr. by Nicholas Kolumban).
        MalR (63) O 82, p. 51.
        "The Smile of My Exile" (tr. by Nicholas Kolumban).
        NewOR (9:1) Spr-Sum 82, p. 12.

907. CUERVO, Jose S.
        "Los Estragos del Progreso." Maize (5:1/2) Aut-Wint
        81-82, p. 51.

908. CUMMINS, James
        from The Perry Mason Sestinas: (4, 5, 11) AntR
        (40:1) Wint 82, p. p. 48-53.

909. CUNLIFFE, Dave
      "Blackburn Rovers Revisted." Bogg (49) 82, p. 36-37.

910. CURRIE, John
      "A Footnote to Shakespeare's Hamlet" (tr. of Jarkko
         Laine, w. the author). Spirit (6:2/3) 82, p. 177-
         179.

911. CURTIS, Jack
      "The Builder." PoNow (6:4, issue 34) 82, p. 32.
      "Crepuscalo" (from Punta Prieta Desert). StoneC
         (10:1/2) Aut-Wint 82-83, p. 23.

912. CURTIS, Redmond
      "Show-Biz Success." AntigR (49) Spr 82, p. 104.
      "We Are Such Stuff." AntigR (49) Spr 82, p. 105.

913. CURTIS, Tony
      "Andrew Wyeth Poems." SoDakR (20:3) Aut 82, p. 9-11.
      "Jack Watts." MalR (61) F 82, p. 108-109.
      "My Grandmother's Cactus." Confr (23) Wint 82, p.
         39.
      "Tannenbaum." NewYorker (58:44) D 20, 82, p. 38.

914. CUSHMAN, Kathleen
      "Brothers and Sisters." NewYorker (58:26) Ag 16, 82,
         p. 28.

915. CUTLER, Bruce
      "Nights in the Canebrake." KanQ (14:2) Spr 82, p.
         50-51.
      "Rings." KanQ (14:2) Spr 82, p. 42.
      "Things." KanQ (14:2) Spr 82, p. 51.

916. CUZA MALE, Belkis
      "En lo Alto." BelPoJ (32:4) Sum 82, p. 18.
      "On High" (tr. by Ricardo Pau-Llosa). BelPoJ (32:4)
         Sum 82, p. 19.

917. CYNDIAN, Charles London
      "Gospel." CarolQ (34:3) Spr 82, p. 13.

918. CZAPLA, Cathy Young
      "Alvira's Garden." Sam (33:3, issue 131) 82, p. 57.
      "Counting the Casualties." Sam (33:3, issue 131) 82,
         p. 57.
      "Fuel Shortage." Bogg (48) 82, p. 12.

      D., H. (DOOLITTLE, Hilda)
      See: H. D.

919. DABNEY, Janice
      "Growing Up Two Miles from WCW." CentR (26:3) Sum
         82, p. 275-276.
      "Photograph: The Mother." CentR (26:3) Sum 82, p.
         275.

920. DABYDEEN, Cyril
      "Flood." Waves (10:3) Wint 82, p. 64-65.
      "Rehearsal." CanLit (95) Wint 82, p. 28-29.

"Snake's Belly Turned Over." <u>CanLit</u> (95) Wint 82, p.
     65-66.
"A Sun's Life." <u>CanLit</u> (95) Wint 82, p. 65.

921. DACEY, Philip
     "August, 1980." <u>AspenJ</u> (1) Wint 82, p. 32.
     "The Blue Moon Ballroom Burns Down." <u>PoNow</u> (6:6,
          issue 36) 82, p. 6.
     "Door-Discipline." <u>SouthernPR</u> (22:1) Spr 82, p. 27.
     "Hamlet Revealed." <u>Chelsea</u> (41) 82, p. 110-111.
     "Owning a Wife." <u>Chelsea</u> (41) 82, p. 111.
     "The Poet Picks Rock." <u>PoNow</u> (6:6, issue 36) 82, p.
          6.
     "The Safe." <u>AspenJ</u> (1) Wint 82, p. 32.
     "Sunset." <u>UnderRM</u> 1(1) Spr 82, p. 12.

922. DACEY, Philip
     "The Triangle." <u>WestB</u> (11) 82, p. 31-32.
     "What It Is." <u>WestB</u> (11) 82, p. 30-31.

923. DACEY, Philip
     "Which Hand." <u>UnderRM</u> 1(1) Spr 82, p. 13.

924. DAIGON, Ruth
     "Old People at the Film Series at the Museum of
          Modern Art." <u>LittleBR</u> (1:3) Spr 81, p. 54.

925. D'ALFONSO, Antonio
     "She." <u>PoetryCR</u> (4:2) Wint 82, p. 7.

926. DALTON, Philip
     "Jarflies." <u>Poem</u> (46) N 82, p. 49.
     "Shadows Divined." <u>Poem</u> (46) N 82, p. 48.
     "Yesterday, or Tomorrow." <u>Poem</u> (46) N 82, p. 50.

927. DALTON, Roque
     "Americalatina." <u>Maize</u> (5:3/4) Spr-Sum 82, p. 45.
     "Latinamerica" (tr. by Edward Baker). <u>Maize</u> (5:3/4)
          Spr-Sum 82, p. 40.
     "Love Poem" (tr. by Edward Baker). <u>Maize</u> (5:3/4) Spr-
          Sum 82, p. 41.
     "Mecanografo." <u>Maize</u> (5:3/4) Spr-Sum 82, p. 44-45.
     "O.A.S." (tr. by Edward Baker). <u>Maize</u> (5:3/4) Spr-Sum
          82, p. 42.
     "O.E.A." <u>Maize</u> (5:3/4) Spr-Sum 82, p. 46.
     "Poema de Amor." <u>Maize</u> (5:3/4) Spr-Sum 82, p. 45-46.
     "Todos." <u>Maize</u> (5:3/4) Spr-Sum 82, p. 43.
     "Typist" (tr. by Edward Baker). <u>Maize</u> (5:3/4) Spr-Sum
          82, p. 39-40.
     "We all" (tr. by Edward Baker). <u>Maize</u> (5:3/4) Spr-Sum
          82, p. 38.

928. DALY, Desmond
     "Before the Keys." <u>Waves</u> (10:4) Spr 82, p. 70.

929. DALY, Mary Ann
     "Women with the Attributes of Their Death." <u>CarolQ</u>
          (34:3) Spr 82, p. 15.

930. DAMACION, Zamora
     "Woman with a Camera" (Diane Arbus: Born 1923 - Died
     1972). PoNow (6:4, issue 34) 82, p. 47.

931. DAMON, Maria
     "Question and Answer." Hangl (43) Wint 82-83, p. 57.

932. DANA, Robert
     "Driving the Coeur d'Alene Without You." NewEngR
     (4:3) Spr 82, p. 448-449.
     "Getting It Right." Ploughs (8:2/3) 82, p. 40-41.
     "Horses." Spirit (6:2/3) 82, p. 21-22.
     "Mating" (found poem). Kayak (58) Ja 82, p. 45.
     "Nine Lives" (for RS, 1921-1981). Ploughs (8:2/3) 82,
     p. 42-43.
     "What the Stones Know." NewEngR (4:3) Spr 82, p.
     450.

933. DANGEL, Leo
     "A Clear Day." PoNow (7:1, issue 37) 82, p. 11.
     "Doreen Has Another Rummage Sale." PoNow (7:1, issue
     37) 82, p. 11.
     "My Father in the Distance." PoNow (7:1, issue 37)
     82, p. 11.

934. DANIEL, Arnaut
     "Amors e Jois e Liocs e Tems" (second version) (tr.
     by Ezra Pound). Antaeus (44) Wint 82, p. 26-27.
     "Amors e Jois e Liocs e Tems" (tr. by Ezra Pound).
     Antaeus (44) Wint 82, p. 24-25.
     "Er Vei Vermeills, Vertz, Blaus, Blancs, Groucs
     (second version)" (tr. by Ezra Pound). Antaeus (44)
     Wint 82, p. 22-23.
     "Er Vei Vermeills, Vertz, Blaus, Blancs, Groucs" (tr.
     by Ezra Pound). Antaeus (44) Wint 82, p. 20-21.
     "Lanquan Vei Fueill' e Flors e Frug (second version)"
     (tr. by Ezra Pound). Antaeus (44) Wint 82, p. 18-
     19.
     "Lanquan Vei Fueill' e Flors e Frug" (tr. by Ezra
     Pound). Antaeus (44) Wint 82, p. 16-17.

935. DANIEL, John
     "At a Party, Three Years Later." Wind (12:44) 82, p.
     18.
     "First Light." PoNow (7:1, issue 37) 82, p. 11.
     "The Longing." CutB (19) Aut-Wint 82, p. 72-73.

936. DANIEL, Lorne
     "There Are No Original Rituals." Dandel (9:2) 82, p.
     5.

937. DANIELS, Jim
     "Baseball Cards #1." Pig (9) 82, p. 46.
     "Baseball Cards #2." Pig (9) 82, p. 46.
     "Bullets." MinnR (NS19) Aut 82, p. 51.
     "Ghazal: 1." WormR (22:3, issue 87) 82, p. 84.
     "Ghazal: 2." WormR (22:3, issue 87) 82, p. 84-85.
     "Ghazal: 3." WormR (22:3, issue 87) 82, p. 85.
     "Hard Times in the Motor City." MinnR (NS19) Aut 82,
     p. 52-53.

"Heart Victim." KanQ (14:3) Sum 82, p. 150.
"Right Fielder." Pig (9) 82, p. 55.
"Shoplifting." HiramPoR (31) Aut-Wint 82, p. 19.
"Something About the Wind." CimR (58) Ja 82, p. 26.

DANIELSON, Anita Endrezze
See: ENDREZZE-DANIELSON, Anita

938. DANKLEFF, Richard
"Bud's Daddy." ColEng 44(1) Ja 82, p. 42.
"Last Winter." ColEng 44(1) Ja 82, p. 41.
"Winter Quarters." HiramPoR (32) Spr-Sum 82, p. 17.
"A Winter's Tale." SewanR (90:3) Sum 82, p. 403.

939. DARGIS, Daniel
"Cette Voix d'Attributs et d'Antitheses." Os (14)
82, p. 12-13.

940. DARLINGTON, Andrew
"Animalisms/Copernicus, City of the Dead." Bogg (48)
82, p. 41.
"Marine Incident." Vis (8) 82, p. 38.

941. DARLINGTON, Chris
"Fisherman's Dreams." Bogg (49) 82, p. 53.

942. DARR, Ann
"At Sixteen." PoNow (6:4, issue 34) 82, p. 7.
"Canned Heat." PoNow (6:6, issue 36) 82, p. 24.
"The Case of the Frightened Bride." Ploughs (8:1)
82, p. 143-144.
"For 65 Thousand Dollars." PoNow (6:6, issue 36) 82,
p. 24.
"Friends." PoNow (6:6, issue 36) 82, p. 24.
"Or Dreaming." PoNow (6:6, issue 36) 82, p. 24.

943. DARUWALLA, Keki N.
"The Lighthouse Paintings." NewL (49:2) Wint 82-83,
p. 44-45.
"The Middle Ages." NewL (48:3/4) Spr-Sum 82, p. 15-
16.
"Migrations." NewL (48:3/4) Spr-Sum 82, p. 16-17.
"The Unrest of Desire." NewL (48:3/4) Spr-Sum 82, p.
17.

944. DARWISH, Mahmud
"Sorrow and Anger" (tr. by Ben Bennani). Paint
(7/8:13/16) 80-81, p. 44-46.

945. DAS, Ashok
"Cuttack." NewL (48:3/4) Spr-Sum 82, p. 183.
"Graveyard." NewL (48:3/4) Spr-Sum 82, p. 183.

946. DAS, Jagannath Prasad
"The Corpse" (tr. by Jayanta Mahapatra). NewL
(48:3/4) Spr-Sum 82, p. 36.

947. DAS, Jibanananda
"Dance of the Twilight Junction" (tr. by Debashish
Banerji). Os (14) 82, p. 23.

"Pakhira/Birds" (tr. by Debashish Banerji). Os (14) 82, p. 24-25.

948. DAS, Kamala
"The Dance of the Eunuchs." NewL (48:3/4) Spr-Sum 82, p. 156-157.
"The Sea Shore." NewL (48:3/4) Spr-Sum 82, p. 156.
"The Testing of the Sirens." NewL (48:3/4) Spr-Sum 82, p. 157-158.

949. DAS, Mahadai
"Awaken my love." Sam (31:2, issue 122) 82, p. 15.
"Birds break through the wall of heaven." Sam (31:2, issue 122) 82, p. 5.
"The Day of Revolution." Sam (31:2, issue 122) 82, p. 16.
"For Walter Rodney & Other Victims." Sam (31:2, issue 122) 82, p. 9-10.
"How soon the cold rain, pellets shatering the thin grass." Sam (31:2, issue 122) 82, p. 6.
"Love, love, I have survived so long." Sam (31:2, issue 122) 82, p. 13.
"My Final Gift to Life." Sam (31:2, issue 122) 82, p. 8.
"My Finer Steel Will Grow." Sam (31:2, issue 122) 82, p. 4.
"O love you silence my words leaping." Sam (31:2, issue 122) 82, p. 11-12.
"Place your hand upon my womb." Sam (31:2, issue 122) 82, p. 14.
"There are eyes that watch behind the shroud of darkness." Sam (31:2, issue 122) 82, p. 3.
"There was always the urgent essentiality." Sam (31:2, issue 122) 82, p. 2.
"While the Sun Is Trapped." Sam (31:2, issue 122) 82, p. 7.

950. DAS, Sisir Kumar
"An Indian Dog Show" (tr. by the author). NewL (48:3/4) Spr-Sum 82, p. 48.

951. DAS, Varsha
"Stars" (tr. of Sitanshu Yashaschandra). NewL (48:3/4) Spr-Sum 82, p. 257.

952. DATTA, Jyotirmoy
"A Poem Smuggled Out of Prison" (tr. by the author). NewL (48:3/4) Spr-Sum 82, p. 207.
"Snail" (tr. by Prithvindra Chakravarti and Ulli Beier). NewL (48:3/4) Spr-Sum 82, p. 236.

953. DAUGHERTY, Michael
"No More Spearmint Kisses." Bogg (49) 82, p. 34.
"Riffraff." Bogg (48) 82, p. 45.

954. DAUGHTER (Anonymous)
"Antecedents." LittleBR (3:2) Wint 82-83, p. 31-33.

955. DAUNT, Jon
    "Another Hitch-Hiker in Galilee" (from The Odin
      Chronicles). Nimrod (26:1) Aut-Wint 82, p. 76-78.
    "Birds fly across sky's changing seasons." WindO
      (40, Anti-Haiku issue) Sum 82, p. 45.
    "The Escape of Jezebel's Daughter." DekalbLAJ
      (14:1/4) Aut 80-Sum 81, p. 71.
    "Lawn Chair on the Plains of Troy" (from The Odin
      Chronicles). Nimrod (26:1) Aut-Wint 82, p. 73-75.
    "Odin Goes to Gettysburg" (from The Odin Chronicles).
      Nimrod (26:1) Aut-Wint 82, p. 79.
    "Odin Meets Another Giant" (from The Odin
      Chronicles). Nimrod (26:1) Aut-Wint 82, p. 80-82.
    "Still Life with Treasure" (from The Odin
      Chronicles). Nimrod (26:1) Aut-Wint 82, p. 78-79.

956. DAVEY, Julie A.
    "Perseverance." WritersL Ag 82, p. 6.

957. DAVID, Sigmund
    "The Deserted Corridor." Vis (9) 82, p. 36.

958. DAVIDSON, Michael
    "Watermark" (part IV for Lou Harrison). Sulfur (2:1,
      issue 4) 82, p. 121-125.
    "The Words Are Trapped in Doxa." Sulfur (2:1, issue
      4) 82, p. 117-118.
    "You Are Not Great You Are Life." Sulfur (2:1, issue
      4) 82, p. 119-120.

959. DAVIDSON, Scott L.
    "The View from Cataldo Mission." CutB (19) Aut-Wint
      82, p. 52-53.

960. DAVIE, Donald
    "Fare Thee Well." AmerS (51:4) Aut 82, p. 550-551.
    "Hope for the Best." Thrpny (10) Sum 82, p. 14-15.
    "Tortoiseshell" (for Ed Dorn). AmerS (51:1) Wint 81-
      82, p. 94.

    DAVILA, Marcos Reyes
    See: REYES DAVILA, Marcos

961. DAVILA MALAVE, Angela Maria
    "Cuando revienta un rayo." Areito (8:31) 82, p. 40.

962. DAVIS, Christine
    "After Moving." Tendril (12) Wint 82, p. 21.

963. DAVIS, Christopher
    "A Journalist Interviews One of Pancho Villa's Widows
      in Mexico, 1968" NewL (49:1) Aut 82, p. 51-53.

964. DAVIS, Duane
    "Daughter." Sam (32:2, issue 126) 82, p. 5.
    "It's a Job, He Said." Sam (32:2, issue 126) 82, p.
      11.
    "Protective Custody, Hold & Treat." Sam (32:2, issue
      126) 82, p. 6-7.
    "Reason with Me." Sam (32:2, issue 126) 82, p. 4.

"She Wanted to Know What Had Happened." Sam (32:2,
    issue 126) 82, p. 12.
"Statement of Witness." Sam (32:2, issue 126) 82, p.
    2-3.
"Winning." Sam (32:2, issue 126) 82, p. 8-10.

965. DAVIS, Ed
    "The Farmer." Sam (32:3, issue 127) 82, p. 29.

966. DAVIS, Glover
    "Even Our Statues Dream for Us." CharR (8:1) Spr 82,
        p. 24-25.
    "Lancelot." CharR (8:1) Spr 82, p. 24.
    "Moon Hull." CharR (8:1) Spr 82, p. 23.
    "Paper Wings." CharR (8:1) Spr 82, p. 25-26.
    "Red Feather." BlackWR (7:2) Spr 81, p. 46-47.

967. DAVIS, Lloyd
    "After Georg Trakl." Annex (4), 82 p. 60.
    "Armstrong Spring Creek." Annex (4), 82 p. 69.
    "At an Esso Station in Dailey, W. Va.." Annex (4),
        82 p. 70.
    "The Bath at Warm Springs." Annex (4), 82 p. 73-74.
    "Bob Hosey Is Dead." Annex (4), 82 p. 75.
    "A Couple in a Car." Annex (4), 82 p. 59-60.
    "Death of the Lower Jackson." Annex (4), 82 p. 78.
    "Driving Down Decker's Creek in the Rain." Annex
        (4), 82 p. 65.
    "Driving into Buffalo at Six O'Clock." Annex (4), 82
        p. 68.
    "Driving to the Bullpasture River by Myself." Annex
        (4), 82 p. 70-71.
    "Driving to Work, Monday." Annex (4), 82 p. 66.
    "Driving West: Diamond Ring, Montana." Annex (4), 82
        p. 69.
    "Eyes." OhioR (27) 82, p. 28.
    "Farmington No. 9." Annex (4), 82 p. 61.
    "The First Day of Spring." Annex (4), 82 p. 59.
    "Fishing Manns Creek." Annex (4), 82 p. 78.
    "Fishing the Lower Jackson." Annex (4), 82 p. 71.
    "Floating the Yellowstone." Annex (4), 82 p. 80.
    "Florida: St. Petersburg Beach." Annex (4), 82 p.
        62.
    "Highway 23, North of Columbus, Ohio." Annex (4), 82
        p. 69.
    "In the Summer Night." Annex (4), 82 p. 61.
    "In Virginia." Annex (4), 82 p. 76.
    "Just West of Bovina, Colorado." Annex (4), 82 p.
        68.
    "Last Day of the Trip." Annex (4), 82 p. 80.
    "Late in the Evening." Annex (4), 82 p. 77.
    "March 24." Annex (4), 82 p. 63.
    "May 2: A Late Spring." Annex (4), 82 p. 63.
    "Mingo Cemetery." Annex (4), 82 p. 67.
    "My Old Blue Sweater." Annex (4), 82 p. 64.
    "Nancy." Annex (4), 82 p. 74.
    "Near Bear Wallow." Annex (4), 82 p. 77.
    "Near Mustoe, Va.." Annex (4), 82 p. 79-80.
    "On the Upper Jackson." Annex (4), 82 p. 73.
    "Opening Doors." OhioR (27) 82, p. 29.

"Panic." <u>Annex</u> (4), 82 p. 72.
"Saturday." <u>Annex</u> (4), 82 p. 62.
"Sewell in June." <u>Annex</u> (4), 82 p. 68.
"The Spring Rain." <u>Annex</u> (4), 82 p. 63.
"There Is Magic." <u>Annex</u> (4), 82 p. 72.
"To Point Marion, December 30." <u>Annex</u> (4), 82 p. 66.
"West Virginia Roadside Park." <u>Annex</u> (4), 82 p. 67.

968. DAVIS, William Virgil
"Another Version of the Same Story." <u>ConcPo</u> (15:2)
Aut 82, p. 68.
"Ashes." <u>MassR</u> (23:3) Aut 82, p. 486.
"At the Ruins." <u>Hudson</u> (35:1) Spr 82, p. 70.
"Depth of Field." <u>StoneC</u> (10:1/2) Aut-Wint 82-83, p.
24.
"Detail." <u>ConcPo</u> (15:2) Aut 82, p. 69.
"The Fall" <u>Im</u> (8:1) 82, p. 7.
"Homage to Joseph Cornell." <u>StoneC</u> (10:1/2) Aut-Wint
82-83, p. 24.
"In the Embassy Waiting Room on Thursday." <u>PoNow</u>
(6:6, issue 36) 82, p. 37.
"The Librarian." <u>PoNow</u> (6:4, issue 34) 82, p. 46.
"Lines for My Mother." <u>NewEngR</u> (4:3) Spr 82, p. 468.
"Memories of Wash Day" (for my mother). <u>CimR</u> (58) Ja
82, p. 24-25.
"The Motorcycle" (for Billy). <u>Poem</u> (44) Mr 82, p. 18.
"The Ohio Poem" (for James Wright). <u>Hudson</u> (35:1) Spr
82, p. 69-70.
"On a Hill in Crete." <u>MassR</u> (23:2) Sum 82, p. 305.
"One Winter Night in a Room." <u>Paint</u> (9:17/18) Spr-
Aut 82, p. 14.
"Pentimento." <u>NewEngR</u> (4:3) Spr 82, p. 468.
"Roses." <u>Poem</u> (44) Mr 82, p. 17.
"The Tree." <u>MalR</u> (61) F 82, p. 20.
"What the Bones Do After Dark." <u>Im</u> (8:1) 82, p. 7.
"Why I Don't Dream." <u>PoNow</u> (6:6, issue 36) 82, p.
37.
"The Witness." <u>PoNow</u> (6:4, issue 34) 82, p. 46.

969. DAVISON, Peter
"The Everlasting." <u>Atl</u> (249:4) Ap 82, p. 96.
"The Money Cry." <u>Poetry</u> (140:5) Ag 82, p. 271.
"Night Watch." <u>Tendril</u> (12) Wint 82, p. 22.
"Not a Dilemma." <u>Poetry</u> (140:5) Ag 82, p. 272-273.
"Stern Stuff." <u>Atl</u> (249:4) Ap 82, p. 96.
"Swimming 1935" (Six sentences for Robert Penn
Warren). <u>Poetry</u> (140:5) Ag 82, p. 269-270.

970. DAY, Robert
"Speaking French in Western Kansas." <u>LittleBR</u> (3:2)
Wint 82-83, p. 64.
"Teal Hunting with Two Old Uncles." <u>LittleBR</u> (2:1)
Aut 81, p. 35.

971. DAYAN, Joan C.
"Myth" (tr. of Aime Cesaire). <u>Paint</u> (7/8:13/16) 80-
81, p. 41.

De ALBA, Alice Gaspar
<u>See</u>: GASPAR de ALBA, Alice

De ANDRADE, Carlos Drummond
    <u>See</u>: ANDRADE, Carlos Drummond de

De ANDRADE, Eugenio
    <u>See</u>: ANDRADE, Eugenio de

De ARELLANO, Olga Ramirez
    <u>See</u>: RAMIREZ de ARELLANO, Olga

De AREVALO, Marta
    <u>See</u>: ISIS

De ARMAS, Jose R.
    <u>See</u>: ARMAS, Jose R. de

De BALMACEDA, Margarita Sastre
    <u>See</u>: SASTRE de BALMACEDA, Margarita

De BIEDMA, Jaime Gil
    <u>See</u>: GIL de BIEDMA, Jaime

972. De BOLT, William Walter
    "Insight." <u>ChrC</u> (99:3) Ja 27, 82, p. 79.
    "Second Thought." <u>ChrC</u> (99:2) Ja 20, 82, p. 45.
    "To a Girl in April." <u>ArizQ</u> (38:1) Spr 82, p. 68.

De BURGOS, Julia
    <u>See</u>: BURGOS, Julia de

De CAMPOS, Alvaro
    <u>See</u>: PESSOA, Fernando

De CRIADO, Yolanda Gracia
    <u>See</u>: GRACIA de CRIADO, Yolanda

De HEREDIA, Jose-Maria
    <u>See</u>: HEREDIA, Jose-Maria de

De HOYOS, Angela
    <u>See</u>: HOYOS, Angela de

De JUANA, Pedro Sevilla
    <u>See</u>: SEVILLA de JUANA, Pedro

De la PUEBLA, Manuel
    <u>See</u>: PUEBLA, Manuel de la

De LEON, Maria de los Angeles Ortiz
    <u>See</u>: ORTIZ de LEON, Maria de los Angeles

De los MILAGROS PEREZ, Maria
    <u>See</u>: PEREZ, Maria de los Milagros

973. De MARIS, Ron
    "The Bath House." <u>SouthernPR</u> (23, i.e. 22:2) Aut 82,
        p. 15.
    "The Echo." <u>EnPas</u> (13) 82, p. 18-19.
    "Lovers." <u>KanQ</u> (14:1) Wint 82, p. 105.
    "My Father Eating Glass." <u>SouthernPR</u> (23, i.e. 22:2)
        Aut 82, p. 16.

"Spoor." CarolQ (34:3) Spr 82, p. 22-24.
"Wind from the Sea" (after Wyeth). CarolQ (35:1) Aut
   82, p. 49.
"Windmills." SouthernPR (23, i.e. 22:2) Aut 82, p.
   17.

De MATOS, Isabel Freire
   See: FREIRE de MATOS, Isabel

De MELLO BREYNER ANDRESEN, Sophia
   See: ANDRESEN, Sophia de Mello Breyner

De MOLINA, Mercedes Gonzalez Vega
   See: GONZALEZ VEGA de MOLINA, Mercedes

De OSBORNE, Elba Diaz
   See: DIAZ de OSBORNE, Elba

De PALCHI, Alfredo
   See: PALCHI, Alfredo de

974. De ROO, Harvey
   "The Dawn Horse Canters." WestCR (17:1) Je 82, p.
      10.
   "Night Picture with Horses." WestCR (17:1) Je 82, p.
      11.
   "Triads." WestCR (17:1) Je 82, p. 11-12.
   "You Ask about Grace." WestCR (17:1) Je 82, p. 10.

De RUBIO, Nieves del Rosario Marquez
   See: MARQUEZ de RUBIO, Nieves del Rosario

De RUBIO, Victor Gil
   See: GIL de RUBIO, Victor

De SENA, Jorge
   See: SENA, Jorge de

975. De SOUZA, Eunice
   "Idyll." NewL (48:3/4) Spr-Sum 82, p. 188.
   "Mrs. Hermione Gonsalvez." NewL (48:3/4) Spr-Sum 82,
      p. 188-189.

976. De STEFANO, John
   "Occasional Poem." PartR (49:3) 82, p. 441.

De TORRES, Rosario Esther Rios
   See: RIOS de TORRES, Rosario Esther

De WOESTIJNE, Karel van
   See: WOESTIJNE, Karel van de

977. DEAL, Susan Strayer
   "Because of All the Air." CentR (26:3) Sum 82, p.
      271.
   "Darkening Lake. The Hush." HiramPoR (31) Aut-Wint
      82, p. 20.
   "Horses in the Rain." PoNow (7:1, issue 37) 82, p.
      12.
   "Muse." CentR (26:3) Sum 82, p. 270-271.

"Noun Clusters and Other Muses." *Pig* (8) 80, p. 33.
"Ritual." *PoNow* (7:1, issue 37) 82, p. 12.
"Woman in a Garden." *Abraxas* (25/26) 82, p. 25.

978. DEAN, Misao
"Finding Language." *CrossC* (4:1) Wint 82, p. 11.

979. DEAVEL, C. Christine
"He Is Unemployed into Fall." *MinnR* (NS19) Aut 82,
p. 42.

980. DEETER, Kay
"The Whipstitch." *CapeR* (18:1) Wint 82, p. 21.

981. DeFOE, Mark
"At a Stoplight in a Small Town." *Shout* (3:1) 82, p.
14.
"Monarch." *Outbr* (10/11) Aut 82-Spr 83, p. 74.
"Running after the Women." *Outbr* (10/11) Aut 82-Spr
83, p. 72-73.
"To the Future Archaeologist." *Outbr* (10/11) Aut 82-
Spr 83, p. 75.
"Wife-Wooing." *SewanR* (90:2) Spr 82, p. 219.

982. DeFord, Sara
"Cross-Word Puzzle." *ChrC* (99:20) Je 2, 82, p. 664.

983. DeFREES, Madeline
"Extended Outlook." *Iowa* (12:2/3) Spr-Sum 81, p. 49.
"Hanging the Pictures." *Iowa* (12:2/3) Spr-Sum 81, p.
48.
"The Light Station on Tillamook Rock." *Shen* (33:4)
82, p. 42-60.
"Recessional from the Cloister." *MassR* (23:2) Sum
82, p. 271-272.
"Scenes from the Great Round." *MassR* (23:2) Sum 82,
p. 270-271.

984. DeGRAVELLES, Charles
"The Happiest Man in Paris." *SenR* (13:1) 82-83, p.
8-9.
"In the Beginning." *SenR* (13:1) 82-83, p. 6-7.
"The Inheritance of Death in the Vesture of Dance."
SenR (13:1) 82-83, p. 3-5.

985. DeGRUSON, Gene
"Warning." *LittleBR* (1:3) Spr 81, p. 33.

986. DELANEY, John
"Walter Mitty in Retirement." *CharR* (8:1) Spr 82, p.
49-50.

987. DELGADO, Abelardo
"From Garden City to Hays." *RevChic* (10:1/2) Wint-
Spr 82, p. 62-63.
"The Last Vow." *RevChic* (10:1/2) Wint-Spr 82, p. 64-
66.

DELIZ, Wenceslao Serra
See: SERRA DELIZ, Wenceslao

988. DELP, Michael
      "The Women Are Coming." PoNow (6:4, issue 34) 82, p.
      14.

989. DeMARIS, Arlene
      "Naming Your Fear." SmPd (19:2, issue 55) Spr 82, p.
      28.
      "Send Help." SmPd (19:1, issue 54) Wint 82, p. 21.

990. DEMUS, Klaus
      "Morning Stillness" (tr. by Beth Bjorklund). LitR
      (25:2) Wint 82, p. 247.
      "Summer Report" (tr. by Beth Bjorklund). LitR (25:2)
      Wint 82, p. 246.

991. DENBERG, Ken
      "Manipulation" (for Lynn). SouthernPR (23, i.e. 22:2)
      Aut 82, p. 31.
      "Rabbits." SouthernPR (23, i.e. 22:2) Aut 82, p. 30.

992. DenBOER, David C.
      "The Night's Heart." HiramPoR (31) Aut-Wint 82, p.
      21.

993. DENHAM, Paula
      "This Is the Nature of a Tree." Hangl (43) Wint 82-
      83, p. 61.

994. DENMAN, David
      "Grace." ChrC (99:21) Je 9-16, 82, p. 692.

995. DENNIS, Carl
      "Charity." AmerPoR (11:2) Mr-Ap 82, p. 38.
      "The Dreamer." AmerPoR (11:2) Mr-Ap 82, p. 38.
      "The Guest." AmerPoR (11:2) Mr-Ap 82, p. 38.
      "Passage to India." PoetryNW (23:1) Spr 82, p. 15-
      16.
      "To Be Continued." MichQR (21:3) Sum 82, p. 443-444.

996. DENT, Dorothy Hill
      "A Leaf to Grow" (To A.G.S.). LittleBR (2:2) Wint 81-
      82, p. 59.

997. DePOY, Phillip
      "If, to the Sparrow, Green" (from The Book of Birds).
      SouthernPR (23, i.e. 22:2) Aut 82, p. 48.

998. DePREIST, James
      "A landscape newly bathed in ambiguous hues." PortR
      (28:2) 82, p. 13.
      "Much of what is." PortR (28:2) 82, p. 12.
      "Tomorrow is fully booked." PortR (28:2) 82, p. 12.
      "We are heirs to unseen legacies of power." PortR
      (28:2) 82, p. 13.

999. DEPTA, Victor
      "Doesn't Look Good on Film." WestB (10) 82, p. 46.
      "Peach Galls." OhioR (28) 82, p. 32-33.
      "Wild Rose." WestB (10) 82, p. 47-48.

Der GRAFT, Guillaume van
  See: GRAFT, Guillaume van der

1000. Der HOVANESSIAN, Diana
      from My Sun, My Artaxerxes: (1-9) (tr. of Vassilis
        Vassilikos, w. the author). PraS (56:1) Spr 82, p.
        28-30.
      "The Old True Story." PoNow (6:6, issue 36) 82, p.
        46.
      "Sometimes." PoNow (6:6, issue 36) 82, p. 46.

      Der MOLEN, W. J. van
      See: MOLEN, W. J. van der

1001. DeREMIGIS, P.
      "A Moment." AntigR (49) Spr 82, p. 42.
      "Reflections on Time and Sunlight." AntigR (49) Spr
        82, p. 43.
      "A Year." AntigR (49) Spr 82, p. 42-43.

1002. DERRICOTTE, Toi
      "Black Letter." OP (33) Spr 82, p. 48.
      "The Creation." OP (33) Spr 82, p. 52-53.
      "The Mirror." OP (33) Spr 82, p. 47.
      from Natural Birth: "II November." Iowa (12:2/3)
        Spr-Sum 81, p. 63-65.
      from Natural Birth: "IV Maternity." Iowa (12:2/3)
        Spr-Sum 81, p. 65.
      from Natural Birth: "VI Transition." Iowa (12:2/3)
        Spr-Sum 81, p. 65-68.
      "Poem for My Father." OP (33) Spr 82, p. 49-51.

1003. DERRY, Alice
      "Clamming with Lanterns." SouthernPR (22:1) Spr 82,
        p. 42.
      "Star Thistle." PortR (28:1) 82, p. 17.

1004. DESAI, S. K.
      "The Gipsy Girl" (tr. of U. R. Ananthamurthy). NewL
        (48:3/4) Spr-Sum 82, p. 149.
      "A Lesson" (tr. of K. S. Nisar Ahmed). NewL (48:3/4)
        Spr-Sum 82, p. 235.
      "A Photographer" (tr. of B. R. Laxman Rao). NewL
        (48:3/4) Spr-Sum 82, p. 144-145.

1005. DesRUISSEAUX, Pierre
      "Barbare Memoire d'Ou." Os (15) 82, p. 10.
      "Rien de Ton Chemin." Os (14) 82, p. 2.
      "Roc par Intemperie." Os (14) 82, p. 3.

1006. DESY, Peter
      "Becoming." CapeR (18:1) Wint 82, p. 30.
      "Coming Home for the Divorce." SouthernPR (23, i.e.
        22:2) Aut 82, p. 41.
      "Consulting the Fruit during a Time of Depression."
        CapeR (18:1) Wint 82, p. 31.
      "Entering." ColEng 44(3) Mr 82, p. 289.
      "March Snowfall." WestB (11) 82, p. 80.
      "The Return." WestB (11) 82, p. 81.

"When I Die and They Find Me." HiramPoR (32) Spr-
Sum 82, p. 18.

1007. DETELA, Lev
"Green" (tr. of Edvard Kocbek, with Herbert Kuhner
and Milena Detela). PortR (28:1) 82, p. 7.

1008. DETELA, Milena
"Green" (tr. of Edvard Kocbek, with Herbert Kuhner
and Lev Detela). PortR (28:1) 82, p. 7.

1009. DEUMER, Joseph
"Prayer." Tendril (12) Wint 82, p. 27-28.
"A Quarry in Indiana." Tendril (12) Wint 82, p. 23-
26.

1010. DEVEAU, Leo
"Consummation" (for Thomas Merton). PottPort (4) 82-
83, p. 42.
"Shuffle." PottPort (4) 82-83, p. 41.

1011. DeVEAUX, Alexis
"And Do You Love Me." OP (34) Aut-Wint 82, p. 42-
43.
"French Doors: A Vignette." OP (34) Aut-Wint 82, p.
40-41.
"Madeleine's Dreads." Iowa (12:2/3) Spr-Sum 81, p.
62.
"The Woman Who Lives in the Botanical Gardens." OP
(34) Aut-Wint 82, p. 44-45.

DEVENTER, George V. van
See: VanDEVENTER, George V.

1012. DEWDNEY, Christopher
"Fashioning crude loopholes with our bare hands."
Dandel (9:2) 82, p. 65.
"Type two words, two inches apart on blank paper."
Dandel (9:2) 82, p. 66.
"We became completely acquainted with every aspect
of evolution." Dandel (9:2) 82, p. 64.

1013. DHARWADKER, Vinay
"On the Beach" (tr. of Mangesh Padgaonkar). CharR
(8:2) Aut 82, p. 46-47.
"Unclouded" (tr. of Mangesh Padgaonkar). CharR (8:2)
Aut 82, p. 47.

1014. DHOOMIL
"A Poem" (tr. by Ajit Khullar). NewL (48:3/4) Spr-
Sum 82, p. 152-153.

1015. Di CICCO, Pier Giorgio
"Lying Low." CanLit (91) Wint 81, p. 80.
"Male Rage Poem." Waves (10:3) Wint 82, p. 68-69.
"Quotidian." CanLit (91) Wint 81, p. 9.

1016. Di MICHELE, Mary
"Beatitude." Waves (10:4) Spr 82, p. 44.
"Pearls." Waves (10:4) Spr 82, p. 47.

"Poem for My Daughter." _Waves_ (10:4) Spr 82, p. 45.
"The Wheat and the Chaff." _Waves_ (10:4) Spr 82, p.
    46.

1017. Di PIERO, W. S.
    "The Arrival." _PoNow_ (6:4, issue 34) 82, p. 38.
    "Canada." _AmerS_ (51:3) Sum 82, p. 316.
    "I'll Remember This Autumn" (tr. of Leonardo
        Sinisgalli). _Pequod_ (14) 82, p. 52.
    "Late Day." _SewanR_ (90:3) Sum 82, p. 398.
    "Likeness." _Pequod_ (14) 82, p. 53.
    "Saxophone." _Telescope_ (1) Spr 81, p. 7-8.
    "Second Horn" (Venice, 1975, Scuola di San Giorgio
        degli Schiavoni). _Agni_ (17) 82, p. 8-9.
    "Settling." _SewanR_ (90:3) Sum 82, p. 397.
    "Strates Shows." _ChiR_ (33:2) 82, p. 124-125.

1018. Di PRISCO, Joseph
    "The Beautiful Country." _PoNow_ (6:6, issue 36) 82,
        p. 31.

1019. Di SALVO, Tommaso Giuseppe
    "Cuatro Meses de Purgatorio, un Mes de Infierno."
        _Os_ (15) 82, p. 24-25.
    "Flores fragiles." _Os_ (15) 82, p. 26.

1020. DIARA, Schavi Mali
    "African Woman." _BlackALF_ (16:2) Sum 82, p. 71.
    "Most Likely to Succeed." _BlackALF_ (16:2) Sum 82,
        p. 71.
    "Struggling and Surviving." _BlackALF_ (16:2) Sum 82,
        p. 71.
    "To a Special Friend." _BlackALF_ (16:2) Sum 82, p.
        71.

1021. DIAZ de OSBORNE, Elba
    "Dimension." _Mairena_ (4:9) Spr 82, p. 37.

1022. DIAZ MARRERO, Andres
    "Ausencia" (from Voces). _Mairena_ (4:9) Spr 82, p.
        85.

1023. DICKEMAN, Nancy
    "Breathing and Dreaming." _PoetryNW_ (23:2) Sum 82,
        p. 19-20.
    "On the Oak Lined Streets." _PoetryNW_ (23:2) Sum 82,
        p. 20-21.

1024. DICKENS, Eric
    "Brueghel" (tr. of Stanislaw Grochowiak). _Stand_
        (23:2) 82, p. 72.
    "The Suicide's Room" (tr. of Wislawa Szymborska).
        Stand (23:2) 82, p. 71.

1025. DICKEY, William
    "Afternoon Evening and Night in the Courtyard of the
        Museum of Modern Art." _PoNow_ (6:6, issue 36) 82,
        p. 21.
    "Constructive Criticism." _PoNow_ (6:4, issue 34) 82,
        p. 23.

"Conversazione." PoNow (6:4, issue 34) 82, p. 23.
"Ezekiel's Rabbit." NewEngR (5:1/2) Aut-Wint 82, p.
    134-135.
"Gloryosky, Zero!" Poetry (140:3) Je 82, p. 164-
    165.
"I Know, Let's Put on a Show Ourselves." MassR
    (23:3) Aut 82, p. 505-506.
"Permissions." NewEngR (5:1/2) Aut-Wint 82, p. 132-
    133.
"Seizure." Poetry (140:3) Je 82, p. 166-167.
"Soon, and in the Company of a Young Gentleman."
    GeoR (36:4) Wint 82, p. 833.
"Those Destroyed by Success." Poetry (140:3) Je 82,
    p. 168-169.
"Warning Keep Fingers Hair Jewelry away from This
    Area." PoNow (6:6, issue 36) 82, p. 21.
"Windows." GeoR (36:4) Wint 82, p. 832.

1026. DICKSON, John
    "1898." Outbr (10/11) Aut 82-Spr 83, p. 95-96.
    "Archer Avenue." StoneC (9:3/4) Spr-Sum 82, p. 35.
    "Cinderella." Poetry (141:3) D 82, p. 146-147.
    "Rose." Outbr (10/11) Aut 82-Spr 83, p. 94.
    "A Tale of Two Cities." Poetry (141:3) D 82, p.
        145-146.

1027. DIDACUS, Brother
    "August Night Qualms" (a sequence). Vis (9) 82, p.
        23, 25.

1028. DIEGO, Eliseo
    "Palabras Escritas un Trece de Octubre." Areito
        (8:32) 82, inside back cover.

1029. DIETZ, Sheila
    "Desert Stargaze." BelPoJ (33:2) Wint 82-83, p. 31-
        36.
    "I dream seagulls gather on the beach." StoneC
        (9:3/4) Spr-Sum 82, p. 15.

1030. DILLARD, Annie
    "Soft Coral." AntigR (48) Wint 82, p. 5.

1031. DIMITROVA, Blaga
    "If" (tr. by Jascha Kessler and Alexander
        Shurbanov). Kayak (59) Je 82, p. 66.
    "If" (tr. by Jascha Kessler and Alexander
        Shurbanov). Nimrod (26:1) Aut-Wint 82, p. 37.
    "What Price Constancy" (tr. by Jascha Kessler and
        Alexander Shurbanov). Kayak (59) Je 82, p. 67.
    "A Woman Pregnant" (tr. by Jascha Kessler and
        Alexander Shurbanov). Nimrod (26:1) Aut-Wint 82,
        p. 38.

1032. DING, Zuxin
    "By the Han and the Yangtze" (tr. of Anonymous, w.
        Burton Raffel). DenQ (17:2) Sum 82, p. 90.
    "The Drum Thunders" (tr. of Anonymous, w. Burton
        Raffel). DenQ (17:2) Sum 82, p. 91.

"A Fisherman's Family" (tr. of Zhen Xie, w. Burton
Raffel). DenQ (17:2) Sum 82, p. 95.
"North Hill" (tr. of Anonymous, w. Burton Raffel).
DenQ (17:2) Sum 82, p. 92.
"On My Way to Jian-men, in a Drizzle" (tr. of Lu
You, w. Burton Raffel). DenQ (17:2) Sum 82, p. 93.
"On the Night of the First Full Moon" (tr. of Zhu
Sushen, w. Burton Raffel). DenQ (17:2) Sum 82, p.
94.
"Poem #123 (1839)" (tr. of Gong Zizhen, w. Burton
Raffel). DenQ (17:2) Sum 82, p. 96.
"To a Japanese Friend" (tr. of Qiu Jin, w. Burton
Raffel). DenQ (17:2) Sum 82, p. 97.

1033. DINGLER, Crystal
"Lying Beside the River." PoetryNW (23:2) Sum 82,
p. 47.

1034. DISCH, Tom
"Ode on the Source of the Foux." AntR (40:1) Wint
82, p. 46-47.
"Symphonic Ode for St. Cecilia's Day" (for Greg
Sandow). Shen (33:1) 81-82, p. 78-82.

1035. DISCHELL, Stuart
"After Rain." Iowa (12:4) Aut 81, p. 57.
"Boston, Winter." Agni (17) 82, p. 31.
"Into the Green Marsh" (off Absecon Island, 1960).
Iowa (12:4) Aut 81, p. 58.

1036. DISKIN, Lahna
"Braids." ColEng 44(5) S 82, p. 491-492.
"House for Sale." EngJ (71:2) F 82, p. 30.
"Traveling Alone." CEAFor (13:1) O 82, p. 8.

1037. DITSKY, John
"The Dispute Over The Dating Of Easter: A Love-
Antiphon." HolCrit (19:2) Ap 82, p. 18.
"Habit." PortR (28:2) 82, p. 17.
"Highwater Mark." WritersL Je 82, p. 23.
"Monkey Mountain, Beppu." KanQ (14:3) Sum 82, p.
93.
"The Orient Express." MalR (61) F 82, p. 235.
"Outpatient Clinic" (for Brian Gamble). PortR (28:2)
82, p. 14-15.
"Rite." PortR (28:2) 82, p. 16.
"West Variations." PortR (28:2) 82, p. 18.
"Whitman Supra Emerson." PortR (28:2) 82, p. 15.

1038. DITTA, Joseph M.
"Argyle Park." Wind (12:44) 82, p. 9-10.
"Markings." Wind (12:44) 82, p. 10-11.
"Poem of Exceptions." ModernPS (11:1/2) 82, p. 86-
88.
"Tottori Sand Dunes." Wind (12:44) 82, p. 11-12.

1039. DIXON, Melvin
"Sightseeing" (for Richard). Obs (7:2/3) Sum-Wint
81, p. 150-151.

1040. DJAGAROV, Georgy
      "Night" (tr. by Jascha Kessler and Alexander
      Shurbanov). Kayak (59) Je 82, p. 69.

1041. DJANIKIAN, Gregory
      "The Journey." Poetry (140:6) S 82, p. 322-323.
      "Literally Speaking." Poetry (140:6) S 82, p. 324.

1042. DOBBERSTEIN, Michael
      "Locations in the Visible World." CimR (61) O 82,
      p. 12-14.
      "The Wish." CutB (18) Spr-Sum 82, p. 93-94.

1043. DOBBS, Jeannine
      "Restoration." MidwQ (24:1) Aut 82, p. 59.

1044. DOBLER, Patricia
      "1920 Photo." Annex (4), 82 p. 88.
      "All Souls Day, 1957." Annex (4), 82 p. 104.
      "Anticipating Her Death, Grandma Dreams about
      Grandpa." Annex (4), 82 p. 106.
      "August." Annex (4), 82 p. 90-91.
      "Brother and Sister." Annex (4), 82 p. 106.
      "Carolyn at 16." Annex (4), 82 p. 99.
      "Carolyn at 20." Annex (4), 82 p. 100.
      "Carolyn at 40." Annex (4), 82 p. 100.
      "Cold Frame." Annex (4), 82 p. 98.
      "Daddy's Hunting Coat." Annex (4), 82 p. 90.
      "Dancing Men." Tendril (12) Wint 82, p. 29.
      "Dancing Men." Annex (4), 82 p. 103.
      "Diet." Annex (4), 82 p. 91.
      "Familiar." Annex (4), 82 p. 105.
      "Family Dream." Annex (4), 82 p. 92.
      "For Mary Cunningham." Annex (4), 82 p. 101-102.
      "The Gazebo." Annex (4), 82 p. 102.
      "Grandma's Hands." Annex (4), 82 p. 107.
      "Gravestone Rubbing." Annex (4), 82 p. 97.
      "Hospital Call." Annex (4), 82 p. 95.
      "How to Winter Out." CapeR (17:2) Sum 82, p. 12.
      "Jealous Wife." Annex (4), 82 p. 94.
      "On Murray Avenue." Annex (4), 82 p. 104.
      "Phoenix" (for my brother). Annex (4), 82 p. 105.
      "Portrait." Annex (4), 82 p. 89.
      "Separations." Annex (4), 82 p. 95-96.
      "Steel Poem, 1912" (for Kevin). Annex (4), 82 p. 89-
      90.
      "Tarot Stew." Annex (4), 82 p. 98.
      "Their Marriage/Memory." Annex (4), 82 p. 92.
      "Undiscovered Rooms" (for John M. Dobler). Annex
      (4), 82 p. 93.
      "The Wall" (for Richard Shelton). Annex (4), 82 p.
      101.
      "Watching the Perseid Shower" (for Bruce). Annex
      (4), 82 p. 95.

1045. DOBYNS, Stephen
      "Art." Antaeus (47) Aut 82, p. 69-70.
      "Birth Report." AmerPoR (11:4) Jl-Ag 82, p. 37.
      "Black Dog, Red Dog." AmerPoR (11:4) Jl-Ag 82, p.
      37.

"Boy with Pigeons." <u>MissouriR</u> (5:2) Wint 81-82, p. 43.
"The Card Game." <u>Kayak</u> (58) Ja 82, p. 18.
"Dream." <u>Kayak</u> (58) Ja 82, p. 17.
"Frenchie." <u>AmerPoR</u> (11:4) Jl-Ag 82, p. 38.
"The Great Doubters of History." <u>AmerPoR</u> (11:4) Jl-Ag 82, p. 39-40.
"The Gun." <u>Antaeus</u> (47) Aut 82, p. 67-68.
"North Wind." <u>AmerPoR</u> (11:4) Jl-Ag 82, p. 39.
"The Turkish Room." <u>Kayak</u> (58) Ja 82, p. 16.

1046. DOCK, Leslie
"Botticelli's Venus." <u>Abraxas</u> (25/26) 82, p. 98.

1047. DODD, Wayne
"And If Someone." <u>CharR</u> (8:1) Spr 82, p. 10-11.
"Beside Mill Creek." <u>CharR</u> (8:1) Spr 82, p. 7-8.
"Driving the Schoolbus." <u>CharR</u> (8:1) Spr 82, p. 5.
"A Morning Poem, Written to Michael Waters' Class, 29 January 1981." <u>CharR</u> (8:1) Spr 82, p. 12.
"Some Mornings When I Wake." <u>CharR</u> (8:1) Spr 82, p. 6-7.
"Tongues." <u>GeoR</u> (36:3) Aut 82, p. 493-495.
"Two Love Poems" (For Joyce). <u>CharR</u> (8:1) Spr 82, p. 8-9.

DOES, Michael vander
<u>See</u>: Vander DOES, Michael

1048. DOLGORUKOV, Florence
"Autochthon." <u>LitR</u> (25:3) Spr 82, p. 354.

1049. DOMINA, Lynn
"Vestiges." <u>KanQ</u> (14:3) Sum 82, p. 198-199.
"Wiseman Monument, Bow Valley, Nebraska." <u>Tendril</u> (13) Sum 82, p. 23-25.

1050. DOMINGUEZ, Jose Angel
"Y si me preguntan de donde vengo les dire." <u>Areito</u> (8:32) 82, p. 26.

1051. DONAVEL, David F.
"Late Fall: Wind." <u>WindO</u> (41) Aut-Wint 82-83, p. 12.

1052. DONEGAN, Nancy
"Terminus." <u>Tendril</u> (13) Sum 82, p. 26.

1053. DONNELL, David
"Evelyn Waugh on the Young Russians." <u>PoetryCR</u> (4:1) Sum 82, p. 9.
"Men." <u>PoetryCR</u> (4:1) Sum 82, p. 8.
"Murks." <u>PoetryCR</u> (4:1) Sum 82, p. 9.
"Open Roads." <u>PoetryCR</u> (4:1) Sum 82, p. 9.
"The Power of Uniforms." <u>PoetryCR</u> (4:1) Sum 82, p. 8.
"West End Livingroom at Night." <u>PoetryCR</u> (4:1) Sum 82, p. 9.
"Wrecked Boats." <u>PoetryCR</u> (4:1) Sum 82, p. 9.

1054. DONNELLY, Dorothy
      "Faces" (For Walter). Poetry (141:1) O 82, p. 7-9.

1055. DONNELLY, Paul
      "Exiles." Bogg (49) 82, p. 33.
      "King Kong Whips It Out." Bogg (48) 82, p. 44.

1056. DONNELLY, Susan
      "Eve Names the Animals." BelPoJ (32:3) Spr 82, p.
      24-25.
      "In Her Dream." PoetryNW (23:4) Wint 82-83, p. 36-
      38.

1057. DONOVAN, Laurence
      "Poet." SoCaR (14:2) Spr 82, p. 33.

      DOOLITTLE, Hilda
      See: H. D.

1058. DOPLICHER, Fabio
      "The Casting" (tr.by Ruth Feldman). Agni (16) 82, p.
      20-22.

1059. DORESKI, William
      "At the Tomb of Mary Baker Eddy." Salm (57) Sum 82,
      p. 137-138.
      "Bar Harbor." LitR (26:1) Aut 82, p. 111-112.
      "Normandy." LitR (26:1) Aut 82, p. 110-111.
      "Working All Day in the Garden." Salm (57) Sum 82,
      p. 135-136.

1060. DORMAN, Sonya
      "Childhood of a Warrior." HiramPoR (31) Aut-Wint
      82, p. 22.
      "Describing Darkness" (on lines by W. S.Merwin).
      PoetryNW (23:2) Sum 82, p. 31-32.
      "I.Q. Tests." PoetryNW (23:2) Sum 82, p. 32-33.

1061. DORNEY, Dennis M.
      "Island." HiramPoR (31) Aut-Wint 82, p. 23.

1062. DOTY, Catherine
      "Nitrous Oxide." Spirit (6:2/3) 82, p. 81.

      DOTY, M. R.
      See: DOTY, Mark

1063. DOTY, Mark
      "It Begins." SouthernPR (22:1) Spr 82, p. 64.
      "Late Conversation." MissR (10:3, issue 30) Wint-
      Spr 82, p. 57-60.
      "Looking at a Photograph." MissR (10:3, issue 30)
      Wint-Spr 82, p. 63-64.
      "March." BlackWR (7:2) Spr 81, p. 56-57.
      "Nepal." MinnR (NS19) Aut 82, p. 26-27.
      "Nocturne in D." MissR (10:3, issue 30) Wint-Spr
      82, p. 61-62.
      "Two Evenings and a Snowy Morning." MissR (10:3,
      issue 30) Wint-Spr 82, p. 65-66.

1064. DOUBIAGO, Sharon
      "Seagull." MendoR (6) Sum 81, p. 138-144.

1065. DOUGHERTY, Mary Ellen
      "State Hospital." ChrC (99:16) My 5, 82, p. 531.

1066. DOUGHERTY, William F.
      "By Owl Light." StoneC (9:3/4) Spr-Sum 82, p. 21.

1067. DOUSKEY, Franz
      "Eddie." PoNow (6:4, issue 34) 82, p. 24.
      "History of Night." GeoR (36:1) Spr 82, p. 67.
      "The Snake." PoNow (6:4, issue 34) 82, p. 24.

1068. DOVE, Rita
      "Anti-Father." MassR (23:2) Sum 82, p. 253.
      "Aurora Borealis." OhioR (28) 82, p. 77.
      "Cameos." Agni (17) 82, p. 67-77.
      "The Charm." OhioR (28) 82, p. 78.
      "Compendium." OhioR (28) 82, p. 75.
      "Courtship." OhioR (28) 82, p. 71-72.
      "Definition in the Face of Unnamed Fury." OhioR
        (28) 82, p. 76.
      "Eastern European Eclogues." OntR (17) Aut-Wint 82,
        p. 25.
      "The Event." OhioR (28) 82, p. 67.
      "Flirtation." Poetry (141:1) O 82, p. 10.
      "Jiving." OhioR (28) 82, p. 69.
      "The Left-Handed Cellist." NewOR (9:1) Spr-Sum 82,
        p. 88.
      "Lines Muttered in Sleep." PoNow (6:4, issue 34)
        82, p. 19.
      "Parsley." OntR (17) Aut-Wint 82, p. 22-24.
      "Receiving the Stigmata." GeoR (36:3) Aut 82, p.
        496.
      "Refrain." OhioR (28) 82, p. 73.
      "The Stroke." OhioR (28) 82, p. 79.
      "Taking in Wash." Ploughs (8:2/3) 82, p. 85.
      "Three Days of a Forest, a River, Free." MassR
        (23:2) Sum 82, p. 254.
      "Tou Wan Speaks to Her Husband, Liu Sheng." PoNow
        (6:5, issue 35) 82, p. 35.
      "Variation on Guilt." OhioR (28) 82, p. 74.
      "Variation on Pain." OhioR (28) 82, p. 68.
      "The Zeppelin Factory." OhioR (28) 82, p. 70.

1069. DOW, Jan Henson
      "The Man Next Door." KanQ (14:3) Sum 82, p. 116.

1070. DOW, Philip
      from Birthmarks: "Faint reflection of my face."
        Pequod (14) 82, p. 36-38.

1071. DOWNES, Gwladys
      "Flotsam at Rose Point." CanLit (94) Aut 82, p.
        113.
      "The Fool in Winter." CanLit (94) Aut 82, p. 95.

1072. DOWNIE, Glen
      "Atlantis." Bogg (49) 82, p. 44.

"Salamander." Quarry (31:4) Aut 82, p. 4-5.

1073. DOXEY, W. S.
      "Pictures by Goya, Words and Music by Me." StoneC
      (10:1/2) Aut-Wint 82-83, p. 60-61.

1074. DOYLE, Donna
      "The Way You Make Love." PottPort (4) 82-83, p. 30.

1075. DOYLE, Suzanne J.
      "In Beaufort." SouthernR (18:2) Spr 82, p. 369.
      "My Mother's Jewels." SouthernR (18:2) Spr 82, p.
      372.
      "Nightsong." SouthernR (18:2) Spr 82, p. 371.
      "Off to the East." SouthernR (18:2) Spr 82, p. 368.
      "On Virtue." SouthernR (18:2) Spr 82, p. 371.
      "The Siren's Song." SouthernR (18:2) Spr 82, p.
      373.
      "Turning Back." SouthernR (18:2) Spr 82, p. 370.

1076. DRABIK, Grazyna
      "Any Case" (tr. of Wislawa Szymborska, w. Sharon
      Olds). QRL (23) 82, p. 16.
      "Astonishment" (tr. of Wislawa Szymborska, w. Sharon
      Olds). QRL (23) 82, p. 14.
      "Children of the Epoch" (tr. of Wislawa Szymborska,
      w. Austin Flint). QRL (23) 82, p. 12-13.
      "The Classic" (tr. of Wislawa Szymborska, w. Sharon
      Olds). QRL (23) 82, p. 53.
      "Clothes" (tr. of Wislawa Szymborska, w. Sharon
      Olds). QRL (23) 82, p. 62.
      "Dream" (tr. of Wislawa Szymborska, w. Sharon Olds).
      QRL (23) 82, p. 21.
      "Drinking Wine" (tr. of Wislawa Szymborska, w.
      Sharon Olds). QRL (23) 82, p. 33-34.
      "Experiment" (tr. of Wislawa Szymborska, w. Sharon
      Olds). QRL (23) 82, p. 29.
      "From an Expedition Which Did Not Take Place" (tr.
      of Wislawa Szymborska, w. Austin Flint). QRL (23)
      82, p. 59-60.
      "The Great Number" (tr. of Wislawa Szymborska, w.
      Austin Flint). QRL (23) 82, p. 19.
      "Hunger Camp at Jaslo" (tr. of Wislawa Szymborska,
      w. Austin Flint). QRL (23) 82, p. 22.
      "I Am Too Near" (tr. of Wislawa Szymborska, w.
      Sharon Olds). QRL (23) 82, p. 30-31.
      "In Praise of a Guilty Conscience" (tr. of Wislawa
      Szymborska, w. Austin Flint). QRL (23) 82, p. 54.
      "In Praise of My Sister" (tr. of Wislawa Szymborska,
      w. Austin Flint). QRL (23) 82, p. 41.
      "In the Tower of Babel" (tr. of Wislawa Szymborska,
      w. Sharon Olds). QRL (23) 82, p. 28.
      "The Joy of Writing" (tr. of Wislawa Szymborska, w.
      Sharon Olds). QRL (23) 82, p. 63-64.
      "Letters of the Dead" (tr. of Wislawa Szymborska, w.
      Sharon Olds). QRL (23) 82, p. 52.
      "Lot's Wife" (tr. of Wislawa Szymborska, w. Austin
      Flint). QRL (23) 82, p. 38-39.
      "Memory Finally" (tr. of Wislawa Szymborska, w.
      Sharon Olds). QRL (23) 82, p. 20.

"Monologue for Cassandra" (tr. of Wislawa
Szymborska, w. Sharon Olds). QRL (23) 82, p. 50-
51.
"Nothingness Turned Over" (tr. of Wislawa
Szymborska, w. Sharon Olds). QRL (23) 82, p. 37.
"The Number Pi" (tr. of Wislawa Szymborska, w.
Austin Flint). QRL (23) 82, p. 44.
"Once We Knew" (tr. of Wislawa Szymborska, w. Sharon
Olds). QRL (23) 82, p. 23.
"Onion" (tr. of Wislawa Szymborska, w. Sharon Olds).
QRL (23) 82, p. 61.
"Poem in Honor of" (tr. of Wislawa Szymborska, w.
Austin Flint). QRL (23) 82, p. 15.
"Portrait of a Woman" (tr. of Wislawa Szymborska, w.
Austin Flint). QRL (23) 82, p. 43.
"Returns" (tr. of Wislawa Szymborska, w. Sharon
Olds). QRL (23) 82, p. 42.
"The Room of a Suicide" (tr. of Wislawa Szymborska,
w. Austin Flint). QRL (23) 82, p. 49.
"Seen from Above" (tr. of Wislawa Szymborska, w.
Sharon Olds). QRL (23) 82, p. 40.
"The Shadow" (tr. of Wislawa Szymborska, w. Sharon
Olds). QRL (23) 82, p. 32.
"Summary" (tr. of Wislawa Szymborska, w. Sharon
Olds). QRL (23) 82, p. 25.
"A Terrorist Is Watching" (tr. of Wislawa
Szymborska, w. Austin Flint). QRL (23) 82, p. 45-
46.
"Thanks" (tr. of Wislawa Szymborska, w. Austin
Flint). QRL (23) 82, p. 35-36.
"Torture" (tr. of Wislawa Szymborska, w. Austin
Flint). QRL (23) 82, p. 26-27.
"The Two Apes of Brueghel" (tr. of Wislawa
Szymborska, w. Sharon Olds). QRL (23) 82, p. 24.
"Under This Little Star" (tr. of Wislawa Szymborska,
w. Sharon Olds). QRL (23) 82, p. 10-11.
"Utopia" (tr. of Wislawa Szymborska, w. Austin
Flint). QRL (23) 82, p. 57-58.
"A View with a Grain of Sand" (tr. of Wislawa
Szymborska, w. Austin Flint). QRL (23) 82, p. 47-
48.
"The Warning" (tr. of Wislawa Szymborska, w. Austin
Flint). QRL (23) 82, p. 55-56.
"Writing a Curriculum Vitae" (tr. of Wislawa
Szymborska, w. Austin Flint). QRL (23) 82, p. 17-
18.

1077. DRAKE, Albert
"Campfire." PoNow (6:5, issue 35) 82, p. 32.
"Gap." Im (8:1) 82, p. 10.

1078. DRAKE, Robert
"Pieta." Sam (33:3, issue 131) 82, p. 16.

1079. DRENNER, D. von R.
"Martha Discovered." LittleBR (2:1) Aut 81, p. 51.
"Martha Remembered." LittleBR (2:1) Aut 81, p. 50.
"No sorrow Is So Bad As That Which Quite Goes By."
LittleBR (2:1) Aut 81, p. 50-51.

1080. DRINNAN, Marjorie
      "Concerned Citizens." <u>PottPort</u> (4) 82-83, p. 41.

1081. DRISCOLL, Jack
      "Boxing towards My Birth." <u>QW</u> (15) Aut-Wint 82-83,
      p. 61.
      "Playing Piano at the Old Folks Home." <u>Kayak</u> (59)
      Je 82, p. 34.
      "There Are Reasons to Lie." <u>Kayak</u> (59) Je 82, p.
      34-35.

      DRUMMOND de ANDRADE, Carlos
      <u>See</u>: ANDRADE, Carlos Drummond de

1082. DRURY, John
      "Exhibitionist on a Rainy Day" (from The Ghost
      Story). <u>PoetC</u> (14:1) 82, p. 8.
      "The Fear of Taking Off the Mask." <u>Iowa</u> (12:4) Aut
      81, p. 65.
      "Stake Out" (from The Ghost Story). <u>PoetC</u> (14:1) 82,
      p. 7-8.

1083. Du PASSAGE, Mary
      "For Sisyphus." <u>HolCrit</u> (19:5) D 82, p. 19.

1084. DUBIE, Norman
      "At Midsummer" (for Jeannine). <u>AmerPoR</u> (11:6) N-D
      82, p. 20.
      "An Old Woman's Vision." <u>NewYorker</u> (58:22) Jl 19,
      82, p. 38.

1085. DUBIE, William
      "Great-Uncle in the Beach House." <u>NewRena</u> (5:1, 15)
      Aut 82, p. 48-49.
      "The Madrigal of Waters." <u>NewRena</u> (5:1, 15) Aut 82,
      p. 47.
      "Rainbow." <u>Bogg</u> (49) 82, p. 16.

1086. DuBOIS, Harold J.
      "The Memphis Express." <u>LittleBR</u> (1:2) Wint 80-81,
      p. 21-25.

1087. DUCKETT, Ian
      "Poem: Every summer it is the same." <u>Bogg</u> (48) 82,
      p. 46.
      "Western Dream." <u>Bogg</u> (49) 82, p. 40.

1088. DUDLEY, Michael
      "Innocence." <u>Quarry</u> (31:3) Sum 82, p. 43-44.
      "Magic." <u>Quarry</u> (31:3) Sum 82, p. 44.
      "Snowy Owls at Toronto International Airport" (for
      Frank). <u>Quarry</u> (31:3) Sum 82, p. 43.

1089. DUEMER, Joseph
      "Four Flat Songs." <u>AntR</u> (40:1) Wint 82, p. 54-55.
      "Three for Mike Cummings." <u>Iowa</u> (12:4) Aut 81, p.
      67-68.

      DUENAS, Jorge Ruiz
      <u>See</u>: RUIZ DUENAS, Jorge

1090. DUGAN, Alan
       "The Decimation Before Phraata" (A variation after
         the Greek). Antaeus (47) Aut 82, p. 145.
       "The Monarchs, the butterflies, are commanded."
         Antaeus (47) Aut 82, p. 144.
       "Untitled Poem: One tries to be sober and
         respectable." NowestR (20:1) 82, p. 74.
       "What a Circus." Antaeus (47) Aut 82, p. 143.
       "When the window glass blows in." Antaeus (47) Aut
         82, p. 142.

1091. DUGGAN, M. B.
       "Fist of Flowers." CapilR (22) 82, p. 43-48.

1092. DUKES, Norman
       "Freud." Agni (17) 82, p. 14.
       "To the Shore, and the Shore Thereof" (Phrase from a
         real estate document). Agni (17) 82, p. 12-13.

1093. DUMITRIU van SAANEN, Christine
       "La Fille des Bois." Dandel (9:1) 82, p. 52, 54.
       "La Fille des Bois" (tr. by Barbara Belyea). Dandel
         (9:1) 82, p. 53, 55.
       "J'irai Loin." Dandel (9:1) 82, p. 48.
       "J'irai Loin" (tr. by Barbara Belyea). Dandel (9:1)
         82, p. 49.
       "Neiges." Dandel (9:1) 82, p. 50.
       "Neiges/Snows" (tr. by Barbara Belyea). Dandel (9:1)
         82, p. 51.
       "Un Point." Dandel (9:1) 82, p. 48.
       "Un Point" (tr. by Barbara Belyea). Dandel (9:1) 82,
         p. 49.

1094. DUNCAN, Judith
       "Leaving." StoneC (9:3/4) Spr-Sum 82, p. 63.

1095. DUNN, Douglas
       "A Summer Night." NewYorker (58:29) S 6, 82, p. 36.

1096. DUNN, Millard
       "Directions." KanQ (14:1) Wint 82, p. 62.
       from Marriage Group: "II. The Clerk's Tale."   Stand
         (23:2) 82, p. 70.
       from Marriage Group: "III. The Merchant's Tale."
         Stand (23:2) 82, p. 70.

1097. DUNN, Si
       "How Nippon Froze Over." Vis (10) 82, p. 33.

1098. DUNN, Stephen
       "An Argument with Wisdom at Montauk." MissouriR
         (6:1) Aut 82, p. 17.
       "Atlantic City." NewEngR (4:3) Spr 82, p. 374-375.
       "The Beginning of the Eighties." PoetryNW (23:2)
         Sum 82, p. 15-16.
       "A Child by the Window." Telescope (2) Aut 81, p.
         52.
       "Climbing Ladders Anyway." PoetryNW (23:3) Aut 82,
         p. 6-7.
       "Corners." Poetry (140:6) S 82, p. 330.

"The Dinner." GeoR (36:4) Wint 82, p. 892-893.
"Eggs." Poetry (140:6) S 82, p. 331-332.
"In Defense of Blowfish." Antaeus (47) Aut 82, p.
    44.
"In the 20th Century." PoetryNW (23:3) Aut 82, p.
    5-6.
"It So Happens" (after Neruda). Pequod (14) 82, p.
    108.
"Kansas." NewEngR (4:3) Spr 82, p. 373.
"Late Summer." Pequod (14) 82, p. 109-110.
"Leaves." Telescope (2) Aut 81, p. 6-7.
"Plumage." Telescope (2) Aut 81, p. 28.
"Praying Mantis on the Screen Door." Telescope (2)
    Aut 81, p. 29.
"Rubbing." Poetry (140:6) S 82, p. 333.
"Wavelengths." PoetryNW (23:3) Aut 82, p. 3-5.
"The Wild." PoetryNW (23:2) Sum 82, p. 14-15.

1099. DUNNING, Stephen
"Anyone Home." NewL (49:2) Wint 82-83, p. 20.
"Burning Poems" (for Robert Hayden, from Good Words:
    Poems on the Theme of Loss). Nimrod (26:1) Aut-
    Wint 82, p. 67.
"Close Scrutiny of Certain Actions." SouthernPR
    (23, i.e. 22:2) Aut 82, p. 41.
"Dear Uncle." Nimrod (26:1) Aut-Wint 82, p. 68.
"Leaves" (for Yehuda Amichai). MichOR (21:2) Spr 82,
    p. 343-344.
"Melvin's Boy." MichOR (21:2) Spr 82, p. 342-343.
"Otter Dream." NewL (48:2) Wint 81-82, p. 34.
"Plague, Frothy and Sure." AmerPoR (11:5) S-O 82,
    p. 28.
"Turns." NewL (48:2) Wint 81-82, p. 35.

1100. DUNSMORE, Roger
"Teepee Rings" (For the old ones, for Stephen). CutB
    (18) Spr-Sum 82, p. 88-89.

1101. DUPREE, Edison
"The Barn." MissouriR (6:1) Aut 82, p. 40-41.
"Down at the Creek, Mussels" (for Ryan). SouthernPR
    (22:1) Spr 82, p. 40.
"I Fool the Cats." PoNow (7:1, issue 37) 82, p. 13.
"A Man" (For Joe C.). PoNow (7:1, issue 37) 82, p.
    13.

1102. DURAK, Carol
"The Bean Eater." NowestR (20:1) 82, p. 96.

1103. DUTCHER, Roger
"Pieces of the sun." Northeast (3:12) Wint 81-82,
    p. 39.
"The Plains." Northeast (3:12) Wint 81-82, p. 39.

1104. DUVAL, Quinton
"The Last River." CharR (8:2) Aut 82, p. 40-41.
"Over and Done." CharR (8:2) Aut 82, p. 41.

DUYN, Mona van
See: Van DUYN, Mona

1105. DWYER, Cynthia Brown
       "The Blue-eyed Persian Plumber." PoNow (6:4, issue
         34) 82, p. 19.
       "In a Persian Garden." PoNow (6:4, issue 34) 82, p.
         19.
       "January 20, 1981." PoNow (6:4, issue 34) 82, p.
         19.

1106. DWYER, Deirdre
       "Truth Is What Most Contradicts Itself in Time."
         PottPort (4) 82-83, p. 18.

1107. DWYER, Frank
       "Miss Subways." CentR (26:4) Aut 82, p. 358.
       "Ploughing on Sunday." Salm (56) Spr 82, p. 145-
         146.
       "Prologue." Salm (56) Spr 82, p. 145.

1108. DWYER, T. J.
       "Change." HiramPoR (33) Aut-Wint 82, p. 12.
       "A Lover's Plea." HiramPoR (33) Aut-Wint 82, p. 12.

1109. DYBEK, Stuart
       "Belly Button." Sky (10-12) Aut 82, p. 20.
       "Curtains." Sky (10-12) Aut 82, p. 18.
       "Lost." Sky (10-12) Aut 82, p. 20.
       "Lover." Sky (10-12) Aut 82, p. 16-17.
       "Papayas." PoNow (6:4, issue 34) 82, p. 30.
       "Three Windows." Sky (10-12) Aut 82, p. 19.

1110. DYC, Gloria
       "Language Barrier." Spirit (6:2/3) 82, p. 166.

1111. DYCK, E. F.
       "Goose, in Love." CanLit (95) Wint 82, p. 109.

1112. DYER, Dan
       "Beetroot." PoNow (7:1, issue 37) 82, p. 12.

       DYKE, Patricia van
       See: Van DYKE, Patricia

1113. EADY, Cornelius
       "Living with Genius." PoNow (6:5, issue 35) 82, p.
         40.

1114. EASON, Alethea
       "Divining Rods." Wind (12:45) 82, p. 13-14.

1115. EASTMAN, Bruce
       "Foundered." Thrpny (9) Spr 82, p. 11.

1116. EASTWOOD, D. J.
       "Anything But Loving." PottPort (4) 82-83, p. 28.
       "Untitled: I knew a potter who used piss for
         bleach." PottPort (4) 82-83, p. 51.

1117. EATON, Charles Edward
       "The Art of Quotation." MidwQ (23:4) Sum 82, p.
         392.

"The Barbarian." <u>SouthernHR</u> (16:4) Aut 82, p. 318.
"The Blood Paintings." <u>SouthernPR</u> (22:1) Spr 82, p. 74-75.
"Butterfly Sheets." <u>Poem</u> (45) Jl 82, p. 37.
"The Diapason." <u>CentR</u> (26:4) Aut 82, p. 355-356.
"The Fan." <u>DenQ</u> (16:4) Wint 82, p. 89.
"Figure of Speech." <u>SouthernPR</u> (23, i.e. 22:2) Aut 82, p. 47.
"The Gestalt." <u>Salm</u> (57) Sum 82, p. 119.
"The Image Exit." <u>MidwQ</u> (23:4) Sum 82, p. 391.
"Incidence of Ormolu." <u>WebR</u> (7:1) Spr 82, p. 108-109.
"Lizard Shoes." <u>ModernPS</u> (11:1/2) 82, p. 57.
"The Manuscript Collection." <u>Paint</u> (9:17/18) Spr-Aut 82, p. 10.
"The Philter." <u>ArizQ</u> (38:2) Sum 82, p. 100.
"Pictograph." <u>Im</u> (8:1) 82, p. 9.
"The Plethora." <u>SouthernPR</u> (23, i.e. 22:2) Aut 82, p. 46.
"River Job." <u>ModernPS</u> (11:1/2) 82, p. 56-57.
"The Thallophyte." <u>Poem</u> (45) Jl 82, p. 39.
"A Tin of Sardines." <u>Poem</u> (45) Jl 82, p. 38.
"Two-Way Stretch." <u>GeoR</u> (36:3) Aut 82, p. 527.
"View from a Balloon." <u>SouthernR</u> (18:1) Wint 82, p. 191-192.
"The Winch." <u>Chelsea</u> (41) 82, p. 112-113.

1118. EBERHART, Richard
"As We Go." <u>PoNow</u> (6:5, issue 35) 82, p. 2.
"Configuration." <u>PoNow</u> (6:4, issue 34) 82, p. 4.
"Emerson's Concord." <u>Paint</u> (7/8:13/16) 80-81, p. 15.
"Fantasy of a Small Idea." <u>PoNow</u> (6:5, issue 35) 82, p. 2.
"Hysteria of Communication." <u>Paint</u> (7/8:13/16) 80-81, p. 14.
"The Ideal and the Real." <u>LitR</u> (25:4) Sum 82, p. 523.
"John Finley." <u>PoNow</u> (6:5, issue 35) 82, p. 3.
"Man and Nature." <u>PoNow</u> (6:5, issue 35) 82, p. 3.
"New Marriage." <u>LitR</u> (25:4) Sum 82, p. 526.
"Old Dichotomy: Choosing Sides." <u>LitR</u> (25:4) Sum 82, p. 525.
"Shiftings." <u>LitR</u> (25:4) Sum 82, p. 524.
"Shiftings." <u>PoNow</u> (6:5, issue 35) 82, p. 3.
"Somwhere Else." <u>LitR</u> (25:4) Sum 82, p. 527.

1119. EBERLY, David
"Carriere's Verlaine." <u>HangL</u> (41) 82, p. 29.
"To Weldon Kees." <u>HangL</u> (41) 82, p. 28.

1120. EBNER, Jeannie
"Dialogue" (tr. by Beth Bjorklund). <u>LitR</u> (25:2) Wint 82, p. 190.
"Hunger" (tr. by Beth Bjorklund). <u>LitR</u> (25:2) Wint 82, p. 190.

1121. ECKRICH, Catherine
"Ipso Jure." <u>Poetry</u> (140:1) Ap 82, p. 27.

1122. ECONOMOU, George
        from Amerikh Two: (IV, V). Sulfur (2:2, issue 5) 82,
        p. 109-112.

1123. EDELMAN, Sandra Prewitt
        "Cezanne's Apples." SouthwR (67:4) Aut 82, p. 369.

1124. EDGERTON, Larry
        "Death of a Boy in a Rockslide." BelPoJ (33:1) Aut
        82, p. 18-19.

1125. EDMUNDSON, Lee
        "Pam's Poem." MendoR (5) Sum 81, p. 63.

1126. EDSON, Russell
        "The Bachelor's Hand." Antaeus (44) Wint 82, p.
        187.
        "The Belching." PoNow (6:6, issue 36) 82, p. 16.
        "The Brute." Antaeus (44) Wint 82, p. 185.
        "Buying a Baby." PoNow (6:6, issue 36) 82, p. 16.
        "The Closed Coffin." PoNow (6:6, issue 36) 82, p.
        16.
        "Dirt Lesson." PoNow (6:6, issue 36) 82, p. 16.
        "Dr. Broken's Last Trip to the Moon." PoNow (6:5,
        issue 35) 82, p. 18.
        "Elephant Dormitory." Ploughs (8:2/3) 82, p. 194.
        "Elephant Tears." PoNow (6:4, issue 34) 82, p. 13.
        "Father and Son Sharing Grandmother." PoNow (6:6,
        issue 36) 82, p. 17.
        "The Feet of the Fallen Man." PoNow (6:6, issue 36)
        82, p. 17.
        "The Half-and-Half Man." Antaeus (44) Wint 82, p.
        185.
        "The Having to Love Something Else." Antaeus (47)
        Aut 82, p. 47.
        "The Hourglass." Antaeus (44) Wint 82, p. 187.
        "The Love Affair." Antaeus (44) Wint 82, p. 186.
        "The Manure Book." Antaeus (44) Wint 82, p. 186.
        "The Melting." Ploughs (8:2/3) 82, p. 192.
        "Mr. San Marino's Underwear." PoNow (6:5, issue 35)
        82, p. 18.
        "On the Eating of Mice." Ploughs (8:2/3) 82, p.
        193.
        "The Rat's Tight Schedule." Antaeus (47) Aut 82, p.
        46.
        "The Tunnel." Antaeus (47) Aut 82, p. 45.
        "What the Old Grandmother Dreamed." PoNow (6:5,
        issue 35) 82, p. 18.

1127. EDWARDS, Nancy
        "Ali." LittleBR (1:3) Spr 81, p. 53.

1128. EGGERT, Jim
        "Changing Oil." Abraxas (25/26) 82, p. 94.

1129. EGGLESTON, Simon
        "Committing Lowell." Bogg (48) 82, p. 48.

1130. EGLETON, Andy
        "The Printed Work of Time." Bogg (48) 82, p. 63.

1131. EGYEDI, Bela
"The Air-Rider" (for "joe magic", anciennement:
Fletcher's Field and Vieux-Montreal). AntigR (50)
Sum 82, p. 102-103.
"The Black Madonna." AntigR (48) Wint 82, p. 45.
"Harvest of a Beach Forsaken." AntigR (51) Aut 82,
p. 56.
"Waiting As If." AntigR (51) Aut 82, p. 57-58.

1132. EHRHART, W. D.
"The Blizzard of Sixty-Six." StoneC (10:1/2) Aut-
Wint 82-83, p. 72.
"The Christmas Party." Sam (32:3, issue 127) 82, p.
36-37.
"Helpless." UnderRM 1(1) Spr 82, p. 19.
"Photograph." UnderRM 1(1) Spr 82, p. 19.

1133. EHRLICH, Shelley
"Love Poem." Northeast (3:12) Wint 81-82, p. 10.
"On Seeing a Painted Bunting in Everglades Nat'l
Park." Tendril (12) Wint 82, p. 30.

1134. EHRMAN, Sally
"Before It Happens." Sam (32:3, issue 127) 82, p.
2.

1135. EIDUS, Janice
"The Growth of Trees." LittleM (13:3/4) 82, p. 98.
"Hearts." LittleM (13:3/4) 82, p. 99.

1136. EIGNER, Larry
"Between bedrooms is the can." PoNow (6:4, issue
34) 82, p. 28.
"Everybody from the phonebook." PoNow (6:6, issue
36) 82, p. 20.
"The fast sudden slow." PoNow (6:5, issue 35) 82,
p. 30.
"Street corners." PoNow (6:6, issue 36) 82, p. 20.

1137. EIKENBERRY, Gary
"The Seasonally Adjusted Unemployment Rate."
PottPort (4) 82-83, p. 29.

1138. EINBOND, Bernard Lionel
"A Bit of an Englishman." Bogg (48) 82, p. 29.

1139. EINHORN, Linda
"Language." EngJ (71:6) O 82, p. 86.

1140. EINZIG, Barbara
"For November's Clear Sun." Pig (9) 82, p. 84.

1141. EISENBERG, Susan
"Asbestos." Hangl (43) Wint 82-83, p. 56-57.
"Hanging in, Solo." Hangl (43) Wint 82-83, p.
54-55.

1142. EKHOLM, John
"Great Blue Heron." Northeast (3:14) Wint 82-83, p.
12.

1143. EKLUND, Jane
      "After Supper." MassR (23:3) Aut 82, p. 488.
      "Hawthorne Poem." MassR (23:3) Aut 82, p. 487.

1144. ELENKOV, Luchezar
      "Concerned with Something Else While Turnovo's
      Dying" (tr. by Jascha Kessler and Alexander
      Shurbanov). Nimrod (26:1) Aut-Wint 82, p. 39-40.
      "Sauna" (tr. by Jascha Kessler and Alexander
      Shurbanov). Kayak (59) Je 82, p. 65.

1145. ELIAS, Vic
      "Fifteen." AntigR (48) Wint 82, p. 55.

1146. ELIASON, Shirley
      from Formal Garden Series: "Motableautin II"
      (Acrylic on paper, 1979). Iowa (12:2/3) Spr-Sum
      81, p. 70-71.
      from Formal Garden Series: "Motableautin III"
      (Watercolor, 1979). Iowa (12:2/3) Spr-Sum 81, p.
      72-73.
      from Formal Garden Series: "Motableautin IV"
      (Watercolor, 1979). Iowa (12:2/3) Spr-Sum 81, p.
      74-75.

1147. ELIOT, Eileen
      "Alternative Psychiatry." PikeF (4) Spr 82, p. 25.
      "Alternative Psychiatry." Vis (10) 82, p. 16.
      "First Day." Wind (12:46) 82, p. 12.
      "Four to a Room." Vis (10) 82, p. 17.
      "Suicide (to Her Children)." Vis (10) 82, p. 20.

1148. ELIOT, T. S.
      "Macavity: The Mystery Cat." AmerPoR (11:4) Jl-Ag
      82, p. 8.
      "The Naming of Cats." AmerPoR (11:4) Jl-Ag 82, p.
      9.

1149. ELIZONDO Sergio
      "Cantar de las Gentiles Damas." RevChic (10:1/2)
      Wint-Spr 82, p. 67.
      "Este Es un Cuento." RevChic (10:1/2) Wint-Spr 82,
      p. 68.
      "He Sabido, Carnala." RevChic (10:1/2) Wint-Spr 82,
      p. 69.

1150. ELKIND, Sue Saniel
      "After Impact." Wind (12:46) 82, p. 13-14.
      "Camps." KanQ (14:3) Sum 82, p. 163.
      "Down the Corridor." Wind (12:46) 82, p. 14.
      "Hues." KanQ (14:3) Sum 82, p. 163.
      "No Signposts." Wind (12:46) 82, p. 13.
      "Starving." Shout (3:1) 82, p. 44.

1151. ELLENBOGEN, George
      "A Letter from Ierapetra." KanQ (14:3) Sum 82, p.
      202-203.

1152. ELLENWOOD, Ray
        from Entrails: "Apolnixede between Heaven and Earth"
        (tr. of Claude Gauvreau). Sulfur (2:3, issue 6)
        82, p. 95-100.
        from Entrails: "The Shadow on the Hoop" (tr. of
        Claude Gauvreau). Sulfur (2:3, issue 6) 82, p.
        102-104.

1153. ELLICK, Heather A.
        "Bait Set." PottPort (4) 82-83, p. 27.
        "Left Overs." PottPort (4) 82-83, p. 27.
        "Rooster." PottPort (4) 82-83, p. 28.

1154. ELLIOTT, David L.
        "Half-Hearted Elegy" (for Charles Olson). WindO (41)
        Aut-Wint 82-83, p. 18.
        "Hands." PikeF (4) Spr 82, p. 33.
        "Illinois Farm." WindO (41) Aut-Wint 82-83, p. 19.
        "Inheritance." WindO (41) Aut-Wint 82-83, p. 19.
        "July Morning." WindO (41) Aut-Wint 82-83, p. 18.
        "Night Presences." WindO (41) Aut-Wint 82-83, p.
        19.
        "September Birth." WindO (41) Aut-Wint 82-83, p.
        18.

1155. ELLIOTT, Harley
        "The Iris." Spirit (6:2/3) 82, p. 97.

1156. ELLIOTT, William I.
        "Passing." ChrC (99:21) Je 9-16, 82, p. 686.

1157. ELON, Florence
        "The No-Neck Monster" (age: one month). PoNow (6:4,
        issue 34) 82, p. 29.

1158. ELOVIC, Barbara
        "Afterwards." Poetry (140:3) Je 82, p. 162-163.
        "Clinton Street." PoNow (7:1, issue 37) 82, p. 13.
        "Common Objects." SmPd (19:3, issue 56) Aut 82, p.
        19.
        "On a Photograph by Robert Capa." PoNow (7:1, issue
        37) 82, p. 13.

1159. ELSBERG, John
        "The Art of Rowing" (w. George Cairncross). Bogg
        (48) 82, p. 65.
        "At the Other Side of the Bed" (for Trevor Greenley,
        w. George Cairncross). Bogg (48) 82, p. 65.
        "Complexity." Gargoyle (17/18) 81, p. 34.
        "Conceit." Bogg (48) 82, p. 62-63.
        "Interlude." Bogg (49) 82, p. 60.
        "Item" (w. George Cairncross). Bogg (48) 82, p. 65.
        "On Taking a Shower Together." PoNow (6:5, issue
        35) 82, p. 46.

1160. ELSON, Virginia
        "If Satan in Falling from Heaven Had Swerved
        Slightly as He Fell" (from John Hollander's review
        of Harold Bloom's Anxiety of Influence). PraS
        (56:3) Aut 82, p. 26.

1161. ELSTON, A. W.
        "Five Poems in Search of Form." MalR (61) F 82, p.
        143-145.
        "The Home-Grown Child." MalR (61) F 82, p. 143.
        "Myth." MalR (61) F 82, p. 144.
        "Pastoral." MalR (61) F 82, p. 144.
        "Ritual." MalR (61) F 82, p. 145.
        "Street." MalR (61) F 82, p. 145.

1162. ELUARD, Paul
        "The Excellent Moments" (tr. by Lisa Gruberg-
        Piccione). Kayak (60) O 82, p. 14.

1163. ELYTIS, Odysseus
        from The Primal Sun (Helios o Protos): (IX, XIV)
        (tr. by Edward Moran and Lefteris Pavlides). CharR
        (8:1) Spr 82, p. 51-52.

1164. EMANS, Elaine V.
        "Elegy for a Dead Beetle." KanQ (14:3) Sum 82, p.
        132.
        "For a Barn Owl." KanQ (14:3) Sum 82, p. 132.

1165. EMANUEL, Lynn
        "The Daughter Who Killed Herself." PraS (56:2) Sum
        82, p. 54.
        "Silence. She Is Six Years Old." Iowa (12:2/3) Spr-
        Sum 81, p. 77.
        "The Sleeping." Iowa (12:2/3) Spr-Sum 81, p. 76.
        "You Tell Me." GeoR (36:1) Spr 82, p. 113.

1166. EMERSON, John
        "Like a fish on a line." PortR (28:2) 82, p. 32.
        "Of what I have to offer." PortR (28:2) 82, p. 31.
        "Picking his step, his step." PortR (28:2) 82, p.
        32.
        "Weaving one another's wrong sides." PortR (28:2)
        82, p. 32.

1167. EMKE, Stacey
        "Untitled: The soft waterfall silently flows."
        MendoR (5) Sum 81, p. 67.

1168. EMMANUEL, Pierre
        "Funeral Home" (tr. by Bruce Berlind). PoNow (6:6,
        issue 36) 82, p. 42.
        "Thomas" (tr. by Bruce Berlind). PoNow (6:6, issue
        36) 82, p. 42.

1169. EMMETT, Elaine
        "On the Death of the Farmer Poet of Lone Star
        Township." LittleBR (3:1) Aut 82, p. 43.

1170. EMMOTT, Kirsten
        "A Virgin Asks for Birth Control Pills." PoetryCR
        (3:4) Sum 82, p. 15.

        EMRE, Yunus
        See: YUNUS EMRE

1171. ENDREZZE-DANIELSON, Anita
"Helix Aspersa." PoetryNW (23:4) Wint 82-83, p. 42-
43.
"Sanctuary." PoetryNW (23:4) Wint 82-83, p. 43-44.

1172. ENGEL, Bernard F.
"Poet Steals Gems, Buys Caddy." CEAFor (12:3) F 82,
p. 15.

1173. ENGEL, Kathy
"Displacement." Pequod (14) 82, p. 74-75.
"In My Father's Cabin." Iowa (12:2/3) Spr-Sum 81,
p. 78-79.
"The Sculptors." Pequod (14) 82, p. 76.

1174. ENGEL, Mary
"Consensus." NewRena (5:1, 15) Aut 82, p. 73.

1175. ENGELS, John
"Anniversary: a November poem." NewEngR (5:1/2)
Aut-Wint 82, p. 20-22.
"Autumn Poem." NewEngR (5:1/2) Aut-Wint 82, p. 18.
"Cardinals." NewYorker (58:6) Mr 29, 82, p. 121.
"Damp Rot." NewEngR (5:1/2) Aut-Wint 82, p. 19-20.
"`Darlin Corey' on the Autoharp." QW (15) Aut-Wint
82-83, p. 74-75.
"Pilgrimage." NewEngR (5:1/2) Aut-Wint 82, p. 16-
17.

1176. ENSLIN, Theodore
"Poem: Out of the years' rehearsals." Harp
(265:1586) Jl 82, p. 66.

1177. EPPLE, Juan Armando
"Tiempo Chicano" (himno nacional, a un cuadro futuro
de Rene Castro). Maize (6:1/2) Aut-Wint 82-83, p.
100-101.

1178. EPSTEIN, Daniel Mark
"Miami." AmerS (51:2) Spr 82, p. 202-203.

1179. EPSTEIN, Elaine
"What Comes Back." GeoR (36:2) Sum 82, p. 369.

1180. ERICKSON, Jon
"Come around the edge of the wall into the square"
(for Ralph Gibson). Abraxas (25/26) 82, p. 77.

1181. ERICKSON, Lorene
"Water." Pig (8) 80, p. 75.

1182. ERICKSON, Stephanie
"A Dream of Flying." MendoR (6) Sum 81, p. 64.

1183. ERON, Don
"The Clockbuilder." PraS (56:3) Aut 82, p. 23.
"Getting It Right." PraS (56:3) Aut 82, p. 24.

1184. ERSKINE, Ron
"On This Green Earth." WritersL D 82, p. 8.

161   ERWIN

1185. ERWIN, Paul C.
      "Continuity" (for Andrew Lytle). Poem (46) N 82, p.
      42-44.
      "Desire." Poem (46) N 82, p. 46-47.
      "Mother at the Kitchen Window." Poem (46) N 82, p.
      45.

1186. ESCALANTE, Evodio
      "Borges." BelPoJ (32:4) Sum 82, p. 30.
      "Borges" (tr. by Ricardo Pau-Llosa). BelPoJ (32:4)
      Sum 82, p. 31.

1187. ESCOBAR GALINDO, David
      "Desde una Grieta de la Luz." BelPoJ (32:4) Sum 82,
      p. 24, 26.
      "Through a Crack in the Light" (tr. by Ricardo Pau-
      Llosa). BelPoJ (32:4) Sum 82, p. 25, 27.

1188. ESHLEMAN, Clayton
      "But There Is This Hurt" (tr. of Aime Cesaire, w.
      Annette Smith). Sulfur (2:2, issue 5) 82, p. 43-
      44.
      "Corpse of a Frenzy" (tr. of Aime Cesaire, w.
      Annette Smith). Sulfur (2:2, issue 5) 82, p. 44-
      45.
      "Debris" (tr. of Aime Cesaire, w. Annette Smith).
      Sulfur (2:2, issue 5) 82, p. 34-35.
      "I Perseus Centuplicating Myself" (tr. of Aime
      Cesaire, w. Annette Smith). Sulfur (2:2, issue 5)
      82, p. 45.
      "Lost Body" (from Lost Body, 1950, tr. of Aime
      Cesaire, w. Annette Smith). Sulfur (2:2, issue 5)
      82, p. 41-43.
      "Noon Knives" (from Solar Throat Slashed, 1948, tr.
      of Aime Cesaire, w. Annette Smith). Sulfur (2:2,
      issue 5) 82, p. 39-41.
      "The Oubliettes of the Sea and the Deluge" (from The
      Miraculous Weapons, 1946, tr. of Aime Cesaire, w.
      Annette Smith). Sulfur (2:2, issue 5) 82, p. 36-
      37.
      "Redemption" (tr. of Aime Cesaire, w. Annette
      Smith). Sulfur (2:2, issue 5) 82, p. 38.
      "Tangible Disaster" (tr. of Aime Cesaire, w. Annette
      Smith). Sulfur (2:2, issue 5) 82, p. 37.
      "Terrestrial." Sulfur (2:2, issue 5) 82, p. 73-76.
      "Tom-Tom II" (for Wifredo, tr. of Aime Cesaire, w.
      Annette Smith). Sulfur (2:2, issue 5) 82, p. 35.
      "Tomb of Paul Eluard" (from Ferraments, 1960, tr. of
      Aime Cesaire, w. Annette Smith). Sulfur (2:2,
      issue 5) 82, p. 46-49.
      "Visitation" (tr. of Aime Cesaire, w. Annette
      Smith). Sulfur (2:2, issue 5) 82, p. 33-34.
      "Voluntary Prayer." PartR (49:1) 82, p. 137-138.
      "Your Hair" (tr. of Aime Cesaire, w. Annette Smith).
      Sulfur (2:2, issue 5) 82, p. 38-39.

1189. ESPADA, Martin
      "Manuel Is Quiet Sometimes." Abraxas (25/26) 82, p.
      78-79.

1190. ESPAILLAT, Rhina
      "Metrics." Comm (109:18) O 22, 82, p. 563.

1191. ESPEJO-SAAVEDRA, Fernando
      "El Loco." Mester (11:2) 82 [i.e. My 83], p. 38.

1192. ESPINOLA, Lourdes
      "Asuncion." LetFem (8:2) 82, p. 82.
      "Dialogo." LetFem (8:2) 82, p. 85.
      "Simone, Nina-Mujer." LetFem (8:2) 82, p. 83.
      "Tratar de Ser y No." LetFem (8:2) 82, p. 84.

1193. ESPINOZA, Danny J.
      "Life Is." Maize (6:1/2) Aut-Wint 82-83, p. 52.
      "Videogames videogames videogames videogames."
      Maize (6:1/2) Aut-Wint 82-83, p. 53.

1194. ESPOSITO, Nancy
      "Dorothy, Destination: Oz." PoetC (14:2) 82, p. 49.
      "In My Ascendancy." PoetC (14:2) 82, p. 46-48.
      "Modalities." Tendril (13) Sum 82, p. 27-28.

1195. ESTAVER, Paul
      "How High the Moon." Vis (9) 82, p. 33-34.
      "Night of the Salamander." StoneC (9:3/4) Spr-Sum
      82, p. 48.

1196. ESTES, Carolyn
      "On Being the World's Greatest English Teacher"
      (inspired by an advertising button). EngJ (71:5) S
      82, p. 63.

1197. ESTEVES, Sandra Maria
      "For Noel Rico." RevChic (10:1/2) Wint-Spr 82, p.
      71.
      "Let my spirit fly in time." RevChic (10:1/2) Wint-
      Spr 82, p. 70.
      "So you want me to be your mistress." RevChic
      (10:1/2) Wint-Spr 82, p. 71-72.

1198. ETTER, Dave
      "Body." Poetry (139:4) Ja 82, p. 207.
      "Carl Yelenich: One Tough Hombre." NewL (48:2) Wint
      81-82, p. 95.
      "Guy Hansen: Nothing to Do, Nothing to Be." PoNow
      (6:4, issue 34) 82, p. 24.
      "Karen Hicks: Loony." PoNow (6:6, issue 36) 82, p.
      20.
      "Kyle Trowbridge: Birds-Eye View." PoNow (6:5,
      issue 35) 82, p. 37.
      "Leonard Massingail: Fatherly Advice." NewL (48:2)
      Wint 81-82, p. 94.
      "Oliver Briggs: Night Work." NewL (48:2) Wint 81-
      82, p. 93.
      "Pamela Dooley: High Jumper." PoNow (6:5, issue 35)
      82, p. 37.
      "Rex Agee: Getting at the Truth." PoNow (6:4, issue
      34) 82, p. 24.
      "Rose Garabaldi: Real Estate." PoNow (6:5, issue
      35) 82, p. 37.

"Tanya." PoNow (6:4, issue 34) 82, p. 44.
"Valerie Mayhew: Cornfield Virgin." PoNow (6:4,
    issue 34) 82, p. 24.
"When Sister Pearl Does Her Homework." Poetry
    (139:4) Ja 82, p. 206.

1199. EVANS, Abbie Huston
    "Letter to Sandra McPherson." Iowa (12:2/3) Spr-Sum
        81, p. 80.

1200. EVANS, David Allan
    "Cattle at Night." NewOR (9:2) Aut 82, p. 84.

1201. EVANS, Frank
    "Political Acumen Test." Bogg (49) 82, p. 15.

1202. EVANS, James
    "The Biggest." WindO (41) Aut-Wint 82-83, p. 24.
    "The Going." KanQ (14:3) Sum 82, p. 202.
    "Now the Buds." WindO (41) Aut-Wint 82-83, p. 24.
    "Poem to My Daughter." WindO (41) Aut-Wint 82-83,
        p. 24.

1203. EVANS, Merrill
    "Orpheus Ascending." Pig (8) 80, p. 57.

1204. EVARTS, P.
    "Coming to Colonus." BelPoJ (33:2) Wint 82-83, p.
        39-40.

1205. EVARTS, Prescott, Jr.
    "A Christian Childhood." Hudson (35:4) Wint 82-83,
        p. 598.
    "Counters." KanQ (14:3) Sum 82, p. 192-193.
    "Dingleton Hill, Transcendental." KanQ (14:3) Sum
        82, p. 192.
    "Hunting." Hudson (35:4) Wint 82-83, p. 597.
    "Morning in Vermont, Evening in New York." CimR
        (60) Jl 82, p. 60-61.

1206. EVERHARD, Jim
    "Memory of Roanoke" (for Tom)." PoNow (7:1, issue
        37) 82, p. 22.
    "Sailor." PoNow (7:1, issue 37) 82, p. 22.

1207. EVERMAN, Welch D.
    "Five Fictions." Pequod (15) 82, p. 45-47.
    "Minneapolis and Its People." Pequod (15) 82, p.
        43-44.

1208. EWART, Gavin
    "In Another Country." AmerS (51:4) Aut 82, p. 511-
        512.

1209. EWICK, David
    "The Double." CutB (19) Aut-Wint 82, p. 20.
    "Grandmother's Revival." MidwQ (23:3) Spr 82, p.
        298.
    "An Old Man Playing a Pipe." MidwQ (23:3) Spr 82,
        p. 297.

1210. EXNER, Richard
"Gmy" (tr. by Ewald Osers). Stand (23:1) 81-82, p. 4-7.

1211. EZEKIEL, Nissim
"For Elkana." NewL (48:3/4) Spr-Sum 82, p. 12-13.
"Guru." NewL (48:3/4) Spr-Sum 82, p. 9.
"In the Country Cottage." NewL (48:3/4) Spr-Sum 82, p. 10-11.
"In the Garden." NewL (48:3/4) Spr-Sum 82, p. 10.
"A Morning Walk." NewL (48:3/4) Spr-Sum 82, p. 11-12.

1212. FABIAN, R. Gerry
"The Spectator." Pig (9) 82, p. 34.
"Suicide Squeeze." Pig (9) 82, p. 27.

1213. FACKLER, Herb
"From the Window." RevIn (11:1) Spr 81, p. 131.
"Murphy at Night." RevIn (11:1) Spr 81, p. 130.

1214. FAGAN, Kathy
"Sheet of Miscellaneous Studies of Destruction Falling on the Earth, with Notes -- DaVinci." AntR (40:4) Aut 82, p. 444.

1215. FAHEY, William A.
"Broccoli." WormR (22:3, issue 87) 82, p. 83.
"Celery." WormR (22:3, issue 87) 82, p. 82.
"Cherries." WormR (22:3, issue 87) 82, p. 81.
"Peaches." WormR (22:3, issue 87) 82, p. 82.
"Plums." WormR (22:3, issue 87) 82, p. 81.
"Tomatoes." WormR (22:3, issue 87) 82, p. 82-83.

1216. FAHRENTHOLD, Lisa
"Skirmish at the H.E.B." StoneC (10:1/2) Aut-Wint 82-83, p. 74-75.

1217. FAIERS, Chris
"Farley Hill, Barbados." Grain (10:3) Ag 82, p. 33.
"Fluttering white egret on palm fronds." PoetryCR (4:1) Sum 82, p. 5.
"Hurricane." Grain (10:3) Ag 82, p. 31.
"Jessie, Maisie and Pat." Grain (10:3) Ag 82, p. 31.

1218. FAINLIGHT, Ruth
"Calcutta." NewL (48:3/4) Spr-Sum 82, p. 184-185.
"Judgment at Marble Arch." Thrpny (9) Spr 82, p. 3.
"Observations of the Tower Block." Hudson (35:2) Sum 82, p. 253.

1219. FAIR, Ronald
"Black Writer's Prayer." BlackALF (16:2) Sum 82, p. 76.
"Stockholders' Meeting and Menu." BlackALF (16:2) Sum 82, p. 76.

1220. FAIRCHILD, B. H.
        "For Junior Gilliam (1928-1978)." LittleM (13:3/4)
        82, p. 27.
        "Night Shift." SouthernPR (22:1) Spr 82, p. 5.
        "Otello." LittleM (13:3/4) 82, p. 26.
        "Shooting." QW (14) Spr-Sum 82, p. 69.

1221. FAIRLEY, Bruce
        "Cape Scott in the Summer of '72." Waves (10:4) Spr
        82, p. 62.

1222. FAIZ, Faiz Ahmed
        "Ghazal" (tr. by Agha Shahid Ali). Kayak (60) O 82,
        p. 25.
        "Ghazal #2" (tr. by Agha Shahid Ali). DenQ (17:2)
        Sum 82, p. 75.
        "Ghazal #3" (tr. by Agha Shahid Ali). DenQ (17:2)
        Sum 82, p. 76.
        "Ghazal #4" (tr. by Agha Shahid Ali). DenQ (17:2)
        Sum 82, p. 77.
        "Ghazal #6" (tr. by Agha Shahid Ali). DenQ (17:2)
        Sum 82, p. 78.
        "Ghazal: In the Sahara of longing" (tr. by Agha
        Shahid Ali). Paint (9:17/18) Spr-Aut 82, p. 29.
        "Ghazal: Let me again assess my destiny" (tr. by
        Agha Shahid Ali). Paint (9:17/18) Spr-Aut 82, p.
        28.

1223. FALCONE, James
        "Postal Code." PottPort (4) 82-83, p. 49.
        "To the Gray Ladies." CrossC (4:4) 82, p. 11.

1224. FALKEID, Kolbein
        "Occupation" (tr. by Erik Strand and John Morrow).
        Stand (23:3) 82, p. 32.

1225. FANDEL, John
        "A Darwinian Scruple." Confr (23) Wint 82, p. 40.
        "Greening." Confr (23) Wint 82, p. 40.
        "Telling Time." Confr (23) Wint 82, p. 41.

1226. FARBER, Norma
        "A New Haggadah." PoNow (6:4, issue 34) 82, p. 34-
        35.
        "Poem in the Form of a Cheetah." ConcPo (15:2) Aut
        82, p. 16.

1227. FAREWELL, Patricia
        "On Becoming an Ex-Alcoholic." Spirit (6:2/3) 82,
        p. 124.

1228. FARGNOLI, Joseph
        "Sunrise Service." Paint (7/8:13/16) 80-81, p. 18-
        19.

1229. FARGUE, Leon-Paul
        "The Railway Station" (tr. by Francis Golffing).
        EnPas (13) 82, p. 4-6.

1230. FARIDI, Shams
       "A Nazm" (tr. by K. K. Khullar). NewL (48:3/4) Spr-
       Sum 82, p. 230.

1231. FARLEY, Melanie
       "Bees." KanQ (14:1) Wint 82, p. 103.
       "Carne." LittleBR (2:3) Spr 82, p. 59.

1232. FARNSWORTH, Robert L.
       "Blaming the Swan." GeoR (36:1) Spr 82, p. 163.
       "Grenouillere, or The Princess and the Frog."
       SouthernR (18:2) Spr 82, p. 378-379.
       "Seven Stanzas in Praise of Patience." PoetryNW
       (23:4) Wint 82-83, p. 29-30.
       "Speech to a Dog." SouthernR (18:2) Spr 82, p. 380.
       "Still Life." SouthernR (18:2) Spr 82, p. 377-378.

1233. FARRELL, James
       "Bajo la Calle." Mester (11:2) 82 [i.e. My 83], p.
       51.
       "Melar la Noche." Mester (11:2) 82 [i.e. My 83], p.
       51.

1234. FARRELL, Katy
       "Dali/Painting Man." AntigR (49) Spr 82, p. 28.
       "Watching the Knife." AntigR (49) Spr 82, p. 28.

1235. FARROKHZAD, Forugh
       "In an Eternity of Setting Sun: A Dialogue Between
       Lovers" (tr. by Jascha Kessler and Amin Banani).
       MichQR (21:2) Spr 82, p. 246-248.

1236. FARUQI, S. R.
       "Urban Expansion" (tr. of Majid Amjad, w. F. W.
       Pritchett). NewL (48:3/4) Spr-Sum 82, p. 214.

1237. FAUCHER, Real
       "A Civilized Dinner." Sam (32:3, issue 127) 82, p.
       7.
       "The Great General." WritersL O-N 82, p. 16.
       "Wings of Thunder." Sam (32:3, issue 127) 82, p.
       44.
       "Wo(man)." Bogg (48) 82, p. 71.

1238. FAULKNER, D. W.
       "Poem Written in Afternoon toward Twilight in Sudden
       and Unexpected Praise of Molly, a Cat." PoetryNW
       (23:2) Sum 82, p. 43.
       "Thanksgiving at Cutchogue" (for D and L) NewEngR
       (4:3) Spr 82, p. 436.

1239. FAULKNER, Karin
       "On Saying No to Unicorns." MendoR (5) Sum 81, p.
       60.

1240. FAULKNER, Leigh
       from The Celebrant Cycle: "I. Bass River." Germ
       (6:1) Spr-Sum 82, p. 7.
       from The Celebrant Cycle: "II. Risser's Beach."
       Germ (6:1) Spr-Sum 82, p. 8.

from The Celebrant Cycle: "IV. Pugwash." <u>Germ</u> (6:1)
Spr-Sum 82, p. 9.
from The Celebrant Cycle: "VI. Mira River." <u>Germ</u>
(6:1) Spr-Sum 82, p. 10.
from The Celebrant Cycle: "VII. Cape Split." <u>Germ</u>
(6:1) Spr-Sum 82, p. 11.
from The Celebrant Cycle: "VIII. Castlereagh." <u>Germ</u>
(6:1) Spr-Sum 82, p. 12.
from The Celebrant Cycle: "XI. Gulf Shore." <u>Germ</u>
(6:1) Spr-Sum 82, p. 13.
from The Celebrant Cycle: "XII. Lake Ellenwood."
<u>Germ</u> (6:1) Spr-Sum 82, p. 14.
from The Celebrant Cycle: "XIII. Grand Lake." <u>Germ</u>
(6:1) Spr-Sum 82, p. 15.
"Overcoming Stasis at Petite." <u>Germ</u> (6:2) Aut-Wint
82, p. 16.
"Spring Hiking near Frozen Ocean Lake." <u>Germ</u> (6:2)
Aut-Wint 82, p. 15.

1241. FAULKNER, Margherita (Margherita Woods)
"The Basement Potatoes" (In Memory of Emily
Dickinson). <u>Northeast</u> (3:14) Wint 82-83, p. 16.
"The Beehive." <u>Spirit</u> (6:2/3) 82, p. 63.
"My Tongue." <u>HolCrit</u> (19:3) Je 82, p. 12.
"The Still Unborn" (For Ann). <u>Outbr</u> (8/9) Aut 81-Spr
82, p. 15.
"These Innocents." <u>Outbr</u> (8/9) Aut 81-Spr 82, p.
14.
"The Waitress." <u>Northeast</u> (3:14) Wint 82-83, p. 16.

1242. FAWCETT, Brian
"Christmas Day 1980." <u>Waves</u> (10:3) Wint 82, p. 56-
57.

1243. FAWCETT, Susan
"The Locust Talks to Its Skin." <u>MichQR</u> (21:3) Sum
82, p. 405.

1244. FAY, Julie
"1943." <u>PoetC</u> (14:2) 82, p. 29-32.
"Birthday Poem." <u>AmerPoR</u> (11:3) My-Je 82, p. 18.
"Statue at Gila Pueblo, Globe, Arizona." <u>PoetC</u>
(14:2) 82, p. 33-34.

1245. FEDER, Chris
"The Swimmers." <u>Thrpny</u> (11) Aut 82, p. 19.

1246. FEDO, David
"The Burden of Psychoanalysis." <u>CapeR</u> (18:1) Wint
82, p. 19.
"Eros Reconsidered." <u>KanQ</u> (14:3) Sum 82, p. 113.
"The Invasion." <u>KanQ</u> (14:3) Sum 82, p. 112.
"Trying to Imagine Vermont." <u>KanQ</u> (14:3) Sum 82, p.
114.

1247. FEDOR, Michael
"Practitioner." <u>ChrC</u> (99:24) Jl 21-28, 82, p. 791.

1248. FEDULLO, Mick
"Ira Hayes." <u>Telescope</u> (2) Aut 81, p. 71-72.

"An Old Woman's Cottage Burns." Telescope (2) Aut
81, p. 65-68.

1249. FEE, Dan
"Northern California Weather." KanQ (14:1) Wint 82,
p. 38-39.

1250. FEENY, Thomas
"Summers." FourQt (31:4) Sum 82, p. 22.

1251. FEILER, Eva
"Death in the Well" (tr. of Nina Cassian). Chelsea
(41) 82, p. 135.
"Impervious" (tr. of Nina Cassian). Chelsea (41) 82,
p. 134.
"Music by Varese" (tr. of Nina Cassian). Chelsea
(41) 82, p. 134.
"Tongue of Cold" (tr. of Nina Cassian). Chelsea (41)
82, p. 135.

1252. FEIRSTEIN, Frederick
"Siddhartha Dove." Salm (55) Wint 82, p. 131-132.

1253. FELDMAN, Irving
"Adventures in the Postmodern Era." Shen (33:2) 82,
p. 98-99.
"Albert Feinstein." Antaeus (47) Aut 82, p. 75-76.
"The Epiphanies." YaleR (71:4) Sum 82, p. 582.
"The Grand Magic Theater Finale" (To Katharine). Nat
(235:5) Ag 21-28, 82, p. 154.
"Just Another Smack." Poetry (139:4) Ja 82, p. 198-
199.
"The Salon of Famous Babies." VirQR (58:2) Spr 82,
p. 268-270.
"To What's-Her-Name." Shen (33:3) 82, p. 47.

1254. FELDMAN, Ruth
"At Portici" (tr. of Rocco Scotellaro, w. Brian
Swann). PoNow (6:5, issue 35) 82, p. 43.
"Beggars" (tr. of Rocco Scotellaro, w. Brian Swann).
PoNow (6:4, issue 34) 82, p. 41.
"La Bussola" (tr. of Luciano Marrucci, w. Martin
Robbins). StoneC (10:1/2) Aut-Wint 82-83, p. 25.
"The Casting" (tr. of Fabio Doplicher). Agni (16)
82, p. 20-22.
"The Compass" (tr. of Luciano Marrucci, w. Martin
Robbins). StoneC (10:1/2) Aut-Wint 82-83, p. 25.
"Evening in Potenza" (tr. of Rocco Scotellaro, w.
Brian Swann). PoNow (6:5, issue 35) 82, p. 43.
"Return Trip" (tr. of Rocco Scotellaro, w. Brian
Swann). PoNow (6:4, issue 34) 82, p. 41.
"Stones." PoNow (6:5, issue 35) 82, p. 46.
"Ticket for Turin" (tr. of Rocco Scotellaro, w.
Brian Swann). PoNow (6:4, issue 34) 82, p. 41.
"To My Father" (tr. of Rocco Scotellaro, w. Brian
Swann). PoNow (6:5, issue 35) 82, p. 43.

1255. FELICIANO MENDOZA, Ester
"Cielo Marinero" (from Ronda del Mar). Mairena (4:9)
Spr 82, p. 84.

"Hermano Francisco" (Para Francisco Matos Paoli, hermano en el verso). Mairena (4:11/12) Wint 82, p. 147.

1256. FELICIANO SANCHEZ, Francisco
"No Morire." Mairena (4:10) Sum-Aut 82, p. 77.

1257. FELL, Mary
"Ah Ho, Chinatown 1873." Tendril (12) Wint 82, p. 33.

1258. FENSTERMAKER, Vesle
"Itinerant." Wind (12:45) 82, p. 15.
"Old Wives Tale." Wind (12:45) 82, p. 16-17.

1259. FENZA, David
"A Letter to Apollinaire Long after His Death on Armistice Day, 1918." AntR (40:4) Aut 82, p. 438-439.

1260. FEREN, David
"Alike as Two." LitR (25:3) Spr 82, p. 378.
"Evening." KanQ (14:3) Sum 82, p. 133.
"Heroes." KanQ (14:3) Sum 82, p. 133.
"Ode to Frank O'Hara." LitR (25:3) Spr 82, p. 379.
"Winter City." KanQ (14:1) Wint 82, p. 106.

1261. FERICANO, Paul
"Channel Seven Newscene." PoNow (6:4, issue 34) 82, p. 38.
"A Telegram to the Reviewers." PoNow (6:6, issue 36) 82, p. 41.

1262. FERNANDEZ, Pablo Armando
"Trajan" (tr. by Michael L. Johnson). PortR (28:2) 82, p. 41.

1263. FERNANDEZ RETAMAR, Roberto
"Haydee." Areito (8:32) 82, inside front cover.

1264. FERNEAU, Brenda
"Gaea." CharR (8:1) Spr 82, p. 43.

1265. FERRARELLI, Rina
"And Suddenly It's Evening" (tr. of Salvatore Quasimodo). PoNow (6:4, issue 34) 82, p. 41.
"A Boy Dies a Little" (tr. of Leonardo Sinisgalli). DenQ (17:2) Sum 82, p. 123.
"The Council" (tr. of Giorgio Chiesura). Chelsea (41) 82, p. 74-81.
"The Crooked Birch" (tr. of Giorgio Chiesura). DenQ (17:2) Sum 82, p. 128.
"Green Drift" (tr. of Salvatore Quasimodo). PoNow (6:4, issue 34) 82, p. 41.
"The Hospital" (tr. of Leonardo Sinisgalli). DenQ (17:2) Sum 82, p. 124.
"Mirror" (tr. of Salvatore Quasimodo). PoNow (6:4, issue 34) 82, p. 41.
"Narni-Amelia Scalo" (tr. of Leonardo Sinisgalli). DenQ (17:2) Sum 82, p. 125.

"On a Road to Florence" (tr. of Franco Fortini).
DenQ (17:2) Sum 82, p. 126.
"One September Evening" (tr. of Franco Fortini).
DenQ (17:2) Sum 82, p. 127.
"Poetry." BallSUF (23:2) Spr 82, p. 80.
"The Streetcar." BallSUF (23:2) Spr 82, p. 80.
"The Survivors" (tr. of Giorgio Chiesura). NewQR
(9:3) Wint 82, p. 88.
"Waiting Outside the Wright Brothers Memorial
Museum." PoNow (7:1, issue 37) 82, p. 13.

1266. FERRY, Dick
"Open House." PikeF (4) Spr 82, p. 12.
"A Pencilled Saga." PikeF (4) Spr 82, p. 12.

1267. FEWELL, Richard
"The 2nd Coming." Obs (7:2/3) Sum-Wint 81, p. 160.
"Black Baby." Obs (7:2/3) Sum-Wint 81, p. 161.
"The Dark Ages." Obs (7:2/3) Sum-Wint 81, p. 162-
163.
"Grandmama Spolke in Tongues (& Raised the Living)."
Obs (7:2/3) Sum-Wint 81, p. 161.
"What It Is." Obs (7:2/3) Sum-Wint 81, p. 164.

1268. FIALKOWSKI, Barbara
"Christopher's Garden." NoAmR (267:3) S 82,p. 30.
"Literacy Begins." Abraxas (25/26) 82, p. 43.

1269. FICKERT, Kurt J.
"The Outsider." Wind (12:45) 82, p. 31.

1270. FIELDER, William A.
"Bequest" (tr. of Cahit Kulebi, w. Ozcan Yalim and
Dionis Coffin Riggs). StoneC (10:1/2) Aut-Wint 82-
83,p. 31.
"The Lamp" (tr. of Behcet Necatigil, w. Ozcan Yalim
and Dionis Coffin Riggs).DenQ (17:1) Spr 82, p.
85.
"A Lesson" (tr. of Ulku Tamer, w. Ozcan Yalim and
Dionis Coffin Riggs).DenQ (17:1) Spr 82, p. 87.
"To Live" (tr. of Orhan Veli, w. Ozcan Yalim and
Dionis Coffin Riggs).DenQ (17:1) Spr 82, p. 86.

1271. FIELDS, Kenneth
"Going Out." ChiR (33:2) 82, p. 120.
"In the Wain." ChiR (33:2) 82, p. 119.
"Realizations." ChiR (33:2) 82, p. 121.
"Separate Camp." ChiR (33:2) 82, p. 118.

1272. FIFER, Elizabeth
"Visiting My Great-Grandmother Bella in Brownsville
(1950)." WestB (11) 82, p. 102-103.

1273. FIFER, Ken
"According to the Baal Shem Toad." NewL (48:2) Wint
81-82, p. 50.
"Near the Susquehanna." WestB (10) 82, p. 65.
"Swallows by the New Street Bridge." WestB (10) 82,
p. 64.

171   FIFER

"Waiting for the Sea to Join Them." StoneC (9:3/4)
    Spr-Sum 82, p. 63.
"What It Might Be." WestB (10) 82, p. 65.

1274. FIGUEROA-MELENDEZ, Manuel
    "Ha sentido otra vez." Mester (11:2) 82 [i.e. My
        83], p. 37.
    "Hoy estoy triste y no he llorado." Mester (11:2)
        82 [i.e. My 83], p. 36.

1275. FILSON, Bruce K.
    "A Fortune of Unicorns." PoetryCR (3:3) Spr 82, p.
        16.
    "Once Upon a Hill." PoetryCR (3:3) Spr 82, p. 16.

1276. FINALE, Frank
    "The Animals." Poem (45) Jl 82, p. 22.
    "Stranger Passing." NewRena (5:1, 15) Aut 82, p.
        46.
    "Visiting." NewRena (5:1, 15) Aut 82, p. 45.
    "The Woman in the Window." KanQ (14:1) Wint 82, p.
        126.

1277. FINCH, Roger
    "The Child in the Escalator." HiramPoR (33) Aut-
        Wint 82, p. 13.
    "Condensed and Largely Revised Edition." WebR (7:2)
        Aut 82, p. 69.
    "The Earth Quails before Her Sister Moon." SoDakR
        (20:2) Sum 82, p. 38.
    "Gardens of the Hand" (after Sakutaro Hagiwara).
        DekalbLAJ (14:1/4) Aut 80-Sum 81, p. 72-73.
    "Haiku, 'That Zen Thing'." WindO (41) Aut-Wint 82-
        83, p. 13.
    "Hunting Macaws" (A drawing by Riou, based on J.
        Crevaux). LitR (25:3) Spr 82, p. 352-354.
    "The Mirror of Matsuyama." LitR (26:1) Aut 82, p.
        122-123.
    "Morning Glory." Waves (11:1) Aut 82, p. 75.
    "A Mote in the Eye of the Woods." Confr (24) Sum
        82, p. 82.
    "A Rare and Precious Fabric Woven of Friends."
        HiramPoR (31) Aut-Wint 82, p. 24.
    "Scene with Tulip Bed and Classical Allusion."
        CapeR (17:2) Sum 82, p. 30.
    "View from the Top of Unfinished Stairs." CapeR
        (17:2) Sum 82, p. 31.

1278. FINCKE, Gary
    "The Avenue E Thief's Recorded Message." Outbr
        (8/9) Aut 81-Spr 82, p. 65.
    "The Child Who Is Wounded by Fear." SouthernPR (23,
        i.e. 22:2) Aut 82, p. 20.
    "Closet Child." WormR (22:3, issue 87) 82, p. 87.
    "Design." Pequod (15) 82, p. 42.
    "Digestible Toy." Outbr (8/9) Aut 81-Spr 82, p. 64.
    "The Foreman, Sixty." WestB (10) 82, p. 32.
    from Generic Life: (10-14). Pig (8) 80, p. 32.
    "Home Run." Pig (9) 82, p. 25.
    "Leaving Town." PoNow (6:6, issue 36) 82, p. 15.

"The Man in the Pipe." WormR (22:3, issue 87) 82,
     p. 87.
"May 26th." Wind (12:45) 82, p. 18.
"The Reactionary Ache." FourQt (31:3) Spr 82, p.
     10.
"Sale." PikeF (4) Spr 82, p. 11.
"Seance." FourQt (32:1) Aut 82, p. 2.
"Shelter." SouthernPR (23, i.e. 22:2) Aut 82, p.
     18-19.
"The Vibration in the Land." Wind (12:45) 82, p.
     18.
"Weekend." FourQt (31:3) Spr 82, p. 10.
"Wind." PoNow (6:6, issue 36) 82, p. 15.

1279. FINE, Janice
     "To Take Root in Rock." BallSUF (23:2) Spr 82, p.
          54.

1280. FINERAN, Mary C.
     "Foundering." CutB (18) Spr-Sum 82, p. 9.

1281. FINGUERET, Manuela
     "Jerusalem" (tr. by Ricardo Pau-Llosa). BelPoJ
          (32:4) Sum 82, p. 3.
     "Jerusalen." BelPoJ (32:4) Sum 82, p. 2.

1282. FINKEL, Donald
     "Concerning the Transmission." Kayak (59) Je 82, p.
          37.
     from The Detachable Man: "A Home Away." PoNow (6:6,
          issue 36) 82, p. 5.
     from The Detachable Man: "If People Had Roots."
          PoNow (6:5, issue 35) 82, p. 4.
     from The Detachable Man: "Metastasis." PoNow (6:5,
          issue 35) 82, p. 4.
     from The Detachable Man: "Night Flight." PoNow
          (6:5, issue 35) 82, p. 4.
     from The Detachable Man: "Solitaire." PoNow (6:5,
          issue 35) 82, p. 4.
     "Hitting the Road." Kayak (59) Je 82, p. 36.
     "In the Valley of Giants." PoNow (6:5, issue 35)
          82, p. 23.
     "Resources." PoNow (6:5, issue 35) 82, p. 23.

1283. FINKELSTEIN, Caroline
     "Married Dreams." Ploughs (8:2/3) 82, p. 156.
     "More and More Married." Tendril (12) Wint 82, p.
          32.
     "My Father's Store." Ploughs (8:2/3) 82, p. 154-
          155.
     "Runaway Marriage." Tendril (12) Wint 82, p. 31.

1284. FINLAY, John
     "Audubon at Oakley" (in Memory of Yvor Winters).
          SouthernR (18:2) Spr 82, p. 357.
     "The Black Earth." SouthernR (18:3) Sum 82, p. 532-
          533.
     "Odysseus" (in Memory of Yvor Winters). SouthernR
          (18:2) Spr 82, p. 356.

1285. FINLEY, C. Stephen
      "Gestures." SouthernHR (16:2) Spr 82, p. 153.

1286. FINNE, Diderik
      "The Last Communique." Shen (33:3) 82, p. 80.
      "Leaving the Lazaretto." Shen (33:3) 82, p. 79.

1287. FINNEGAN, James
      "The Cafe." CapeR (18:1) Wint 82, p. 20.
      "Stars and Blossoms." CutB (18) Spr-Sum 82, p. 41.

1288. FINNELL, Dennis
      "Bucolic" (tr. of Aime Cesaire). AmerPoR (11:5) S-O
        82, p. 8.
      "From My Weariness" (tr. of Aime Cesaire). AmerPoR
        (11:5) S-O 82, p. 8.
      "It Is the Courage of Men Which Is Disjointed" (tr.
        of Aime Cesaire). AmerPoR (11:5) S-O 82, p. 8.
      "Marine Intimacy" (tr. of Aime Cesaire). AmerPoR
        (11:5) S-O 82, p. 8.
      "Oscar Tries to Have Children." PoetryNW (23:1) Spr
        82, p. 29-30.
      "Oscar's Birth and Early Years." PoetryNW (23:1)
        Spr 82, p. 27-28.
      "Oscar's Confession." PoetryNW (23:1) Spr 82, p.
        28-29.
      "Oscar's Last Will and Testament." PoetryNW (23:1)
        Spr 82, p. 30-31.
      "Oscar's Note from Limbo." PoetryNW (23:1) Spr 82,
        p. 31-32.

1289. FINNIGAN, Joan
      from The Watershed Collection: (III, IV, VII, V).
        Waves (11:1) Aut 82, p. 56-59.

1290. FINUCANE, Martin L.
      "Fragment." PraS (56:3) Aut 82, p. 77.
      "Old Friends from a Tough School." PraS (56:3) Aut
        82, p. 76.

1291. FIORITO, Joe
      "I Have a Picture." PoetryCR (3:4) Sum 82, p. 15.
      "Lament." PoetryCR (4:1) Sum 82, p. 5.

1292. FIRER, Susan
      "Footsteps." Abraxas (25/26) 82, p. 90.

1293. FISH, Karen
      "The Lake." NewYorker (58:26) Ag 16, 82, p. 69.

1294. FISHER, David
      "An Old Man." Kayak (58) Ja 82, p. 35.
      "The Tailor of Warsaw." Kayak (58) Ja 82, p. 34.
      "The Virgin of Guadalupe." Kayak (58) Ja 82, p. 33.

1295. FISHER, Harrison
      "Bewilderness." OP (33) Spr 82, p. 21.
      "Deputized." OP (33) Spr 82, p. 23.
      "Dog Democracy." Pig (8) 80, p. 28.
      "Serious Muzak." OP (33) Spr 82, p. 22.

"Target Future F." OP (33) Spr 82, p. 20.

1296. FISHER, Nancy M.
    "Rapunsel--Twenty Years Later." Wind (12:45) 82, p.
      6.

1297. FISHMAN, Charles
    "Hit and Run." Pig (9) 82, p. 26.
    "Moon Gold." PoNow (6:5, issue 35) 82, p. 33.
    "A Stop on the Tour." PoetryE (8) Aut 82, p. 45.
    "The Storm." PoNow (6:5, issue 35) 82, p. 33.

1298. FITZGERALD, Robert
    "Aeneid III, 1-72." YaleR (71:2) Wint 82, p. 238-
      240.
    from The Aeneid, Book IV, lines 1-53, 68-89, 136-
      172: "Dido in Love" (tr. of Virgil). NewYRB
      (28:21/22) Ja 21, 82, p. 14-15.

1299. FIXEL, Lawrence
    "Leaving the City." PoNow (6:5, issue 35) 82, p.
      18.

1300. FIXEL, Michael
    "The Freedom of the Dreamer." Catalyst (Erotica
      Issue) 82, p. 20-21.

1301. FLAMM, Matthew
    "Neighbors." NewYorker (58:3) Mr 8, 82, p. 137.
    "The New Co-Op Owners in Their Living Room."
      PoetryE (8) Aut 82, p. 33.
    "Takako in New York." PoetryE (8) Aut 82, p. 34.

1302. FLANDERS, Jane
    "Ancestors (A Daguerreotype)." MassR (23:3) Aut 82,
      p. 412.
    "August Philosophers." Atl (250:1) Jl 82, p. 55.
    "Grandfather Mountain." LitR (25:3) Spr 82, p. 358-
      359.
    "The House That Fear Built: Warsaw, 1943)." Chelsea
      (41) 82, p. 88-89.
    "I Have Beheld Such Splendors." WestB (10) 82, p.
      8.
    "In an Accelerated Time Frame." Chelsea (41) 82, p.
      89.
    "Late Report from Miss Harriet Robinson's Third
      Grade." Poetry (140:3) Je 82, p. 137-138.
    "Picasso's Blue Period." Nat (234:22) Je 5, 82, p.
      694.
    "The Scholar's Stone Garden." WestB (10) 82, p. 9.
    "Special Friends." PoNow (6:4, issue 34) 82, p. 18.
    "Twigs." Confr (24) Sum 82, p. 14.
    "Van Gogh's Bed Is." Comm (109:16) S 24, 82, p.
      503.
    "The Water-Garden, Giverny." LitR (25:3) Spr 82, p.
      356-357.
    "Your Name in Greek." LitR (25:3) Spr 82, p. 357.

1303. FLANNER, Hildegarde
    "The Blackberry Picker." Salm (57) Sum 82, p. 114.

"The Island." <u>Salm</u> (57) Sum 82, p. 117-118.
"Junction." <u>Salm</u> (57) Sum 82, p. 118.
"One Dark Night." <u>Salm</u> (57) Sum 82, p. 115.
"Public Beach, California." <u>Salm</u> (57) Sum 82, p. 116.

1304. FLAVIN, Jack
      "Dunbar's Lament for the Makaris." <u>MidwQ</u> (23:3) Spr 82, p. 294-296.

1305. FLECK, Polly
      "Subway into Autumn" (Eglinton Station 10:00). <u>Waves</u> (10:4) Spr 82, p. 71.

1306. FLECK, Richard F.
      "Thunder Beings." <u>Paint</u> (7/8:13/16) 80-81, p. 22.

1307. FLEITES, Alex
      "Double Spaced" (tr. by Margaret Randell). <u>SeC</u> (9:1/2) 80, p. 30-31.

1308. FLEMING, Gerald
      "At a Science Lecture." <u>Pequod</u> (14) 82, p. 104.

1309. FLEMING, Harold
      "At Night, in the Mental Hospital." <u>WestB</u> (11) 82, p. 58-59.
      "In Memory of Ann Belfry." <u>StoneC</u> (10:1/2) Aut-Wint 82-83, p. 9.
      "The Way Time Is." <u>WestB</u> (10) 82, p. 53.

1310. FLEMING, Harold Lee
      "Now It Is Morning." <u>Poetry</u> (140:3) Je 82, p. 151.

1311. FLETCHER, Luellen
      "A Father's Tryst." <u>Spirit</u> (6:2/3) 82, p. 180.

1312. FLINT, Austin
      "Children of the Epoch" (tr. of Wislawa Szymborska, w. Grazyna Drabik). <u>QRL</u> (23) 82, p. 12-13.
      "From an Expedition Which Did Not Take Place" (tr. of Wislawa Szymborska, w. Grazyna Drabik). <u>QRL</u> (23) 82, p. 59-60.
      "The Great Number" (tr. of Wislawa Szymborska, w. Grazyna Drabik). <u>QRL</u> (23) 82, p. 19.
      "Hunger Camp at Jaslo" (tr. of Wislawa Szymborska, w. Grazyna Drabik). <u>QRL</u> (23) 82, p. 22.
      "In Praise of a Guilty Conscience" (tr. of Wislawa Szymborska, w. Grazyna Drabik). <u>QRL</u> (23) 82, p. 54.
      "In Praise of My Sister" (tr. of Wislawa Szymborska, w. Grazyna Drabik). <u>QRL</u> (23) 82, p. 41.
      "Lot's Wife" (tr. of Wislawa Szymborska, w. Grazyna Drabik). <u>QRL</u> (23) 82, p. 38-39.
      "The Number Pi" (tr. of Wislawa Szymborska, w. Grazyna Drabik). <u>QRL</u> (23) 82, p. 44.
      "Poem in Honor of" (tr. of Wislawa Szymborska, w. Grazyna Drabik). <u>QRL</u> (23) 82, p. 15.
      "Portrait of a Woman" (tr. of Wislawa Szymborska, w. Grazyna Drabik). <u>QRL</u> (23) 82, p. 43.

"The Room of a Suicide" (tr. of Wislawa Szymborska,
   w. Grazyna Drabik). QRL (23) 82, p. 49.
"A Terrorist Is Watching" (tr. of Wislawa
   Szymborska, w. Grazyna Drabik). QRL (23) 82, p.
   45-46.
"Thanks" (tr. of Wislawa Szymborska, w. Grazyna
   Drabik). QRL (23) 82, p. 35-36.
"Torture" (tr. of Wislawa Szymborska, w. Grazyna
   Drabik). QRL (23) 82, p. 26-27.
"Utopia" (tr. of Wislawa Szymborska, w. Grazyna
   Drabik). QRL (23) 82, p. 57-58.
"A View with a Grain of Sand" (tr. of Wislawa
   Szymborska, w. Grazyna Drabik). QRL (23) 82, p.
   47-48.
"The Warning" (tr. of Wislawa Szymborska, w. Grazyna
   Drabik). QRL (23) 82, p. 55-56.
"Writing a Curriculum Vitae" (tr. of Wislawa
   Szymborska, w. Grazyna Drabik). QRL (23) 82, p.
   17-18.

1313. FLINT, Roland
"Aubade." TriQ (55) Aut 82, p. 73.
"Echo from the Woods" (tr. of Krassin Himmersky, w.
   the author). Vis (9) 82, p. 11.
"Glen Allen Delvo." GeoR (36:3) Aut 82, p. 654.
"God Bless Invention Pigeon." TriQ (55) Aut 82, p.
   76.
"He Didn't Even Know He Was a." TriQ (55) Aut 82,
   p. 74.
"It Seems That after Writing Twenty-Eight Days
   without a Pause." TriQ (55) Aut 82, p. 78.
"Last Words." TriQ (55) Aut 82, p. 71-72.
"Nearing Their Official." TriQ (55) Aut 82, p. 77.
"Pigeon Wonders Again." TriQ (55) Aut 82, p. 75.

1314. FLINTOFF, Eddie
"Childhood Storm." Bogg (48) 82, p. 58.
"Knocked Sideways." Bogg (48) 82, p. 54.

1315. FLOOK, Maria
"Ants in a White Peony." Agni (16) 82, p. 81.
"Apology for John." Agni (16) 82, p. 87-88.
"Diving Alone." Agni (16) 82, p. 80.
"For a Father." Iowa (12:4) Aut 81, p. 54.
"In Love." Agni (16) 82, p. 83-84.
"Poem for Prevention." Agni (16) 82, p. 82.
"Radio Request." Agni (16) 82, p. 76-77.
"Reunion." Agni (16) 82, p. 85-86.
"Snow Statement." Agni (16) 82, p. 78-79.
"Years of This." Iowa (12:4) Aut 81, p. 55.

1316. FLORIAN, Miroslav
"Report on the Flood" (tr. by Dana Habova and Stuart
   Friebert). Field (27) Aut 82, p. 79.

1317. FLORSCHUTZ, Roger Johannes
"The Death of Her before Dying." Waves (11:1) Aut
   82, p. 62-63.

1318. FLORY, Sheldon
       "Snapshot" (Crow Hill Road, Early April, 1937).
       NewYorker (58:16) Je 7, 82, p. 135.

       FOE, Mark de
       See: DeFOE, Mark

1319. FOERSTER, Richard
       "Oscar Wilde at Hotel d'Alsace, 1900." SouthernHR
       (16:1) Wint 82, p. 60.

1320. FOGARTY, Susan
       "The Calamity of Man." CutB (19) Aut-Wint 82, p.
       56.

1321. FOGEL, Daniel Mark
       "Darkcast." WestHR (36:2) Sum 82, p. 164.

1322. FOGEL, Ephim
       "The Age of the Wolfdog" (tr. of Osip Mandelshtam).
       NewL (48:2) Wint 81-82, p. 44.
       "Leningrad" (tr. of Osip Mandelshtam). NewL (48:2)
       Wint 81-82, p. 43.
       "To Nadezhda Mandelshtam" (tr. of Osip Mandelshtam).
       NewL (48:2) Wint 81-82, p. 44.
       "The Uncollected Works of Osip Mandelshtam (1972)."
       NewL (48:2) Wint 81-82, p. 45.

1323. FOLKS, Jeffrey
       "Major John Cartwright to His Friend, Thomas
       Jefferson, 14 June 1824." Poem (46) N 82, p. 6.
       "The Piltdown Man." Poem (46) N 82, p. 5.

1324. FOLLANSBEE, Peter
       "Pantoum: The Salmon Ladder." NoAmR (267:1) Mr
       82,p. 33.

       FOLLETTE, Melvin Walker la
       See: La FOLLETTE, Melvin Walker

1325. FOLTZ-GRAY, Dorothy
       "Chimes." MissR (10:3, issue 30) Wint-Spr 82, p.
       46.
       "Economics in Wartime." MissR (10:3, issue 30)
       Wint-Spr 82, p. 45.

1326. FORBES, Marjorie V.
       "The blizzard rages" (Haiku). LittleBR (2:2) Wint
       81-82, p. 70.
       "Foggy winter day" (Haiku). LittleBR (2:2) Wint 81-
       82, p. 70.
       "Hoarfrost everywhere" (Haiku). LittleBR (2:2) Wint
       81-82, p. 70.
       "In crisp autumn chill" (Haiku). LittleBR (1:3) Spr
       81, p. 55.
       "White feathery flakes" (Haiku). LittleBR (2:2) Wint
       81-82, p. 70.
       "Windy, moonlit night" (Haiku). LittleBR (2:2) Wint
       81-82, p. 70.

1327. FORCHE, Carolyn
    "Because One Is Always Forgotten" (in memoriam, Jose
        Rudolfo Viera, 1939-1981, El Salvador). Iowa
        (12:2/3) Spr-Sum 81, p. 85.
    "Endurance." Iowa (12:2/3) Spr-Sum 81, p. 83-84.
    "Expatriate." Iowa (12:2/3) Spr-Sum 81, p. 82.
    "Message." Iowa (12:2/3) Spr-Sum 81, p. 86.
    "Poem for Maya." Iowa (12:2/3) Spr-Sum 81, p. 81.
    "Selective Service." Iowa (12:2/3) Spr-Sum 81, p.
        87.

1328. FORD, Cathy
    "Beauty razed like the countryside." Dandel (9:1)
        82, p. 32.
    "Paternoster." PoetryCR (3:3) Spr 82, p. 13.
    "Returning to the Same Places." Dandel (9:1) 82, p.
        31.

    FORD, Sara de
    See: DeFORD, Sara

1329. FORD, William
    "Forth of July" (Juniper Beach, Washington). WestB
        (10) 82, p. 70.

1330. FORSTROM, Martha
    "Old Horse." Wind (12:45) 82, p. 8.

1331. FORT, Charles
    "Something Called a City" (New Orleans). GeoR (36:1)
        Spr 82, p. 166.

1332. FORTINI, Franco
    "On a Road to Florence" (tr. by Rina Ferrarelli).
        DenQ (17:2) Sum 82, p. 126.
    "One September Evening" (tr. by Rina Ferrarelli).
        DenQ (17:2) Sum 82, p. 127.

1333. FOSTER, Linda Nemec
    "The Abandoned Children." Nimrod (26:1) Aut-Wint
        82, p. 44.
    "The Baba Yaga Poems." Nimrod (26:1) Aut-Wint 82,
        p. 41-47.
    "Baba Yaga Tells the Story of the Hanged Man."
        Nimrod (26:1) Aut-Wint 82, p. 45.
    "Baba Yaga." Nimrod (26:1) Aut-Wint 82, p. 41-42.
    "The Chant of the Three Sisters." Nimrod (26:1)
        Aut-Wint 82, p. 45.
    "The Flight." Nimrod (26:1) Aut-Wint 82, p. 43.
    "For My Sister." Tendril (12) Wint 82, p. 35.
    "The Night Songs." Nimrod (26:1) Aut-Wint 82, p.
        47.
    "The Peasant Woman Tells How Baba Yaga Took Her
        Grandmother." Nimrod (26:1) Aut-Wint 82, p. 44.
    "Quarry." Tendril (12) Wint 82, p. 34.
    "The Reader Speaks to Baba Yaga." Nimrod (26:1)
        Aut-Wint 82, p. 46.
    "Spring." PoNow (7:1, issue 37) 82, p. 14.
    "The Unending Vigil" Nimrod (26:1) Aut-Wint 82, p.
        41.

"The Woman Taken in Adultery." Tendril (12) Wint
    82, p. 36.

1334. FOTOPOULOS, Niki
    "Creation." UnderRM 1(1) Spr 82, p. 22.

1335. FOWLER, Barbara
    "Loving." Abraxas (25/26) 82, p. 88.
    "Sounion." Abraxas (25/26) 82, p. 89.

1336. FOWLER, Gene
    "Not Macho, Just Mucho." SeC (9:1/2) 80, p. 35.

1337. FOWLER, Jay Bradford, Jr.
    "The Heart Harangue." Shen (33:1) 81-82, p. 38.
    "Letter North." Shen (33:1) 81-82, p. 39.

1338. FOX, Gail
    "The Lover." Waves (10:4) Spr 82, p. 55.
    "Neruda" (for Ted). Waves (10:4) Spr 82, p. 55.
    "The Question" (for Betty Jane Wylie). Waves (10:4)
        Spr 82, p. 54.
    "Thomas Merton." Quarry (31:3) Sum 82, p. 14-15.

1339. FOX, Hugh
    "51." Spirit (6:2/3) 82, p. 64.
    "Following Strangers." Abraxas (25/26) 82, p. 48.
    "Kit-Kat." Abraxas (25/26) 82, p. 47.
    "Veterans of the Medical Wars." PoNow (6:5, issue
        35) 82, p. 31.

1340. FOX, Lucia
    "Ellos y Ellas: Poetas." LetFem (8:1) 82, p. 94.
    "Maga." LetFem (8:1) 82, p. 96.
    "Pesadilla." LetFem (8:1) 82, p. 95.

1341. FOX, Nancy Ann
    "Lady." FourQt (32:1) Aut 82, p. 18.

1342. FOX, Susan
    "Cong under Saigon,1974." MinnR (NS19) Aut 82, p.
        15-16.
    "War Baby." MinnR (NS19) Aut 82, p. 14.

1343. FRANCIS, Pat Therese
    "The Burning Factory." AmerPoR (11:3) My-Je 82, p.
        32.
    "Marriage." AmerPoR (11:3) My-Je 82, p. 32.

1344. FRANCIS, Reynold S.
    "Cost Efficiency." Maize (6:1/2) Aut-Wint 82-83, p.
        106.

1345. FRANK, Adassa
    "En Route, Boston." NewRena (5:1, 15) Aut 82, p.
        56-57.

1346. FRANK, Bernhard
    "The End of the Fall" (tr. of Daliah Rabikovich).
        PoNow (6:4, issue 34) 82, p. 42.

1347. FRANK, Mark
"Drought." Sam (32:3, issue 127) 82, p. 26.

1348. FRANKSTON, Jay
"They." MendoR (6) Sum 81, p. 14-15.

1349. FRASER, Kathleen
"1930." Ploughs (8:1) 82, p. 58-59.
from Leda. & Swan: "Energy Unavailable for Useful
Work in a System Undergoing Change." Iowa (12:2/3)
Spr-Sum 81, p. 88-96.

1350. FRATE, Frank C.
"Investigation for Warren." CapeR (17:2) Sum 82, p.
16.

1351. FRATICELLI, Marco
"3 Erotic Haiku." Catalyst (Erotica Issue) 82, p.
27.

1352. FRATUS, David
"The Bee Tree: A Local Legend." HiramPoR (32) Spr-
Sum 82, p. 19.
"The Garden." HiramPoR (32) Spr-Sum 82, p. 20-21.
"The High-Wire Clown." HiramPoR (32) Spr-Sum 82, p.
22.
"Wrists." HiramPoR (32) Spr-Sum 82, p. 23.

1353. FRAZEE, C. Mann
"In Remembrance of Eve's Curse." WindO (41) Aut-
Wint 82-83, p. 25.
"Second Sister." WindO (41) Aut-Wint 82-83, p. 25.

1354. FRAZEE, James
"Dead Man's Float." AspenJ (1) Wint 82, p. 31.
"Lighthouse." AspenJ (1) Wint 82, p. 31.
"The Motel." SouthernPR (22:1) Spr 82, p. 76.

1355. FRAZIER, Robert
"Telephone Ghosts." Pig (10) 82, p. 93.

FREES, Madeline de
See: DeFREES, Madeline

1356. FREIRE de MATOS, Isabel
"Haremos una Isla" (w. Francisco Matos Paoli, from
Isla para los Ninos). Mairena (4:9) Spr 82, p. 84.

1357. FREIVALDS, Karlis
"Color Drawn on Weather and Season." Vis (9) 82, p.
17.

1358. FRENCH, Donna
"Photo, Age 3." PraS (56:4) Wint 82-83, p. 27.

FRESE, Marcos Rodriguez
See: RODRIGUEZ FRESE, Marcos

1359. FRETWELL, Kathy Vaughan
"Ghazal." PottPort (4) 82-83, p. 34.

"Rose Garden." PottPort (4) 82-83, p. 28.
"What Norman Rockwell Never Realized." PottPort (4)
   82-83, p. 15.

1360. FREY, Cecelia
   "The Ballad of Lucy Labelle." Quarry (31:4) Aut 82,
      p. 11.
   "Metamorphosis." PoetryCR (3:4) Sum 82, p. 15.

1361. FREY, Janice
   "Swatting a Diaphanous Fly." HiramPoR (33) Aut-Wint
      82, p. 14-15.

1362. FREYTAG-LORINGHOVEN, Elsa von, Baroness
   "A Dozen Cocktails--Please." Sulfur (2:3, issue 6)
      82, p. 133-134.
   "Enchantment." Sulfur (2:3, issue 6) 82, p. 148.
   "Fluency." Sulfur (2:3, issue 6) 82, p. 139-140.
   "Game (Legend)." Sulfur (2:3, issue 6) 82, p. 149-
      150.
   "History. Dim." Sulfur (2:3, issue 6) 82, p. 136-
      137.
   "In the Midst." Sulfur (2:3, issue 6) 82, p. 142-
      144.
   "Jigg." Sulfur (2:3, issue 6) 82, p. 137-138.
   "Skin of Faith." Sulfur (2:3, issue 6) 82, p. 135-
      136.
   "Sunsong." Sulfur (2:3, issue 6) 82, p. 138-139.
   "Ultramundanity." Sulfur (2:3, issue 6) 82, p. 144-
      147.
   "Untitled: Whatever you think about jesus christ."
      Sulfur (2:3, issue 6) 82, p. 140-142.

1363. FRIAR, Kimon
   "1949 A.D" (tr. of Tasos Livadhitis). Kayak (58) Ja
      82, p. 4.
   "Able to Work" (tr. of Tasos Livadhitis). Kayak (58)
      Ja 82, p. 7.
   "Afternoon in Athens" (tr. of Yannis Kondos). Kayak
      (60) O 82, p. 17.
   "Disengaged" (tr. of Tasos Livadhitis). Kayak (58)
      Ja 82, p. 6.
   "Etesian Winds" (tr. of Yannis Ritsos). PoNow (6:6,
      issue 36) 82, p. 43.
   "The Fingernails" (tr. of Yannis Kondos). Kayak (60)
      O 82, p. 16.
   "In the Half Dark" (tr. of Yannis Kondos). Kayak
      (60) O 82, p. 17.
   "Indiscretions" (tr. of Tasos Livadhitis). Kayak
      (58) Ja 82, p. 5.
   "The Lamp" (tr. of Tasos Livadhitis). Kayak (58) Ja
      82, p. 4.
   "The Last Command" (tr. of Tasos Livadhitis). Kayak
      (58) Ja 82, p. 6.
   "Painting by an Unknown Artist" (tr. of Tasos
      Livadhitis). Kayak (58) Ja 82, p. 7.
   "The Perfect Crime" (tr. of Tasos Livadhitis). Kayak
      (58) Ja 82, p. 5.
   "Precautions" (tr. of Tasos Livadhitis). Kayak (58)
      Ja 82, p. 7.

"Ragpickers." (tr. of Tasos Livadhitis). <u>Kayak</u> (58)
Ja 82, p. 4.
"Self-Knowledge" (tr. of Yannis Patilis). <u>PoNow</u>
(6:5, issue 35) 82, p. 44.
"Small Existentialist Parenthesis" (tr. of Tasos
Livadhitis). <u>Kayak</u> (58) Ja 82, p. 5.
"Sonorous Page" (tr. of Lefteris Poulios). <u>PoNow</u>
(6:4, issue 34) 82, p. 40.
"Succession" (tr. of Yannis Ritsos). <u>PoNow</u> (6:6,
issue 36) 82, p. 43.
"Suddenly" (tr. of Yannis Ritsos). <u>PoNow</u> (6:6, issue
36) 82, p. 43.
"The Summer Is" (tr. of Yannis Patilis). <u>PoNow</u> (6:5,
issue 35) 82, p. 44.
"Various Thoughts of a Rising Poet" (tr. of Yannis
Patilis). <u>PoNow</u> (6:5, issue 35) 82, p. 44.
"Your Eyes Are an Empty Distance" (tr. of Yannis
Kondos). <u>Kayak</u> (60) O 82, p. 18.

1364. FRIEBERT, Stuart
"Aria for Tenor" (tr. of Giovanni Raboni, w. Vinio
Rossi). <u>MalR</u> (62) Jl 82, p. 62.
"Biodrama" (tr. of Miroslav Holub, w. Dana
Ha'bova'). <u>MalR</u> (62) Jl 82, p. 92.
"The Check Room" (tr. of Giovanni Raboni, w. Vinio
Rossi). <u>MalR</u> (62) Jl 82, p. 62.
"Dreams" (tr. of Miroslav Holub, w. Dana Ha'bova').
<u>MalR</u> (62) Jl 82, p. 89.
"Dudley Blue." <u>KanQ</u> (14:1) Wint 82, p. 112.
"Elements of an Urban Landscape" (tr. of Giovanni
Raboni, w. Vinio Rossi). <u>MalR</u> (62) Jl 82, p. 64.
"Exposed Persons." <u>CimR</u> (58) Ja 82, p. 36.
"The First Sentence" (tr. of Donat Sajner, w. Dana
Habova). <u>Field</u> (27) Aut 82, p. 78.
"The Fisherman (Perpetuum Mobile)" (tr. of Josef
Simon, w. Dana Habova). <u>Field</u> (27) Aut 82, p. 80.
"From the Hospital" (tr. of Bettina Behn). <u>Tendril</u>
(12) Wint 82, p. 15.
"Hominization" (tr. of Miroslav Holub, w. Dana
Ha'bova'). <u>MalR</u> (62) Jl 82, p. 93.
"In Memory of Light." <u>AmerPoR</u> (11:4) Jl-Ag 82, p.
40.
"The Jewish Cemetery at Olsany, Kafka's Tomb, April,
Sunny Weather" (tr. of Miroslav Holub, w. Dana
Ha'bova'). <u>MalR</u> (62) Jl 82, p. 90.
"Judas' Oration" (tr. of Giovanni Raboni, w. Vinio
Rossi). <u>MalR</u> (62) Jl 82, p. 64.
"Like a Man." <u>CentR</u> (26:2) Spr 82, p. 178-179.
"Lovers I" (tr. of Vladimir Holan, w. Dana Habova).
<u>Field</u> (27) Aut 82, p. 74.
"Meditation in the Orchard" (tr. of Giovanni Raboni,
w. Vinio Rossi). <u>MalR</u> (62) Jl 82, p. 63.
"My Father's Heart." <u>AmerPoR</u> (11:4) Jl-Ag 82, p.
40.
"A Natural History of Arthropods" (tr. of Miroslav
Holub, w. Dana Ha'bova'). <u>MalR</u> (62) Jl 82, p. 91.
"Night of Sleep" (in memory of a friend's child).
<u>KanQ</u> (14:1) Wint 82, p. 111.
"The Nightly News in Jerusalem" (for Shirley &
Bill). <u>WestB</u> (11) 82, p. 22.

"The Pope's Desire for Children." WestB (10) 82, p. 63.
"Report on the Flood" (tr. of Miroslav Florian, w. Dana Habova). Field (27) Aut 82, p. 79.
"Serenade" (tr. of Giovanni Raboni, w. Vinio Rossi). LittleBR (2:4) Sum 82, p. 73.
"Simulated & Dissimulated" (for my son) (tr. of Giovanni Raboni, w. Vinio Rossi). MalR (62) Jl 82, p. 63.
"Without Looking Ahead." Tendril (12) Wint 82, p. 37.

1365. FRIED, Erich
"Deserted Room" (tr. by Beth Bjorklund). LitR (25:2) Wint 82, p. 211.
"Rural" (tr. by Beth Bjorklund). LitR (25:2) Wint 82, p. 210.
"Speechless" (tr. by Beth Bjorklund). LitR (25:2) Wint 82, p. 212.

1366. FRIED, Philip
"Above the Friction." PortR (28:1) 82, p. 8.
"Ballad of the Little Boy." Im (8:1) 82, p. 11.
"Rudich's Demon" (For Lynn). BelPoJ (32:3) Spr 82, p. 23.

1367. FRIEDLAND, Linda
"The coffee vendor." Dandel (9:1) 82, p. 85.
"Dancing Hair." Dandel (9:1) 82, p. 86.
"Gas Station Ladies' Room." Dandel (9:1) 82, p. 85.
"I was here when the lilacs." Dandel (9:1) 82, p. 87.
"There is a kind man in the orchestra." Dandel (9:1) 82, p. 84.

1368. FRIEDMAN, Debbie
"Shea Stadium Revisited." Pig (9) 82, p. 65.

1369. FRIEDMAN, Jacob
"Who Brings the Songs?" (tr. by Aaron Kramer). NewEngR (4:4) Sum 82, p. 557.

1370. FRIEDMAN, Norman
"Father to Son." CentR (26:4) Aut 82, p. 360.
"Son to Father." CentR (26:4) Aut 82, p. 359-360.

1371. FRIEDMAN, Racelle
"Cosmetic Surgery." PoNow (7:1, issue 37) 82, p. 14.

1372. FRIEDMANN, Elizabeth
"Take Some Time to Be Alone, As Your Drive Is Intense." UTR (7:2) 82?, p. 20.

1373. FRITSCH, Gerhard
"Afternoon" (tr. by Beth Bjorklund). LitR (25:2) Wint 82, p. 221.
"Fear" (tr. by Beth Bjorklund). LitR (25:2) Wint 82, p. 217.

"I Thought Myself to Be Guest" (tr. by Beth
    Bjorklund). LitR (25:2) Wint 82, p. 218.
"Judas" (tr. by Beth Bjorklund). LitR (25:2) Wint
    82, p. 221.
"Saint Maria Maggiore" (tr. by Beth Bjorklund). LitR
    (25:2) Wint 82, p. 220.
"Why the Many Words?" (tr. by Beth Bjorklund). LitR
    (25:2) Wint 82, p. 219.
"Words Persistently" (tr. by Beth Bjorklund). LitR
    (25:2) Wint 82, p. 219.

1374. FRITSCH, Janice
"Breastplate" (tr. of Joyce Mansour, w. Elton
    Glaser). CharR (8:2) Aut 82, p. 44.
"I've Gone Deep into." (tr. of Joyce Mansour, w.
    Elton Glaser). CharR (8:2) Aut 82, p. 43.
"You Don't Know My Night-Face" (tr. of Joyce
    Mansour, w. Elton Glaser). CharR (8:2) Aut 82, p.
    43.

1375. FROSCH, Thomas
"Bluefish." BelPoJ (33:2) Wint 82-83, p. 20-21.

1376. FROST, Carol
"Frost." Agni (17) 82, p. 158.
"Passage." AmerPoR (11:1) Ja-F 82, p. 17.
"The Secret." AmerPoR (11:1) Ja-F 82, p. 17.
"To Fish." CimR (60) Jl 82, p. 56-57.

1377. FROST, Celestine
"Tomatoes." LittleM (13:3/4) 82, p. 21.

1378. FROST, Joseph B.
"After All This." Poem (45) Jl 82, p. 51.
"Mourningless the Morning." Poem (45) Jl 82, p. 50.
"Two Little Thoughts of Green." Poem (45) Jl 82, p.
    52.

1379. FROST, Kenneth
"Mountain Climber." Outbr (10/11) Aut 82-Spr 83, p.
    4.
"Soloing." Outbr (10/11) Aut 82-Spr 83, p. 6.
"The Speculator." Outbr (10/11) Aut 82-Spr 83, p.
    5.
"Tightrope Walker." Outbr (10/11) Aut 82-Spr 83, p.
    3.

1380. FROST, Richard
"The Answer." PoNow (6:4, issue 34) 82, p. 31.
"The Basket Case." CimR (59) Ap 82, p. 8.
"Heat." LitR (26:1) Aut 82, p. 126.
"Marriage." Poetry (140:3) Je 82, p. 139-140.
"The Standing Broad Jump." Poetry (140:3) Je 82, p.
    140.
"Winter Flies." CimR (59) Ap 82, p. 56.
"You." PraS (56:3) Aut 82, p. 72.

1381. FRUMKIN, Gene
"Arbitrary Design." Sulfur (2:3, issue 6) 82, p.
    86.

"Crises." Chelsea (41) 82, p. 97.
"Disquiet of Reason." Chelsea (41) 82, p. 97.
"Elusive." PoNow (6:6, issue 36) 82, p. 28.
"The Explanation." Chelsea (41) 82, p. 96.
"Faith." Chelsea (41) 82, p. 96.
"Following." Chelsea (41) 82, p. 96-97.
"For Those Who Dream of Love." Sulfur (2:3, issue 6) 82, p. 82-83.
"Reject from a Marxist Anthology." Sulfur (2:3, issue 6) 82, p. 83-84.
"The Renaturing Cycle." Sulfur (2:3, issue 6) 82, p. 84-85.
"Script." Sulfur (2:3, issue 6) 82, p. 88-89.
"Something." Sulfur (2:3, issue 6) 82, p. 87.
"The Style." NewL (48:2) Wint 81-82, p. 88.
"The Tape." PoNow (6:4, issue 34) 82, p. 20.
"A Trick of Memory." Chelsea (41) 82, p. 97.
"The Woman." PoNow (6:4, issue 34) 82, p. 20.

1382. FRUTKIN, Mark
    "Hunter." AntigR (51) Aut 82, p. 119.

1383. FRY, Susie
    "After the Thunderstorm." KanQ (14:1) Wint 82, p. 20.
    "The Lover." KanQ (14:1) Wint 82, p. 21.

1384. FUHRINGER, Sandra
    "November's grey dawn." Waves (11:1) Aut 82, p. 77.

1385. FUJIWARA no KACHIOMU
    "The Direction of Autumn" (from the Kokinshu, tr. by Graeme Wilson). WestHR (36:3) Aut 82, p. 264.

1386. FULKER, Tina
    "Call Me Wreckless Too." Vis (9) 82, p. 12.
    "Poem for Dari." Bogg (48) 82, p. 50.

1387. FULLER, Winston
    "Genetics." OhioR (29) 82, p. 102.
    "Reckoning." OhioR (29) 82, p. 102.

1388. FULMER, Patrick
    "Amarume." PortR (28:1) 82, p. 62.
    "Birth of the Demon's Child" (for Jesus Christ, tr. of Murano Shino). PortR (28:1) 82, p. 62.
    "Rainy Season, Song" (tr. of Murano Shino). PortR (28:1) 82, p. 62.
    "A Washbasin" (tr. of Mitsuharu Kaneko PortR (28:1) 82, p. 63.

1389. FULTON, Alice
    "Body-Surfing." AntigR (49) Spr 82, p. 44.
    "The Breakers." AntigR (49) Spr 82, p. 44.
    "Chance Music." Confr (24) Sum 82, p. 88.
    "Second-Sight." PoNow (7:1, issue 37) 82, p. 14.
    "Toward Clairvoyance." PoNow (7:1, issue 37) 82, p. 14.

1390. FULTON, Robin
       "Company" (tr. of Olav Hauge). Stand (23:3) 82, p.
       15.
       "The Grasshopper" (tr. of Werner Aspenstrom). Field
       (26) Spr 82, p. 16.
       "The House Sparrow" (tr. of Werner Aspenstrom).
       Field (26) Spr 82, p. 19.
       "I Pause beneath the Old Oak One Rainy Day" (tr. of
       Olav Hauge). Stand (23:3) 82, p. 14.
       "If There Were Only Two Words" (tr. of Werner
       Aspenstrom). Field (26) Spr 82, p. 21.
       "Many Years' Experience with Bow and Arrow" (tr. of
       Olav Hauge). Stand (23:3) 82, p. 13.
       "New Table-Cloth" (tr. of Olav Hauge). Stand (23:3)
       82, p. 12.
       "Paul Celan" (tr. of Olav Hauge). Stand (23:3) 82,
       p. 13.
       "Portrait" (tr. of Werner Aspenstrom). Field (26)
       Spr 82, p. 17.
       "Shoes Long to be Out" (tr. of Werner Aspenstrom).
       Field (26) Spr 82, p. 20.
       "The Snowflake" (tr. of Werner Aspenstrom). Field
       (26) Spr 82, p. 18.
       "Up through the River Valley" (tr. of Olav Hauge).
       Stand (23:3) 82, p. 14.

1391. FULVIO
       "Poem: Lightning hand fleet foot." CrossC (4:2/3)
       82, p. 37.

1392. FUNGE, Robert
       "The Room in March." MidwQ (23:4) Sum 82, p. 393.
       "Sometimes I Feel Like My Father Looked." MidwQ
       (23:4) Sum 82, p. 395.
       "A Way of Saying." MidwQ (23:4) Sum 82, p. 394.

1393. FUNKHOUSER, Erica
       "December, New England." NewEngR (4:3) Spr 82, p.
       424-425.
       "Earth Day in Provincetown." Poetry (139:4) Ja 82,
       p. 200.
       "For a Man Who Never Dreamed." NewEngR (4:3) Spr
       82, p. 425-426.

1394. FUSSELL, Edwin Sill
       "A Suite of Locals." Maize (6:1/2) Aut-Wint 82-83,
       p. 28-29.

1395. FUTORANSKY, Luisa
       "Viatraux de Exilio." Mairena (4:10) Sum-Aut 82, p.
       70.

1396. GABBARD, G. N.
       "Flowers from Enna." HiramPoR (31) Aut-Wint 82, p.
       25.

1397. GADEA, Gerardo
       "La Escuela antes de la Revolucion." Maize (5:3/4)
       Spr-Sum 82, p. 75.

1398. GAFFNEY, Elizabeth
      "9/1" (for Joe). ColEng 44(7) N 82, p. 717.

1399. GAFFORD, Charlotte
      "Midsummer." SouthernPR (23, i.e. 22:2) Aut 82, p.
      38.

1400. GAIK, Frank
      "In Lafayette, Louisiana to Judge My First High
      School Debate Tournament." SouthernR (18:3) Sum
      82, p. 545-546.
      "The Walls of Connemara." SouthernR (18:3) Sum 82,
      p. 546.

1401. GALASSI, Jonathan
      "Our Wives." Nat (235:17) N 20, 82, p. 526.
      "You're Not a Flash." Ploughs (8:2/3) 82, p. 35.

1402. GALE, Zona
      "Gravel Sunset" (for Anwar Sadat). Vis (10) 82, p.
      12.

1403. GALEF, David
      "Chiaroscuro." DekalbLAJ (14:1/4) Aut 80-Sum 81, p.
      74.

1404. GALEF, Jack
      "Nolan Ryan's 4th No-Hitter." Pig (9) 82, p. 34.

      GALINDO, David Escobar
      See: ESCOBAR GALINDO, David

      GALINDO, Jose Maria Rius
      See: RIUS GALINDO, Jose Maria

1405. GALL, Sally M.
      "Home from the Outer Hebrides." Confr (23) Wint 82,
      p. 144.

1406. GALLAGHER, Brian
      "Just Plane Haiku." WormR (22:3, issue 87) 82,
      p.110-111.
      "To Repeal the Invention of Surgical Necessity."
      WormR (22:3, issue 87) 82, p.110.

1407. GALLAGHER, Tess
      "Death of the Horses by Fire." AmerPoR (11:6) N-D
      82, p. 21.
      "Each Bird Walking." Iowa (12:2/3) Spr-Sum 81, p.
      97-98.
      "The Hug." AmerPoR (11:6) N-D 82, p. 20.
      "Reading Aloud." AmerPoR (11:6) N-D 82, p. 21.
      "Sudden Journey." Atl (250:5) N 82, p. 108.

1408. GALLER, David
      "Rotten Dreams." Confr (24) Sum 82, p. 13.
      "To My Wife." Poetry (140:3) Je 82, p. 144-145.

1409. GALVIN, Brendan
      "Mole." SouthernR (18:3) Sum 82, p. 552.

"An Old One." PraS (56:3) Aut 82, p. 50.
"Old Woman Telling Another Version." GeoR (36:2)
    Sum 82, p. 332-333.
"Pack Ice." SouthernR (18:3) Sum 82, p. 551-552.
"Transmigration." NewYorker (58:24) Ag 2, 82, p.
    34-35.

1410. GALVIN, James
"Anthropology." Field (26) Spr 82, p. 26.
"For the Time Being." AmerPoR (11:2) Mr-Ap 82, p.
    6.
"Fragments Written While Traveling through a
    Midwestern Heat Wave." AmerPoR (11:2) Mr-Ap 82, p.
    6.
"High Plains Rag". AmerPoR (11:2) Mr-Ap 82, p. 6.
"Misericord." Antaeus (47) Aut 82, p. 43.
"A Poem from the Edge of America." MissouriR (6:1)
    Aut 82, p. 9.
"Still Here." MissouriR (6:1) Aut 82, p. 10.
"Three Sonnets." AmerPoR (11:2) Mr-Ap 82, p. 6.
"Virga." MissouriR (6:1) Aut 82, p. 11.

1411. GALVIN, Martin
"Pine Barrens." KanQ (14:3) Sum 82, p. 66.
"Rural Free Delivery." HiramPoR (31) Aut-Wint 82,
    p. 26.

1412. GANT, Shaun
"Bird-Girl in Winter." SoDakR (20:4) Wint 82-83, p.
    57.

1413. GARAY, Mary Sanders
"I Am None of Shakespeare's Women." CEACritic
    (44:3) Mr 82, p. 31.

1414. GARCIA, Dwight
"A Brazilian Catholic Priest's Prayer upon the Death
    of a Young Fighter" (To Rogelio Paulo, tr. of Luis
    Rogelio Nogueras). RevIn (11:2) Sum 81, p. 256.
"Coincidence" (tr. of Luis Rogelio Nogueras). RevIn
    (11:2) Sum 81, p. 254.
"Litany for R. M. V.: The Blood Which Flees Us" (tr.
    of Luis Rogelio Nogueras). RevIn (11:2) Sum 81, p.
    255.
"Monsieur Julian (del Casal)" (tr. of Luis Rogelio
    Nogueras). RevIn (11:2) Sum 81, p. 252.
"Oh, Rains for Whom" (tr. of Luis Rogelio Nogueras).
    RevIn (11:2) Sum 81, p. 253.

GARCIA, Raul Ramirez
See: RAMIREZ GARCIA, Raul

1415. GARCIA ALONSO, Agustin
"A Candelas Ranz Hormazabal." Mairena (4:10) Sum-
    Aut 82, p. 74.
"Meditacion." Mairena (4:10) Sum-Aut 82, p. 74-75.

1416. GARCIA-CAMARILLO, Cecilio
"Chivo." RevChic (10:1/2) Wint-Spr 82, p. 76.

"Compassionate Heart." RevChic (10:1/2) Wint-Spr
     82, p. 75.
"Juvencio." RevChic (10:1/2) Wint-Spr 82, p. 73-74.
"Rancho." RevChic (10:1/2) Wint-Spr 82, p. 74.

1417. GARCIA SARAVI, Gustavo
     "La Gaviota." Mairena (4:10) Sum-Aut 82, p. 57.

1418. GARDELS, Susan
     "Plains Song." Poetry (140:4) Jl 82, p. 201.
     "Warblers at Eve." Poetry (140:4) Jl 82, p. 199-
     200.

1419. GARDNER, John
     "Songs for the End of the World." Paint (7/8:13/16)
     80-81, p. 6-11.

1420. GARDON, Margarita
     "He Venido a Esta Tierra." Mairena (4:10) Sum-Aut
     82, p. 85.

1421. GAREBIAN, Keith
     "For Kath Walker." Grain (10:3) Ag 82, p. 47-48.
     "Illustrated Lady." Grain (10:3) Ag 82, p. 48.
     "A sister, Dying." Grain (10:3) Ag 82, p. 47.

1422. GARGI, Balwant
     "Loona" (A dramatic poem, tr. of Shiv Kumar
     Batalvi). NewL (48:3/4) Spr-Sum 82, p. 164-165.
     "My Village Girl" (tr. of Mohan Singh). NewL
     (48:3/4) Spr-Sum 82, p. 143.

1423. GARLAND, Max
     "Dandelions." Wind (12:44) 82, p. 14.
     "First-Born." SouthernPR (22:1) Spr 82, p. 28-29.
     "The Flooding of Lusk Canyon." Wind (12:44) 82, p.
     13.
     "In Summer." Wind (12:44) 82, p. 14.
     "Remains." Wind (12:44) 82, p. 13.

1424. GARMON, John
     "Grandfathers." SoDakR (20:1) Spr 82, p. 47-48.
     "Growing Older." SoDakR (20:1) Spr 82, p. 48-49.

1425. GARRISON, David
     "The Boundaries" (tr. of Gabriel Celaya). DenQ
     (17:3) Aut 82, p. 23.
     "Every Morning" (tr. of Jose Bergamin). DenQ (17:3)
     Aut 82, p. 24.
     "I Touch in My Heart" (tr. of Jose Bergamin). DenQ
     (17:3) Aut 82, p. 25.
     "Sparrow" (tr. of Claudio Rodriguez). DenQ (17:3)
     Aut 82, p. 46.
     "The Unemployment Office." CapeR (18:1) Wint 82, p.
     15.

1426. GARRISON, Joseph
     "Adjusting the Antenna Mast." KanQ (14:3) Sum 82,
     p. 148-149.
     "Healing by Hand." KanQ (14:3) Sum 82, p. 148.

1427. GARSON, Karl
       "Warning." PoNow (7:1, issue 37) 82, p. 14.
       "Wisconsin February." Northeast (3:14) Wint 82-83,
          p. 10.

1428. GARTNER, Paul
       "Big Top Brand, Little Gavinka, and the Bee
          Threars." Pig (8) 80, p. 16-17.

1429. GARTON, Victoria
       "Dimensions of the Avocado." KanQ (14:1) Wint 82,
          p. 81.
       "I Am the Puzzle of Hollows." KanQ (14:3) Sum 82,
          p. 184.
       "North of Chanute, Kansas." LittleBR (2:2) Wint 81-
          82, p. 30.
       "The Pumpkin Eater's Shut-In." KanQ (14:3) Sum 82,
          p. 185.
       "Rabbit Luck." WebR (7:2) Aut 82, p. 41.

       GASCON, Antonio Ramos
       See: RAMOS-GASCON, Antonio

1430. GASPAR de ALBA, Alice
       "Easter: The Lame Bull." RevChic (10:3) Sum 82, p.
          13.

1431. GASPARINI, Len
       "The Book Reviewer." CanLit (93) Sum 82, p. 59.
       "Hometown." CanLit (94) Aut 82, p. 66.
       "In the Tropics." WestCR (16:4) Ap 82, p. 25.
       "On Dostoevsky's 'Notes from the Underground'."
          CanLit (94) Aut 82, p. 9.

1432. GATES, Edward
       "Baptism." PottPort (4) 82-83, p. 49.
       "Falling." AntigR (49) Spr 82, p. 121.
       "The Moose." PottPort (4) 82-83, p. 52.

1433. GAUER, Jim
       "As Sure As I'm Sitting Here." Iowa (13:1) Wint 82,
          p. 122-123.
       "Lullaby." Iowa (13:1) Wint 82, p. 121.

1434. GAUVREAU, Claude
       from Entrails: "Apolnixede between Heaven and Earth"
          (tr. by Ray Ellenwood). Sulfur (2:3, issue 6) 82,
          p. 95-100.
       from Entrails: "The Shadow on the Hoop" (tr. by Ray
          Ellenwood). Sulfur (2:3, issue 6) 82, p. 102-104.
       from Entrails: "Trustful Fatigue and Reality."
          Sulfur (2:3, issue 6) 82, p. 101.

1435. GAY, Gary
       "Misting." WindO (40, Anti-Haiku issue) Sum 82, p.
          42.
       "Restless the sparrows change trees." WindO (40,
          Anti-Haiku issue) Sum 82, p. 42.
       "Timberline sunset." WindO (40, Anti-Haiku issue)
          Sum 82, p. 42.

"Woodland trail." <u>WindO</u> (40, Anti-Haiku issue) Sum 82, p. 42.

1436. GEARING, Barry Jay
"Baseball and the Business Child." <u>Pig</u> (9) 82, p. 69.

1437. GEBHARD, Christine
"Birthday." <u>GeoR</u> (36:3) Aut 82, p. 618.
"Every Sixty Seconds, the Train Moves Forward." <u>Agni</u> (16) 82, p. 116.
"Last Night." <u>PoetryNW</u> (23:4) Wint 82-83, p. 44.
"To a Suitable Stranger." <u>PoetryNW</u> (23:4) Wint 82-83, p. 44-45.
"To My Reader." <u>PoetryNW</u> (23:4) Wint 82-83, p. 45-46.

1438. GEHRING, Wes
"Comparing Two Clowns: Charlie Chaplin & Peter Sellers." <u>BallSUF</u> (23:2) Spr 82, p. 60-61.

1439. GEIER, Joan Austin
"My Mother's Smile." <u>Vis</u> (10) 82, p. 19.

1440. GEIGER, Geoff
"Brown Bag." <u>Sam</u> (32:3, issue 127) 82, p. 49.
"Nostalgia." <u>Sam</u> (32:3, issue 127) 82, p. 63.

1441. GELETA, Greg
"Enemy Zone." <u>Wind</u> (12:46) 82, p. 12.

1442. GENEGA, Paul
"Descent and Sentiment." <u>Outbr</u> (10/11) Aut 82-Spr 83, p. 11.
"Essay on My Name." <u>CimR</u> (61) O 82, p. 39-40.
"The Rainmaker." <u>Outbr</u> (10/11) Aut 82-Spr 83, p. 9-10.

1443. GENGE, Fred
"Poem for Painting by Rouault." <u>MendoR</u> (5) Sum 81, p. 65.

1444. GENSLER, Kinereth
"Car Country." <u>Ploughs</u> (8:1) 82, p. 158-159.

1445. GENT, Andrew
"Epitaph for Bice Donetti" (after Salvatore Quasimodo). <u>MissouriR</u> (5:3) Sum 82, p. 29.

1446. GENTRY, Jane
"Washing Sheets in July." <u>HolCrit</u> (19:2) Ap 82, p. 19.

1447. GEORGE, Emery
"Admiralty Building" (tr. of Osip Mandelstam). <u>Spirit</u> (6:2/3) 82, p. 39.
"Auden in Old Age" (tr. of Agnes Gergely). <u>PoNow</u> (6:5, issue 35) 82, p. 44.
"Outskirts, Afternoon" (tr. of Judit Toth). <u>PoNow</u> (6:6, issue 36) 82, p. 42.

"Rest on the Flight to Egypt." MichOR (21:1) Wint
82, p. 153.

1448. GEORGE, Stefan
"After the Gleaning" (tr. by Peter Viereck). LitR
(26:1) Aut 82, p. 95.
"Song" (tr. by Peter Viereck). PoNow (6:6, issue 36)
82, p. 43.

1449. GERBASI, Vicente
"Cobre Pulido." BelPoJ (32:4) Sum 82, p. 40.
"Forehead Resting upon the Table" (tr. by Ricardo
Pau-Llosa). BelPoJ (32:4) Sum 82, p. 43.
"Frente Apoyada en la Mesa." BelPoJ (32:4) Sum 82,
p. 42.
"New Day" (tr. by Ricardo Pau-Llosa). BelPoJ (32:4)
Sum 82, p. 43.
"Nuevo Dia." BelPoJ (32:4) Sum 82, p. 42.
"Polished Copper" (tr. by Ricardo Pau-Llosa). BelPoJ
(32:4) Sum 82, p. 41.

1450. GERBER, Dan
"In the Winter Dark." GeoR (36:4) Wint 82, p. 754.

1451. GERBERICK, Marlene Ekola
"The Gossip's Tea Party." KanQ (14:1) Wint 82, p.
31.

1452. GERGELY, Agnes
"Auden in Old Age" (tr. by Emery George). PoNow
(6:5, issue 35) 82, p. 44.

1453. GERLACH, Lee
"After a Long Illness." MichOR (21:1) Wint 82, p.
154.

1454. GERNES, Sonia
"The Mushroom-Eaters." GeoR (36:3) Aut 82, p. 601.
"Rites of Women." BelPoJ (33:1) Aut 82, p. 2-3.

1455. GERRY, David
"Dream: 1953." StoneC (10:1/2) Aut-Wint 82-83, p.
22.

1456. GERSHATOR, Phillis
"Irreversible Damage." Confr (24) Sum 82, p. 122.

1457. GERSHGOREN, Sid
"To Sarah in Your Squirrels's Body." UnderRM 1(1)
Spr 82, p. 21.

1458. GERY, John
"The Game of the Week." Pig (9) 82, p. 17.

1459. GESSWEIN, Alfred
"The Days Count Again" (tr. by Beth Bjorklund). LitR
(25:2) Wint 82, p. 178.
"Watteau's Coloration" (tr. by Beth Bjorklund). LitR
(25:2) Wint 82, p. 177.

1460. GETTY, Sarah
      "Music Cruise." Shen (33:1) 81-82, p. 20-21.

1461. GHIGNA, Charles
      "Bareback City Nights." PoNow (6:4, issue 34) 82,
      p. 29.
      "The Blue Haired Ladies." PoNow (6:4, issue 34) 82,
      p. 29.
      "Gumption." ColEng 44(3) Mr 82, p. 288-289.
      "Home Run Voyeur." Pig (9) 82, p. 21.

1462. GHISELIN, Olive
      "Mazatlan Jungle." Poetry (140:1) Ap 82, p. 12.
      "Sarcophagi." Poetry (140:1) Ap 82, p. 13.

1463. GHITELMAN, David
      "In Early Spring." Agni (17) 82, p. 27-28.
      "Survivors." Agni (17) 82, p. 25-26.

1464. GIAMMATTEO, Hollis
      "Touch Nothing." Nimrod (26:1) Aut-Wint 82, p. 83.

1465. GIBB, Robert
      "Aubade." MissouriR (5:2) Wint 81-82, p. 26-27.
      "The Broadwings." PraS (56:3) Aut 82, p. 52.
      "The Brown Thrasher." PraS (56:3) Aut 82, p. 51.
      "Dove Hunting in Burks County." HiramPoR (31) Aut-
      Wint 82, p. 27.
      "Fathers and Sons." MissouriR (5:2) Wint 81-82, p.
      32-33.
      "Home." MissouriR (5:2) Wint 81-82, p. 28.
      "Seeing Pittsburgh." MissouriR (5:2) Wint 81-82, p.
      29-31.

1466. GIBBONS, Ruark
      "Words to Accompany a Leaf from Sirmione." PoetryNW
      (23:1) Spr 82, p. 13-14.

1467. GIBBS, Jeanne Osborne
      "Ode to the Paper Mite." DekalbLAJ (14:1/4) Aut 80-
      Sum 81, p. 107.
      "Power Failure in Ice Storm." DekalbLAJ (14:1/4)
      Aut 80-Sum 81, p. 108.

1468. GIBBS, Joan
      "Internal Geography -- Part One." Iowa (12:2/3)
      Spr-Sum 81, p. 99-100.

1469. GIBBS, Robert
      "Nocturne." PottPort (4) 82-83, p. 34.
      "Requiem for a Spanner." PottPort (4) 82-83, p. 26.

1470. GIBSON, Morgan
      "Bicycleman and Telegraphman." PoNow (6:6, issue
      36) 82, p. 40.
      "Lazarus." PoNow (6:6, issue 36) 82, p. 40.

1471. GIBSON, Stephen M.
      "Florida Sinkhole,1981." MinnR (NS18) Spr 82, p.
      22.

1472. GIBSON, William
         "Deposition." LittleBR (2:1) Aut 81, p. 19.
         "A Musicbox Clock." LittleBR (2:1) Aut 81, p. 18.
         "Short Story." LittleBR (1:4) Sum 81, p. 19.
         "Stonewall." LittleBR (2:1) Aut 81, p. 17.

1473. GIGUERE, Roland
         "A la Suite." Os (15) 82, p. 2.
         "Nous ne Mourrons Pas." Os (15) 82, p. 5.
         "Vu du Dedans." Os (15) 82, p. 4.

1474. GJELSNESS, Barent
         "Arcanum." Kayak (59) Je 82, p. 58.
         "In the Key of C." Kayak (59) Je 82, p. 59.
         "Mexico City, a Busy Street." Kayak (59) Je 82, p.
         59.
         "Song for Spring." Kayak (60) O 82, p. 68.
         "To Each His Own." Kayak (59) Je 82, p. 58.
         "Two White Snowbirds." PoNow (6:4, issue 34) 82, p.
         31.

1475. GIL de BIEDMA, Jaime
         "De Senectute" (tr. by Anthony Kerrigan). DenQ
         (17:3) Aut 82, p. 83.
         "A Family Chat" (tr. by Anthony Kerrigan). DenQ
         (17:3) Aut 82, p. 84.
         "T'Introduire Dans Mon Histoire" (tr. by Anthony
         Kerrigan). DenQ (17:3) Aut 82, p. 85.

1476. GIL de RUBIO, Victor
         from Decimas Puertorriquenas: (III). Mairena (4:9)
         Spr 82, p. 86.

1477. GILBERT, Celia
         "Narcissi in Winter." Atl (249:1) Ja 82, p. 39.

1478. GILBERT, Christopher
         from Horizontal Cosmology: "5. Speaking Things."
         Nimrod (26:1) Aut-Wint 82, p. 88.
         from Horizontal Cosmology: "6. The Facts." Nimrod
         (26:1) Aut-Wint 82, p. 88-92.

1479. GILBERT, Jack
         "Alone on Christmas Eve in Japan." AmerPoR (11:2)
         Mr-Ap 82, p. 4.
         "Burning and Fathering: Accounts of My Country."
         Nat (234:12) Mr 27, 82, p. 378.
         "Don Giovanni in Trouble." NewYorker (58:2) Mr 1,
         82, p. 44.
         "Farming by Instinct." AmerPoR (11:6) N-D 82, p.
         22.
         "Getting Ready." AmerPoR (11:2) Mr-Ap 82, p. 5.
         "Heart Skidding." AmerPoR (11:2) Mr-Ap 82, p. 5.
         "Leaving Monolithos." AmerPoR (11:2) Mr-Ap 82, p.
         4.
         "The Lord Sits with Me out in Front." AmerPoR
         (11:6) N-D 82, p. 22.
         "Losing." AmerPoR (11:2) Mr-Ap 82, p. 4.
         "Meaning Well." AmerPoR (11:2) Mr-Ap 82, p. 5.
         "More Than Friends." AmerPoR (11:2) Mr-Ap 82, p. 4.

"Night after Night." AmerPoR (11:2) Mr-Ap 82, p. 3.
"Not Part of Literature." AmerPoR (11:2) Mr-Ap 82,
    p. 4.
"Playing House." AmerPoR (11:6) N-D 82, p. 22.
"Prospero Listens to the Night." AmerPoR (11:6) N-D
    82, p. 22.
"Prospero on the Mountain Gathering Wood." AmerPoR
    (11:6) N-D 82, p. 22.
"Registration." AmerPoR (11:2) Mr-Ap 82, p. 4.
"The Revolution." AmerPoR (11:2) Mr-Ap 82, p. 4.
"Siege." Nat (234:12) Mr 27, 82, p. 378.
"Song." AmerPoR (11:2) Mr-Ap 82, p. 5.
"Textures." AmerPoR (11:2) Mr-Ap 82, p. 5.
"They Call It Attempted Suicide." AmerPoR (11:2)
    Mr-Ap 82, p. 4.
"Threshing the Fire." AmerPoR (11:2) Mr-Ap 82, p.
    3.
"Walking Home Across the Island." AmerPoR (11:2)
    Mr-Ap 82, p. 4.

1480. GILBERT, Sandra M.
    "Autumn Song." PoetC (14:2) 82, p. 10.
    "Blood Pressure." Poetry (139:6) Mr 82, p. 339.
    "Easter 1949." PoetC (14:2) 82, p. 9.
    "Eating Your Words." Poetry (139:6) Mr 82, p. 338.
    "Jackson Heights Apartment Kitchen, 1948." PoetC
        (14:2) 82, p. 8.
    "Late Beethoven." AmerS (51:4) Aut 82, p. 508-510.
    "The Love Sequence." Iowa (12:2/3) Spr-Sum 81, p.
        101-108.
    "Sitting" (For Carole Peel). Poetry (139:6) Mr 82,
        p. 336-337.
    "The Wild Grasses." PoetC (14:2) 82, p. 11.

1481. GILBERT, Virginia
    "The Field." PoNow (6:6, issue 36) 82, p. 21.

1482. GILCHRIST, Ellen
    "Clanking to Byzantium" (for Gwen). Iowa (12:2/3)
        Spr-Sum 81, p. 123-124.

1483. GILDZEN, Alex
    "Morning after the Worm Moon." Hangl (43) Wint 82-
        83, p. 30.

1484. GILES, Dolores
    "Etude in Fear Sharp." Wind (12:45) 82, p. 19-20.
    "It Happens Every Twenty Four Hours." Wind (12:45)
        82, p. 19.

1485. GILES, Laurence T.
    "Once Love." Abraxas (25/26) 82, p. 84.

1486. GILL, John
    "The Lover." PoNow (6:5, issue 35) 82, p. 24.
    "Silence." PoNow (6:5, issue 35) 82, p. 24.
    "There's a Song in His Throat, Buried." PoNow (6:5,
        issue 35) 82, p. 24.

1487. GILL, Stephen
      "Ask Me Not What Is Love." WritersL O-N 82, p. 33.
      "Dreams for Sale." WritersL Jl 82, p. 8.
      "If There Is a Third World War." WritersL S 82, p.
         20.
      "Let Us Hibernate." WritersL Jl 82, p. 8.
      "A Strange Request." WritersL Je 82, p. 10.
      "To Mother." WritersL Je 82, p. 15.
      "To War-Mongers." WritersL D 82, p. 26.
      "War Is Fraud." WritersL D 82, p. 26.
      "Where Love Resides?" WritersL O-N 82, p. 32.

1488. GILLETTE, Richard
      "The jewels of life." MendoR (6) Sum 81, p. 32.

1489. GILLILAN, Pamela
      "Daphne Morse." Stand (23:4) 82, p. 64.

1490. GIMENEZ SALDIVIA, Lulu
      "Escritura." Prismal (7/8) Spr 82, p. 80.
      "No Tengo la Luna Hoy." Prismal (7/8) Spr 82, p.
         81-82.

1491. GINSBERG, Allen
      "Verses Written for Student Anti Draft-Registration
         Rally 1980." Shout (3:1) 82, p. 70.

1492. GIOIA, Dana
      "Bix Beiderbecke (1903-1931)" (January, 1926). OntR
         (17) Aut-Wint 82, p. 79.
      "California Hills in August." NewYorker (58:25) Ag
         9, 82, p. 30.
      "Daily Horoscope." Hudson (35:2) Sum 82, p. 221-
         224.
      "Insomnia." OntR (17) Aut-Wint 82, p. 78.
      "The Journey, the Arrival, and the Dream" (The Tyrol
         above Merano). Poetry (141:3) D 82, p. 142-144.
      "Mottetti XVII" (tr. of Eugenio Montale). Field (27)
         Aut 82, p. 23.
      "My Secret Life." Poetry (139:4) Ja 82, p. 203-205.

1493. GIROUX, Robert
      "Le Soleil Ebloui." Os (15) 82, p. 30.

1494. GIRRI, Alberto
      "Alfombra Como Lirica." BelPoJ (32:4) Sum 82, p. 2,
         4.
      "Rug As Lyric" (tr. by Ricardo Pau-Llosa). BelPoJ
         (32:4) Sum 82, p. 3, 5.

1495. GITTINGS, Robert
      "Gilbert White at Selborne." Stand (23:4) 82, p. 6.

1496. GLADDING, Jody
      "Letter to Michael from New York." Epoch (31:3) Sum
         82, p. 198-199.

1497. GLANCY, Diane
      "Great Bend, Kansas." EnPas (13) 82, p. 9.

"Museum of the American Indian, New York City."
Nimrod (25:2) Spr-Sum 82, p. 11.

1498. GLASER, Elton
"Breastplate" (tr. of Joyce Mansour, w. Janice
Fritsch). CharR (8:2) Aut 82, p. 44.
"Circus Master." Ploughs (8:1) 82, p. 85.
"Elegy for Professor Longhair." CutB (19) Aut-Wint
82, p. 57.
"Festive Songs on Lesser Occasions." PoetryNW
(23:3) Aut 82, p. 25.
"I've Gone Deep into." (tr. of Joyce Mansour, w.
Janice Fritsch). CharR (8:2) Aut 82, p. 43.
"March." Ploughs (8:1) 82, p. 82.
"Mosquito Hawks." Ploughs (8:1) 82, p. 83-84.
"Sunday Evenings with Calvin Coolidge." PoNow (6:6,
issue 36) 82, p. 13.
"You Don't Know My Night-Face" (tr. of Joyce
Mansour, w. Janice Fritsch). CharR (8:2) Aut 82,
p. 43.

1499. GLASOV, Marina
"127. Why am I again on the same circuit?" (tr. by
John Barnstead). Germ (6:1) Spr-Sum 82, p. 31.

1500. GLASS, Malcolm
"Carpentry." NewL (49:2) Wint 82-83, p. 68.
"Goodwill." NewL (49:2) Wint 82-83, p. 69.
"Ice" (for my father, from Bone Love). Vis (8) 82,
p. 7.
"In the Mirror." StoneC (9:3/4) Spr-Sum 82, p. 37.
"Mowing" (from Bone Love). Vis (9) 82, p. 21.
"P-38 `Lightning'." PoNow (6:4, issue 34) 82, p.
27.
"Roller Coaster." Catalyst (Erotica Issue) 82, p.
10.
"Sixth Grade." PoNow (6:4, issue 34) 82, p. 27.

1501. GLAZE, Andrew
"Delmore." PoNow (6:4, issue 34) 82, p. 5.
"Doubleknit Socks." PoNow (6:4, issue 34) 82, p. 5.
"Getting Old." PoNow (6:6, issue 36) 82, p. 45.
"Islands among Us." QP (33) Spr 82, p. 11.
"Night Walk to a Country Theatre." NewYorker
(57:49) Ja 25, 82, p. 40.
"Notes." QP (33) Spr 82, p. 15.
"Patsy." SouthernPR (23, i.e. 22:2) Aut 82, p. 25.
"To a Han Horse." QP (33) Spr 82, p. 14.
"Wink." QP (33) Spr 82, p. 12-13.

1502. GLEB, Thomas
"I was born without a name" (tr. by Martin Zeidner).
PortR (28:2) 82, p. 42-44.

1503. GLEN, Emilie
"Nickname." Wind (12:45) 82, p. 17.
"Poinsettia at Four Above." StoneC (10:1/2) Aut-
Wint 82-83, p. 21.
"Rose Guard." Wind (12:45) 82, p. 17.
"Sadly Out Over." Spirit (6:2/3) 82, p. 98.

"Undisclosed Date in Summer." StoneC (10:1/2) Aut-
Wint 82-83, p. 21.

1504. GLENN, Laura
"Halloween Is a Drag." Chelsea (41) 82, p. 165.
"Impatience." Epoch (32:1) Aut 82, p. 41.
"Verisimilitude." Chelsea (41) 82, p. 164.

1505. GLICKMAN, Susan
"Complicity." Hangl (43) Wint 82-83, p. 62-65.
"The Sadness of Mothers." Hangl (43) Wint 82-83, p.
66.

1506. GLOTZER, David
"Ergo, Home at Last" (for Sukey). SeC (9:1/2) 80, p.
20.
"If I Didn't Love You, You Couldn't Leave Me" (For
V.). SeC (9:1/2) 80, p. 21.
"Mother's Day." SeC (9:1/2) 80, p. 16.

1507. GLOVER, Jon
"The Wall and the Candle." Stand (23:2) 82, p. 42.

1508. GLOWNEY, John
"On a Country Road After Midnight: a Rabbit in My
Headlights." PoetryNW (23:3) Aut 82, p. 40.
"Two Stanzas from November." Northeast (3:14) Wint
82-83, p. 9.

1509. GLUSKER, Peter
"Birth of a Moment" (The Time-Space Cliff, for
Robert Bly). MendoR (6) Sum 81, p. 23.

1510. GOAD, Craig M.
"Setting Off." KanQ (14:3) Sum 82, p. 67.

1511. GOEBEL, Ulf
"Drift of Speech." Agni (17) 82, p. 131.

1512. GOEDICKE, Patricia
"Across the Water." PoetryNW (23:3) Aut 82, p. 37-
39.
"After the First Embrace." NewL (49:1) Aut 82, p.
54-55.
"El Dorado." NewEngR (4:4) Sum 82, p. 570-572.
"Green Harbor." PoetryNW (23:3) Aut 82, p. 34-36.
"In the Aquarium." NewYorker (58:26) Ag 16, 82, p.
34.
"In the Middle of the Worst Sickness." Ploughs
(8:2/3) 82, p. 147-150.
"Letter from D. S." NowestR (20:2/3) 82, p. 254-
255.
"The Moving Van." NewL (48:2) Wint 81-82, p. 86-87.
"This Man (Who Wants to Forget the Nightmare)."
PoetryNW (23:3) Aut 82, p. 36-37.
"Whether a Bright Stranger." AmerPoR (11:2) Mr-Ap
82, p. 35.

1513. GOETHE, Johann Wolfgang von
      "Traver's Evening Song II" (tr. by Nathaniel B.
      Smith). Paint (7/8:13/16) 80-81, p. 40.

      GOGISGI
      See: ARNETT, Carroll

1514. GOINGS, Margaret
      "Progress." Sam (32:3, issue 127) 82, p. 64.

1515. GOJMERAC-LEINER, Georgia
      "Of Soap." VirQR (58:1) Wint 82, p. 56-57.
      "On the Other Side of the Ocean." VirQR (58:1) Wint
      82, p. 56.

1516. GOLAS, Irene
      "Scavenger." Germ (6:1) Spr-Sum 82, p. 39.

1517. GOLD, Edward
      "Une Femme Comique." Gargoyle (17/18) 81, p. 14.

1518. GOLD, Herman
      "Sol and Beatrice." PoNow (6:4, issue 34) 82, p.
      12.
      "Solomon and David." PoNow (6:4, issue 34) 82, p.
      12.

1519. GOLDBARTH, Albert
      "8 Hrs." Kayak (60) O 82, p. 44.
      "The Accountings." OntR (16) Spr-Sum 82, p. 42-43.
      "After Reading Basho and Company I Enter the Comic
      Book Store." SouthernPR (23, i.e. 22:2) Aut 82, p.
      44-45.
      "After the Wreck." Salm (56) Spr 82, p. 135-136.
      "Ambassador." Agni (16) 82, p. 61-62.
      "Anybody's Poem." NoAmR (267:2) Je 82, p. 7.
      "Blame and Maybe Exorcise." DenQ (17:1) Spr 82, p.
      14-15.
      "A Corner." CarolQ (34:3) Spr 82, p. 21.
      "Edgewater Hospital." Poetry (140:1) Ap 82, p. 5.
      "The Faces." AntR (40:4) Aut 82, p. 432.
      "A Film." Poetry (141:2) N 82, p. 97-98.
      "Getting Ugly." PraS (56:2) Sum 82, p. 21-28.
      "Grandma's." Confr (23) Wint 82, p. 80.
      "Halos." AmerPoR (11:6) N-D 82, p. 23.
      "He Is Convinced That" MissouriR (5:3) Sum 82, p.
      10-11.
      "Houdin." Kayak (60) O 82, p. 45.
      "The Hum." GeoR (36:3) Aut 82, p. 556.
      "The Importance of Artists' Biographies." Poetry
      (141:2) N 82, p. 91-96.
      "In Pain." OntR (16) Spr-Sum 82, p. 44.
      "Incomplete." PoetryNW (23:3) Aut 82, p. 21-23.
      "Legends." OntR (16) Spr-Sum 82, p. 35-44.
      "Lepidoptera Etc." Salm (56) Spr 82, p. 137-138.
      "M = L/T." OntR (16) Spr-Sum 82, p. 39-40.
      "Mist." CharR (8:1) Spr 82, p. 31.
      "Musics and Vegetables." CharR (8:1) Spr 82, p. 31-
      32.
      "Off." SouthernPR (22:1) Spr 82, p. 8-9.

"On a Quiet Street." AmerS (51:4) Aut 82, p. 533-
    534.
"One Story." CarolQ (34:3) Spr 82, p. 18-20.
"Oxidation ,--> Reduction." PoetryNW (23:3) Aut 82,
    p. 20-21.
"Praise / Complaint." NewEngR (5:1/2) Aut-Wint 82,
    p. 88-89.
"Reel Estate." Poetry (140:1) Ap 82, p. 4.
"The Relative Proportions of." AmerPoR (11:6) N-D
    82, p. 23.
"Return to the World." PoetryNW (23:1) Spr 82, p.
    46-47.
"A Sanguinary." BelPoJ (33:1) Aut 82, p. 20-36.
"Sitting in the Margin." Poetry (140:1) Ap 82, p.
    3.
"The Song of: England/China/Austin, Texas" (May 17,
    1980). Pequod (15) 82, p. 49-53.
"Sorry, It Just Won't Work Out -- Goodbye." OntR
    (16) Spr-Sum 82, p. 41.
"Stretch." MissouriR (5:3) Sum 82, p. 8-9.
"A Theory of Wind." Poetry (141:2) N 82, p. 99-100.
"There Is a Legend about a Piano That Somehow Got
    Flushed into the Sewers of Chicago." OntR (16)
    Spr-Sum 82, p. 36-38.
"Toward a Texas Haiku." Agni (16) 82, p. 60.
"The Well" (A poem about Edward Hicks with a quote
    about Millet). Poetry (141:2) N 82, p. 101-104.
"Whelp." PoetryNW (23:1) Spr 82, p. 45-46.
"Which Everybody." CharR (8:1) Spr 82, p. 30.
"The World of Expectations." NewEngR (5:1/2) Aut-
    Wint 82, p. 87.
"Worlds." Poetry (140:1) Ap 82, p. 1-2.

1520. GOLDBERG, Barbara
    "Ghazal: Low Down on the Food Chain." Bogg (48) 82,
        p. 15.
    from Writings from the Quattrocento: "Journal
        Entry, All Saints' Day, 1427." Nimrod (25:2) Spr-
        Sum 82, p. 50-51.

1521. GOLDBERG, Beckian Fritz
    "Cranes." SenR (13:1) 82-83, p. 71-72.
    "Trajectory" (For Thomas James). SenR (13:1) 82-83,
        p. 73-74.

1522. GOLDEN, Doug
    "Barn Building." Poem (44) Mr 82, p. 9.
    "Movement in a Field." Poem (44) Mr 82, p. 10.

1523. GOLDEN, Gail
    "Waiting for Jacob" (Genesis 29:18). Vis (8) 82, p.
        36-37.

1524. GOLDEN, John J.
    "Mens Sana." Comm (109:5) Mr 12, 82, p. 158.

1525. GOLDENSOHN, Barry
    "Misalliance Committee Report." Salm (56) Spr 82,
        p. 133.

1526. GOLDENSOHN, Lorrie
      "Clytie." NoAmR (267:3) S 82,p. 74.
      "The Disappearance: Argentina, 1979" (for Dr. Laura
         Bonaparte). NewL (48:2) Wint 81-82, p. 42-43.
      "The Survivor." NoAmR (267:3) S 82,p. 75.

1527. GOLDMAN, Mark
      "Bright Morning at the Tennis Court." KanQ (14:3)
         Sum 82, p. 117.

1528. GOLDSTEIN, Laurence
      "The Three Musketeers, Illustrated Edition."
         SouthernR (18:1) Wint 82, p. 166-168.

1529. GOLEMBIEWSKI, Alison
      "The Moral Code of Athens." PoetryNW (23:1) Spr 82,
         p. 6-7.
      "The Plantation Mistress." AmerPoR (11:4) Jl-Ag 82,
         p. 30.
      "Woman Trapped in Burning Building." AmerPoR (11:4)
         Jl-Ag 82, p. 30.

1530. GOLFFING, Francis
      "Into all sceneries" (tr. of Georg Heym). PoNow
         (6:5, issue 35) 82, p. 42.
      "Missed Opportunities for Dying" (tr. of Peter
         Handke). PoNow (6:4, issue 34) 82, p. 40.
      "The Railway Station" (tr. of Leon-Paul Fargue).
         EnPas (13) 82, p. 4-6.
      "Sleep" (tr. of Georg Trakl). PoNow (6:6, issue 36)
         82, p. 43.
      "The Sun" (tr. of Georg Trakl). PoNow (6:6, issue
         36) 82, p. 43.

1531. GOLL, Yvan
      "Morgue" (tr. by Paul Morris). Pequod (15) 82, p.
         57.

1532. GOM, Leona
      "All." PoetryCR (4:1) Sum 82, p. 7.
      "Candid Shot." WestCR (17:1) Je 82, p. 26.
      "Hotel Dieu." PoetryCR (4:2) Wint 82, p. 11.
      "I Love Money." WestCR (17:1) Je 82, p. 25.
      "Nostalgia." WestCR (17:1) Je 82, p. 26.

1533. GOMES, Olivinho
      "The Wound" (tr. of Madhav Borkar). NewL (48:3/4)
         Spr-Sum 82, p. 89.

1534. GOMEZ-CORREA, Enrique
      "La Pareja Real." BelPoJ (32:4) Sum 82, p. 10, 12.
      "The Royal Couple" (tr. by Ricardo Pau-Llosa).
         BelPoJ (32:4) Sum 82, p. 11, 13.

1535. GOMEZ LANCE, Betty Rita
      "No Se Le Puede Dejar Morir." LetFem (8:2) 82, p.
         81.
      "Un Rio de Tinta." LetFem (8:2) 82, p. 80.

1536. GOMEZ PINEDA, Victor Manuel
      "Rosa Argentina Montes." Maize (5:3/4) Spr-Sum 82,
      p. 74.

1537. GONG, Zizhen
      "Poem #123 (1839)" (tr. by Zuxin Ding and Burton
      Raffel). DenQ (17:2) Sum 82, p. 96.

1538. GONZALEZ, Angel
      "Counter-Order (Poetics I favor on Certain Days)"
      (tr. by Anthony Kerrigan). DenQ (17:3) Aut 82, p.
      34.
      "Four Sides to Every Issue" (tr. by Anthony
      Kerrigan). DenQ (17:3) Aut 82, p. 32-35.
      "Order (The Poetics to Which Others Apply
      Themselves)" (tr. by Anthony Kerrigan). DenQ
      (17:3) Aut 82, p. 33.
      "Poetics (To Which I Sometimes Apply Myself)" (tr.
      by Anthony Kerrigan). DenQ (17:3) Aut 82, p. 32.
      "Poetics No. 4" (tr. by Anthony Kerrigan). DenQ
      (17:3) Aut 82, p. 35.

      GONZALEZ, Francisco Jose Ramos
      See: RAMOS-GONZALEZ, Francisco Jose

1539. GONZALEZ, Jose Emilio
      "A Francisco Matos Paoli en la Prision: Genio
      Inmortal de la Poesia Puertorriquena." Mairena
      (4:11/12) Wint 82, p. 146.

1540. GONZALEZ BIGAS, Guelcia M.
      "Voz Mia" (from Voces de Mi Silencio). Mairena (4:9)
      Spr 82, p. 86.

1541. GONZALEZ CRUZ, Luis
      "Al Regreso" (from Disgregaciones). Mairena (4:10)
      Sum-Aut 82, p. 38.
      "Nueva Perdida" (from Disgregaciones). Mairena
      (4:10) Sum-Aut 82, p. 39.

1542. GONZALEZ VEGA de MOLINA, Mercedes
      from Con o Sin Nombre: (I, VII). Mairena (4:9) Spr
      82, p. 87.

1543. GOOD, Ruth
      "Relativity." SouthernPR (22:1) Spr 82, p. 62-63.

1544. GOODENOUGH, J. B. (Judith B.)
      "After Bright Rain." Ascent (7:2) 82, p. 30-31.
      "Among Vines." EnPas (13) 82, p. 20.
      "Ball." LitR (26:1) Aut 82, p. 123.
      "Birthing." Confr (24) Sum 82, p. 105.
      "Children at Full Moon." WestB (10) 82, p. 49.
      "Curing." Ascent (7:2) 82, p. 30.
      "Dead Letters." HolCrit (19:4) O 82, p. 18.
      "Disciple." CentR (26:4) Aut 82, p. 356.
      "Dream Circus in Rain." HiramPoR (32) Spr-Sum 82,
      p. 24.
      "The Gates of the Town." PortR (28:2) 82, p. 49.
      "Grandmothers." CapeR (18:1) Wint 82, p. 6.

"In the Wood." FourQt (31:3) Spr 82, p. 9.
"In This Town." CapeR (18:1) Wint 82, p. 7.
"Planting." SmPd (19:1, issue 54) Wint 82, p. 23.
"Steps of the Church." CentR (26:4) Aut 82, p. 356-
357.
"Summer in the Evening." HiramPoR (31) Aut-Wint 82,
p. 28.
"Terms." Northeast (3:12) Wint 81-82, p. 3.
"This Woman Your Wife." SmPd (19:1, issue 54) Wint
82, p. 22.
"Walking with Shadows." CapeR (18:1) Wint 82, p. 5.

1545. GOODMAN, Alice
"The Chemical Blonde." Poetry (139:5) F 82, p. 251-
257.

1546. GOODMAN, Jeffrey
"Demonology" (for Helen Trimpi). SouthernR (18:2)
Spr 82, p. 397.
"On a Skull" (Museum of Natural History, Denver).
SouthernR (18:2) Spr 82, p. 396.
"Three Epigrams." SouthernR (18:2) Spr 82, p. 395-
396.

1547. GOODMAN, Mark D.
"3 Visions of a Night in July." Pig (9) 82, p. 18.

1548. GOODMAN, Michael
"Deja Vu." MendoR (5) Sum 81, p. 57.
"I sit, poet in the breeze." MendoR (5) Sum 81, p.
58.
"In Flight." MendoR (5) Sum 81, p. 58.
"Of Love and Loving." MendoR (5) Sum 81, p. 58-59.

1549. GOODMAN, Miriam
"Coming to Chicago." Tendril (13) Sum 82, p. 30-31.
"Longing." Tendril (13) Sum 82, p. 29.

1550. GORCZYNSKI, Renata
"Separate Notebooks: A Mirrored Gallery" (tr. of
Czeslaw Milosz w. Robert Hass). Antaeus (47) Aut
82, p. 7-15.

1551. GORDON, Guanetta
"The Heart's Choice." LittleBR (1:3) Spr 81, p. 50.

1552. GORDON, Jack
"The Bridge Reverberates Each Step We Take" (tr. by
Aaron Kramer). NewEngR (4:4) Sum 82, p. 556.

1553. GORDON, Kirpal
"Breaking the Face of Extinction" (for Lonnie
Landrum, prisoner). Wind (12:46) 82, p. 15-16.

1554. GORHAM, Sarah
"The Changeling" (For Beckie). PoNow (7:1, issue 37)
82, p. 15.
"In the Vestibule." Paint (9:17/18) Spr-Aut 82, p.
13.

"Portrait in Blue: A Family Death, 1910." PoNow
(7:1, issue 37) 82, p. 15.

1555. GORLIN, Debra
"California." NewEngR (4:4) Sum 82, p. 573.

1556. GORMLEY, Gregg J.
"Farming with Boustrophedon." Poetry (139:5) F 82,
p. 276-277.

1557. GOSSETT, Hattie
"Dakar/Samba." Cond (8) 82, p. 22-26.
"On the Question of Fans/the Slave Quarters Are
Never Air Conditioned." Cond (8) 82, p. 19-21.

1558. GOTRO, Paul Edmund
"Absence: The Living Room." Quarry (31:4) Aut 82,
p. 47.
"On Beaches." Quarry (31:4) Aut 82, p. 48-49.
"The Only Man Alive." Quarry (31:4) Aut 82, p. 48.
"Taking the Evening" (for Rex). PoetryCR (3:4) Sum
82, p. 15.

1559. GOTTLIEB, Bonnie
"Butterfly." Outbr (10/11) Aut 82-Spr 83, p. 85-86.
"A Sonnet from the New Yorkese." Outbr (10/11) Aut
82-Spr 83, p. 84.
"To Know a Leaf." Outbr (10/11) Aut 82-Spr 83, p.
87.

1560. GOTTLIEB, Elaine
"Elegy." PoetryNW (23:4) Wint 82-83, p. 47.

1561. GOUMAS, Yannis
"If I am Elected, When I am Elected." MalR (61) F
82, p. 14-15.

1562. GOWAN, Lee
"Under the Road." Grain (10:2) My 82, p. 50.

1563. GRABILL, James
"Night Work." NewL (49:2) Wint 82-83, p. 71.
"Tomato Season." NewL (49:2) Wint 82-83, p. 71-72.

GRACE, Lois Mathieu
See: MATHIEU-GRACE, Lois

1564. GRACIA de CRIADO, Yolanda
"El Sueno de Mis Hijos." Mairena (4:9) Spr 82, p.
42.

1565. GRAFT, Guillaume van der
"While Writing" (tr. by John Stevens Wade). WebR
(7:1) Spr 82, p. 38.

1566. GRAHAM, Allan
"The Textbook Pine." PottPort (4) 82-83, p. 40.

1567. GRAHAM, Chael
"Roads." PoNow (7:1, issue 37) 82, p. 15.

"Zanesville Still Life." PoNow (7:1, issue 37) 82, p. 15.

1568. GRAHAM, David
"Paul Celan." Iowa (12:4) Aut 81, p. 62.
"Worcester, Next Nine Exits." Iowa (12:4) Aut 81, p. 61.

1569. GRAHAM, Jorie
"At the Exhumed Body of Santa Chiara, Assisi." NewEngR (5:1/2) Aut-Wint 82, p. 14-15.
"Daily." BlackWR (7:2) Spr 81, p. 11-12.
"Erosion." Agni (17) 82, p. 173-175.
"Game." BlackWR (7:2) Spr 81, p. 15-16.
"In What Manner the Body Is United with the Soule." AmerPoR (11:4) Jl-Ag 82, p. 18.
"Masaccio's Expulsion." Antaeus (47) Aut 82, p. 79-82,.
"Mother in Daylight." BlackWR (7:2) Spr 81, p. 13-14.
"Of Unevenness." Pequod (14) 82, p.34-35.
"On Form for Berryman" (January 7, 1982). NewEngR (5:1/2) Aut-Wint 82, p. 13-14.
"Reading Plato." AmerPoR (11:4) Jl-Ag 82, p. 19.
"Salmon." MissouriR (6:1) Aut 82, p. 18-19.
"Scirocco." Antaeus (47) Aut 82, p. 83-86.
"The Sense of an Ending" (for Jim). AmerPoR (11:6) N-D 82, p. 24-25.
"Still Life with Fish and Window." Pequod (14) 82, p. 32-33.
"Tapestry." AmerPoR (11:4) Jl-Ag 82, p. 19.
"To a Friend Going Blind." Iowa (12:2/3) Spr-Sum 81, p. 125-126.

1570. GRAHAM, Matthew
"To a Friend Killed in the Fighting." AntR (40:2) Spr 82, p. 174-175.

1571. GRAHAM, Neile
"Cassandra." AntigR (51) Aut 82, p. 17.
"Heart of Stone." CutB (19) Aut-Wint 82, p. 38-40.
"The Man's Dark Voice." Dandel (9:2) 82, p. 43-44.
"Photograph." AntigR (51) Aut 82, p. 18.
"The Seasons Break Their Shapes." MalR (61) F 82, p. 185-186.
"Sky Dark, Cloudless and Starless." MalR (61) F 82, p. 183-184.
"St. Maudlin (La Folle)." MalR (61) F 82, p. 186-187.

1572. GRAHN, Judy
"I, Boudica." Iowa (12:2/3) Spr-Sum 81, p. 127-131.

1573. GRAPENTINE, Rachel
"Thomas Lake." HiramPoR (32) Spr-Sum 82, p. 25.

1574. GRASS, Gunter
"Saturn" (tr. by Steven Polgar and Nicholas Kolumban). AmerPoR (11:1) Ja-F 82, p. 31.

GRAVELLES, Charles de
     See: DeGRAVELLES, Charles

1575. GRAVES, Michael
     "Aubade." HolCrit (19:2) Ap 82, p. 12.

1576. GRAVES, Tom
     "Who Knows Better." WritersL D 82, p. 18.

1577. GRAY, Cecile
     "My Father's Woods." HiramPoR (31) Aut-Wint 82, p.
     29.

1578. GRAY, Darrell
     "An Old Southern Critic Takes a Look at My Poems."
     Spirit (6:2/3) 82, p. 77-78.

     GRAY, Dorothy Foltz
     See: FOLTZ-GRAY, Dorothy

1579. GRAY, John
     "Morning As It Waits." Pig (8) 80, p. 87.
     "Out Back, in Their Eyes." Pig (8) 80, p. 89.

1580. GRAY, Mary Holstine
     "A Fisherwoman's Tale." LittleBR (1:4) Sum 81, p.
     57-58.

1581. GRAY, Patrick Worth
     "Child Bride." SouthernHR (16:1) Wint 82, p. 13.
     "Depths." Nimrod (25:2) Spr-Sum 82, p. 22.
     "House above the Sea." MalR (63) O 82, p. 205.
     "Jungle." Poem (46) N 82, p. 10-11.
     "Moving Day." CapeR (17:2) Sum 82, p. 4.
     "Omaha" (for Jim Evans). KanQ (14:3) Sum 82, p. 159.
     "Puzzle." ConcPo (15:2) Aut 82, p. 56-57.
     "Searching for the Captain." CapeR (17:2) Sum 82,
     p. 5.
     "Vanishing Point." SouthwR (67:4) Aut 82, p. 428-
     429.

1582. GRAYWOOD, John
     "Death Is a Lady." Paint (9:17/18) Spr-Aut 82, p.
     16.
     "The Disappearing Rainbow." Paint (9:17/18) Spr-Aut
     82, p. 17.

1583. GRAZIANO, Frank
     "After the Lecture on Dionysus of Paris." CharR
     (8:1) Spr 82, p. 48.

1584. GREEN, George Dawes
     "But Not Yet." CarolQ (35:1) Aut 82, p. 74-75.

1585. GREEN, Jessie Lee
     "In a garden row" (Haiku). LittleBR (1:3) Spr 81,
     p. 55.

1586. GREENBERG, Alvin
      "Another Poem that Returns Him to His Beginnings."
      GeoR (36:2) Sum 82, p. 354.
      "Poem with Nothing in It." UnderRM 1(1) Spr 82, p.
      26.
      "Postcard." UnderRM 1(1) Spr 82, p. 25.

1587. GREENE, Johnathan
      "Back." Sulfur (2:1, issue 4) 82, p. 50.
      "Concert." Sulfur (2:1, issue 4) 82, p. 51.
      "History of the Great Poem." Sulfur (2:1, issue 4)
      82, p. 52-53.

1588. GREENLEAF, Cynthia
      "Legacy." Maize (5:3/4) Spr-Sum 82, p. 81-84.

1589. GREGER, Debora
      "A Corner for Breughel." GeoR (36:4) Wint 82, p.
      732.
      "The Shallows." Iowa (12:2/3) Spr-Sum 81, p. 133.
      "Well Enough Alone." Iowa (12:2/3) Spr-Sum 81, p.
      132.

1590. GREGERSON, Linda
      "De Arte Honeste Amandi." Iowa (12:2/3) Spr-Sum 81,
      p. 134-136.
      "Ex Machina." NewEngR (4:4) Sum 82, p. 594.
      "Goering at Nuremberg." Antaeus (47) Aut 82, p. 87-
      88.
      "Maudlin, or, The Magdalen's Tears." Antaeus (47)
      Aut 82, p. 89-90.
      "Russia, Morocco, Peru." PoNow (7:1, issue 37) 82,
      p. 23.
      "Wife." PoNow (7:1, issue 37) 82, p. 23.

1591. GREGG, Linda
      "After What Came After Ended." Ploughs (8:2/3) 82,
      p. 137.
      "Four Photographs for a Quarter." Pequod (15) 82,
      p. 54.
      "The Ghosts Poem." AmerPoR (11:5) S-O 82, p. 19-20.
      "Knowing Our Bodies Wear Out." Pequod (15) 82, p.
      56.
      "Maybe." Pequod (15) 82, p. 55.
      "Trying to Believe." Ploughs (8:2/3) 82, p. 136.
      "Without Design All Beauty Melts Away." Ploughs
      (8:2/3) 82, p. 137.

1592. GREGG, Rosalind J.
      "The Clematis, Clinging to Life." WritersL Ag 82,
      p. 4.

1593. GREGORY, Carole E.
      "A Letter from Home." Obs (7:2/3) Sum-Wint 81, p.
      219.
      "Lotus Women." Obs (7:2/3) Sum-Wint 81, p. 220.
      "Singing Exercise in the U.S. Army." Obs (7:2/3)
      Sum-Wint 81, p. 219.
      "A Vacation." Obs (7:2/3) Sum-Wint 81, p. 221.

"Writers and Lovers." Obs (7:2/3) Sum-Wint 81, p.
220.

1594. GREGORY, Carolyn Holmes
"Cowgirl Moving On." PikeF (4) Spr 82, p. 11.
"The Depression" (After Edward Steichen). Sky (10-
12) Aut 82, p. 55.
"Eclipse" (for Bill Costley). AmerPoR (11:3) My-Je
82, p. 16.
"Painting the House." AmerPoR (11:3) My-Je 82, p.
16.
"Travellers" (For Thomas Ward Miller). Sky (10-12)
Aut 82, p. 56.

1595. GREGORY, Robert
"Sermon with a Mobile Letter R." ModernPS (11:1/2)
82, p. 35.
"Souvenir." ModernPS (11:1/2) 82, p. 33.
"A Typological Difficulty." ModernPS (11:1/2) 82,
p. 33-34.
"Walking Home by the Side of the Road." ModernPS
(11:1/2) 82, p. 34.

1596. GREY, Lucinda
"Clinch River Pearls." Poem (44) Mr 82, p. 41.
"Seed." Poem (44) Mr 82, p. 42.
"Settling for Less." SouthernPR (22:1) Spr 82, p.
44.

1597. GRIECO, Joseph
"Churchill Downs Touts." MissR (10:3, issue 30)
Wint-Spr 82, p. 42.
"Instructions at Sea." MissR (10:3, issue 30) Wint-
Spr 82, p. 43.

1598. GRIEG, Andrew
"Exiles." AntigR (50) Sum 82, p. 121.
"In the Tool-Shed." AntigR (50) Sum 82, p. 120.

1599. GRIER, Eldon
"Charcoal and Acrylic on Hornby Island by Jack
Shadbolt." PoetryCR (4:2) Wint 82, p. 12.

1600. GRIFFITH, Benjy
"Landslide." FourQt (32:1) Aut 82, p. 12.

1601. GRIFFITH, E. V.
"Hart Crane: 1899-1932." PoNow (6:5, issue 35) 82,
p. 33.

1602. GRIM, Scott R.
"The palms of your hand." MendoR (6) Sum 81, p.
169.
"Self-Portrait." MendoR (6) Sum 81, p. 24.
"When you looked me in the eyes." MendoR (6) Sum
81, p. 169.

1603. GRIMES, Michael
"An Endorsement for Pudding." Spirit (6:2/3) 82, p.
52-53.

1604. GRIMSON, Todd
      "Dazzling of the Splash." PortR (28:2) 82, p. 50-
      55.

1605. GRIMSSON, Stefan Hordur
      "The Car That Brakes by the Glade" (tr. by Alan
      Boucher). Vis (8) 82, p. 12.

1606. GRINDAL, Gracia
      "The Christian Religion Is the Most Physical of
      Religions." ChrC (99:29) S 29, 82, p. 948.

1607. GRINDE, Olav
      "Landscape with Steam Shovels" (tr. of Rolf
      Jacobsen). PoNow (6:5, issue 35) 82, p. 42.

1608. GROCHOWIAK, Stanislaw
      "Brueghel" (tr. by Eric Dickens). Stand (23:2) 82,
      p. 72.

1609. GROFF, David
      "The Saddle River." NoAmR (267:2) Je 82, p. 52.

1610. GRONOWICZ, Antoni
      "Christ." PoetryCR (3:3) Spr 82, p. 6.
      "Hope." PoetryCR (3:3) Spr 82, p. 6.
      "You and I." PoetryCR (3:3) Spr 82, p. 6.

1611. GROSHOLZ, Emily
      "Galerie Orphee." Hudson (35:1) Spr 82, p. 71.
      "In the Light of October" (for V. G. M.). Hudson
      (35:1) Spr 82, p. 72.
      "On the Balcony." NewEngR (4:4) Sum 82, p. 590-591.

1612. GROSSMAN, Allen
      "An Inventory of Destructions." Poetry (140:1) Ap
      82, p. 14-17.
      "The Slave." Salm (57) Sum 82, p. 127-130.

1613. GROSSMAN, Florence
      "Relations." NewL (49:2) Wint 82-83, p. 36.

1614. GROSSMAN, Richard
      "Against the Upcoming War." Kayak (58) Ja 82, p.
      44.
      "Blue Ghosts." Kayak (58) Ja 82, p. 44.
      "Forgetting." SoDakR (20:1) Spr 82, p. 41.

1615. GROUNDSTAFF, Lance
      "I (it) do(wi)n't wan(ll)t." WindO (41) Aut-Wint
      82-83, p. 52.

1616. GROVER-ROGOFF, Jay
      "Labor." MinnR (NS19) Aut 82, p. 40.

1617. GROW, Eric
      "Darling." WormR (22:1, issue 85) 82, p. 11.
      "My Mustache." WormR (22:1, issue 85) 82, p. 11.
      "A Natural." WormR (22:1, issue 85) 82, p. 11.

1618. GRUBERG-PICCIONE, Lisa
"The Excellent Moments" (tr. of Paul Eluard). Kayak
(60) O 82, p. 14.

1619. GRUHN, Hollace
"On the Missouri." SoDakR (20:1) Spr 82, p. 45-46.

GRUSON, Gene de
See: DeGRUSON, Gene

GUARDIA, Armando Rojas
See: ROJAS GUARDIA, Armando

1620. GUDE, Michael
"Becoming Prayer." NoAmR (267:2) Je 82,p. 13.

1621. GUERNELLI, Adelaide L.
"La Catacumba." Mairena (4:9) Spr 82, p. 38.

1622. GUERNSEY, Bruce
"Back Road." PoNow (7:1, issue 37) 82, p. 23.
"The Bat." NewL (49:1) Aut 82, p. 75.
"The Dump Pickers." PoNow (7:1, issue 37) 82, p.
23.
"The Icehouse." PoNow (7:1, issue 37) 82, p. 23.
"Moss." Ascent (8:1) 82, p. 17.
"My Father's Voice." NewL (49:1) Aut 82, p. 76.
"The Owl." Poetry (141:3) D 82, p. 137.
"The Photographer of Funerals." Poetry (141:3) D
82, p. 139.
"The Seeing-Eye Dog." Poetry (141:3) D 82, p. 138.
"The Well." Ascent (7:3) 82, p. 35.

1623. GUIGNON, Valery
"The Sheep Don't Dream." MendoR (5) Sum 81, p. 27.

1624. GUILFORD, Chuck
"In February by a River." KanQ (14:1) Wint 82, p.
80.

1625. GUILLEN, Nicolas
"Problemas del subdesarrollo." Areito (8:30) 82,
inside back cover.

GUIN, Ursula K. le
See: Le GUIN, Ursula K.

1626. GUISTA, Michael
"Give Me." Bogg (48) 82, p. 30.

1627. GULICK, Charles
"Music Man." Poem (45) Jl 82, p. 1.
"To Count." Poem (45) Jl 82, p. 2.
"Walter's Brother II." CarolQ (35:1) Aut 82, p. 50-
52.
"Zero." Poem (45) Jl 82, p. 3.

1628. GULLANS, Charles
"Local Winds." SouthernR (18:2) Spr 82, p. 350-355.
"The Source." Poetry (140:5) Ag 82, p. 283.

1629. GUMILEV, Nikolai
        "The Sixth Sense" (tr. by Jack Marshall). Spirit
        (6:2/3) 82, p. 83.

1630. GUNDERSON, Carol
        "Getting Towards Noon." UnderRM (1:2) Aut 82, p.
        17.

1631. GUNDY, Jeff
        "The Archetypal Experience of C. Wordsworth
        Crockett." PikeF (4) Spr 82, p. 13.
        "C.W. Finds an Organization Pome." PikeF (4) Spr
        82, p. 13.
        "C.W. Searches for a Pome of the Deep Image" (for
        William Stafford). PikeF (4) Spr 82, p. 13.

1632. GUNN, Thom
        "The Girls Next Door." NewYorker (58:11) My 3, 82,
        p. 153.
        "Hell's Angel Listening to Jefferson Airplane."
        MassR (23:1) Spr 82, p. 131.
        "The Inside-Outside Game" (based on an idea by
        Donald Moyer). MassR (23:1) Spr 82, p. 129.
        "The Libertine." MassR (23:1) Spr 82, p. 129.
        "Nice Thing." MassR (23:1) Spr 82, p. 132.
        "Silence." MassR (23:1) Spr 82, p. 133.
        "Song of a Camera" (for Robert Mapplethorpe). Thrpny
        (9) Spr 82, p. 3.
        "Waitress." Thrpny (8) Wint 82, p. 21.
        "The Wart." MassR (23:1) Spr 82, p. 130.

1633. GUNNARS, Kristjana
        "Milky Way Vegetation II." Waves (11:1) Aut 82, p.
        70.

1634. GUNTHER, C.
        "A Beloved Wreckage in the Wilderness." Im (8:2)
        82, p. 4.

1635. GUREVITZ, Zali
        "Light Fever" (tr. by Linda Zisquit). BaratR (8:2)
        Wint 81, p. 92.
        "Morning with" (tr. by Linda Zisquit). BaratR (8:2)
        Wint 81, p. 93.

1636. GURLEY, George H., Jr.
        "In the Cities of Stone." LittleBR (2:4) Sum 82, p.
        49-50.
        "A Room in the Dust." NewL (48:2) Wint 81-82, p.
        92.

1637. GUSS, David
        "Empty" (for Blaise Cendrars, tr. of Vicente
        Huidobro). Kayak (60) O 82, p. 58.
        "Horizon" (tr. of Vicente Huidobro). Kayak (60) O
        82, p. 59.
        "Spring" (tr. of Vicente Huidobro). Kayak (60) O 82,
        p. 60.
        "Swimmer" (tr. of Vicente Huidobro). Kayak (60) O
        82, p. 61.

1638. GUSTAFSSON, Lars
"Africa (3)" (tr. by Philip Martin). QRL (23) 82, p. 54.
"Africa (4)" (tr. by Philip Martin). QRL (23) 82, p. 54.
"After Rain" (tr. by Philip Martin). QRL (23) 82, p. 13.
"At Cologne Cathedral" (tr. by Philip Martin). QRL (23) 82, p. 52.
"Ballad of Philip Martin" (tr. by Philip Martin and John Stanley Martin). QRL (23) 82, p. 64-65.
"Ballad of the Dogs" (tr. by Philip Martin). QRL (23) 82, p. 62-63.
"Ballad of the Stone Forest in Yunnan" (tr. by Philip Martin). QRL (23) 82, p. 66-68.
"The Balloonists" (tr. by Philip Martin). QRL (23) 82, p. 14-15.
"Bar-Girl, Memphis, Tennessee" (tr. by Philip Martin). QRL (23) 82, p. 57.
"The Chinese Painter" (tr. by Philip Martin). QRL (23) 82, p. 55.
"The Crows" (tr. by Philip Martin). QRL (23) 82, p. 42.
"The Decisive Battle" (tr. by Philip Martin). QRL (23) 82, p. 59.
from Declaration of Love to a Sephardic Lady: "Events in 1939" (lines 1-41, tr. by Philip Martin). QRL (23) 82, p. 27-28.
from Declaration of Love to a Sephardic Lady: "Humaniora" (tr. by Philip Martin). QRL (23) 82, p. 29-31.
"The Didapper" (tr. by Philip Martin). QRL (23) 82, p. 41.
"The Dog" (tr. by Philip Martin). QRL (23) 82, p. 17.
"The Dogs" (tr. by Philip Martin). QRL (23) 82, p. 39-40.
"Eel and Well" (tr. by Philip Martin). QRL (23) 82, p. 44.
"Elegy" (from The Brothers Wright in Search of Kitty Hawk, 1968, tr. by Philip Martin). QRL (23) 82, p. 26.
"Elegy on a Dead Labrador" (tr. by Philip Martin). QRL (23) 82, p. 60-61.
"A Fantasy on Wolfgang Amadeus Mozart" (tr. by Philip Martin). QRL (23) 82, p. 45.
"Inscription on a Stone" (from Journey to the Centre of the Earth, 1966, tr. by Philip Martin). QRL (23) 82, p. 19.
"A Landscape" (from Journey to the Centre of the Earth, 1966, tr. by Philip Martin). QRL (23) 82, p. 20-24.
"A Love Poem" (tr. by Philip Martin). QRL (23) 82, p. 58.
"The Meeting" (tr. by Philip Martin). QRL (23) 82, p. 43.
"The Night" (tr. by Philip Martin). QRL (23) 82, p. 50.
"The Old Dry Tree" (tr. by Philip Martin). QRL (23) 82, p. 47.

"On Certain Evenings" (tr. by Philip Martin). QRL
    (23) 82, p. 46.
"Poem on Revisionism" (from Warm Rooms and Cold,
    1972, tr. by Philip Martin). QRL (23) 82, p. 32.
"The Silence of the World before Bach" (tr. by
    Philip Martin). QRL (23) 82, p. 48.
"Snow" (from Journey to the Centre of the Earth,
    1966, tr. by Philip Martin). QRL (23) 82, p. 18.
"A Solemn Morning" (tr. by Philip Martin). QRL (23)
    82, p. 16.
from Sonnets (1977): I. "The Desert at Rio Grande"
    (tr. by Philip Martin). QRL (23) 82, p. 34.
from Sonnets (1977): (XVI, XVII, XXIII, XXVIII) (tr.
    by Philip Martin). QRL (23) 82, p. 35-38.
"The Starred Sky" (tr. by Philip Martin). QRL (23)
    82, p. 49.
"Streams of Particles" (tr. by Philip Martin). QRL
    (23) 82, p. 51.
"Veduta. Embarcamento. Golfo di Rapallo" (tr. by
    Philip Martin). QRL (23) 82, p. 53.
"Warm Rooms and Cold" (from Warm Rooms and Cold,
    1972, tr. by Philip Martin). QRL (23) 82, p. 33.
"A Wind in Texas" (tr. by Philip Martin). QRL (23)
    82, p. 56.
"The Window-Pane" (from The Brothers Wright in
    Search of Kitty Hawk, 1968, tr. by Philip Martin).
    QRL (23) 82, p. 25.

1639. GUSTAVSON, Jeffrey
    "Nervous Forces." Agni (17) 82, p. 123-127.

1640. GUTHRIE, Hamish
    "Blue Heron." AntigR (49) Spr 82, p. 77.

1641. GUTIERREZ, Guillermo
    "Toro de Minos" (from Quilla a la Nada). Mairena
        (4:10) Sum-Aut 82, p. 92.

1642. GUTIERREZ, L. Houle
    "The Divorce." VirQR (58:4) Aut 82, p. 697.
    "Visiting." VirQR (58:4) Aut 82, p. 698.

1643. GUTIERREZ-REVUELTAS, Pedro
    "Una Dos y Tres." Maize (5:3/4) Spr-Sum 82, p. 80.
    "No Draft, No War, U.S. Out of El Salvador." Maize
        (5:3/4) Spr-Sum 82, p. 78-79.

1644. GUTTENBRUNNER, Michael
    "Dead Poet in the Mountains" (tr. by Beth
        Bjorklund). LitR (25:2) Wint 82, p. 199.
    "The Guardian Angel" (tr. by Beth Bjorklund). LitR
        (25:2) Wint 82, p. 199.
    "The Landing" (tr. by Beth Bjorklund). LitR (25:2)
        Wint 82, p. 198.
    "Reflection" (tr. by Beth Bjorklund). LitR (25:2)
        Wint 82, p. 197.
    "The Snake Star" (tr. by Beth Bjorklund). LitR
        (25:2) Wint 82, p. 197.

GUZMAN BOUVARD, Marguerite
<u>See</u>: BOUVARD, Marguerite Guzman

1645. GWYNN, R. S.
"Letter from Carthage." <u>SewanR</u> (90:3) Sum 82, p. 404.

1646. H. D.
"Delphi." <u>Poetry</u> (139:4) Ja 82, p. 223-228.
"Dodona." <u>SouthernR</u> (18:2) Spr 82, p. 338-343.
"Helios and Athene." <u>Iowa</u> (12:2/3) Spr-Sum 81, p. 150-154.
"I Said" (1919). <u>SouthernR</u> (18:2) Spr 82, p. 344-347.
"Other Sea-Cities." <u>YaleR</u> (71:2) Wint 82, p. 165-171.
"Sigil VIII-XIX <u>Antaeus</u> (44) Wint 82, p. 37-45.

1647. HABOVA, Dana
"And There" (tr. of Vladimir Holan, w. David Young). <u>Field</u> (27) Aut 82, p. 75.
"Biodrama" (tr. of Miroslav Holub, w. Stuart Friebert). <u>MalR</u> (62) Jl 82, p. 92.
"Dreams" (tr. of Miroslav Holub, w. Stuart Friebert). <u>MalR</u> (62) Jl 82, p. 89.
"The First Sentence" (tr. of Donat Sajner, w. Stuart Friebert). <u>Field</u> (27) Aut 82, p. 78.
"The Fisherman (Perpetuum Mobile)" (tr. of Josef Simon, w. Stuart Friebert). <u>Field</u> (27) Aut 82, p. 80.
"Hominization" (tr. of Miroslav Holub, w. Stuart Friebert). <u>MalR</u> (62) Jl 82, p. 93.
"Interferon" (tr. of Miroslav Holub, w. David Young). <u>Field</u> (26) Spr 82, p. 61-67.
"The Jewish Cemetery at Olsany, Kafka's Tomb, April, Sunny Weather" (tr. of Miroslav Holub, w. Stuart Friebert). <u>MalR</u> (62) Jl 82, p. 90.
"Lovers I" (tr. of Vladimir Holan, w. Stuart Friebert). <u>Field</u> (27) Aut 82, p. 74.
"A Natural History of Arthropods" (tr. of Miroslav Holub, w. Stuart Friebert). <u>MalR</u> (62) Jl 82, p. 91.
"Report on the Flood" (tr. of Miroslav Florian, w. Stuart Friebert). <u>Field</u> (27) Aut 82, p. 79.
"Resurrection" (tr. of Vladimir Holan, w. David Young). <u>Field</u> (27) Aut 82, p. 76.

1648. HACKER, Marilyn
"Graffiti from the Gare Saint-Manque" (for Zed Bee). <u>Shen</u> (33:2) 82, p. 13-17.
"July Fifth." <u>OP</u> (34) Aut-Wint 82, p. 33-36.
"Saturday Night Bile." <u>Cond</u> (8) 82, p. 51.
"Visiting Chaldon Down" (for Jeanne Wordsworth). <u>Shout</u> (3:1) 82, p. 85-86.
"The Witch's Garden." <u>NewEngR</u> (5:1/2) Aut-Wint 82, p. 23-24.

1649. HADAS, Pamela White
"The Ballad of Baseball Annie" (for Ron Powers). <u>NewEngR</u> (5:1/2) Aut-Wint 82, p. 188-191.

"Dear Lydia E. Pinkham." <u>TriQ</u> (55) Aut 82, p. 14-22.
"Queen Charming." <u>Iowa</u> (12:2/3) Spr-Sum 81, p. 164-166.
"Ringling Bros. Present: The Lucky Lucie Lamort."
<u>Poetry</u> (140:5) Ag 82, p. 264-266.
"To Make a Dragon Move: From the Diary of an Anorexic." <u>Poetry</u> (140:5) Ag 82, p. 261-263.

1650. HADAS, Rachel
"Black Light." <u>YaleR</u> (71:3) Spr 82, p. 391-392.
"From Sickness." <u>NewEngR</u> (4:3) Spr 82, p. 372.
"Rhapsody for Thanksgiving 1981." <u>SenR</u> (13:1) 82-83, p. 56-59.
"Speaking in Tongues." <u>Thrpny</u> (10) Sum 82, p. 17.
"Three Angers." <u>Agni</u> (17) 82, p. 128-130.

1651. HAGGARTY, Zoe
"Fears." <u>HangL</u> (42) 82, p. 10.

1652. HAGIWARA, Sakutaro
"Death" (tr. by Kiyoko Miura). <u>StoneC</u> (10:1/2) Aut-Wint 82-83, p. 18.
"A Murder Case" (tr. by Kiyoko Miura). <u>StoneC</u> (10:1/2) Aut-Wint 82-83, p. 18.

1653. HAGUE, Richard
"Haircut." <u>Wind</u> (12:44) 82, p. 15-16.
"Sparrows Drinking." <u>HiramPoR</u> (31) Aut-Wint 82, p. 30.

1654. HAHN, Kimiko
"A Girl Combs Her Hair" (after Li Ho). <u>Agni</u> (16) 82, p. 101-102.
"Roost." <u>SoDakR</u> (20:3) Aut 82, p. 63.

1655. HAHN, Steve
"Lines for My Mother, at 55." <u>SouthernPR</u> (23, i.e. 22:2) Aut 82, p. 37.

1656. HAINES, John
from Forest without Leaves: (V, X, XXIII, XXV, XXXII, XXXV). <u>KanQ</u> (14:2) Spr 82, p. 75-78.
"Mineral Heritage." <u>KanQ</u> (14:3) Sum 82, p. 48.
"Shadows." <u>Telescope</u> (1) Spr 81, p. 64.

1657. HAINES, John Francis
"Another Elm." <u>Bogg</u> (48) 82, p. 59.

1658. HAISLIP, John
from Storm Journal: "Been alone now for a week."
<u>CutB</u> (18) Spr-Sum 82, p. 74.

1659. HALDEMAN, Jill Breckenridge
"Cashmere Sweaters." <u>PoNow</u> (7:1, issue 37) 82, p. 16.
"Putting Up Applesauce" (For Julie). <u>PoNow</u> (7:1, issue 37) 82, p. 16.

1660. HALE, Amanda
       "Ritual Sacrifice." PoetryCR (4:2) Wint 82, p. 15.

1661. HALL, Donald
       "Great Day in the Cows' House." AmerPoR (11:6) N-D
          82, p. 27.
       "The Henyard Round." Ploughs (8:1) 82, p. 24-26.

1662. HALL, Frances
       "A Ceremonial of Artichokes." Outbr (8/9) Aut 81-
          Spr 82, p. 5.
       "Earthquake Fault." SouthwR (67:1) Wint 82, p. 77.

1663. HALL, Heidi
       "Untitled: My grandmother is a blob of love."
          MendoR (5) Sum 81, p. 67.

1664. HALL, James Baker
       "At Such Times." CharR (8:2) Aut 82, p. 38-39.
       "I Have an Address." CharR (8:2) Aut 82, p. 39-40.
       "I Move." Poetry (140:3) Je 82, p. 135-136.
       "The Lesson." CharR (8:2) Aut 82, p. 35-40.
       "The Lesson of Hope." CharR (8:2) Aut 82, p. 39.
       "Listening." CharR (8:2) Aut 82, p. 35-36.
       "The Shape of a Man." CharR (8:2) Aut 82, p. 36-37.
       "Sitting between Two Mirrors." Poetry (140:3) Je
          82, p. 133-134.
       "Stopping on the Edge to Wave." NewYorker (58:14)
          My 24, 82, p. 36.
       "To Get There." NewYorker (57:48) Ja 18, 82, p.
          111.
       "The Voices." CharR (8:2) Aut 82, p. 37-38.

1665. HALL, Jim
       "False Statements." Poetry (140:4) Jl 82, p. 205-
          206.
       "Feeding the Horse." CimR (61) O 82, p. 34.
       "The First One." Poetry (140:4) Jl 82, p. 207.
       "Hand Shadows: To Be Thrown upon the Wall." PoNow
          (6:5, issue 35) 82, p. 38.
       "Winter in Texas." QW (14) Spr-Sum 82, p. 66-67.

1666. HALL, Joan Joffe
       "The Astronaut." DenQ (17:1) Spr 82, p. 67.
       "For J -- Age Eight." BelPoJ (32:3) Spr 82, p. 4-6.
       "Kansas, Sunstruck." SouthernPR (22:1) Spr 82, p.
          53.
       "Plumb Bob." DenQ (17:1) Spr 82, p. 66.

1667. HALL, Judith
       "Hunger Issue: Lunch at the East Wing." SouthernPR
          (22:1) Spr 82, p. 46-47.
       "The Legend of Salt-Mary." LittleM (13:3/4) 82, p.
          16-19.
       "Sestina Set in an Antique Shop." Shen (33:3) 82,
          p. 78-79.

1668. HALL, Natalie Grace
       "Envy the Hippo." FourQt (32:1) Aut 82, p. 28.

1669. HALL, Rodney
       "Calcutta." NewL (48:3/4) Spr-Sum 82, p. 81.

1670. HALL, Thelma R.
       "The Victim." DekalbLAJ (14:1/4) Aut 80-Sum 81, p.
       75.

1671. HALL, Tommy
       "Courtship." Poem (46) N 82, p. 53.
       "Ladies of the Easter Morn." Poem (46) N 82, p. 52.
       "Sanctuary." Poem (46) N 82, p. 51.

1672. HALLERMAN, Victoria
       "The Wonderful Laurice." PoNow (7:1, issue 37) 82,
       p. 16.

1673. HALLEY, Anne
       "News from Another Province." Poetry (141:2) N 82,
       p. 80-82.
       "Oh a Quick Man." Poetry (141:2) N 82, p. 83.

1674. HALLGREN, Stephanie
       "Whales." NoAmR (267:1) Mr 82,p. 43.
       "A Wife on the Roof." NoAmR (267:1) Mr 82,p. 43.

1675. HALLIDAY, David
       from The House That Loved Children No. 1: "The lawn
       in front of the old house was made out of long red
       hair." Grain (10:2) My 82, p. 38.
       from The House That Loved Children No. 2:
       "Christiane turned around quickly." Grain (10:2)
       My 82, p. 38-39.
       from The House That Loved Children No. 3: "Mr.
       Krattle coughed and cleared his throat." Grain
       (10:2) My 82, p. 39.

1676. HALLIDAY, Mark
       "Casualty Report." MassR (23:1) Spr 82, p. 156-158.
       "Lunch at Bruno's." Ploughs (8:1) 82, p. 75-77.

1677. HALPERIN, Mark
       "Anti-Haiku/Uncle Howyou." WindO (40, Anti-Haiku
       issue) Sum 82, p. 11.
       "Dreyfus Pleads for the Lives of Sacco and
       Vanzetti." Tendril (12) Wint 82, p. 38-39.
       "A Letter" (For Steve Orien). PoNow (6:4, issue 34)
       82, p. 7.
       "The Performance Medium." SouthernPR (22:1) Spr 82,
       p. 72-73.
       "Time's Arrow." PoNow (6:4, issue 34) 82, p. 7.

1678. HALPERN, Daniel
       "Calling West" (for Bob). OhioR (28) 82, p. 60-61.
       "The Dwelling Air." NewEngR (5:1/2) Aut-Wint 82, p.
       144.
       "The Last Days of the Year." AntR (40:1) Wint 82,
       p. 86-87.
       "Leaving Summer." AmerPoR (11:5) S-O 82, p. 9.
       "Nude." OhioR (28) 82, p. 60.

"Snapshot of Hue" (for Robert Stone). NewEngR
(5:1/2) Aut-Wint 82, p. 145.

1679. HALPERN, Peter
"Down-island." DenQ (17:2) Sum 82, p. 106.

HALTEREN, Marjorie van
See: Van HALTEREN, Marjorie

1680. HAMBLIN, Robert W.
"My Daughter at Her Guitar" (Christmas 1981). CapeR
(17:2) Sum 82, p. 40.

1681. HAMBURGER, Michael
"Dying." Stand (23:4) 82, p. 4.
"A Silence" (i.m. L.M.H. 1887-1980). Stand (23:4)
82, p. 4-5.

1682. HAMEL, Guy
"Renewed Humanity." WritersL O-N 82, p. 21.

1683. HAMERMESH, Madeline
"Pas de Deux" (For M.J.). MendoR (6) Sum 81, p. 77.

1684. HAMILL, Paul
"Specifically Themselves." Poetry (139:5) F 82, p.
281-282.

1685. HAMILL, Sam
"The Body of Winter" (after Elytis). CutB (18) Spr-
Sum 82, p. 4.
"In the Company of Men." Hangl (43) Wint 82-83, p.
42-43.
"Loyalty: a Letter." Hangl (43) Wint 82-83, p. 44-
47.
"On Calligraphy" (homage to Girvin). MalR (62) Jl
82, p. 158-159.

1686. HAMILTON, Alfred Starr
"Arms." NewL (48:2) Wint 81-82, p. 74.
"Baloney, and the Moon." Peb (22, special issue:
The Big Parade) 82, p. 37.
"Banners." Peb (22, special issue: The Big Parade)
82, p. 1.
"The Big Parade" (special issue, published by the
Best Cellar Press). Peb (22) 82, 41 p.
"Bread and Butter." Peb (22, special issue: The Big
Parade) 82, p. 28.
"Bushel of Potatoes." Peb (22, special issue: The
Big Parade) 82, p. 20.
"A Carrot." NewL (48:2) Wint 81-82, p. 74.
"Christmas Eve." Peb (22, special issue: The Big
Parade) 82, p. 19.
"Cinderella." Peb (22, special issue: The Big
Parade) 82, p. 27.
"City." Peb (22, special issue: The Big Parade) 82,
p. 39.
"Criss Cross." NewL (48:2) Wint 81-82, p. 72-73.
"Dark Continent." Peb (22, special issue: The Big
Parade) 82, p. 3.

"Dark Corner." <u>Peb</u> (22, special issue: The Big Parade) 82, p. 2.
"Dime." <u>Peb</u> (22, special issue: The Big Parade) 82, p. 4.
"Dynamo." <u>PoNow</u> (6:5, issue 35) 82, p. 32.
"Eire." <u>PoNow</u> (6:6, issue 36) 82, p. 36.
"Electra." <u>PoNow</u> (6:5, issue 35) 82, p. 32.
"The Flag." <u>Peb</u> (22, special issue: The Big Parade) 82, p. 30-31.
"Flocks." <u>Peb</u> (22, special issue: The Big Parade) 82, p. 35.
"Foolscap Bay." <u>Peb</u> (22, special issue: The Big Parade) 82, p. 9.
"Forbidden." <u>Peb</u> (22, special issue: The Big Parade) 82, p. 5.
"Forsythia Vine." <u>Peb</u> (22, special issue: The Big Parade) 82, p. 33.
"Free." <u>Peb</u> (22, special issue: The Big Parade) 82, p. 7.
"Free." <u>WormR</u> (22:1, issue 85) 82, p. 36.
"A Girl's Command." <u>PoNow</u> (6:6, issue 36) 82, p. 36.
"Harmonica." <u>Peb</u> (22, special issue: The Big Parade) 82, p. 6.
"Judith and Her Maidservant." <u>Peb</u> (22, special issue: The Big Parade) 82, p. 12-13.
"Laffs." <u>Peb</u> (22, special issue: The Big Parade) 82, p. 40.
"Lefty." <u>Peb</u> (22, special issue: The Big Parade) 82, p. 34.
"The Little Shop around the Corner." <u>Peb</u> (22, special issue: The Big Parade) 82, p. 25.
"MacGregor's Gardens." <u>Peb</u> (22, special issue: The Big Parade) 82, p. 23.
"The Moon Is Down." <u>WormR</u> (22:1, issue 85) 82, p. 35.
"Newark." <u>Peb</u> (22, special issue: The Big Parade) 82, p. 24.
"Night." <u>Peb</u> (22, special issue: The Big Parade) 82, p. 29.
"Nine." <u>WormR</u> (22:1, issue 85) 82, p. 35.
"The Papermill Playhouse." <u>Peb</u> (22, special issue: The Big Parade) 82, p. 15.
"Pink Ponds." <u>Peb</u> (22, special issue: The Big Parade) 82, p. 10-11.
"The Pool." <u>Peb</u> (22, special issue: The Big Parade) 82, p. 41.
"Potatoes." <u>Peb</u> (22, special issue: The Big Parade) 82, p. 21.
"Salvation Army." <u>Peb</u> (22, special issue: The Big Parade) 82, p. 17.
"Shoe." <u>Peb</u> (22, special issue: The Big Parade) 82, p. 38.
"Shoe Factory." <u>Peb</u> (22, special issue: The Big Parade) 82, p. 14.
"Sibelius." <u>Peb</u> (22, special issue: The Big Parade) 82, p. 8.
"Sixteen Peons." <u>WormR</u> (22:1, issue 85) 82, p. 35.
"Sky." <u>Peb</u> (22, special issue: The Big Parade) 82, p. 18.

"Suburbia." Peb (22, special issue: The Big Parade)
    82, p. 36.
"Telephone." NewL (48:2) Wint 81-82, p. 74.
"Tenement." Peb (22, special issue: The Big Parade)
    82, p. 32.
"Thanksgiving." Peb (22, special issue: The Big
    Parade) 82, p. 16.
"Thursday." Peb (22, special issue: The Big Parade)
    82, p. 22.
"Underground." PoNow (6:5, issue 35) 82, p. 32.
"War Years Ahead." Peb (22, special issue: The Big
    Parade) 82, p. 26.
"Yeast Kentucky." PoNow (6:6, issue 36) 82, p. 36.

1687. HAMILTON, Carol
    "By Definition." Poem (44) Mr 82, p. 33.
    "I Am Kangaroo Rat." Poem (44) Mr 82, p. 34-35.
    "My Children Come to Visit Me and Wonder Who I Am."
        Poem (44) Mr 82, p. 36.
    "Pushing Past the Labor Room." SmPd (19:3, issue
        56) Aut 82, p. 22.

1688. HAMILTON, Fritz
    "At the Seaman's Hall." CentR (26:4) Aut 82, p.
        357.
    "Man of Spice." Bogg (48) 82, p. 13.
    "Seeing My Father." Wind (12:46) 82, p. 17.

1689. HAMMOND, Karla M.
    "Abortions." UnderRM (1:2) Aut 82, p. 11.
    "Bigfoot." UnderRM (1:2) Aut 82, p. 11-12.
    "Grandmother Hex." UnderRM (1:2) Aut 82, p. 10.
    "Juggernaut" (in reply to James Tate's "Dark
        Street"). Paint (7/8:13/16) 80-81, p. 25.
    "The Palm Reader." PortR (28:2) 82, p. 57.
    "Self-Portrait." Paint (7/8:13/16) 80-81, p. 24.
    "Voices of the Moon." PortR (28:2) 82, p. 56.

1690. HAMPL, Patricia
    "Leading to Your Hands." Iowa (13:1) Wint 82, p.
        106-108.
    "The Loon." Iowa (13:1) Wint 82, p. 104-105.

    HAN, Yong-Woon
    See: MANHAE

1691. HANDKE, Peter
    "Missed Opportunities for Dying" (tr. by Francis
        Golffing). PoNow (6:4, issue 34) 82, p. 40.

1692. HANDLIN, Jim
    "The fog lifts." WindO (40, Anti-Haiku issue) Sum
        82, p. 30.
    "A History of Landscape." PraS (56:3) Aut 82, p.
        43.
    "I hit the target that dunks my wife." WindO (40,
        Anti-Haiku issue) Sum 82, p. 30.
    "Inside my muddy footprint." WindO (40, Anti-Haiku
        issue) Sum 82, p. 30.

"Molly's Resurrection: A Triptych." PraS (56:3) Aut
    82, p. 43-44.
"Watching her green eyes as she eats a grape."
    WindO (40, Anti-Haiku issue) Sum 82, p. 30.

1693. HANE, Norman
    "Ishmael: Last Words." EnPas (13) 82, p. 16.

1694. HANEBURY, Derek
    "The Battle of Boredom." PoetryCR (3:4) Sum 82, p.
    15.

1695. HANKLA, Cathryn
    "Flight Luck." MissouriR (5:3) Sum 82, p. 16.
    "Lighting the Dark Side of the Moon." MissouriR
    (5:3) Sum 82, P 17.

1696. HANLEY, Patricia
    "Turning." PoetryCR (4:2) Wint 82, p. 15.

1697. HANLY, Ken
    "Cabbages." Bogg (48) 82, p. 72.
    "In the Bank." PoetryCR (4:2) Wint 82, p. 15.

1698. HANNAN, Greg
    "The Fish Shop." Shout (3:1) 82, p. 31-33.
    "The Night Clerk." Shout (3:1) 82, p. 29-30.

1699. HANNS, Genine
    "Swampwater." CrossC (4:2/3) 82, p. 50.

1700. HANSEN, Joseph
    "The Gap." SoDakR (20:2) Sum 82, p. 35.
    "The Worriers." SoDakR (20:2) Sum 82, p. 34.

1701. HANSEN, Matthew
    "Clearing." KanQ (14:3) Sum 82, p. 130-131.

1702. HANSEN, Tom
    "Another Wooden Angel Poem." WebR (7:2) Aut 82, p.
    40.
    "The Decline of Evil." PoNow (6:5, issue 35) 82, p.
    45.
    "Killing All Evil Dragons, My Son." VirQR (58:4)
    Aut 82, p. 688-689.
    "November." PoNow (6:5, issue 35) 82, p. 45.
    "When The Severely Retarded Die." Im (8:1) 82, p.
    3.

1703. HANSEN, Toralf Moller
    "Music: of Earth, and Stone, and the People" (tr. of
    Paal-Helge Haugen, w. Jon Silkin and David
    McDuff). Stand (23:3) 82, p. 45.

1704. HANSON, Alice Taylor
    "Words, Words, Words." EngJ (71:4) Ap 82, p. 62.

1705. HANSON, Charles
    "Earth." KanQ (14:3) Sum 82, p. 147.

"Instructions to Sleepwalkers." LittleM (13:3/4)
    82, p. 65.
"The Nostrums." Outbr (10/11) Aut 82-Spr 83, p. 13.
"Silver Seclusion." CapeR (18:1) Wint 82, p. 26.
"Swine." LittleM (13:3/4) 82, p. 64.

1706. HANSON, Erik P.
    "Katrina Are You Seriously Dead?" UnderRM 1(1) Spr
        82, p. 5.

1707. HANSON, Howard G.
    "After Heraclitus." ArizQ (38:2) Sum 82, p. 146.

1708. HANSON, Kenneth O.
    "Amphora (A-1311)." MalR (63) O 82, p. 94.
    "At Ringside (Modesto)." MalR (63) O 82, p. 93.
    "At the Edge of the Sea Song." MalR (63) O 82, p.
        98-99.
    "It Was Not Quite Immediate." MalR (63) O 82, p.
        96.
    "Ithaka (Later)." MalR (63) O 82, p. 95.
    "Lighting the Night Sky." NowestR (20:2/3) 82, p.
        211-213.
    "Near Nea Smyrni." MalR (63) O 82, p. 89-90.
    "Summer Solstice." MalR (63) O 82, p. 97.
    "The Weather They Live for." MalR (63) O 82, p. 90-
        91.
    "What Would It Take to Convince You?" MalR (63) O
        82, p. 92-93.

    HAO-JAN, Meng
    See: MENG, Hao-jan

1709. HARA, Ed
    "Fringe Benefit: Teaching English." EngJ (71:7) N
        82, p. 70.

1710. HARDING, Gunnar
    "Lightning in the ground" (tr. of Lars Lundkvist, w.
        Anselm Hollo). Spirit (6:2/3) 82, p. 122.
    "Man across the moor" (tr. of Lars Lundkvist, w.
        Anselm Hollo). Spirit (6:2/3) 82, p. 122.
    "Once much ice was here" (tr. of Lars Lundkvist, w.
        Anselm Hollo). Spirit (6:2/3) 82, p. 122-123.

1711. HARGITAI, Peter
    "Weary Man" (tr. of Attila Jozsef). PraS (56:1) Spr
        82, p. 43.

1712. HARKNESSS, Edward
    "Tonight." PoetryNW (23:1) Spr 82, p. 11-12.

1713. HARLOW, Christopher
    "Harbour." Bogg (48) 82, p. 61.

1714. HARMON, William
    "Invoices." SouthernR (18:1) Wint 82, p. 152-160.
    "Not Exactly an Impromptu But Also Not Exactly Not
        One, Either." Kayak (60) O 82, p. 56-57.
    "One Woman, Four Lights." Agni (17) 82, p. 170-171.

1715. HARMSTON, Richard
      "Snowfall." EngJ (71:4) Ap 82, p. 76.

1716. HARN, John
      "Obviously." NowestR (20:1) 82, p. 100.

1717. HARNACK, Curtis
      "Figures in a Stranger's Dream." Salm (57) Sum 82,
      p. 123-126.
      "Rain Saturday Night." (49:1) Aut 82, p. 33.

1718. HARPER, Elizabeth
      "East End." PottPort (4) 82-83, p. 12.

1719. HARPER, Michael S.
      "Homage to Lyal Buffington" (for Ruth). WorldO
      (16:2) Wint 82, p. 18-19.
      "In Hayden's Collage" (Amsterdam). MichQR (21:1)
      Wint 82, p. 187-188.

1720. HARR, Lorraine Ellis
      "Autumn winds" (Haiku). LittleBR (1:3) Spr 81, p.
      55.

1721. HARRIMAN, Eddie
      "Exposure." Bogg (49) 82, p. 43.

1722. HARRIS, Brian
      "Sentence." DenQ (16:4) Wint 82, p. 86.
      "The Thought of It." DenQ (16:4) Wint 82, p. 85.

1723. HARRIS, Claire K.
      "Perhaps to this poem as to a tapestry." Waves
      (11:1) Aut 82, p. 52-54.
      "There are days when no shout in the streets."
      Waves (10:3) Wint 82, p. 31.

1724. HARRIS, Judith
      "Song for the Horses Unlocked at Night." Nimrod
      (25:2) Spr-Sum 82, p. 60.
      "Song of the Fisherman without Hours." Nimrod
      (25:2) Spr-Sum 82, p. 23.
      "Song of the Night." Nimrod (25:2) Spr-Sum 82, p.
      60.
      "Song of the Rain in the Graveyard." Nimrod (25:2)
      Spr-Sum 82, p. 61.

1725. HARRIS, Marie
      "Killing Time." PoNow (6:4, issue 34) 82, p. 32.

1726. HARRIS, Sandra
      "I Stayed Up 'till Five AM" (To my Students). EngJ
      (71:6) O 82, p. 39.

1727. HARRIS, William J.
      "The Flower and the Bee." PoNow (6:5, issue 35) 82,
      p. 10.

1728. HARRISON, Jeanne
        "This May Not Be a Dream." Waves (10:3) Wint 82, p.
        66.

1729. HARRISON, Jim
        "After Reading Takahashi" (for Lucien and Peter).
        AmerPoR (11:4) Jl-Ag 82, p. 4.
        "Epithalamium" (for Peter and Maria). AmerPoR (11:4)
        Jl-Ag 82, p. 4.
        "Followers." AmerPoR (11:4) Jl-Ag 82, p. 4.
        "Not Writing My Name." AmerPoR (11:4) Jl-Ag 82, p.
        3.
        "Rooster" (to Pat Ryan). AmerPoR (11:4) Jl-Ag 82, p.
        4.
        "Waiting." AmerPoR (11:4) Jl-Ag 82, p. 3.
        "Walter of Battersea" (for Anjelica Huston). AmerPoR
        (11:4) Jl-Ag 82, p. 3.
        "The Woman from Spiritwood." AmerPoR (11:4) Jl-Ag
        82, p. 3.

1730. HARRISON, Pamela
        "Blue Rug." SenR (13:1) 82-83, p. 62-63.
        "Clear Through." SenR (13:1) 82-83, p. 64-65.
        "Original Sin." SenR (13:1) 82-83, p. 66-67.
        "The Pipes." PoNow (7:1, issue 37) 82, p. 17.
        "Pirates." PoNow (7:1, issue 37) 82, p. 17.

1731. HARROLD, William
        "The Formula Einstein Missed" (from the Leona Larkey
        Prose Poems series). SeC (9:1/2) 80, p. 27.
        "Jukebox Roulette" (from the Leona Larkey Prose
        Poems series). SeC (9:1/2) 80, p. 26.
        "Pauline." Abraxas (25/26) 82, p. 84.

1732. HART, James
        "Wings." CharR (8:1) Spr 82, p. 46.

1733. HART, John
        "Runner Heard in Illness." SouthernPR (22:1) Spr
        82, p. 19-20.

1734. HART, Paul J.
        "Depression." KanQ (14:2) Spr 82, p. 66.
        "For a Friend, Autumn 1978." KanQ (14:2) Spr 82, p.
        65.

1735. HARTEIS, Richard
        "Ageing." SenR (13:1) 82-83, p. 38.
        "Christmas with the Premees." SenR (13:1) 82-83, p.
        41.
        "The Hermit's Curse." SenR (13:1) 82-83, p. 42-43.
        "Work in Progress." SenR (13:1) 82-83, p. 39-40.

1736. HARTMAN, Charles O.
        "In the Mean Time." NewYorker (57:52) F 15, 82, p.
        42-43.
        "Plain Grass." Kayak (58) Ja 82, p. 48.
        "Things to Attend to." SouthernR (18:3) Sum 82, p.
        549-550.

1737. HARTMAN, Renee G.
      "Paris." MassR (23:2) Sum 82, p. 306.
      "A Stone in Hand" (for A. R. Ammons). MassR (23:2)
         Sum 82, p. 307.

1738. HARTMAN, Susan
      "Reminding my Enemies." KanQ (14:1) Wint 82, p. 82.

1739. HARTOG, Diana
      "The Common Man. " MalR (62) Jl 82, p. 149.
      "The Exception." MalR (62) Jl 82, p. 145.
      "The Man Who Loved Ordinary Objects." MalR (62) Jl
         82, p. 148.
      "Produit du Canadodo." MalR (62) Jl 82, p. 146-147.
      "Tuolumne River." MalR (62) Jl 82, p. 144.

1740. HARVEY, Gayle Elen
      "After an Argument." Bogg (49) 82, p. 18.
      "The Canal" (Seurat). Im (8:1) 82, p. 12.
      "Dog Tied to a Tree" (for Jim ------). SouthernPR
         (23, i.e. 22:2) Aut 82, p. 57.
      "Family." Nimrod (25:2) Spr-Sum 82, p. 61.
      "Fog, Late Zinnias." CapeR (17:2) Sum 82, p. 37.
      "In the Dream, Even This Poem." StoneC (9:3/4) Spr-
         Sum 82, p. 65.
      "Poem for a Man Born under the Moon of Strong Cold."
         StoneC (10:1/2) Aut-Wint 82-83, p. 15.
      "Rabid Dog." CapeR (18:1) Wint 82, p. 39.

1741. HARVEY, Helen Bohlen
      "Jaded." Poem (44) Mr 82, p. 15.
      "Waiting." Poem (44) Mr 82, p. 16.

1742. HARVEY, Ken J.
      "A Drink of Water." PottPort (4) 82-83, p. 51.
      "A Statement of Denial." PottPort (4) 82-83, p. 51.

1743. HARWAY, Judith
      "Bats." CanLit (94) Aut 82, p. 8-9.
      "Chiaroscuro." CanLit (94) Aut 82, p. 94-95.

1744. HASHMI, Alamgir
      "Binoculars after Sunset." PortR (28:1) 82, p. 42.

1745. HASKINS, Lola
      "Castings: A Sequence." Nimrod (26:1) Aut-Wint 82,
         p. 54-55.
      "Clara and the Law." BelPoJ (33:2) Wint 82-83, p.
         36-38.
      "Dedication" (for Jane). BelPoJ (32:3) Spr 82, p. 8-
         14.
      "Dracula's Deserted Lady." Nimrod (26:1) Aut-Wint
         82, p. 57.
      "Freezer." BelPoJ (33:2) Wint 82-83, p. 38-39.
      "Mary in His Chamber." Nimrod (26:1) Aut-Wint 82,
         p. 56.
      "On the Death of Fanny." CharR (8:1) Spr 82, p. 35-
         37.
      "Scene." Nimrod (26:1) Aut-Wint 82, p. 57-58.

"Speaking with Lucy (d. 1736): Her Answers." <u>Nimrod</u>
(26:1) Aut-Wint 82, p. 57.
"A Study in Time." <u>Nimrod</u> (26:1) Aut-Wint 82, p.
56.

1746. HASRAT, Sukhpal Vir Singh
"Miss Tanuja Is All Tenderness" (tr. by Pritam
Singh). <u>NewL</u> (48:3/4) Spr-Sum 82, p. 233.

1747. HASS, Robert
"Le Monde--C'est Terrible, Cezanne" (From the
Separate Notebooks, tr. of Czeslaw Milosz, w. the
author). <u>Pequod</u> (15) 82, p. 11-14.
"The Separate Notebooks: A Mirrored Gallery" (tr. of
Czeslaw Milosz w. Renata Gorczynski). <u>Antaeus</u> (47)
Aut 82, p. 7-15.

1748. HASTINGS, Tom
"How silly this time of day." <u>WindO</u> (40, Anti-Haiku
issue) Sum 82, p. 24.

1749. HASTY, Palmer
"The Candles." <u>Confr</u> (24) Sum 82, p. 123-124.

1750. HATHAWAY, James
"In the Library." <u>Epoch</u> (31:2) Spr 82, p. 136.
"On the Potty." <u>Epoch</u> (31:2) Spr 82, p. 137.

1751. HATHAWAY, Jeanine
"Preparing the Way." <u>BelPoJ</u> (33:1) Aut 82, p. 12.

1752. HATHAWAY, Lodene Brown
"And a Little Child." <u>ChrC</u> (99:40) D 15, 82, p.
1278.

1753. HATHAWAY, William
"Crab in the Hole, Crab in the Hand" (for Simone).
<u>Hudson</u> (35:2) Sum 82, p. 228-229.
"Dear Wordsworth." <u>PoNow</u> (6:6, issue 36) 82, p. 24.
"The Gibbon's Hoot." <u>NewEngR</u> (4:3) Spr 82, p. 452.
"Hunting Agates at Big Creek" (for Michael Colvin).
<u>Hudson</u> (35:2) Sum 82, p. 229-230.
"I Tell My Sons." <u>MidwQ</u> (24:1) Aut 82, p. 64.
"The Iceball." <u>MidwQ</u> (24:1) Aut 82, p. 62-63.
"Incoming Squall at Twilight." <u>PoNow</u> (6:6, issue
36) 82, p. 24.
"The Mating of the Anurans." <u>Telescope</u> (1) Spr 81,
p. 78.
"Nate's Dimple." <u>PoNow</u> (6:4, issue 34) 82, p. 7.
"Tardiness Lecture" (for Jesse). <u>MidwQ</u> (24:1) Aut
82, p. 60-61.

1754. HAUGE, Olav N.
"Company" (tr. by Robin Fulton). <u>Stand</u> (23:3) 82, p.
15.
"Harvest Time" (tr. by Robert Bly). <u>Ploughs</u> (8:2/3)
82, p. 212.
"I Pause beneath the Old Oak One Rainy Day" (tr. by
Robin Fulton). <u>Stand</u> (23:3) 82, p. 14.

"Looking at an Old Mirror" (tr. by Robert Bly).
   Ploughs (8:2/3) 82, p. 211.
"Many Years' Experience with Bow and Arrow" (tr. by
   Robin Fulton). Stand (23:3) 82, p. 13.
"New Table-Cloth" (tr. by Robin Fulton). Stand
   (23:3) 82, p. 12.
"Paul Celan" (tr. by Robin Fulton). Stand (23:3) 82,
   p. 13.
"There Is Nothing So Scary" (tr. by Robert Bly).
   Ploughs (8:2/3) 82, p. 211.
"Up on Top" (tr. by Robert Bly). Stand (23:3) 82, p.
   15.
"Up through the River Valley" (tr. by Robin Fulton).
   Stand (23:3) 82, p. 14.

1755. HAUGEN, Paal-Helge
      "Bees, Honey" (tr. by Jon Silkin and David McDuff).
         Stand (23:3) 82, p. 44.
      "For Olav H. Hauge" (tr. by Jon Silkin and David
         McDuff). Stand (23:3) 82, p. 44.
      "Music: of Earth, and Stone, and the People" (tr. by
         Jon Silkin, David McDuff and Toralf Moller
         Hansen). Stand (23:3) 82, p. 45.

1756. HAUGHAWOUT, Margaret E.
      "Wild Things." LittleBR (1:2) Wint 80-81, p. 53.

1757. HAUPTFLEISCH, Susan
      "In the Suburbs of Summer." PoetC (14:2) 82, p. 36-
         37.
      "You Are Free to Resume Your Maiden Name." PoetC
         (14:2) 82, p. 35.

1758. HAUSMANN, Raoul
      "Cauchemar." Sulfur (2:3, issue 6) 82, p. 52-53.
      "Present Inter Noumenal" (w. Kurt Schwitters).
         Sulfur (2:3, issue 6) 82, p. 50-51.
      "Three Little Pine Trees." Sulfur (2:3, issue 6)
         82, p. 54-58.

      HAVELIN, Jim LaVilla
      See: LaVILLA-HAVELIN, Jim

1759. HAVEN, Stephen
      "The Sense of Calm Hours" (for Cathy). CutB (19)
         Aut-Wint 82, p. 74-75.

1760. HAVINS, Peter J. Neville
      "War's Winter Is." Bogg (49) 82, p. 52-53.

      HAWK, Red
      See: RED HAWK

1761. HAWKINS, Hunt
      "Divorce." MinnR (NS19) Aut 82, p. 48-49.
      "The Grand Canyon." WormR (22:3, issue 87) 82, p.
         103.
      "The Havana Psychiatric Hospital." MinnR (NS19) Aut
         82, p. 47.
      "My Wife's Shoes." MinnR (NS18) Spr 82, p. 10-11.

HAWKINS   228

"Remembering the Tidy Town Laundromat." WormR
(22:3, issue 87) 82, p. 104-105.
"We Buy Our Couch." WormR (22:3, issue 87) 82, p.
103-104.

1762. HAWKINS, Tom
"Malinda." KanQ (14:3) Sum 82, p. 191.

1763. HAWLEY, Beatrice
"The Ballad of Butter." Ploughs (8:1) 82, p. 135-
137.

1764. HAWLEY-MEIGS, James
"From a Room in Lausanne." Telescope (3) Sum 82, p.
33-34.
"Josiah." Telescope (3) Sum 82, p. 35.

1765. HAXTON, Brooks
"Breakfast Ex Animo." Poetry (140:2) My 82, p. 63-
73.

1766. HAYES, Ann
"For a School of Dolphins." SouthernR (18:2) Spr
82, p. 393.
"On Seeing the Mountains" (The Jungfrau, from
Wengen). SouthernR (18:2) Spr 82, p. 390-391.
"South Door, Chartres." SouthernR (18:2) Spr 82, p.
394.
"To Accommodated Man." SouthernR (18:2) Spr 82, p.
391.
"To Cluny." SouthernR (18:2) Spr 82, p. 391-392.
"To Dinner." SouthernR (18:2) Spr 82, p. 389.

1767. HAYES, Diana
"Choosing the Miracle." Quarry (31:1) Wint 82, p.
13-14.
"The Mirror and the Wand." PoetryCR (4:2) Wint 82,
p. 6.

1768. HAZARD, James
"Negroes in Whiting, Indiana" (for Paul Cebar).
NoAmR (267:4) D 82, p. 6.

1769. HEALD, James D.
"Please Teacher, Tell Me Why." EngJ (71:1) Ja 82,
p. 44.

1770. HEANEY, Seamus
"Brigid." Tendril (13) Sum 82, p. 32-34.

1771. HEARST, James
"Anyone Can See." PoNow (6:5, issue 35) 82, p. 36.
"Double Talk." PoNow (6:5, issue 35) 82, p. 36.
"How Good Is Good Enough." PoNow (6:4, issue 34)
82, p. 37.
"Let It Shine." WormR (22:1, issue 85) 82, p. 38.
"No Advice Today, Thank You." KanQ (14:3) Sum 82,
p. 128.
"Now Hear This." PoNow (6:6, issue 36) 82, p. 11.

"Only Flowers Seem Not to Die." PoNow (6:6, issue
    36) 82, p. 11.
"Shelter Under Glass." NewL (49:2) Wint 82-83, p.
    70.
"Sign Directed." PoNow (6:6, issue 36) 82, p. 11.
"Subscription to Salvation." WormR (22:1, issue 85)
    82, p. 38-39.
"This Is the Way It Seems." EngJ (71:1) Ja 82, p.
    69.
"Whither Away, Friend." Grain (10:2) My 82, p. 31.
"Witnesses." SoDakR (20:1) Spr 82, p. 44.

1772. HEATH, Terrence
    "Once upon a Time in Atlantis." Grain (10:3) Ag 82,
        p. 38.
    "Sons of the Morning Singing Together." Grain
        (10:3) Ag 82, p. 39.

1773. HEBALD, Carol
    "How a Living Bird Became a Jewel in the Sweet
        Mirror of God" (For St. Teresa, For Beethoven).
        Confr (24) Sum 82, p. 53.

1774. HECHT, Anthony
    "Anthem." Poetry (141:1) O 82, p. 12.
    "Horatian Virtue" (Horace I:22). Poetry (141:1) O
        82, p. 13.
    "On Translation" (For Robert Fitzgerald). Poetry
        (141:1) O 82, p. 11.
    "Recyclings." Atl (250:5) N 82, p. 153.

1775. HEDIN, Robert
    "On Tuesdays They Open the Local Pool to the Stroke-
        Victims" (For my sons). Poetry (140:1) Ap 82, p.
        29.
    "Tornado." Poetry (140:1) Ap 82, p. 28.

1776. HEFFERNAN, Michael
    "Argument from Design." LittleBR (1:2) Wint 80-81,
        p. 64.
    "For an Epiphany." NewL (48:2) Wint 81-82, p. 95.

1777. HEFFERNAN, Thomas
    "From Her Letters." SouthernPR (22:1) Spr 82, p.
        65-68.

    HEHIR, Diana O'
    See: O'HEHIR, Diana

1778. HEIDSIECK, Bernard
    "Le Carrefour de la Chaussee d'Antin." Sulfur (2:3,
        issue 6) 82, p. 113-127.

1779. HEIMAN, Frances
    "My Brother, the Wolf." HiramPoR (32) Spr-Sum 82,
        p. 26.

1780. HEINEMAN, W. F.
    "Southern Border Desert." Os (15) 82, p. 28.

"The stonework stopped." SmPd (19:3, issue 56) Aut
   82, p. 7.

1781. HEISTAND, Anita
   "Guardians." LittleBR (1:4) Sum 81, p. 51.

1782. HEJINIAN, Lyn
   "The blue-green northeast lake props its aureole."
      Sulfur (2:2, issue 5) 82, p. 119.
   "The inanimate are rocks, desks, bubble, mineral,
      ramps." Sulfur (2:2, issue 5) 82, p. 117.
   "It rained all afternoon." Sulfur (2:2, issue 5)
      82, p. 119-120.
   "The lighter the sky the less depth is apparent."
      Sulfur (2:2, issue 5) 82, p. 121-122.
   "Mental watchdog, the brainstorm's over." Sulfur
      (2:2, issue 5) 82, p. 120-121.
   "Pandemonium hews no clouds." Sulfur (2:2, issue 5)
      82, p. 123.
   "Rain on the macadam quaver ticks." Sulfur (2:2,
      issue 5) 82, p. 117-118.
   "The tidal throughway from a distance." Sulfur
      (2:2, issue 5) 82, p. 122.
   "Under the radio roof, a mere wisp." Sulfur (2:2,
      issue 5) 82, p. 118.

1783. HEJNA, Jim
   "China Fortress." Ploughs (8:2/3) 82, p. 250-251.
   "Train Crash." Ploughs (8:2/3) 82, p. 249.
   "Troths Told." Ploughs (8:2/3) 82, p. 252.

1784. HELDENBRAND, Sheila
   "There Is a Little House." Spirit (6:2/3) 82, p.
      80.

1785. HELLE, Anita
   "Bait." PoetC (14:2) 82, p. 25.
   "Sauvie's Island." PoetC (14:2) 82, p. 24.
   "Snow Angels: Postcard for Tana." PoetC (14:2) 82,
      p. 23.

1786. HELLER, Janet Ruth
   "Wedding Guest." Wind (12:46) 82, p. 18.

1787. HELLER, Michael
   "3 AM, the Muse." OhioR (29) 82, p. 6.
   "In Central Park." Im (8:2) 82, p. 12.
   "Montaigne." Pequod (14) 82, p. 50-51.
   "Partitions. The War." Im (8:2) 82, p. 12.

1788. HELWIG, David
   "Counterpoint, the flutes of fire." Quarry (31:3)
      Sum 82, p. 9.

1789. HELWIG, Maggie
   "Fragments for a Time." Dandel (9:1) 82, p. 81-83.
   from Gothic Church, North Italy: "First Voice,
      Second Voice." Grain (10:3) Ag 82, p. 11.
   "With Angels and Archangels." AntigR (48) Wint 82,
      p. 9.

1790. HEMSCHEMEYER, Judith
       "Indulgence and Accidents." Iowa (12:2/3) Spr-Sum
       81, p. 187-188.

1791. HENAO, Raul
       "Retorno de Nietzsche." BelPoJ (32:4) Sum 82, p.
       16.
       "The Return of Nietzsche" (tr. by Ricardo Pau-
       Llosa). BelPoJ (32:4) Sum 82, p. 17.

1792. HENDERSON, Archibald
       "Bibles." Sam (33:3, issue 131) 82, p. 60.
       "Revelation." PoNow (6:6, issue 36) 82, p. 46.

1793. HENDERSON, Brian
       "A White Wall Under the Wallpaper." PoetryCR (4:2)
       Wint 82, p. 12.

1794. HENDLER, Earl
       "An Impromptu for Natie." Poem (45) Jl 82, p. 6.
       "In Transit." Poem (45) Jl 82, p. 5.
       "Suburbia." Poem (45) Jl 82, p. 7.

1795. HENDRIX, Nancy
       "Riverside Romance Recycled." Wind (12:46) 82, p.
       19.

1796. HENISCH, Peter
       "Three Poems" (tr. by Beth Bjorklund). LitR (25:2)
       Wint 82, p. 292-293.

1797. HENLEY, Lloyd
       "Answering the Census." CapeR (17:2) Sum 82, p. 41.
       "The Cabbage Seedlings." Poem (44) Mr 82, p. 11.
       "Calling in the Plumber." CapeR (17:2) Sum 82, p.
       43.
       "Cartoon: Through a Glass, Darkly." CapeR (17:2)
       Sum 82, p. 42.
       "Coloring." Poem (44) Mr 82, p. 12.
       "Last Person on the Walkway" (Kansas City, Missouri,
       7/17/81). CharR (8:1) Spr 82, p. 38-39.
       "News Footage from Africa." CharR (8:1) Spr 82, p.
       37-38.

1798. HENN, Mary Ann, Sister
       "White Moods." Wind (12:46) 82, p. 20.

1799. HENNEBERRY, Rosemary
       "The Betrayal." PottPort (4) 82-83, p. 18.
       "Tongue-Tide." PottPort (4) 82-83, p. 43.

1800. HENNESSEY, Michael F.
       "Old Pete: A Memory." PottPort (4) 82-83, p. 43.

1801. HENNIG, Sharon
       "Mountainscape." Germ (6:2) Aut-Wint 82, p. 12.

1802. HENRI, Raymond
       "Trafalgar Square." Confr (24) Sum 82, p. 50.

1803. HENRIE, Carol
      "Limits." Poetry (140:2) My 82, p. 77-78.
      "Sacrifices." PoNow (7:1, issue 37) 82, p. 17.

1804. HENRIKSSON, Mats
      "Akallan Av Hemlandet" (ur Luz de los Heroes 1954,
         tr. of Francisco Matos Paoli). Mairena (4:11/12)
         Wint 82, p. 157.
      "En Poets Biografi" (ur El Viento y la Paloma 1963-
         65, tr. of Francisco Matos Paoli). Mairena
         (4:11/12) Wint 82, p. 157.
      "Ge Mig Hjarta" (ur La marea sube 1971, tr. of
         Francisco Matos Paoli). Mairena (4:11/12) Wint 82,
         p. 156.
      "Hyllning Till Pedro Albizu Campos" (ur La Marea
         sube 1971, tr. of Francisco Matos Paoli). Mairena
         (4:11/12) Wint 82, p. 156.
      "Vaggvisa" (ur Teoria de Olvido 1944, tr. of
         Francisco Matos Paoli). Mairena (4:11/12) Wint 82,
         p. 156.

1805. HENRY, Michael
      "Ball Park." Bogg (48) 82, p. 55.
      "Grand Guignol." AntigR (50) Sum 82, p. 54.
      "Prairie Gold." Bogg (49) 82, p. 50.
      "Record Rap." AntigR (50) Sum 82, p. 54.

1806. HENRY, Sarah
      "Painted Leaves" (For Fen). HolCrit (19:3) Je 82, p.
         12.

1807. HENSON, David
      "Loch Ness / Monster / Moon." Pig (10) 82, p. 19.

1808. HENSON, Lance
      "Journal Entry." Telescope (3) Sum 82, p. 51.
      "The Room" (for my son). Telescope (3) Sum 82, p.
         50.

1809. HEPBURN, Jamie
      "Nationality." NewL (48:2) Wint 81-82, p. 71.
      "Victorian Photograph." NewL (48:2) Wint 81-82, p.
         70.

1810. HEPBURN, Margaret
      "Not Looking." NewL (49:1) Aut 82, p. 58-59.
      "Seeing Things." NewL (49:1) Aut 82, p. 56-58.

1811. HEREDIA, Jose-Maria de
      "Antony and Cleopatra" (tr. by Michael L. Johnson).
         LitR (25:3) Spr 82, p. 373.
      "La Trebbia." LittleBR (3:2) Wint 82-83, p. 28.
      "The Trebbia" (tr. by Michael L. Johnson). LittleBR
         (3:2) Wint 82-83, p. 29.
      "The Vision of Khem" (tr. by Michael L. Johnson).
         LitR (26:1) Aut 82, p. 106.

1812. HERMSEN, Terry
      "October/the Suburbs Moving Out/the Harvest Coming
         in." Pig (8) 80, p. 88.

1813. HERNAN, Owen
        from: "Home." HiramPoR (33) Aut-Wint 82, p. 16-17.

1814. HERNANDEZ, Alberto
        "Yo era la piedra furtiva" (from Instantes). Prismal
        (7/8) Spr 82, p. 89.

        HERNANDEZ, Victor de Leon
        See: LEON HERNANDEZ, Victor de

1815. HERNANDEZ AQUINO, Luis
        "La Aldea." Mairena (4:11/12) Wint 82, p. 147.

1816. HERRERA, Juan Felipe
        "Photo-Poem of the Chicano Moratorium 1980/L.A."
        RevChic (10:3) Sum 82, p. 5-9.

1817. HERRERA SOBEK, Maria
        "Abuelas Revolucionarias." RevChic (10:1/2) Wint-
        Spr 82, p. 128.
        "Colores de un Hombre Fuerte." RevChic (10:1/2)
        Wint-Spr 82, p. 129.
        "Mantillas." RevChic (10:1/2) Wint-Spr 82, p. 130.
        "Nos Encontramos." RevChic (10:1/2) Wint-Spr 82, p.
        131.

1818. HERSHMAN, M. F.
        "For Aleichem." MassR (23:3) Aut 82, p. 430.

1819. HERSHON, Elizabeth
        "Babylon." HangL (42) 82, p. 12.
        "The Balloons Drift in from the North." HangL (42)
        82, p. 13-14.
        "A War by the Ocean." HangL (42) 82, p. 11-12.

1820. HERSHON, Robert
        "Broward County." PoetryNW (23:1) Spr 82, p. 3-4.
        "Everybody and Everything." HangL (42) 82, p. 16-
        17.
        "Saturday Morning Extra Early." HangL (42) 82, p.
        15.
        "Shop Talk." HangL (42) 82, p. 18-19.
        "Walking around Downtown." PoNow (6:5, issue 35)
        82, p. 30.
        "Would You Cheat at Cards?" HangL (42) 82, p. 15.

1821. HESKETH, Phoebe
        "On Being Seventy." Stand (23:1) 81-82, p. 44.
        "Waiting." Stand (23:1) 81-82, p. 44.

1822. HESTER, M. L.
        "Lurlene." PoNow (6:4, issue 34) 82, p. 20.
        "Maria Concita Chihauhau a la Douch." Wind (12:44)
        82, p. 17.
        "The Octopus." ConcPo (15:1) Spr 82, p. 60.
        "The Price of Motels." Wind (12:44) 82, p. 17-18.
        "What My Father Said to the Statue of Liberty."
        MinnR (NS19) Aut 82, p. 41.
        "What the Rock Said." Bogg (49) 82, p. 21.

"The Young Roaches." StoneC (9:3/4) Spr-Sum 82, p.
   21.

1823. HETTICH, Michael
      "The Dance." Sam (32:3, issue 127) 82, p. 62.

1824. HEWETT, Greg
      "Gravity." PoNow (7:1, issue 37) 82, p. 18.

1825. HEWITT, Geof
      "December 8, 1980" (in Memory of John Lennon). NewL
      (48:2) Wint 81-82, p. 103.

1826. HEYM, Georg
      "The Demons of the Cities" (tr. by Peter Viereck).
         LitR (26:1) Aut 82, p. 92-93.
      "Into all sceneries" (tr. by Francis Golffing).
         PoNow (6:5, issue 35) 82, p. 42.

1827. HICKEY, Dona J.
      "Not for the Best." CarolQ (35:1) Aut 82, p. 30.

1828. HICKEY, Mark
      "Ash." KanQ (14:3) Sum 82, p. 43.

1829. HICKS, John V.
      "Flight at Sunset." Quarry (31:1) Wint 82, p. 57.
      "It Needs Still Water." Grain (10:3) Ag 82, p. 60.
      "A Song for Sylvia." KanQ (14:1) Wint 82, p. 150.
      "Wandering in an Owlery." Quarry (31:1) Wint 82, p.
         57.

1830. HIGGINBOTHAM, Keith
      "Babysitters." HangL (42) 82, p. 22.
      "Electricity." Wind (12:44) 82, p. 19.
      "Switzerland" (for Rick). HangL (42) 82, p. 20-21.

1831. HIGGINS, Anne, Sister
      "The Roofless Church." AntigR (50) Sum 82, p. 64.

1832. HIGGINS, Dick
      "Wedding Bells in 100 Words" (for Jackson in
         Vermont, August 12, 1970). Ploughs (8:2/3) 82, p.
         89.

1833. HIGH, John
      "A Voyage." HolCrit (19:5) D 82, p. 19-20.

1834. HIKEL, Trina M.
      "Fight." NoAmR (267:3) S 82,p. 53-55..

1835. HILBERRY, Conrad
      "The Dog." VirQR (58:1) Wint 82, p. 59-60.
      "A Procession of Ants, Chanting." Poetry (140:5) Ag
         82, p. 277-278.

1836. HILDEBIDLE, John
      "Das Ewig-Weibliche." Ploughs (8:1) 82, p. 157.

1837. HILL, Gerald
       "Hillside, New Brunswick, Elevation 339 Feet,
       C.P.R." Dandel (9:2) 82, p. 27.

1838. HILLERT, Margaret
       "Quick Solution." BallSUF (23:1) Wint 82, p. 56.

1839. HILLMAN, Brenda
       "Changement" (for Maxine). Field (27) Aut 82, p. 59.
       "Fossil." Field (27) Aut 82, p. 60.
       "Ophelia." Thrpny (10) Sum 82, p. 9.
       "Recital." CharR (8:1) Spr 82, p. 45-46.

1840. HILLMAN, William S.
       "Schedule." SouthwR (67:2) Spr 82, p. 196.

1841. HILTON, David
       "Black Stallion." PoNow (6:5, issue 35) 82, p. 22.
       "I Try to Turn in My Jock." Spirit (6:2/3) 82, p.
       70.
       "Listening to the Orioles - 1." Pig (9) 82, p. 17.
       "Listening to the Orioles - 2." Pig (9) 82, p. 20.
       "On the Floating Petroglyphs" (w. Jim Stephens).
       Abraxas (25/26) 82, p. 74.
       "The Raft." PoNow (6:6, issue 36) 82, p. 7.
       "We Lie Back." PoNow (6:4, issue 34) 82, p. 10.
       "Your Hair." Bogg (49) 82, p. 18.

1842. HILTON, William C.
       "Days That Grow in Dry Places." AntigR (50) Sum 82,
       p. 47.
       "Entropy." AntigR (50) Sum 82, p. 48.

1843. HIMMERSKY, Krassin
       "Echo from the Woods" (tr. by the author and Roland
       Flint). Vis (9) 82, p. 11.

1844. HIMMIRSKY, Krassin
       "The Cricket" (tr. by Denise Levertov). Hudson
       (35:4) Wint 82-83, p. 580.
       "The Men from My Childhood" (tr. by the author and
       Edward Weismiller). Vis (10) 82, p. 28.

1845. HIND, Steven
       "Familiar Ground." LittleBR (1:2) Wint 80-81, p.
       66-67.
       "Good Morning" (For Wim). LittleBR (1:4) Sum 81, p.
       20.
       "Night Driving." LittleBR (3:1) Aut 82, p. 46.

1846. HINDLEY, Norman
       "Slaughter" (for Bill Aki). PraS (56:4) Wint 82-83,
       p. 78-80.

1847. HINE, Daryl
       "The First Snowflake." PartR (49:2) 82, p. 246-248.
       "Sapphics." Poetry (141:1) O 82, p. 14.
       "Window or Wall." Poetry (141:1) O 82, p. 15.

1848. HINEGARDNER, Verna Lee
        "Silent old cricket" (Haiku). LittleBR (1:3) Spr
          81, p. 55.
        "To the Ghost of Robert Frost." LittleBR (1:3) Spr
          81, p. 48.

1849. HINESLEY, Cristin
        "Someday Madonna." Poem (46) N 82, p. 60.

1850. HINRICHSEN, Dennis
        "Ancestors" (after Pavese). Tendril (13) Sum 82, p.
          35.
        "Chincoteague." Tendril (13) Sum 82, p. 36.
        "November Streets." Agni (17) 82, p. 29-30.

1851. HIROSHI, Kashiwagi
        "Haircut." SeC (9:1/2) 80, p. 34.
        "Tofu." SeC (9:1/2) 80, p. 33.

1852. HIRSCH, Edward
        "The Bluebird Is a Fist." Sky (10-12) Aut 82, p.
          50.
        "Dawn Walk." NewYorker (58:38) N 8, 82, p. 159.
        "Edward Hopper and the House by the Railroad
          (1925)." Poetry (140:4) Jl 82, p. 219-220.
        "Fall." NewYorker (58:40) N 22, 82, p. 50.
        "In the Middle of August." Nat (235:4) Ag 7-14, 82,
          p. 120.
        "Message from Artaud." PoetryNW (23:2) Sum 82, p.
          9.
        "Moving toward a Blue Unicorn." Poetry (140:4) Jl
          82, p. 221-223.
        "My Grandfather Loved Storms." Sky (10-12) Aut 82,
          p. 51.
        "The Night of My Conception." Sky (10-12) Aut 82,
          p. 52.
        "The Night Parade" (Homage to Charles Ives). GeoR
          (36:1) Spr 82, p. 68-70.

1853. HIRSCHFIELD, Robert
        "El Salvador." ChrC (99:7) Mr 3, 82, p. 228.
        "Mr. John Ficken, Dead of Cancer, St. Rose's Home."
          Comm (109:16) S 24, 82, p. 503.

1854. HIRSCHFIELD, Ted
        "Comment on Job." CapeR (17:2) Sum 82, p. 11.

1855. HIRSHFIELD, Jane
        "5 P.M., As We Talk." QRL (23) 82, p. 36.
        "Alaya." QRL (23) 82, p. 9-10.
        "And." QRL (23) 82, p. 44.
        "Black Hag Mountain/Sotoba Komachi." QRL (23) 82, p.
          11.
        "The Conquerors of Troy." QRL (23) 82, p. 51.
        "December 13, Two." QRL (23) 82, p. 71.
        "December Solstice, '73." QRL (23) 82, p. 43.
        "December Solstice, '75." QRL (23) 82, p. 39-40.
        "Dragon Poem." QRL (23) 82, p. 70.
        "Epilogue." QRL (23) 82, p. 16.
        "Everything That Is Not You." QRL (23) 82, p. 12.

"For B.H." QRL (23) 82, p. 13.
"For P." QRL (23) 82, p. 54.
"For Wang Wei." QRL (23) 82, p. 57.
"Fuyu Persimmon." QRL (23) 82, p. 41.
"The Garden" (for Alan Chadwick). QRL (23) 82, p. 58.
"Ghazal IV." QRL (23) 82, p. 69.
"Ghazal for Ghalib." QRL (23) 82, p. 49.
"The Gift." QRL (23) 82, p. 37.
"Grandmother: a Still Life." QRL (23) 82, p. 17.
"How to Give." QRL (23) 82, p. 8.
"Hunting Song." QRL (23) 82, p. 35.
"The Landscape Painter's Dream." QRL (23) 82, p. 55-56.
"Like Salt." QRL (23) 82, p. 42.
"Lineage." QRL (23) 82, p. 50.
"Love Poem--Autumn." QRL (23) 82, p. 20.
"Mary." QRL (23) 82, p. 46.
"Norway." QRL (23) 82, p. 38.
"On a Picture of Ansel Adams." QRL (23) 82, p. 53.
"One Version." QRL (23) 82, p. 32.
"The Path of Least Resistance." QRL (23) 82, p. 67.
"Picnic." PoNow (7:1, issue 37) 82, p. 24.
"Picnic." QRL (23) 82, p. 15.
"Poems for a Stranger." QRL (23) 82, p. 25-28.
"Remnants" (for James Wright). QRL (23) 82, p. 47.
"A Riddle." QRL (23) 82, p. 18.
"River." QRL (23) 82, p. 68.
"Rye Grass Poems." QRL (23) 82, p. 21-22.
"SF Afternoon Rerun Haiku." QRL (23) 82, p. 31.
"Songs to the Nirmanakaya World." QRL (23) 82, p. 62-66.
"The Sound of Tires." PoNow (7:1, issue 37) 82, p. 24.
"The Sound of Tires." QRL (23) 82, p. 30.
"Spring Cleaning." QRL (23) 82, p. 48.
"Stranger Now." QRL (23) 82, p. 29.
"The Stream of It." QRL (23) 82, p. 72.
"Suite for Four Hands"(for May Miller). QRL (23) 82, p. 59-60.
"Surveying." QRL (23) 82, p. 33-34.
"Tanabata." QRL (23) 82, p. 19.
"Those Chinese Poems." QRL (23) 82, p. 24.
"To a Mare." QRL (23) 82, p. 52.
"Vermont: Hunting." QRL (23) 82, p. 14.

1856. HISE, Jesse
"To Those in Charge." EngJ (71:4) Ap 82, p. 30.

1857. HIXON, Jane
"The Old Widow." SoCaR (14:2) Spr 82, p. 77.

HO, Hon Leung
See: LEUNG, Ho Hon

1858. HOAGLAND, Tony
"When Travelling." Spirit (6:2/3) 82, p. 36-37.

1859. HOAR, Deidre
"Annunciation." Comm (109:22) D 17, 82, p. 687.

1860. HOBBY, Bernard
        "Lament." Bogg (48) 82, p. 71.
        "Remainder Bin." Bogg (49) 82, p. 35.

1861. HOBERMAN, Mary Ann
        "Parting Moment." SouthernPR (22:1) Spr 82, p. 55.
        "So I Open the Novel." SmPd (19:3, issue 56) Aut
        82, p. 24.
        "Suddenly." SmPd (19:3, issue 56) Aut 82, p. 23.
        "Tenth Year." SouthernPR (23, i.e. 22:2) Aut 82, p.
        24.

1862. HODGES, Charles
        "Last Day in Paradise." MendoR (5) Sum 81, p. 11.
        "Prophecy of Frogs and Owls." KanQ (14:3) Sum 82,
        p. 93.

1863. HODGKINSON, Edith
        "You, you're a space case running downhill." HangL
        (41) 82, p. 31.
        "You're Not Home." HangL (41) 82, p. 30.

1864. HOEFER, David
        "The Regular Monthly Long Distance Call to a
        Friend." PoNow (7:1, issue 37) 82, p. 18.
        "Vision of Neal and Jack." PoNow (7:1, issue 37)
        82, p. 18.

1865. HOEFT, Robert D.
        "Thirty Days of Snow on the Ground." Poem (44) Mr
        82, p. 5.
        "The Winter As Villain." Poem (44) Mr 82, p. 6.

1866. HOFER, Mariann
        "Fall in Reily, Ohio." Wind (12:45) 82, p. 21.

1867. HOFFMAN, Carla
        "Lord Randal's Lady." PoNow (6:6, issue 36) 82, p.
        36.

1868. HOFFMAN, Cindy
        "Faculty Lounge." EngJ (71:6) O 82, p. 25.

1869. HOFFMAN, Dan
        "Bwana." ChrC (99:26) Ag 18-25, 82, p. 858.

1870. HOFFMAN, Daniel
        "At Fontaine-Les-Dijon." PoetryNW (23:4) Wint 82-
        83, p. 35-36.
        "The Battle of Hastings." PoetryNW (23:4) Wint 82-
        83, p. 33-35.
        "A Letter to W. H. Auden." YaleR (71:2) Wint 82, p.
        236-237.

1871. HOFMANN, Michael
        "Fates of the Expressionists." AmerS (51:3) Sum 82,
        p. 338.
        "White Noise." Poetry (140:2) My 82, p. 91.

1872. HOGAN, Michael
          "How a Planet Stays in Orbit." PoNow (6:4, issue
          34) 82, p. 21.
          "Two Childhood Friends." PoNow (6:4, issue 34) 82,
          p. 12.

1873. HOGG, Ian
          "Surrey on a Sunday." Bogg (48) 82, p. 46.

1874. HOHEISEL, Peter
          "At Lake Superior." CentR (26:2) Spr 82, p. 174-
          175.

      HOLADAY, Woon-Ping Chin
      See: CHIN, Woon Ping

1875. HOLAN, Vladimir
          "And There" (tr. by Dana Habova and David Young).
          Field (27) Aut 82, p. 75.
          "Lovers I" (tr. by Dana Habova and Stuart Friebert).
          Field (27) Aut 82, p. 74.
          "Resurrection" (tr. by Dana Habova and David Young).
          Field (27) Aut 82, p. 76.

1876. HOLDEN, Jonathan
          "An American Boyhood." MissouriR (5:2) Wint 81-82,
          p. 42.
          "Buying a Baseball." MinnR (NS19) Aut 82, p. 43.
          "Deathbed." MidwQ (23:2) Wint 82, p. 185.
          "Filling the Ruts." AspenJ (1) Wint 82, p. 31.
          "In a Cloud." WestB (10) 82, p. 67.
          "In Memory of Dale Long." ColEng 44(3) Mr 82, p.
          286-287.
          "Losers." Poetry (140:4) Jl 82, p. 210-211.
          "The Man Who Is Finished." MassR (23:4) Wint 82, p.
          750-751.
          "The Names of the Rapids." GeoR (36:2) Sum 82, p.
          414.
          "School-Yard." MissouriR (5:2) Wint 81-82, p. 40-
          41.
          "'The Swing,' by Honore Fragonard." MinnR (NS18)
          Spr 82, p. 18.
          "The Third Party." Poetry (140:4) Jl 82, p. 212-
          213.
          "To Father." StoneC (9:3/4) Spr-Sum 82, p. 10-11.
          "Visiting Pre-school." MidwQ (23:2) Wint 82, p.
          184.
          "Visiting Pre-School." WestB (10) 82, p. 66.
          "Watching the Snow, I Give Up." MidwQ (23:2) Wint
          82, p. 183.

1877. HOLDERLIN, Friedrich
          "Summer" (tr. by David Rattray). Sulfur (2:3, issue
          6) 82, p. 111.

1878. HOLLADAY, Hilary W.
          "Mary, Queen of Scots." WestB (10) 82, p. 69.
          "The Sleepless Night." WestB (10) 82, p. 68.

1879. HOLLAHAN, Eugene
        "The Lighthouse at St. Augustine." UTR (7:2) 82?,
        p. 10-12.

1880. HOLLAND, Barbara A.
        "Advance upon Canaan." StoneC (10:1/2) Aut-Wint 82-
        83, p. 10-11.
        "The Circle of Chalk." Im (8:1) 82, p. 4.
        "UFO." PoNow (6:4, issue 34) 82, p. 43.

1881. HOLLAND, Gill
        "Shot on the Radioactive Set: Our Countdown with the
        Duke." SouthernPR (22:1) Spr 82, p. 70-71.

1882. HOLLAND, Walter
        "For Franz Kline." LitR (26:1) Aut 82, p. 119.
        "For Georgia O'Keefe." LitR (26:1) Aut 82, p. 120.
        "Poems for Marsden Hartley." LitR (26:1) Aut 82, p.
        121.

1883. HOLLANDER, John
        "Behold!" Nat (235:17) N 20, 82, p. 522.
        "Disagreements" Antaeus (44) Wint 82, p. 181.
        "Figuring It Out." Nat (235:17) N 20, 82, p. 523.
        "Hidden Rhymes." Antaeus (44) Wint 82, p. 180.
        "On the Way to Summer." Shen (33:3) 82, p. 48-50.
        "Refrains." Antaeus (44) Wint 82, p. 182.
        "Rites of Passage." Nat (235:17) N 20, 82, p. 523.
        "Some Walks with You." AmerPoR (11:5) S-O 82, p.
        21-23.
        "When Blood Is Nipped." Nat (235:17) N 20, 82, p.
        522.

1884. HOLLANDER, Martha
        "Venetian Blinds." Hudson (35:1) Spr 82, p. 89.

1885. HOLLO, Anselm
        "Lightning in the ground" (tr. of Lars Lundkvist, w.
        Gunnar Harding). Spirit (6:2/3) 82, p. 122.
        "Man across the moor" (tr. of Lars Lundkvist, w.
        Gunnar Harding). Spirit (6:2/3) 82, p. 122.
        "Once much ice was here" (tr. of Lars Lundkvist, w.
        Gunnar Harding). Spirit (6:2/3) 82, p. 122-123.
        "Song of the Tusk." Spirit (6:2/3) 82, p. 67.

1886. HOLLOWAY, David
        "Thick Days in Miami." Kayak (60) O 82, p. 48.

1887. HOLLOWAY, Geoffrey
        "April Dusk." Bogg (49) 82, p. 55.
        "Gaol Transcript." Stand (23:1) 81-82, p. 28-29.

1888. HOLLOWAY, John
        "Cleanness." Stand (23:1) 81-82, p. 68.
        "Singing Is Believing." Hudson (35:4) Wint 82-83,
        p. 574.
        "Sleeping and Waking." Hudson (35:4) Wint 82-83, p.
        572.
        "Sunbathing Talk." Hudson (35:4) Wint 82-83, p.
        573.

1889. HOLMES, John Clellon
    "Our Minotaur Is Gone" (For Henry Miller). PoNow
    (6:5, issue 35) 82, p. 9.

1890. HOLMES, Olivia
    "Fresco: The Battle of Milvio Bridge." Shen (33:1)
    81-82, p. 62.
    "Helen in Bed." Hudson (35:4) Wint 82-83, p. 601.
    "Sentences" (for M. G.). Shen (33:1) 81-82, p. 63.

1891. HOLMGREN, Mark
    "Waiting for Eggs." PoNow (6:4, issue 34) 82, p.
    47.

1892. HOLUB, Miroslav
    "At the Bottom of the Day" (tr. Oldrich Vyhlidal, w.
    David Young). Field (27) Aut 82, p. 77.
    "Biodrama" (tr. by Dana Ha'bova' and Stuart
    Friebert). MalR (62) Jl 82, p. 92.
    "Dreams" (tr. by Dana Ha'bova' and Stuart Friebert).
    MalR (62) Jl 82, p. 89.
    "The Grave of Casanova" (tr. of Jaroslav Seifert, w.
    David Young). Field (27) Aut 82, p. 71-73.
    "Hominization" (tr. by Dana Ha'bova' and Stuart
    Friebert). MalR (62) Jl 82, p. 93.
    "Interferon" (tr. by Dana Habova and David Young).
    Field (26) Spr 82, p. 61-67.
    "The Jewish Cemetery at Olsany, Kafka's Tomb, April,
    Sunny Weather" (tr. by Dana Ha'bova' and Stuart
    Friebert). MalR (62) Jl 82, p. 90.
    "A Natural History of Arthropods" (tr. by Dana
    Ha'bova' and Stuart Friebert). MalR (62) Jl 82, p.
    91.

1893. HOLZER, Max
    "He Let the House Be" (tr. by Beth Bjorklund). LitR
    (25:2) Wint 82, p. 189.
    "Mysterious Geometry" (tr. by Beth Bjorklund). LitR
    (25:2) Wint 82, p. 187.
    "The Summer's Cold" (tr. by Beth Bjorklund). LitR
    (25:2) Wint 82, p. 187-188.

1894. HOLZMAN, Michael
    "Tar." Maize (5:3/4) Spr-Sum 82, p. 57-61.

1895. HOMER, Art
    "Collage Not Culled from the Pages of History Books
    or Newspapers." Tendril (13) Sum 82, p. 38-39.
    "Old Stories, the Morning News." ColEng 44(7) N 82,
    p. 716-717.
    "Rainy View from Second Story." Tendril (13) Sum
    82, p. 37.
    "Ten A.M. Highway." QW (14) Spr-Sum 82, p. 41.

1896. HONECKER, George J.
    "Glass Bottom Boat" (for Sina Richards). LittleM
    (13:3/4) 82, p. 46-51.

1897. HONGO, Garrett Kaoru
        "And Your Soul Shall Dance" (for Wakako Yamauchi).
        Spirit (6:2/3) 82, p. 147.

1898. HONIG, Edwin
        "After the Letter." Salm (55) Wint 82, p. 133-134.
        "By Sea Stone." Im (8:2) 82, p. 7.
        "Three Desperate Love Songs." PoNow (6:6, issue 36)
        82, p. 13.

1899. HOOD, Michael
        "Black Diamonds" (Wenham, from an untitled work-in-
        progress). StoneC (10:1/2) Aut-Wint 82-83,p. 29.
        "February Feeling" (Barnstable, from an untitled
        work-in-progress). StoneC (10:1/2) Aut-Wint 82-
        83,p. 28.
        "View from a Porch" (Bourne, from an untitled work-
        in-progress). StoneC (10:1/2) Aut-Wint 82-83,p.
        28.

1900. HOOPER, Patricia
        "At Evening." SouthernPR (23, i.e. 22:2) Aut 82, p.
        21.
        "Money." MichQR (21:1) Wint 82, p. 159-160.

1901. HOOVER, Paul
        "Bright Surviving Actual Scene." Epoch (31:3) Sum
        82, p. 219.
        "The Chinese Notebook." Sulfur (2:3, issue 6) 82,
        p. 24-28.
        "In a Suburb of the Spirit." NewOR (9:1) Spr-Sum
        82, p. 36.
        "Out of Sight, Out of Mind." Epoch (31:3) Sum 82,
        p. 220.
        "Ships Arriving, Puget Sound." NowestR (20:1) 82,
        p. 88-89.
        "Somebody Talks a Lot." Epoch (31:3) Sum 82, p.
        218-219.

1902. HOPE, A. D.
        "Salabhanjika." NewL (48:3/4) Spr-Sum 82, p. 116-
        117.

1903. HOPE, Akua Lezli
        "Getting to Know, or Stepping Out in an Entirely
        Different Way" (for Swan). Iowa (12:2/3) Spr-Sum
        81, p. 189.
        "Gowanus Canal (Because You Said Look Again)." Iowa
        (12:2/3) Spr-Sum 81, p. 190.

1904. HOPES, David
        "And At Sea it Is Like This." PoetryNW (23:1) Spr
        82, p. 43-44.
        "Dust." WestB (10) 82, p. 5-6.
        "In That Heaven." Poem (45) Jl 82, p. 8.
        "Sunday Bells." WestB (10) 82, p. 7.
        "Three Songs for Saint Valentine's Day." Poem (45)
        Jl 82, p. 10-11.
        "Two for Farewell." Poem (45) Jl 82, p. 9.

1905. HOPKINS, Gerard Manley
      "The Windhover: To Christ Our Lord." AntigR (49)
      Spr 82, p. 22.

1906. HOPKINS, Mark
      "August." Tendril (13) Sum 82, p. 40.

1907. HORACE
      "1.25." StoneC (9:3/4) Spr-Sum 82, p. 26.
      "1.25" (tr. by Joseph Salemi). StoneC (9:3/4) Spr-
      Sum 82, p. 27.

1908. HORNE, Lewis
      "Gymnasts in Woods." Quarry (31:1) Wint 82, p. 10.
      "Lines from a Prairie City." MichQR (21:1) Wint 82,
      p. 155.
      "Marionette Circus." Quarry (31:1) Wint 82, p. 10-
      11.
      "My Grandmother's Clock." Quarry (31:1) Wint 82, p.
      11-12.

1909. HORNER, Jan
      "Cyclist." Dandel (9:2) 82, p. 23-24.

1910. HORNIG, Doug
      "Long Time Coming, Got to Be a Long Time Gone."
      Bogg (49) 82, p. 7.

1911. HOROVITZ, Bruce
      "Like the Year Richie Schienbloom Went 0 for 64."
      Pig (9) 82, p. 56.

1912. HOROWITZ, Mikhail
      "Equation." Pig (9) 82, p. 39.
      "A Meditation on the Death of Thurman Munson." Pig
      (9) 82, p. 41.
      "One for the Monk." Abraxas (25/26) 82, p. 44.

1913. HORSTING, Eric
      "Making Omelettes." DenQ (17:2) Sum 82, p. 15.

1914. HORVATH, Brooke
      "I'll Always Remember You Sweet in the Grass." Poem
      (44) Mr 82, p. 40.

1915. HORVATH, John
      "Apalachee Twister." AntigR (50) Sum 82, p. 28.
      "How Baba Earned Her Hump." PoetC (14:1) 82, p. 36-
      37.
      "Strikers' Sunday." PoetC (14:1) 82, p. 35-36.

1916. HOSKIN, William D.
      "Jesse Plays for Dancing." HiramPoR (33) Aut-Wint
      82, p. 18.
      "Uncle Lou." HiramPoR (31) Aut-Wint 82, p. 31.

1917. HOTCH, Phyllis
      "The Frugal Repast" (Picasso, Paris, Autumn 1904).
      Thrpny (10) Sum 82, p. 20.

1918. HOTHAM, Gary
"Fresh snow." Northeast (3:14) Wint 82-83, p. 21.
"Last night's snow." Northeast (3:14) Wint 82-83,
p. 21.

HOVANESSIAN, Diana der
See: Der HOVANESSIAN, Diana

1919. HOUCHIN, Ron
"Pagasus." Poem (45) Jl 82, p. 20-21.
"A Surveyor Considers the Clouds." Poem (45) Jl 82,
p. 19.

1920. HOUGHTON, Tim
"Legend of the Black Gods." DenQ (16:4) Wint 82, p.
54.
"Those Who Were Left." DenQ (16:4) Wint 82, p. 52-
53.

1921. HOUSE, Tom
"Anima." Bogg (48) 82, p. 10-11.
"The Pick-Up." Catalyst (Erotica Issue) 82, p. 30.
"Roughting It." Vis (9) 82, p. 9.

1922. HOUSLEY, Kathleen
"Directions for Reading the Bible." ChrC (99:24) Jl
21-28, 82, p. 788.

1923. HOVDE, A. J.
"Sleeping Dragon." Wind (12:44) 82, p. 7.
"What Wonders Are in Store As We Grow Old."
SouthernHR (16:2) Spr 82, p. 144.

1924. HOWARD, Lynne Cawood
"The Miner's Son." Telescope (3) Sum 82, p. 52.

1925. HOWE, Fanny
"Onlie X." Ploughs (8:2/3) 82, p. 157.
"Poem for Potential." Ploughs (8:2/3) 82, p. 158.

1926. HOWELL, Bill
"Ode to the Thirteen Confederate Generals Secretly
Buried in Halifax, N.S." PoetryCR (4:1) Sum 82, p.
7.

1927. HOWELL, Christopher
"Notes." MinnR (NS19) Aut 82, p. 56.
"The Search for Stephen Skjei." MinnR (NS19) Aut
82, p. 54-55.

1928. HOWELL, Sue
"On Re-Reading Paradise Lost." EngJ (71:3) Mr 82,
p. 40.

1929. HOWELL, William
"Believing on Skyline Drive." CimR (58) Ja 82, p.
61.
"Practicing in the Bottomland." SouthernR (18:1)
Wint 82, p. 179-180.

1930. HOYOS, Angela de
"The Final Laugh." RevChic (10:1/2) Wint-Spr 82, p. 78.
"Un Llanto en Seco." RevChic (10:1/2) Wint-Spr 82, p. 77.
"The Missing Ingredient." RevChic (10:1/2) Wint-Spr 82, p. 79.

1931. HRV
"Time and Time Again." Maize (5:3/4) Spr-Sum 82, p. 52.

1932. HRYCIUK, Marshall
"On the Lisp." Quarry (31:3) Sum 82, p. 41-42.
"The Shield of Canada." Quarry (31:3) Sum 82, p. 39-41.
"Thousand Island Dressing." Quarry (31:3) Sum 82, p. 38-39.

1933. HRYNIUK, Angela
"Brain Cancer." WritersL D 82, p. 14.

HUALING, Nieh
See: NIEH, Hualing

1934. HUCHEL, Peter
"Chiesa del Soccorso" (tr. by Rich Ives). PortR (28:1) 82, p. 33.
"Dream in the Trap" (tr. by Rich Ives). PortR (28:1) 82, p. 33.
"Fog" (for Ludvik Kundera, tr. by Rich Ives). PortR (28:1) 82, p. 33.
"Sibyl of Summer" (tr. by Rich Ives). PortR (28:1) 82, p. 33.

1935. HUDGINS, Andrew
"Audubon Examines a Bittern." Poetry (140:2) My 82, p. 84.
"Burial Detail." SouthernR (18:4) Aut 82, p. 825-827.
"He Imagines His Wife Dead: Sidney Lanier, 1878." Hudson (35:2) Sum 82, p. 225.
"Sidney Lanier: His Wife." Hudson (35:2) Sum 82, p. 227.
"The Winter's Dance" (for Olivia). SouthernHR (16:1) Wint 82, p. 45-46.
"The Yellow Steeple." Hudson (35:2) Sum 82, p. 226.

1936. HUFF, Robert
"Boy in the Suburbs" (In Memory of Ben Shahn). PoNow (6:5, issue 35) 82, p. 8.
"For a Man Who Died Quickly on a Road in Mexico." PoNow (6:5, issue 35) 82, p. 8.
"On the Morning of the Death of Robert Hillyer." PoNow (6:4, issue 34) 82, p. 28.

1937. HUFF, Roland
"Crazy Like a Fox for Anne Sexton." CapeR (17:2) Sum 82, p. 20.

"Epitaph" (for a convicted rapist). _Wind_ (12:46) 82,
p. 21.

1938. HUFFSTICKLER, Albert
"Madonna of the Dispossessed." _Nimrod_ (25:2) Spr-
Sum 82, p. 13.
"South of Saltillo." _Abraxas_ (25/26) 82, p. 45.

1939. HUGO, Richard
"Ashville." _AmerPoR_ (11:6) N-D 82, p. 28.
"Bannerman's Island" (for Chris). _NowestR_ (20:2/3)
82, p. 127.
"Bannerman's Island" (for Chris). _NewEngR_ (5:1/2)
Aut-Wint 82, p. 11.
"Distances." _Atl_ (250:2) Ag 82, p. 54.
"Gray Stone." _AmerPoR_ (11:6) N-D 82, p. 29.
"Making Certain It Goes On." _AmerPoR_ (11:6) N-D 82,
p. 29.
"Poem for Zen Hofman." _NewEngR_ (5:1/2) Aut-Wint 82,
p. 12.
"Red Stone." _AmerPoR_ (11:6) N-D 82, p. 29.
"Saltwater Story." _NewYorker_ (58:39) N 15, 82, p.
52.

HUIDOBRO, Matias Montes
See: MONTES HUIDOBRO, Matias

1940. HUIDOBRO, Vicente
"Empty" (for Blaise Cendrars, tr. by David Guss).
Kayak (60) O 82, p. 58.
"Horizon" (tr. by David Guss). _Kayak_ (60) O 82, p.
59.
"Spring" (tr. by David Guss). _Kayak_ (60) O 82, p.
60.
"Swimmer" (tr. by David Guss). _Kayak_ (60) O 82, p.
61.

1941. HULL, Gloria
"Blues Snatch." _Obs_ (7:2/3) Sum-Wint 81, p. 191.
"Movin' and Steppin'." _Obs_ (7:2/3) Sum-Wint 81, p.
188-189.
"The Prison and the Park." _Obs_ (7:2/3) Sum-Wint 81,
p. 189-190.

1942. HUMES, Harry
"Adultery." _StoneC_ (9:3/4) Spr-Sum 82, p. 52-53.
"Adultery" (The Phillips Poetry Award--Spring/Summer
1982). _StoneC_ (10:1/2) Aut-Wint 82-83, p. 38.
"All the Way Back." _CimR_ (58) Ja 82, p. 60.
"Baking Bread during a Drought." _BelPoJ_ (33:2) Wint
82-83, p. 1.
"Building a Tower" (for Rachel). _MassR_ (23:4) Wint
82, p. 706-708.
"The Deacon's Arm." _KanQ_ (14:3) Sum 82, p. 64.
"The Garden in Ruins." _KanQ_ (14:3) Sum 82, p. 63.
"Reading Late by a Simple Light." _KanQ_ (14:3) Sum
82, p. 63.
"Ridge Music." _PoetryNW_ (23:3) Aut 82, p. 27-28.
"Safety Zone." _KanQ_ (14:3) Sum 82, p. 62.
"The Sermon Stump." _KanQ_ (14:3) Sum 82, p. 65.

"Through the Ice Tree." <u>Comm</u> (109:5) Mr 12, 82, p.
    158.
"The Ways of Water." <u>PoetryNW</u> (23:3) Aut 82, p. 26-
    27.
"While You Are Watching." <u>MissouriR</u> (5:3) Sum 82,
    p. 20.
"Woman in the Herb Garden." <u>PoetryNW</u> (23:3) Aut 82,
    p. 28.

1943. HUMMA, John
    "Drowning, Friendship, a Girlfriend." <u>Poem</u> (45) Jl
        82, p. 60.
    "El Salvador." <u>MinnR</u> (NS18) Spr 82, p. 19.
    "Sleep and Dreams." <u>Poem</u> (45) Jl 82, p. 61.

1944. HUMMER, T. R.
    "Correspondence: Faded Love" (For George Woodward
        and Nannie Carlisle: lovers and correspondents:
        married 1856). <u>QW</u> (15) Aut-Wint 82-83, p. 65-72.
    "Love Poem: The Dispossessed." <u>NewYorker</u> (58:5) Mr
        22, 82, p. 44.
    "Train Wreck, 1890: My Grandmother Lies Down with
        the Dead." <u>PraS</u> (56:4) Wint 82-83, p. 28-29.
    "Voice and Room, in the Course of Time." <u>CharR</u>
        (8:2) Aut 82, p. 28-29.
    "What Shines in Winter Burns." <u>NoAmR</u> (267:4) D
        82, p. 34.

1945. HUMPHREYS, Helen
    "Circumstantial Removal." <u>MalR</u> (62) Jl 82, p. 61.

1946. HUNT, Evelyn Tooley
    "Advent." <u>ChrC</u> (99:38) D 1, 82, p. 1230.
    "The Street." <u>ChrC</u> (99:1) Ja 6-13, 82, p. 13.

1947. HUNT, William
    "After a Theme by Houdini." <u>Salm</u> (56) Spr 82, p.
        132.

1948. HUNTER, Bruce
    "After She Has Left." <u>CrossC</u> (4:2/3) 82, p. 38.
    "The Sad Man Muses on the Sad State of Things."
        <u>CrossC</u> (4:2/3) 82, p. 38.
    "Strong Women" (after Marg Piercy). <u>PoetryCR</u> (3:3)
        Spr 82, p. 15.

1949. HUNTER, Deena
    "Driller." <u>Quarry</u> (31:3) Sum 82, p. 70-71.
    "Sudden Wind." <u>Quarry</u> (31:3) Sum 82, p. 69-70.

1950. HUNTER, Donnell
    "Friday Morning Trivia." <u>ColEng</u> 44(7) N 82, p. 715.

1951. HUNTINGTON, Cynthia
    "Accidental." <u>Ploughs</u> (8:2/3) 82, p. 13-14.
    "At Tut's Store." <u>Nimrod</u> (26:1) Aut-Wint 82, p.
        103.
    "Calm." <u>Ploughs</u> (8:2/3) 82, p. 19-20.
    "Climbing Long Mountain." <u>Nimrod</u> (26:1) Aut-Wint
        82, p. 102-103.

"Fire." <u>Nimrod</u> (26:1) Aut-Wint 82, p. 105-106.
"From Exile." <u>Ploughs</u> (8:2/3) 82, p. 15-18.
"Here Come the Men My Mother Warned Me of." <u>VirQR</u>
   (58:2) Spr 82, p. 270-272.
"The House among Pines." <u>Nimrod</u> (26:1) Aut-Wint 82,
   p. 97-107.
"The Lake." <u>Nimrod</u> (26:1) Aut-Wint 82, p. 100-101.
"The Length of the Hour." <u>Ploughs</u> (8:1) 82, p. 145-
   146.
"Migraine." <u>VirQR</u> (58:2) Spr 82, p. 272-274.
"Moorings." <u>Nimrod</u> (26:1) Aut-Wint 82, p. 97-100.
"Night." <u>Nimrod</u> (26:1) Aut-Wint 82, p. 106-107.
"Return." <u>Nimrod</u> (26:1) Aut-Wint 82, p. 104-105.
"A Visit." <u>Nimrod</u> (26:1) Aut-Wint 82, p. 101.

1952. HURD, Michael Robert
   "To a Former Professor." <u>KanQ</u> (14:1) Wint 82, p.
   59.

1953. HURLEY, Andrew
   "Legacies" (tr. of Heberto Padilla, w. Alastair
   Reid). <u>NewYorker</u> (57:46) Ja 4, 82, p. 36-37.
   "A Prayer for the End of the Century" (tr. of
   Heberto Padilla, w. Alastair Reid). <u>NewYorker</u>
   (57:46) Ja 4, 82, p. 36.
   "Returning to Bright Places" (tr. of Heberto
   Padilla, w. Alastair Reid). <u>NewYorker</u> (57:46) Ja
   4, 82, p. 36.
   "Song of the Navigator" (tr. of Heberto Padilla, w.
   Alastair Reid). <u>NewYorker</u> (57:46) Ja 4, 82, p. 36.
   "Walking" (tr. of Heberto Padilla, w. Alastair
   Reid). <u>NewYorker</u> (57:46) Ja 4, 82, p. 36.

1954. HUSEBOE, Arthur R.
   "Sioux Land." <u>SoDakR</u> (20:4) Wint 82-83, p. 35.

1955. HUTCHINGS, Pat
   "After the Wedding They Move to Missouri." <u>SmPd</u>
   (19:3, issue 56) Aut 82, p. 22.
   "Al's Tropical Fish Paradise." <u>Abraxas</u> (25/26) 82,
   p. 102.
   "Perfect Match." <u>PoNow</u> (7:1, issue 37) 82, p. 18.
   "Redecorating." <u>SmPd</u> (19:2, issue 55) Spr 82, p.
   21.
   "Thirty-One and Wondering about Eighty." <u>SmPd</u>
   (19:2, issue 55) Spr 82, p. 21.
   "Winter Keeps Us Close." <u>Poetry</u> (141:2) N 82, p.
   67.

1956. HUTCHINSON, Robert
   "Grief in Blackhawk, Colorado" (L. A. H., 1884-
   1968). <u>Telescope</u> (3) Sum 82, p. 69-70.

1957. HUTCHISON, Joseph
   "Couplets." <u>Catalyst</u> (Erotica Issue) 82, p. 27.
   "Interlude at Green Mountain Park." <u>Northeast</u>
   (3:14) Wint 82-83, p. 11.

1958. HUTCHMAN, Laurence
   "Enchantress." <u>PoetryCR</u> (4:2) Wint 82, p. 6.

"The Garden." AntigR (51) Aut 82, p. 106-108.

1959. HUTCHMAN, Lawrence
       "La Tempete." PoetryCR (4:1) Sum 82, p. 5.

1960. HYETT, Barbara Helfgott
       "The Keeper of the Light." MassR (23:4) Wint 82, p.
         705.
       "Kick the Can." PoetryNW (23:2) Sum 82, p. 34-35.

1961. HYLAND, Gary
       "The Last Sermon of the 14th Dalai Lama." Grain
         (10:3) Ag 82, p. 49.

1962. IACONO, Eva
       "7:40-2:19 Weekdays." HangL (41) 82, p. 54.

1963. IBACH, Howard
       "Listening to Myself." UTR (7:2) 82?, p. 7.
       "Orange Eyes of Flight." UTR (7:2) 82?, p. 8-9.

1964. IGNATOW, David
       "Above and Within." Pequod (15) 82, p. 77.
       "And in Pity." Im (8:2) 82, p. 6.
       "Beyond That." UnderRM (1:2) Aut 82, p. 8.
       "Credo." Pequod (15) 82, p. 75.
       "Dear Homer." Agni (17) 82, p. 48.
       "A Double Grace." Pequod (15) 82, p. 76.
       "Each Stone." Telescope (2) Aut 81, p. 49.
       "For Now." Nat (235:13) O 23, 82, p. 405.
       "From Across the Room." Telescope (2) Aut 81, p.
         48.
       "The Garden and the Store." UnderRM (1:2) Aut 82,
         p. 9.
       "His Own Grave." PoNow (6:6, issue 36) 82, p. 12.
       "I Am." NewL (48:2) Wint 81-82, p. 39.
       "I Wish." Im (8:2) 82, p. 6.
       "Knowledge." Im (8:2) 82, p. 6.
       "The Language." Nat (235:13) O 23, 82, p. 405.
       "The Machine." Agni (17) 82, p. 49.
       "The Need." Im (8:2) 82, p. 6.
       "On Quantitative Analysis." PoNow (6:6, issue 36)
         82, p. 12.
       "On the Bowery." UnderRM (1:2) Aut 82, p. 8.
       "Popcorn." Im (8:2) 82, p. 6.
       "Sacrates in Hades." UnderRM (1:2) Aut 82, p. 10.
       "A Sequence for James Wright." OhioR (29) 82, p.
         100-101.
       "Silent." PoetryE (7) Spr 82, p. 20.
       "The Storm." Im (8:2) 82, p. 6.
       "Survivors." PoNow (6:6, issue 36) 82, p. 12.
       "That Car." Im (8:2) 82, p. 6.
       "Who Knows?" PoetryE (7) Spr 82, p. 19.

1965. IGNATOW, Yaedi
       "Suicide." Confr (23) Wint 82, p. 119.

1966. IKAN, Ron
       "All-Nite Diner." PoNow (6:4, issue 34) 82, p. 30.
       "Corona Borealis." KanQ (14:3) Sum 82, p. 99.

"Eleven Right, Seventeen Left, Twenty-three Right."
StoneC (9:3/4) Spr-Sum 82, p. 34.
"Fifty Thousand Watts." MinnR (NS18) Spr 82, p. 68.
"The Man Who Sprang from Clay." PoNow (6:4, issue
34) 82, p. 30.
"My Grandfather." AspenJ (1) Wint 82, p. 27.
"North American Rites." KanQ (14:3) Sum 82, p. 98.
"Powder River Country." AspenJ (1) Wint 82, p. 27.
"Special Theory." KanQ (14:3) Sum 82, p. 100.
"Stud Barn." CapeR (17:2) Sum 82, p. 21.

1967. IKEDA, Patricia Y.
"A Card Game: Kinjiro Sawada." Field (27) Aut 82,
p. 64-65.
"Dated." Field (27) Aut 82, p. 63.
"Imagine Paris" (for Mathis Szykowski). Field (27)
Aut 82, p. 66-67.

1968. INADA, Lawson Fusao
"Japan I: To Be." NowestR (20:2/3) 82, p. 57-58.
"Japan XVI: Swift Ness." NowestR (20:2/3) 82, p.
58-59.

1969. INEZ, Colette
"All Things Are One Said Empedocles in a Light as
Probable as Hume." PartR (49:3) 82, p. 429-430.
"The Auras around Our Bodies." LittleM (13:3/4) 82,
p. 68.
"Grandma Moses Painted from the Topside Down, First,
the Sky, People, Last." BlackWR (7:2) Spr 81, p.
39.
"Lake Song." YaleR (72:1) Aut 82, p. 62.
"Sylvia and Annie." NoAmR (267:4) D 82,p. 16.
"Things Dream of Their Likenesses and Needs." MassR
(23:2) Sum 82, p. 201-202.
"Without Toys at the Home." WestB (10) 82, p. 44-
45.
"Word Songs." Im (8:2) 82, p. 10.

1970. INGALLS, Jeremy
"Epitome." PoNow (6:5, issue 35) 82, p. 21.
"Millenial Parable." PoNow (6:6, issue 36) 82, p.
29.

1971. INGALLS, Russell
"My Babysitter's Threats." PoNow (7:1, issue 37)
82, p. 18.

1972. INKSTER, Tim
"The Daisies in the Field." MalR (61) F 82, p. 148.
"Something is Always Left." MalR (61) F 82, p. 149.
"You Know My Love of Tea." MalR (61) F 82, p. 148.

1973. INMAN, Will
"Estaban" (a lorca night). Abraxas (25/26) 82, p.
52-53.
"Freedom." Sam (33:3, issue 131) 82, p. 10-13.
"Meantime We Shall Weave." Im (8:1) 82, p. 11.
"Territories and Realms." Abraxas (25/26) 82, p.
54.

1974. IOANNOU, Susan
      "Editorial." PoetryCR (3:3) Spr 82, p. 13.

1975. IRIE, Kevin
      "Apartment Bicycles." AntigR (50) Sum 82, p. 43.
      "Cat-Tails." Germ (6:2) Aut-Wint 82, p. 14.
      "Cottage Country, Winter." AntigR (48) Wint 82, p.
        93-94.
      "June Trillium." Germ (6:2) Aut-Wint 82, p. 13.
      "Skinner's Rock." PoetryCR (3:3) Spr 82, p. 13.
      "The Wasp Nest." Waves (11:1) Aut 82, p. 69.
      "Winter Earth, Winter Sky." AntigR (48) Wint 82, p.
        94.

1976. IRWIN, G.
      "The river changed its mind." Bogg (49) 82, p. 35.

1977. IRWIN, Mark
      "Augustifolia." AntR (40:4) Aut 82, p. 442.
      "The Bell." PoNow (7:1, issue 37) 82, p. 19.
      "Elegy." PoNow (7:1, issue 37) 82, p. 19.
      "The Keys" (tr. of Nichita Stanescue, w. Mariana
        Carpinisan). Pequod (15) 82, p. 74.
      "Lesson on the Circle" (tr. of Nichita Stanescue, w.
        Mariana Carpinisan). Pequod (15) 82, p. 73.

1978. ISIS
      "Ojo de Leopardo." LetFem (8:1) 82, p. 102-105.
      "Requiem por Mi." LetFem (8:1) 82, p. 106.

1979. ISSAIA, Nana
      "Instant Love." Dandel (9:1) 82, p. 56.
      "Note of Dust." Dandel (9:1) 82, p. 57.
      "Self." Grain (10:2) My 82, p. 55.

1980. ISSENHUTH, Jean-Pierre
      "L'Asclepiade." Os (15) 82, p. 29.
      "Foret de St-Lin." Os (15) 82, p. 29.

1981. ITZIN, Charlie
      "Bienvenido, America. America March 1973." NewL
        (49:1) Aut 82, p. 78.

1982. IVES, Rich
      "The Answer Man." VirQR (58:2) Spr 82, p. 276-277.
      "Chiesa del Soccorso" (tr. of Peter Huchel). PortR
        (28:1) 82, p. 33.
      "A Delivery." PortR (28:2) 82, p. 58.
      "Dream in the Trap" (tr. of Peter Huchel). PortR
        (28:1) 82, p. 33.
      "Fog" (for Ludvik Kundera, tr. of Peter Huchel).
        PortR (28:1) 82, p. 33.
      "Landscape with Sailors" (for Peter Huchel). QW (14)
        Spr-Sum 82, p. 35.
      "Sibyl of Summer" (tr. of Peter Huchel). PortR
        (28:1) 82, p. 33.
      "Unnatural Attractions." PortR (28:2) 82, p. 59.

1983. IZAGUIRRE, Marcelo
      "Palabras Silenciosas." Prismal (7/8) Spr 82, p.
      90.

1984. J. M.
      "The End." SouthernPR (22:1) Spr 82, p. 69.

1985. JACKSON, Fleda Brown
      "Jumping from Rock to Rock along the Route to
      Salvation." WindO (41) Aut-Wint 82-83, p. 50-52.
      "Provisions." HiramPoR (32) Spr-Sum 82, p. 29-30.

1986. JACKSON, Haywood
      "The Cold Woman in the Trees and Snow." Confr (24)
      Sum 82, p. 52.
      "Holidays." StoneC (10:1/2) Aut-Wint 82-83, p. 15.
      "Lines of Force." Confr (24) Sum 82, p. 51.
      "On the Playing Fields with Boswell, Rehearsing for
      a 'Cruex' Commercial." PoNow (6:4, issue 34) 82,
      p. 45.
      "Out of the Deepness." Spirit (6:2/3) 82, p. 152.
      "Queen Medb and the Brown Bull of Cooley." KanQ
      (14:3) Sum 82, p. 167.
      "Venus Descending." SouthernPR (23, i.e. 22:2) Aut
      82, p. 34.

1987. JACKSON, Richard
      "Echo Lake." PraS (56:2) Sum 82, p. 81-82.
      "My Daughter's Dream." PraS (56:2) Sum 82, p. 80-
      81.

      JACKSON, William Haywood
      See: JACKSON, Haywood

1988. JACO, Roger
      "Brogues." HangL (41) 82, p. 32.
      "Capitalistic." HangL (41) 82, p. 32.

1989. JACOB, John
      "I Heard the Birds." Abraxas (25/26) 82, p. 55.

1990. JACOBOWITZ, Judah L.
      "Apart." DekalbLAJ (14:1/4) Aut 80-Sum 81, p. 76.

1991. JACOBS, M. G.
      "Funeral." Poem (45) Jl 82, p. 44.
      "Model Railroad." Poem (45) Jl 82, p. 43.

1992. JACOBS, Maria
      "Remember the Strait of Calais?" (tr. of Patricia
      Lasoen). Waves (10:4) Spr 82, p. 43.

1993. JACOBS, Sondra Dunner
      "Grammar Lesson." DekalbLAJ (14:1/4) Aut 80-Sum 81,
      p. 77.
      "In My Nightmare." DekalbLAJ (14:1/4) Aut 80-Sum
      81, p. 77.

1994. JACOBSEN, Josephine
"The Night Watchman." PoNow (6:5, issue 35) 82, p. 24.
"Rainy Night at the Writers' Colony." PoNow (6:5, issue 35) 82, p. 24.
"The Rich Old Woman." PoNow (6:5, issue 35) 82, p. 7.

1995. JACOBSEN, Rolf
"Landscape with Steam Shovels" (tr. by Olav Grinde). PoNow (6:5, issue 35) 82, p. 42.
"Shopping Precinct" (tr. by Anne Born). Stand (23:3) 82, p. 9.
"The Silence Afterwards" (tr. by Robert Bly). Stand (23:3) 82, p. 10.
"Slowly" (tr. by David McDuff). Stand (23:3) 82, p. 11.

1996. JAFFE, Maggie
"Joseph Conrad" (for W. Francis Browne). Confr (23) Wint 82, p. 90.

1997. JAGODZINSKE, Marcia
"After Saturday Cleaning." UnderRM (1:2) Aut 82, p. 5.
"Memory of Getting Older." UnderRM (1:2) Aut 82, p. 4.
"My Brother Is a Farmer." UnderRM (1:2) Aut 82, p. 5.

1998. JAMES, David
"The Ending of October." KanO (14:3) Sum 82, p. 166.
"Initiation." HiramPoR (31) Aut-Wint 82, p. 32-33.

1999. JAMES, Thomas
"Gangrene." SenR (13:1) 82-83, p. 20-21.
"In Fever." SenR (13:1) 82-83, p. 19.
"Pears on the Windowsill." SenR (13:1) 82-83, p. 24.
"Suicide." SenR (13:1) 82-83, p. 18.
"Tom O'Bedlam Makes Love." SenR (13:1) 82-83, p. 22-23.
"The Wharf." SenR (13:1) 82-83, p. 25-26.

2000. JAMMES, Francis
"Down That Way" (tr. by Gary Wilson). AmerPoR (11:4) Jl-Ag 82, p. 7.
"Elle Va A La Pension." HolCrit (19:4) O 82, p. 19.
"She Goes To The Boarding School." (tr.by Gary Wilson) HolCrit (19:4) O 82, p. 19-20.
"With Your Umbrella" (tr. by Gary Wilson). AmerPoR (11:4) Jl-Ag 82, p. 7.

2001. JANDL, Ernst
"Concerning Rainy Shadows" (tr. by Beth Bjorklund). LitR (25:2) Wint 82, p. 239.
"Figure of Speech" (tr. by Beth Bjorklund). LitR (25:2) Wint 82, p. 236.

"Four Attempts at Definition" (tr. by Beth Bjorklund). LitR (25:2) Wint 82, p. 236.
"Jupiter uninhabited" (tr. by Beth Bjorklund). LitR (25:2) Wint 82, p. 234.
"On the Life of Trees" (tr. by Beth Bjorklund). LitR (25:2) Wint 82, p. 240.
"Perfection" (tr. by Beth Bjorklund). LitR (25:2) Wint 82, p. 237.
"Travelogue" (tr. by Beth Bjorklund). LitR (25:2) Wint 82, p. 235.
"Verdict" (tr. by Beth Bjorklund). LitR (25:2) Wint 82, p. 238.

2002. JANDL, Hermann
"Successful Attempt" (tr. by Beth Bjorklund). LitR (25:2) Wint 82, p. 273.

2003. JANES, Percy
"Sana." PottPort (4) 82-83, p. 15.

2004. JANOWITZ, Phyllis
"Giant Step." PraS (56:2) Sum 82, p. 58.
"Roles." PraS (56:2) Sum 82, p. 60.
"Sardines." PraS (56:2) Sum 82, p. 59.
"Tree in Autumn, Lawrence, N.J., 1979." OhioR (29) 82, p. 128-129.

2005. JANZEN, Jean
"Communion." ChrC (99:27) S 1-8, 82, p. 891.
"The Way the Leaf Falls." ChrC (99:35) N 10, 82, p. 1133.

2006. JAQUISH, Karen I.
"The Man Who Stayed." CapeR (18:1) Wint 82, p. 27.

JARAMILLO, Miguel A. Salinas
See: SALINAS JARAMILLO, Miguel

2007. JARMAN, Mark
"By-Blows." NewYorker (58:28) Ag 30, 82, p. 67.
"Far and Away." NewYorker (58:20) Jl 5, 82, p. 30.
"Half Sonnets." OhioR (28) 82, p. 16-17.
"In Her Dream the Sun Was on the Islands." Grain (10:2) My 82, p. 26.
"The Medium." MissouriR (5:3) Sum 82, p. 13.
"When the Time Comes." PoNow (6:4, issue 34) 82, p. 38.
"Whiskey Head." Grain (10:2) My 82, p. 25.

2008. JASON, Philip K.
"Goodbye Brentanos." Confr (24) Sum 82, p. 110.
"Sometimes, Late in the Night." SouthernPR (22:1) Spr 82, p. 6.
"The Woman Who Feared Statues." PoNow (6:6, issue 36) 82, p. 29.

2009. JEBB, Keith
"To the Head in Your Hands." Bogg (49) 82, p. 48.

2010. JEFFERS, Lance
      "The Arson to this Age." Obs (7:2/3) Sum-Wint 81,
         p. 159.
      "Deacons." Obs (7:2/3) Sum-Wint 81, p. 159.

2011. JELLEMA, Rod
      "Flieger's Barn." PoNow (6:4, issue 34) 82, p. 22.
      "On Edge." PoNow (6:4, issue 34) 82, p. 22.

2012. JENA, Bibek
      "Moonlight Poem" (tr. by Jayanta Mahapatra). NewL
         (48:3/4) Spr-Sum 82, p. 179.

2013. JENCKES, Norma
      "More." AntigR (51) Aut 82, p. 74.

2014. JENDRZEJCZYK, L. M.
      "Bag Lady." ChrC (99:17) My 12, 82, p. 570.

2015. JENKINS, Louis
      "Cold." PoetryE (8) Aut 82, p. 21.
      "Cumulus." Ascent (7:3) 82, p. 55-56.
      "Doing Nothing." PoetryE (8) Aut 82, p. 17.
      "Down to the River." Ascent (7:3) 82, p. 56-57.
      "Driftwood." PoetryE (8) Aut 82, p. 18.
      "The Dutch Shoe." PoetryE (8) Aut 82, p. 16.
      "First Snow." PoetryE (8) Aut 82, p. 22.
      "Fishing below the Dam." PoetryE (8) Aut 82, p. 19.
      "The Flood." PoNow (6:6, issue 36) 82, p. 17.
      "The House at the Lake." PoetryE (8) Aut 82, p. 20.
      "In a Tavern." PoetryE (8) Aut 82, p. 26.
      "Invisible." PoNow (6:4, issue 34) 82, p. 16.
      "The Lake." PoetryE (8) Aut 82, p. 13.
      "Library." PoetryE (8) Aut 82, p. 31.
      "Life Is So Complex." PoetryE (8) Aut 82, p. 32.
      "The Lighthouse." PoetryE (8) Aut 82, p. 14.
      "Motorcycle." PoetryE (8) Aut 82, p. 25.
      "November." PoetryE (8) Aut 82, p. 12.
      "Palisade Head." PoetryE (8) Aut 82, p. 11.
      "A Photograph." PoetryE (8) Aut 82, p. 23.
      "Restaurant Overlooking Lake Superior." PoetryE (8)
         Aut 82, p. 9.
      "Sailors." PoetryE (8) Aut 82, p. 15.
      "Sergeant Norquist." PoetryE (8) Aut 82, p. 24.
      "Tamaracks." PoetryE (8) Aut 82, p. 10.
      "Twins." PoetryE (8) Aut 82, p. 28.
      "Violence on Television." PoetryE (8) Aut 82, p. 8.
      "Walking through a Wall." PoetryE (8) Aut 82, p.
         29.
      "The Way." PoetryE (8) Aut 82, p. 30.
      "The Well Digger's Wife." PoetryE (8) Aut 82, p.
         27.

2016. JENNINGS, Kate
      "Bitch." LitR (25:3) Spr 82, p. 383.
      "Fall" (Jura). Hudson (35:2) Sum 82, p. 249-250.
      "Headache." FourQt (31:3) Spr 82, p. 8-9.
      "March Poem." SouthernPR (22:1) Spr 82, p. 25-26.
      "Poem for the Broken Cup" (for David and Anne).
         Hudson (35:2) Sum 82, p. 248-249.

"Severe." LittleM (13:3/4) 82, p. 25.
"She Dreams about Hatteras." Confr (23) Wint 82, p.
    60-61.

2017. JENNINGS, Lane
    "Undress Parade." Bogg (49) 82, p. 20-21.

2018. JENNINGS, Michael
    "The Table Spread." SouthernHR (16:3) Sum 82, p.
        200.

2019. JENSEN, Laura
    "Cats That Are Not Mine, in Black and White." Field
        (27) Aut 82, p. 106.
    "Coit Tower." PoetC (14:2) 82, p. 19.
    "Crowsong." Field (27) Aut 82, p. 105.
    "Dull Brown." Field (27) Aut 82, p. 107-108.
    "Dull Winter." Field (27) Aut 82, p. 104.
    "Hungry." PoetC (14:2) 82, p. 18.
    "Kite." NowestR (20:2/3) 82, p. 77-78.
    "Like Swallows at the Pilings of the Ferry." PoetC
        (14:2) 82, p. 17.
    "Mouse." Iowa (12:2/3) Spr-Sum 81, p. 191.
    "Untitled: Although I am very tired." PoetC (14:2)
        82, p. 16.
    "Whale." Iowa (12:2/3) Spr-Sum 81, p. 192-193.

2020. JESSYE, Eva
    "A Bag of Peanuts." LittleBR (1:4) Sum 81, p. 17-
        18.

2021. JILES, Paulette
    "Griffon Poems" (Where they disembarked). OP (34)
        Aut-Wint 82, p. 27.
    "The Looney Bin." OP (34) Aut-Wint 82, p. 28.
    "Mackinak Island." OP (34) Aut-Wint 82, p. 22-23.
    "The Nature of Trains." OP (34) Aut-Wint 82, p. 26.
    "Paul Revere." OP (34) Aut-Wint 82, p. 24-25.
    "Poetry Review." CrossC (4:1) Wint 82, p. 11.
    "Poetry Review." OP (34) Aut-Wint 82, p. 29.

2022. JIMENEZ, Vita
    "Poetry Dream Journal." LittleM (13:3/4) 82, p.
        102.
    "Sestina." LittleM (13:3/4) 82, p. 103-104.

2023. JITU, Almasi Sidu
    "The Man Can't Understand It." Obs (7:2/3) Sum-Wint
        81, p. 179.
    "My Country 'Tis of Thee." Obs (7:2/3) Sum-Wint 81,
        p. 180.

2024. JOGLAR CACHO, Manuel
    "Soneto." Mairena (4:11/12) Wint 82, p. 146.

    JOHN, Richard St.
    See: ST. JOHN, Richard

2025. JOHNSEN, Gretchen
    "How to Write (A Primer for Young Men)." <u>Gargoyle</u>
        (19) 82, p. 10.
    "Interior." <u>Gargoyle</u> (19) 82, p. 17.
    "Interiors." <u>Gargoyle</u> (19) 82, p. 7.
    "Intermission." <u>Gargoyle</u> (19) 82, p. 14.
    "Matisse." <u>Gargoyle</u> (19) 82, p. 8.
    "Needlepoint." <u>Gargoyle</u> (19) 82, p. 16.
    "Private Eye." <u>Gargoyle</u> (19) 82, p. 13.
    "Pygmalion." <u>Gargoyle</u> (19) 82, p. 9.
    "Stars." <u>Gargoyle</u> (19) 82, p. 11.
    "Swim." <u>Gargoyle</u> (19) 82, p. 18.
    "Trapeze." <u>Gargoyle</u> (19) 82, p. 15.
    "Wedlock." <u>Gargoyle</u> (19) 82, p. 12.

2026. JOHNSON, David
    "Daughter of Eve." <u>ChrC</u> (99:11) Mr 31, 82, p. 360.
    "Driving Home at Night." <u>KanQ</u> (14:3) Sum 82, p.
        162.

2027. JOHNSON, Denis
    "Customers." <u>CarolQ</u> (34:3) Spr 82, p. 10.
    "Enough." <u>AmerPoR</u> (11:2) Mr-Ap 82, p. 29.
    "The Honor." <u>AmerPoR</u> (11:2) Mr-Ap 82, p. 29.
    "The Monk's Insomnia." <u>NewYorker</u> (58:35) O 18, 82,
        p. 56.
    "The Spectacle." <u>AntR</u> (40:4) Aut 82, p. 445-447.
    "Street Scene." <u>CarolQ</u> (34:3) Spr 82, p. 9.

2028. JOHNSON, Don
    "Home Game." <u>PoetC</u> (14:1) 82, p. 18--19.
    "Kona Weather" (for Chester Mahelona). <u>BelPoJ</u> (32:3)
        Spr 82, p. 31-32.

2029. JOHNSON, Greg
    "Traces." <u>SouthernHR</u> (16:3) Sum 82, p. 210-211.

2030. JOHNSON, Helen
    "Query." <u>Poem</u> (46) N 82, p. 40-41.
    "Request." <u>Poem</u> (46) N 82, p. 39.

2031. JOHNSON, Jean Youell
    "Drying Time." <u>Bogg</u> (49) 82, p. 30.

2032. JOHNSON, Julie A.
    "Hunter Orion." <u>KanQ</u> (14:3) Sum 82, p. 26-27.

2033. JOHNSON, Karen
    "Some Clouds, No Wind." <u>Tendril</u> (13) Sum 82, p. 42.
    "The Stroke." <u>Tendril</u> (13) Sum 82, p. 41.

2034. JOHNSON, Kate Knapp
    "Anniversary." <u>Poetry</u> (140:5) Ag 82, p. 275-276.
    "For Now." <u>Poetry</u> (140:5) Ag 82, p. 274.

2035. JOHNSON, Kathryn Hyden
    "The Feast." <u>Tendril</u> (13) Sum 82, p. 43.

2036. JOHNSON, Larry
"Modern Poet and Calypso." Iowa (12:4) Aut 81, p. 50.

2037. JOHNSON, Michael L.
"Adagio." UnderRM 1(1) Spr 82, p. 58.
"Antony and Cleopatra" (tr. of Jose-Maria de Heredia). LitR (25:3) Spr 82, p. 373.
"The Clock" (tr. of Jorge Carrera Andrade). PortR (28:1) 82, p. 22.
"Deep Blankness Verses Ignorant Bliss." UnderRM (1:2) Aut 82, p. 27.
"Deer Stand." Wind (12:45) 82, p. 22.
"Derelict." Im (8:1) 82, p. 5.
"An Elegy." UnderRM 1(1) Spr 82, p. 59.
"Homage to Oppenheimer." UnderRM (1:2) Aut 82, p. 27.
"The Magpie Laughs, Black against the Orange Trees" (tr of Salvatore Quasimodo). LitR (26:1) Aut 82, p. 107.
"Maiden Lady in August." Wind (12:45) 82, p. 22.
"Movies." LittleBR (1:3) Spr 81, p. 38.
"Some Beasts" (tr. of Pablo Neruda). PortR (28:2) 82, p. 84-85.
"Summer" (tr. of Cesare Pavese). LitR (25:3) Spr 82, p. 372.
"To L.W. at 35." UnderRM (1:2) Aut 82, p. 28.
"Trajan" (tr. of Pablo Armando Fernandez). PortR (28:2) 82, p. 41.
"The Trebbia" (tr. of Jose-Maria de Heredia). LittleBR (3:2) Wint 82-83, p. 29.
"Veterrima Laurus" (tr. of Enrique Banchs). PortR (28:1) 82, p. 23.
"The Vision of Khem" (tr. of Jose-Maria de Heredia). LitR (26:1) Aut 82, p. 106.
"Wrigley's Spearmint." LittleBR (3:1) Aut 82, p. 68.

2038. JOHNSON, Nancy
"Winter 2 a.m." Vis (9) 82, p. 28.

2039. JOHNSON, Nick
"For the Record." Epoch (32:1) Aut 82, p. 60-61.
"Maybe This Country." Epoch (32:1) Aut 82, p. 58-59.

2040. JOHNSON, Peter M.
"A Crowd of People Looks into a Miror Whereupon It Sees a Strange Man." Tendril (12) Wint 82, p. 40.

2041. JOHNSON, Ronald
"Ark 39: The Roswell Spire" (for Donald Anderson). Sulfur (2:3, issue 6) 82, p. 68-72.

2042. JOHNSON, Tom
"Artifacts." SewanR (90:4) Aut 82, p. 516-517.
"Jedediah Strong Smith 1799-1831." SewanR (90:4) Aut 82, p. 517.

2043. JOHNSTON, Mark
        "Attrition." CentR (26:3) Sum 82, p. 274.
        "Bomb." BallSUF (23:1) Wint 82, p. 41.
        "Chopping." AspenJ (1:2) Sum 82, p. 44.
        "My Connection with Pancho Villa" (To the Memory of
            My Uncle Donald, 1897-1935). AspenJ (1:2) Sum 82,
            p. 44.
        "The Scream (after Munch)." LittleM (13:3/4) 82, p.
            67.

2044. JOINER, Lawrence D.
        "Finale." DekalbLAJ (14:1/4) Aut 80-Sum 81, p. 79.
        "Great Grandmother." PikeF (4) Spr 82, p. 33.

2045. JOLY, Greg
        "Heavily in Air." HangL (41) 82, p. 55.

2046. JONES, Andrew McCord
        "A-Poet - A-Love Lost A-Part - A-lone." Wind
            (12:45) 82, p. 11.

2047. JONES, D. G.
        "Atlantic Ranger." Dandel (9:2) 82, p. 8-9.
        "For E. J. Pratt." Dandel (9:2) 82, p. 9.
        "For Robert Kroetsch." Dandel (9:2) 82, p. 10.
        "The Wanderer." Dandel (9:2) 82, p. 6-7.

2048. JONES, Judith Clare
        "After last night's storm" (Haiku). LittleBR (1:3)
            Spr 81, p. 55.

2049. JONES, Patricia Thuner
        "Meeting" (With special thanks to Peter
            Matthiessen). MalR (63) O 82, p. 130-131.

2050. JONES, Richard
        "The Letter." PoNow (7:1, issue 37) 82, p. 19.
        "Poem for My Friends." PoNow (7:1, issue 37) 82, p.
            19.
        "The Spiders." KanQ (14:3) Sum 82, p. 92.

2051. JONES, Robert
        "What Sad Story." ChrC (99:21) Je 9-16, 82, p. 700.

2052. JONES, Rodney
        "A Hill of Chestnuts." PoetryNW (23:4) Wint 82-83,
            p. 4-5.
        "A History of Speech." PoetryNW (23:4) Wint 82-83,
            p. 7-8.
        "Love Songs." PoetryNW (23:4) Wint 82-83, p. 6.
        "Remembering Fire." PoetryNW (23:4) Wint 82-83, p.
            3.

2053. JONES, Roger
        "The Track" (for Bag). Wind (12:45) 82, p. 20.

      JONES, Sylvia
      See: BARAKA, Amina

2054. JONKER, Peter
       "Two at Solo." Dandel (9:2) 82, p. 62-63.

2055. JORDAN, June
       "Problems of Translation: Problems of Language"
           (dedicated to Myriam Diaz Diocaretz). Iowa
           (12:2/3) Spr-Sum 81, p. 194-197.
       "A Right to Lifer in Grand Forks, North Dakota"
           (Poem for Sandy Donaldson). Shout (3:1) 82, p. 52.

2056. JORGENSEN, Kyle S.
       "Diamond Tree." LittleBR (2:3) Spr 82, p. 81.

2057. JORON, Andrew
       "A Beautiful Disease." Pig (10) 82, p. 33.

2058. JOSELOW, Beth
       "No Artistic Unity of Opposed Curves." Gargoyle
           (15/16) 80, p. 26.
       "Static." MissR (10:3, issue 30) Wint-Spr 82, p.
           56.

2059. JOSEPH, Lawrence
       "It Will Rain All Day." MichQR (21:1) Wint 82, p.
           156-157.

2060. JOSEPHS, Laurence
       "Genre Painting." Salm (57) Sum 82, p. 108.
       "Poem: In Memory of the Painter Norris Embry."
           Salm (57) Sum 82, p. 107-108.
       "Poet." Salm (57) Sum 82, p. 109.

2061. JOSHI, Dhruvakumar
       "Homecoming." NewL (48:3/4) Spr-Sum 82, p. 14.

2062. JOUBERT
       from Mathematics of the Heart: "The world has always
           been full of artists..." (tr. by Andre Lefevere).
           Paint (9:17/18) Spr-Aut 82, p. 20-21.

2063. JOY, Donna
       "Finches, Moths, Herons." NewYorker (58:14) My 24,
           82, p. 66.

2064. JOYCE, James
       "The Rule of Participation in Loving an Only
           Sister." MissouriR (6:1) Aut 82, p. 36-37.

2065. JOYCE, Jim
       "Aesthetic Credo Pebble No. 5." Quarry (31:3) Sum
           82, p. 28.
       "Dandelion." Germ (6:2) Aut-Wint 82, p. 6.
       "Directions." Germ (6:2) Aut-Wint 82, p. 7.
       "Fashionable Compliment." PoetryCR (3:3) Spr 82, p.
           7.
       "Metalbeasts." MalR (61) F 82, p. 110-114.
       "Restigouche, August." Germ (6:2) Aut-Wint 82, p.
           9.
       "Trout Song." Germ (6:2) Aut-Wint 82, p. 8.

2066. JOYCE, Thomas
        "Beauty's Beast." Grain (10:3) Ag 82, p. 30.
        "Katsuno." Waves (10:3) Wint 82, p. 63.
        "Sea Changes." Grain (10:2) My 82, p. 36.
        "We hear the oldest silences." Dandel (9:2) 82, p.
        68.

2067. JOZSEF, Attila
        "Dumb Poet" (tr. by John Batki). PoNow (6:4, issue
        34) 82, p. 42.
        "Dusk" (tr. by John Batki). Spirit (6:2/3) 82, p.
        82.
        "Weary Man" (tr. by Peter Hargitai). PraS (56:1) Spr
        82, p. 43.

      JUANA, Pedro Sevilla de
      See: SEVILLA de JUANA, Pedro

2068. JUARROZ, Roberto
        "Nocturnal Being" (tr. by Ricardo Pau-Llosa). BelPoJ
        (32:4) Sum 82, p. 7.
        "Ser Nocturno." BelPoJ (32:4) Sum 82, p. 6.

2069. JUDGE, Frank
        "Don't Shut My Eyes" (tr. of Alfredo Bonazzi). PoNow
        (6:5, issue 35) 82, p. 43.
        "Woman of the South" (tr. of Alfredo Bonazzi). PoNow
        (6:5, issue 35) 82, p. 43.

2070. JUDSON, John
        "6 Februrary: Psalm for Burrs." KanQ (14:3) Sum 82,
        p. 46.
        "22 October." Sparrow (42) 82, p. 21.
        "28 April 78." KanQ (14:2) Spr 82, p. 37.
        "After the Hysterectomy." Sparrow (42) 82, p. 17.
        "Checking the Fire" (9 Feb 80). KanQ (14:2) Spr 82,
        p. 36.
        "Dear Loved Ones." Sparrow (42) 82, p. 20.
        "Fairy Tale." Abraxas (25/26) 82, p. 86.
        "For the Benefit of the County Sheriff's
        Association." Sparrow (42) 82, p. 12.
        "Master Charge." Sparrow (42) 82, p. 15.
        "Moss" (3 December 79). KanQ (14:3) Sum 82, p. 48.
        "On the Occasion of My 44th Birthday." Sparrow (42)
        82, p. 10.
        "Only Scotch Pine Grows in This Sand" (23 Feb 80).
        KanQ (14:2) Spr 82, p. 37.
        "Reasons Why I Am Not Perfect No. 1." Sparrow (42)
        82, p. 7.
        "Reasons Why I Am Not Perfect No. 2." Sparrow (42)
        82, p. 8.
        "Reasons Why I Am Not Perfect No. 3." Sparrow (42)
        82, p. 9.
        "Reasons Why I Am Not Perfect No. 4." Sparrow (42)
        82, p. 11.
        "Reasons Why I Am Not Perfect No. 5." Sparrow (42)
        82, p. 13.
        "Reasons Why I Am Not Perfect No. 6" (variation on
        Plato's cave & my apple cut the wrong way).
        Sparrow (42) 82, p. 14.

"Reasons Why I Am Not Perfect No. 7." <u>Sparrow</u> (42)
    82, p. 16.
"Reasons Why I Am Not Perfect No. 8." <u>Sparrow</u> (42)
    82, p. 19.
"The Second Week." <u>Sparrow</u> (42) 82, p. 18.
"Untitled: Catullus, I love it." <u>KanQ</u> (14:3) Sum
    82, p. 47.

2071. JUNKINS, Donald
    "Playing with Fire." <u>OhioR</u> (27) 82, p. 30-31.
    "Reaching Out" (After reading MacLeish Succumbs at
        eight-nine). <u>MassR</u> (23:4) Wint 82, p. 680.

2072. JURCEKA, Judy
    "As I Walk." <u>DekalbLAJ</u> (14:1/4) Aut 80-Sum 81, p.
        80.
    "Momma Used to Love Me." <u>DekalbLAJ</u> (14:1/4) Aut 80-
        Sum 81, p. 80.
    "Sadness Is a Smoke Filled Glass." <u>DekalbLAJ</u>
        (14:1/4) Aut 80-Sum 81, p. 81.

2073. JUSSAWALLA, Adil
    "Nine Poems on Arrival." <u>NewL</u> (48:3/4) Spr-Sum 82,
        p. 18.

2074. JUSTICE, Donald
    "In the Cemetery." <u>Atl</u> (250:3) S 82, p. 76.
    "On the Porch." <u>Atl</u> (250:1) Jl 82, p. 75.
    "Tremayne Autumnal." <u>NewYorker</u> (58:32) S 27, 82, p.
        118.

2075. KABBANI, Rana
    "Boreham Road." <u>Nimrod</u> (25:2) Spr-Sum 82, p. 14.
    "The Road to Damascus." <u>Nimrod</u> (25:2) Spr-Sum 82,
        p. 15-16.

    KACHIOMU, Fujiwara no
    <u>See</u>: FUJIWARA no KACHIOMU

2076. KAHN, Hannah
    "Checkmate." <u>UTR</u> (7:2) 82?, p. 17.

2077. KALAMARAS, George
    "Low Wind on the Hill." <u>KanQ</u> (14:3) Sum 82, p. 164.

    KALAMU ya SALAAM
    <u>See</u>: SALAAM, Kalamu ya

2078. KALDESTAD, Per Olav
    from Mammy, Blue: "The ancient streams" (tr. of
        Eldrid Lunden, w. Andrew Kennedy). <u>Stand</u> (23:3)
        82, p. 33.

2079. KALIKOFF, Beth
    "Juanita Bink." <u>SoDakR</u> (20:1) Spr 82, p. 38-40.

2080. KALLSEN, T. J.
    "Citation." <u>KanQ</u> (14:3) Sum 82, p. 168.
    "Minnesota River." <u>KanQ</u> (14:3) Sum 82, p. 168.

2081. KALOGERIS, George
      "Bums' Rush." Tendril (13) Sum 82, p. 44.

2082. KAMENETZ, Roger
      "Confessions of an Apartment Manager." PoNow (6:5,
      issue 35) 82, p. 46.

2083. KANDINSKY, Carla
      "Blackberries." PikeF (4) Spr 82, p. 11.
      "Double." Pig (8) 80, p. 75.

2084. KANE, Katherine
      "Drowned Woman." PoNow (7:1, issue 37) 82, p. 20.
      "Moonbath." VirQR (58:3) Sum 82, p. 444.
      "Under a Rim of Shade." Iowa (12:4) Aut 81, p. 51.
      "We'll to the Woods No More" (for Ticia). VirQR
      (58:3) Sum 82, p. 443-444.

      KANEKO, Mitsuharu
      See: MITSUHARU, Kaneko

2085. KANFER, Allen
      "Our Wounds Invisible." SouthernHR (16:2) Spr 82,
      p. 128.

2086. KANN, Kevin F.
      "Summer Sidewalks." PoNow (6:6, issue 36) 82, p.
      47.

2087. KANNAN, Lakshmi
      "Kanya Kumari." NewL (48:3/4) Spr-Sum 82, p. 164.

2088. KAO, Chu-Ch'ing
      "Pure Brightness" (tr. by Robert Branham and Daniel
      Stevenson). PraS (56:1) Spr 82, p. 30.

2089. KAPLAN, Ed
      "A Confusion of People Inside." Sulfur (2:1, issue
      4) 82, p. 36-38.

2090. KAPPEL, Andrew
      "Her Son." ModernPS (11:1/2) 82, p. 106.

2091. KARLEN, Arno
      "Telegrams." NewL (48:2) Wint 81-82, p. 82-83.

2092. KARP, Vickie
      "How Peace, after Asking Its Question, Becomes War."
      NewYRB (28:21/22) Ja 21, 82, p. 24.
      "Police Sift New Clues in Search for Beauty"
      (Headline in the Post). NewYorker (58:18) Je 21,
      82, p. 42-43.

2093. KARR, Mary
      "The Distance." Poetry (140:4) Jl 82, p. 230-231.
      "The Magnifying Mirror." Poetry (140:4) Jl 82, p.
      233.
      "Predictions." Poetry (140:4) Jl 82, p. 232.
      "Report." Poetry (140:4) Jl 82, p. 235.

"Witnessing My Father's Will." Poetry (140:4) Jl
    82, p. 234.

KASHIWAGI, Hiroshi
    See: HIROSHI, Kashiwagi

2094. KASTMILER, Peter
    "The Blood of My Grandfather Flows in Me." Vis (10)
        82, p. 27.

2095. KATES, J.
    "Aaron (Exodus 4:10-32:18)" (for Chip Bamberger).
        KanQ (14:1) Wint 82, p. 175.
    "Akhmatova's Egg." PoetryE (8) Aut 82, p. 46.
    "Birds and Cats." Outbr (10/11) Aut 82-Spr 83, p.
        8.
    "The Cherubim." KanQ (14:3) Sum 82, p. 44-45.
    "Night People." KanQ (14:1) Wint 82, p. 174-175.

2096. KATRAK, Kersy D.
    "Woman on the Beach." NewL (48:3/4) Spr-Sum 82, p.
        254-246.

2097. KATROVAS, Richard
    "Drink." MissouriR (5:3) Sum 82, p. 14-15.
    "God, It Is Like a Man." NewEngR (4:4) Sum 82, p.
        595-596.
    "Leaving the French Quarter." BlackWR (7:2) Spr 81,
        p. 44-45.

2098. KATZ, Susan
    "Too Near a Certain Death." AmerS (51:3) Sum 82, p.
        390.

2099. KAUFMAN, Shirley
    "Abishag." Iowa (12:2/3) Spr-Sum 81, p. 198-199.
    "Annunciation." Poetry (140:4) Jl 82, p. 208-209.
    "Appearances." Nat (235:3) Jl 24-31, 82, p. 88.
    "Arches." MassR (23:4) Wint 82, p. 572.
    "As the Reel Turns." Field (26) Spr 82, p. 58.
    "Bearings." Nat (235:20) D 11, 82, p. 634.
    "The Blue Shirt." Field (26) Spr 82, p. 59.
    "Chosen." OhioR (29) 82, p. 106.
    from Claims: "I might have had a sister." Iowa
        (12:2/3) Spr-Sum 81, p. 202.
    from Claims: "I wanted to grow up somewhere else."
        Iowa (12:2/3) Spr-Sum 81, p. 202.
    from Claims: "Look at the map." Iowa (12:2/3) Spr-
        Sum 81, p. 200.
    from Claims: "My mother remembered how she sat."
        Iowa (12:2/3) Spr-Sum 81, p. 200-201.
    from Claims: "Snow in the winter." Iowa (12:2/3)
        Spr-Sum 81, p. 201.
    "Daughters." GeoR (36:4) Wint 82, p. 804.
    "The Dome." Field (26) Spr 82, p. 60.
    "For the Sin." MassR (23:2) Sum 82, p. 308.

2100. KAUL, J. L.
    "The Moon" (tr. of Dina Nath Nadim). NewL (48:3/4)
        Spr-Sum 82, p. 46.

KAVAFIS, Constantine
See: CAVAFY, Constantin

2101. KAY, Guy Gavriel
"After the Ball." AntigR (50) Sum 82, p. 109-110.
"Your Voice and Hers." AntigR (50) Sum 82, p. 108.

2102. KAZUK, A. R.
"One of the Things." PoetryCR (4:2) Wint 82, p. 15.

2103. KEATING, Diane
"Benediction." MalR (61) F 82, p. 10.
"Bottom of the Garden." MalR (61) F 82, p. 13.
"Fall." MalR (61) F 82, p. 10.
"Mooncalf." MalR (61) F 82, p. 9.
"Qu'Appelle Valley." MalR (61) F 82, p. 7.
"Sticks and Stones." MalR (61) F 82, p. 11.
"Tintinnabulation." MalR (61) F 82, p. 8-9.
"Towers." MalR (61) F 82, p. 12.
"Wolfskin." MalR (61) F 82, p. 11.

2104. KEENAN, Leanne
"Canvas Tears." AntigR (51) Aut 82, p. 38.

2105. KEENAN, Terrance
"Dragons in the Field." PoNow (7:1, issue 37) 82,
p. 20.

2106. KEENER, LuAnn
"Alfred Russell Wallace, Naturalist, Leaves the
Amazon: July 1852 with Thirty-Four Specimens
Surviving of the Hundred He'd Collected." AspenJ
(1) Wint 82, p. 31.
"Carefully." CutB (19) Aut-Wint 82, p. 71.

2107. KEGG, Martin Matthew
"Pow-Wow Shots." Poetry (139:4) Ja 82, p. 221.

2108. KEHL, D. G.
"Literary Lexiconoclasm." EngJ (71:1) Ja 82, p. 60.

2109. KEIN, Sybil
"A La Veuve Paris." Obs (7:2/3) Sum-Wint 81, p.
142-143.
"Aseteur." Obs (7:2/3) Sum-Wint 81, p. 144-145.
"Honteu." Obs (7:2/3) Sum-Wint 81, p. 145.
"Now" (tr. by the author). Obs (7:2/3) Sum-Wint 81,
p. 144.
"The River" (for Rudy, tr. by the author). Obs
(7:2/3) Sum-Wint 81, p. 143.
"La Riviere" (pour Rudolphe). Obs (7:2/3) Sum-Wint
81, p. 143-144.
"Shame" (tr. by the author). Obs (7:2/3) Sum-Wint
81, p. 145.
"To the Widow Paris" (tr. by the author). Obs
(7:2/3) Sum-Wint 81, p. 142.

2110. KEITH, Lara
"The Conquest." PottPort (4) 82-83, p. 30.

2111. KEITHLEY, George
          "Blizzard." LitR (25:4) Sum 82, p. 540.
          "The Bridge." LitR (25:4) Sum 82, p. 537.
          "The Children Who Left." NewL (48:2) Wint 81-82, p.
              76.
          "Owl Has Closed His Eyes." PoNow (6:5, issue 35)
              82, p. 28.
          "Proverbs." NewL (48:2) Wint 81-82, p. 77.
          "Rain." NewL (48:2) Wint 81-82, p. 75.
          "Something New." NewL (48:2) Wint 81-82, p. 78.
          "Spoor." LitR (25:4) Sum 82, p. 538.
          "Spring Snow." LitR (25:4) Sum 82, p. 535-536.
          "The Storm." LitR (25:4) Sum 82, p. 539.
          "This Field, This Lake." NewL (48:2) Wint 81-82, p.
              79.
          "Wolf." LitR (25:4) Sum 82, p. 541.

2112. KELLER, David
          "After the Movie" (for Robert Hass). Annex (4) 82,
              p. 19-20.
          "And So On into the Light" (for Glenn, for Bette).
              Annex (4) 82, p. 27.
          "Beauty, in the Present Sense." Annex (4) 82, p.
              38-39.
          "Before the Separation." Annex (4) 82, p. 38.
          "Circling the Site." Annex (4) 82, p. 15-52.
          "Closing the Sutures." BelPoJ (33:1) Aut 82, p. 16-
              18.
          "Diccionario." Annex (4) 82, p. 23.
          "The Discovery of March." Annex (4) 82, p. 26.
          "The Discovery of March." Tendril (13) Sum 82, p.
              45.
          "The Dream before Sleep" (for Dina). Annex (4) 82,
              p. 51.
          "Each Night before Sleep I Turn." Annex (4) 82, p.
              50.
          "February Afternoon." Annex (4) 82, p. 51-52.
          "The Feel of the Place." Annex (4) 82, p. 32.
          "How It Should Have Been." Annex (4) 82, p. 43-44.
          "How the Sioux Invented Cold." Annex (4) 82, p. 36.
          "In the Dream of the Body." Annex (4) 82, p. 41.
          "In the New Year." MinnR (NS19) Aut 82, p. 30.
          "In the Schoolroom." Annex (4) 82, p. 46.
          "Last Letter to a Son." Annex (4) 82, p. 24-25.
          "Leaving Town Again." Annex (4) 82, p. 37.
          "Lessons." Annex (4) 82, p. 29-30.
          "Moving Away." Annex (4) 82, p. 48.
          "Nightfall." Annex (4) 82, p. 25.
          "Not Speaking." Annex (4) 82, p. 22-23.
          "One of the Old Songs." Annex (4) 82, p. 45.
          "The Plants Started the Hunger Strike." Annex (4)
              82, p. 31.
          "Pockets of Ice." Annex (4) 82, p. 43.
          "Reading by Firelight." Annex (4) 82, p. 34.
          "Shaking Off the Maple." Annex (4) 82, p. 18-19.
          "Sinking in August." Annex (4) 82, p. 18.
          "Still Life with Bears." Annex (4) 82, p. 42.
          "Sumac." Annex (4) 82, p. 28.
          "Teaching It Cold." Annex (4) 82, p. 30-31.

"Thinking What to Say, for C.M." Annex (4) 82, p.
   47.
"The Time Takes Hold." Annex (4) 82, p. 49.
"A Visit Up-River." Annex (4) 82, p. 35.
"A Visit Up-River." QW (14) Spr-Sum 82, p. 21.
"Walking It Off." Annex (4) 82, p. 39-40.
"Why I Come Back to You." Annex (4) 82, p. 33.
"Workmen." Annex (4) 82, p. 21.
"Wyrd" (for my father). Annex (4) 82, p. 40.

2113. KELLER, Emily
   "The Birthday Party." FourQt (32:1) Aut 82, p. 18.
   "Vega Nor" (A Painting by Victor Vasarely). KanQ
   (14:4) Aut 82, p. 54.

2114. KELLER, Hans
   "Poem: To pray is to beat language out of lead" (tr.
   by John Stevens Wade). WebR (7:1) Spr 82, p. 39.

2115. KELLER, Madeleine
   "Ancestria." Spirit (6:2/3) 82, p. 85.

2116. KELLER, Mike
   "Living for the Long Weekend" (for my grandfather).
   Telescope (3) Sum 82, p. 59-61.
   from White-Collar Erotica: "The Proofreader's
   Lament." Telescope (2) Aut 81, p. 46.
   from White-Collar Erotica: "The Proofreader's Lament
   II." Telescope (2) Aut 81, p. 47.

2117. KELLUM, D. F.
   "Our Way with Her." PottPort (4) 82-83, p. 18.
   "Pee-Eye Spud Farmer." PottPort (4) 82-83, p. 52.

2118. KELLY, Dave
   "Three Meditations." PoNow (6:4, issue 34) 82, p.
   35.

2119. KELLY, Emma A.
   "The Old/The New." Obs (7:2/3) Sum-Wint 81, p. 214.
   "Wombs for Rent." Obs (7:2/3) Sum-Wint 81, p. 214.

2120. KELLY, Joseph
   "First Anniversary." HiramPoR (32) Spr-Sum 82, p.
   31.
   "Sunday at the Nursing Home." CharR (8:2) Aut 82,
   p. 42.

2121. KELLY, Kevin
   "Day 480, Final Edit." Obs (7:2/3) Sum-Wint 81, p.
   177.

2122. KELLY, Robert (of Bard College)
   "Variations on a Poem of Stefan George." Epoch
   (31:2) Spr 82, p. 117-122.

2123. KELLY, Robert A. (of Macon, GA)
   "Spring Rains in Louisiana, 1973." AntigR (50) Sum
   82, p. 9.

2124. KELLY, T. J.
      "Coventry, Dresden and Richard Rodgers." StoneC
      (10:1/2) Aut-Wint 82-83, p. 47.

2125. KELLY, Terence
      "Runners at Night." Bogg (49) 82, p. 43.

2126. KELLY, Tracey
      "The Petrol Pump Man." Bogg (49) 82, p. 10.

2127. KELLY-DeWITT, Susan
      "Making Love Outside a Cemetery Somewhere near
      Marysville under a Full Moon." NewL (48:2) Wint
      81-82, p. 97.

2128. KEMMETT, Bill
      "A Poet Who Asks, What Is the Process: In Answer
      to." StoneC (10:1/2) Aut-Wint 82-83, p. 34.
      "Sonnet of Bones." StoneC (10:1/2) Aut-Wint 82-83,
      p. 35.
      "Three Haiku." HangL (41) 82, p. 33.

2129. KEMP, P. J.
      "Batting, Average." Sam (32:4, issue 128) 82, back
      cover.
      "Portrait in Space/Summer '82." Sam (34:1, issue
      133) 82 or 83, p. 5-7.
      "Send Back Pictures." Sam (34:1, issue 133) 82 or
      83, p. 9-10.
      "Thallium Glass." Sam (34:1, issue 133) 82 or 83,
      p. 12.
      "Thought Processed." Sam (34:1, issue 133) 82 or
      83, p. 11.
      "A Trick of Time." Sam (34:1, issue 133) 82 or 83,
      p. 2-4.
      "The Word Became Device." Sam (34:1, issue 133) 82
      or 83, p. 8.

2130. KEMP, Penny
      "The Question." PoetryCR (4:1) Sum 82, p. 12.

2131. KEMPHER, Ruth Moon
      "Do-It-Yourself Villanelle." WindO (40, Anti-Haiku
      issue) Sum 82, p. 23.

2132. KENDRICK, Dolores
      "Catching Water." OP (34) Aut-Wint 82, p. 12-13.
      "Dead Asters" (for Cabot Lyford). OP (34) Aut-Wint
      82, p. 14.
      "Jesus, Looking for an Aspirin." OP (34) Aut-Wint
      82, p. 15-16.
      "The Snow Bird." OP (34) Aut-Wint 82, p. 10-11.

2133. KENNEDY, Andrew
      from Mammy, Blue: "The ancient streams" (tr. of
      Eldrid Lunden, w. Per Olav Kaldestad). Stand
      (23:3) 82, p. 33.

2134. KENNEDY, Jo
      "Footbridge." KanQ (14:3) Sum 82, p. 195.

2135. KENNEDY, Terry
"A Poem for Writers Written under a Full Moon While
Feeling Totally Exhausted." SeC (9:1/2) 80, p. 18.
"The Years Were Hours." SeC (9:1/2) 80, p. 19.

2136. KENNEDY, X. J.
"On the Proposed Seizure of Twelve Graves in a
Colonial Cemetery." Ploughs (8:2/3) 82, p. 244-
245.

2137. KENSETH, Arnold
"Seasons and Sceneries." MassR (23:2) Sum 82, p.
221-225.

2138. KENYON, Jane
"Briefly It Enters, and Briefly Speaks." Iowa
(12:2/3) Spr-Sum 81, p. 204.
"Camp Evergreen." Ploughs (8:1) 82, p. 41.
"Frost Flowers." Ploughs (8:1) 82, p. 39-40.
"Mud Season." Ploughs (8:2/3) 82, p. 200-201.
"Philosophy in Warm Weather." Iowa (12:2/3) Spr-Sum
81, p. 203.
"Photograph of a Child on a Vermont Hillside."
Ploughs (8:1) 82, p. 41.
"The Pond at Dusk." Iowa (12:2/3) Spr-Sum 81, p.
205.

2139. KENYON, Michael C.
"Contacts." Dandel (9:2) 82, p. 67.
"Grey Wings Applaud the Crash." Dandel (9:2) 82, p.
67.
"Matins." Quarry (31:1) Wint 82, p. 54.
"Recalling the Fourth Month the Ninth Symptom."
Quarry (31:1) Wint 82, p. 55.

2140. KERLIKOWSKE, Elizabeth
"William Jennings Bryan Watches an Eclipse." Sky
(10-12) Aut 82, p. 36.

2141. KERR, Grace
"Untitled: They were mostly bright days." MendoR
(5) Sum 81, p. 67.

2142. KERR, Louella
"Seattle Saga." MalR (63) O 82, p. 126-129.
"Thetis Lake." MalR (63) O 82, p. 125.

2143. KERR, Nora (Nora F.)
"Diffugere Nives." UnderRM (1:2) Aut 82, p. 28.
"Hecuba to Me." UnderRM (1:2) Aut 82, p. 29.
"Language." UnderRM (1:2) Aut 82, p. 30.
"Salads." UnderRM 1(1) Spr 82, p. 11.
"Wrestling Match." UnderRM 1(1) Spr 82, p. 12.

2144. KERRIGAN, Anthony
"Ante Diem" (tr. of Jose Manuel Caballero Bonald).
DenQ (17:3) Aut 82, p. 61.
"Counter-Order (Poetics I favor on Certain Days)"
(tr. of Angel Gonzalez). DenQ (17:3) Aut 82, p.
34.

"De Senectute" (tr. of Jaime Gil de Biedma). DenQ
(17:3) Aut 82, p. 83.
"Dead City" (tr. of Antonio Colinas). DenQ (17:3)
Aut 82, p. 74.
"A Family Chat" (tr. of Jaime Gil de Biedma). DenQ
(17:3) Aut 82, p. 84.
"Fear of Impotence" (tr. of Jose Manuel Caballero
Bonald). DenQ (17:3) Aut 82, p. 62.
"Four Sides to Every Issue" (tr. of Angel Gonzalez).
DenQ (17:3) Aut 82, p. 32-35.
"In Attitude of Oasis" (tr. of Juan Antonio
Masoliver Rodenas). DenQ (17:3) Aut 82, p. 75.
"Order (The Poetics to Which Others Apply
Themselves)" (tr. of Angel Gonzalez). DenQ (17:3)
Aut 82, p. 33.
"Perpetual Confinement" (tr. of Francisco Brines).
DenQ (17:3) Aut 82, p. 47.
"Piano Trio" (for Karen Buranskas, cello). MalR (61)
F 82, p. 48.
"Poetics (To Which I Sometimes Apply Myself)" (tr.
of Angel Gonzalez). DenQ (17:3) Aut 82, p. 32.
"Poetics No. 4" (tr. of Angel Gonzalez). DenQ (17:3)
Aut 82, p. 35.
"T'Introduire Dans Mon Histoire" (tr. of Jaime Gil
de Biedma). DenQ (17:3) Aut 82, p. 85.

2145. KERSLAKE, Susan
"Magma." Germ (6:1) Spr-Sum 82, p. 29.
"Sometimes, before I sleep." Germ (6:1) Spr-Sum 82,
p. 30.

2146. KESSEL, Amy
"Bathing Kari in the Blue Tub." BelPoJ (33:1) Aut
82, p. 1.

2147. KESSLER, Clyde
"Robert Hawby." Im (8:2) 82, p. 7.

2148. KESSLER, Jascha
"And June?" (Complement to a poem by Holderlin, tr.
of Gyorgy Somlyo, w. Maria Korosy). MichOR (21:1)
Wint 82, p. 160-161.
"Concerned with Something Else While Turnovo's
Dying" (tr. of Luchezar Elenkov, w. Alexander
Shurbanov). Nimrod (26:1) Aut-Wint 82, p. 39-40.
"If" (tr. of Blaga Dimitrova, w. Alexander
Shurbanov). Kayak (59) Je 82, p. 66.
"If" (tr. of Blaga Dimitrova, w. Alexander
Shurbanov). Nimrod (26:1) Aut-Wint 82, p. 37.
"In an Eternity of Setting Sun: A Dialogue Between
Lovers" (tr. of Forugh Farrokhzad, w. Amin
Banani). MichOR (21:2) Spr 82, p. 246-248.
"Lilies" (tr. of Bozhidar Bozhilov, w. Alexander
Shurbanov). Kayak (59) Je 82, p. 71.
"Night" (tr. of Georgy Djagarov, w. Alexander
Shurbanov). Kayak (59) Je 82, p. 69.
"No Denying" (tr. of Mihalyi Ladanyi). Spirit
(6:2/3) 82, p. 19-20.
"River Run" (tr. of Elisaveta Bagryana, w. Alexander
Shurbanov). Kayak (59) Je 82, p. 68-69.

"Sauna" (tr. of Luchezar Elenkov, w. Alexander
  Shurbanov). Kayak (59) Je 82, p. 65.
"Secret Love" (tr. of Lyubomir Levchev, w. Alexander
  Shurbanov). Kayak (59) Je 82, p. 63-64.
"Troubles" (tr. of Bozhidar Bozhilov, w. Alexander
  Shurbanov). Kayak (59) Je 82, p. 71.
"What Price Constancy" (tr. of Blaga Dimitrova, w.
  Alexander Shurbanov). Kayak (59) Je 82, p. 67.
"The Wise Ones" (tr. of Bozhidar Bozhilov, w.
  Alexander Shurbanov). Kayak (59) Je 82, p. 70-71.
"A Woman Pregnant" (tr. of Blaga Dimitrova, w.
  Alexander Shurbanov). Nimrod (26:1) Aut-Wint 82,
  p. 38.

2149. KESSLER, Milton
  "Found on Rehov Sinai." Im (8:2) 82, p. 10.

2150. KEYES, Claire
  "After the Funeral." Vis (10) 82, p. 23.

2151. KEYES, Robert Lord
  "Baseball." MassR (23:4) Wint 82, p. 739-740.
  "Radio Comics" (For Jerry Siegal and Joe Shuster).
  MassR (23:4) Wint 82, p. 738-739.

2152. KEYISHIAN, Marjorie Deiter
  "Alchemy." LitR (25:3) Spr 82, p. 362.
  "Climbing the Greased Pole." LitR (25:3) Spr 82, p.
  363.

2153. KHARE, Vishnu
  "Towards Delhi" (tr. of Kunwar Narayan). NewL
  (48:3/4) Spr-Sum 82, p. 190.

2154. KHOT, Chandrakant
  "God: Two Moods" (tr. by Prabhakar Machwe). NewL
  (48:3/4) Spr-Sum 82, p. 231.

2155. KHOURY, Alexis
  "The Owego Transport Museum." CimR (59) Ap 82, p.
  28-29.

2156. KHULLAR, Ajit
  "Aquarium" (tr. of Vijay Dev Narain Sahi). NewL
  (48:3/4) Spr-Sum 82, p. 237.
  "A Hieroglyph of Lost Intents." NewL (48:3/4) Spr-
  Sum 82, p. 161.
  "A Poem" (tr. of Dhoomil). NewL (48:3/4) Spr-Sum 82,
  p. 152-153.

2157. KHULLAR, K. K.
  "Haridwar (The Door to God)" (tr. of Nadaan). NewL
  (48:3/4) Spr-Sum 82, p. 86.
  "A Nazm" (tr. of Shams Faridi). NewL (48:3/4) Spr-
  Sum 82, p. 230.

2158. KIEFER, Rita Brady
  "Exorcism." WindO (41) Aut-Wint 82-83, p. 23.
  "I Never Even Knew the Semi-Colon Existed." WindO
  (41) Aut-Wint 82-83, p. 22.

"Continental Trailway to Denver." WindO (41) Aut-
Wint 82-83, p. 22.

2159. KIMBRO, Harriet
"Copper-coated sea" (Haiku). LittleBR (2:3) Spr 82,
p. 50.

2160. KIME, Peter
"The Fishing Room" (For Roy). PoNow (7:1, issue 37)
82, p. 20.
"Good Shepherd Home." PoNow (7:1, issue 37) 82, p.
20.

2161. KIND, Anne
"A String of Pearls." Stand (23:2) 82, p. 7.

2162. KING, Harley
"Breeze stirs the grass." Northeast (3:14) Wint 82-
83, p. 38.
"A buzzing fly." Northeast (3:14) Wint 82-83, p.
38.
"Fruit cellar." Northeast (3:14) Wint 82-83, p. 38.
"Full moon silvers the icy fields." Northeast
(3:14) Wint 82-83, p. 38.
"Moonlight rushes over the dam." Northeast (3:14)
Wint 82-83, p. 38.
"Walnut darkness." Northeast (3:14) Wint 82-83, p.
38.

2163. KING, Robert S.
"The Black Lady." Poem (44) Mr 82, p. 27.
"Burying a Mute." Poem (44) Mr 82, p. 25.
"The Death of Magic." Poem (44) Mr 82, p. 25.
"Feeding the Body of Earth." CharR (8:1) Spr 82, p.
41.
"The Gravedigger Prays for Sunset." Poem (44) Mr
82, p. 25.
"Karma of the Gravedigger." Poem (44) Mr 82, p. 22-
23.
"A Matter of Time" (from Karma of a Gravedigger).
CapeR (18:1) Wint 82, p. 32.
"The Old Deeds of the Gravedigger." Poem (44) Mr
82, p. 24.
"Snowhaunt." Poem (44) Mr 82, p. 26.
"The Well of Aguas Calientes." EnPas (13) 82, p.
10-11.
"A Wingbeat of Hope" (from Karma of a Gravedigger).
CapeR (18:1) Wint 82, p. 33.

2164. KINGSTON, Maxine Hong
"Absorption of Rock." Iowa (12:2/3) Spr-Sum 81, p.
207-208.
"Restaurant" (for Lilah Kan). Iowa (12:2/3) Spr-Sum
81, p. 206.

2165. KINSLEY, Robert
"Geography." OhioR (29) 82, p. 103-104.
"Grasshoppers." Ploughs (8:2/3) 82, p. 122.
"Keep-Away." OhioR (29) 82, p. 103.
"On Poetry." OhioR (29) 82, p. 104-105.

"Sometimes the Dead." OhioR (29) 82, p. 105.

2166. KINZIE, Mary
"Gabriel" (for Peg and Bob). Salm (55) Wint 82, p.
119.
"Strawberry Pipe" (for my mother). AmerPoR (11:6) N-
D 82, p. 30.
"Summers of Vietnam." SouthernR (18:3) Sum 82, p.
528-531.

2167. KIRCHER, Pamela
"The Market." OhioR (29) 82, p. 14.

2168. KIRK, Dorothy Arlene Bates
"Courtroom Drama: Europa, Victim or Perpetrator?"
LittleBR (2:2) Wint 81-82, p. 64.
"Nobody." LittleBR (2:1) Aut 81, p. 72.

2169. KIRKLAND, Lyn
"I pulled a lung for a cripple in a damaged car."
DekalbLAJ (14:1/4) Aut 80-Sum 81, p. 81.

2170. KIRKPATRICK, Kathryn
"Groping for Trout in a Peculiar River." Epoch
(31:2) Spr 82, p. 134-135.
"Sigune to Parzival: A Discourse on Grief." Shen
(33:1) 81-82, p. 48-50.
"To Fear Death by Water." Telescope (2) Aut 81, p.
50-51.

2171. KIRKWOOD, Judith
"Last Born." Thrpny (11) Aut 82, p. 16.
"Summer Nights." Abraxas (25/26) 82, p. 73.

2172. KIRSCH, Sarah
"Confusione" (tr. by C. Maurice Taylor). MalR (62)
Jl 82, p. 94.
"The Empty String" (tr. by C. Maurice Taylor). MalR
(62) Jl 82, p. 95.
"The Smell of Snow is in the Air" (tr. by C. Maurice
Taylor). MalR (62) Jl 82, p. 94.
"The Village" (tr. by Wayne Kvam). PoNow (6:6, issue
36) 82, p. 43.

2173. KIRSTEIN, Lincoln
"Mr. Clean." MichQR (21:4) Aut 82, p. 597-599.

2174. KISSICK, Gary
"At Paliku." PraS (56:4) Wint 82-83, p. 76.
"Honolulu." PoNow (6:4, issue 34) 82, p. 29.
"Yukiko." PraS (56:4) Wint 82-83, p. 75.

2175. KISTLER, Suzanne F.
"A Poststructuralist Tale." SewanR (90:4) Aut 82,
p. 568.

2176. KISTNER, Toni
"A Meal." HangL (42) 82, p. 58-59.
"Salesman after the Sit." HangL (42) 82, p. 56-57.

2177. KITAGAWA, Kurtis Gene
    "Empty Slowly Out the Holler." Dandel (9:1) 82, p.
    79.

2178. KITCHEN, Judith
    "Letter to California." OhioR (28) 82, p. 45.
    "Monday Morning." GeoR (36:4) Wint 82, p. 810.

    KIYOKO, Miura
    See: MIURA, Kiyoko

2179. KIZER, Carolyn
    "Fanny." Antaeus (47) Aut 82, p. 52-58.

2180. KLECK, Judith
    "The Makers of Ceremony (for Julie). PoetryNW
    (23:1) Spr 82, p. 7-8.

2181. KLEIN, Arnold
    "After Cendrars." Hudson (35:4) Wint 82-83, p. 600.

2182. KLEIN, Jim
    "Blue Chevies." WormR (22:3, issue 87) 82, p. 91-
    102.
    "Jerry." WormR (22:4, issue 88) 82, p. 124.

2183. KLEIN, Susie
    "Poem for a Painting, Georgia O'Keefe." MendoR (5)
    Sum 81, p. 66.

2184. KLEINSCHMIDT, Edward
    "At Dreamland in Alabama." PoetryNW (23:4) Wint 82-
    83, p. 32-33.
    "Backing Up On the Freeway." PoetryNW (23:4) Wint
    82-83, p. 30.
    "Two Women Who Die Each January, Two Women Who Die
    Every February" (for my grandmothers). PoetryNW
    (23:4) Wint 82-83, p. 30-31.
    "What's Yellow." PoetryNW (23:4) Wint 82-83, p. 31-
    32.

2185. KLEINZAHLER, August
    "Good Sound at Lake Fork." Thrpny (11) Aut 82, p.
    27.

2186. KLEPFISZ, Irena
    "Work Sonnets" (with Notes and a Monologue). Cond
    (8) 82, p. 76-85.

2187. KLINE, Shaya
    "Reb Baruch" (For M. S.) HolCrit (19:3) Je 82, p.
    17.

2188. KLINGER, Kurt
    "The Cats" (tr. by Beth Bjorklund). LitR (25:2) Wint
    82, p. 251.
    "Cinema" (tr. by Beth Bjorklund). LitR (25:2) Wint
    82, p. 250.
    "The Crazy Lady" (tr. by Beth Bjorklund). LitR
    (25:2) Wint 82, p. 251.

"Mattina" (tr. by Beth Bjorklund). LitR (25:2) Wint
   82, p. 251.
"We Think Farewell" (tr. by Beth Bjorklund). LitR
   (25:2) Wint 82, p. 250.

2189. KLOEFKORN, William
   "from Platte Valley Homestead." CarolQ (34:3) Spr
      82, p. 28-33.
   "Out-and-Down Pattern." Spirit (6:2/3) 82, p. 134-
      135.
   "Sleeping with Grandmother." Telescope (3) Sum 82,
      p. 48-49.
   "Taking the Milk to Grandmother." GeoR (36:3) Aut
      82, p. 616-617.
   "Whatever Is Elevated and Pure, Precisely on Key."
      PraS (56:3) Aut 82, p. 45.

2190. KNIBESTOL, Leiv
   "The Builder" (tr. by Anne Born). Stand (23:3) 82,
      p. 48.

2191. KNIES, Elizabeth
   "The First Hot Night." Hudson (35:2) Sum 82, p.
      247.
   "The Great Loves." Hudson (35:2) Sum 82, p. 246.
   "Summer." Hudson (35:2) Sum 82, p. 246-247.

2192. KNIGHT, Ann
   "In their silent joydance." Quarry (31:1) Wint 82,
      p. 65.
   "Odetta." Quarry (31:1) Wint 82, p. 66.

2193. KNIGHT, Arthur Winfield
   "Friends with the Poor." Bogg (49) 82, p. 10.
   "The Man Who Never Slept with Marlon Brando" (for
      Harold Norse). CrossC (4:1) Wint 82, p. 22.
   "Secret Pain" (for Mom). Bogg (48) 82, p. 16-18.

2194. KNIGHT, Jeff
   "The Movies." Thrpny (9) Spr 82, p. 25.

2195. KNOEPFLE, John
   "Amtrack Station, Lincoln." Northeast (3:12) Wint
      81-82, p. 9.
   "Concert at Normal." Northeast (3:12) Wint 81-82,
      p. 9.

2196. KNOLL, J. T. (James T.)
   "At the Other Side." MidwQ (23:3) Spr 82, p. 303.
   "The Hill." LittleBR (2:3) Spr 82, p. 82-83.
   "Letter to My Brothers." MidwQ (23:3) Spr 82, p.
      303.
   "Lightning." LittleBR (1:2) Wint 80-81, p. 32.
   "Quilting." LittleBR (2:2) Wint 81-82, p. 44.
   "Waiting." Wind (12:46) 82, p. 22.

2197. KNOLL, John
   "Bird" (for Norberta Wachter). LittleBR (3:1) Aut
      82, p. 45.

2198. KNOLL, Linda O'Nelio
"Prairie Schooner." LittleBR (3:2) Wint 82-83, p. 15.

2199. KNOLL, Michael
"Vivaldi on the Far Side of the Bars" (for William Aberg). GeoR (36:4) Wint 82, p. 831.

2200. KNOTT, Tom
"The universe of physical reality." WestCR (16:2/3) O 81-Ja 82, p. 31.

2201. KNOWLTON, Lindsay
"Narrowing the Blue." Tendril (12) Wint 82, p. 41.

2202. KNUTSON, Nancy Roxbury
"A Calm." PoNow (6:5, issue 35) 82, p. 47.

2203. KOCBEK, Edvard
"Green" (tr. by Herbert Kuhner, Lev Detela, and Milena Detela). PortR (28:1) 82, p. 7.

2204. KOCH, Michael
"The Game." Pig (9) 82, p. 56.

2205. KOEHLER, Stanley
"Contours of Greece." MassR (23:2) Sum 82, p. 273.
"Dodona." MassR (23:2) Sum 82, p. 287.
"An Early Classical Head." MassR (23:2) Sum 82, p. 275.
"Eleusinian." MassR (23:2) Sum 82, p. 280.
"Figures for a White Ground." MassR (23:2) Sum 82, p. 288.
"Fisherman: Tolo." MassR (23:2) Sum 82, p. 283.
"In the Stadium: Delphi." MassR (23:2) Sum 82, p. 282.
"Odysseus Speaks of Asphodel." MassR (23:2) Sum 82, p. 277.
"On the Acropolis." MassR (23:2) Sum 82, p. 279.
"Poseidon of Artemision." MassR (23:2) Sum 82, p. 274.
"Theater: Epidauros." MassR (23:2) Sum 82, p. 281.
"Thermopylae." MassR (23:2) Sum 82, p. 278.
"Tipota: Variations on a Dance." MassR (23:2) Sum 82, p. 284-286.
"Two Sides of an Urn for Leagros Kalos." MassR (23:2) Sum 82, p. 276.

2206. KOEHN, Lala
"The Ice Bird." PoetryCR (4:2) Wint 82, p. 12.

2207. KOEHNE, David
"Loup-Garou." Spirit (6:2/3) 82, p. 111-112.

2208. KOERTGE, Ronald
"Dear John." PoNow (6:5, issue 35) 82, p. 25.
"Demands of the Molars." Spirit (6:2/3) 82, p. 132.
"Every Bird Is My Rival" (Lucy Bakewell Audubon). PoNow (6:5, issue 35) 82, p. 37.

"Further Adventures of Gulliver." PoNow (6:6, issue
  36) 82, p. 18.
"Girls With Older Brothers." WormR (22:1, issue 85)
  82, p. 12.
"Gretel." PoNow (6:5, issue 35) 82, p. 25.
"The Seed Bulls." PoNow (6:6, issue 36) 82, p. 18.
"Sidekicks." PoNow (6:5, issue 35) 82, p. 25.
"The Time I Put on My Mother's Underwear." PoNow
  (6:4, issue 34) 82, p. 21.
"The Voice of the Heron." PoNow (6:5, issue 35) 82,
  p. 37.
"West Coast Romance." PoNow (6:4, issue 34) 82, p.
  21.
"The Whores Were Taking Vitamins." SeC (9:1/2) 80,
  p. 28.
"You Can Never Tell." WormR (22:1, issue 85) 82, p.
  12.

2209. KOESTENBAUM, Phyllis
  "Considerations." NowestR (20:1) 82, p. 40-43.
  "Crazy December." NowestR (20:1) 82, p. 48-49.
  "Right Side Up." NowestR (20:1) 82, p. 50-52.
  "Sentences." NowestR (20:1) 82, p. 44-47.
  "The Trout." NowestR (20:1) 82, p. 37-39.

2210. KOKICH, Kimble
  "Esmeralda and Her First Phone." Gargoyle (17/18)
  81, p. 23.

2211. KOLATKAR, Arun
  from Six Jejuri Poems: "The Door." NewL (48:3/4)
  Spr-Sum 82, p. 124.
  from Six Jejuri Poems: "The Horseshoe Shrine." NewL
  (48:3/4) Spr-Sum 82, p. 124-125.
  from Six Jejuri Poems: "Manohar." NewL (48:3/4)
  Spr-Sum 82, p. 126.
  from Six Jejuri Poems: "An Old Woman." NewL
  (48:3/4) Spr-Sum 82, p. 125-126.
  from Six Jejuri Poems: "A Scratch." NewL (48:3/4)
  Spr-Sum 82, p. 123.
  from Six Jejuri Poems: "Yeshwant Rao." NewL
  (48:3/4) Spr-Sum 82, p. 127-128.

2212. KOLIAS, Helen
  "Afternoon" (tr. of Yannis Ritsos). CarolQ (34:3)
  Spr 82, p. 26.
  "The Graves of Our Forefathers" (tr. of Yannis
  Ritsos). CarolQ (34:3) Spr 82, p. 27.

2213. KOLLERITSCH, Alfred
  "Five Poems" (tr. by Beth Bjorklund). LitR (25:2)
  Wint 82, p. 268-273.

2214. KOLUMBAN, Nicholas
  "At a Wedding." CutB (18) Spr-Sum 82, p. 42-43.
  "At Home, in the Night" (tr. of Sandor Csoori). MalR
  (63) O 82, p. 54.
  "I Can Do Nothing" (tr. of Elizabeth Borchers, w.
  Steven Polgar). AmerPoR (11:1) Ja-F 82, p. 31.

"Poem for Two Women at the Same Time" (tr. of Sandor
Csoori). MalR (63) O 82, p. 52-53.
"Saturn" (tr. of Gunter Grass, w. Steven Polgar).
AmerPoR (11:1) Ja-F 82, p. 31.
"September Confessions" (tr. of Sandor Csoori). MalR
(63) O 82, p. 51.
"The Smile of My Exile" (tr. of Sandor Csoori).
NewOR (9:1) Spr-Sum 82, p. 12.
"The Tourist." CharR (8:1) Spr 82, p. 49.

2215. KOMUNYAKAA, Yusef
"Audacity." Nimrod (26:1) Aut-Wint 82, p. 59.
"Copacetic Mingus." MissouriR (6:1) Aut 82, p. 32.
"In God We Trust." Kayak (58) Ja 82, p. 49.
"In the Labor Camp of Good Intentions." PoNow (6:4,
issue 34) 82, p. 17.
"Newport Beach, 1979." PartR (49:3) 82, p. 434-435.
"Sorrow." Kayak (58) Ja 82, p. 50.
"Speaking of Luck." Nimrod (26:1) Aut-Wint 82, p.
59.
"The Thorn Merchant's Wife." PoNow (6:4, issue 34)
82, p. 17.

2216. KONDOS, Yannis
"Afternoon in Athens" (tr. by Kimon Friar). Kayak
(60) O 82, p. 17.
"The Fingernails" (tr. by Kimon Friar). Kayak (60) O
82, p. 16.
"In the Half Dark" (tr. by Kimon Friar). Kayak (60)
O 82, p. 17.
"Your Eyes Are an Empty Distance" (tr. by Kimon
Friar). Kayak (60) O 82, p. 18.

2217. KOOSER, Ted
"Geronimo's Mirror." PoNow (6:5, issue 35) 82, p.
10.
"Goodbye." PoNow (6:6, issue 36) 82, p. 20.
"Just Now." GeoR (36:2) Sum 82, p. 404.
"Uncle Tubby." PoNow (6:5, issue 35) 82, p. 10.
"Voyager II." PoNow (6:4, issue 34) 82, p. 10.

2218. KOPEC, Carol
"Summer Nights." DekalbLAJ (14:1/4) Aut 80-Sum 81,
p. 82.

2219. KOPELKE, Kendra
"Blue." AntR (40:1) Wint 82, p. 88-89.
"Eager Street." Iowa (12:2/3) Spr-Sum 81, p. 209-
210.
"Green." AntR (40:1) Wint 82, p. 90.
"Pardons." AntR (40:1) Wint 82, p. 91.

2220. KOPP, Karl
"Reunion." NewL (48:2) Wint 81-82, p. 100-101.
"Thorndyke Reflects with Distaste upon His Culture."
NewL (48:2) Wint 81-82, p. 99.

2221. KORAL, Mary
"Eight Add on Eight." Shen (33:1) 81-82, p. 23.

2222. KORNBLUM, Allan
        "Her Hair Is Wet." Spirit (6:2/3) 82, p. 74.

2223. KORNBLUM, Cinda
        "The Honeymooners." Spirit (6:2/3) 82, p. 73.

2224. KORNEGAY, Burt
        "Pattie Place's Pride (Another True Story)."
        DekalbLAJ (14:1/4) Aut 80-Sum 81, p. 83-84.

2225. KOROSY, Maria
        "And June?" (Complement to a poem by Holderlin, tr.
        of Gyorgy Somlyo, w. Jascha Kessler). MichQR
        (21:1) Wint 82, p. 160-161.

2226. KORSTANGE, Gordon
        "Let Them Eat Children." NewL (48:3/4) Spr-Sum 82,
        p. 210-211.
        "Murugesan's Daughter" (for Rathanam). NewL (48:3/4)
        Spr-Sum 82, p. 210.

2227. KOSHAREK, Pat
        "We Crossed the Field." SmPd (19:3, issue 56) Aut
        82, p. 21.

2228. KOST, Virginia
        "Christian Fields." SouthernR (18:3) Sum 82, p.
        553.
        "Waiting for the Men to Come Home from War."
        SouthernR (18:3) Sum 82, p. 554.

2229. KOSTELANETZ, Richard
        "Indistinct face, with or without glasses." Spirit
        (6:2/3) 82, p. 115.
        "Short Fiction: `I Walked'." PoNow (6:6, issue 36)
        82, p. 11.
        "Silver, Gold, Bronze, Lead." Abraxas (25/26) 82,
        p. 50.
        "Spectacularly long very dark hair." Spirit (6:2/3)
        82, p. 116.

2230. KOSTINER, Eileen
        "Spring Vacation." SouthernPR (22:1) Spr 82, p. 26.

2231. KOTEK, Jo-Anna
        "Canvas." PoetryCR (4:2) Wint 82, p. 15.
        "Tonight." PoetryCR (4:2) Wint 82, p. 15.

2232. KOTLUM, Johannes ur
        "Climacteric" (tr. by Alan Boucher). Vis (8) 82, p.
        22.

2233. KOVADLOFF, Santiago
        "Country" (tr. by Ricardo Pau-Llosa). BelPoJ (32:4)
        Sum 82, p. 9.
        "Es Decir." BelPoJ (32:4) Sum 82, p. 8.
        "Pais." BelPoJ (32:4) Sum 82, p. 8.
        "Which Is to Say" (tr. by Ricardo Pau-Llosa). BelPoJ
        (32:4) Sum 82, p. 9.

2234. KOWIT, Steve
      "A Vote for Harold." PoNow (6:6, issue 36) 82, p.
      28.

2235. KOZER, Jose
      "He's Still Alive, Grown Small My Father" (tr. by
      Selim-Roberto Picciotto). Im (8:2) 82, p. 5.
      "Remember Sylvia" (tr. by Selim-Roberto Picciotto).
      Im (8:2) 82, p. 5.
      "Syllogism" (tr. by Selim-Roberto Picciotto). Im
      (8:2) 82, p. 5.
      "Welcome" (tr. by Selim-Roberto Picciotto). Im (8:2)
      82, p. 5.

2236. KRAFTNER, Hertha
      "Litanies" (tr. by Beth Bjorklund). LitR (25:2) Wint
      82, p. 248-249.

2237. KRAKANER, Romy
      "Untitled: Dreaming tastes like raw powder." MendoR
      (5) Sum 81, p. 66.

2238. KRAMER, Aaron
      "All-Star Neutron Day: Aug. 9, 1981." Vis (8) 82,
      p. 21.
      "At the Wheel." Vis (8) 82, p. 10.
      "Booom!! Vis (8) 82, p. 20.
      "The Bridge Reverberates Each Step We Take" (tr. of
      Jack Gordon). NewEngR (4:4) Sum 82, p. 556.
      "Dental Appointment." Confr (24) Sum 82, p. 54-55.
      "Friends." AntigR (50) Sum 82, p. 80.
      "Had I Not." Vis (9) 82, p. 20.
      "In the Cage." NewEngR (4:4) Sum 82, p. 555.
      "Line of Vision." AntigR (50) Sum 82, p. 80.
      "A Neighbor Dies." Wind (12:44) 82, p. 20-21.
      "The News." NewEngR (4:4) Sum 82, p. 555.
      "Nocturne." NewEngR (4:4) Sum 82, p. 554.
      "Phone Call." AntigR (49) Spr 82, p. 94.
      "Suite." Wind (12:44) 82, p. 21-23.
      "Who Brings the Songs?" (tr. of Jacob Friedman).
      NewEngR (4:4) Sum 82, p. 557.

2239. KRAMER, Larry
      "A Chant for Waugh Street." HiramPoR (31) Aut-Wint
      82, p. 34-35.

2240. KRAPF, Norbert
      "The American Dream." PoNow (6:5, issue 35) 82, p.
      16.
      "Bookends" Im (8:1) 82, p. 10.
      "Circus Songs, 6." Confr (23) Wint 82, p. 44.
      "Circus Songs, 9." Confr (23) Wint 82, p. 46.
      "Circus Songs, 10." Confr (23) Wint 82, p. 48.
      "Currents." Im (8:1) 82, p. 10.

2241. KRATT, Mary
      "Don't Tell the Lazarus Story This Morning." ChrC
      (99:21) Je 9-16, 82, p. 692.

2242. KRAUSE, Judith
        "Elephantiasis." Grain (10:2) My 82, p. 27.
        "The Storytellers." Grain (10:2) My 82, p. 28.

2243. KRAUSS, Janet
        "Let Us Fly." PikeF (4) Spr 82, p. 18.
        "The Rabbit" (after "A Rabbit among the Fairies" by
        John Anster Fitzgerald). PikeF (4) Spr 82, p. 18.

2244. KRAUSS, Ruth
        "Duet and Sunrise." PoNow (6:6, issue 36) 82, p.
        34.
        "I Love You with the Aid of Brecht." Confr (24) Sum
        82, p. 34.

2245. KREITER-KURYLO, Carolyn
        "From the Cloister, Saint-Remy." Vis (8) 82, p. 31-
        32.

2246. KREMER, Henry G.
        "Memorable Days." LittleBR (1:3) Spr 81, p. 49.

2247. KRESH, David
        "Dreams of You Persist." Salm (56) Spr 82, p. 140.
        "High Summer at Zebe's." WebR (7:2) Aut 82, p. 42-
        43.
        "Round Faces." Salm (56) Spr 82, p. 141.
        "Tinsel Eyes." Salm (56) Spr 82, p. 142.
        "View of Spring Garden Street." Spirit (6:2/3) 82,
        p. 16.

2248. KRETZ, Thomas
        "A December Chill in Frascati." HolCrit (19:4) O
        82, p. 14.

2249. KRIDLER, David
        "Appleseed" (for John Chapman, 1775-1845). Ploughs
        (8:1) 82, p. 60-67.

2250. KRISAK, Len
        "Counting Pentecosts." Comm (109:11) Je 4, 82, p.
        341.

2251. KRISHNAN, S.
        "To Golconda, with William Meredith." NewL (48:3/4)
        Spr-Sum 82, p. 180-181.

2252. KROLL, Ernest
        "Aftermath." PoNow (6:4, issue 34) 82, p. 15.
        "At the Funeral of Thomas Hardy (1928)." WebR (7:2)
        Aut 82, p. 45.
        "Booth at Bay." PoNow (6:6, issue 36) 82, p. 37.
        "Flying Foreign." BelPoJ (32:3) Spr 82, p. 7.
        "Moonshine." CapeR (17:2) Sum 82, p. 50.
        "Retorts." BelPoJ (32:3) Spr 82, p. 6.
        "Tradition" (Wankinquoah River, Wareham, Mass.).
        WebR (7:2) Aut 82, p. 44.

2253. KROLL, Judith
        "From the Plains" (Hyderabad, India). NewL (49:2)
        Wint 82-83, p. 54-56.

2254. KRONENBERG, Susan
        "Release." PoNow (7:1, issue 37) 82, p. 20.

2255. KRYSS, T. L.
        "Magi." Abraxas (25/26) 82, p. 8.
        "Unicorn Sugar." Abraxas (25/26) 82, p. 9.

2256. KUBICEK, J. L.
        "Solicited Blurbs." Bogg (49) 82, p. 12.

2257. KUFFEL, Frances
        "The Blind Man's Poem." CutB (18) Spr-Sum 82, p. 7.

2258. KUHNER, Herbert
        "Green" (tr. of Edvard Kocbek, with Lev Detela, and
        Milena Detela). PortR (28:1) 82, p. 7.

2259. KUJAWINSKI, Frank
        "Because Only this World of Pain" (tr. of Stanislaw
        Baranczak). ManhatR (2:1) 81, p. 29.
        "I'm Through with These" (tr. of Stanislaw
        Baranczak). ManhatR (2:1) 81, p. 36.
        "If Porcelain, Then Only the Kind" (tr. of Stanislaw
        Baranczak). ManhatR (2:1) 81, p. 35.
        "In Principle, It's Not Possible" (tr. of Stanislaw
        Baranczak). ManhatR (2:1) 81, p. 32.
        "Lullaby" (tr. of Stanislaw Baranczak). ManhatR
        (2:1) 81, p. 33.
        "These Words" (tr. of Stanislaw Baranczak). ManhatR
        (2:1) 81, p. 28.
        "Together with Dust" (tr. of Stanislaw Baranczak).
        ManhatR (2:1) 81, p. 34.
        "Where Did I Wake Up?" (tr. of Stanislaw Baranczak).
        ManhatR (2:1) 81, p. 27.
        "Window" (tr. of Stanislaw Baranczak). ManhatR (2:1)
        81, p. 30-31.

2260. KULEBI, Cahit
        "Bequest" (tr. by Ozcan Yalim, William A. Fielder,
        and Dionis Coffin Riggs). StoneC (10:1/2) Aut-Wint
        82-83,p. 31.
        "Tereke." StoneC (10:1/2) Aut-Wint 82-83, p. 30.

2261. KUMAR, Sati
        "Stormward" (tr. by Manohar Bandhyopadhyay). NewL
        (48:3/4) Spr-Sum 82, p. 209.

2262. KUMAR, Shiv K.
        "At the Ghats of Benares." NewL (48:3/4) Spr-Sum
        82, p. 88.
        "Crematorium in Adikmet, Hyderabad." NewL (49:2)
        Wint 82-83, p. 49.
        "A Dark Mood." NewL (48:3/4) Spr-Sum 82, p. 88-89.

2263. KUMIN, Maxine
        "Appetite." AmerPoR (11:6) N-D 82, p. 31.

"At a Private Showing in 1982." NewYorker (58:32) S
27, 82, p. 48.
"Grandchild" (For Yann). Poetry (141:3) D 82, p.
148-149.
"In the Pea Patch." Tendril (12) Wint 82, p. 5.
"Leaving My Daughter's House." Iowa (12:2/3) Spr-
Sum 81, p. 211-212.
"Out-of-the-Body-Travel." Ploughs (8:1) 82, p. 27.
"Retrospect in the Kitchen." Ploughs (8:1) 82, p.
28.
"You Are in Bear Country." AmerPoR (11:6) N-D 82,
p. 31.

2264. KUNITZ, Stanley
"The Abduction." Atl (250:5) N 82, p. 130.

KURYLO, Carolyn Kreiter
See: KREITER-KURYLO, Carolyn

2265. KUZMA, Greg
"Bach." LitR (25:4) Sum 82, p. 542.
"Dark." SouthernPR (22:1) Spr 82, p. 75.
"Death in Crete." OhioR (29) 82, p. 13.
"Evening, and Morning." MidwQ (23:4) Sum 82, p.
398.
"Face." LitR (25:4) Sum 82, p. 543.
"A Farewell To Arms." MinnR (NS18) Spr 82, p. 47-
48.
"The First Day of the Week." BaratR (8:2) Wint 81,
p. 101.
"For My Brother Four Years Dead." MidwQ (23:4) Sum
82, p. 399.
"Hands." LitR (25:4) Sum 82, p. 543.
"Hands." VirQR (58:2) Spr 82, p. 274.
"Hearing." CutB (18) Spr-Sum 82, p. 23-25.
"The Lake." OhioR (29) 82, p. 12.
"Midwest Harvest." OhioR (29) 82, p. 12.
"Monday." Epoch (31:3) Sum 82, p. 216.
"Pain." Northeast (3:12) Wint 81-82, p. 17.
"Plants." Epoch (31:3) Sum 82, p. 217.
"The Sailors." MidwQ (23:4) Sum 82, p. 396.
"Seeing the Photographs." PoetryE (8) Aut 82, p.
42-44.
"September 1980" (For Jeff). LitR (25:4) Sum 82, p.
544.
"These Are Interesting Times." NewL (49:1) Aut 82,
p. 71-72.
"The True Fish." LitR (25:4) Sum 82, p. 542.
"When You Died" (For my brother). LitR (25:4) Sum
82, p. 544.
"William Carlos Williams." MidwQ (23:4) Sum 82, p.
397.
"You Had to Be Persuaded to Return." OhioR (28) 82,
p. 18.

2266. KVAM, Wayne
"The Village" (tr. of Sarah Kirsch). PoNow (6:6,
issue 36) 82, p. 43.

2267. KWIATEK, JoEllen
       "Field in November." AmerPoR (11:2) Mr-Ap 82, p.
       19.

2268. KYLER, Inge Logenburg
       "The Alm." WritersL O-N 82, p. 11.

2269. La FOLLETTE, Melvin Walker
       "Ash Wednesday." ChrC (99:6) F 24, 82, p. 206.

      La PUEBLA, Manuel de
      See: PUEBLA, Manuel de la

2270. La ROSA, Pablo
       "Lullaby." KanQ (14:3) Sum 82, p. 28.

2271. LACHMAN, Sol P.
       "Elegy for Irving 11-9-79." Sky (10-12) Aut 82, p.
       43.
       "The Story of the Bride, Laughing." Sky (10-12) Aut
       82, p. 44.

2272. LADANYI, Mihalyi
       "No Denying" (tr. by Jascha Kessler). Spirit (6:2/3)
       82, p. 19-20.

2273. LADER, Bruce
       "Behold." AntigR (51) Aut 82, p. 24.
       "Panic." AntigR (51) Aut 82, p. 24-25.
       "Recital." MalR (63) O 82, p. 164.

2274. LaFLEUR, William R.
       "So Much Spume." LitR (25:3) Spr 82, p. 342-344.

2275. LAINE, Jarkko
       "A Footnote to Shakespeare's Hamlet" (tr. by John
       Currie and the author). Spirit (6:2/3) 82, p. 177-
       179.

2276. LAKE, Paul Robert
       "Waiting for Grandma." Bogg (48) 82, p. 41-42.

2277. LALOUETTE, J.
       "Le Telephone Noir." PoetryCR (3:4) Sum 82, p. 6.

2278. LAMB, Elizabeth Searle
       "Shimmer of dawn" (Haiku). LittleBR (2:3) Spr 82, p.
       50.

2279. LAMBERT, Nancy
       "Billions of Books." LittleM (13:3/4) 82, p. 108.

2280. LAMMON, Marty
       from Migrations: "Today a man pulled an ear of
       corn." NewL (48:2) Wint 81-82, p. 69.

2281. LAMON, Laurie
       "Lament." CutB (18) Spr-Sum 82, p. 77-78.
       "To the Last Artful Man." CutB (18) Spr-Sum 82, p.
       75-76.

2282. LAMORTE, Pat
      "Closing Over." <u>Salm</u> (57) Sum 82, p. 134.
      "Hypnos in Egypt." <u>WebR</u> (7:1) Spr 82, p. 16-17.
      "Rain." <u>Salm</u> (57) Sum 82, p. 133.

2283. LAMSTEIN, Sarah
      "Last Moments." <u>Paint</u> (9:17/18) Spr-Aut 82, p. 15.

      LANCE, Betty Rita Gomez
      <u>See</u>: GOMEZ LANCE, Betty Rita

2284. LANDALE, Zoe
      "Ballad of the Reluctant Fisherman" (for
         Bill). <u>PoetryCR</u> (3:4) Sum 82, p. 4.
      "Success." <u>PoetryCR</u> (3:3) Spr 82, p. 12.

2285. LANE, Donna M.
      "The Orphans." <u>AspenJ</u> (1) Wint 82, p. 28.
      "Pygmalion." <u>AspenJ</u> (1) Wint 82, p. 28.

2286. LANE, Erskine
      "They Had No Electricity There" (tr. of Alvaro de
         Campos [Fernando Pessoa]). <u>Spirit</u> (6:2/3) 82, p.
         183.

2287. LANE, John
      "Four Old Graves in the Virginia Woods" (errata:
         Kennedy is not the author, as printed). <u>Ploughs</u>
         (8:2/3) 82, p. 246-247.
      "Seeing Wild Horses" (errata: Kennedy is not the
         author, as printed). <u>Ploughs</u> (8:2/3) 82, p. 248.

2288. LANE, M. Travis
      "Any Day Now." <u>PoetryCR</u> (4:2) Wint 82, p. 13.
      "Need." <u>CanLit</u> (93) Sum 82, p. 58.
      "Road Ending." <u>CanLit</u> (92) Spr 82, p. 45.

2289. LANE, Patrick
      "Monarch I-IV." <u>Grain</u> (10:2) My 82, p. 5-9.
      "Old Mother." <u>Grain</u> (10:3) Ag 82, p. 29.

2290. LANG, Stephen
      "Batik." <u>Poem</u> (46) N 82, p. 59.
      "A Cloud in Neutral." <u>Poem</u> (44) Mr 82, p. 53.
      "Hider." <u>Poem</u> (44) Mr 82, p. 54.
      "L.W." <u>Poem</u> (46) N 82, p. 58.
      "To Mr. Kirkpatrick." <u>Poem</u> (44) Mr 82, p. 52.

2291. LANG, Warren
      "In the Silence on a Winter Night." <u>Abraxas</u> (25/26)
         82, p. 75.

2292. LANGDALE, Allan
      "Nostoi II." <u>Dandel</u> (9:1) 82, p. 75.
      "Nostoi VII." <u>Dandel</u> (9:1) 82, p. 76.

2293. LANGDON, Keith
      "Teaching." <u>EngJ</u> (71:8) D 82, p. 42.

2294. LANGTON, Charles
       "Environmental Impact Statement." <u>NewL</u> (48:2) Wint
          81-82, p. 65.
       "To Tom about the Apple Trees." <u>NewL</u> (48:2) Wint
          81-82, p. 66.

2295. LANGTON, Daniel J.
       "Flight." <u>CentR</u> (26:2) Spr 82, p. 174.
       "The Unbroken Chain." <u>PoNow</u> (6:6, issue 36) 82, p.
          7.

2296. LANOUE, David
       "Blue." <u>HiramPoR</u> (32) Spr-Sum 82, p. 32.

2297. LANSING, Gerrit
       "3 Poems of the Underworld(s)." <u>Sulfur</u> (2:3, issue
          6) 82, p. 128-129.

2298. LANTEIGNE, M. P.
       "When You Open Your Hands." <u>PottPort</u> (4) 82-83, p.
          8.

2299. LAPPIN, Linda
       "Fragment of the Oranges." <u>Kayak</u> (59) Je 82, p. 14-
          15.
       "Miracle of the Bus Stop." <u>Kayak</u> (59) Je 82, p. 16.

2300. LARDAS, Konstantinos
       "Tellings." <u>ModernPS</u> (11:1/2) 82, p. 151.

2301. LARKIN, Jonah
       "Untitled: Being mad feels like a sliver inside your
          hand." <u>MendoR</u> (5) Sum 81, p. 66.

2302. LARSON, Clinton F.
       "A View of History." <u>SoDakR</u> (20:1) Spr 82, p. 51.

2303. LaSALLE, Peter
       "Blue Snow." <u>MinnR</u> (NS18) Spr 82, p. 46.
       "Juxtaposition." <u>AspenJ</u> (1:2) Sum 82, p. 46.

2304. LASARTE, Javier
       "Casablanca." <u>Prismal</u> (7/8) Spr 82, p. 76.
       "Qerida fulana." <u>Prismal</u> (7/8) Spr 82, p. 75.

2305. LASDUN, James
       "Above Laggan." <u>Waves</u> (11:1) Aut 82, p. 12.
       "Vindice at the Oyster Bar." <u>Waves</u> (11:1) Aut
          82, p. 13.
       "Widow Music." <u>Waves</u> (11:1) Aut 82, p. 12.

2306. LASH, Kenneth
       "La Nausee." <u>NoAmR</u> (267:1) Mr 82,p. 11.
       "Xmas Shopping Guide." <u>NoAmR</u> (267:4) D 82,p. 7.

2307. LASHER, Darlene
       "Gypsy." <u>Tendril</u> (13) Sum 82, p. 46.

2308. LASNIER, Rina
       "Joie de Mourir." <u>Os</u> (15) 82, p. 15.

2309. LASOEN, Patricia
"Remember the Strait of Calais?" (tr. by Maria
Jacobs). Waves (10:4) Spr 82, p. 43.
"Weet Je Het Nog: Het Nauw Van Calais?" Waves (10:4)
Spr 82, p. 43.

2310. LATHAM, J.
"The Pain of Adolescence." Bogg (48) 82, p. 40.

2311. LATORRE, Carlos
"To-Be-America" (tr. by Mary Crow). DenQ (16:4) Wint
82, p. 39.

2312. LAU-MANNING, Carolyn
"For the Mission Beach Marvel." Catalyst (Erotica
Issue) 82, p. 4.
"I Didn't Write This Poem." Shout (3:1) 82, p. 89-
94.
"Usual Method for Orgasm" (for Pat Wolf). Catalyst
(Erotica Issue) 82, p. 5.

2313. LAUGHLIN, James
"After Martial." Ploughs (8:2/3) 82, p. 80.
"The Child." Poetry (139:4) Ja 82, p. 222.
"I Like You." Ploughs (8:2/3) 82, p. 78.
"If You Stare." Ploughs (8:2/3) 82, p. 79.

2314. LAUTERMILCH, Steven
"The Catechism of the Fire." CentR (26:2) Spr
82, p. 175-176.
"Like Water" (tr. of Ranier Maria Rilke). ArizQ
(38:4) Wint 82, p. 335.

2315. LAVALLE, Tomas Guido
"Matter of Friends" (for Alfredo Plank, tr. by Jason
Weiss). PraS (56:1) Spr 82, p. 42-43.

2316. LAVANT, Christine
"Five Poems" (tr. by Beth Bjorklund). LitR (25:2)
Wint 82, p. 184-186.
"Seit Heute, Aber fur Immer." AspenJ (1:2) Sum
82, p. 29.
"Since Today, But Forever" (tr. by Johannes
Beilharz). AspenJ (1:2) Sum 82, p. 29.
"Wer Wird Mir Hungern Helfer Diese Nacht." AspenJ
(1:2) Sum 82, p. 29.
"Who Will Help Me Starve This Night?" (tr. by
Johannes Beilharz). AspenJ (1:2) Sum 82, p. 29.

2317. LAVAZZI, Thomas
"Impressions" Catalyst (Erotica Issue) 82, p. 21.

2318. LAVELLE, Tom
"Domestic." Abraxas (25/26) 82, p. 101.

2319. LAVIERA, Tato
"Angelito's Eulogy in Anger." RevChic (10:1/2)
Wint-Spr 82, p. 83-85.
"The Song of an Oppressor." RevChic (10:1/2) Wint-
Spr 82, p. 80-82.

"Standards." RevChic (10:1/2) Wint-Spr 82, p. 86.
"Tito Madera Smith" (for Dr. Juan Flores). RevChic
   (10:1/2) Wint-Spr 82, p. 87-88.

2320. LAVIGNE, Su
       "Janice." WritersL Jl 82, p. 23.

2321. LaVILLA-HAVELIN, Jim
       "Simon's Masterpiece." Pig (9) 82, p. 81.

2322. LAVIN CERDA, Hernan
       "Diaspora con Colmillos" Inti(12) Aut 80, p. 80-82.
       "Monologo del Esqueleto." Inti(12) Aut 80, p. 80.

2323. LAWDER, Donald
       "O the Great English Iambic!" KanQ (14:3) Sum
          82, p. 75-80.
       "Slaughtering a Bull" (Five years ago this June, in
          Dalton, Pennsylvania, for my neighbor Jim) AmerS
          (51:3) Sum 82, p. 368.
       "There Is a Way." AmerS (51:2) Spr 82, p. 244.
       "The Wild Bird (II)" (an old story retold for my son
          Wally and his bride Pat). KanQ (14:3) Sum 82, p.
          74.

2324. LAWDER, Douglas
       "Jogging the Lake." Telescope (2) Aut 81, p. 14.
       "Sun after Three Days of Rain." Telescope (2) Aut
          81, p. 9.

2325. LAWRENCE, David
       "Letter to Kelly." DekalbLAJ (14:1/4) Aut 80-Sum
          81, p. 84.

2326. LAWSON, David
       "Ex-GI Writes Poem for Young Instructor." QW (14)
          Spr-Sum 82, p. 44-45.

2327. LAWTON, Susan
       "Free Admission, Name Dropping, Love, Lust, Incest &
          Cultism within the Ranks of Small Pressers." Bogg
          (49) 82, p. 14-15.

2328. LAX, Lenny
       "All for the Love (of a Sixteen Year Old
          Girl)." MendoR (6) Sum 81, p. 92.

2329. LAYTON, Elizabeth
       "The House of Glass." LittleBR (2:2) Wint 81-82, p.
          29.
       "A New Dress for Debbie." LittleBR (3:2) Wint 82-
          83, p. 17.

2330. LAYTON, Irving
       "Comrade Undershaftsky." PoetryCR (4:2) Wint 82, p.
          10.
       "Day in Court." PottPort (4) 82-83, p. 34.
       "Fabrizio" (for William Goodwin). CanLit (95) Wint
          82, p. 6.

"For the Wife of John Milton." CanLit (91) Wint
   81, p. 96.
"Portrait of a Modern Woman." PoetryCR (3:4) Sum
   82, p. 5.
"The Swamp." PottPort (4) 82-83, p. 25.
"The Vacuum." PoetryCR (4:1) Sum 82, p. 11.

2331. Le GUIN, Ursula K.
      "The Basalt." OP (33) Spr 82, p. 30.
      "For Katya." OP (33) Spr 82, p. 28.
      "To St George." OP (33) Spr 82, p. 29.
      "Wild Oats and Fireweed" (Para mi hermana Diana). OP
         (33) Spr 82, p. 31-32.

2332. LEA, Sydney
      "The One White Face in the Place." SouthernR (18:1)
         Wint 82, p. 169-172.
      "There Should Have Been" (for Alastair Reid). OhioR
         (28) 82, p. 34-35.
      "Trajectory" (for M. R. B.). Hudson (35:2) Sum
         82, p. 254-255.

2333. LEACH, Chet
      "Recollections in Tranquility." WestB (10) 82, p.
         78.

2334. LEALE, B. C.
      "Attack." Bogg (48) 82, p. 62.

2335. LEAMON, Marlene
      "Upstairs." Iowa (12:2/3) Spr-Sum 81, p. 213-214.

2336. LEAMON, Warren
      "It Ended Like This." SoCaR (14:2) Spr 82, p. 99.

2337. LEBECK, Michael
      "Black Sheep." WormR (22:3, issue 87) 82, p.111-
         112.
      "Kaddish." WormR (22:3, issue 87) 82, p.111.

2338. LEBOURDAIS, Vanessa
      "The Blanket." CrossC (4:2/3) 82, p. 36.

2339. LEBRON, Lolita
      from Poema de Recuerdo: (fragmento). Mairena
         (4:11/12) Wint 82, p. 152.

2340. LeCOMPTE, Kendall
      "Newton's Ghost Considers the Bicyclist
         Descending." AspenJ (1:2) Sum 82, p. 47.

2341. LEE, Adam
      "Untitled: Laughing sounds like burnt hic-
         cups." MendoR (5) Sum 81, p. 66.

2342. LEE, Alice
      "Burial Instructions." SouthernHR (16:4) Aut 82, p.
         302.

2343. LEE, Ann
        "Fairy Tale." SmPd (19:3, issue 56) Aut 82, p. 7.
        "The Message." Wind (12:44) 82, p. 23.

2344. LEE, John B.
        "Confrontation." Quarry (31:1) Wint 82, p. 48-49.
        "The Town Drunk." PoetryCR (4:1) Sum 82, p. 11.

2345. LEE, Lance
        "What She Takes from Me." PoetryNW (23:4) Wint 82-
        83, p. 25.
        "Windtossed, the Oranges." Poem (46) N 82, p. 7-9.

2346. LEE, Mattie
        "Churchyard Games." SoDakR (20:4) Wint 82-83, p.
        58.
        "Raphael Lies." SoDakR (20:4) Wint 82-83, p. 59.

2347. LEED, Jacob
        from Looking at Chinese Pictures: "After the
        Rain." Hangl (43) Wint 82-83, p. 67.
        from Looking at Chinese Pictures: "Mr Huang." Hangl
        (43) Wint 82-83, p. 67.

2348. LEFCOWITZ, Barbara
        "Letter to Marina" (for D.M. Thomas). Bogg (49)
        82, p. 8.

2349. LEFCOWITZ, Barbara F.
        "Gretel's Story." WebR (7:1) Spr 82, p. 10-15.

2350. LEFEVERE, Andre
        "The Ladder and the Rope" (tr. of Karel van de
        Woestijne). Paint (7/8:13/16) 80-81, p. 47.
        from Mathematics of the Heart: "The world has always
        been full of artists..." (tr. of Joubert). Paint
        (9:17/18) Spr-Aut 82, p. 20-21.

2351. LEFFLER, Merrill
        "A Snub for Mr. and Ms. Exegesis." PoNow (7:1,
        issue 37) 82, p. 24.
        "To the Failed Suicides." PoNow (7:1, issue 37)
        82, p. 24.

2352. LeFORGE, P. V.
        "At First." Pig (9) 82, p. 26.

2353. LEGARE, Huguette
        "Cheval Semi-figuratif." Os (14) 82, p. 19-22.

2354. LEGGAT, Graham
        "Wood Hymn." Hangl (43) Wint 82-83, p. 58.

2355. LEGLER, Philip
        "Stopping to Relieve Myself." PoNow (6:5, issue 35)
        82, p. 28.
        "The Survivor." SouthwR (67:3) Sum 82, p. 300-301.

2356. LEHMAN, David
        "The Ideal Subway." Shen (33:1) 81-82, p. 24.

2357. LeMASTER, J. R.
"Beyond" (tr. of Claude Vigee, w. Kenneth Lawrence
Beaudoin). WebR (7:2) Aut 82, p. 18-19.
"King of Our Years" (tr. of Claude Vigee, w. Kenneth
Lawrence Beaudoin). WebR (7:2) Aut 82, p. 17.
"Nothing Is Wholly Lost" (tr. of Claude Vigee, w.
Kenneth Lawrence Beaudoin). WebR (7:2) Aut 82, p.
19.

2358. LENT, John
"Pastoral No. 1: St. Albert Sideroad, 1961" (for my
sister, Susan). Waves (10:3) Wint 82, p. 67.

LEON, Maria de los Angeles Ortiz
See: ORTIZ de LEON, Maria de los Angeles

2359. LEON HERNANDEZ, Victor de
"Recuerdos de Manolo." RevChic (10:3) Sum 82, p.
18-20.

2360. LERNER, Laurence
"Solving the Riddle." NewL (49:1) Aut 82, p. 59.

2361. LERNER, Linda
"Another Country." Shout (3:1) 82, p. 24-25.
"When the Mind." PoNow (6:4, issue 34) 82, p. 38.

2362. LESLIE, Nate
"Hard Soul Hats Heads and Soul." Pig (8) 80, p. 18.

2363. LESSING, Karin
"Dunes." Sulfur (2:1, issue 4) 82, p. 97-101.

2364. LESTER-MASSMAN, Gordon
"Acid." Sam (31:4, issue 124) 82, p.4.
"For Mary Kay Harmon." Sam (31:4, issue 124)
82, p.12.
"Gomorrah: Two Views." Sam (31:4, issue 124)
82, p.13-14.
"Icarus." HolCrit (19:2) Ap 82, p. 17.
"Mr. Poor." Sam (31:4, issue 124) 82, p.2.
"My Sister Scares Me." StoneC (9:3/4) Spr-Sum
82, p. 69.
"The Peaceable Kingdom." Shen (33:2) 82, p. 72.
"Poetica Verita." Sam (31:4, issue 124) 82, p.10-
11.
"Some Portraits of My Colleagues." Sam (31:4, issue
124) 82, p.5-8.
"Whores." Sam (31:4, issue 124) 82, p.15.
"Why Certain Conversations Lapse." Sam (31:4, issue
124) 82, p.9.
"The Work Song." Sam (31:4, issue 124) 82, p.3.
"The Worker's Lament." Sam (31:4, issue 124)
82, p.16.

2365. LEUNG, Ho Hon
"I was part of the O's thrid son." AntigR (48) Wint
82, p. 73-74.

2366. LEVANT, Howard
        "The Novelist." PoNow (6:4, issue 34) 82, p. 17.

2367. LEVCHEV, Lyubomir
        "Secret Love" (tr. by Jascha Kessler and Alexander
          Shurbanov). Kayak (59) Je 82, p. 63-64.

2368. LEVENSON, Christopher
        "Communications." Epoch (32:1) Aut 82, p. 80.
        "Ghost." Epoch (32:1) Aut 82, p. 81.
        "Scranton, PA." Epoch (32:1) Aut 82, p. 81.

2369. LEVER, Bernice
        "A Dream of Dying" (April 28, 1980 -- 5 a.m.). MalR
          (63) O 82, p. 162-163.
        "How to Weather a Marriage." CrossC (4:2/3) 82, p.
          32.
        "Out to Lunch." CrossC (4:2/3) 82, p. 32.

2370. LEVER, Melanie
        "King Henry IV: Reflections on Stratford." Waves
          (10:4) Spr 82, p. 72.
        "Quiet Thoughts." Waves (10:4) Spr 82, p. 72.

2371. LEVERING, Donald
        "Notes from the Arroyo." PortR (28:1) 82, p. 32.
        "The Sun Has Fallen." PortR (28:2) 82, p. 60-61.

2372. LEVERTOV, Denise
        "The Cricket" (tr. of Krassin Himmirsky). Hudson
          (35:4) Wint 82-83, p. 580.
        "Seeing for a Moment." HangL (42) 82, p. 24.
        "Sneers." HangL (42) 82, p. 23.

2373. LEVI, Jan Heller
        "Bradley Beach" (for Michael). Pequod (14) 82, p.
          81.
        "The Broadway Local." Pequod (14) 82, p. 80.
        "A Sequence for My Mother." Iowa (12:2/3) Spr-Sum
          81, p. 215-219.
        "Sylvia Is Grinding." BelPoJ (32:3) Spr 82, p. 19.

2374. LEVI, Toni Mergentime
        "Daylight Savings." Poem (45) Jl 82, p. 46.
        "Gardener." Poem (45) Jl 82, p. 45.

2375. LEVIN, Arthur
        "The Aged Trustee Relinquishes His Trust." Pequod
          (14) 82, p. 82-84.

2376. LEVIN, Harriet
        "Sustenance" (for Saley Nong and Ed Dinger). Nimrod
          (26:1) Aut-Wint 82, p. 11-12.

2377. LEVIN, John
        "A Stand." WormR (22:1, issue 85) 82, p. 10.
        "To The Point." WormR (22:1, issue 85) 82, p. 9.

2378. LEVINE, Ellen
        "Double Exposure." Vis (10) 82, p. 10.

"Early September" (for my father). CarolQ (34:3) Spr
82, p. 25.

2379. LEVINE, Philip
"Been Here Before." Ploughs (8:2/3) 82, p. 37-38.
"Last Words." NewYorker (58:43) D 13, 82, p. 44.
"The Man Who Lost His Name." NewEngR (5:1/2) Aut-
Wint 82, p. 61-63.
"On the Language of Dust." NewYorker (58:36) O 25,
82, p. 46.
"Shore." NewYorker (58:25) Ag 9, 82, p. 36.
"Voyages." NewYorker (58:40) N 22, 82, p. 44.
"When the Shift Was Over." Ploughs (8:2/3) 82, p.
39.

2380. LEVINE, Rachel A.
"Lobotomy." Tendril (12) Wint 82, p. 42.

2381. LEVINSON, Alan
"Dinner for Two." UnderRM 1(1) Spr 82, p. 53.
"If." UnderRM 1(1) Spr 82, p. 53.

2382. LEVIS, Larry
"1974: My Story in a Late Style of Fire." AmerPoR
(11:6) N-D 82, p. 33.
"Adolescence." AntR (40:3) Sum 82, p. 322-323.
"The Cry." AntR (40:3) Sum 82, p. 324-325.
"Irish Music." AntR (40:3) Sum 82, p. 319-321.
"Sensationalism." AntR (40:3) Sum 82, p. 328-329.
"Though His Name Is Infinite, My Father Is
Asleep." AntR (40:3) Sum 82, p. 326-327.

2383. LEVITIN, Alexis
"Ariadne" (tr. of Eugenio de Andrade). PoNow (6:4,
issue 34) 82, p. 42.
"Cars Pass" (tr. of Jorge de Sena). Chelsea (41)
82, p. 131.
"The Dangers of Innocence" (tr. of Jorge de
Sena). AmerPoR (11:2) Mr-Ap 82, p. 28.
"Dissonances" (tr. of Eugenio de Andrade). NewOR
(9:3) Wint 82, p. 62.
"Farewell" (tr. of Augusto Frederico
Schmidt). PoetryE (8) Aut 82, p. 81.
"The First Flower" (tr. of Carmen Conde, w. Jose R.
de Armas). WebR (7:2) Aut 82, p. 23.
"First Night on Earth" (from Mujer sin Eden, tr. of
Carmen Conde w. Jose R. de Armas). PraS (56:1) Spr
82, p. 40-41.
"Fourth Canto" (tr. of Carmen Conde, w. Jose R. de
Armas). Confr (24) Sum 82, p. 78.
"The Great Moment" (tr. of Augusto Frederico
Schmidt). PoetryE (8) Aut 82, p. 80.
"In Crete with the Minotaur" (tr. of Jorge de
Sena). AmerPoR (11:2) Mr-Ap 82, p. 28.
"Initial" (tr. of Sophia de Mello Breyner
Andresen). PraS (56:1) Spr 82, p. 38.
"Lately" (tr. of Sophia de Mello Breyner
Andresen). PraS (56:1) Spr 82, p. 39.
"Lisbon--1971" (tr. of Jorge de Sena). Chelsea (41)
82, p. 130.

"Litany" (tr. of Eugenio de Andrade). PoetryE (8)
     Aut 82, p. 76.
"Metamorphosis of the House" (tr. of Eugenio de
     Andrade). PortR (28:1) 82, p. 63.
"The Murder of Simonetta Vespucci" (tr. of Sophia de
     Mello Breyner Andresen). PraS (56:1) Spr 82, p.
     38-39.
"On Nudity" (tr. of Jorge de Sena). DenQ (16:4) Wint
     82, p. 38.
"Origin Of Epic Poetry" (tr. of Jorge de Sena).
     DenQ (16:4) Wint 82, p. 35.
"A Pale Winter" (tr. of Sophia de Mello Bryner
     Andresen). PortR (28:1) 82, p. 34.
"Penniless Lovers" (tr. of Eugenio de
     Andrade). MissR (10:3, issue 30) Wint-Spr 82, p.
     44.
"Prayer" (tr. of Carmen Conde, w. Jose R. de
     Armas). WebR (7:2) Aut 82, p. 24.
"Premonition" (tr. of Carmen Conde, w. Jose R. de
     Armas). Confr (24) Sum 82, p. 79.
"Sonnet 49" (tr. of Augusto Frederico
     Schmidt). PoetryE (8) Aut 82, p. 82.
"Summer Days" (tr. of Sophia de Mello Breyner
     Andresen). DenQ (17:1) Spr 82, p. 84.
"Thanksgiving" (tr. of Jorge de Sena). DenQ (16:4)
     Wint 82, p. 37.
"Three or Four Syllables" (tr. of Eugenio de
     Andrade). PoetryE (8) Aut 82, p. 77.
"To My Mother" (tr. of Eugenio de Andrade). PoetryE
     (8) Aut 82, p. 78-79.
"To Piaf" (tr. of Jorge de Sena). DenQ (16:4) Wint
     82, p. 36.
"The Tragic Poet" (tr. of Sophia de Mello Bryner
     Andresen). PortR (28:1) 82, p. 34.
"Voice of the Old Eve in Mary" (tr. of Carmen Conde,
     w. Jose R. de Armas). WebR (7:2) Aut 82, p. 22.

2384. LEVY, Howard
     "Hands." AmerPoR (11:1) Ja-F 82, p. 30.
     "Montauk and the World Revealed through the Magic of
     New Orleans." AmerPoR (11:1) Ja-F 82, p. 30.
     "The Spanish Poets" (for David Ungar). AmerPoR
     (11:1) Ja-F 82, p. 30.

2385. LEVY, Robert J.
     "The English Garden." Outbr (10/11) Aut 82-Spr
     83, p. 65-66.
     "Soft Focus." Kayak (59) Je 82, p. 57.
     "The Tristan Chord." Outbr (10/11) Aut 82-Spr
     83, p. 67-68.
     "Window Dressing." Kayak (59) Je 82, p. 56.

2386. LEWANDOWSKI, Stephen
     "The Bouncing Interchangeable Puppycat." PoNow
     (6:5, issue 35) 82, p. 40.
     "Rural Eloquence." PoNow (6:6, issue 36) 82, p. 22.
     "Versus." PoNow (6:6, issue 36) 82, p. 22.
     "Waitress." PoNow (6:6, issue 36) 82, p. 22.

2387. LEWIN, Rebecca
   "Lover with Rita.";;Catalyst (Erotica Issue) 82,;p.
      7.
   "Your Hands.";;Catalyst (Erotica Issue) 82,;p. 7.

2388. LEWIS, Janet
   "For Carl Rippin";(Sunmount Sanatorium,
      1922);SouthernR (18:2) Spr 82,;p. 348.
   "Spring Night.";;Thrpny (8) Wint 82,;p. 11.
   "Ulysses in the Land of the Phaeacians.";;SouthernR
      (18:2) Spr 82,;p. 349.

2389. LEWIS, Kevin
   "The Night Desk.";;ChrC (99:25) Ag 4-11, 82,;p. 822.

2390. LEWISOHN, James
   "The Birds.";;PoNow (6:5, issue 35) 82,;p. 28.
   "The Blind Man.";;PoNow (6:6, issue 36) 82,;p. 27.

2391. LEYDEN, Rosemary L.
   "A Pastoral Scene.";;ChrC (99:33) O 27, 82,;p. 1079.

2392. LIBERTO, Anita
   "Frustration and Subsequent Acceptance." Bogg (48)
      82, p. 29.

2393. LIEBERMAN, Laurence
   "Ago Bay: The Regatta in the Skies." NewYorker
      (58:19) Je 28, 82, p. 40-41.
   "Death." KanQ (14:3) Sum 82, p. 67.
   "Draft Dodger's American Dream." SoCaR (15:1) Aut
      82, p. 22.
   "Eros at the World Kite Pageant" (Santiago,
      Dominican Republic). AmerPoR (11:1) Ja-F 82, p. 6-
      9.
   "In American Meadows." KanQ (14:2) Spr 82, p. 38.
   "Kashikojima: The Grave Rubbings" (for Laurence
      Donovan and Dee Clark). Hudson (35:1) Spr 82, p.
      39-46.
   "The Mensch." SoCaR (15:1) Aut 82, p. 23.
   "My Father's Place." KanQ (14:2) Spr 82, p. 38.
   "Ode to the Runaway Caves" (Ochos Rios, Jamaica,
      1980). QW (15) Aut-Wint 82-83, p. 139-161.
   "Saltcod Red." Nat (235:1) Jl 3, 82, p. 22.
   "Soba Noodles and Gun Buffs." KanQ (14:2) Spr 82,
      p. 39-42.
   "Song of the River Sweep" (Dunn's River Falls,
      Jamaica). CharR (8:2) Aut 82, p. 5-23.
   "The Tilemaker's Hill Fresco." AmerPoR (11:1) Ja-F
      82, p. 3-5.
   "Two Koto Songs." MichQR (21:1) Wint 82, p. 110-
      112.
   "The Used Car Lot." KanQ (14:2) Spr 82, p. 39.
   "When I." KanQ (14:3) Sum 82, p. 66.
   "Yokosuka Churl." NewEngR (5:1/2) Aut-Wint 82, p.
      167-168.

2394. LIETZ, Robert
        "Afternoon Movies at the Catholic Grade School"
          (from The Lindbergh Half-Century). OntR (16) Spr-
          Sum 82, p. 70.
        "The Baby Sitter." CharR (8:1) Spr 82, p. 28-29.
        "Daughter of the Empire" (from The Lindbergh Half-
          Century). OntR (16) Spr-Sum 82, p. 65-66.
        "A Dream" (for Bob Borke). KanQ (14:1) Wint 82, p.
          173.
        "For Matthew Clarkson, for Luke Moore Clarkson (In
          Memoriam)" (from The Lindbergh Half-Century). OntR
          (16) Spr-Sum 82, p. 62-63.
        "In Flood Country." CharR (8:1) Spr 82, p. 26-27.
        "In the Back House" (from The Lindbergh Half-
          Century). OntR (16) Spr-Sum 82, p. 68-69.
        "The Patriarch's Last Days" (from The Lindbergh
          Half-Century). OntR (16) Spr-Sum 82, p. 64.
        "Reflections on Her Father, 1946" (from The
          Lindbergh Half-Century). OntR (16) Spr-Sum 82, p.
          67.
        "Thanksgiving Weekend: The Last Touch Football for
          the Twenty-Fifth Season." MissouriR (5:3) Sum 82,
          p. 24-25.
        "Women Drinking Beer" (after Manet). MissouriR (5:3)
          Sum 82, p. 26.
        "Wyoming Entry." CutB (19) Aut-Wint 82, p. 55.

2395. LIFSHIN, Lyn
        "As If There Was a Fault Line." AmerPoR (11:2) Mr-
          Ap 82, p. 29.
        "Back Door Madonna." WormR (22:4, issue 88) 82, p.
          147.
        "Ballet Madonna." WormR (22:3, issue 87) 82, p. 88.
        "Beaver Madonna." WormR (22:3, issue 87) 82, p. 88.
        "Bit Tits Thin Legs or." WindO (41) Aut-Wint 82-83,
          p. 15.
        "Black Sweater in May." WormR (22:1, issue 85) 82,
          p. 27.
        "Blue Pieces of China, Silver of Spoon." SouthernPR
          (22:1) Spr 82, p. 13.
        "Books I Brought to the Last Poetry Readings."
          PoNow (6:6, issue 36) 82, p. 35.
        "Brisbee." WormR (22:1, issue 85) 82, p. 28.
        "Cabbage Madonna." WindO (41) Aut-Wint 82-83, p.
          15.
        "The Candidate." WormR (22:1, issue 85) 82, p. 17.
        "Cat Pee Smell Madonna." WormR (22:3, issue 87) 82,
          p. 88.
        "Caterpillars." ConcPo (15:1) Spr 82, p. 25.
        "The Day after the First Day of Spring." AntigR
          (49) Spr 82, p. 74.
        "Deer." WormR (22:1, issue 85) 82, p. 15.
        "Depression." WormR (22:1, issue 85) 82, p. 26.
        "Didn't Know They Have." WindO (41) Aut-Wint 82-83,
          p. 14.
        "Editing Poems For The Anthology." WormR (22:1,
          issue 85) 82, p. 14.
        "Everything Steaming." WormR (22:1, issue 85) 82,
          p. 28.

"Extension Cord Madonna." WormR (22:3, issue 87)
82, p. 88.
"February 7." WormR (22:1, issue 85) 82, p. 20.
"The Feeling." WormR (22:1, issue 85) 82, p. 23.
"First Sunday in Three without Your Mouth." AntigR
(49) Spr 82, p. 73.
"For An Anthology On Being Fat." WormR (22:1, issue
85) 82, p. 21.
"The Forties The Fifties." WormR (22:1, issue 85)
82, p. 22.
"Fragments of Doctors." WormR (22:1, issue 85) 82,
p. 25.
"Fuzz From My Bathrobe." WormR (22:1, issue 85) 82,
p. 16.
"Games." WormR (22:1, issue 85) 82, p. 27.
"Goodby Yellow Maverick." WormR (22:1, issue 85)
82, p. 28.
"He Makes You Never Forget He's There." WindQ (41)
Aut-Wint 82-83, p. 15.
"He Was Like That." PoNow (6:6, issue 36) 82, p.
35.
"Her Words Startle." PoNow (6:6, issue 36) 82, p.
35.
"Hotel Lifshin." PoNow (6:4, issue 34) 82, p. 33.
"The Hotel Lifshin." WormR (22:3, issue 87) 82, p.
88.
"The Hotel Lifshin - 3." Bogg (49) 82, p. 4.
"The Hotel Lifshin - 4." Bogg (49) 82, p. 4.
"I Think I Understand A Little Of That." WormR
(22:1, issue 85) 82, p. 22.
"In Black Grass." Vis (9) 82, p. 4.
"Indian Summer Madonna." WormR (22:3, issue 87) 82,
p. 87.
"Isadora Duncan." WormR (22:1, issue 85) 82, p. 14.
"It Never Ends In Real Life The Way It Ends In The
Movies." WormR (22:1, issue 85) 82, p. 25.
"It Was Like." AmerPoR (11:2) Mr-Ap 82, p. 29.
"It Was Like." WormR (22:1, issue 85) 82, p. 24.
"Jealousy's." Pequod (15) 82, p. 48.
"Jogging Madonna." WormR (22:3, issue 87) 82, p.
89.
"The Journal." WormR (22:1, issue 85) 82, p. 15.
"July 4 1980." WormR (22:1, issue 85) 82, p. 27.
"Kaleidoscope Madonna." WormR (22:3, issue 87) 82,
p. 87.
"The Koertge-Lifshin-Locklin Sandwich" (after a
short note from Gerry Locklin and with one image
stolen from him). WormR (22:1, issue 85) 82, p.
15.
"Kristallnacht November 9-10 1938." WormR (22:1,
issue 85) 82, p. 21.
"Leaning Tower or Pisa Madonna." WormR (22:4, issue
88) 82, p. 147.
"Let Down Madonna." WormR (22:3, issue 87) 82, p.
88.
"Like Dogs Left Out Near The Crumbling Adobes."
WormR (22:1, issue 85) 82, p. 19.
"Like So Much This Summer." WormR (22:1, issue 85)
82, p. 27.

"The Lion Tamer's Wife: or This is Your Life."
WormR (22:1, issue 85) 82, p. 23.
"Loose Madonna." WormR (22:3, issue 87) 82, p. 88.
"Love in the Midwest." PoNow (6:5, issue 35) 82, p.
34.
"Madonna of the Bathroom." WormR (22:3, issue 87)
82, p. 88.
"Madonna of the Cold House." WormR (22:4, issue 88)
82, p. 147.
"Madonna of the Mail." WormR (22:3, issue 87) 82,
p. 88.
"Madonna of the Pot Roast." WormR (22:3, issue 87)
82, p. 88.
"Madonna Who Knows Something Is Up or Down When."
WormR (22:3, issue 87) 82, p. 89.
"Madonna Who Makes the Most Out of Nothing." WindO
(41) Aut-Wint 82-83, p. 17.
"Madonna Who Writes Ten Poems a Day." WormR (22:1,
issue 85) 82, p. 26.
"Making Poems and Making Men." WormR (22:1, issue
85) 82, p. 19.
"Marriage is Like Collecting Stamps--Scotty Woolf."
WormR (22:1, issue 85) 82, p. 17.
"May 16, 1979." Bogg (48) 82, p. 8.
"Medical Journal Ads For Women's Tranquilizers."
WormR (22:1, issue 85) 82, p. 22.
"Midwest." PoNow (6:5, issue 35) 82, p. 34.
"Model Home." WormR (22:1, issue 85) 82, p. 28.
"More Soaps." PoNow (6:5, issue 35) 82, p. 34.
"Musee Cluny." WormR (22:1, issue 85) 82, p. 22.
"Naked Joy Riding Sisters Will Get Psycho Exams."
PoNow (6:6, issue 36) 82, p. 34.
"Near Troublesome Creek Southeastern Kentucky."
WormR (22:1, issue 85) 82, p. 26.
"Night Deposit Madonna." WormR (22:3, issue 87) 82,
p. 89.
"November 1 Boogie." NewL (48:2) Wint 81-82, p. 48.
"Nymphomaniac Madonna of the Mails." WormR (22:4,
issue 88) 82, p. 147.
"Of Course Madonna." WormR (22:1, issue 85) 82, p.
26.
"Oh Yes." WormR (22:1, issue 85) 82, p. 24.
"Old Homesteads in Canada." NewL (48:2) Wint 81-82,
p. 48.
"Olympic Flame Madonna." PoNow (6:6, issue 36) 82,
p. 35.
"Olympic Flame Madonna." WormR (22:4, issue 88) 82,
p. 147.
"One Stop Shop Convenience Modonna." WormR (22:1,
issue 85) 82, p. 18.
"Over Reacting Madonna." WormR (22:1, issue 85) 82,
p. 17.
"Pavarotti and Mehta." WormR (22:1, issue 85) 82,
p. 15.
"The Pearls." Chelsea (41) 82, p. 160-161.
"Playing Doctor." Catalyst (Erotica Issue) 82, p.
14.
"Poetry Reading Benefit." KanQ (14:1) Wint 82, p.
128-129.

"Poetry Reading Benefit." WormR (22:1, issue 85) 82, p. 20.
"Red Hot Mama Madonna." ConcPo (15:1) Spr 82, p. 26.
"Rural Madonna." WormR (22:4, issue 88) 82, p. 147.
"Salad Madonna." WormR (22:3, issue 87) 82, p. 88.
"Second Dream of February 23 1979." WormR (22:1, issue 85) 82, p. 24.
"Soap Opera." PoNow (6:5, issue 35) 82, p. 34.
"Something In Me." WormR (22:1, issue 85) 82, p. 20.
"Split Infinitive Madonna." WormR (22:3, issue 87) 82, p. 88.
"The Strange toward Morning Dream." Catalyst (Erotica Issue) 82, p. 5.
"Stuck Car Thermostat Madonna." WormR (22:4, issue 88) 82, p. 147.
"Students." Paint (7/8:13/16) 80-81, p. 31.
"Stuffed Madonna." WormR (22:4, issue 88) 82, p. 147.
"Sunday." PoNow (6:6, issue 36) 82, p. 34.
"Tennessee." Abraxas (25/26) 82, p. 37.
"The The Man Who is Married to Siamese Twins Joined at the Skull." WormR (22:1, issue 85) 82, p. 16.
"There is No Swearing." WormR (22:1, issue 85) 82, p. 14.
"Thinking About Anne Sexton's Letter In Ms." WormR (22:1, issue 85) 82, p. 23.
"Three Days before You Leave Town." WindO (41) Aut-Wint 82-83, p. 17.
"Thru Blue Dust." Vis (9) 82, p. 4.
"To the Man Who Asked Me Why I Took So Many Showers." Abraxas (25/26) 82, p. 42.
"Today, Writing Any More Poems." WormR (22:1, issue 85) 82, p. 19.
"Tongue Depressor Madonna." WindO (41) Aut-Wint 82-83, p. 17.
"Too Hot Madonna." Bogg (49) 82, p. 11.
"Too Many Readings Too Many Men." PoNow (6:6, issue 36) 82, p. 35.
"Towards the End." PoNow (6:6, issue 36) 82, p. 35.
"Tuesday." AntigR (49) Spr 82, p. 72.
"Tunnel Vision Madonna." WormR (22:1, issue 85) 82, p. 16.
"Unassessed Madonna." WormR (22:1, issue 85) 82, p. 18.
"Unease." WormR (22:1, issue 85) 82, p. 24.
"Vincent." PoNow (6:4, issue 34) 82, p. 33.
"Wanted." WormR (22:1, issue 85) 82, p. 15.
"The Way I Write." WormR (22:1, issue 85) 82, p. 21.
"With One Love It Was Things That Grow That Flower Up Like Cream in Those Old Glass." WormR (22:1, issue 85) 82, P. 18.
"With You Lying There on the Other Side of the Bed." PoNow (6:6, issue 36) 82, p. 35.
"Write from the Point of View of a Woman If You're a Man I Tell the Class and Vice Versa." WindO (41) Aut-Wint 82-83, p. 16.

2396. LIFSHITZ, Leatrice
      "Art." StoneC (9:3/4) Spr-Sum 82, p. 30.

2397. LIGHT, Joanne
      "The Colour of the Water in Lake Atitlan." PottPort
      (4) 82-83, p. 13.
      "Friday Night." PottPort (4) 82-83, p. 8.

2398. LIGI
      "Hey." Agni (16) 82, p. 35.

2399. LIGNELL, Kathleen
      "The Letter, 1891." KanQ (14:4) Aut 82, p. 84.
      "Paper Fish." NoAmR (267:3) S 82,p. 35.
      "The Sighting." Nimrod (25:2) Spr-Sum 82, p. 7-9.
      "Tarzan in the Home for Retired Actors." PoNow
      (6:4, issue 34) 82, p. 36.

2400. LILLYWHITE, Harvey
      "The Choice." PoetryE (8) Aut 82, p. 39.
      "First Vision." PoetryE (8) Aut 82, p. 38.
      "Homage to Sisyphus." PoetryE (8) Aut 82, p. 40.
      "Memorial Day." CutB (18) Spr-Sum 82, p. 26.
      "Repair." PoetryE (8) Aut 82, p. 41.

2401. LIMON, Mercedes
      "Esperame en la Historia Che Guevara." Maize
      (6:1/2) Aut-Wint 82-83, p. 103-104.
      "Mentira." Maize (6:1/2) Aut-Wint 82-83, p. 102.

2402. LINDEMAN, Jack
      "Persian." KanQ (14:1) Wint 82, p. 112.
      "Quandary." Comm (109:5) Mr 12, 82, p. 158.
      "Snow Season." SouthwR (67:1) Wint 82, p. 17.

2403. LINDHOLDT, Paul
      "The Blue Mission." Tendril (13) Sum 82, p. 47.
      "Shaker Indian Churchyard." SouthernPR (23, i.e.
      22:2) Aut 82, p. 52-53.

2404. LINDNER, Carl
      "First Frost." PoNow (7:1, issue 37) 82, p. 29.
      "Helping an Old Lady Across the Street." PoNow
      (7:1, issue 37) 82, p. 29.
      "Why I Gave Up Jogging." PoNow (7:1, issue 37) 82,
      p. 29.

2405. LINDSAY, Fran
      "Singing the Pachelbel Canon." Pequod (14) 82, p.
      85.

2406. LINDSAY, Frannie
      "Bedside Lamp." PikeF (4) Spr 82, p. 12.
      "Candle As Phoenix." PikeF (4) Spr 82, p. 12.
      "Deer in Spring." PikeF (4) Spr 82, p. 12.
      "Ithaca, N.Y." PikeF (4) Spr 82, p. 12.
      "The Unfinished Ships." Tendril (12) Wint 82, p.
      43.

2407. LINDSEY, Alison
    "Salt Wind, Creaking Snow, Daisies." <u>PottPort</u> (4)
      82-83, p. 40.
    "There's Blood on My Hands." <u>PottPort</u> (4) 82-83, p.
      23.
    "To His Ex-Wife, with Love." <u>PottPort</u> (4) 82-83, p.
      13.

2408. LINDSTROM, Naomi
    "The Ants Clasp Hands" (tr. of Jaime Sabines). <u>DenQ</u>
      (16:4) Wint 82, p. 44.
    "They Get Me in the Head" (tr. of Jaime Sabines).
      <u>DenQ</u> (16:4) Wint 82, p. 43.
    "The Trees are Swaying" (tr. of Jaime Sabines). <u>NewL</u>
      (48:2) Wint 81-82, p. 98.

2409. LINEHAN, Don
    "April 11." <u>Germ</u> (6:1) Spr-Sum 82, p. 17.
    "August 28." <u>Germ</u> (6:1) Spr-Sum 82, p. 19.
    "The Competition." <u>PottPort</u> (4) 82-83, p. 16.
    "One of My Chromosomes Remembers." <u>Germ</u> (6:1) Spr-
      Sum 82, p. 20.
    "Peskawa: May." <u>Germ</u> (6:1) Spr-Sum 82, p. 18.
    "Roses and Stars." <u>AntigR</u> (51) Aut 82, p. 86-87.
    "Untitled: Definition of Canadian artist." <u>PottPort</u>
      (4) 82-83, p. 32.

2410. LIPOWSKI, Mike
    "Gallowed." <u>WritersL</u> Jl 82, p. 23.
    "Tracks." <u>WritersL</u> Jl 82, p. 19.

2411. LIPSITZ, Lou
    "The Poem That Goes Two Ways." <u>Kayak</u> (58) Ja 82, p.
      29.

2412. LISOWSKI, Joseph
    "Duckweed Pond" (tr. of Wang Wei). <u>WestB</u> (11) 82, p.
      99.
    "Gold Dust Spring" (tr. of Wang Wei). <u>WestB</u> (11) 82,
      p. 98.
    "Spring Street Blues." <u>Vis</u> (9) 82, p. 22.

2413. LIT, Peter D.
    "Destruction of Friendship against Our Will, a
      Dissembling." <u>MendoR</u> (6) Sum 81, p. 84.
    "How Is Today Different Than Any Other Day?" (for
      ayn). <u>MendoR</u> (6) Sum 81, p. 84.

2414. LITOWINSKY, Olga
    "Eternity" (tr. of Arthur Rimbaud, w. Edward Babun).
      <u>StoneC</u> (9:3/4) Spr-Sum 82, p. 23.

2415. LITTAUER, Andrew
    "At the Whale Road's End." <u>SewanR</u> (90:4) Aut 82,
      p. 518.
    "Spleen." <u>SewanR</u> (90:4) Aut 82, p. 519.

2416. LITTLE, Billy
    "Ardent Iceholes." <u>CapilR</u> (22) 82, p. 57.
    "The First Canadian Pope." <u>CapilR</u> (22) 82, p. 58.

2417. LITTLE, Geraldine C. (Geraldine Clinton)
    "Canzone for Constellations." PraS (56:4) Wint 82-
      83, p. 53-54.
    "Early Spring in the Pine Barrens, N.J." StoneC
      (9:3/4) Spr-Sum 82, p. 9.
    "Last Thoughts, April 9, 1945, Flossenburg, Germany:
      Dietrich Bonhoeffer. PraS (56:4) Wint 82-83, p.
      51-52.
    "One of Medea's Sons." Nimrod (25:2) Spr-Sum 82, p.
      53-54.
    "The Other Son." Nimrod (25:2) Spr-Sum 82, p. 56-
      57.
    "Simplicities in White Snow." StoneC (10:1/2) Aut-
      Wint 82-83, p. 78.
    "Triptych: Psychology of Aftermath -- Shadrach,
      Meshach, Abednego LitR (25:3) Spr 82, p. 336-337.

2418. LIU, Tsung-yuan
    "River Snow" (tr. by Arthur Bull). Dandel (9:1) 82,
      p. 22.

2419. LIVADHITIS, Tasos
    "1949 A.D" (tr. by Kimon Friar). Kayak (58) Ja 82,
      p. 4.
    "Able to Work" (tr. by Kimon Friar). Kayak (58) Ja
      82, p. 7.
    "Disengaged" (tr. by Kimon Friar). Kayak (58) Ja 82,
      p. 6.
    "Indiscretions" (tr. by Kimon Friar). Kayak (58) Ja
      82, p. 5.
    "The Lamp" (tr. by Kimon Friar). Kayak (58) Ja 82,
      p. 4.
    "The Last Command" (tr. by Kimon Friar). Kayak (58)
      Ja 82, p. 6.
    "Painting by an Unknown Artist" (tr. by Kimon
      Friar). Kayak (58) Ja 82, p. 7.
    "The Perfect Crime" (tr. by Kimon Friar). Kayak (58)
      Ja 82, p. 5.
    "Precautions" (tr. by Kimon Friar). Kayak (58) Ja
      82, p. 7.
    "Ragpickers." (tr. by Kimon Friar). Kayak (58) Ja
      82, p. 4.
    "Small Existentialist Parenthesis" (tr. by Kimon
      Friar). Kayak (58) Ja 82, p. 5.

2420. LIVESAY, Dorothy
    "Wintering." PoetryCR (4:2) Wint 82, p. 13.

    LLOSA, Ricardo Pau
    See: PAU-LLOSA, Ricardo

2421. LLOYD, D. H.
    "Names." WormR (22:4, issue 88) 82, p. 150.
    "The Widow." WormR (22:4, issue 88) 82, p. 150.

2422. LLOYD, Roseann
    "Southeast Asia, Second Grade." CutB (18) Spr-Sum
      82, p. 72-73.

303   LLUCH MORA

2423. LLUCH MORA, Francisco
      "Sonidos." _Mairena_ (4:11/12) Wint 82, p. 148.

2424. LOCKE, Duane
      "Alleys." _UTR_ (7:2) 82?, p. 31.
      "At 4 PM on a Rural Pennsylvania Road." _Vis_ (9) 82,
      p. 26.
      "Beetle." _UTR_ (7:2) 82?, p. 30.
      "The Camera di Psiche Palazzo del Te, Mantova."
      Abraxas (25/26) 82, p. 57.
      "Ludwig II." _LitR_ (26:1) Aut 82, p. 113-115.
      "When I Decided to Be Born." _UTR_ (7:2) 82?, p. 32.
      "The Word." _UTR_ (7:2) 82?, p. 29.

2425. LOCKLIN, Gerald
      "Also, My Shoes Still Come Untied." _WormR_ (22:4,
      issue 88) 82, p. 133.
      "Another Rubric Down the W.C." _Wind_ (12:46) 82, p.
      24.
      "A Brief Hiatus." _Wind_ (12:46) 82, p. 24-25.
      "The Circuits Are in Danger of Overloading." _WormR_
      (22:4, issue 88) 82, p. 139.
      "Class." _WormR_ (22:1, issue 85) 82, p. 31-32.
      "D-Day, 1980." _WormR_ (22:4, issue 88) 82, p. 132-
      133.
      "The Death of Jean-Paul Sartre." _WormR_ (22:4, issue
      88) 82, p. 131-132.
      "Drowning the Hatchet." _WormR_ (22:4, issue 88) 82,
      p. 144.
      "Fathers and Sons." _WormR_ (22:1, issue 85) 82, p.
      29-30.
      "Goldie Girl." _WormR_ (22:4, issue 88) 82, p. 138-
      139.
      "Growing Up Alive." _WormR_ (22:4, issue 88) 82, p.
      136.
      "I Suspect Our Future Conversation Will Be Altered."
      WormR (22:4, issue 88) 82, p. 134-135.
      "I Taught Her Too Well." _WormR_ (22:3, issue 87) 82,
      p.113.
      "Last of the Big Spenders." _WormR_ (22:4, issue 88)
      82, p. 134.
      "The Leader of the Pack." _WormR_ (22:4, issue 88)
      82, p. 142.
      "Locklin Versus Locklin." _Wind_ (12:46) 82, p. 23.
      "Mindlessness Over Matter." _WormR_ (22:4, issue 88)
      82, p. 143-144.
      "My Aunts and Uncles." _WormR_ (22:1, issue 85) 82,
      p. 29.
      "Off to a Great Start." _WormR_ (22:3, issue 87) 82,
      p.114.
      "On Violence: A Note to Reviewers." _WormR_ (22:4,
      issue 88) 82, p. 139.
      "Patriotic Poem." _WormR_ (22:4, issue 88) 82, p.
      139.
      "A Piece of Unsolicited Advice." _WormR_ (22:3, issue
      87) 82, p.113.
      "The Pornographer's Favorite Antacid." _WormR_ (22:4,
      issue 88) 82, p. 141.
      "Rip." _WormR_ (22:4, issue 88) 82, p. 141.

"The Roar of the Greasepaint." WormR (22:4, issue
    88) 82, p. 135.
"Roger Hotspur Strikes Back." WormR (22:4, issue
    88) 82, p. 142.
"She Didn't Like Us Much Even Before the Ayatollah."
    WormR (22:1, issue 85) 82, p. 30-31.
"Six of One." WormR (22:4, issue 88) 82, p. 137-
    138.
"Something's Happening." WormR (22:4, issue 88) 82,
    p. 136-137.
"The Stars and Stripes Forever: A Meditation upon
    Patriotic Utterances." WormR (22:3, issue 87) 82,
    p.114.
"Succubus." Abraxas (25/26) 82, p. 41.
"Theory and Practice." WormR (22:4, issue 88) 82,
    p. 140.
"We Can Do It Too." Abraxas (25/26) 82, p. 41.
"We'll Never Know How Much of Life Is Learned
    Behavior." Abraxas (25/26) 82, p. 40.
"The Women Have Won." WormR (22:4, issue 88) 82, p.
    130.

2426. LOCKWOOD BARLETTA, Naomi
    "Elegia." Mairena (4:10) Sum-Aut 82, p. 79.

2427. LOCKWOOD, Margo
    "Dublin Streets." Ploughs (8:1) 82, p. 108.
    "Gaze." Ploughs (8:1) 82, p. 110.
    "Grey Paris." Ploughs (8:1) 82, p. 109.

2428. LODGE, Michael O.
    "Elegy for Laura" (for R.N. Murray). Telescope (1)
    Spr 81, p. 49-50.

2429. LOGAN, John (John B.)
    "The Assessment" (for Tom Lucas). GeoR (36:3) Aut
    82, p. 528.
    "Believe It" (for Tina Logan after visiting the
    Believe It or Not Museum with her in San
    Francisco, 1980). Nat (235:12) O 16, 82, p. 372.
    "The Feast of Friends" (For Tom Lucas). NewL (49:2)
    Wint 82-83, p. 91-92.
    "Happening on Aegina" (for Al and Daphne Poulin).
    AmerPoR (11:5) S-O 82, p. 48.
    "Impressions of Ydra." AmerPoR (11:5) S-O 82, p.
    48.
    "Lines on His Birthday" (from Only the Dreamer Can
    Change the Dream, 1981). Nat (235:12) O 16, 82, p.
    373.
    "Only the Dreamer Can Change the Dream" (from Only
    the Dreamer Can Change the Dream, 1981). Nat
    (235:12) O 16, 82, p. 373.
    "The Piano Scholar." MassR (23:2) Sum 82, p. 349-
    351.
    "The Search" (from Only the Dreamer Can Change the
    Dream, 1981). Nat (235:12) O 16, 82, p. 373.
    "A Visit to Bill Merwin at His Hawaiian Home."
    Antaeus (47) Aut 82, p. 41-42.
    "The Yellow Christ" (After Gauguin). NewL (49:2)
    Wint 82-83, p. 91.

2430. LOGAN, William
       "Dream Contract." GeoR (36:1) Spr 82, p. 21.
       "Florida" (a postcard). Agni (17) 82, p. 47.
       "In Exile." Antaeus (47) Aut 82, p. 59-60.

2431. LONDON, Jonathan
       "The Boy Who Persisted Despite Great Odds." PoNow
       (6:6, issue 36) 82, p. 15.
       "The Retired Contractor." PoNow (6:4, issue 34) 82,
       p. 14.

2432. LONE, A. M.
       "Jealousy" (tr. of Rafeeque Raaz). NewL (48:3/4)
       Spr-Sum 82, p. 232-233.

2433. LONG, Robert
       "December." AmerS (51:1) Wint 81-82, p. p. 52-53.

2434. LONGO, Louise
       "After the First Cigarette." MalR (63) O 82, p.
       158-159.
       "High-School Photo." MalR (63) O 82, p. 159.

2435. LOO, Katie Wong
       "En tu Penetrante Ausencia" (from Rosa Falica).
       Mairena (4:10) Sum-Aut 82, p. 45-46.

2436. LOPES, Michael
       "September Song." Hangl (43) Wint 82-83, p. 31.
       "Spring Forward, Fall Back." Hangl (43) Wint 82-83,
       p. 32-33.

2437. LOPEZ, Emy
       "Los Que Lo Saben Lo Ignoran, Los Que Lo Ignoran, Yo
       Se Los Cuento. Maize (6:1/2) Aut-Wint 82-83, p.
       94-95.

2438. LOPEZ SURIA, Violeta
       "Canto de la Locura" (A Francisco Matos Paoli,
       Viviendo su poesia). Mairena (4:11/12) Wint 82, p.
       148.

2439. LORDE, Audre
       "A Poem for Women in Rage." Iowa (12:2/3) Spr-Sum
       81, p. 220-222.

       LORINGHOVEN, Elsa von Freytag, Baroness
       See: FREYTAG-LORINGHOVEN, Elsa von, Baroness

       Los MILAGROS PEREZ, Maria de
       See: PEREZ, Maria de los Milagros

2440. LOTT, Clarinda Harriss
       "Discoveries." Vis (8) 82, p. 14.
       "Talismen" (Hamsa fi ainek). Vis (8) 82, p. 16.
       "The Untouched." Vis (9) 82, p. 39.

2441. LOURIE, Richard
    "Advice from an Experienced Prisoner: Don't Figure
    the Date" (tr. of Wiktor Woroszylski). PartR
    (49:4) 82, p. 517.
    "Bromide" (tr. of Wiktor Woroszylski). PartR (49:4)
    82, p. 516-517.
    "Christmas Eve '81" (tr. of Adam Zagajewski). PartR
    (49:4) 82, p. 520-521.
    "Court" (tr. of Adam Zagajewski). PartR (49:4) 82,
    p. 521-522.
    "Diary of an Internment" (December 1981--February
    1982, Bialoleka--Jaworze) (tr. of Wiktor
    Woroszylski). PartR (49:4) 82, p. 514-520.
    "Dreaming and Awake" (tr. of Wiktor Woroszylski).
    PartR (49:4) 82, p. 519-520.
    "I'm Not Upset" (tr. of Wiktor Woroszylski). PartR
    (49:4) 82, p. 515.
    "The Loudspeaker" (tr. of Wiktor Woroszylski). PartR
    (49:4) 82, p. 516.
    "A Meeting" (tr. of Wiktor Woroszylski). PartR
    (49:4) 82, p. 518.
    "Notes Smuggled to and from Prison" (tr. of Wiktor
    Woroszylski). PartR (49:4) 82, p. 518-519.
    "Overheard" (tr. of Wiktor Woroszylski). PartR
    (49:4) 82, p. 515.
    "A Picture" (tr. of Wiktor Woroszylski). PartR
    (49:4) 82, p. 519.
    "A Polish Day" (tr. of Wiktor Woroszylski). PartR
    (49:4) 82, p. 520.
    "The Prisonrs' Walk" (tr. of Wiktor Woroszylski).
    PartR (49:4) 82, p. 518.
    "Reeducators" (tr. of Wiktor Woroszylski). PartR
    (49:4) 82, p. 516.
    "Sign Here Please" (tr. of Wiktor Woroszylski).
    PartR (49:4) 82, p. 515.
    "Still Nothing" (tr. of Wiktor Woroszylski). PartR
    (49:4) 82, p. 514.
    "With Full Respect" (tr. of Wiktor Woroszylski).
    PartR (49:4) 82, p. 517.

2442. LOUTHAN, Robert
    "The Answer." Ploughs (8:2/3) 82, p. 125.
    "The Delivery." Ploughs (8:2/3) 82, p. 123.
    "A Flaw in Death." PoNow (6:5, issue 35) 82, p. 38.
    "Lost" (after Rafael Alberti). Kayak (58) Ja 82, p.
    24.
    "Material Written by the Ventriloquist for His Dummy
    to Recite." AmerPoR (11:1) Ja-F 82, p. 29.
    "The Mistake." Ploughs (8:2/3) 82, p. 124.
    "Mother's Routine." MassR (23:4) Wint 82, p. 714.
    "The New Contemporary Poem." NoAmR (267:3) S 82,p.
    33.
    "None of Us." Hudson (35:1) Spr 82, p. 90.
    "A Postcard from Hell." Ploughs (8:2/3) 82, p. 125.
    "The Same" (for W. E. Butts). Hudson (35:1) Spr 82,
    p. 91.
    "The Second Coming." Kayak (58) Ja 82, p. 24.
    "So Much Work." AmerPoR (11:1) Ja-F 82, p. 29.
    "Testimonial" (for T. G.). AmerPoR (11:1) Ja-F 82,
    p. 29.

2443. LOVEID, Cecilie
        "Captive Wild Rose" (tr. by Anne Born). Stand (23:3)
        82, p. 47.
        "Song behind the House (Puberty)" (tr. by Anne
        Born). Stand (23:3) 82, p. 47.

2444. LOW, Denise
        "Indian Burial Pit" (New Cambria, Kansas). Abraxas
        (25/26) 82, p. 46.
        "Mt. Saint Helens Day." KanQ (14:3) Sum 82, p. 26.
        "Picking Wild Strawberries." LittleBR (2:1) Aut 81,
        p. 71.
        "Snakes." LittleBR (1:4) Sum 81, p. 35.
        "Views of the Kansas Turnpike: Flint Hills" (for
        Dzidka). Abraxas (25/26) 82, p. 47.

        LOW, Jackson Mac
        See: Mac LOW, Jackson

2445. LOWE, Frederick
        "Epithalamion" (for T. deB. and R. M.). BelPoJ
        (32:3) Spr 82, p. 3.

2446. LOWENSTEIN, Alice Adelman
        "Elegy for John." Ploughs (8:2/3) 82, p. 138-139.

2447. LOWENSTEIN, Robert
        "A Closed Door Always Says Open." Poem (45) Jl 82,
        p. 54.
        "Drought Makes Everything Clear." Wind (12:46) 82,
        p. 26.
        "The Good Life." SmPd (19:3, issue 56) Aut 82, p.
        8.
        "The Language of Bone." StoneC (9:3/4) Spr-Sum 82,
        p. 36.
        "A Ride on the Ferry." Poem (45) Jl 82, p. 53.

2448. LOWERY, Jeannette
        "First Frost." PikeF (4) Spr 82, p. 20.
        "October." PikeF (4) Spr 82, p. 20.

2449. LOWEY, Mark
        "Every Death a Dance." AntigR (49) Spr 82, p. 27.
        "A Partner for Nureyev." AntigR (49) Spr 82, p. 26.
        "Stage Fright." AntigR (49) Spr 82, p. 25.

2450. LOWREY, John
        "Special Forces." PoNow (6:4, issue 34) 82, p. 14.

2451. LOWRY, Betty
        "Mother Sorrow." ChrC (99:12) Ap 7, 82, p. 404.
        "To an Expunged Saint: February 14." ChrC (99:4) F
        3-10, 82, p. 114.

2452. LOWRY, John
        "From the Journals of Felix Gomez" (Four entries).
        Confr (24) Sum 82, p. 106.

2453. LOWTHER, Catherine
        "Franz Joseph." MalR (62) Jl 82, p. 204-205.

"Testament at Aachen, 814." <u>MalR</u> (62) Jl 82, p.
206-209.

2454. LOY, Sandra
"Botany." <u>PraS</u> (56:3) Aut 82, p. 19.
"Buddha's Arms/Broken/Clattering." <u>PraS</u> (56:3) Aut
82, p. 19.
"Carny, Seattle Waterfront." <u>PraS</u> (56:3) Aut 82, p.
17-18.
"Humanities." <u>PraS</u> (56:3) Aut 82, p. 17.
"Lima Beans." <u>LittleM</u> (13:3/4) 82, p. 20.
"Which Is/ the Original Sin?" <u>PraS</u> (56:3) Aut 82,
p. 18.

2455. LU, You
"On My Way to Jian-men, in a Drizzle" (tr. by Zuxin
Ding and Burton Raffel). <u>DenQ</u> (17:2) Sum 82, p.
93.

2456. LUCE, Gregory
"Goya: 'Don Manuel Osorio de Zuniga'." <u>KanQ</u> (14:4)
Aut 82, p. 19.

LUCERO, Myrna Marina Vera
<u>See</u>: VERA LUCERO, Myrna Marina

2457. LUCIANI, Oscar
"Acto Literario." <u>Mairena</u> (4:10) Sum-Aut 82, p. 58.

2458. LUCINA, Mary, Sister
"Off the Thruway a Falling Star." <u>Nimrod</u> (25:2)
Spr-Sum 82, p. 48.
"Riding." <u>SouthernPR</u> (23, i.e. 22:2) Aut 82, p. 60.

2459. LUCKHARDT, Jennifer
"Fantasy Dream." <u>ArizQ</u> (38:1) Spr 82, p. 36.

2460. LUDVIGSON, Susan
"After He Called Her a Witch." <u>Poetry</u> (141:2) N 82,
p. 79.
"Conquering the Night Jasmine." <u>GeoR</u> (36:2) Sum 82,
p. 372.
"Departures." <u>Telescope</u> (1) Spr 81, p. 13.
"The Sabotage of Dreams." <u>SouthernPR</u> (22:1) Spr 82,
p. 10.
"Slow Learner." <u>Telescope</u> (1) Spr 81, p. 9.
"Some Notes on Courage." <u>Poetry</u> (139:4) Ja 82, p.
210.

2461. LUHRMANN, Tom
"Manifest Destiny." <u>MichQR</u> (21:2) Spr 82, p. 348-
349.
"Winter Nihilism." <u>MichQR</u> (21:2) Spr 82, p. 347-
348.

LUM, Wing Tek
<u>See</u>: WING, Tek Lum

2462. LUNDE, David
"The Lesson." <u>PoNow</u> (6:4, issue 34) 82, p. 13.

"Lump." PoNow (6:4, issue 34) 82, p. 13.
"The Taxi-Dancer's Dream." PortR (28:1) 82, p. 7.

2463. LUNDEN, Eldrid
from Anna: (3-7, 9) (tr. by Nadia Christensen).
Stand (23:3) 82, p. 35.
from Mammy, Blue: "The ancient streams" (tr. by Per
Olav Kaldestad and Andrew Kennedy). Stand (23:3)
82, p. 34.

2464. LUNDKVIST, Artur
"Darkforest Wolves" (tr. by Diane Wormuth). Confr
(23) Wint 82, p. 83.
"The Glory of the World, the Shark in Love" (tr. by
Diane Wormuth). Confr (23) Wint 82, p. 83.

2465. LUNDKVIST, Lars
"Lightning in the ground" (tr. by Gunnar Harding and
Anselm Hollo). Spirit (6:2/3) 82, p. 122.
"Man across the moor" (tr. by Gunnar Harding and
Anselm Hollo). Spirit (6:2/3) 82, p. 122.
"Once much ice was here" (tr. by Gunnar Harding and
Anselm Hollo). Spirit (6:2/3) 82, p. 122-123.

2466. LUTHER, Susan M.
"Doll Museum" (Jekyll Island). Poem (44) Mr 82, p.
58-59.
"The Renovater." SmPd (19:1, issue 54) Wint 82, p.
8.
"Traveling (Via?) Iceland." SmPd (19:1, issue 54)
Wint 82, p. 6-7.

2467. LYLES, Peggy Willis
"The Breather." DekalbLAJ (14:1/4) Aut 80-Sum 81,
p. 85.
"Rough Idling." CapeR (17:2) Sum 82, p. 38.

2468. LYNCH, Marie C.
"An Education Poem." EngJ (71:1) Ja 82, p. 44.

2469. LYNCH, Thomas P.
"A Dog with Character." Poetry (139:6) Mr 82, p.
326.
"The Grandmothers." Poetry (139:6) Mr 82, p. 324.
"In Her Bright Flesh." MidwQ (23:2) Wint 82, p.
189.
"The Orient." MidwQ (23:2) Wint 82, p. 187-188.
"Rotary Album." MidwQ (23:2) Wint 82, p. 186.
"The Widow." Poetry (139:6) Mr 82, p. 325.

2470. LYNE, Sandford
"The Flower-Pool." Ploughs (8:2/3) 82, p. 166.
"Separation: The Centipede." Ploughs (8:2/3) 82, p.
165.
"Separation: The Daily Life." Ploughs (8:2/3) 82,
p. 165.
"What It Is Hard to Give." Ploughs (8:2/3) 82, p.
166.

2471. LYNSKEY, Edward C.
      "Fallen Angels" (for Weldon Kees). ColEng 44(5) S
         82, p. 492.
      "Inside the Gun Factory." Atl (250:1) Jl 82, p. 55.
      "Teeth of the Hydra." Shout (3:1) 82, p. 35.

2472. LYON, George Ella
      "The Courtship." PoetC (14:1) 82, p. 33-34.
      "A Testimony" (for L.H.). PoetC (14:1) 82, p. 32.

2473. LYONS, Richard J.
      "Ophelia." Salm (56) Spr 82, p. 144.
      "UXB. For my Grandfather." Telescope (3) Sum 82, p.
         46-47.

      M., J.
      See: J. M.

2474. Mac LOW, Jackson
      "Winds/Instruments." Sulfur (2:3, issue 6) 82, p.
         4-23.

2475. MacBAIN, Walter (Walter D.)
      "Evening into Night." Bogg (48) 82, p. 4.
      "A Man Named Mallory." PoNow (7:1, issue 37) 82, p.
         29.
      "Motel." Wind (12:45) 82, p. 23-24.
      "Snowstorm." Bogg (49) 82, p. 19.
      "Why." SmPd (19:1, issue 54) Wint 82, p. 29.
      "The Yellow Buoy." Wind (12:45) 82, p. 23.

2476. MacBETH, George
      "The Little Ghosts." Stand (23:1) 81-82, p. 45.

2477. MacDONALD, Bruce
      "Crackers Looks for Deadman's Island." Quarry
         (31:4) Aut 82, p. 10.

2478. MacDONALD, Charlie
      "Hopper's 'The Artist's Mother'." SmPd (19:2, issue
         55) Spr 82, p. 24.
      "Once a Year." SmPd (19:2, issue 55) Spr 82, p. 25.

2479. MacDONALD, Cynthia
      "My Familiar Lover." Iowa (12:2/3) Spr-Sum 81, p.
         234-235.
      "The River Honey Queen Bess." Iowa (12:2/3) Spr-Sum
         81, p. 232-233.
      "The Tune He Saw." NewYorker (58:12) My 10, 82, p.
         44.

2480. MacDONALD, Gay
      "Midmorning Ride." PoetryCR (3:3) Spr 82, p. 10.

2481. MacDONALD, Greg
      "These wine-dark nights." Os (14) 82, p. 18.

2482. MacDONALD, Kathryn
      "Annalise, Probing the Past, Learns Why She Fears
         Men." PoetryNW (23:2) Sum 82, p. 11-12.

311   MacDONALD

2483. MacDONALD, W. B.
      "The Wetness of a Dog's Nose." MalR (63) O 82, p.
      157.

2484. MACHWE, Prabhakar
      "God: Two Moods" (tr. of Chandrakant Khot). NewL
      (48:3/4) Spr-Sum 82, p. 231.
      "If Return You Must" (tr. of Vasant Bapat). NewL
      (48:3/4) Spr-Sum 82, p. 158-159.

2485. MacINNES, Mairi
      "April at Ash Lawn, Monroe's Farm in Virginia." QRL
      (22) 81, p. 65-66.
      "Articles of Belief." QRL (22) 81, p. 23.
      "Blessings." QRL (22) 81, p. 37.
      "A Celebration." QRL (22) 81, p. 57.
      "Chickenpox." QRL (22) 81, p. 30.
      "Death Was." QRL (22) 81, p. 13.
      "Flowered Sheets." QRL (22) 81, p. 59.
      "Fraud." QRL (22) 81, p. 28-29.
      "Genesis." QRL (22) 81, p. 55-56.
      "Grandfather." QRL (22) 81, p. 10-11.
      "Hardly Anything Bears Watching." QRL (22) 81, p.
      17.
      "I Object, Said the Object." QRL (22) 81, p. 34-35.
      "The Invasion." QRL (22) 81, p. 62.
      "Learning Another Language." QRL (22) 81, p. 16.
      "The Moorland Road." QRL (22) 81, p. 22.
      "Mother." QRL (22) 81, p. 36.
      "Possession." QRL (22) 81, p. 26-27.
      "The Present Tense of Machines." QRL (22) 81, p.
      63-64.
      "Reading Cavafy in Translation." QRL (22) 81, p.
      18.
      "The Recognitions." QRL (22) 81, p. 70-71.
      "A Run by the Lake." QRL (22) 81, p. 60-61.
      "Running in the Park." QRL (22) 81, p. 21.
      "A Sailor on the Minch." QRL (22) 81, p. 12.
      "The Scots in America." QRL (22) 81, p. 8-9.
      "The Sculptress." QRL (22) 81, p. 20.
      "Sunrise after Sunrise." QRL (22) 81, p. 14-15.
      "Three Cat Poems." QRL (22) 81, p. 31-33.
      "Three Poems about Places." QRL (22) 81, p. 67-69.
      "A Truth or Two." QRL (22) 81, p. 24.
      "View under the Horse's Belly." QRL (22) 81, p. 19.
      "Views of the Conjuror's Trade." QRL (22) 81, p.
      58.
      "VJ Day." QRL (22) 81, p. 25.

2486. MacKENZIE, Ginny
      "Getting Through." Nat (235:6) S 4, 82, p. 184.

2487. MACKIN, Michael
      "One Dozen Long-Stem Roses for a Lady Love." MendoR
      (5) Sum 81, p. 41.

2488. MacKINNON, John
      "Pumpkin Bloom." AntigR (48) Wint 82, p. 56.

2489. MacKINNON, M.
       "Social Activist's Secretary." PottPort (4) 82-83,
          p. 12.

       MacLOW, Jackson
       See: Mac LOW, Jackson

2490. MacSWEEN, R. J.
       "Arctic Day." AntigR (48) Wint 82, p. 16.
       "Called from Darkness." AntigR (48) Wint 82, p. 19.
       "The Cathedral." AntigR (50) Sum 82, p. 88.
       "Caves." AntigR (51) Aut 82, p. 36-37.
       "Learning." AntigR (48) Wint 82, p. 17.
       "Obituaries." AntigR (48) Wint 82, p. 18.
       "So Long Denied." AntigR (50) Sum 82, p. 90.
       "Stillness." AntigR (51) Aut 82, p. 37.
       "Waves." AntigR (50) Sum 82, p. 89.

2491. MADDOCK, Mary (Marija)
       "In the High Stars" (tr. of Anna Akhmatova, w.
          Willis Barnstone). NewL (48:2) Wint 81-82, p. 51.
       "It's All Been Taken Away" (tr. of Anna Akhmatova).
          DenQ (17:2) Sum 82, p. 122.
       from Verses to Blok: "Your name is a bird in my
          hand" (tr. of Marina Tsvetayeva). LitR (26:1) Aut
          82, p. 104-105.
       "Winter Day" (tr. of Bella Akhmadulina). LitR (26:1)
          Aut 82, p. 102.
       "Zhaleyka" (tr. of Bella Akhmadulina). LitR (26:1)
          Aut 82, p. 103-104.

2492. MADSON, Jerry
       "Burgundy Red." UnderRM 1(1) Spr 82, p. 51.
       "When the Well Runs Dry." UnderRM 1(1) Spr 82, p.
          52.

2493. MAGALY QUINONES, Marta
       "La Toma de Conciencia." Areito (8:31) 82, p. 39.

2494. MAGARRELL, Elaine
       "Assignation." Vis (8) 82, p. 38.

2495. MAGDALENO, Celia
       "Paredes." Os (15) 82, p. 20.
       "A Ti, Joven." Os (15) 82, p. 21.

2496. MAGGS, Randall
       "Blackbears and Girls." Quarry (31:1) Wint 82, p.
          16-17.
       "The Daffodil Kid." Quarry (31:1) Wint 82, p. 18-
          19.

2497. MAGORIAN, James
       "Bronzed Baby Shoes." UnderRM (1:2) Aut 82, p. 37.
       "Cellar." UnderRM (1:2) Aut 82, p. 36.

2498. MAGOWAN, Robin
       "Last Evening at Namche Bazaar." Kayak (60) O 82,
          p. 50.

"The Panoply" (tr. of Saint-Pol Roux). <u>Kayak</u> (59) Je
    82, p. 28.
"Sherpa Villagers on Texi Lapcha." <u>Kayak</u> (60) O 82,
    p. 51.
"While Falling Asleep." <u>Kayak</u> (59) Je 82, p. 42-43.

2499. MAHAPATRA, Jayanta
"Birthday" (tr. of Devdas Chhotray). <u>NewL</u> (48:3/4)
    Spr-Sum 82, p. 115.
"The Corpse" (tr. of Jagannath Prasad Das). <u>NewL</u>
    (48:3/4) Spr-Sum 82, p. 36.
"Fear" (tr. of Devdas Chhotray). <u>NewL</u> (48:3/4) Spr-
    Sum 82, p. 114-115.
from Four Stolen Glances at Time: "I am no good at
    discussing space rockets" (tr. of Ramakanta Rath).
    <u>NewL</u> (48:3/4) Spr-Sum 82, p. 97-98.
"The Ghost of the Unborn" (tr. of Prasanna Kumar
    Mishra). <u>NewL</u> (48:3/4) Spr-Sum 82, p. 212.
"The Hour before Dawn." <u>Hudson</u> (35:2) Sum 82, p.
    220.
"Hunger." <u>NewL</u> (49:2) Wint 82-83, p. 43.
"An Impotent Poem." <u>NewL</u> (48:3/4) Spr-Sum 82, p.
    40-41.
"An Indian Journal." <u>NewL</u> (48:3/4) Spr-Sum 82, p.
    40.
"Indian Summer Poem." <u>NewL</u> (49:2) Wint 82-83, p.
    42.
"The Kerosene Lamp" (tr. of Ramakanta Rath). <u>NewL</u>
    (48:3/4) Spr-Sum 82, p. 97.
"A Monsoon Day Fable." <u>NewEngR</u> (4:4) Sum 82, p.
    574-575.
"Moonlight Poem" (tr. of Bibek Jena). <u>NewL</u> (48:3/4)
    Spr-Sum 82, p. 179.
"Needs." <u>SewanR</u> (90:2) Spr 82, p. 221.
"Of This Evening." <u>Hudson</u> (35:2) Sum 82, p. 219.
"A Poem at Fifty-One." <u>Hudson</u> (35:2) Sum 82, p.
    218.
"Robinson Crusoe" (tr. of Soubhagaya Kumar Misra).
    <u>NewL</u> (48:3/4) Spr-Sum 82, p. 50.
"Sarita." <u>NewL</u> (48:3/4) Spr-Sum 82, p. 38.
"Shapes by the Daya." <u>SewanR</u> (90:2) Spr 82, p. 220.
"Sunday" (tr. of Devdas Chhotray). <u>NewL</u> (48:3/4)
    Spr-Sum 82, p. 114.
"Total Solar Eclipse" (February 16, 1980, Puri,
    India). <u>NewL</u> (48:3/4) Spr-Sum 82, p. 37-38.
"The Vase." <u>NewL</u> (48:3/4) Spr-Sum 82, p. 39.
"The Whorehouse in a Calcutta Street." <u>NewL</u> (49:2)
    Wint 82-83, p. 41-42.

2500. MAHER, James
"Body of Water." <u>Gargoyle</u> (17/18) 81, p. 42.

2501. MAHLER, David
"Composed Outbursts." <u>PortR</u> (28:2) 82, p. 63.
"Pacific International." <u>PortR</u> (28:2) 82, p. 64.
"Time Piece." <u>PortR</u> (28:2) 82, p. 65.

2502. MAHON, Derek
"How to Live" (Horace, Odes, Book One, 11). <u>Hudson</u>
    (35:2) Sum 82, p. 251.

"A Lighthouse in Maine." Hudson (35:2) Sum 82, p.
    251-253.

2503. MAHONY, Phillip
      "Anjali." PoetryE (8) Aut 82, p. 35-37.
      "The Rematch." PoNow (6:6, issue 36) 82, p. 47.

2504. MAIER, Carol
      "Blind Man's Dream" (tr. of Octavio Armand). NewOR
          (9:2) Aut 82, p. 56-57.
      "Braille for Left Hand" (To My Translator, tr. of
          Octavio Armand). NewOR (9:1) Spr-Sum 82, p. 77.

2505. MAILMAN, Leo
      "The Stripper." PoNow (6:4, issue 34) 82, p. 43.

2506. MAINO, Jeannette
      "Ceres to Her Daugher Persephone." Poem (45) Jl 82,
          p. 4.

2507. MAJOR, Clarence
      "Bernardston." LitR (25:4) Sum 82, p. 551-554.
      "The Other Side of the Wall." LitR (25:4) Sum 82,
          p. 546-550.

2508. MAKELL, Lawrence
      "The Poet Surrealist" (for Jim Grabill). PortR
          (28:2) 82, p. 66.

2509. MAKOLKINA, Anna
      "Dreams." WritersL S 82, p. 11.

2510. MAKUCK, Peter
      "My Father's Back." OhioR (27) 82, p. 101.

      MALAVE, Angela Maria Davila
      See: DAVILA MALAVE, Angela Maria

      MALE, Belkis Cuza
      See: CUZA MALE, Belkis

2511. MALIK, Keshav
      "The Date." NewL (48:3/4) Spr-Sum 82, p. 47-48.
      "In Praise of Guns." NewL (48:3/4) Spr-Sum 82, p.
          47.

2512. MALINOWITZ, Michael
      "Address." Shen (33:2) 82, p. 95.
      "All the Subjects on the Threshold." MassR (23:1)
          Spr 82, p. 192.
      "Disintegrating the Polemic." OP (33) Spr 82, p.
          39.
      "Dromophobia." OP (33) Spr 82, p. 40.
      "Neat Compartments." OP (33) Spr 82, p. 41.
      "Pictures of Alex and Nick." Shen (33:2) 82, p. 95.
      "The Poet Writes about Death." OP (33) Spr 82, p.
          40.

2513. MALTMAN, Kim
      "Circa 1930, Cool Dawns." Dandel (9:2) 82, p. 46.

"Comfort." Waves (11:1) Aut 82, p. 67.
"The Gatherers of Dead Wood." Waves (11:1) Aut 82,
    p. 66.
"Labor, after Dawn." Grain (10:2) My 82, p. 21.
"Nihilism." Grain (10:2) My 82, p. 20.
"Owl." PoetryCR (4:2) Wint 82, p. 11.
"Owl." Quarry (31:1) Wint 82, p. 34-36.
"People Who Don't Understand." Quarry (31:1) Wint
    82, p. 31-34.
"Snow and Coal." Dandel (9:2) 82, p. 45.
"Warmth." Dandel (9:2) 82, p. 47.

2514. MALYON, Carol
    "Buckminster Fuller Seems to Be a Verb." Waves
    (11:1) Aut 82, p. 71.

2515. MANDEL, Charlotte
    "Letter to Lynn." StoneC (9:3/4) Spr-Sum 82, p. 68.

    MANDELSHTAM, Osip
    See: MANDELSTAM, Osip

2516. MANDELSTAM, Osip
    "Admiralty Building" (tr. by Emery George). Spirit
    (6:2/3) 82, p. 39.
    "The Age" (tr. by Marianne Andrea). DenQ (16:4) Wint
    82, p. 47.
    "The Age of the Wolfdog" (tr. by Ephim Fogel). NewL
    (48:2) Wint 81-82, p. 44.
    "Leningrad" (tr. by Ephim Fogel). NewL (48:2) Wint
    81-82, p. 43.
    "The Stream of Golden Honey" (for Vera Stravinsky,
    from Tristia, 1922, tr. by Robert Tracy). NewYRB
    (29:19) D 2, 82, p. 22.
    "To Nadezhda Mandelshtam" (tr. by Ephim Fogel). NewL
    (48:2) Wint 81-82, p. 44.
    "Tristia" (from Tristia, 1922, tr. by Robert Tracy).
    NewYRB (29:19) D 2, 82, p. 22.

2517. MANFRED, Freya
    "My Basketball Brother Versus Windom." Spirit
    (6:2/3) 82, p. 108-110.

2518. MANGAN, Kathy
    "Lament: Forsythia." AntR (40:2) Spr 82, p. 171.
    "Solo." AntR (40:2) Spr 82, p. 172-173.

2519. MANHAE
    "Awake" (tr. by Bruce Taylor). NewOR (9:3) Wint 82,
    p. 73.

2520. MANN, Paul
    "Codicil." NewOR (9:2) Aut 82, p. 88.

    MANNING, Carolyn Lau
    See: LAU-MANNING, Carolyn

2521. MANNING, Nichola
    "Dear Mummy." UnderRM (1:2) Aut 82, p. 13.
    "Gratitude." UnderRM (1:2) Aut 82, p. 16.

"Mother." UnderRM (1:2) Aut 82, p. 14.
"Mutt!" WormR (22:1, issue 85) 82, p. 32-33.
"One More Round for Hiroshima." WormR (22:1, issue 85) 82, p. 34.
"Punk Buttons." WormR (22:1, issue 85) 82, p. 33-34.
"Sarah Kassem Zadeh." WormR (22:1, issue 85) 82, p. 33.
"To Whom It May Concern." UnderRM (1:2) Aut 82, p. 15.

2522. MANSOUR, Joyce
"Breastplate" (tr. by Elton Glaser and Janice Fritsch). CharR (8:2) Aut 82, p. 44.
"I've Gone Deep into." (tr. by Elton Glaser and Janice Fritsch). CharR (8:2) Aut 82, p. 43.
"You Don't Know My Night-Face" (tr. by Elton Glaser and Janice Fritsch). CharR (8:2) Aut 82, p. 43.

2523. MAQUELANI, O. T. (Orson T.)
"Lean Black Faces." BlackALF (16:2) Sum 82, p. 75.
"Oracles of Strength." DekalbLAJ (14:1/4) Aut 80-Sum 81, p. 85.

2524. MARANO, Russell
"Night Boy." Wind (12:45) 82, p. 25.

2525. MARCANO MONTANEZ, Jaime
"A Francisco Matos Paoli." Mairena (4:11/12) Wint 82, p. 151.

2526. MARCELLO, Leo Luke
"Burning Leaves." PoNow (7:1, issue 37) 82, p. 29.
"The Parking Lot." SouthernR (18:1) Wint 82, p. 188-190.

2527. MARCHAELLE, Ilona
"Pompeii." Germ (6:1) Spr-Sum 82, p. 26.

2528. MARCUS, Marne
"Working in the Light." KanQ (14:1) Wint 82, p. 139.

2529. MARCUS, Mordecai
"Emily Dickinson Receives a Visit from King Kong." SouthernPR (23, i.e. 22:2) Aut 82, p. 66.
"An Explanation." WebR (7:2) Aut 82, p. 64.
"Hardened Delicacy." WebR (7:2) Aut 82, p. 65.
"Rack and Cane." NoAmR (267:1) Mr 82,p. 30.
"Restorations." ChrC (99:18) My 19, 82, p. 596.

2530. MARCUS, Morton
"Credo." PoNow (6:4, issue 34) 82, p. 13.
"What It's All About." Kayak (60) O 82, p. 33.

2531. MAREY, Juan
"Antisonnet a la Mer Vierge" (tr. of Francisco Matos Paoli). Mairena (4:11/12) Wint 82, p. 95.
"Biographie d'un Poete" (tr. of Francisco Matos Paoli). Mairena (4:11/12) Wint 82, p. 105-106.

from Chant de la Folie: (1-4) (tr. of Francisco
Matos Paoli). Mairena (4:11/12) Wint 82, p. 95-
103.
"Immanence" (tr. of Francisco Matos Paoli). Mairena
(4:11/12) Wint 82, p. 103-105.

2532. MARGGRAFF, Roberta
"Making the Word Known." HiramPoR (31) Aut-Wint 82,
p. 36.

2533. MARGOLIS, Gary
"Across the Grain." PraS (56:4) Wint 82-83, p. 26-
27.
"August." GeoR (36:3) Aut 82, p. 602.
"The Sitter Moves." ColEng 44(6) O 82, p. 614.
"Town Meeting." Poetry (140:6) S 82, p. 334-335.

2534. MARGOSHES, Dave
"Length of Reach." Waves (11:1) Aut 82, p. 73.

2535. MARGULIES, Ronnie
"Often Yours" (tr. of Turgut Uyar). Stand (23:1) 81-
82, p. 67.

2536. MARIANI, Paul
"Baudelaire at Gamma Level." Agni (16) 82, p. 17-
19.
"The Girl who Learned to Sing in Crow." Tendril
(12) Wint 82, p. 44-45.
"In the Boiler." NewEngR (5:1/2) Aut-Wint 82, p.
171-173.
"A Walk in Early March" (for Mark). NewEngR (5:1/2)
Aut-Wint 82, p. 173-175.

2537. MARION, Paul
"Winterport." CaroIQ (35:1) Aut 82, p. 19.

MARIS, Arlene de
See: DeMARIS, Arlene

MARIS, Ron de
See: De MARIS, Ron

2538. MARISCAL, Jose Luis
"Ayer." Mairena (4:10) Sum-Aut 82, p. 52.
"Surco y Arabesco." Mairena (4:10) Sum-Aut 82, p.
53.

2539. MARKERT, Lawrence
"Two Questions for Richard." Wind (12:45) 82, p.
26.

2540. MARLATT, Daphne
"June near the River Clyst, Clust, Clear. Clystmois
This Holding Wet & Clear." Dandel (9:2) 82, p. 53.
"To Ilfracombe." Dandel (9:2) 82, p. 54-55.
"Under Poltimore or Clystmois ('Some Confusion about
the Name')." Dandel (9:2) 82, p. 52.

2541. MARLIS, Stefanie
        "History, Opening and Closing."   AspenJ (1) Wint
            82, p. 32.
        "The Powerless." PoNow (7:1, issue 37) 82, p. 30.
        "The Single Feather." PoNow (7:1, issue 37) 82, p.
            30.
        "Sunday." PoNow (7:1, issue 37) 82, p. 30.

2542. MARQUEZ de RUBIO, Nieves del Rosario
        "Busqueda" (Desde Tejas). LetFem (8:1) 82, p. 91.
        "Juego." LetFem (8:1) 82, p. 90.

        MARRERO, Andres Diaz
        See: DIAZ MARRERO, Andres

2543. MARRIOTT, Anne
        "Burned Woodlot." PoetryCR (3:4) Sum 82, p. 13.

2544. MARRUCCI, Luciano
        "La Bussola" (tr. by Ruth Feldman and Martin
            Robbins). StoneC (10:1/2) Aut-Wint 82-83, p. 25.
        "The Compass" (tr. by Ruth Feldman and Martin
            Robbins). StoneC (10:1/2) Aut-Wint 82-83, p. 25.

2545. MARSH, Bill
        "Bait Shop Postcard." WormR (22:1, issue 85) 82, p.
            6.
        "Playing Dead." WormR (22:1, issue 85) 82, p. 7.
        "Rape." WormR (22:1, issue 85) 82, p. 7.

2546. MARSH, Kirk
        "Plus Ca Change." Sam (33:3, issue 131) 82, p. 55.
        "The Seaside Marathon." Sam (33:3, issue 131) 82,
            p. 9.
        "Veteran on the Mound." Sam (33:3, issue 131) 82,
            p. 55.

2547. MARSHALL, Benjamin V.
        "December." Obs (7:2/3) Sum-Wint 81, p. 166.
        "From the Kitchen." Obs (7:2/3) Sum-Wint 81, p.
            169.
        "Lent." Obs (7:2/3) Sum-Wint 81, p. 165-166.
        "The Village." Obs (7:2/3) Sum-Wint 81, p. 167.
        "White Bread." Obs (7:2/3) Sum-Wint 81, p. 167-168.

2548. MARSHALL, Jack
        "The Life and Times of Erik Satie." AmerPoR (11:5)
            S-O 82, p. 27-28.
        "The Sixth Sense" (tr. of Nikolai Gumilev). Spirit
            (6:2/3) 82, p. 83.

2549. MARSHALL, Niobe
        "Fifteen." Obs (7:2/3) Sum-Wint 81, p. 208.
        "Love + Love, on Losing Someone Dear to Me." Obs
            (7:2/3) Sum-Wint 81, p. 207.
        "Talk Is Cheap." Obs (7:2/3) Sum-Wint 81, p. 207.
        "Under the Sky." Obs (7:2/3) Sum-Wint 81, p. 206.

2550. MARSHALL, Renie
        "Corfu." WritersL O-N 82, p. 16.

2551. MARSHALL, Tom
"Field Syllabics" (for Dennis Lee). <u>Quarry</u> (31:3)
Sum 82, p. 11-12.
"The Mythmakers: Poet and Novelist." <u>Quarry</u> (31:3)
Sum 82, p. 12-13.

2552. MARTEAU, Robert
"Fragments de la France." <u>Os</u> (15) 82, p. 16-19.

2553. MARTELLO, Jacqueline
"I Sit Here." <u>AntigR</u> (49) Spr 82, p. 118.
"Kate." <u>AntigR</u> (49) Spr 82, p. 117.

2554. MARTI, Jose
"Amor Errante." <u>NotArte</u> (7:1) Ja 82, p. 12.
from La Bailarina Espanola: (X). <u>NotArte</u> (7:1) Ja
82, p. 17.
"Brazos Fragantes." <u>NotArte</u> (7:1) Ja 82, p. 10.
"Hijo del Alma." <u>NotArte</u> (7:1) Ja 82, p. 12.
"Hijo: Espantado de todo, me refugio en ti."
<u>NotArte</u> (7:1) Ja 82, p. 10.
"Mi Caballero." <u>NotArte</u> (7:1) Ja 82, p. 10.
"Mi Despensero." <u>NotArte</u> (7:1) Ja 82, p. 13.
"Mi Reyecillo." <u>NotArte</u> (7:1) Ja 82, p. 12.
"Musa Traviesa." <u>NotArte</u> (7:1) Ja 82, p. 11.
"Penachos Vividos." <u>NotArte</u> (7:1) Ja 82, p. 12.
"Principe Enano." <u>NotArte</u> (7:1) Ja 82, p. 10-11.
"Rosilla Nueva." <u>NotArte</u> (7:1) Ja 82, p. 13.
"Sobre Mi Hombro." <u>NotArte</u> (7:1) Ja 82, p. 12.
"Sueno Despierto." <u>NotArte</u> (7:1) Ja 82, p. 10.
"Tabanos Fieros." <u>NotArte</u> (7:1) Ja 82, p. 12-13.
"Tortola Blanca." <u>NotArte</u> (7:1) Ja 82, p. 13.
from Tortola Blanca: "Un baile parece de copas
exhaustas!" <u>NotArte</u> (7:1) Ja 82, p. 17.
"Valle Lozano." <u>NotArte</u> (7:1) Ja 82, p. 13.

2555. MARTIN, Charles
"Grace, Secrets, Mysteries ..." (Fatima, 1917).
<u>Hudson</u> (35:1) Spr 82, p. 87-88.
"Three Passages from Friday." <u>NewEngR</u> (5:1/2) Aut-
Wint 82, p. 56-60.

2556. MARTIN, Charles Casey
"Almost Persuaded" (from the spiritual by P.P.
Bliss). <u>Telescope</u> (2) Aut 81, p. 53-54.
"Elvis." <u>Telescope</u> (2) Aut 81, p. 55-56.
"Sixpoint Five." <u>Iowa</u> (12:4) Aut 81, p. 44-45.

MARTIN, D. Roger
<u>See</u>: MARTIN, Don Roger

2557. MARTIN, Don Roger
"20,000 Crazy People Roaring." <u>Sam</u> (31:3, issue
123) 82, p. 11.
"The Auxiliary Squad." <u>Sam</u> (31:3, issue 123) 82, p.
9.
"Be a Man, Kid" (Little League As Teacher). <u>Sam</u>
(31:3, issue 123) 82, p. 10.
"A Day in the Bleachers." <u>Sam</u> (31:3, issue 123) 82,
p. 5.

"Five Bucks a Game." Sam (31:3, issue 123) 82, p.
     3.
"Glen Hobbie." Sam (31:3, issue 123) 82, p. 6.
"Graduate." Sam (32:3, issue 127) 82, p. 12.
"No Dreams for Sale." Sam (31:3, issue 123) 82, p.
     12.
"Out in Boston." Sam (31:3, issue 123) 82, p. 4.
"Remembering Kenny Hubbs." Sam (31:3, issue 123)
     82, p. 7.
"Roger Maris: 61 in '61." Sam (31:3, issue 123) 82,
     p. 2.
"Small Town Chimney Fire." Sam (33:3, issue 131)
     82, p. 56.
"Washed Up at 30." Sam (31:3, issue 123) 82, p. 8.

2558. MARTIN, Herbert Woodward
     "On Julia's Birth." Im (8:1) 82, p. 8.

2559. MARTIN, James
     "Concessions."   MassR (23:3) Aut 82, p. 387-388.

2560. MARTIN, John Stanley
     "Ballad of Philip Martin" (tr. of Lars Gustafsson,
     w. Philip Martin). QRL (23) 82, p. 64-65.

2561. MARTIN, Philip
     "Africa (3)" (tr. of Lars Gustafsson). QRL (23) 82,
          p. 54.
     "Africa (4)" (tr. of Lars Gustafsson). QRL (23) 82,
          p. 54.
     "After Rain" (tr. of Lars Gustafsson). QRL (23) 82,
          p. 13.
     "At Cologne Cathedral" (tr. of Lars Gustafsson). QRL
          (23) 82, p. 52.
     "Ballad of Philip Martin" (tr. of Lars Gustafsson,
          w. John Stanley Martin). QRL (23) 82, p. 64-65.
     "Ballad of the Dogs" (tr. of Lars Gustafsson). QRL
          (23) 82, p. 62-63.
     "Ballad of the Stone Forest in Yunnan" (tr. of Lars
          Gustafsson). QRL (23) 82, p. 66-68.
     "The Balloonists" (tr. of Lars Gustafsson). QRL (23)
          82, p. 14-15.
     "Bar-Girl, Memphis, Tennessee" (tr. of Lars
          Gustafsson). QRL (23) 82, p. 57.
     "The Chinese Painter" (tr. of Lars Gustafsson). QRL
          (23) 82, p. 55.
     "The Crows" (tr. of Lars Gustafsson). QRL (23) 82,
          p. 42.
     "The Decisive Battle" (tr. of Lars Gustafsson). QRL
          (23) 82, p. 59.
     from Declaration of Love to a Sephardic Lady:
          "Events in 1939" (lines 1-41, tr. of Lars
          Gustafsson). QRL (23) 82, p. 27-28.
     from Declaration of Love to a Sephardic Lady:
          "Humaniora" (tr. of Lars Gustafsson). QRL (23) 82,
          p. 29-31.
     "The Didapper" (tr. of Lars Gustafsson). QRL (23)
          82, p. 41.
     "The Dog" (tr. of Lars Gustafsson). QRL (23) 82, p.
          17.

"The Dogs" (tr. of Lars Gustafsson). QRL (23) 82, p.
    39-40.
"Eel and Well" (tr. of Lars Gustafsson). QRL (23)
    82, p. 44.
"Elegy" (tr. of Lars Gustafsson). QRL (23) 82, p.
    26.
"Elegy on a Dead Labrador" (tr. of Lars Gustafsson).
    QRL (23) 82, p. 60-61.
"A Fantasy on Wolfgang Amadeus Mozart" (tr. of Lars
    Gustafsson). QRL (23) 82, p. 45.
"Inscription on a Stone" (tr. of Lars Gustafsson).
    QRL (23) 82, p. 19.
"A Landscape" (tr. of Lars Gustafsson). QRL (23) 82,
    p. 20-24.
"A Love Poem" (tr. of Lars Gustafsson). QRL (23) 82,
    p. 58.
"The Meeting" (tr. of Lars Gustafsson). QRL (23) 82,
    p. 43.
"The Night" (tr. of Lars Gustafsson). QRL (23) 82,
    p. 50.
"The Old Dry Tree" (tr. of Lars Gustafsson). QRL
    (23) 82, p. 47.
"On Certain Evenings" (tr. of Lars Gustafsson). QRL
    (23) 82, p. 46.
"Poem on Revisionism" (tr. of Lars Gustafsson). QRL
    (23) 82, p. 32.
"The Silence of the World before Bach" (tr. of Lars
    Gustafsson). QRL (23) 82, p. 48.
"Snow" (tr. of Lars Gustafsson). QRL (23) 82, p. 18.
"A Solemn Morning" (tr. of Lars Gustafsson). QRL
    (23) 82, p. 16.
from Sonnets (1977): I. "The Desert at Rio Grande"
    (tr. of Lars Gustafsson). QRL (23) 82, p. 34.
from Sonnets (1977): (XVI, XVII, XXIII, XXVIII) (tr.
    of Lars Gustafsson). QRL (23) 82, p. 35-38.
"The Starred Sky" (tr. of Lars Gustafsson). QRL (23)
    82, p. 49.
"Streams of Particles" (tr. of Lars Gustafsson). QRL
    (23) 82, p. 51.
"Veduta. Embarcamento. Golfo di Rapallo" (tr. of
    Lars Gustafsson). QRL (23) 82, p. 53.
"Warm Rooms and Cold" (tr. of Lars Gustafsson). QRL
    (23) 82, p. 33.
"A Wind in Texas" (tr. of Lars Gustafsson). QRL (23)
    82, p. 56.
"The Window-Pane" (tr. of Lars Gustafsson). QRL (23)
    82, p. 25.

2562. MARTIN, Stephen-Paul
    "Bob Gets There." SmPd (19:2, issue 55) Spr 82, p.
    20.
    "Still Life with Monkey, Mandolin, and Bananas."
    KanQ (14:4) Aut 82, p. 19.

2563. MARTINEZ, Renato
    "Cancion de Cuna para una Nina Que No Comio Pan."
    Maize (5:3/4) Spr-Sum 82, p. 35-36.

    MARTINEZ, Tomas Rivera
    See: RIVERA MARTINEZ, Tomas

2564. MARTINEZ CASTRO, Sara
        "Malgastada de Suenos" (from Vitrina al Sueno).
        Mairena (4:10) Sum-Aut 82, p. 43.
        "Mi Padre" (from Vitrina al Sueno). Mairena (4:10)
        Sum-Aut 82, p. 44.
        "Ofertorio" (from Vitrina al Sueno). Mairena (4:10)
        Sum-Aut 82, p. 44.

2565. MARTONE, Michael
        "French Lick." AntR (40:4) Aut 82, p. 440.

2566. MARTY, Miriam
        "Rogation Days." GeoR (36:1) Spr 82, p. 114.

2567. MARZOLF, Laurel
        "Acquaintances of a Four-Year-Old." Grain (10:2) My
        82, p. 42.

2568. MASOLIVER RODENAS, Juan Antonio
        "In Attitude of Oasis" (tr. by Anthony Kerrigan).
        DenQ (17:3) Aut 82, p. 75.

2569. MASON-BROWNE, Nicholas
        "I Killed a Bird in Andalucia." SouthernPR (22:1)
        Spr 82, p. 11.

      MASSMAN, Gordon Lester
      See: LESTER-MASSMAN, Gordon

      MASTER, J. R. le
      See: LeMASTER, J. R.

2570. MASTERSON, Dan
        "Calling Home." NewYorker (57:49) Ja 25, 82, p. 79.
        "The End of Things." PoetryNW (23:1) Spr 82, p. 24-
        26.
        "Pencil." PoetryNW (23:1) Spr 82, p. 26-27.

2571. MASUD, Iqbal
        "Pain" (tr. of Padma Sachdev). NewL (48:3/4) Spr-Sum
        82, p. 99.

2572. MATCHETT,William H.
        "Chores." Ploughs (8:2/3) 82, p. 152-153.

2573. MATHERNE, Beverly M.
        "Cane Field." KanQ (14:2) Spr 82, p. 94.
        "Rite de Passage." KanQ (14:2) Spr 82, p. 94.

2574. MATHESON, Jeff
        "Untitled: Way down down below." MendoR (5) Sum 81,
        p. 66.

2575. MATHIEU-GRACE, Lois
        "Gesuitengarten." PortR (28:2) 82, p. 83.

2576. MATHIS, Cleopatra
        "From a Summer Journal: Running." PoNow (6:5, issue
        35) 82, p. 29.

MATOS, Isabel Freire de
See: FREIRE de MATOS, Isabel

2577. MATOS-CINTRON, Nemir
"Este poema nacio de la inconciencia" (from A Traves
del Aire y del Fuego Pero No del Cristal). Mairena
(4:9) Spr 82, p. 87.

2578. MATOS PAOLI, Francisco
"A Juan Ramon Jimenez." Mairena (4:9) Spr 82, p.
51.
"Akallan Av Hemlandet" (ur Luz de los Heroes 1954,
tr. by Mats Henriksson). Mairena (4:11/12) Wint
82, p. 157.
"Antisoneto al Mar Doncel." Mairena (4:11/12) Wint
82, p. 94.
"Antisonnet a la Mer Vierge" (tr. by Juan Marey)
Mairena (4:11/12) Wint 82, p. 95.
"Biografia de un Poeta." Mairena (4:11/12) Wint 82,
p. 104-106.
"Biographie d'un Poete" (tr. by Juan Marey) Mairena
(4:11/12) Wint 82, p. 105-106.
from Canto de la Locura: (1-4). Mairena (4:11/12)
Wint 82, p. 94-102.
from Canto de la Locura: (Fragmentos) Mairena
(4:11/12) Wint 82, p. 38-50.
from Chant de la Folie: (1-4) (tr. by Juan Marey)
Mairena (4:11/12) Wint 82, p. 95-103.
"En Poets Biografi" (ur El Viento y la Paloma 1963-
65, tr. by Mats Henriksson). Mairena (4:11/12)
Wint 82, p. 157.
"Ge Mig Hjarta" (ur La marea sube 1971, tr. by Mats
Henriksson). Mairena (4:11/12) Wint 82, p. 156.
"Haremos una Isla" (w. Isabel Freire de Matos, from
Isla para los Ninos). Mairena (4:9) Spr 82, p. 84.
"Hyllning Till Pedro Albizu Campos" (ur La Marea
sube 1971, tr. by Mats Henriksson). Mairena
(4:11/12) Wint 82, p. 156.
"Immanence" (tr. by Juan Marey) Mairena (4:11/12)
Wint 82, p. 103-105.
"La Inmanencia." Mairena (4:11/12) Wint 82, p. 102-
104.
"El Simbolo Poetico" (from Cancionero IX). Mairena
(4:9) Spr 82, p. 89.
from Song of Madness: (Fragments) (tr. by Frances
Aparicio). Mairena (4:11/12) Wint 82, p. 39-51.
"Soy fiel: milito en la adversidad" (from Antologia
minuto). Mairena (4:9) Spr 82, p. 88-89.
"Vaggvisa" (ur Teoria de Olvido 1944, tr. by Mats
Henriksson). Mairena (4:11/12) Wint 82, p. 156.

2579. MATSON, Suzanne
"Fossils." PoetryNW (23:4) Wint 82-83, p. 39-40.
"Leaving Garibaldi." PoetryNW (23:4) Wint 82-83, p.
40-41.
"Love in the Coal Mine." PoetryNW (23:2) Sum 82, p.
26.
"Newspaper Pictures Out of Poland" (December 1981).
PoetryNW (23:2) Sum 82, p. 28-29.
"Scotch Coulee." PoetryNW (23:2) Sum 82, p. 26-27.

"Widow Aunts." PoetryNW (23:2) Sum 82, p. 28.

2580. MATTESON, Fredric
"Samba." SouthwR (67:4) Aut 82, p. 399-400.

2581. MATTHEWS, Sebastian
"Hide Away, Closing Act." HangL (42) 82, p. 61.
"Hideaway Revisited." Hangl (43) Wint 82-83, p. 79.
"Night Thoughts." HangL (42) 82, p. 60.

2582. MATTHEWS, William
"Arrogant." Tendril (12) Wint 82, p. 49.
"Charming." Atl (249:5) My 82, p. 80.
"Civilization and Its Discontents." Antaeus (47)
    Aut 82, p. 61-62.
"Closure." PoNow (6:5, issue 35) 82, p. 11.
"Descriptive Passages." AmerPoR (11:2) Mr-Ap 82, p.
    19.
"Disclosure." PoNow (6:5, issue 35) 82, p. 11.
"Flood Plain." Tendril (12) Wint 82, p. 47.
"Four Small Laments." Tendril (12) Wint 82, p. 46.
"Good Company." AmerPoR (11:2) Mr-Ap 82, p. 18.
"Hello." PoNow (6:4, issue 34) 82, p. 9.
"Inquiline." NewEngR (5:1/2) Aut-Wint 82, p. 79.
"The Interpretation of Dreams." Antaeus (47) Aut
    82, p. 63-64.
"Jilted." NewEngR (5:1/2) Aut-Wint 82, p. 80.
"Loyal." Atl (250:4) O 82, p. 37.
"Make It New." Telescope (1) Spr 81, back cover.
"Office Life." Telescope (1) Spr 81, p. 20.
"On the Porch at the Frost Place, Franconia, N.H."
    Atl (249:2) F 82, p. 51.
"Prurient." NewEngR (5:1/2) Aut-Wint 82, p. 78.
"The Psychopathology of Everyday Life." Antaeus
    (47) Aut 82, p. 65-66.
"Sentimental." Tendril (12) Wint 82, p. 48.
"Strangers on a Train." PoNow (6:5, issue 35) 82,
    p. 11.
"Unrelenting Flood." AmerPoR (11:2) Mr-Ap 82, p.
    18.
"We Shall All Be Born Again But We Shall Not All Be
    Saved." MissouriR (6:1) Aut 82, p. 30-31.

2583. MATTHIAS, John
"Northern Summer: Nine Poems." Bound (10:3) Spr 82,
    p. 303-317.

2584. MATTISON, Alice
"Hunter Radiation Center: Halloween." Ploughs (8:1)
    82, p. 30-32.
"No Harm." Ploughs (8:1) 82, p. 33-38.

2585. MATYAS, Cathy
"The Conversation" (title of a drawing by Francisco
    Zuniga). Quarry (31:3) Sum 82, p. 63.
"Skipping Stones." Quarry (31:3) Sum 82, p. 64.
"Vienna." Quarry (31:3) Sum 82, p. 63-64.

2586. MAUCH, James
        "Dawn" (tr. of Shamsher Bahadur Singh). NewL
        (48:3/4) Spr-Sum 82, p. 99.

2587. MAURA, Sister
        "Christmas, with a Bowl of Paperwhite Narcissus."
        ChrC (99:40) D 15, 82, p. 1277.
        "Night Walk: Kyoto." SouthernHR (16:2) Spr 82, p.
        164.

2588. MAXMIN, Jody
        "Lays of Ancient Rome" (For Ray). PraS (56:3) Aut
        82, p. 85.

2589. MAXSON, Gloria (Gloria A.)
        "Executive." ChrC (99:21) Je 9-16, 82, p. 696.
        "Fashionable." ChrC (99:17) My 12, 82, p. 556.
        "Frank." ChrC (99:1) Ja 6-13, 82, p. 8.
        "Modern." ChrC (99:22) Je 23-30, 82, p. 722.
        "Snow Angels." ChrC (99:39) D 8, 82, p. 1247.
        "Spared." ChrC (99:10) Mr 24, 82, p. 325.
        "Stepchild." ChrC (99:16) My 5, 82, p. 525.
        "The Two Feastings." ChrC (99:37) N 24, 82, p.
        1196.

2590. MAXWELL, Anna
        "The Woman Who Wants." Tendril (12) Wint 82, p. 50.

2591. MAY, Kerry Paul
        "Leaving Oregon." NewL (48:2) Wint 81-82, p. 66.

2592. MAYER, John Eleanor, Sister
        "How Easy Some Days to Beowulf It." EngJ (71:3) Mr
        82, p. 69.

2593. MAYER, Liz
        "The First Chilly Night." MidwQ (23:3) Spr 82, p.
        299.

2594. MAYES, Frances
        "In the Dreams of Exiles." NewEngR (5:1/2) Aut-Wint
        82, p. 136-137.
        "The Poem with No End." BlackWR (7:2) Spr 81, p.
        42-43.

2595. MAYFIELD, Carl
        "I forgot everybody's name." WindO (40, Anti-Haiku
        issue) Sum 82, p. 45.
        "Spring, summer, autumn, winter." WindO (40, Anti-
        Haiku issue) Sum 82, p. 45.

2596. MAYHALL, Jane
        "Landfill Hours" (Saratoga, Dec. 26). NewL (48:2)
        Wint 81-82, p. 98.
        "To a Blind Jogger." AmerS (51:2) Spr 82, p. 263.

2597. MAYROCKER, Friederike
        "Five Poems" (tr. by Beth Bjorklund). LitR (25:2)
        Wint 82, p. 229-231.

2598. MAZUR, Gail
"Daylight." Shen (33:1) 81-82, p. 22-23.
"Dutch Tulips." Pequod (15) 82, p. 36.
"In the Dark Our Story." Ploughs (8:1) 82, p. 56-
57.

2599. MAZZA, Antonino
"Falsetto" (tr. of Eugenio Montale). Waves (10:4)
Spr 82, p. 50-51.
"Giovannina." Waves (10:4) Spr 82, p. 48.

2600. MAZZARO, Jerome
"Departing Buffalo." Hudson (35:4) Wint 82-83, p.
547-548.
"Intensities." LitR (25:4) Sum 82, p. 555.
"Sunlight." Hudson (35:4) Wint 82-83, p. 548.
"Sushi/Sashimi." Hudson (35:4) Wint 82-83, p. 546.
"Yesterday's Children." LitR (25:4) Sum 82, p. 556.

2601. MAZZOCCO, Robert
"Au Club." NewYorker (58:3) Mr 8, 82, p. 44.
"Midnight at Gstaad." Ploughs (8:2/3) 82, p. 185.
"Sanctuary." Ploughs (8:2/3) 82, p. 183-184.

2602. McALEAVEY, David
"Arriving Lost." Gargoyle (15/16) 80, p. 41.
"Bonsai, Seisuke (National Arboretum)." Gargoyle
(17/18) 81, p. 7.
"Burning Burning." Gargoyle (17/18) 81, p. 7.
"What It Felt Like." Gargoyle (15/16) 80, p. 42.
"Written Next to a Page of Emerson." Gargoyle
(15/16) 80, p. 40.

2603. McAULEY, James J.
"The Boy Who Knew Nine Languages." Poetry (141:3) D
82, p. 140-141.

2604. McBRIDE, Elizabeth
"Immortal Longings." MinnR (NS19) Aut 82, p. 50.
"South Pacific Stars and Stripes." CapeR (17:2) Sum
82, p. 35.

2605. McBRIDE, Mekeel
"The Arrival of the Unexpected" (for Philip
Metzner). Tendril (12) Wint 82, p. 78-79.
"As She Has Been Taught." Kayak (58) Ja 82, p. 40.
"Clues." Kayak (58) Ja 82, p. 43.
"The Delicacy of Freedom" (for Fred). PoetryE (7)
Spr 82, p. 38-40.
"The Form and Theory of Ordinary Joy." Tendril (12)
Wint 82, p. 90-91.
"How It Begins." Tendril (12) Wint 82, p. 84.
"Ice Fishing" (for Ian MacKenzie). Tendril (12) Wint
82, p. 76-77.
"The Language of Goodbye." PoetryE (7) Spr 82, p.
37-38.
"Letter to My Sister in California." Tendril (12)
Wint 82, p. 86-87.
"Loneliness." Tendril (12) Wint 82, p. 73.
"Marriage." Tendril (12) Wint 82, p. 80.

"Metaphor for the Past." Kayak (58) Ja 82, p. 41.
"One River Story." Tendril (12) Wint 82, p. 72.
"The Pain Sweepstakes." Tendril (12) Wint 82, p.
   81.
"Relations." Tendril (12) Wint 82, p. 88-89.
"Summer." Tendril (12) Wint 82, p. 71.
"The Waiting Room." Tendril (12) Wint 82, p. 85.
"Walking on This Earth" (for Larkin Warren). Tendril
   (12) Wint 82, p. 74-75.
"Water Music." Kayak (58) Ja 82, p. 43.
"Whether or Not." Tendril (12) Wint 82, p. 82-83.

2606. McCABE, Victoria
"Aunt." NewL (49:2) Wint 82-83, p. 35-36.
"The Women in the Photograph." NewL (49:2) Wint 82-
   83, p. 34-35.

2607. McCAFFREY, Phillip
"Aglaia ('Brilliance')." SouthernPR (22:1) Spr 82,
   p. 24.
"Euphrosyne ('Joy')." SouthernPR (22:1) Spr 82, p.
   23.
"Picasso's Ear." SouthernPR (23, i.e. 22:2) Aut 82,
   p. 61-65.
"The Source." ColEng 44(2) F 82, p. 160.

2608. McCANN, David R.
"Air Shimmering" (tr. of So Chongju). QRL (22) 81,
   p. 35.
"At a Wine House Near Taegu" (tr. of So Chongju).
   QRL (22) 81, p. 79-80.
"An Autumn Day" (tr. of So Chongju). QRL (22) 81, p.
   61.
"Barley Summer" (tr. of So Chongju). QRL (22) 81, p.
   16.
"Beside a Chrysanthemum" (tr. of So Chongju). QRL
   (22) 81, p. 34.
"Blue Days" (tr. of So Chongju). QRL (22) 81, p. 27.
"The Bride" (tr. of So Chongju). QRL (22) 81, p. 70.
"By the Gate at Sonun Temple" (tr. of So Chongju).
   QRL (22) 81, p. 55.
"Ch'unhyang's Testament" (tr. of So Chongju). QRL
   (22) 81, p. 37.
"Ch'usok" (tr. of So Chongju). QRL (22) 81, p. 51.
"Crane" (tr. of So Chongju). QRL (22) 81, p. 33.
"The Cuckoo Makes a River" (tr. of So Chongju). QRL
   (22) 81, p. 66.
"Dandelion" (tr. of So Chongju). QRL (22) 81, p. 30.
"Dry Rapids" (tr. of So Chongju). QRL (22) 81, p.
   53.
"A Flower Blooms" (tr. of So Chongju). QRL (22) 81,
   p. 48.
"Flower-Patterned Snake" (tr. of So Chongju). QRL
   (22) 81, p. 15.
"Four A.M." (tr. of So Chongju). QRL (22) 81, p. 63.
"Go Back to Shu" (tr. of So Chongju). QRL (22) 81,
   p. 25.
"Homing Song" (tr. of So Chongju). QRL (22) 81, p.
   78.

"The Huge Wave" (tr. of So Chongju). QRL (22) 81, p. 71.

"If I Became a Stone" (tr. of So Chongju). QRL (22) 81, p. 59.

"Kimch'i Song" (tr. of So Chongju). QRL (22) 81, p. 81.

"Like a Wind from Lotus Blossoms" (tr. of So Chongju). QRL (22) 81, p. 47.

"Looking at Mount Peerless" (tr. of So Chongju). QRL (22) 81, p. 32.

"Marching Song" (tr. of So Chongju). QRL (22) 81, p. 29.

"Monologue to the Flowerbed" (tr. of So Chongju). QRL (22) 81, p. 40.

"My Eternity" (tr. of So Chongju). QRL (22) 81, p. 50.

"My Love's Fingertip" (tr. of So Chongju). QRL (22) 81, p. 57.

"My Poems" (tr. of So Chongju). QRL (22) 81, p. 38.

"New Year's Prayer 1976" (tr. of So Chongju). QRL (22) 81, p. 75-76.

"The Old Man's Song" (tr. of So Chongju). QRL (22) 81, p. 41-43.

"Old-Fashioned Hours" (tr. of So Chongju). QRL (22) 81, p. 60.

"Peony Afternoon" (tr. of So Chongju). QRL (22) 81, p. 49.

"Poem of Sudae-Dong" (tr. of So Chongju). QRL (22) 81, p. 17.

"Poetics" (tr. of So Chongju). QRL (22) 81, p. 73.

"Postcard to a Friend" (tr. of So Chongju). QRL (22) 81, p. 18.

"Rhododendron" (tr. of So Chongju). QRL (22) 81, p. 58.

"Screech-Owl" (tr. of So Chongju). QRL (22) 81, p. 19.

"The Sea" (tr. of So Chongju). QRL (22) 81, p. 20-21.

"The Secret" (tr. of So Chongju). QRL (22) 81, p. 23.

"Self Portrait" (tr. of So Chongju). QRL (22) 81, p. 14.

"The Shaman: Her Face, Her Food" (tr. of So Chongju). QRL (22) 81, p. 77.

"Sister's House" (tr. of So Chongju). QRL (22) 81, p. 26.

"A Sneeze" (tr. of So Chongju). QRL (22) 81, p. 56.

"Snow Days" (tr. of So Chongju). QRL (22) 81, p. 52.

"Song" (tr. of So Chongju). QRL (22) 81, p. 28.

"Spring Lean" (tr. of So Chongju). QRL (22) 81, p. 67.

"Stone Orchid: The Birthday of Gautama" (tr. of So Chongju). QRL (22) 81, p. 74.

"Such a Land" (tr. of So Chongju). QRL (22) 81, p. 65.

"Swing Song: Ch'unhyang's words" (tr. of So Chongju). QRL (22) 81, p. 36.

"Thought/Fragment" (tr. of So Chongju). QRL (22) 81, p. 64.

"Twilight" (tr. of So Chongju). QRL (22) 81, p. 54.

"Untitled: Pine flower's blooming" (tr. of So
    Chongju). QRL (22) 81, p. 68.
"Untitled: Somehow this place becomes an exceedingly
    hard stone interior" (tr. of So Chongju). QRL (22)
    81, p. 24.
"Whispers" (tr. of So Chongju). QRL (22) 81, p. 44.
"Winter Hail" (tr. of So Chongju). QRL (22) 81, p.
    69.
"Winter Sky" (tr. of So Chongju). QRL (22) 81, p.
    46.

2609. McCANN, Janet
    "Academic Kids." KanQ (14:1) Wint 82, p. 149.

2610. McCANN, K. P.
    "The Trouble with Wings." Bogg (48) 82, p. 55-56.

2611. McCANN, Pat
    "The Dregs." WestCR (16:4) Ap 82, p. 35.
    "Exodus." WestCR (16:4) Ap 82, p. 36.

2612. McCARRISTON, Linda
    "Bucked." Poetry (140:3) Je 82, p. 157.
    "Driveway." Poetry (140:3) Je 82, p. 158.
    "On Horseback" (For the McFauns). Poetry (140:3) Je
        82, p. 156.
    "Quincey's Harvest Moon." Poetry (140:3) Je 82, p.
        155.
    "Riding out at Evening." Poetry (140:3) Je 82, p.
        153-154.

2613. McCARTIN, James T.
    "James Abbott McNeill Whistler." KanQ (14:4) Aut
        82, p. 83.

2614. McCLANE, Kenneth A.
    "Albatross." Shout (3:1) 82, p. 36.
    "At Winter's Solstice." CapeR (17:2) Sum 82, p. 9.
    "The Lilies." StoneC (10:1/2) Aut-Wint 82-83, p.
        27.
    "Meditation at Jones River." Wind (12:44) 82, p.
        24.
    "Morning." Wind (12:44) 82, p. 24.
    "Vineyard Morning." Wind (12:44) 82, p. 26.
    "When Light Hunkers In." Wind (12:44) 82, p. 25-26.
    "A World of Hedges." StoneC (10:1/2) Aut-Wint 82-
        83, p. 27.

2615. McCLATCHY, J. D.
    "Hummingbird." NewYorker (58:19) Je 28, 82, p. 105.
    "Three Conversations with the Sculptor" (for Natalie
        Charkow). Shen (33:1) 81-82, p. 46-47.

2616. McCLELLAND, Bruce
    "Petersburg 1982." Sulfur (2:2, issue 5) 82, p. 54-
        55.
    "Swerves." Sulfur (2:2, issue 5) 82, p. 56.

2617. McCLOSKEY, Mark
    "He Is the Same." PoNow (6:6, issue 36) 82, p. 30.

"I Pretended to Be a Girl." PoetryNW (23:3) Aut 82,
    p. 18.
"In Person." PoetryNW (23:3) Aut 82, p. 17.
"The Jews Have Thanksgiving Dinner." PoetryNW
    (23:3) Aut 82, p. 18-19.
"My Life in the Boots." PoetryNW (23:3) Aut 82, p.
    16-17.
"The Picture Book of the Dead." PoetryNW (23:3) Aut
    82, p. 19.
"The Second Marriage." PoNow (6:5, issue 35) 82, p.
    22.

2618. McCLURE, Andrew
    "Dream Song" (w. Susan McMaster). Grain (10:3) Ag
        82, p. 34-35.
    "Shadowless on black spruce" (w. Susan McMaster).
        Grain (10:3) Ag 82, p. 36-37.

2619. McCLURE, Michael
    "Blues." PortR (28:1) 82, p. 20.
    "Hymn to Kwannon." PortR (28:1) 82, p. 19.
    "Poem: Sure, let's celebrate the black side of joy."
        PortR (28:1) 82, p. 20.

2620. McCLURE, Mitch
    "The Retarded Boy Visits a Pentecostal Church."
        HolCrit (19:1) F 82, p. 20.
    "Retriever." QW (15) Aut-Wint 82-83, p. 64.

2621. McCOLLUM, Eric (Eric E.)
    from Miles from Town: 4 Stanzas. LittleBR (1:4) Sum
        81, p. 49-51.
    "Storm." KanO (14:3) Sum 82, p. 179.

2622. McCONNELL, Michael
    "Creation." Poem (44) Mr 82, p. 8.
    "Winter As Revelation." Poem (44) Mr 82, p. 7.

2623. McCOWN, Clint
    "Columbus." PoNow (7:1, issue 37) 82, p. 30.
    "Missing Link Sausages." PoNow (7:1, issue 37) 82,
        p. 30.

2624. McCOY, Joan
    "On Digressing (from Interstate 70)." LittleBR
        (2:4) Sum 82, p. 19.

2625. McCRACKEN, Kathleen
    "Before the Storm." PoetryCR (4:2) Wint 82, p. 12.

2626. McCULLOUGH, Ken
    "Looking Out on the Strait of Juan De Fuca." NewL
        (48:2) Wint 81-82, p. 49.

2627. McCURDY, Harold
    "Beside the Still Waters." ChrC (99:26) Ag 18-25,
        82, p. 855.

2628. McDANIEL, Wilma Elizabeth
"After a Divorce." WormR (22:2, issue 86) 82, p. 43.
"Assessment." WormR (22:2, issue 86) 82, p. 42.
"Barter System." WormR (22:2, issue 86) 82, p. 71.
"Battered Stetsons." WormR (22:2, issue 86) 82, p. 65.
"Birthday Gift." WormR (22:2, issue 86) 82, p. 64.
"Celebrating the Fourth of July." WormR (22:2, issue 86) 82, p. 44.
"Change of Clothing." WormR (22:2, issue 86) 82, p. 65.
"The Collector." WormR (22:2, issue 86) 82, p. 47.
"Conversion." WormR (22:2, issue 86) 82, p. 60.
"Credibility." WormR (22:2, issue 86) 82, p. 57.
"Day after a Divorce." WormR (22:2, issue 86) 82, p. 61.
"December 28th." WormR (22:2, issue 86) 82, p. 62.
"Diet for One Day." WormR (22:2, issue 86) 82, p. 62.
"Equals." WormR (22:2, issue 86) 82, p. 52.
"Expenses." WormR (22:2, issue 86) 82, p. 72.
"A Father's Insight." WormR (22:2, issue 86) 82, p. 66.
"Flowers In a Tin Can." WormR (22:2, issue 86) 82, p. 41.
"Going Away Costume." WormR (22:2, issue 86) 82, p. 50.
"Grooming." WormR (22:2, issue 86) 82, p. 48.
"Habits." WormR (22:2, issue 86) 82, p. 49.
"Headgear." WormR (22:2, issue 86) 82, p. 69.
"Homicide." WormR (22:2, issue 86) 82, p. 46.
"Horticulture." WormR (22:2, issue 86) 82, p. 49.
"Ignorance." WormR (22:2, issue 86) 82, p. 54.
"Insight." WormR (22:2, issue 86) 82, p. 63.
"January Passage." WormR (22:2, issue 86) 82, p. 71.
"Jared's Candy." WormR (22:2, issue 86) 82, p. 63.
"The Jester." WormR (22:2, issue 86) 82, p. 47.
"Library." WormR (22:2, issue 86) 82, p. 64.
"Litany." WormR (22:2, issue 86) 82, p. 74.
"Memorials." WormR (22:2, issue 86) 82, p. 45.
"Messenger." WormR (22:2, issue 86) 82, p. 76.
"Miser." WormR (22:2, issue 86) 82, p. 54.
"Nightmares." WormR (22:2, issue 86) 82, p. 55.
"Obese Neighbor." WormR (22:2, issue 86) 82, p. 73.
"Old Times of 1950." WormR (22:2, issue 86) 82, p. 42.
"Phonies." WormR (22:2, issue 86) 82, p. 51.
"Poor Street Journal." WormR (22:2, issue 86) 82, p. 74.
"Prisoner." WormR (22:2, issue 86) 82, p. 76.
"Question." WormR (22:2, issue 86) 82, p. 52.
"Ritual." WormR (22:2, issue 86) 82, p. 75.
"Royalty." WormR (22:2, issue 86) 82, p. 75.
"Selecting Christmas Cards." WormR (22:2, issue 86) 82, p. 68.
"Social Climber." WormR (22:2, issue 86) 82, p. 56.
"Spendthrift." WormR (22:2, issue 86) 82, p. 53.
"Stood Up." WormR (22:2, issue 86) 82, p. 67.

"Style." WormR (22:2, issue 86) 82, p. 53.
"Surprises." WormR (22:2, issue 86) 82, p. 46.
"Then and Now." WormR (22:2, issue 86) 82, p. 55.
"Travel." WormR (22:2, issue 86) 82, p. 48.
"Ultimatum." WormR (22:2, issue 86) 82, p. 43.
"Visitors." WormR (22:2, issue 86) 82, p. 68.
"Wars." WormR (22:2, issue 86) 82, p. 69.
"A Widow's Game." WormR (22:2, issue 86) 82, p. 70.
"Wishes." WormR (22:2, issue 86) 82, p. 70.

2629. McDONALD, Kevin
"Chris, the Joey (1958-1968)." LittleBR (2:4) Sum
82, p. 87.
"A Visit to Osawatomie State Hospital: Paul."
LittleBR (2:4) Sum 82, p. 87.

2630. McDONALD, L. M.
"Lines for Girl on a Californian Highway." PottPort
(4) 82-83, p. 39.
"Thoughts on an Unborn Child." PottPort (4) 82-83,
p. 32.

2631. McDONOUGH, Robert E.
"Grounder." Pig (9) 82, p. 21.

2632. McDOWELL, Robert
"Put Your Hand Up to the TV and Touch Mine." Kayak
(59) Je 82, p. 13.

2633. McDUFF, David
"Bees, Honey" (tr. of Paal-Helge Haugen, w. David
McDuff). Stand (23:3) 82, p. 44.
"For Olav H. Hauge" (tr. of Paal-Helge Haugen, w.
David McDuff). Stand (23:3) 82, p. 44.
"Going Back Again." Stand (23:2) 82, p. 60.
"Music: of Earth, and Stone, and the People" (tr. of
Paal-Helge Haugen, w. David McDuff and Toralf
Moller Hansen). Stand (23:3) 82, p. 45.
"Slowly" (tr. of Rolf Jacobsen). Stand (23:3) 82, p.
11.

2634. McELROY, Colleen J.
"The Ways of Women." KanQ (14:3) Sum 82, p. 45.

2635. McFADDEN, David
"Adults at Play." AntigR (51) Aut 82, p. 51-52.

2636. McFADDEN, Mary Ann
"The Heron." Kayak (59) Je 82, p. 27.
"Tar Queen." Kayak (59) Je 82, p. 26.

2637. McFARLAND, Ron
"No Demand." PoNow (7:1, issue 37) 82, p. 31.
"Remains of Icarus Uncovered." PoNow (7:1, issue
37) 82, p. 31.
"There's Something Suspicious." NewL (49:1) Aut 82,
p. 28.

2638. McFEE, Michael
"Bean Arbor." WestHR (36:2) Sum 82, p. 134.

"Doves." Poem (46) N 82, p. 19.
"Eclogue." Poem (46) N 82, p. 18.
"Twice in the Same Place." KanQ (14:1) Wint 82, p.
113.

2639. McFERREN, Martha
"The Burning of The Crystal Palace, May 2, 1851."
LitR (25:3) Spr 82, p. 380-381.
"Louisiana Buzz." CharR (8:1) Spr 82, p. 47.

2640. McFERRIN, Terri
"Drawing a Breath." CutB (19) Aut-Wint 82, p. 58-
59.

2641. McGANN, Jerome
"The Roland Park Poems." Shen (33:3) 82, p. 60-65.

2642. McGORMAN, Don
"Intervals, with Shakespeare" (for J.). MalR (61) F
82, p. 150-152.

2643. McGOWAN, James
"For a Creole Lady" (tr. of Charles Baudelaire).
SouthernHR (16:2) Spr 82, p. 116.
"A Former Life" (tr. of Charles Baudelaire).
HiramPoR (32) Spr-Sum 82, p. 33.
"Sorrows of the Moon" (tr. of Charles Pierre
Baudelaire). Northeast (3:12) Wint 81-82, p. 15.
"Spleen (I)" (tr. of Charles Baudelaire). HiramPoR
(32) Spr-Sum 82, p. 34.
"Spleen (II)" (tr. of Charles Baudelaire). HiramPoR
(32) Spr-Sum 82, p. 35.

2644. McGOWAN, Jim
"Apologie for John Donne." Bogg (48) 82, p. 70.
"Sweetest love, I did thee wronge." Bogg (49) 82,
p. 36.

2645. McGRATH, Thomas
"Letter to an Imaginary Friend: Christmas Section
(III)." TriQ (55) Aut 82, p. 181-197.

2646. McGUIGAN, Dana
"Francesca." HolCrit (19:2) Ap 82, p. 11.

2647. McHUGH, Heather
"Fast and Straight." Kayak (59) Je 82, p. 8.
"I Knew I'd Sing." Kayak (59) Je 82, p. 6.
"Mean Mother." Kayak (59) Je 82, p. 9.
"On Faith." Iowa (12:2/3) Spr-Sum 81, p. 236.
"Person and Number." Kayak (59) Je 82, p. 7.

2648. McHUGH, Paul
"Interlude to Doeschka." MendoR (6) Sum 81, p. 68.
"Michigan Winter: TheEnd of an Affair" (a poetic
sequence). MendoR (6) Sum 81, p. 66-70.

2649. McILROY, Brian
"To Bron Whilst at Home." Bogg (49) 82, p. 52.

2650. McINTYRE, Sandra
      "To a First Love." Bogg (48) 82, p. 62.

2651. McKAIN, David
      "The Birdcarver." CentR (26:2) Spr 82, p. 173.
      "The Death of Six Horses." ModernPS (11:1/2) 82, p.
      58.

2652. McKEAN, James
      "Bindweed." PoetryNW (23:3) Aut 82, p. 39.
      "Bull Slaughter." Atl (250:1) Jl 82, p. 54.
      "Rowing for Water." Agni (16) 82, p. 121.

2653. McKENZIE-PORTER, Patricia
      "On Seing the '81 Portfolio." PottPort (4) 82-83,
      p. 28.
      "Out of Season." PottPort (4) 82-83, p. 23.

2654. McKEOWN, Tom
      "Alone in Autumn." MichQR (21:1) Wint 82, p. 162-
      163.
      "Hymn to the Marvelous." Kayak (59) Je 82, p. 47.
      "Octopus Wheelchair." Kayak (59) Je 82, p. 46.

2655. McKERNAN, John
      "The Ballad of Foreknowledge." VirQR (58:1) Wint
      82, p. 61.
      "The Early Map." OhioR (29) 82, p. 34-35.
      "Loud Chant in the Darkness." VirQR (58:1) Wint 82,
      p. 62.
      "Platform." OhioR (29) 82, p. 34.
      "The Song of Light." VirQR (58:1) Wint 82, p. 60.
      "Victory Cry of the Unconscious Flagpole." VirQR
      (58:1) Wint 82, p. 61.

2656. McKINNEY, Irene
      "Death-Person." Confr (24) Sum 82, p. 31-32.
      "An Invitation to My Body." MassR (23:1) Spr 82, p.
      152.
      "Little Sister I." Confr (24) Sum 82, p. 31.

2657. McKINNEY, Paul
      "How I hate haiku." WindO (40, Anti-Haiku issue)
      Sum 82, p. 24.

2658. McKINSEY, Martin
      "A Day Will Come" (tr. of Manolis Anagnostakis).
      Chelsea (41) 82, p. 126.
      "The Great Decisions" (tr. of Manolis Anagnostakis).
      Chelsea (41) 82, p. 122.
      "Not This Way" (tr. of Manolis Anagnostakis).
      Chelsea (41) 82, p. 124.
      "Now, I Speak Again" (tr. of Manolis Anagnostakis).
      Chelsea (41) 82, p. 123.
      "There Is Not the Many" (tr. of Manolis
      Anagnostakis). Chelsea (41) 82, p. 125.

2659. McKNIGHT, Frances Elizabeth
      "A Mother." WritersL Jl 82, p. 22.

2660. McLAIN, Geoffrey
      "Winter Lambing." <u>Grain</u> (10:2) My 82, p. 14.

2661. McLAUGHLIN, Dorothy
      "The Kiln." <u>StoneC</u> (10:1/2) Aut-Wint 82-83, p. 33.

2662. McLAUGHLIN, Joe-Anne
      "Great-Aunt Francesca." <u>Ploughs</u> (8:2/3) 82, p. 151.

2663. McLAUGHLIN, William
      "Conversation among Five Frescoed Warrior Saints"
         (tr. of Anonymous). <u>CapeR</u> (17:2) Sum 82, p. 29.
      "Down the Tube." <u>WestB</u> (10) 82, p. 58-59.
      "Ein Blick auf einem Blick." <u>WestB</u> (10) 82, p. 60-
         61.
      "Ice on the Pond." <u>PraS</u> (56:3) Aut 82, p. 49.

2664. McLAURIN, Ken
      "Iron." <u>WindO</u> (41) Aut-Wint 82-83, p. 23.
      "Storm Pit." <u>Wind</u> (12:46) 82, p. 48.

2665. McLEAN, Reg
      "My Great Grandmother." <u>MendoR</u> (5) Sum 81, p. 65.

2666. McLEOD, John
      "A Vision of Being." <u>Bogg</u> (48) 82, p. 60-61.

2667. McMAHON, Lynne
      "Asthma." <u>Iowa</u> (12:2/3) Spr-Sum 81, p. 237.

2668. McMAHON, Michael Beirne
      "Of Hubris and Guiness." <u>Bogg</u> (48) 82, p. 28.

2669. McMASTER, Susan
      "Canadian Spring." <u>WritersL</u> Ag 82, p. 4.
      "Dream Song" (w. Andrew McClure). <u>Grain</u> (10:3) Ag
         82, p. 34-35.
      "Letter to Silence." <u>Quarry</u> (31:4) Aut 82, p. 45-
         46.
      "Shadowless on black spruce" (w. Andrew McClure).
         <u>Grain</u> (10:3) Ag 82, p. 36-37.
      "Spring Over Grown." <u>Quarry</u> (31:4) Aut 82, p. 45.

2670. McMULLEN, Richard E.
      "The Damned Voices." <u>Comm</u> (109:12) Je 18, 82, p.
         375.

2671. McNAIR, Wesley
      "Calling Harold." <u>Ploughs</u> (8:2/3) 82, p. 23.
      "The Fat People of the Old Days." <u>Ploughs</u> (8:2/3)
         82, p. 22-23.
      "Old Trees." <u>Ploughs</u> (8:2/3) 82, p. 21.

2672. McNAMARA, Eugene
      "The Gift." <u>PoetryCR</u> (4:2) Wint 82, p. 13.
      "History." <u>CrossC</u> (4:4) 82, p. 6.

2673. McNEES, Eleanor
      "Embalming." <u>CapeR</u> (17:2) Sum 82, p. 47.

"For Christopher and Tolouse-Lautrec." <u>CapeR</u> (17:2)
     Sum 82, p. 46.

2674. McPHEE, Linda
     "Bread & Roses." <u>Hangl</u> (43) Wint 82-83, p. 34-35.

2675. McPHERSON, Sandra
     "The Anointing." <u>Iowa</u> (13:1) Wint 82, p. 116.
     "Earthstars, Birthparents' House." <u>Antaeus</u> (47) Aut
          82, p. 28.
     "Helen Todd: My Birthname." <u>Iowa</u> (13:1) Wint 82, p.
          115.
     "If the Cardinals Were Like Us." <u>NowestR</u> (20:2/3)
          82, p. 27-28.
     "Ode Near the Aspen Music School." <u>Antaeus</u> (47) Aut
          82, p. 29-31.
     "Only Once." <u>Poetry</u> (140:4) Jl 82, p. 190.
     "Peter is Here." <u>Poetry</u> (140:4) Jl 82, p. 189.
     "Pornography, Nebraska." <u>Antaeus</u> (44) Wint 82, p.
          84-85.
     "Trap-shooting Range" (Additional Lines for Johannes
          Bobrowski) <u>Antaeus</u> (44) Wint 82, p. 83.
     "Unitarian Easter." <u>Antaeus</u> (44) Wint 82, p. 81.
     "Urban Ode." <u>Poetry</u> (140:4) Jl 82, p. 187-188.
     "Utanikki, August 1978 (for A.K.). <u>Iowa</u> (12:2/3)
          Spr-Sum 81, p. 238-239.
     "The White Shirt." <u>Antaeus</u> (44) Wint 82, p. 82.
     "Wings and Seeds: For My Birth Mother." <u>Poetry</u>
          (140:4) Jl 82, p. 191.

2676. McQUADE, Molly
     "Beach Plums." <u>Tendril</u> (13) Sum 82, p. 49.
     "He Comes Home after a Business Trip." <u>Tendril</u> (13)
          Sum 82, p. 48.
     "Secret People." <u>NoAmR</u> (267:2) Je 82, p. 28.

2677. McQUILKIN, Rennie
     "Black Ice." <u>KanQ</u> (14:4) Aut 82, p. 98.
     "Carnival." <u>PoNow</u> (7:1, issue 37) 82, p. 32.
     "The Flower Man." <u>SmPd</u> (19:3, issue 56) Aut 82, p.
          6.
     "For an Edwardian Lady, Drowned While Picking a
          Chestnut Flower." <u>ColEng</u> 44(8) D 82, p. 809.
     "Her Will." <u>LitR</u> (25:3) Spr 82, p. 366.
     "Isobel at 87." <u>Poetry</u> (139:4) Ja 82, p. 219.
     "Lester." <u>BelPoJ</u> (33:1) Aut 82, p. 13.
     "Miss Caroline." <u>Poetry</u> (139:4) Ja 82, p. 220.
     "Prayer." <u>SmPd</u> (19:2, issue 55) Spr 82, p. 23.
     "Rendezvous in a Country Churchyard." <u>Poetry</u>
          (140:3) Je 82, p. 152.
     "Song of My Selves" (for Lewis Thomas). <u>HiramPoR</u>
          (32) Spr-Sum 82, p. 38.
     "Thief." <u>PoNow</u> (7:1, issue 37) 82, p. 32.
     "Tucker, Truman, Drill Sergeant, U.S.M.C." <u>PoNow</u>
          (7:1, issue 37) 82, p. 32.
     "Wild Grapes." <u>ColEng</u> 44(8) D 82, p. 809.

2678. McROBERTS, Robert
     "Apples." <u>PoetryCR</u> (3:3) Spr 82, p. 15.

2679. McWHIRTER, George
"The Voyeur and the Countess Wielopolska." PoetryCR
(4:2) Wint 82, p. 7.

2680. MEARS, Charlotte
"Old Man in a Garret Room." Nimrod (26:1) Aut-Wint
82, p. 69.

2681. MEATS, Stephen
"Elephants Attack Village." LittleBR (2:4) Sum 82,
p. 13.
"Prairie Winter." LittleBR (3:2) Wint 82-83, p. 30.

2682. MECHCATIE, Oliver
"Bloodstones." Os (15) 82, p. 6.
"Night Ensemble." Os (15) 82, p. 9.

2683. MECKEL, Christoph
"Primeval Forest" (tr. by Carol Bedwell). WebR (7:2)
Aut 82, p. 21.
"Song of Lademli Lolle" (tr. by Carol Bedwell). WebR
(7:2) Aut 82, p. 20.

2684. MEDINA, Pablo
"The Ivory Tower." Poetry (140:2) My 82, p. 97.
"Return to Dunbarton Oaks" (For Barbara Selig).
Poetry (140:2) My 82, p. 98.

2685. MEEKS, Dodie
"If I Mail Seashells." SouthwR (67:3) Sum 82, p.
281.

2686. MEHREN, Stein
"Apple Tree" (tr. by Goran Printz-Pahlson). Stand
(23:3) 82, p. 37.
"Nr 58" (tr. by Goran Printz-Pahlson). Stand (23:3)
82, p. 38.
"The Old Barn" (tr. by Goran Printz-Pahlson). Stand
(23:3) 82, p. 39.

2687. MEHROTRA, Arvind Krishna
"All Alone" (tr. of Nirala). NewL (48:3/4) Spr-Sum
82, p. 93.
"The Betrayal" (tr. of Nirala). NewL (48:3/4) Spr-
Sum 82, p. 93.b:
"Don't Tie the Skiff" (tr. of Nirala). NewL (48:3/4)
Spr-Sum 82, p. 92.
"Engraving of a Bison on Stone." NewL (48:3/4) Spr-
Sum 82, p. 96.
"His Touch Woke Up" (tr. of Nirala). NewL (49:2)
Wint 82-83, p. 52.
"Ignorance" (tr. of Nirala). NewL (48:3/4) Spr-Sum
82, p. 94.
"It Sits Everywhere" (tr. of Nirala). NewL (49:2)
Wint 82-83, p. 54.
"The King Gets Away" (tr. of Nirala). NewL (49:2)
Wint 82-83, p. 53.
"Love Song" (tr. of Nirala). NewL (48:3/4) Spr-Sum
82, p. 92.

"Poem in Five Parts" (tr. of Nirala). NewL (49:2)
Wint 82-83, p. 53-54.
"River Stop." NewL (48:3/4) Spr-Sum 82, p. 95-96.
"Soundings (A Fragment)" (tr. of Nirala). NewL
(48:3/4) Spr-Sum 82, p. 94.
"The Telegram" (for A. J.). NewL (48:3/4) Spr-Sum
82, p. 95.
"There Was Mist" (tr. of Nirala). NewL (48:3/4) Spr-
Sum 82, p. 94.
"You Aren't Him" (tr. of Nirala). NewL (49:2) Wint
82-83, p. 52.

2688. MEIER, Kay
"Finalist." EngJ (71:5) S 82, p. 76.
"Night Rooms." CapeR (17:2) Sum 82, p. 36.

MEIGS, James Hawley
See: HAWLEY-MEIGS, James

2689. MEINKE, Peter
"The Gift of the Magi." Poetry (141:3) D 82, p.
127-128.
"Greta Garbo Poem #41." PoNow (6:5, issue 35) 82,
p. 25.
"The Laughter of Dead Poets." PoNow (6:5, issue 35)
82, p. 25.
"Miss Arbuckle." PoNow (6:5, issue 35) 82, p. 25.

2690. MEISSNER, William
"The Baseball Lover." KanQ (14:3) Sum 82, p. 181.
"Champions." PoNow (6:4, issue 34) 82, p. 44.
"The Education of Martin Halsted." Northeast (3:12)
Wint 81-82, p. 19.
"Hunting at the End of the Wilderness." SouthernPR
(22:1) Spr 82, p. 33.
"Husband Shoveling Snow from the Roof." QW (14)
Spr-Sum 82, p. 16-17.

2691. MELAKOPIDES, Costas
"Sophist Leaving Syria" (1926, tr. of Constantin
Cavafy). Quarry (31:4) Aut 82, p. 42.
"To Stay" (1918, tr. of Constantin Cavafy). Quarry
(31:4) Aut 82, p. 40-41.
"When They Are Aroused" (1913, tr. of Constantin
Cavafy). Quarry (31:4) Aut 82, p. 41.

MELENDEZ, Manuel Figueroa
See: FIGUEROA-MELENDEZ, Manuel

2692. MELHEM, D. H.
"Aphasia." Confr (23) Wint 82, p. 81.
"Retrieval." Confr (23) Wint 82, p. 81.

MELLO BREYNER ANDRESEN, Sophia de
See: ANDRESEN, Sophia de Mello Breyner

2693. MELNYCZUK, Askold
"Never the Kind." Agni (17) 82, p. 172.

"We Who Have No Future: Fragments of a Credo, in Verse" (tr. of Valentyn Vorog). _Agni_ (16) 82, p. 133-145.

2694. MELVIN, Gregg
"From the Science Library" (found poem). _Kayak_ (58) Ja 82, p. 15.

2695. MENASHE, Samuel
"Grief." _Im_ (8:2) 82, p. 9.
"Non-Stop Flight." _Im_ (8:2) 82, p. 9.
"The Oracle." _Im_ (8:2) 82, p. 9.
"Prowess." _Im_ (8:2) 82, p. 9.
"Waterfall." _Im_ (8:2) 82, p. 9.
"Waves." _Im_ (8:2) 82, p. 9.

2696. MENDEZ, Luis
"La Muerte Que Adelanto." _Maize_ (6:1/2) Aut-Wint 82-83, p. 86.

2697. MENDINI, Douglas A.
"Dad." _SmPd_ (19:3, issue 56) Aut 82, p. 27.

MENDOZA, Ester Feliciano
See: FELICIANO MENDOZA, Ester

2698. MENDOZA, Rafael
"Secreto Profesional." _Maize_ (6:1/2) Aut-Wint 82-83, p. 88.

2699. MENEBROKER, Ann
"The Blue Fish." _Bogg_ (48) 82, p. 33.
"Love." _Bogg_ (48) 82, p. 33.
"Manuscripts." _WormR_ (22:4, issue 88) 82, p. 150.
"The Marathon Man & the Aging Poet." _WormR_ (22:4, issue 88) 82, p. 148-149.
"Old Times." _WormR_ (22:4, issue 88) 82, p. 148.
"Paul F." _WormR_ (22:4, issue 88) 82, p. 149.
"Realization." _WormR_ (22:4, issue 88) 82, p. 149.
"Script." _Bogg_ (49) 82, p. 11.
"Torch Song." _Bogg_ (48) 82, p. 33.
"Valley Living." _WormR_ (22:4, issue 88) 82, p. 148.

2700. MENEN DESLEAL, Alvaro
"Oracion Que Ayuda a Bien Condenarse a un Tirano" (Recese tres veces diarias y se tendran 90 dias indulgencia plenaria). _Maize_ (6:1/2) Aut-Wint 82-83, p. 80-81.

2701. MENG, Hao-jan
"Spring Dawn" (tr. by Arthur Bull). _Dandel_ (9:1) 82, p. 22.

2702. MENZA, Claudia
"Lunch on the Sand." _Confr_ (23) Wint 82, p. 97.

2703. MERCER, Anthony
"Among the Amish." _FourQt_ (31:4) Sum 82, p. 28.

2704. MEREDITH, Bernard
       "At a Small Cemetery on the Pennsylvania Border."
       SewanR (90:2) Spr 82, p. 222.

2705. MEREDITH, William
       "The Seasons' Difference." Paint (7/8:13/16) 80-81,
       p. 39.

2706. MERRILL, Christopher
       "A Boy Juggling His Soccer Ball." PoetryNW (23:2)
       Sum 82, p. 12-13.

2707. MERRILL, James
       "After the Ball." Poetry (141:1) O 82, p. 17.
       "The Blue Grotto." Poetry (141:1) O 82, p. 16.
       "The House Fly." NewYRB (29:8) My 13, 82, p. 6.
       "The 'Metro'." NewYorker (58:12) My 10, 82, p. 38.
       "Palme" (tr. of Paul Ambroise Valery). NewYRB (29:4)
       Mr 18, 82, p. 10.
       "Processional." Atl (250:5) N 82, p. 68.
       "Santorini: Stopping the Leak." NewYorker (58:31) S
       20, 82, p. 36-37.
       "An Upset." NewYorker (58:1) F 22, 82, p. 38.

2708. MERRILL, Tim
       "Early Fall." MalR (62) Jl 82, p. 214.

2709. MERRIMAN, Conrad
       "Tasteful." Germ (6:2) Aut-Wint 82, p. 27.

2710. MERTZ, Lisa
       "Unemployed." Shout (3:1) 82, p. 43.

2711. MERWIN, W. S.
       "After a Storm." NewYorker (58:8) Ap 12, 82, p. 44.
       "Ali." Iowa (13:1) Wint 82, p. 28-29.
       "Birdie." Iowa (13:1) Wint 82, p. 19-20.
       "The Black Jewel." Iowa (13:1) Wint 82, p. 22.
       "The Burnt Child." Iowa (13:1) Wint 82, p. 21.
       "The Cart." Nat (234:19) My 15, 82, p. 600.
       "Coming Back in the Spring." NewYorker (58:13) My
       17, 82, p. 42-43.
       "Dark Side." AmerPoR (11:5) S-O 82, p. 4.
       "The Fields." NewYorker (58:33) O 4, 82, p. 42.
       "Green Island." AmerPoR (11:5) S-O 82, p. 4.
       "Hearing." NewYorker (58:37) N 1, 82, p. 46.
       "The Houses." Iowa (13:1) Wint 82, p. 23-26.
       "Living Together." AmerPoR (11:5) S-O 82, p. 4-5.
       "The Middle of Summer." YaleR (71:4) Sum 82, p.
       579.
       "One Night." YaleR (71:4) Sum 82, p. 579.
       "The Quoit." NewYorker (58:30) S 13, 82, p. 40.
       "The Shore." Iowa (13:1) Wint 82, p. 27.
       "St. Valentine's Eve." AmerPoR (11:5) S-O 82, p. 3.
       "Turning to You." AmerPoR (11:5) S-O 82, p. 3.
       "Unknown Forebear." Nat (234:15) Ap 17, 82, p. 472.

2712. MESCHERY, Tom
       "Drinks All Around." PoNow (6:5, issue 35) 82, p.
       47.

2713. MESSER, Richard E.
      "Explaining the Rise in Infant Mortality around
         Three Mile Island." <u>Pig</u> (8) 80, p. 78.
      "Interiors." <u>Pig</u> (8) 80, p. 60.

2714. MESSERLI, Douglas
      "Skinning the Deer." <u>Gargoyle</u> (15/16) 80, p. 61.

2715. METRAS, Gary
      "Coming to Water." <u>UnderRM</u> 1(1) Spr 82, p. 14.
      "Deceits of Animals." <u>Sam</u> (33:3, issue 131) 82, p.
         24.
      "Teaching the Children." <u>UnderRM</u> 1(1) Spr 82, p.
         16.

2716. METZ, Roberta
      "Home Movies." <u>PoNow</u> (6:6, issue 36) 82, p. 15.
      "One-Colored Chameleon." <u>KanO</u> (14:3) Sum 82, p. 43.
      "Oscar." <u>PoNow</u> (6:6, issue 36) 82, p. 15.
      "Some Ducks." <u>PoNow</u> (6:6, issue 36) 82, p. 15.
      "Why I Always Keep Stones in My Pockets." <u>Pig</u> (8)
         80, p. 27.

2717. METZGER, Jonathan
      "I touched the knife." <u>PoNow</u> (7:1, issue 37) 82, p.
         32.

2718. MEUDT, Edna
      "Report to Robert Frost." <u>Abraxas</u> (25/26) 82, p.
         112.

2719. MEYERS, Christene Cosgriffe
      "Garage Sale." <u>Tendril</u> (13) Sum 82, p. 50.

2720. MEZEY, Robert
      "The Owl." <u>Kayak</u> (59) Je 82, p. 10.

2721. MICHAEL, Christine
      "A Petrol Bomb." <u>Vis</u> (8) 82, p. 19.

      MICHELE, Mary di
      <u>See</u>: Di MICHELE, Mary

2722. MICHELINE, Jack
      "Go Home and Blow" (from Skinny Dynamite). <u>SeC</u> (8:2)
         80, p. 49-50.
      "Homage to Mickey" (from Skinny Dynamite). <u>SeC</u> (8:2)
         80, p. 32.
      "Let's Ride on the Angel, Goodbye" (from Skinny
         Dynamite). <u>SeC</u> (8:2) 80, p. 79-80.

2723. MICHELSON, Richard
      "From the Bench." <u>PoetryNW</u> (23:1) Spr 82, p. 42-43.
      "The Latest Fashions." <u>SouthernPR</u> (23, i.e. 22:2)
         Aut 82, p. 40.

2724. MICKLEY, Loretta
      "In June." <u>CarolO</u> (34:3) Spr 82, p. 14.

2725. MIDDLETON, David
    "Compline." SouthernR (18:2) Spr 82, p. 367.
    "The Sirens." SouthernR (18:2) Spr 82, p. 365-366.

2726. MIKLITSCH, Robert
    "The Bait." MissR (10:3, issue 30) Wint-Spr 82, p.
        47-48.
    "Domestic Vision." MissR (10:3, issue 30) Wint-Spr
        82, p. 49-50.
    "Hesitation Waltz." SouthernPR (23, i.e. 22:2) Aut
        82, p. 26-27.
    "Paris Recherche." MissR (10:3, issue 30) Wint-Spr
        82, p. 51.
    "Pear." SouthernPR (23, i.e. 22:2) Aut 82, p. 28.

    MILAGROS PEREZ, Maria de los
    See: PEREZ, Maria de los Milagros

2727. MILBURN, Michael
    "Amiens 1977." Agni (17) 82, p. 99.
    "Days of 1974." Agni (17) 82, p. 98.
    "The Far Frame." PraS (56:3) Aut 82, p. 75-76.
    "Girl Asleep in Library." Agni (17) 82, p. 95.
    "The Hunter." Agni (17) 82, p. 102.
    "The Letters." Agni (17) 82, p. 96-97.
    "Mussels." Agni (17) 82, p. 93-94.
    "Narragansett." PraS (56:3) Aut 82, p. 73.
    "Portrait." Agni (17) 82, p. 91-92.
    "Such Silence." Agni (17) 82, p. 100-101.
    "The View." PraS (56:3) Aut 82, p. 74.

2728. MILES, Josephine
    "Afternoon Walk." Iowa (12:2/3) Spr-Sum 81, p. 240.
    "Capitol" (indexed from (32:1), p. 89). Epoch (31:1)
        Aut 81, p. 90 ff.
    "For Magistrates" (indexed from (32:1), p. 89).
        Epoch (31:1) Aut 81, p. 90 ff.
    "He Said" (indexed from (32:1), p. 89). Epoch (31:1)
        Aut 81, p. 90 ff.
    "Ions" (indexed from (32:1), p. 89). Epoch (31:1)
        Aut 81, p. 90 ff.
    "My House is Afire" (tr. of Balakrishna Sharma).
        NewL (48:3/4) Spr-Sum 82, p. 189.
    "Vigils." Shen (33:3) 82, p. 92.
    "West from Ithaca" (indexed from (32:1), p. 89).
        Epoch (31:1) Aut 81, p. 90 ff.

2729. MILES, Ron
    "Forest." CanLit (93) Sum 82, p. 25.
    "Old Man Falling." CanLit (93) Sum 82, p. 176.

2730. MILES, Sara
    "Doing Time" (for Michael Fury). Iowa (12:2/3) Spr-
        Sum 81, p. 241-242.

2731. MILLEN, Alan
    "Harewood Field." PoetryCR (3:3) Spr 82, p. 13.
    "Scrag Fight." PoetryCR (4:1) Sum 82, p. 11.

2732. MILLEN, Ivan
    "Blueberry Highway." <u>PottPort</u> (4) 82-83, p. 45.
    "Missing Person." <u>PottPort</u> (4) 82-83, p. 43.
    "These Chains." <u>PottPort</u> (4) 82-83, p. 41.

2733. MILLER, A. McA.
    "Confession" (from Patton). <u>StoneC</u> (10:1/2) Aut-Wint
        82-83, p. 49.
    "Miss Paam" (Ben Cat., Vietnam). <u>Spirit</u> (6:2/3) 82,
        p. 151.
    "The War Come Home." <u>StoneC</u> (10:1/2) Aut-Wint 82-
        83, p. 76-77.

2734. MILLER, Brown
    "These Are Not Words and You Are Not Reading." <u>NewL</u>
        (48:2) Wint 81-82, p. 67.
    "We Dance Birth/We Relax Death." <u>SeC</u> (9:1/2) 80, p.
        3-4.
    "When Both Mayors of San Francisco Were Killed."
        <u>SeC</u> (9:1/2) 80, p. 13.
    "When You Touch the H on Any Typewriter Please
        Think." <u>NewL</u> (48:2) Wint 81-82, p. 67.

2735. MILLER, Carl
    "Charles Darwin Facing Innocence." <u>Chelsea</u> (41) 82,
        p. 90.
    "Jim Gibbs." <u>Shout</u> (3:1) 82, p. 27.
    "Walter Alves Pereira." <u>Shout</u> (3:1) 82, p. 26.

2736. MILLER, Carolyn Reynolds
    "At Night, New Suburbs, Their Streetlamps Salty."
        <u>PoetryNW</u> (23:4) Wint 82-83, p. 12-13.
    "Home Repairs." <u>PoetryNW</u> (23:4) Wint 82-83, p. 11-
        12.
    "Ma Bete." <u>PoetryNW</u> (23:4) Wint 82-83, p. 10-11.
    "Passing Spectres near Prescott, Washington" (for
        Scott and the town boys). <u>PoetryNW</u> (23:2) Sum 82,
        p. 17-18.
    "Surface Tension Around the Heart, Like Heaven."
        <u>PoetryNW</u> (23:4) Wint 82-83, p. 13-14.

2737. MILLER, Chuck
    "Requiem: A Surrealist Graveyard." <u>Spirit</u> (6:2/3)
        82, p. 71.

2738. MILLER, David
    "Ten Trees." <u>SouthernPR</u> (22:1) Spr 82, p. 35.

2739. MILLER, E. S.
    "A Rub-A-Dub Rubbing." <u>WebR</u> (7:2) Aut 82, p. 67-68.

2740. MILLER, Hugh
    "All Hail to Our Underseas Forces!" (for Daniel S.
        Silvia). <u>AntigR</u> (48) Wint 82, p. 82.
    "At the Artifactorie" (for Elinor Distler). <u>AntigR</u>
        (50) Sum 82, p. 12.
    "Economic History of Geology" (for John T. Alfors).
        <u>AntigR</u> (48) Wint 82, p. 83.

"Elegy for Giant Oranges, 15 July 1973" (for Prof. Richard T. Curley & Sue). <u>AntigR</u> (51) Aut 82, p. 23.
"Ginny's Science" (for Ginny on her birthday). <u>AntigR</u> (50) Sum 82, p. 11-12.
"Patience in the Central Valley." <u>AntigR</u> (51) Aut 82, p. 22.
"To the Aging Painter" (for Bill Melton). <u>AntigR</u> (50) Sum 82, p. 13.

2741. MILLER, John N.
"Epigram: Daphne and Friend." <u>PikeF</u> (4) Spr 82, p. 11.
"Fetishes." <u>PikeF</u> (4) Spr 82, p. 13.

2742. MILLER, Leslie Adrienne
"After the Commemoration." <u>OP</u> (33) Spr 82, p. 42-43.
"American Summer." <u>NowestR</u> (20:1) 82, p. 86-87.
"The Bass Player's Wife." <u>OP</u> (33) Spr 82, p. 45-46.
"Jealousy." <u>GeoR</u> (36:2) Sum 82, p. 427.
"Spring Fever." <u>OP</u> (33) Spr 82, p. 44.
"The Ventriloquist." <u>KanQ</u> (14:3) Sum 82, p. 186.

2743. MILLER, Lorna H.
"Flying Lesson." <u>ConcPo</u> (15:2) Aut 82, p. 58.

2744. MILLER, Margot
"Les Nympheas." <u>Harp</u> (265:1586) Jl 82, p. 66.

2745. MILLER, Marya F.
"A Polite Good Morning." <u>CrossC</u> (4:4) 82, p. 28.

2746. MILLER, Michael
"Shark." <u>PoNow</u> (7:1, issue 37) 82, p. 33.

2747. MILLER, Pamela
"Letter from Another Hemisphere." <u>Sky</u> (10-12) Aut 82, p. 30-31.
"The Zoology Professor on His Honeymoon." <u>Sky</u> (10-12) Aut 82, p. 29.

2748. MILLER, Philip
"Cats in the House." <u>Confr</u> (23) Wint 82, p. 137.

2749. MILLER, Stephen M.
"Captured" (for Frank King). <u>Abraxas</u> (25/26) 82, p. 81.

2750. MILLER, Vassar
"First Intimation." <u>Iowa</u> (12:2/3) Spr-Sum 81, p. 243.
"Progression." <u>PoNow</u> (6:4, issue 34) 82, p. 31.

2751. MILLER, Walter James
"Z" (In Memory of Louis Zukofsky). <u>LitR</u> (26:1) Aut 82, p. 116-118.

2752. MILLER, Warren C.
"Loop-the-Loop." <u>Wind</u> (12:45) 82, p. 27-28.

"Upstairs." <u>Wind</u> (12:45) 82, p. 27.

MILLER, Wilfredo Cruz
  <u>See</u>: CRUZ MILLER, Wilfredo

2753. MILLIS, Christopher
  "Confessions of a Dinosaur." <u>SoDakR</u> (20:2) Sum 82,
    p. 33.
  "The Perfect Pteradactyl." <u>SoDakR</u> (20:2) Sum 82, p.
    32.

2754. MILLS, George
  "Fisherman." <u>StoneC</u> (10:1/2) Aut-Wint 82-83, p. 26.
  "Road." <u>StoneC</u> (10:1/2) Aut-Wint 82-83, p. 26.

2755. MILLS, Ralph J., Jr.
  "11/80." <u>Telescope</u> (2) Aut 81, p. 12-13.
  "In Early September." <u>Poem</u> (44) Mr 82, p. 2-3.
  "No Moon." <u>Poem</u> (44) Mr 82, p. 1.
  "Winters." <u>Poem</u> (44) Mr 82, p. 4.

2756. MILLS, Sparling
  "7th Floor Flat." <u>AntigR</u> (49) Spr 82, p. 11.
  "Holiday in Chester." <u>PottPort</u> (4) 82-83, p. 35.
  "My Cousin Rachel." <u>PoetryCR</u> (4:1) Sum 82, p. 11.
  "An Old Professor Comes to Town." <u>AntigR</u> (49) Spr
    82, p. 10.
  "Peggy, Growing Old." <u>PoetryCR</u> (3:3) Spr 82, p. 12.
  "Tolkien's Tale." <u>Bogg</u> (49) 82, p. 38.
  "With My Hickory Stick." <u>CrossC</u> (4:4) 82, p. 10.

2757. MILOSZ, Czeslaw
  "Le Monde--C'est Terrible, Cezanne" (From the
    Separate Notebooks, tr. by the author and Robert
    Hass). <u>Pequod</u> (15) 82, p. 11-14.
  "The Separate Notebooks: A Mirrored Gallery" (tr. by
    Robert Hass and Renata Gorczynski). <u>Antaeus</u> (47)
    Aut 82, p. 7-15.

2758. MINER, Ken
  "Untitled: On a clear night." <u>KanQ</u> (14:4) Aut 82,
    p. 97.

2759. MINER, Virginia Scott
  "Apropos of a Japanese Print." <u>NewL</u> (48:2) Wint 81-
    82, p. 49.

2760. MINGUEZ "OREJANILLA," Luis
  "Fuencisla del Amor." <u>Mairena</u> (4:10) Sum-Aut 82, p.
    75.

2761. MINTY, Judith
  "Meditation on Friendship: Getting Lost in the Woods
    with Deena -- Jamesville, NY." <u>Iowa</u> (12:2/3) Spr-
    Sum 81, p. 244-245.

2762. MIRABAL, Mili
  "En Tu Oido." <u>Mairena</u> (4:9) Spr 82, p. 44.

"No soy poeta pero si artesana de suenos y de
fantasias" (from Apuntes de Servilletas). <u>Mairena</u>
(4:9) Spr 82, p. 90.
"Responso." <u>Mairena</u> (4:10) Sum-Aut 82, p. 89.

2763. MIRANDA, Gary
"Clackamas River Suite" (For Clyde Rice, and for
Nicolas). <u>Salm</u> (57) Sum 82, p. 110-113.

2764. MIRE, Stephanie Pearl
"The Fight." <u>BlackALF</u> (16:2) Sum 82, p. 74.
"Like Then, I Don't Need You Now." <u>BlackALF</u> (16:2)
Sum 82, p. 74.
"That Good Ol' Unshaded Nigga." <u>BlackALF</u> (16:2) Sum
82, p. 75.

2765. MIROLLA, Michael
"The Fit." <u>Dandel</u> (9:1) 82, p. 58.
"I'm in No Way." <u>CanLit</u> (94) Aut 82, p. 84.

2766. MISHA, S. S.
"At Crossroads" (tr. by Gulzar Singh Sandhu). <u>NewL</u>
(48:3/4) Spr-Sum 82, p. 186.

2767. MISHKIN, Julia
"Ice Water." <u>Poetry</u> (139:5) F 82, p. 260.
"A Man Who Plays Billiards Well Is a Gentleman."
<u>AntR</u> (40:4) Aut 82, p. 443.
"On Reading Certain Novels of Henry James." <u>Poetry</u>
(139:5) F 82, p. 258-259.
"Perspectives on Moving Backwards." <u>Iowa</u> (12:4) Aut
81, p. 52-53.
"The Sin-Eater." <u>MissouriR</u> (6:1) Aut 82, p. 38.
"Sleeper and Luck." <u>PoetryNW</u> (23:4) Wint 82-83, p.
14-15.
"Sleeper Asleep." <u>PoetryNW</u> (23:4) Wint 82-83, p.
15.
"To a Painter Who Can't Paint." <u>PraS</u> (56:2) Sum 82,
p. 84-85.
"Women Love to Pose." <u>PraS</u> (56:2) Sum 82, p. 85.
"You Hate Water, But." <u>PraS</u> (56:2) Sum 82, p. 83.

2768. MISHLER, Richard M.
"Attrition." <u>StoneC</u> (10:1/2) Aut-Wint 82-83, p. 68.
"The Bell Telephone Hour." <u>Sam</u> (33:3, issue 131)
82, p. 15.
"The Bell Telephone Hour." <u>Shout</u> (3:1) 82, p. 7.
"Blizzard." <u>Shout</u> (3:1) 82, p. 71.
"Ceremony." <u>Shout</u> (3:1) 82, p. 9.
"Dark Friend." <u>Shout</u> (3:1) 82, p. 8.
"In His Image." <u>Shout</u> (3:1) 82, p. 69.
"Wound Factory." <u>Shout</u> (3:1) 82, p. 10.

2769. MISHRA, Prasanna Kumar
"The Ghost of the Unborn" (tr. by Jayanta
Mahapatra). <u>NewL</u> (48:3/4) Spr-Sum 82, p. 212.

2770. MISRA, Soubhagaya Kumar
"The Hill" (tr. by the author). <u>NewL</u> (48:3/4) Spr-
Sum 82, p. 51-52.

"Robinson Crusoe" (tr. by Jayanta Mahapatra). NewL
(48:3/4) Spr-Sum 82, p. 50.

2771. MITCHAM, Judson
"After Losing My Daughter." SouthernPR (22:1) Spr
82, p. 31.
"Memory of Frances Solomon." Wind (12:44) 82, p.
29.
"To Keep It Holy." Wind (12:44) 82, p. 27.
"Tryouts." PoNow (7:1, issue 37) 82, p. 33.
"What You Really Want." Wind (12:44) 82, p. 28-29.

2772. MITCHELL, Lionel A.
"Daylight." PottPort (4) 82-83, p. 17.

2773. MITCHELL, Roger
"1872." PoetC (14:1) 82, p. 26-28.
"1898." PoetC (14:1) 82, p. 28.
"In the Hounslow Chinese Take-Away." Shen (33:2)
82, p. 67.
"Lightning Rod." PoNow (6:5, issue 35) 82, p. 38.
"Variations." NoAmR (267:4) D 82,p. 45.

2774. MITCHELL, Stephen
"Alcestis" (tr. of Rainer Maria Rilke). AmerPoR
(11:1) Ja-F 82, p. 14.
"Before Summer Rain" (tr. of Rainer Maria Rilke).
AmerPoR (11:1) Ja-F 82, p. 14.
"Death" (tr. of Rainer Maria Rilke). AmerPoR (11:1)
Ja-F 82, p. 15.
"Evening" (tr. of Rainer Maria Rilke). NewYRB
(29:16) O 21, 82, p. 10.
"The Flamingos" (Jardin des Plantes, Paris, tr. of
Rainer Maria Rilke). AmerPoR (11:1) Ja-F 82, p.
15.
"Going Blind" (tr. of Rainer Maria Rilke). AmerPoR
(11:1) Ja-F 82, p. 13.
"The Grownup" (tr. of Rainer Maria Rilke). AmerPoR
(11:1) Ja-F 82, p. 13.
"The Last Evening" (By permission of Frau Nonna, tr.
of Rainer Maria Rilke). AmerPoR (11:1) Ja-F 82, p.
13.
"Tombs of the Hetaerae" (tr. of Rainer Maria Rilke).
NewYRB (29:16) O 21, 82, p. 10.
"Washing the Corpse" (tr. of Rainer Maria Rilke).
AmerPoR (11:1) Ja-F 82, p. 13.

2775. MITCHELL, Susan
"Elegy for a Child's Shadow." NewYorker (58:9) Ap
19, 82, p. 164.
"Maps" (for my father). Nat (235:11) O 9, 82, p.
346.
"Once, Driving West of Billings, Montana." Nat
(235:10) O 2, 82, p. 314.
"The Road." Kayak (60) O 82, p. 49.

2776. MITSUHARU, Kaneko
"A Washbasin" (tr. by Patrick Fulmer). PortR (28:1)
82, p. 63.

2777. MIURA, Kiyoko
      "Death" (tr. of Sakutaro Hagiwara). StoneC (10:1/2)
      Aut-Wint 82-83, p. 18.
      "A Murder Case" (tr. of Sakutaro Hagiwara). StoneC
      (10:1/2) Aut-Wint 82-83, p. 18.

2778. MIZEJEWSKI, Linda
      "Travellers' Advisory." CarolQ (34:3) Spr 82, p.
      17.

2779. MLS
      from The Suite of the Un-Made Children: "A box of
      crayons." Quarry (31:3) Sum 82, p. 18-19.
      "Without words there are still the sounds." Quarry
      (31:3) Sum 82, p. 18.

2780. MOFFEIT, Tony
      "Robert Johnson." Vis (9) 82, p. 32.
      "Voodoo Snake Woman Blues." Vis (9) 82, p. 32.

2781. MOFFETT, Judith
      "Key West (Triple Ballade with Enjambed Refrain,
      Plus Envoy)." Iowa (12:2/3) Spr-Sum 81, p. 246-
      249.
      "Rainforest." Shen (33:2) 82, p. 36.

2782. MOHR, Bill
      "Doubleheader." PoNow (7:1, issue 37) 82, p. 25.
      "Flat." PoNow (7:1, issue 37) 82, p. 25.

2783. MOLEN, W. J. van der
      "Dusk" (tr. by John Stevens Wade). AntigR (48) Wint
      82, p. 39.
      "Farewell" (tr. by John Stevens Wade). AntigR (48)
      Wint 82, p. 40.

2784. MOLESWORTH, Charles
      "Coming Down the Mountain." Shout (3:1) 82, p. 72-
      73.
      "An Ode to Dragonflies." Shout (3:1) 82, p. 74-75.

      MOLINA, Mercedes Gonzalez Vega de
      See: GONZALEZ VEGA de MOLINA, Mercedes

2785. MOLLA, Roxana
      "Calle de Sol al Sur." LetFem (8:2) 82, p. 87.
      "Poema de Noche Vieja en Ano Nuevo." LetFem (8:2)
      82, p. 86.

2786. MOLLENKOTT, Virginia Ramey
      "Fall Planting." ChrC (99:38) D 1, 82, p. 1220.

2787. MOLTON, Warren Lane
      "Ascent." ChrC (99:41) D 22-29, 82, p. 1303.

2788. MOMBOURQUETTE, Jocelyn
      "December." PottPort (4) 82-83, p. 10.
      "Detritus." PottPort (4) 82-83, p. 24.

2789. MONAGHAN, E. A.
    "The Crazy Indian beside the Glades Oak and the US27
    Sign." UTR (7:2) 82?, p. 6.
    "The Eye of the Pea." UTR (7:2) 82?, p. 5.

2790. MONK, Patricia
    "Firmness." PottPort (4) 82-83, p. 48.
    "Nightsounds." PottPort (4) 82-83, p. 10.
    "The Poet." PottPort (4) 82-83, p. 34.

2791. MONROE, Jonathan
    "Gold Beach." MassR (23:3) Aut 82, p. 504.
    "Polemic." KanQ (14:3) Sum 82, p. 146.
    "Waiting for Sleep." PortR (28:1) 82, p. 6.

2792. MONTAG, Tom
    from The Affliction of Goody Clason: "4. The
    Testimony of Sarah Kecham." Spirit (6:2/3) 82, p.
    113-114.

2793. MONTAGUE, John
    "Border Question." NewEngR (5:1/2) Aut-Wint 82, p.
    210.
    "Cassandra's Answer." NewEngR (5:1/2) Aut-Wint 82,
    p. 211-212.
    "Foreign Field." NewEngR (5:1/2) Aut-Wint 82, p.
    209-210.
    "Invocation to the Guardian." NewEngR (5:1/2) Aut-
    Wint 82, p. 212-213.
    "Sword Land." NewEngR (5:1/2) Aut-Wint 82, p. 208.

2794. MONTALE, Eugenio
    "Buffalo" (tr. by William Arrowsmith). Pequod (15)
    82, p. 108.
    "The Custom-House" (tr. by Vinio Rossi and David
    Young). Field (27) Aut 82, p. 11.
    "Dora Markus" (tr. by Charles Wright). Field (27)
    Aut 82, p. 52-54.
    "Dora Markus" (tr. by Reg Saner). Field (27) Aut 82,
    p. 41-42.
    "The Eel" (tr. by Charles Wright). Field (27) Aut
    82, p. 50-51.
    "Falsetto" (tr. by Antonino Mazza). Waves (10:4) Spr
    82, p. 50-51.
    "Fiesole Window" (tr. by Charles Wright). Field (27)
    Aut 82, p. 54.
    "In the Greenhouse" (tr. by Charles Wright). Field
    (27) Aut 82, p. 8.
    "Iris" (tr. by Sonia Raiziss and Alfredo de Palchi).
    Field (27) Aut 82, p. 29-30.
    "Keepsake" (tr. by William Arrowsmith). Pequod (15)
    82, p. 109.
    "Lemons" (tr. by Vinio Rossi and David Young). Field
    (27) Aut 82, p. 14-15.
    "Mottetti VII." Field (27) Aut 82, p. 27.
    "Mottetti VII" (tr. by Irma Brandeis). Field (27)
    Aut 82, p. 27.
    "Mottetti XVII" (tr. by Dana Gioia). Field (27) Aut
    82, p. 23.

"News from Mount Amiata" (tr. by David Young and
    Vinio Rossi). Field (27) Aut 82, p. 35-36.
"On a Letter Never Written" (from La Bufera e Altro,
    tr. by Edward Babun). StoneC (9:3/4) Spr-Sum 82,
    p. 25.
"Su una Lettera Non Scritta" (from La Bufera e
    Altro). StoneC (9:3/4) Spr-Sum 82, p. 24.
"Syria" (tr. by Charles Wright). Field (27) Aut 82,
    p. 50.
"Two in Twilight" (tr. by Charles Wright). Field
    (27) Aut 82, p. 18-19.
"Visit to Fadin" (tr. by Charles Wright). Field (27)
    Aut 82, p. 46-47.

MONTANEZ, Jaime Marcano
See: MARCANO MONTANEZ, Jaime

2795. MONTAZZOLI, Paul
    "Aeneas." ManhatR (2:1) 81, p. 56-57.
    "Nineteen-Fifty-Five." ManhatR (2:2) Sum 82, p. 27.
    "To Christina." LittleM (13:3/4) 82, p. 44-45.

2796. MONTEMAYOR, Carlos
    "Encounter" (tr. by Ricardo Pau-Llosa). BelPoJ
        (32:4) Sum 82, p. 33.
    "Encuentro." BelPoJ (32:4) Sum 82, p. 32.

2797. MONTENEGRO-CALVELLO, Raquel
    "Ausencia" (para los refugiados). Maize (5:3/4) Spr-
        Sum 82, p. 53.

2798. MONTES HUIDOBRO, Matias
    "Vacio Estoy del Verso y del Poema." Mairena (4:10)
        Sum-Aut 82, p. 66.

2799. MONTGOMERY, George
    "About You--for Linda." PoNow (6:4, issue 34) 82,
        p. 37.
    "The Recipe." PoNow (6:4, issue 34) 82, p. 37.

2800. MONTGOMERY, John
    "There Were Hoof Beats at Sunset." SeC (9:1/2) 80,
        p. 38-39.

2801. MONTGOMERY, Marion
    "At Al Johnson's Lake" (May-June 1979). SouthernR
        (18:4) Aut 82, p. 839-859.
    "Emeritus in the Halls." SouthernR (18:4) Aut 82,
        p. 838-839.

2802. MOOD, Stephanie
    "Loss" (for Michelle). Poem (45) Jl 82, p. 59.
    "Promise." Poem (45) Jl 82, p. 58.
    "Sleep." Poem (45) Jl 82, p. 57.

2803. MOODY, Rodger
    "Today Is the Day." Wind (12:44) 82, p. 30.

2804. MOODY, Shirley
       "Views After 'the Art of Love'." SouthernPR (22:1)
       Spr 82, p. 73.

2805. MOONEY, Kathaleen Kirk
       "Stage Write." EngJ (71:3) Mr 82, p. 52.

2806. MOORE, Barbara
       "Almost Greek." GeoR (36:4) Wint 82, p. 803.
       "Angel." MissouriR (5:3) Sum 82, p. 12.

2807. MOORE, Dinty
       "Smelly Baby Jesus." Pig (8) 80, p. 44.

2808. MOORE, Elizabeth
       "Prophet." PraS (56:3) Aut 82, p. 78.
       "Repeated Demand." PraS (56:3) Aut 82, p. 79.

2809. MOORE, George B.
       "The Benllech Trials." Atl (250:1) Jl 82, p. 55.
       "The Branch" (tr. of Jose Emilio Pacheco). Chelsea
       (41) 82, p. 132.
       "Tulum" (tr. of Jose Emilio Pacheco). Chelsea (41)
       82, p. 133.

2810. MOORE, Honor
       "In Mrs. N's Place." Iowa (12:2/3) Spr-Sum 81, p.
       250-251.

2811. MOORE, Janice Townley
       "All Those Nights." SouthernHR (16:2) Spr 82, p.
       154.

2812. MOORE, Jonathan
       "Sang's Market Mission Street." Abraxas (25/26) 82,
       p. 76.

2813. MOORE, Richard
       "Poets." Poetry (139:4) Ja 82, p. 211-216.

2814. MOORE, Roy Benjamin
       "Fisherman's Luck." WritersL Je 82, p. 8.

2815. MOORE, Tom
       "Newfoundland." Germ (6:1) Spr-Sum 82, p. 32.

2816. MOORHEAD, Andrea
       "All Skin All Fire" Os (14) 82, p. 10.
       "From an Imaginary Journal." Os (15) 82, p. 32-38.
       "Hesitation." Os (14) 82, p. 14-15.
       "March Snow." Confr (24) Sum 82, p. 111.
       "Peau Fragile." Os (14) 82, p. 4.

2817. MOORTHY, P. Rama
       "Blue Eyes." NewL (48:3/4) Spr-Sum 82, p. 150.
       "A Song" (tr. of Siddalingaiah). NewL (48:3/4) Spr-
       Sum 82, p. 204.

2818. MOOSE, Ruth
       "The Narrows." Nat (235:20) D 11, 82, p. 630.

2819. MORA, Daisy
"Cotidianidad." Mairena (4:10) Sum-Aut 82, p. 96.

MORA, Francisco Lluch
See: LLUCH MORA, Francisco

MORA, Jorge Aguilar
See: AGUILAR MORA, Jorge

2820. MORA, Pat
"Chuparrosa: Hummingbird." " RevChic (10:3) Sum
82, p. 11.
"Cool Love." RevChic (10:3) Sum 82, p. 10.
"Sola." RevChic (10:3) Sum 82, p. 12.

2821. MORAGA, Cherrie
"It Got Her Over." Cond (8) 82, p. 72-75.
"Passage." Maize (6:1/2) Aut-Wint 82-83, p. 105.

2822. MORAGO, Kristina
"Mother's Vase." Telescope (2) Aut 81, p. 123.

2823. MORALES, Carlos
"Un Borracho Cargado a Tu Cuenta Bancaria." Maize
(5:1/2) Aut-Wint 81-82, p. 69.
"Hoy." Maize (5:1/2) Aut-Wint 81-82, p. 70-71.

2824. MORALES, Jorge A.
"El Tic Tac del Reloj Pasa Como Los Anos" (from
Baladas de Vellonera). Mairena (4:9) Spr 82, p.
91.
"Vine en busca de tu voz hablandome de ausencias"
(from Vine en Busca de Tu Voz). Mairena (4:9) Spr
82, p. 90-91.

2825. MORALES, Jorge Luis
"Francisco Matos Paoli." Mairena (4:11/12) Wint 82,
p. 150.

2826. MORAN, Edward
from The Primal Sun (Helios o Protos): (IX, XIV)
(tr. of Odysseus Elytis, w. Lefteris Pavlides).
CharR (8:1) Spr 82, p. 51-52.

2827. MORAN, Leo
"Brides of El Salvador." Comm (109:22) D 17, 82, p.
694.

2828. MOREJON, Nancy
"Melancolia en San Juan." Areito (8:32) 82, p. 25.

2829. MORELAND, Jane P.
"About Gloria." PoetryNW (23:3) Aut 82, p. 31-32.
"Growings." PoetryNW (23:3) Aut 82, p. 32-33.
"The Proof of Age." SouthernPR (23, i.e. 22:2) Aut
82, p. 39.
"Prunings." Poetry (140:3) Je 82, p. 141.
"Revisiting Home." PoetryNW (23:3) Aut 82, p. 33.
"Watching for Signs." Poetry (140:3) Je 82, p. 143.

"With Nan in My Garden." Poetry (140:3) Je 82, p.
142.

2830. MORENO TORRES, Gerardo
"Angelus" (A Maria, mi esposa). Mairena (4:10) Sum-
Aut 82, p. 72.

2831. MORGAN, David
"Mirror Mood." Bogg (49) 82, p. 56.

2832. MORGAN, David R.
"Admiration." Bogg (48) 82, p. 59.

2833. MORGAN, Elizabeth
"Caravati's Junkyard." Iowa (12:4) Aut 81, p. 59.

2834. MORGAN, Frederick
"1904." AmerS (51:4) Aut 82, p. 462.
"Abiding." SewanR (90:1) Wint 82, p. 25.
"Captain Blaze." Kayak (58) Ja 82, p. 10-11.
"Gawain." SewanR (90:1) Wint 82, p. 23-24.
"The Gift." AmerS (51:2) Spr 82, p. 201.
"His Last Case." NewYorker (57:50) F 1, 82, p. 40.
"The Master." AmerS (51:1) Wint 81-82, p. 14.
"The Skulls." NewEngR (4:3) Spr 82, p. 434-435.

2835. MORGAN, John
"At Lindberg's Grave." PoNow (6:4, issue 34) 82, p.
8.
"Barnstorming." MassR (23:4) Wint 82, p. 554.
"For the Yiddish Poets of New York." NoAmR (267:3)
S 82, p. 78.
"I Begin to Feel My Way." KanQ (14:1) Wint 82, p.
140-141.
"The Slingshot." PoNow (6:5, issue 35) 82, p. 5.
"Travis McGee: The Half-Life of a Hero." KanQ
(14:1) Wint 82, p. 140.

2836. MORGAN, Kay
"For Elvis, Back Then." CapeR (17:2) Sum 82, p. 32-
33.
"On Love." CapeR (17:2) Sum 82, p. 34.

2837. MORGAN, Robert
"Peers." PoNow (6:4, issue 34) 82, p. 39.

2838. MORGENTHALER, Sharon
"Oh My Darling Psychopath." Bogg (49) 82, p. 3.

2839. MORICE, Dave
"The Cat People" (for B. Kliban). Abraxas (25/26)
82, p. 49.
"In the Middle of a Wind Tunnel." Spirit (6:2/3)
82, p. 86.

2840. MORITZ, A. F.
"Amazement." WestCR (17:2) O 82, p. 35.
"The Chinese Writing Academy." PoetryCR (4:1) Sum
82, p. 6.
"Deaf Presence." WestCR (17:2) O 82, p. 33.

"Life of Determination." <u>WestCR</u> (17:2) O 82, p. 34-
35.
"To Set Love in Order." <u>WestCR</u> (17:2) O 82, p. 32.

2841. MORLEY, Hilda
"Hobble-Dance." <u>Chelsea</u> (41) 82, p. 109.

2842. MORRA, Lynn
"Morning after Blues." <u>Maize</u> (6:1/2) Aut-Wint 82-
83, p. 43.
"Recipe for Hatred." <u>Maize</u> (6:1/2) Aut-Wint 82-83,
p. 42.

2843. MORRIS, Herbert
"After the Reading." <u>NewEngR</u> (5:1/2) Aut-Wint 82,
p. 81-85.
"Descending." <u>Kayak</u> (58) Ja 82, p. 59-61.
"For the Look of the Wounded and Their Wounds."
<u>NewEngR</u> (4:3) Spr 82, p. 353-357.
"Lost." <u>Kayak</u> (59) Je 82, p. 38-40.
"A Photograph by August Sander" (Road construction
workers, Westerwald 1927). <u>Shen</u> (33:1) 81-82, p.
64-68.
"Waiting for Marguerite." <u>NewEngR</u> (4:3) Spr 82, p.
349-352.

2844. MORRIS, Matt
"Aspects of Dagwood." <u>PoNow</u> (6:5, issue 35) 82, p.
47.

2845. MORRIS, Michael
"Porque Te Quiero" (from Telaranas). <u>Mairena</u> (4:9)
Spr 82, p. 92.

2846. MORRIS, Paul
"Morgue" (tr. of Yvan Goll). <u>Pequod</u> (15) 82, p. 57.
"Salome." <u>Telescope</u> (3) Sum 82, p. 32.

2847. MORRIS, Richard
"The Pearly Gates." <u>Spirit</u> (6:2/3) 82, p. 65.

2848. MORRISON, Lee N.
"Rivitting on the Suncoast Seaboard Railroad Bridge
over the Hillsborough River." <u>UTR</u> (7:2) 82?, p.
24.

2849. MORRISSEY, Stephen
"For Chery." <u>PoetryCR</u> (3:3) Spr 82, p. 7.

2850. MORROW, Bradford
"Posthumes." <u>Ploughs</u> (8:2/3) 82, p. 76.

2851. MORROW, John
"Invitation" (tr. of Tarjei Vesaas, w. Erik Strand
and Michael Blakburn). <u>Stand</u> (23:3) 82, p. 8.
"Man on Fire" (tr. of Einar Okland, w. Erik Strand).
<u>Stand</u> (23:3) 82, p. 33.
"Occupation" (tr. of Kolbein Falkeid, w. Erik
Strand). <u>Stand</u> (23:3) 82, p. 32.

2852. MORSE, Samuel French
    "Song: To October." Paint (7/8:13/16) 80-81, p. 12.

2853. MORSHAUSER, Bodo
    "Blues at Lunch Break" (tr. by Michael Mundhenk).
    WestCR (16:4) Ap 82, p. 18.
    "A Day, Grey on Grey" (tr. by Michael Mundhenk).
    MinnR (NS19) Aut 82, p. 24.
    "Going through Films" (tr. by Michael Mundhenk).
    WestCR (16:4) Ap 82, p. 17.
    "Letter from Berlin" (tr. by Michael Mundhenk).
    WestCR (16:4) Ap 82, p. 19.
    "Music of Broken Pieces" (from Alle Tage, tr. by
    Michael Mundhenk). WestCR (16:4) Ap 82, p. 20.
    "Sun at the Stove" (tr. by Michael Mundhenk). MinnR
    (NS19) Aut 82, p. 25.

2854. MORTON, Grace
    "Twisting the Dragon's Tail." BelPoJ (32:3) Spr 82,
    p. 20-21.

2855. MOSBY, George, Jr.
    "As Flies Come Out." HangL (41) 82, p. 37.
    "The Breeze Visits as She Sleeps." Im (8:1) 82, p.
    11.
    "Following Icarus." HangL (41) 82, p. 34.
    "Grandpa Sam" (a poem from childhood). Shout (3:1)
    82, p. 28.
    "The Pack." HangL (41) 82, p. 35.
    "Showdown #2." HangL (41) 82, p. 36.

2856. MOSES, Daniel David
    "Highway above Vancouver." AntigR (48) Wint 82, p.
    6-7.
    "Highway Ninety-Nine." AntigR (49) Spr 82, p. 119-
    120.
    "Meteor." AntigR (48) Wint 82, p. 7.
    "A Room above Rain." AntigR (48) Wint 82, p. 8.

2857. MOSES, W. R.
    "Boy at Target Practice: A Contemplation." KanQ
    (14:2) Spr 82, p. 12.
    "Double View." KanQ (14:2) Spr 82, p. 155.
    "Genre Picture." PoNow (6:6, issue 36) 82, p. 22.
    "Geoffrey: Didactics and Entreaties." KanQ (14:2)
    Spr 82, p. 152-154.
    "Gleaning." PoNow (6:4, issue 34) 82, p. 11.
    "Grass wasn't very lush, but healthy." KanQ (14:2)
    Spr 82, p. 13.
    "The Inarticulate." KanQ (14:2) Spr 82, p. 155.
    "Knowledge of Death." CimR (58) Ja 82, p. 35.
    "Long, Long Trail." PoNow (6:4, issue 34) 82, p.
    11.
    "Rival in the Dooryard." PoNow (6:4, issue 34) 82,
    p. 11.
    "Rose Poem." KanQ (14:2) Spr 82, p. 149-150.
    "Spring Clean-Up." KanQ (14:2) Spr 82, p. 151.
    "Transfer." KanQ (14:2) Spr 82, p. 154.
    "Turtle-Back." KanQ (14:2) Spr 82, p. 156.
    "Unwritten." KanQ (14:2) Spr 82, p. 151.

2858. MOSKOWITZ, Faye
        "Junkyard." Shout (3:1) 82, p. 60-61.
        "Woman's Home." Shout (3:1) 82, p. 58-59.

2859. MOSS, Howard
        "The Gallery Walk: Art and Nature." NewYorker
          (58:45) D 27, 82, p. 44.
        "In Traffic." NewYorker (58:9) Ap 19, 82, p. 42.
        "Rules of Sleep." NewYorker (57:49) Ja 25, 82, p.
          32.
        "Upstate." NewYorker (57:52) F 15, 82, p. 36.

2860. MOUL, Keith
        "Friday's Sickness." Wind (12:44) 82, p. 31.
        "The Rise of Heat." Wind (12:44) 82, p. 31-32.

2861. MOULTON, Carlyn
        "I Don't Believe in Ghosts." PoetryCR (3:4) Sum 82,
          p. 15.

2862. MOULTON-BARRETT, Donalee
        "The Canadian Application." PottPort (4) 82-83, p.
          24.

2863. MOURE, Erin
        "All-Night Groceries." Waves (11:1) Aut 82, p. 64.
        "Angelus Domini." CanLit (93) Sum 82, p. 58-59.
        "Being Carpenter." MalR (62) Jl 82, p. 210-211.
        "Parts of Speech." CanLit (93) Sum 82, p. 118.
        "White Rabbit." Waves (11:1) Aut 82, p. 65.

2864. MOUW, Gudrun
        "21. October, 1945/Wormditt" (from Frozen Souls,
          based on Ostpreussisches Tagebuch by Hans von
          Lehndorff). PraS (56:1) Spr 82, p. 45-46.
        "April, 1945/Camp Rothenstein" (from Frozen Souls,
          based on Ostpreussisches Tagebuch by Hans von
          Lehndorff). PraS (56:1) Spr 82, p. 44.
        "Full Moon." Nimrod (26:1) Aut-Wint 82, p. 24.
        "June Beginning, 1945" (from Frozen Souls, based on
          Ostpreussisches Tagebuch by Hans von Lehndorff).
          PraS (56:1) Spr 82, p. 45.
        "October Ending, 1945/Grasnitz" (from Frozen Souls,
          based on Ostpreussisches Tagebuch by Hans von
          Lehndorff). PraS (56:1) Spr 82, p. 46.
        "A Portrait of Water." Nimrod (26:1) Aut-Wint 82,
          p. 25.
        "The Process." Nimrod (26:1) Aut-Wint 82, p. 25.
        "Two Kinds of Music." Nimrod (26:1) Aut-Wint 82, p.
          24.

2865. MUELLER, Lisel
        "Blood Oranges." Ploughs (8:1) 82, p. 161.
        "A Day Like Any Other." Ploughs (8:1) 82, p. 160.
        "Five for Country Music." Ploughs (8:1) 82, p. 162-
          163.
        "Fracture." Iowa (12:2/3) Spr-Sum 81, p. 253.
        "In the Beginning." NewEngR (5:1/2) Aut-Wint 82, p.
          54.
        "Stone Soup." Iowa (12:2/3) Spr-Sum 81, p. 252.

"The Thousand and First Night." NewEngR (5:1/2)
   Aut-Wint 82, p. 55.
"Tidings." OhioR (27) 82, p. 105.

2866. MUHRINGER, Doris
   "Do Not Lock Your House" (tr. by Beth Bjorklund).
      LitR (25:2) Wint 82, p. 206.
   "Lost Goldfish in Dream" (tr. by Beth Bjorklund).
      LitR (25:2) Wint 82, p. 207.
   "Waiting" (tr. by Beth Bjorklund). LitR (25:2) Wint
      82, p. 207.

2867. MUKHERJEE, Satyabrata
   "A Whirl" (tr. of Mriganka Roy). NewL (48:3/4) Spr-
      Sum 82, p. 160.

2868. MUKHOPADHYAY, Pranabkumar
   "Inheritance" (tr. by the author). NewL (48:3/4)
      Spr-Sum 82, p. 121.

2869. MUKHOPADHYAY, Saratkumar
   "Friends" (tr. by the author). NewL (48:3/4) Spr-Sum
      82, p. 238.

2870. MULAC, Jim
   "Elegy for Duke Ellington." Spirit (6:2/3) 82, p.
      75.

2871. MULLEN, Laura
   "Mirror, Mirror." PoetryNW (23:2) Sum 82, p. 8.
   "Sestina in Which My Grandmother Is Going Deaf."
      PoetryNW (23:2) Sum 82, p. 7-8.

2872. MULLINS, Cecil J.
   "Grandfather." BallSUF (23:4) Aut 82, p. 80.

2873. MULLINS, Terence Y.
   "Mending Stoves." ChrC (99:5) F 17, 82, p. 176.

2874. MULRANE, Scott H.
   "Flood." Nimrod (25:2) Spr-Sum 82, p. 23.
   "Mid-October." Iowa (12:4) Aut 81, p. 64.
   "The Sins of the Fathers." Iowa (12:4) Aut 81, p.
      63.

2875. MUMFORD, Erika
   "Gold Bangles: for my Indian Daughter" (from Bombay
      Journal). PraS (56:1) Spr 82, p. 83.
   "Take Nothing Out" (from Bombay Journal). PraS
      (56:1) Spr 82, p. 84-85.
   "Taking the Waters" (from Bombay Journal). PraS
      (56:1) Spr 82, p. 82.
   "Water Seller" (from Bombay Journal). PraS (56:1)
      Spr 82, p. 85.

2876. MUMM, D.
   "God Comes to Northville" (from The Smudge). SeC
      (9:1/2) 80, p. 23.

2877. MUNDEN, Susan
    "I've Called It Everything." CimR (58) Ja 82, p.
        16.

2878. MUNDHENK, Michael
    "Blues at Lunch Break" (tr. of Bodo Morshauser).
        WestCR (16:4) Ap 82, p. 18.
    "A Day, Grey on Grey" (tr. of Bodo Morshauser).
        MinnR (NS19) Aut 82, p. 24.
    "Going through Films" (tr. of Bodo Morshauser).
        WestCR (16:4) Ap 82, p. 17.
    "Letter from Berlin" (tr. of Bodo Morshauser).
        WestCR (16:4) Ap 82, p. 19.
    "Music of Broken Pieces" (from Alle Tage, tr. of
        Bodo Morshauser). WestCR (16:4) Ap 82, p. 20.
    "Sun at the Stove" (tr. of Bodo Morshauser). MinnR
        (NS19) Aut 82, p. 25.

2879. MUNDT, Gladys M.
    "March." LittleBR (1:3) Spr 81, p. 40.
    "Pursuit." LittleBR (1:3) Spr 81, p. 40.

2880. MUNOZ, Elias Miguel
    "Guernica 1980." Maize (5:1/2) Aut-Wint 81-82, p.
        48-50.

    MUNOZ, Gabriel Trujillo
    See: TRUJILLO MUNOZ, Gabriel

2881. MUNOZ MOLINA, Teodosio
    "Busqueda de la Poesia" (tr. of Carlos Drummond de
        Andrade). Mairena (4:10) Sum-Aut 82, p. 64-65.

2882. MURA, David
    "History: The Craft of the Czar." Quarry (31:3) Sum
        82, p. 65.
    "Morning at the Marsh's Edge." Quarry (31:3) Sum
        82, p. 65-66.
    "The Natives." AmerPoR (11:4) Jl-Ag 82, p. 30.

2883. MURABITO, S. J.
    "Big Plans." PoNow (7:1, issue 37) 82, p. 33.

2884. MURANO, Shino
    "Birth of the Demon's Child" (for Jesus Christ, tr.
        by Patrick Fulmer). PortR (28:1) 82, p. 62.
    "Rainy Season, Song" (tr. by Patrick Fulmer). PortR
        (28:1) 82, p. 62.

2885. MURATORI, Fred
    "The Screen." CharR (8:1) Spr 82, p. 40.

2886. MURAWSKI, Elisabeth
    "Goat Girl." CutB (19) Aut-Wint 82, p. 24.
    "Honoring." VirQR (58:1) Wint 82, p. 64.
    "In His Father's House." WestB (10) 82, p. 50.
    "Inner City." WestB (10) 82, p. 51.
    "The More the Rope Wears." SoCaR (14:2) Spr 82, p.
        87.

2887. MURCKO, Terry
"The Rules of Baseball." _Pig_ (9) 82, p. 8.
"The Termination of Basebal." _Pig_ (9) 82, p. 91.

2888. MURILLO, Rosario
"Azules y Negros Campos." _Maize_ (5:3/4) Spr-Sum 82,
p. 68-69.

2889. MURPHY, Barbara
"Atlanta, 1981." _Poem_ (46) N 82, p. 65.
"Trading Passports." _Poem_ (46) N 82, p. 66.

2890. MURPHY, James
"The Clammer." _BelPoJ_ (32:3) Spr 82, p. 16-17.

2891. MURPHY, Kevin
"Equinox, at 35." _CarolQ_ (35:1) Aut 82, p. 7.

2892. MURPHY, Mary P.
"The Graduate." _CapeR_ (18:1) Wint 82, p. 22.
"Poet's Penance." _CapeR_ (18:1) Wint 82, p. 23.

2893. MURPHY, Rich
"The Adulthood Hollow." _Bogg_ (48) 82, p. 11.
"The Alarm Clock." _SmPd_ (19:1, issue 54) Wint 82,
p. 24.

2894. MURPHY, Sheila E.
"Bedtime." _HangL_ (41) 82, p. 38.
"Hiccup." _Waves_ (10:3) Wint 82, p. 13.
"Precious." _CapeR_ (18:1) Wint 82, p. 38.

2895. MURRAY, G. E.
"Never Like This" (for the father and child). _Ascent_
(8:1) 82, p. 30.
"The Squaw Trade." _OP_ (34) Aut-Wint 82, p. 17-21.
"Two Children." _Ascent_ (8:1) 82, p. 31.

2896. MURRAY, Joan
"The Cicada's Song." _AmerPoR_ (11:1) Ja-F 82, p. 16.
"Coming of Age on the Harlem" (for Kathy). _Hudson_
(35:4) Wint 82-83, p. 540-545.
"The Gathering" (Southold NY). _LittleM_ (13:3/4) 82,
p. 105-107.
"Horseshoe." _AmerPoR_ (11:1) Ja-F 82, p. 16.
"The Natural Life of a Woman." _PraS_ (56:4) Wint 82-
83, p. 81-83.

2897. MURRAY, Les A.
"The Emu and the Nobilities of Interest." _NewYorker_
(58:23) Jl 26, 82, p. 36-37.

2898. MUSHER, Andrea
"In Black Earth, Wisconsin" (from Ocooch Mountain
News). _Abraxas_ (25/26) 82, p. 72-73.

2899. MUSKE, Carol
"Afterwards." _AmerPoR_ (11:4) Jl-Ag 82, p. 6.
"Chattel." _PoetryE_ (7) Spr 82, p. 15-16.
"China White." _NewEngR_ (5:1/2) Aut-Wint 82, p. 50.

"Coming over Coldwater." AmerPoR (11:4) Jl-Ag 82,
    p. 6.
"De-Icing the Wings." MissouriR (6:1) Aut 82, p.
    20-21.
"Fairy Tale." Iowa (12:2/3) Spr-Sum 81, p. 254.
"Iowa: March." NewEngR (5:1/2) Aut-Wint 82, p. 51.
"Panis Angelicus." AmerPoR (11:4) Jl-Ag 82, p. 5.
"Set of Works." PoetryE (7) Spr 82, p. 16-17.
"White Key" (for David). AmerPoR (11:4) Jl-Ag 82, p.
    5.

    MUTANABBI, Abu Tayyib al-
    See: Al-MUTANABBI, Abu Tayyib

2900. MYERS, Douglas
    "Birth of a Brush War, 1877." QW (14) Spr-Sum 82,
        p. 18-19.
    "Learning to Play Left Field." PoNow (7:1, issue
        37) 82, p. 33.

2901. MYERS, Jack
    "The Diaspora." OhioR (27) 82, p. 26-27.

2902. MYERS, Joan Rohr
    "Abandoned School-House." DekalbLAJ (14:1/4) Aut
        80-Sum 81, p. 86.
    "Blanche's Song." DekalbLAJ (14:1/4) Aut 80-Sum 81,
        p. 87.
    "Chill." Abraxas (25/26) 82, p. 99.
    "Love Poem." PortR (28:1) 82, p. 8.

2903. MYERS, Neil
    "Seasonal." PoNow (6:6, issue 36) 82, p. 46.

2904. NADAAN
    "Haridwar (The Door to God)" (tr. by K. K. Khullar).
        NewL (48:3/4) Spr-Sum 82, p. 86.

2905. NADIG, Sumatheendra
    "A Song" (tr. of Siddalingaiah, w. David Ray). NewL
        (48:3/4) Spr-Sum 82, p. 204-205.

2906. NADIM, Dina Nath
    "The Moon" (tr. by J. L. Kaul). NewL (48:3/4) Spr-
        Sum 82, p. 46.

2907. NAG, Ramendra Narayan
    "In Front of the Visa Office" (tr. of Birendra
        Chattopadhyay). NewL (48:3/4) Spr-Sum 82, p. 166.

2908. NAGARJUNA
    "No Troublemaker" (tr. by Mrinal Parde). NewL
        (48:3/4) Spr-Sum 82, p. 203.

2909. NAGEL, Gwen Lindberg
    "Signs of Spring." Paint (7/8:13/16) 80-81, p. 21.

2910. NAIBERG, Lisa
    "His Slide Show." PoetryCR (4:1) Sum 82, p. 5.

2911. NAMEROFF, Rochelle
      "The Desire to be Personal: 1." Telescope (3) Sum
      82, p. 16.
      "Information." Tendril (13) Sum 82, p. 52.
      "Object Lesson." Telescope (3) Sum 82, p. 73-74.
      "Teen Angel." Tendril (13) Sum 82, p. 51.

2912. NAMJOSHI, Suniti
      "From Caliban's Notebook." PoetryCR (4:2) Wint 82,
      p. 10.

2913. NANFITO, Bryanne
      "Anatomy." HiramPoR (33) Aut-Wint 82, p. 19.

2914. NAPIER, Alan
      "The Father." Confr (23) Wint 82, p. 72.
      "Two Wasted Words." WebR (7:2) Aut 82, p. 66.

2915. NARAYAN, Kunwar
      "Towards Delhi" (tr. by Vishnu Khare). NewL (48:3/4)
      Spr-Sum 82, p. 190.

2916. NASH, Jesse, O.S.B.
      "Icon." ChrC (99:5) F 17, 82, p. 171.

2917. NASH, Roger
      "The Kite That Flew a Boy." Germ (6:2) Aut-Wint 82,
      p. 25.
      "The Lake That Became a Hawk." AntigR (49) Spr 82,
      p. 40.
      "Sermon of a Cricket in an Empty Bucket." Quarry
      (31:4) Aut 82, p. 39.
      "Settlement in a School of Whales." Quarry (31:4)
      Aut 82, p. 37-38.
      "Snow Rot." Germ (6:2) Aut-Wint 82, p. 24.
      "Stella Almeida Reads Her Shopping List." Quarry
      (31:1) Wint 82, p. 15.
      "What a Warm Night Tonight." AntigR (49) Spr 82, p.
      41.

2918. NASH, Valery
      "Late Alchemists." PoetryNW (23:2) Sum 82, p. 45.
      "World Going Away." Field (26) Spr 82, p. 13.

2919. NATHAN, Leonard
      "The Almond in Flower." NewEngR (5:1/2) Aut-Wint
      82, p. 138.
      "Coffee." NewEngR (5:1/2) Aut-Wint 82, p. 140.
      "Feeding the Ducks." GeoR (36:2) Sum 82, p. 428.
      "Last Watch." Spirit (6:2/3) 82, p. 172.
      "Meadow Foam." Salm (55) Wint 82, p. 120-124.
      "Missing Persons." NewEngR (5:1/2) Aut-Wint 82, p.
      139.

2920. NATHAN, Norman
      "At the Shadowy Center." MalR (63) O 82, p. 84.
      "Chinese Screen 4." MalR (63) O 82, p. 81-82.
      "Chinese Screen 28." MalR (63) O 82, p. 82.
      "The Cow Queen Speaks." KanQ (14:3) Sum 82, p. 131.
      "The Dignity of Words." MalR (63) O 82, p. 80.

"One Cloth." MalR (63) O 82, p. 83.
"Painted Panels." MalR (63) O 82, p. 80-81.
"Perpetuity." MalR (63) O 82, p. 84.
"The Spirit in Ink and Colors." SoCaR (15:1) Aut 82, p. 57.

2921. NATHANSON, Tenney
"Veiled Landscape with Cows." MassR (23:1) Spr 82, p. 153-155.

2922. NAYAK, Pandav
"Love Knows No Logic." NewL (48:3/4) Spr-Sum 82, p. 151-152.

2923. NEALE, Tom
"The Spider." Abraxas (25/26) 82, p. 95.

2924. NECATIGIL, Behcet
"The Lamp" (tr. by Ozcan Yalim, William A. Fielder, and Dionis Coffin Riggs). DenQ (17:1) Spr 82, p. 85.

2925. NECKER, Robert
"In the Park--the Old Guys." StoneC (9:3/4) Spr-Sum 82, p. 59.

2926. NEEDHAM, Shirley Stanley
"Fog." LittleBR (2:1) Aut 81, p. 68.
"May/Samoa 1943." LittleBR (2:3) Spr 82, p. 30.
"Of Growth." LittleBR (2:3) Spr 82, p. 32.
"Spring Day in Kansas." LittleBR (2:3) Spr 82, p. 31.

2927. NEELD, Judith
"Sentences for the Slow." Outbr (8/9) Aut 81-Spr 82, p. 44-45.
"There Is Nothing to Do about the Tunnel under Your Garden But Wait for the Woodchuck to Come Out." CapeR (17:2) Sum 82, p. 23.

2928. NEJAR, Carlos
"About This Place" (from Canga: Jesualdo Monte, 1971, tr. by Madeleine Picciotto). QRL (22) 81, p. 48-49.
"The Animals That Give Milk" (from Canga: Jesualdo Monte, 1971, tr. by Madeleine Picciotto). QRL (22) 81, p. 30.
"Between Two Reigns" (from Canga: Jesualdo Monte, 1971, tr. by Madeleine Picciotto). QRL (22) 81, p. 28.
"Chant" (from Canga: Jesualdo Monte, 1971, tr. by Madeleine Picciotto). QRL (22) 81, p. 35.
"Cultivation" (from Canga: Jesualdo Monte, 1971, tr. by Madeleine Picciotto). QRL (22) 81, p. 14.
"Edict" (from Canga: Jesualdo Monte, 1971, tr. by Madeleine Picciotto). QRL (22) 81, p. 37.
"Enlistment" (from Canga: Jesualdo Monte, 1971, tr. by Madeleine Picciotto). QRL (22) 81, p. 10-11.
"Exile" (from Canga: Jesualdo Monte, 1971, tr. by Madeleine Picciotto). QRL (22) 81, p. 15.

"Falling Down" (from Canga: Jesualdo Monte, 1971,
   tr. by Madeleine Picciotto). QRL (22) 81, p. 43-
   44.
"Getting Ready" (from Canga: Jesualdo Monte, 1971,
   tr. by Madeleine Picciotto). QRL (22) 81, p. 40-
   41.
"Inheritance" (from Canga: Jesualdo Monte, 1971, tr.
   by Madeleine Picciotto). QRL (22) 81, p. 34.
"Machine" (from Canga: Jesualdo Monte, 1971, tr. by
   Madeleine Picciotto). QRL (22) 81, p. 24-25.
"The Master of the Land" (from Canga: Jesualdo
   Monte, 1971, tr. by Madeleine Picciotto). QRL (22)
   81, p. 31.
"The Metal of Hope" (from Canga: Jesualdo Monte,
   1971, tr. by Madeleine Picciotto). QRL (22) 81, p.
   33.
"Obstacle Course" (from Canga: Jesualdo Monte, 1971,
   tr. by Madeleine Picciotto). QRL (22) 81, p. 38-
   39.
"Oil Lamps" (from Canga: Jesualdo Monte, 1971, tr.
   by Madeleine Picciotto). QRL (22) 81, p. 23.
"Poem about Disaster" (from Canga: Jesualdo Monte,
   1971, tr. by Madeleine Picciotto). QRL (22) 81, p.
   45.
"Premonition" (from Canga: Jesualdo Monte, 1971, tr.
   by Madeleine Picciotto). QRL (22) 81, p. 42.
"Protest" (from Canga: Jesualdo Monte, 1971, tr. by
   Madeleine Picciotto). QRL (22) 81, p. 36.
"Setting Off" (from Canga: Jesualdo Monte, 1971, tr.
   by Madeleine Picciotto). QRL (22) 81, p. 52.
"Smoothness" (from Canga: Jesualdo Monte, 1971, tr.
   by Madeleine Picciotto). QRL (22) 81, p. 54-64.
"Solid Food" (from Canga: Jesualdo Monte, 1971, tr.
   by Madeleine Picciotto). QRL (22) 81, p. 32.
"The Stable" (from Canga: Jesualdo Monte, 1971, tr.
   by Madeleine Picciotto). QRL (22) 81, p. 26.
"Testimony" (from Canga: Jesualdo Monte, 1971, tr.
   by Madeleine Picciotto). QRL (22) 81, p. 16.
"This Creature, Death" (from Canga: Jesualdo Monte,
   1971, tr. by Madeleine Picciotto). QRL (22) 81, p.
   50-51.
"Visitor" (from Canga: Jesualdo Monte, 1971, tr. by
   Madeleine Picciotto). QRL (22) 81, p. 12-13.
"Water Clock" (from Canga: Jesualdo Monte, 1971, tr.
   by Madeleine Picciotto). QRL (22) 81, p. 46-47.
"What Can Be Changed" (from Canga: Jesualdo Monte,
   1971, tr. by Madeleine Picciotto). QRL (22) 81, p.
   17-19.
"Work" (from Canga: Jesualdo Monte, 1971, tr. by
   Madeleine Picciotto). QRL (22) 81, p. 27.
"Yoke" (from Canga: Jesualdo Monte, 1971, tr. by
   Madeleine Picciotto). QRL (22) 81, p. 21-22.

2929. NELMS, Sheryl L.
   "Dead dog." HiramPoR (33) Aut-Wint 82, p. 20.
   "Evangelist." Vis (9) 82, p. 38.
   "Fresh Day." HiramPoR (33) Aut-Wint 82, p. 21.
   "Horned Toad." Abraxas (25/26) 82, p. 27.
   "State Hospital Disco." CapeR (17:2) Sum 82, p. 45.

2930. NELSON, Bonnie J.
"The Dreamwalker." CutB (19) Aut-Wint 82, p. 21.

2931. NELSON, Eric
"Last Page." Nimrod (25:2) Spr-Sum 82, p. 59.
"Prologue to a Poem in Forty Years." Nimrod (25:2)
Spr-Sum 82, p. 68.
"The Weatherwoman." NewL (49:1) Aut 82, p. 73-74.

2932. NELSON, Gary
"The Pieces Drop." CapeR (17:2) Sum 82, p. 19.

2933. NELSON, Howard
"A Life" (for Robert Francis). PoetryE (8) Aut 82,
p. 47-48.

2934. NEMARICH, Patricia
"Just Seconds." Wind (12:45) 82, p. 29.

2935. NEMEROV, Howard
"Adam and Eve in Later Life." Poetry (141:1) O 82,
p. 20.
"Disseverings, Divorces." Poetry (141:1) O 82, p.
20.
"Learning." Poetry (141:1) O 82, p. 19.
"A Moon Eclipsed." Poetry (141:1) O 82, p. 18.
"Poetics." Poetry (141:1) O 82, p. 21.
"A Sprig of Dill." Poetry (141:1) O 82, p. 19.

2936. NEPO, Mark
"Oxenholme." Antaeus (44) Wint 82, p. 183-184.
"Through Thick Green Groves." EnPas (13) 82, p. 8.

2937. NERUDA, Pablo
"The Heights of Macchu Picchu" (tr. by David Young).
Field (27) Aut 82, p. 81-100.
"Some Beasts" (tr. by Michael L. Johnson). PortR
(28:2) 82, p. 84-85.

2938. NEUBERG, Karen
"Cheshire." LittleM (13:3/4) 82, p. 88.

NEVILLE HAVINS, Peter J.
See: HAVINS, Peter J. Neville

2939. NEWALL, Liz
"Sense or Censor." EngJ (71:3) Mr 82, p. 64.

2940. NEWLOVE, John
"For Th--." Quarry (31:3) Sum 82, p. 29-30.

2941. NEWMAN, F. E.
"Chichen Itza." Quarry (31:4) Aut 82, p. 12.

2942. NEWMAN, Michael
"Letter to a Loved One." Bogg (48) 82, p. 47-48.

2943. NEWMAN, P. B.
"The Cape Romain Light." KanQ (14:2) Spr 82, p.
113.

"Starting in New England." SouthernPR (23, i.e.
22:2) Aut 82, p. 55.
"Washington Hunts Bear." KanQ (14:2) Spr 82, p. 93-
94.

2944. NEWMAN, P. D.
"Inhibiting the Night on a Lustful Evening." UTR
(7:2) 82?, p. 25.
"Some Things I Never Get Strait." UTR (7:2) 82?, p.
26.

2945. NEWMAN, Sol
"In Commemoration of Fellow, Ma'm, Brought Telegram
before Telephone Said Scram." Pig (8) 80, p. 79.

2946. NEWMAN, Wade
"The Ants." KanQ (14:3) Sum 82, p. 149.
"Digging Potatoes in February" (Lackandaragh Upper,
Wicklow, Ireland). Nimrod (25:2) Spr-Sum 82, p.
24.

2947. NEWTH, Rebecca
"Red Setter Morning." PoNow (6:6, issue 36) 82, p.
30.
"The Tuxedo." PoNow (6:6, issue 36) 82, p. 30.

2948. NIBBELINK, Cynthia
"If Tomorrow I Am Totally Insane." PoNow (6:6,
issue 36) 82, p. 20.

2949. NICHOL, B. P.
"Hour 17" (5:35 to 6:35 p.m., from A Book of Hours).
CanLit (94) Aut 82, p. 22-24.

2950. NICHOLS, Elizabeth
"Symphonic Senryu." Northeast (3:14) Wint 82-83, p.
14.

2951. NICHOLS, Martha
"White Girl." Sam (33:3, issue 131) 82, p. 33.
"Winter Trees." Bogg (48) 82, p. 5.

2952. NICHOLS, Nell Elaine
"June Bride." LittleBR (2:3) Spr 82, p. 57.

2953. NICHOLS-VELLIOS, Marta
"Corona." Vis (9) 82, p. 16.
"East of Eden." Vis (8) 82, p. 13.
"Penelope: Blind Weaver." Vis (10) 82, p. 8.

2954. NICHOLSON, Joseph
"The Good Little White Donkey That Trots and Trots
Over the Acres of the Moon." PoNow (6:6, issue 36)
82, p. 19.
"In Freaksburg." PoNow (6:6, issue 36) 82, p. 19.
"The Wallpaper Works." PoNow (6:6, issue 36) 82, p.
19.

2955. NIDITCH, B. Z.
"An Artist's Field." UnderRM (1:2) Aut 82, p. 6.

"Auschwitz, 1943." <u>StoneC</u> (10:1/2) Aut-Wint 82-83,
p. 48.
"A Bird in Hand." <u>AntigR</u> (49) Spr 82, p. 114.
"Buchenwald." <u>StoneC</u> (10:1/2) Aut-Wint 82-83, p.
48.
"Child Prodigy." <u>Poem</u> (45) Jl 82, p. 47.
"Ezra Pound." <u>Confr</u> (24) Sum 82, p. 64.
"Flannery O'Connor." <u>Poem</u> (45) Jl 82, p. 48.
"Initiates." <u>Os</u> (15) 82, p. 27.
"Jerusalem Twilight." <u>WebR</u> (7:2) Aut 82, p. 60.
"Power Outage." <u>UnderRM</u> (1:2) Aut 82, p. 6.
"Return to Dachau." <u>WebR</u> (7:2) Aut 82, p. 60.
"A Street in Madrid." <u>Os</u> (15) 82, p. 27.
"U Haul." <u>Poem</u> (45) Jl 82, p. 49.

2956. NIEBAUER, Abby
"Circling the House." <u>Hangl</u> (43) Wint 82-83, p. 47.

2957. NIEH, Hualing
"The Translucent Night" (tr. of Ai Qing). <u>Spirit</u>
(6:2/3) 82, p. 175-176.

2958. NIELSEN, Gretchen
"Rapist." <u>Sam</u> (33:3, issue 131) 82, p. 31.

2959. NIEMANN, Ernst
"Night Wine Thoughts." <u>KanQ</u> (14:1) Wint 82, p. 130.

NIETZCHE, Vicente Rodriguez
<u>See</u>: RODRIGUEZ NIETZCHE, Vicente

2960. NIMMO, Kurt
"Alcohol and a Coffin without Nails" (from The
Smudge). <u>SeC</u> (9:1/2) 80, p. 25.
"Odds and Ends" (from The Smudge). <u>SeC</u> (9:1/2) 80,
p. 24.

2961. NIMS, John Frederick
"Finisterre." <u>GeoR</u> (36:1) Spr 82, p. 148-149.
"Tide Turning." <u>Atl</u> (249:1) Ja 82, p. 45.

2962. NIRALA
"All Alone" (tr. by Arvind Krishna Mehrotra). <u>NewL</u>
(48:3/4) Spr-Sum 82, p. 93.
"The Betrayal" (tr. by Arvind Krishna Mehrotra).
<u>NewL</u> (48:3/4) Spr-Sum 82, p. 93.
"Don't Tie the Skiff" (tr. by Arvind Krishna
Mehrotra). <u>NewL</u> (48:3/4) Spr-Sum 82, p. 92.
"His Touch Woke Up" (tr. by Arvind Krishna
Mehrotra). <u>NewL</u> (49:2) Wint 82-83, p. 52.
"Ignorance" (tr. by Arvind Krishna Mehrotra). <u>NewL</u>
(48:3/4) Spr-Sum 82, p. 94.
"It Sits Everywhere" (tr. by Arvind Krishna
Mehrotra). <u>NewL</u> (49:2) Wint 82-83, p. 54.
"The King Gets Away" (tr. by Arvind Krishna
Mehrotra). <u>NewL</u> (49:2) Wint 82-83, p. 53.
"Love Song" (tr. by Arvind Krishna Mehrotra). <u>NewL</u>
(48:3/4) Spr-Sum 82, p. 92.
"Poem in Five Parts" (tr. by Arvind Krishna
Mehrotra). <u>NewL</u> (49:2) Wint 82-83, p. 53-54.

"Soundings (A Fragment)" (tr. by Arvind Krishna
Mehrotra). NewL (48:3/4) Spr-Sum 82, p. 94.
"There Was Mist" (tr. by Arvind Krishna Mehrotra).
NewL (48:3/4) Spr-Sum 82, p. 94.
"You Aren't Him" (tr. by Arvind Krishna Mehrotra).
NewL (49:2) Wint 82-83, p. 52.

2963. NIXON, Colin
"Harlot for Hire." Bogg (48) 82, p. 45.
"Only Onwards." ChrC (99:31) O 13, 82, p. 1015.

2964. NIXON, David Michael
"Red ants invade the aardvark dark." Gargoyle
(17/18) 81, p. 18.

2965. NOBLE, Charles
"The Moon: II. Atlanta." Grain (10:4) N 82, p. 18-
19.

2966. NOETHE, Sherry
"Billy." OhioR (27) 82, p. 102-103.
"Telescoping." UnderRM 1(1) Spr 82, p. 23.

2967. NOGUERAS, Luis Rogelio
"A Brazilian Catholic Priest's Prayer upon the Death
of a Young Fighter" (To Rogelio Paulo, tr. by
Dwight Garcia). RevIn (11:2) Sum 81, p. 256.
"Coincidence" (tr. by Dwight Garcia). RevIn (11:2)
Sum 81, p. 254.
"Coincidencia" (en imitacion de William Carlos
Williams). RevIn (11:2) Sum 81, p. 254.
"Letania por R. M. V.: Sangre Que Se Nos Va." RevIn
(11:2) Sum 81, p. 255.
"Litany for R. M. V.: The Blood Which Flees Us" (tr.
by Dwight Garcia). RevIn (11:2) Sum 81, p. 255.
"Monsieur Julian (del Casal)" (tr. by Dwight
Garcia). RevIn (11:2) Sum 81, p. 252.
"Monsieur Julian (del Casal)." RevIn (11:2) Sum 81,
p. 252.
"Oh Lluvias por Quien!" RevIn (11:2) Sum 81, p.
253.
"Oh, Rains for Whom" (tr. by Dwight Garcia). RevIn
(11:2) Sum 81, p. 253.
"Oracion de un Sacerdote Catolico Brasileno por la
Muerte de un Joven Combatiente" (a Rogelio Paulo).
RevIn (11:2) Sum 81, p. 256.

2968. NOIPROX, Max
"Elsewhere." Bogg (48) 82, p. 49.

2969. NOLAN, James
"After the French." NewL (48:3/4) Spr-Sum 82, p.
176-177.
"Catalan" (per a Sebastia Camps). NewOR (9:2) Aut
82, p. 25.
"How I Set Myself Free at the Temple of the
Reclining Buddha." WestB (11) 82, p. 25-26.
"The Leftover Seed." WestB (11) 82, p. 26-28.
"The Pilgrim & the Monkey." NewL (48:3/4) Spr-Sum
82, p. 177-178.

"The Secret Air." PoNow (6:6, issue 36) 82, p. 30.
"Tiger Watch." NewL (48:3/4) Spr-Sum 82, p. 178-179.

2970. NOLAND, John
"Exiles in Paradise Bay." BelPoJ (32:3) Spr 82, p. 18.

2971. NOLL, Bink
"A Vision -- The Pulitzer Prizes in Poetry 1918-1974." Abraxas (25/26) 82, p. 110-111.

2972. NORDGREN, Joe
"Postcard from Key West." CimR (59) Ap 82, p. 4.
"Salmon Run" (Cape Addington,Alaska). SouthernPR (22:1) Spr 82, p. 39.

2973. NORMAN, Howard
"Arrives without Dogs." Ploughs (8:1) 82, p. 126-127.
"Drowned in Air." Ploughs (8:1) 82, p. 124-125.
from Incident at Quill: Two Conversations. Ploughs (8:2/3) 82, p. 92-94.
from Sarah Greys, Autobiography of a Cree Woman: June 1976. Ploughs (8:2/3) 82, p. 90-91.
"The Sea Tooth." Ploughs (8:1) 82, p. 122-123.

2974. NORRIS, Becky
"Father." SoDakR (20:1) Spr 82, p. 37.
"Postcards." SoDakR (20:1) Spr 82, p. 37-38.

2975. NORRIS, Gunilla
"After the Cancer Diagnosis." Abraxas (25/26) 82, p. 14.
"The Angel in My House." Abraxas (25/26) 82, p. 13.
"In the River." SouthernPR (23, i.e. 22:2) Aut 82, p. 51.

2976. NORRIS, Gunilla Brodde
"Swimming." Shout (3:1) 82, p. 17.

2977. NORRIS, Ken
"The Aesthetics of Drunkenness." CrossC (4:2/3) 82, p. 32.
"Half-Tones." AntigR (50) Sum 82, p. 44.
"Poem: Thinking about you." CrossC (4:2/3) 82, p. 32.
"The Voices." CanLit (93) Sum 82, p. 97.
"Winter." PoetryCR (4:2) Wint 82, p. 13.
"You are reading this too fast." PoetryCR (3:4) Sum 82, p. 12.

2978. NORRIS, Leslie
"Tree, Stone, Water." Atl (250:3) S 82, p. 61.

2979. NORSE, Harold
"In Scranton." PoNow (6:5, issue 35) 82, p. 16.
"Lament for a Spanish Guitar." PoNow (6:5, issue 35) 82, p. 16.

"Water Sports and Sucking Thumbs." PoNow (6:4,
   issue 34) 82, p. 16.

2980. NORTH, Gloria
      "The Clothes Line." SeC (9:1/2) 80, p. 15.

2981. NORTH, Susan
      "Chains." Spirit (6:2/3) 82, p. 44-45.

2982. NORTHSUN, Nila
      "Every Reservation." SoDakR (20:3) Aut 82, p. 64.
      "Mother/Daughter." PoNow (6:4, issue 34) 82, p. 37.

2983. NORTON, John
      "The People One Sees in a Museum" (for Duane
      Hanson). FourQt (31:3) Spr 82, p. 24.

2984. NORVIG, Gerda S.
      "Even before the Mirror Myra." Iowa (12:2/3) Spr-
      Sum 81, p. 255.
      "Hand Fantasy." Iowa (12:2/3) Spr-Sum 81, p. 256.

2985. NOVACK, Robin
      "Grandpa's Favorite." PoNow (7:1, issue 37) 82, p.
      33.

2986. NOVAK, Michael Paul
      "Answering Albee's Question." KanQ (14:3) Sum 82,
      p. 120.
      "Callings." KanQ (14:3) Sum 82, p. 27.
      "The Lives of the Spanish Poets." PoNow (6:6, issue
      36) 82, p. 45.

2987. NOVEMBER, Sharyn
      "Anatomy Lesson." Outbr (8/9) Aut 81-Spr 82, p. 4.
      "Discovering Musicians." Outbr (8/9) Aut 81-Spr 82,
      p. 3.
      "Message for My Brother." NoAmR (267:4) D 82,p. 42.
      "Seashells." NoAmR (267:3) S 82,p. 44.

2988. NOVO PENA, Silvia
      "Sonata Nuevomejicana" (Al Maestro Joaquin Rodrigo).
      RevChic (10:3) Sum 82, p. 16-17.

2989. NOWAK, Nancy
      "Houdini." PikeF (4) Spr 82, p. 33.
      "Zone." PikeF (4) Spr 82, p. 11.

2990. NOWLAN, Alden
      "The Comedians." WestCR (16:4) Ap 82, p. 12.
      "Driving a Hard Bargain." PoetryCR (4:2) Wint 82,
      p. 5.
      "A Pair of Pruning Shears." WestCR (16:4) Ap 82, p.
      10-11.
      "Two Days before His Forty-Eighth Birthday." WestCR
      (16:4) Ap 82, p. 9.

2991. NOWLAN, Michael O.
      "Deposits." PottPort (4) 82-83, p. 49.
      "Too Strong." PottPort (4) 82-83, p. 51.

2992. NOWLIN, W. W.
      "Clotis Barker." ArizQ (38:3) Aut 82, p. 258.
      "Delta Poem: The Levee." CapeR (17:2) Sum 82, p.
      24-25.
      "The Reverend Otis Barker." ArizQ (38:3) Aut 82, p.
      258.
      "Woo the Grocer." ArizQ (38:3) Aut 82, p. 257.

      NUNEZ, Victor Rodriguez
      See: RODRIGUEZ NUNEZ, Victor

      NUNO, Ruben Bonifaz
      See: BONIFAZ NUNO, Ruben

2993. NURKSE, D.
      "Closed Borders." StoneC (10:1/2) Aut-Wint 82-83,
      p. 81.

2994. NYE, Naomi Shihab
      "Catalogue Army." Poetry (140:2) My 82, p. 74.
      "The Man Who Hated Trees." Poetry (140:2) My 82, p.
      75-76.
      "Sure." Telescope (2) Aut 81, p. 63-64.
      "The Use of Fiction." Antaeus (44) Wint 82, p. 88.

2995. NYHART, Nina
      "A Victory." Ploughs (8:1) 82, p. 81.

2996. NYSTROM, Debra
      "Black Street, Wellesley." AmerPoR (11:5) S-O 82,
      p. 9.
      "Late March." AmerPoR (11:5) S-O 82, p. 9.
      "A Reading." AmerPoR (11:5) S-O 82, p. 9.
      "Return." AmerPoR (11:5) S-O 82, p. 9.

2997. OAKEY, Shaun
      "Melancholia 2/ Roots." AntigR (51) Aut 82, p. 21.

2998. OATES, David
      "Gift." SmPd (19:3, issue 56) Aut 82, p. 27.

2999. OATES, Joyce Carol
      "Baby." Harp (264:1582) Mr 82, p. 70.
      "The Current." MichQR (21:4) Aut 82, p. 577-578.
      "Ecstasy of Boredom at the Berlin Wall" (from
      Invisible Woman). OntR (16) Spr-Sum 82, p. 84-85.
      "Ecstasy of Flight" (from Invisible Woman). OntR
      (16) Spr-Sum 82, p. 80-81.
      "Ecstasy of Motion" (from Invisible Woman). OntR
      (16) Spr-Sum 82, p. 82-83.
      "High-Wire Artist." SouthernR (18:2) Spr 82, p.
      382-383.
      "Nightless Nights." SouthernR (18:2) Spr 82, p.
      381-382.
      "The Return." MichQR (21:4) Aut 82, p. 576-577.
      "So Cold, So Icy." MichQR (21:4) Aut 82, p. 578.

3000. OBEJAS, Archy
      "Born in the Heat of Night." AntigR (50) Sum 82, p.
      46.

"Suspension Frost." <u>AntigR</u> (50) Sum 82, p. 45.

3001. OBER, Robert
"No One We Know." <u>Ploughs</u> (8:2/3) 82, p. 121.

3002. O'BRIEN, John
"After the Morning Hunt." <u>StoneC</u> (10:1/2) Aut-Wint
82-83, p. 17.
"Backpacking, Montana, August Eleventh." <u>WebR</u> (7:2)
Aut 82, p. 39.
"The Brown Bears in Alaska." <u>WebR</u> (7:2) Aut 82, p.
37.
"Deer." <u>WebR</u> (7:2) Aut 82, p. 37.
"The Fireworks in Five Parts." <u>WebR</u> (7:2) Aut 82,
p. 38.
"Hampton Harbor before the Storm." <u>Im</u> (8:2) 82, p.
7.
"In Green Bank, West Virginia." <u>Pig</u> (10) 82, p. 60.
"Legal Visit." <u>WebR</u> (7:1) Spr 82, p. 60.
"Poison." <u>HangL</u> (42) 82, p. 25.
"Return." <u>StoneC</u> (10:1/2) Aut-Wint 82-83, p. 17.
"Route 28, North of Oswego, New York." <u>StoneC</u>
(10:1/2) Aut-Wint 82-83, p. 17.
"Ruffed Grouse." <u>WebR</u> (7:2) Aut 82, p. 37.
"Self-Portrait." <u>WebR</u> (7:1) Spr 82, p. 61.
"Shelley's Drawing." <u>Im</u> (8:2) 82, p. 7.
"Story/Poem." <u>WindO</u> (41) Aut-Wint 82-83, p. 39.
"Walking Alone before First Light." <u>WebR</u> (7:1) Spr
82, p. 61.

3003. O'BRIEN, MacGregor
"Noche triste, noche negra." <u>Mairena</u> (4:10) Sum-Aut
82, p. 84.

3004. O'BRIEN, Tom
"I Have Touched the Fish." <u>HiramPoR</u> (32) Spr-Sum
82, p. 39.

3005. OCAMPO, Silvina
"Xerxes' Plane-tree" (tr. by Melanie Bowman). <u>DenQ</u>
(16:4) Wint 82, p. 45.

3006. OCHART, Ivonne
"Esta es otra larga tarde donde las palabras
sucumben." <u>Mairena</u> (4:10) Sum-Aut 82, p. 67.

3007. OCHART, Luz Ivonne
"Mientras otros cantan a la angustia al amor" (from
Este Es Nuestro Paraiso). <u>Mairena</u> (4:9) Spr 82, p.
94.

3008. OCHESTER, Ed
"The Good-bye, Farewell, Auf Wiedersehen Poem" (for
Gar). <u>OhioR</u> (27) 82, p. 120.

3009. O'CONNOR, Robert H.
"Poem of the Man in the Gazebo." <u>CapeR</u> (17:2) Sum
82, p. 26-27.

3010. ODERMAN, Kevin
       "Pedagogics." WestB (11) 82, p. 21.
       "There Is Nothing Tentative." WestB (11) 82, p. 20.

3011. ODLIN, Reno
       "Palimpsest." AntigR (49) Spr 82, p. 12.
       "The Romans in Britain, the Britons in Rome."
       AntigR (49) Spr 82, p. 13.

3012. O'DONNELL, Patti
       "The Newsboy." Maize (5:1/2) Aut-Wint 81-82, p. 90-
       91.

3013. OGDAHL, Karen
       "A Writing Teacher Enrolls in Writing Class." EngJ
       (71:2) F 82, p. 39.

3014. OGDEN, Hugh
       "Winter Trees." Germ (6:2) Aut-Wint 82, p. 23.

3015. O'HAGAN, Jan
       "Two Views of the City." Grain (10:4) N 82, p. 55-
       57.

3016. O'HEHIR, Diana
       "Charlotte." Field (27) Aut 82, p. 103.
       "Final Anatomy." Iowa (12:2/3) Spr-Sum 81, p. 257.
       "Hospital Visiting." Field (27) Aut 82, p. 102.
       "In the Water." PoetryNW (23:2) Sum 82, p. 3-4.
       "Infant." Field (27) Aut 82, p. 101.
       "Payments." PoetryNW (23:2) Sum 82, p. 5.
       "Period Piece." PoetryNW (23:2) Sum 82, p. 6.
       "The Ritual of the Broken Heart." PoetryNW (23:2)
       Sum 82, p. 4.

3017. OIJER, Bruno K.
       "Blue Cup of Snow." SeC (9:1/2) 80, p. 12.
       "The Empress' Daughter." SeC (9:1/2) 80, p. 7-8.
       "Last Poem for Mathilde." SeC (9:1/2) 80, p. 9-11.
       "Sad Eyes." SeC (9:1/2) 80, p. 5-6.

3018. OJEDA, Mirna
       "A Mi Sobrino Haxel." Maize (5:3/4) Spr-Sum 82, p.
       76.

3019. O'KEEFE, Kathy
       "Tense." EngJ (71:7) N 82, p. 55.

3020. OKLAND, Einar
       "Man on Fire" (tr. by Erik Strand and John Morrow).
       Stand (23:3) 82, p. 33.

3021. OKOPENKO, Andreas
       "Edith" (tr. by Beth Bjorklund). LitR (25:2) Wint
       82, p. 261-262.

3022. OLAFSSON, Olafur Haukur
       "White Night" (tr. by Alan Boucher). Vis (10) 82, p.
       9.

3023. OLDKNOW, Antony
"Stations." Abraxas (25/26) 82, p. 80.

3024. OLDS, Sharon
"35/10." MichQR (21:2) Spr 82, p. 280.
"The Abandoned Newborn." YaleR (72:1) Aut 82, p. 58-59.
"Any Case" (tr. of Wislawa Szymborska, w. Grazyna Drabik). QRL (23) 82, p. 16.
"The Argument" (Milan, April 1945). QP (33) Spr 82, p. 4.
"Astonishment" (tr. of Wislawa Szymborska, w. Grazyna Drabik). QRL (23) 82, p. 14.
"The Body" (Dieppe, 1942). MassR (23:1) Spr 82, p. 54.
"The Classic" (tr. of Wislawa Szymborska, w. Grazyna Drabik). QRL (23) 82, p. 53.
"Clothes" (tr. of Wislawa Szymborska, w. Grazyna Drabik). QRL (23) 82, p. 62.
"The Departure" (to my father). QP (33) Spr 82, p. 10.
"Dream" (tr. of Wislawa Szymborska, w. Grazyna Drabik). QRL (23) 82, p. 21.
"Drinking Wine" (tr. of Wislawa Szymborska, w. Grazyna Drabik). QRL (23) 82, p. 33-34.
"The Elder Sister" (For my parents). PoNow (6:6, issue 36) 82, p. 10.
"The End." Ploughs (8:1) 82, p. 138.
"Experiment" (tr. of Wislawa Szymborska, w. Grazyna Drabik). QRL (23) 82, p. 29.
"Gerbil Funeral." QP (33) Spr 82, p. 8-9.
"The Germans Put the Torch to the Ukraine, 1939." Agni (16) 82, p. 36.
"The Heroine." Shout (3:1) 82, p. 62.
"History: 13." Iowa (12:2/3) Spr-Sum 81, p. 259.
"The House of Fecundity." Iowa (12:2/3) Spr-Sum 81, p. 262-263.
"I Am Too Near" (tr. of Wislawa Szymborska, w. Grazyna Drabik). QRL (23) 82, p. 30-31.
"I Want." MassR (23:1) Spr 82, p. 53.
"In the Tower of Babel" (tr. of Wislawa Szymborska, w. Grazyna Drabik). QRL (23) 82, p. 28.
"The Inheritor" (for Muriel Rukeyser). MassR (23:3) Aut 82, p. 460.
"The Joy of Writing" (tr. of Wislawa Szymborska, w. Grazyna Drabik). QRL (23) 82, p. 63-64.
"The Killer." QP (33) Spr 82, p. 9.
"Letters of the Dead" (tr. of Wislawa Szymborska, w. Grazyna Drabik). QRL (23) 82, p. 52.
"Liddy's Orange." NewYorker (58:24) Ag 2, 82, p. 79.
"Looking at My Father." Agni (17) 82, p. 153-154.
"The Lost." QP (33) Spr 82, p. 5.
"The Meal." Iowa (12:2/3) Spr-Sum 81, p. 261.
"Memory Finally" (tr. of Wislawa Szymborska, w. Grazyna Drabik). QRL (23) 82, p. 20.
"Miscarriage." PoNow (6:5, issue 35) 82, p. 22.
"The Missing Boy" (for Etan Patz). YaleR (72:1) Aut 82, p. 59-60.

"Monologue for Cassandra" (tr. of Wislawa
Szymborska, w. Grazyna Drabik). QRL (23) 82, p.
50-51.
"My Father's Breasts." OP (33) Spr 82, p. 7.
"Nothingness Turned Over" (tr. of Wislawa
Szymborska, w. Grazyna Drabik). QRL (23) 82, p.
37.
"Once We Knew" (tr. of Wislawa Szymborska, w.
Grazyna Drabik). QRL (23) 82, p. 23.
"The One Girl at the Boys' Party." Atl (249:6) Je
82, p. 64.
"Onion" (tr. of Wislawa Szymborska, w. Grazyna
Drabik). QRL (23) 82, p. 61.
"The Partisans and the S. S.." MissouriR (6:1) Aut
82, p. 35.
"Parts of the Body" (Berlin airport, 1932). NewEngR
(5:1/2) Aut-Wint 82, p. 86.
"Pilot Captured by the Japanese, 1942." Iowa
(12:2/3) Spr-Sum 81, p. 258.
"Possessed." PoNow (6:6, issue 36) 82, p. 10.
"Relinquishment." Shout (3:1) 82, p. 63.
"Returns" (tr. of Wislawa Szymborska, w. Grazyna
Drabik). QRL (23) 82, p. 42.
"S.S. Roundup in a Jewish Community Center" (Warsaw,
1939). OP (33) Spr 82, p. 3.
"San Francisco." Kayak (58) Ja 82, p. 26-27.
"Saturn." MissouriR (6:1) Aut 82, p. 34.
"Seen from Above" (tr. of Wislawa Szymborska, w.
Grazyna Drabik). QRL (23) 82, p. 40.
"Sex without Love." Iowa (12:2/3) Spr-Sum 81, p.
264.
"The Shadow" (tr. of Wislawa Szymborska, w. Grazyna
Drabik). QRL (23) 82, p. 32.
"The Sheep" (Italy, 1944). MassR (23:1) Spr 82, p.
53-54.
"The Smart Girl." OP (33) Spr 82, p. 6-7.
"Summary" (tr. of Wislawa Szymborska, w. Grazyna
Drabik). QRL (23) 82, p. 25.
"The Takers." Iowa (12:2/3) Spr-Sum 81, p. 260.
"The Two Apes of Brueghel" (tr. of Wislawa
Szymborska, w. Grazyna Drabik). QRL (23) 82, p.
24.
"Under This Little Star" (tr. of Wislawa Szymborska,
w. Grazyna Drabik). QRL (23) 82, p. 10-11.
"The Woman with the Lettuce" (Poland, 1939). Shout
(3:1) 82, p. 64.

3025. OLES, Carol
"Eating October." PoNow (6:5, issue 35) 82, p. 29.
"The Magic Ring." PoNow (6:5, issue 35) 82, p. 29.

3026. OLES, Carole
"The Cardinal Causes Me to Say Oh." PraS (56:1) Spr
82, p. 78.
"Driving to Worcester in Snow." PraS (56:1) Spr 82,
p. 79.
"Dry Ice." VirQR (58:4) Aut 82, p. 698-699.
"Lady's Writing Desk, Circa 1880." PraS (56:1) Spr
82, p. 77-78.
"Maple in Space." PraS (56:1) Spr 82, p. 76.

"Matters of Grave Consequence." PraS (56:1) Spr 82,
    p. 66-79.
"Quarry." PraS (56:1) Spr 82, p. 71-76.
"Spring." PraS (56:1) Spr 82, p. 68.
"Studying Sky." PraS (56:1) Spr 82, p. 68-70.
"What I Wanted." PraS (56:1) Spr 82, p. 77.

3027. OLIVARES, Arturo
    "Tierra" (from Cantos Materiales). Mairena (4:9) Spr
    82, p. 40.

3028. OLIVER, Mary
    "Bending Metal." WestHR (36:2) Sum 82, p. 132-133.
    "Camping near the Little Holly River." WestHR
    (36:2) Sum 82, p. 131.
    "Feast Poem." WestHR (36:3) Aut 82, p. 262.
    "The Fish." VirQR (58:1) Wint 82, p. 55.
    "Flying." NewEngR (4:3) Spr 82, p. 370.
    "Howard." PraS (56:3) Aut 82, p. 82.
    "John Chapman." AmerS (51:2) Spr 82, p. 242-243.
    "Moles." OhioR (27) 82, p. 119.
    "Morning Song." NewEngR (4:3) Spr 82, p. 371.
    "Music." PraS (56:3) Aut 82, p. 80-81.
    "A Poem for the Blue Heron." NewEngR (4:3) Spr 82,
    p. 368-369.
    "The Sea." Atl (250:3) S 82, p. 84.
    "Skunk Cabbage." GeoR (36:1) Spr 82, p. 23.
    "Tasting the Wild Grapes." WestHR (36:3) Aut 82, p.
    263.
    "Three Poems for James Wright." Ploughs (8:2/3) 82,
    p. 29-32.
    "White Night." VirQR (58:1) Wint 82, p. 54-55.

3029. OLIVER, Merrill
    "The Birthmark." Iowa (12:2/3) Spr-Sum 81, p. 265.

3030. OLIVER, Michael Brian
    "Birds." CanLit (92) Spr 82, p. 6-7.

3031. OLIVER, Raymond
    "Dream Vision." Thrpny (8) Wint 82, p. 3.

3032. OLIVEROS, Chuck
    "Calling the Moon by Name." WormR (22:4, issue 88)
    82, p. 126-127.
    "Refrigerator Gothic I." WormR (22:4, issue 88) 82,
    p. 127-128.

    OLIVIERI, Rafael Colon
    See: COLON OLIVIERI, Rafael

3033. O'LOUGHLIN, Michael
    "The Fugitive." Stand (23:1) 81-82, p. 69.

3034. OLSEN, William
    "Before Words." Tendril (12) Wint 82, p. 52.
    "Five Years." Tendril (12) Wint 82, p. 51.
    "Mules in a Field." NoAmR (267:3) S 82, p. 43.
    "Public Gardens." Nat (234:20) My 22, 82, p. 623.
    "Sundays." Tendril (12) Wint 82, p. 53.

"Vocations." <u>Nat</u> (234:24) Je 19, 82, p. 756.

3035. OLSON, Andrew C.
"In the Spring We Fertilize the Garden with Old
Fish." <u>HiramPoR</u> (32) Spr-Sum 82, p. 40.

3036. OLSON, Charles
"And Melancholy." <u>AmerPoR</u> (11:3) My-Je 82, p. 3.
"As Cabeza de Vaca was given the Guanches gift."
<u>AmerPoR</u> (11:3) My-Je 82, p. 3.
"The boats' lights in the dawn now going so
swiftly." <u>AmerPoR</u> (11:3) My-Je 82, p. 4.
"The hour of evening--supper hour, for my
neighbors." <u>AmerPoR</u> (11:3) My-Je 82, p. 4-5.
"The Land As Haithubu." <u>AmerPoR</u> (11:3) My-Je 82, p.
3.
"O Quadriga." <u>AmerPoR</u> (11:3) My-Je 82, p. 3.
"On the Earth's Edge is alone the Way to Stand."
<u>AmerPoR</u> (11:3) My-Je 82, p. 3.
"The Telesphere." <u>AmerPoR</u> (11:3) My-Je 82, p. 3.

3037. OLSON, Elder
"The Glass Man." <u>NewL</u> (49:1) Aut 82, p. 27.
"The Museum." <u>NewL</u> (49:1) Aut 82, p. 26.
"A Recital by Rudolf Serkin." <u>AmerS</u> (51:2) Spr 82,
p. 218.

3038. OLSON, Sharon
"Interior Decorating." <u>KanQ</u> (14:3) Sum 82, p. 166-
167.

3039. OLSON, Steve
"Coming Home." <u>SoDakR</u> (20:4) Wint 82-83, p. 24-25.

3040. OLYNYK, Charles V.
"Ice Thoughts." <u>Wind</u> (12:46) 82, p. 18.

3041. O'MEARA, Anick
"Winter Legacy" (for my mother, on losing her
mother). <u>Abraxas</u> (25/26) 82, p. 108.

3042. ONDAATJE, Michael
"7 or 8 Things I Know about Her / a Stolen
Biography." <u>Epoch</u> (32:1) Aut 82, p. 86-87.
"The Cinnamon Peeler." <u>Epoch</u> (32:1) Aut 82, p. 84-
85.

3043. O'NEILL, Brian
"Fathers." <u>Epoch</u> (31:2) Spr 82, p. 133.

3044. OPALOV, Leonard
"I Possess" (tr. of Anna Akhmatova). <u>Spirit</u> (6:2/3)
82, p. 187.

3045. OPENGART, Bea
"Nocturne: Narcissus." <u>Agni</u> (17) 82, p. 17.
"Nothing That Can Fly." <u>PoetryNW</u> (23:3) Aut 82, p.
47.
"Opposition to the Angels." <u>Agni</u> (17) 82, p. 19-20.

"To Take Us Further" (for Susan). _Agni_ (17) 82, p. 18.

3046. OPERE, Fernando
"Las Madres de la Plaza de Mayo en Buenos Aires."
RevChic (10:4) Aut 82, p. 11.
"Por Que Se Fue Teresa?" _RevChic_ (10:4) Aut 82, p. 12.
"Por Que Se Marcho Miguel?" _RevChic_ (10:4) Aut 82, p. 13.

OREJANILLA, Luis Minguez
See: MINGUEZ "OREJANILLA," Luis

3047. ORESICK, Peter
"Challenge to the Academy." _MinnR_ (NS18) Spr 82, p. 20.
"Shooting the Governor of Wisconsin." _MinnR_ (NS18) Spr 82, p. 21.

3048. ORIEL-PETERSEN, Anne
"Kairos." _Vis_ (10) 82, p. 7.
"Petition." _Vis_ (10) 82, p. 6.

3049. ORR, Ed
"The Asylum Gardener." _BallSUF_ (23:3) Sum 82, p. 24.
"Bruce Davidson: Portrait of the Steichens." _WindO_ (41) Aut-Wint 82-83, p. 20.
from Love Diary: "March 15." _KanO_ (14:1) Wint 82, p. 162.
"The Wind." _WindO_ (41) Aut-Wint 82-83, p. 21.

3050. ORR, Gregory
"Keats." _Ploughs_ (8:2/3) 82, p. 202-204.
"Leaving the Asylum." _PoetryE_ (7) Spr 82, p. 27-28.
"Nicole at Thirteen." _Ploughs_ (8:2/3) 82, p. 206.
"Poem in New York." _Ploughs_ (8:2/3) 82, p. 205-206.
"Reading Late in the Cottage." _PoetryE_ (7) Spr 82, p. 28.

3051. ORR, Verlena
"Writing Exercise." _PortR_ (28:2) 82, p. 86-87.

3052. ORSZAG-LAND, Thomas
"Only a Girl." _Bogg_ (48) 82, p. 58.
"Public Administration." _Bogg_ (49) 82, p. 39.

ORTIZ COFER, Judith
See: COFER, Judith Ortiz

3053. ORTIZ de LEON, Maria de los Angeles
"Un Dia la Infancia No Amanece." _Mairena_ (4:9) Spr 82, p. 28-29.

3054. ORTIZ RESTO, Jose A.
"Momento." _Mairena_ (4:10) Sum-Aut 82, p. 82.

3055. ORTOLANI, Al
"Jeffers." _LittleBR_ (2:3) Spr 82, p. 49.

"On a Day When I Realized Thoreau Wasn't Enough."
LittleBR (1:4) Sum 81, p. 42.
"Sunlight strikes the pond" (Haiku). LittleBR (2:3)
Spr 82, p. 50.
"Walking the mill dam" (Haiku). LittleBR (2:3) Spr
82, p. 50.

OSBORNE, Elba Diaz de
See: DIAZ de OSBORNE, Elba

3056. OSBORNE, Joanne
"Life Is Still." Dandel (9:1) 82, p. 80.

3057. OSBORNE-McKNIGHT, Juilene
"On Taking My Creative Writing Students for a Winter
Walk." EngJ (71:3) Mr 82, p. 80.

3058. OSERS, Ewald
"Gmy" (tr. of Richard Exner). Stand (23:1) 81-82, p.
4-7.

3059. OSING, Gordon
"Auden." SouthernR (18:3) Sum 82, p. 541.
"The North Fork." CharR (8:2) Aut 82, p. 25-26.
"Ostinato." SouthernR (18:3) Sum 82, p. 540.

3060. OSLANDER, M. Marcuss
"Brush Strokes." NewEngR (4:3) Spr 82, p. 451.

3061. OSTERLUND, Steven
"A routine Investigation." PoNow (6:5, issue 35)
82, p. 45.

3062. OSTRIKER, Alicia
"Message from the Sleeper at Hell's Mouth." Poetry
(139:4) Ja 82, p. 189-194.
"Those Who Know Do Not Speak, Those Who Speak Do Not
Know." LittleM (13:3/4) 82, p. 87.

3063. O'SULLIVAN, Sibbie
"Nightmare Food" (for Eldridge Cleaver). Vis (10)
82, p. 34.

3064. OTERINO, Rafael Felipe
"Rara Materia." Mairena (4:10) Sum-Aut 82, p. 58.

3065. OUELLETTE, Fernand
"A Decouvert" (from En la Nuit, la Mer). AntigR (49)
Spr 82, p. 80.
"The Black Bird" (from En la Nuit, la Mer, tr. by
Gertrude Sanderson). AntigR (50) Sum 82, p. 101.
"La Flute" (A Sylvie, from En la Nuit, la Mer).
AntigR (50) Sum 82, p. 98.
"The Flute" (For Sylvie, from En la Nuit, la Mer,
tr. by Gertrude Sanderson). AntigR (50) Sum 82, p.
99.
"History" (from En la Nuit, la Mer, tr. by Gertrude
Sanderson). AntigR (49) Spr 82, p. 81.
"L'Histoire" (from En la Nuit, la Mer). AntigR (49)
Spr 82, p. 80.

"Nos Yeux" (from Poesie, 1979). StoneC (10:1/2) Aut-
Wint 82-83, p. 36.
"L'Oiseau Noir" (from En la Nuit, la Mer). AntigR
(50) Sum 82, p. 100.
"Openly" (from En la Nuit, la Mer, tr. by Gertrude
Sanderson). AntigR (49) Spr 82, p. 81.
"Our Eyes" (from Poesie, 1979, tr. by Steve
Troyanovich). StoneC (10:1/2) Aut-Wint 82-83, p.
37.
"Les Supplicies" (from En la Nuit, la Mer). AntigR
(49) Spr 82, p. 80.
"Tomb of Ovidiu" (from En la Nuit, la Mer, tr. by
Gertrude Sanderson). AntigR (49) Spr 82, p. 79.
"Tombeau d'Ovidiu" (from En la Nuit, la Mer). AntigR
(49) Spr 82, p. 78.
"The Tortured Ones" (from En la Nuit, la Mer, tr. by
Gertrude Sanderson). AntigR (49) Spr 82, p. 81.

3066. OWEN, John E.
"Suburbia." ArizQ (38:4) Wint 82, p. 302.

3067. OWEN, Sue
"Blood Relatives." PoetryNW (23:1) Spr 82, p. 21-
22.
"Leading the Blind." Ploughs (8:2/3) 82, p. 86.
"Old Wives' Tales." Kayak (60) O 82, p. 47.
"The Prophecy of Ink." NoAmR (267:2) Je 82, p. 45.
"Zero." Kayak (60) O 82, p. 46.

3068. OWENS, Rochelle
"A Sandworm Emerging." Sulfur (2:3, issue 6) 82, p.
73-75.

3069. OWER, John
"A Grace." AntigR (48) Wint 82, p. 86.
"The New Story." AntigR (48) Wint 82, p. 86.

3070. OXENHORN, Harvey
"Us." NewL (49:1) Aut 82, p. 76-77.

3071. OZAROW, Kent Jorgensen
"Approaching Storm." PoNow (7:1, issue 37) 82, p.
34.
"Identity Crisis." PoNow (7:1, issue 37) 82, p. 34.
"Tiny Alice." PoNow (7:1, issue 37) 82, p. 34.

3072. OZICK, Cynthia
"Fire-Foe." LitR (25:4) Sum 82, p. 611.
"In the Yard." LitR (25:4) Sum 82, p. 612.
"Urn-Burial." LitR (25:4) Sum 82, p. 613-616.

3073. PACERNICK, Gary
"Frank O'Hara." Outbr (8/9) Aut 81-Spr 82, p. 16.
"Portrait." Spirit (6:2/3) 82, p. 62.
"Sandbox Burial." PoNow (6:4, issue 34) 82, p. 43.
"Say, Beckett." Outbr (8/9) Aut 81-Spr 82, p. 17.
"Three Sonnets." Sky (10-12) Aut 82, p. 37-38.

3074. PACHECO, Jose Emilio
"The Branch" (tr. by George B. Moore). Chelsea (41)
82, p. 132.
"Tulum" (tr. by George B. Moore). Chelsea (41) 82,
p. 133.

3075. PACK, Robert
"At the Ecology Convention." Agni (16) 82, p. 119-
120.
"Cleaning the Fish." Ploughs (8:2/3) 82, p. 87-88.
"Incurable." DenQ (17:2) Sum 82, p. 27-28.
"Leviathan." MassR (23:4) Wint 82, p. 733-735.
"Prayer for Prayer." AmerS (51:2) Spr 82, p. 180-
182.
"Remains." MassR (23:4) Wint 82, p. 735-737.

3076. PACZUSKI, Joe
"Light Bulb Ode." AntigR (49) Spr 82, p. 82.

3077. PADDOCK, Nancy
"The Greenhouse." UnderRM 1(1) Spr 82, p. 22.

3078. PADGAONKAR, Mangesh
"On the Beach" (tr. by Vinay Dharwadker). CharR
(8:2) Aut 82, p. 46-47.
"Unclouded" (tr. by Vinay Dharwadker). CharR (8:2)
Aut 82, p. 47.

3079. PADHI, Bibhu
"Loss." NewL (48:3/4) Spr-Sum 82, p. 160-161.

3080. PADILLA, Heberto
"Legacies" (tr. by Alastair Reid and Andrew Hurley).
NewYorker (57:46) Ja 4, 82, p. 36-37.
"A Octavio Paz." BelPoJ (32:4) Sum 82, p. 20.
"A Prayer for the End of the Century" (tr. by
Alastair Reid and Andrew Hurley). NewYorker
(57:46) Ja 4, 82, p. 36.
"Returning to Bright Places" (tr. by Alastair Reid
and Andrew Hurley). NewYorker (57:46) Ja 4, 82, p.
36.
"Song of the Navigator" (tr. by Alastair Reid and
Andrew Hurley). NewYorker (57:46) Ja 4, 82, p. 36.
"To Octavio Paz" (tr. by Ricardo Pau-Llosa). BelPoJ
(32:4) Sum 82, p. 21.
"Walking" (tr. by Alastair Reid and Andrew Hurley).
NewYorker (57:46) Ja 4, 82, p. 36.

3081. PADRON, Justo Jorge
"Celebracion de la Palabra." Mairena (4:9) Spr 82,
p. 29-30.
"En las Aguas del Sol." Mairena (4:9) Spr 82, p.
30.

3082. PAGE, P. K.
"After Rain." PoetryCR (3:3) Spr 82, p. 9.
"Dwelling Place." PoetryCR (3:3) Spr 82, p. 9.
"Evening Dance of the Grey Flies" (For Chris)."
PoetryCR (3:3) Spr 82, p. 9.

"Phone Call from Mexico." PoetryCR (3:3) Spr 82, p.
9.
"Star-Gazer." PoetryCR (3:3) Spr 82, p. 9.
"The Stenographers." PoetryCR (3:3) Spr 82, p. 9.
"T-Bar." PoetryCR (3:3) Spr 82, p. 9.

3083. PAGE, William
"Consummation." Poem (46) N 82, p. 1.
"Dust." NoAmR (267:2) Je 82,p. 46.
"Hearing from Home." CimR (60) Jl 82, p. 58-59.
"The Heavens" (for Aunt Pinkie). Poem (46) N 82, p.
2.
"Learning the Basics." KanQ (14:1) Wint 82, p. 76.
"Phosphate." SouthernR (18:4) Aut 82, p. 822-823.
"Saying It All." CimR (60) Jl 82, p. 54-55.
"Taking Care of Its Own." Nimrod (25:2) Spr-Sum 82,
p. 24.
"What We Did before Sex." SouthernR (18:4) Aut 82,
p. 823-824.

PAHLSON, Goran Printz
See: PRINTZ-PAHLSON, Goran

3084. PALADINI, Jorge Hector
"Sueno." Mairena (4:10) Sum-Aut 82, p. 59.

3085. PALADINO, Thomas
"Heraclitus in New Hampshire." NewEngR (4:4) Sum
82, p. 592-593.

3086. PALCHI, Alfredo de
"Iris" (tr. of Eugenio Montale, w. Sonia Raiziss).
Field (27) Aut 82, p. 29-30.

3087. PALEN, John
"Bobby Sands." WindO (41) Aut-Wint 82-83, p. 6.
"Captain Ahab Reads the Daily News." WindO (41)
Aut-Wint 82-83, p. 6.
"Man Burns Car to Celebrate, January 1981." WindO
(41) Aut-Wint 82-83, p. 7.
"Spring Tilling." WindO (41) Aut-Wint 82-83, p. 7.

3088. PALLISTER, Jan
"Le Asine Passavano" (tr. of Umberto Bellintani).
PoNow (6:5, issue 35) 82, p. 43.
"Vera-Cruz" (tr. of Jacques Audiberti). PoNow (6:5,
issue 35) 82, p. 42.

3089. PALMA, Marigloria
"Sola entre mis miradas" (from Aire Habitado).
Mairena (4:9) Spr 82, p. 92-93.
from Versos de Cada Dia: (74). Mairena (4:9) Spr 82,
p. 93.

3090. PALMER, Leslie
"Good, Falling Like Snow at Christmas." Sam (33:3,
issue 131) 82, p. 36.

3091. PALMER, Michael
       "Lies of the Poem." Sulfur (2:2, issue 5) 82, p.
       71-72.
       "The Theory of the Flower." Sulfur (2:2, issue 5)
       82, p. 67-70.

3092. PALMER, William
       "Birthday." WindO (41) Aut-Wint 82-83, p. 29.
       "Night before Mother's Face Lift." WindO (41) Aut-
       Wint 82-83, p. 29.

3093. PALMERO, Carmen
       "Confesion de Amor." LetFem (8:2) 82, p. 76.
       "Imposible Huida." LetFem (8:2) 82, p. 78.
       "Por Que?" LetFem (8:2) 82, p. 79.
       "Rejas." LetFem (8:2) 82, p. 77.

3094. PANIKER, Ayyappa
       "Beograd." NewL (48:3/4) Spr-Sum 82, p. 182.
       "Moskva." NewL (48:3/4) Spr-Sum 82, p. 182-183.

3095. PANKEY, Eric
       "Mute Spirits" (Horatio at Elsinore). CharR (8:1)
       Spr 82, p. 44-45.

       PAOLI, Francisco Matos
       See: MATOS PAOLI, Francisco

3096. PAPE, Greg
       "The Porpoise." NewYorker (57:49) Ja 25, 82, p. 95.
       "Sharks, Caloosahatchee River." Antaeus (47) Aut
       82, p. 73-74.

3097. PARADIS, Philip
       "Night Wish to Elizabeth." Nimrod (25:2) Spr-Sum
       82, p. 69.

3098. PARDE, Mrinal
       "No Troublemaker" (tr. of Nagarjuna). NewL (48:3/4)
       Spr-Sum 82, p. 203.
       "A Poster" (tr. of Kumar Vikal, w. David Ray). NewL
       (48:3/4) Spr-Sum 82, p. 206.

3099. PARHAM, Robert
       "Dialogue between Rousseau and O'Henry." Wind
       (12:46) 82, p. 25.
       "The Domed Glass." KanO (14:1) Wint 82, p. 114.
       "Pig Picking." StoneC (9:3/4) Spr-Sum 82, p. 72.

3100. PARINI, Jay
       "Swimming in Late September." SouthernR (18:1) Wint
       82, p. 187.
       "To His Dear Friend, Bones." SouthernR (18:1) Wint
       82, p. 185-186.

3101. PARIS, Peggy
       "The Color Blue Is Mine." EnPas (13) 82, p. 22-23.

3102. PARISH, Barbara Shirk
      "Cheyenne Bottoms, 1980." LittleBR (2:1) Aut 81, p.
      69.
      "Hinges." SmPd (19:1, issue 54) Wint 82, p. 10.
      "Native Stone." LittleBR (1:4) Sum 81, p. 73.
      "Reclaimed." LittleBR (3:1) Aut 82, p. 17.
      "Settlers." LittleBR (1:4) Sum 81, p. 73.

3103. PARK, Clara Claiborne
      "Advent" (H. S. F, newborn December 1980). AmerS
      (51:1) Wint 81-82, p. 42.

3104. PARLETT, James
      "For Return." PoetryNW (23:1) Spr 82, p. 17-18.
      "The Siamese Twins." PoetryNW (23:1) Spr 82, p. 16-
      17.
      "The Wind-Up Man." CapeR (18:1) Wint 82, p. 18.

3105. PARRIS, Peggy
      "Hypnotist's Pantoum." PoetryNW (23:3) Aut 82, p.
      24-25.

3106. PARSONS, Bruce
      "Untitled: I have the sadness of a young man."
      PottPort (4) 82-83, p. 18.

3107. PARTHASARATHY, R.
      "Delhi." NewL (48:3/4) Spr-Sum 82, p. 82-84.

3108. PARTLOW, Kristel
      "Again Last Night." MalR (63) O 82, p. 56.
      "The Astrologer." MalR (63) O 82, p. 55.

3109. PASCOE, Judith
      "Stranded." StoneC (9:3/4) Spr-Sum 82, p. 14.
      "Tapping on Turtle Shells." HiramPoR (32) Spr-Sum
      82, p. 41.

      PASSAGE, Mary du
      See: Du PASSAGE, Mary

3110. PASSALACQUA, Carlos
      "Lo Que Es" (from Noche, Fuente). Mairena (4:9) Spr
      82, p. 95.

3111. PASTAN, Linda
      "After You Left." TriQ (55) Aut 82, p. 83.
      "Coronary Bypass: for Rod." Agni (17) 82, p. 155.
      "Crimes." Poetry (140:5) Ag 82, p. 289-290.
      "Dido's Farewell." AmerPoR (11:5) S-O 82, p. 28.
      "In the Middle of a Life." Iowa (12:2/3) Spr-Sum
      81, p. 269-270.
      "Lists." Poetry (140:5) Ag 82, p. 287-288.
      "Low Tide." Tendril (12) Wint 82, p. 54.
      "Mosaic." Atl (250:3) S 82, p. 44.
      "A Name: For Susan Who Became Shoshana." TriQ (55)
      Aut 82, p. 84-85.
      "Nostalgia." NewEngR (5:1/2) Aut-Wint 82, p. 49.
      "On the Road to Delphi." PoNow (6:5, issue 35) 82,
      p. 26.

"One Blue Flag." <u>Iowa</u> (12:2/3) Spr-Sum 81, p. 268.
"The Orderly Transfer of Power." <u>PoNow</u> (6:4, issue 34) 82, p. 39.
"The Printer" (for Roland Hoover). <u>GeoR</u> (36:3) Aut 82, p. 516.
"Salt." <u>TriQ</u> (55) Aut 82, p. 81-82.
"Waiting for My Life." <u>PoNow</u> (6:5, issue 35) 82, p. 26.
"Waking." <u>Poetry</u> (140:5) Ag 82, p. 288.
"Water Wheel." <u>Poetry</u> (140:5) Ag 82, p. 291-292.
"A Winter Prothalamion." <u>Tendril</u> (12) Wint 82, p. 55.
"The Writer at 16." <u>PoNow</u> (6:6, issue 36) 82, p. 7.

3112. PASTERNAK, Boris
"The End" (tr. by Mark Rudman and Bohdan Boychuk). <u>Pequod</u> (14) 82, p. 118-119.
"The Mirror" (tr. by Mark Rudman and Bohdan Boychuk). <u>Pequod</u> (15) 82, p. 70-71.
"Postscript" (tr. by Mark Rudman). <u>Sulfur</u> (2:1, issue 4) 82, p. 56.
"Summer" (tr. by Mark Rudman). <u>Sulfur</u> (2:1, issue 4) 82, p. 54-55.

3113. PATAKI, Heidi
"On the Journey to Your Heart" (tr. by Beth Bjorklund). <u>LitR</u> (25:2) Wint 82, p. 290-291.
"You Have Taken My Language Away" (tr. by Beth Bjorklund). <u>LitR</u> (25:2) Wint 82, p. 289.

3114. PATAPIOU, Akis
"Roses Perish One after Another in a Horse's Mouth - Basho." <u>Germ</u> (6:2) Aut-Wint 82, p. 20.

3115. PATCHEN, Kenneth
"But There Was Still Another Pelican in the Breadbox." <u>Pig</u> (8) 80, p. 19.

3116. PATEL, Gieve
"I Am No Good." <u>NewL</u> (48:3/4) Spr-Sum 82, p. 100.
"Just Strain Your Neck." <u>NewL</u> (48:3/4) Spr-Sum 82, p. 100-101.
"Public Hospital." <u>NewL</u> (48:3/4) Spr-Sum 82, p. 101-102.

3117. PATILIS, Yannis
"Self-Knowledge" (tr. by Kimon Friar). <u>PoNow</u> (6:5, issue 35) 82, p. 44.
"The Summer Is" (tr. by Kimon Friar). <u>PoNow</u> (6:5, issue 35) 82, p. 44.
"Various Thoughts of a Rising Poet" (tr. by Kimon Friar). <u>PoNow</u> (6:5, issue 35) 82, p. 44.

3118. PATNAIK, Deba P.
"End of March." <u>NewL</u> (49:2) Wint 82-83, p. 50.
"For Karunya." <u>NewL</u> (48:3/4) Spr-Sum 82, p. 163.
"Karunya's Songs." <u>NewL</u> (49:2) Wint 82-83, p. 50-51.
"My Father's God." <u>NewL</u> (48:3/4) Spr-Sum 82, p. 162.

3119. PATRIARCA, Gianna
"Dolce-Amaro." PoetryCR (4:1) Sum 82, p. 10.

3120. PATTANASHETTI, Siddalinga
"Woman" (tr. by A. K. Ramanujan). NewL (48:3/4) Spr-
Sum 82, p. 253.

3121. PATTEN, Karl
"Dying into the Night." KanQ (14:3) Sum 82, p. 183.
"Finding the Old Chalk Woman." OhioR (28) 82, p.
49-50.
"In Spite of All" (tr. of Charles Cos). CharR (8:1)
Spr 82, p. 53.
"The Loose Cow." KanQ (14:3) Sum 82, p. 182.
"November." OhioR (28) 82, p. 48-49.
"Sonnet" (tr. of Charles Cos). CharR (8:1) Spr 82,
p. 54.
"Testament" (tr. of Charles Cos). CharR (8:1) Spr
82, p. 54.

3122. PATTERSON, Cy
"Haiku: Autumn leaves." Bogg (49) 82, p. 51.
"Haiku: From the sidewalk." Bogg (49) 82, p. 50.
"In the Campaign of Love" (For GC). Bogg (49) 82, p.
49.
"Medical Examination." Bogg (48) 82, p. 57.

3123. PATTERSON, Veronica
"The Dream." CapeR (17:2) Sum 82, p. 8.
"The Woman Who Came Back from the Dead." ConcPo
(15:2) Aut 82, p. 88.

3124. PAU-LLOSA, Ricardo
"12" (tr. of Jorge Ruiz Duenas). BelPoJ (32:4) Sum
82, p. 29, 31.
"Bedside Cyclops." PraS (56:1) Spr 82, p. 86.
"Borges" (tr. of Evodio Escalante). BelPoJ (32:4)
Sum 82, p. 31.
"Capurgana" (tr. of Carlos Bedoya). BelPoJ (32:4)
Sum 82, p. 15.
"Celemania" (tr. of Daniel Sada). BelPoJ (32:4) Sum
82, p. 35, 37.
"Century of Light." DekalbLAJ (14:1/4) Aut 80-Sum
81, p. 87.
"Country" (tr. of Santiago Kovadloff). BelPoJ (32:4)
Sum 82, p. 9.
"Encounter" (tr. of Carlos Montemayor). BelPoJ
(32:4) Sum 82, p. 33.
"The Ends of Days" (tr. of Antonio M. Rivera).
BelPoJ (32:4) Sum 82, p. 23.
"Forehead Resting upon the Table" (tr. of Vicente
Gerbasi). BelPoJ (32:4) Sum 82, p. 43.
"In the Long Run, Like Any Other Life" (tr. of
Javier Sologuren). BelPoJ (32:4) Sum 82, p. 37,
39.
"Jerusalem" (tr. of Manuela Fingueret). BelPoJ
(32:4) Sum 82, p. 3.
"Kandinsky As a Pretext" (tr. of Santiago E.
Sylvester). BelPoJ (32:4) Sum 82, p. 11.

"New Day" (tr. of Vicente Gerbasi). BelPoJ (32:4)
Sum 82, p. 43.
"Nocturnal Being" (tr. of Roberto Juarroz). BelPoJ
(32:4) Sum 82, p. 7.
"On High" (tr. of Belkis Cuza Male). BelPoJ (32:4)
Sum 82, p. 19.
"Once Again the Same Despair" (tr. of Augusto Tamayo
Vargas). BelPoJ (32:4) Sum 82, p. 41.
"Paris Inundated" (for Ron De Maris). Kayak (59) Je
82, p. 41.
"Polished Copper" (tr. of Vicente Gerbasi). BelPoJ
(32:4) Sum 82, p. 41.
"The Red Hole." Kayak (58) Ja 82, p. 57.
"The Return of Nietzsche" (tr. of Raul Henao).
BelPoJ (32:4) Sum 82, p. 17.
"The Royal Couple" (tr. of Enrique Gomez-Correa).
BelPoJ (32:4) Sum 82, p. 11, 13.
"Rug As Lyric" (tr. of Alberto Girri). BelPoJ (32:4)
Sum 82, p. 3, 5.
"Silhouette." Kayak (60) O 82, p. 62.
"Snoring in the Sun, Like a Seal in the Galapagos"
(tr. of J. G. Cobo Borda). BelPoJ (32:4) Sum 82,
p. 15.
"Sorting Metaphors." PoetryNW (23:1) Spr 82, p. 4-
6.
"St. George and the Notary" (after the painting by
David Manzur). PartR (49:3) 82, p. 438-439.
"Sunday" (tr. of Margara Russotto). BelPoJ (32:4)
Sum 82, p. 45, 47.
"Through a Crack in the Light" (tr. of David Escobar
Galindo). BelPoJ (32:4) Sum 82, p. 25, 27.
"To Octavio Paz" (tr. of Heberto Padilla). BelPoJ
(32:4) Sum 82, p. 21.
"Venus." SouthernPR (23, i.e. 22:2) Aut 82, p. 35.
"Which Is to Say" (tr. of Santiago Kovadloff).
BelPoJ (32:4) Sum 82, p. 9.

3125. PAUL, David J.
"Lawren Harris' 'The Ice House, Coldwell, Lake
Superior', c. 1923." Quarry (31:3) Sum 82, p. 72.
"'Maligne Lake, Jasper Park', 1924." Quarry (31:3)
Sum 82, p. 72-73.
"'Pic Island', 1924." Quarry (31:3) Sum 82, p. 73-
74.

3126. PAUL, James
"He Knows He Has a House." Nimrod (25:2) Spr-Sum
82, p. 35.
"Inheritance." Nimrod (25:2) Spr-Sum 82, p. 35.
"Introduction." Nimrod (25:2) Spr-Sum 82, p. 52.
"Islands of Grass." MichQR (21:1) Wint 82, p. 163-
164.
"The Serenade." MissouriR (5:3) Sum 82, p. 27.

3127. PAUL, Jay S.
"Before Snows Silence Everything." CimR (61) O 82,
p. 4.
"We May Have to Cross High Bridges and Bend around
Mountains But." Abraxas (25/26) 82, p. 58.

3128. PAULENICH, Fred
"Eli." HiramPoR (31) Aut-Wint 82, p. 37.

3129. PAVESE, Cesare
"Ancestors" (tr. by Duncan Bush). Stand (23:2) 82,
p. 5.
"Revolt" (tr. by Duncan Bush). Stand (23:2) 82, p.
6.
"Summer" (tr. by Michael L. Johnson). LitR (25:3)
Spr 82, p. 372.
"Two Cigarettes" (tr. by Duncan Bush). Stand (23:2)
82, p. 4.

3130. PAVLIDES, Lefteris
from The Primal Sun (Helios o Protos): (IX, XIV)
(tr. of Odysseus Elytis, w. Edward Moran). CharR
(8:1) Spr 82, p. 51-52.

3131. PAWLAK, Mark
"All the News" (1-7). HangL (42) 82, p. 26-29.

3132. PAYACK, Peter
"Cranial Capacities." PoNow (6:6, issue 36) 82, p.
14.
"The Invention of the Roman Empire." PoNow (6:6,
issue 36) 82, p. 14.
"Monica's Favorite Recipe." PoNow (6:4, issue 34)
82, p. 15.
"The Poverty of the Dead." PoNow (6:6, issue 36)
82, p. 14.
"Researcher Finds 'Death' Site of Socrates." PoNow
(6:6, issue 36) 82, p. 14.

3133. PAYNE, John Burnett
"It's Tough, Jethro, Baby, Real Tough" (for Cid
Hoey). Wind (12:46) 82, p. 27-28.

3134. PEABODY, G. F. (George)
"IV. Brief Thoughts on Human Behavior."
PoetryCR (3:4) Sum 82, p. 15.
"Camp Life #3 - The Water Hauler." PottPort (4) 82-
83, p. 45.
"Some Nights I Dream of Dynamite." PottPort (4) 82-
83, p. 26.

3135. PEABODY, Richard, Jr.
"Homogenized Poetry." PikeF (4) Spr 82, p. 37.

3136. PEACOCK, Molly
"A Bed for a Woman." Shen (33:2) 82, p. 18.
"The Shoulders of Women." LittleM (13:3/4) 82, p.
28.
"This Time." NewL (49:1) Aut 82, p. 74.

3137. PEAK, Mary
"Easter at the Veterans' Hospital." LittleBR (2:3)
Spr 82, p. 71.

3138. PEARCE, Carol Ann
      "The Prison of Streams." SmPd (19:3, issue 56) Aut
      82, p. 25-26.

3139. PEARCE-LEWIS, Kathleen
      "Garden Party." Bogg (48) 82, p. 26.

3140. PEARSON, Helen
      "Greeting Card Rack." LittleBR (1:3) Spr 81, p. 51.

3141. PEASE, Deborah
      "Repercussions." Salm (55) Wint 82, p. 129-130.

3142. PEAVY, Linda
      "Norwegian Liturgy." AntigR (50) Sum 82, p. 119.

3143. PECK, John
      "Jaruzelski Winter." Salm (56) Spr 82, p. 177-178.

3144. PECKENPAUGH, Angela
      "Tulips." Abraxas (25/26) 82, p. 104.

3145. PEDRO, Richard
      "Indian Face." Telescope (2) Aut 81, p. 120.
      "White Buffalo." Telescope (2) Aut 81, p. 121.

3146. PEERADINA, Saleem
      "Landscape with Locomotive." NewL (48:3/4) Spr-Sum
      82, p. 84-85.

3147. PELL, Derek
      "Lolita, over the Hill." Bogg (49) 82, p. 19.

3148. PELLETIER, G.
      "From Sips of Fire on South Lake Shore" (to Ben
      McClary). ConcPo (15:1) Spr 82, p. 59.

3149. PELLETIER, Louise de Gonzague
      "Avec des Mots Courts" (extraits d'une suite
      poetique). Os (14) 82, p. 6.

      PENA, Silvia Novo
      See: NOVO PENA, Silvia

3150. PENN, Rick
      "Coyote." WormR (22:1, issue 85) 82, p. 39.
      "Houses" (for B., in memoriam). Northeast (3:12)
      Wint 81-82, p. 14.
      "Migration." Northeast (3:12) Wint 81-82, p. 14.
      "The Tusked Burrowers." WormR (22:1, issue 85) 82,
      p. 39.

3151. PENNANT, Edmund
      "The Game Plan." PoNow (6:6, issue 36) 82, p. 47.

3152. PENNER, Judith
      "4 Steps in Making a Short Splice." PottPort (4)
      82-83, p. 30.
      "Poem: These blue dreams I am having." Germ (6:2)
      Aut-Wint 82, p. 35.

3153. PENNINGTON, Lee
"James T." Wind (12:45) 82, p. 30-31.

3154. PEPPER, Patric
"Fishing." Gargoyle (15/16) 80, p. 8.

3155. PERCHIK, Simon
"Air laughed in and stored: tires" MinnR (NS18) Spr 82, p. 45.
"The attic is crating itself, I watch." MinnR (NS18) Spr 82, p. 45.
"Awake, words protect me." ModernPS (11:1/2) 82, p. 103-104.
"Beach Blanket Spread." SoDakR (20:2) Sum 82, p. 39.
"A chance, a leg." HolCrit (19:1) F 82, p. 19.
"The dead brag." Confr (24) Sum 82, p. 66.
"Frost nourishes New York." Wind (12:44) 82, p. 33.
"He named each rivet." ModernPS (11:1/2) 82, p. 103.
"His crib offshore." Wind (12:44) 82, p. 33.
"His life oral, pens." Northeast (3:12) Wint 81-82, p. 16.
"I begin with a toss, my nets." Northeast (3:12) Wint 81-82, p. 16.
"I Pray above Each Meal." EnPas (13) 82, p. 21.
"I wait for leftovers." Focus (15:94) O 82, p. 23.
"Poem: Leave it alone!" CentR (26:2) Spr 82, p. 172.
"A safe :three rifles leaning next to next." ModernPS (11:1/2) 82, p. 103.
"Shaking this faucet." Confr (24) Sum 82, p. 67.
"Stale I look for rocks." Confr (24) Sum 82, p. 67.
"Under the soot." PoNow (6:6, issue 36) 82, p. 6.

3156. PEREIRA, Sam
"The Astronomy of the Boulevard" (for Tom Waits). Telescope (1) Spr 81, p. 4-5.
"Fata Morgana." Telescope (1) Spr 81, p. 17-18.
"Sartre." Telescope (1) Spr 81, p. 6.

3157. PEREIRA, Teresinka
"Roberto Santoro, Desaparecido." Maize (5:3/4) Spr-Sum 82, p. 62.

3158. PEREZ, Floridor
"La Autoridad" Inti (12) Aut 80, p. 89.
"Cartas Sin Corregir, Retratos Sin Retocar" Inti (12) Aut 80, p. 86-88.
"Regresos." Inti (12) Aut 80, p. 86.
"Vivir (Tiempo Presente)." Inti (12) Aut 80, p. 88.

3159. PEREZ, Maria de los Milagros
"Tu Instante" (from Brotados de la Sed). Mairena (4:9) Spr 82, p. 41.

3160. PERKINS-ATKINSON, Pamela
"Basil." Im (8:1) 82, p. 12.

3161. PERLMAN, Anne S.
    "Practical Gardener." Hudson (35:4) Wint 82-83, p.
    595-596.

3162. PERONARD, Kai
    "Crisp Golden French Fries and Fat Juicy Spare
    Ribs." HangL (42) 82, p. 62.
    "Myers." HangL (42) 82, p. 63.
    "Rainy Day." HangL (41) 82, p. 58.
    "Teenagerage." HangL (41) 82, p. 59.
    "Uncle Louie." HangL (41) 82, p. 56-57.

3163. PERRY, Ronald
    "Absentee Landlords." NewL (49:2) Wint 82-83, p. 6-
    7.
    "Firing Out." NewL (49:2) Wint 82-83, p. 10-15.
    "Home." AmerPoR (11:6) N-D 82, p. 35.
    "Home." NewL (49:2) Wint 82-83, p. 7-8.
    "Improvisations on Themes Suggested by Sitor
    Situmorang." AmerPoR (11:6) N-D 82, p. 35-36.
    "In the Shallows." AmerPoR (11:6) N-D 82, p. 34-35.
    "An Owl." NewL (49:2) Wint 82-83, p. 9.
    "A Passing Bell." NewL (49:2) Wint 82-83, p. 5-6.
    "Three Dogs." NewL (49:2) Wint 82-83, p. 8-9.
    "Three Poems Against the Mountain." NewL (49:2)
    Wint 82-83, p. 16-19.

3164. PERSONS, Alice
    "Sunday." CapeR (18:1) Wint 82, p. 16.
    "Supermarket, Saturday Midnight." CapeR (18:1) Wint
    82, p. 17.

3165. PESEROFF, Joyce
    "Letter to the Country." Ploughs (8:1) 82, p. 45.
    "October." Ploughs (8:2/3) 82, p. 199.
    "Two Photographs" (for J.H.W.). Ploughs (8:1) 82, p.
    43-44.

3166. PESSOA, Fernando
    "They Had No Electricity There" (tr. by Erskine
    Lane). Spirit (6:2/3) 82, p. 183.

3167. PETER OF BLOIS
    "A Friendly Warning" (tr. by Fleur Adcock). MalR
    (61) F 82, p. 216-217.
    "A New Leaf" (tr. by Fleur Adcock). MalR (61) F 82,
    p. 215.
    "A Touch of Impatience" (tr. by Fleur Adcock). MalR
    (61) F 82, p. 214.

3168. PETERS, Nancy
    "Deer." PraS (56:1) Spr 82, p. 87.

3169. PETERS, Robert
    "Bronze Chains." NewL (48:2) Wint 81-82, p. 29.
    "Departure" (after Heine's "Der Scheidende"). NewL
    (48:2) Wint 81-82, p. 31.
    from Hawker: "Cows." NewL (49:1) Aut 82, p. 31.
    from Hawker: "Hawker Meditates on Birth and Death
    (1850)." NewL (49:1) Aut 82, p. 30-31.

from Hawker: "Needy Family." NewL (49:1) Aut 82, p. 32-33.
from Hawker: "Robert Stephen Hawker, Eccentric Cornish Vicar, to Robert Peters in a Dream." NewL (49:1) Aut 82, p. 29-30.
"Invitation." NewL (48:2) Wint 81-82, p. 31.
"My Father as House-Builder." Abraxas (25/26) 82, p. 70.
"Photograph One." NewL (48:2) Wint 81-82, p. 30.
"Photograph Two." NewL (48:2) Wint 81-82, p. 30.
"Rat." Abraxas (25/26) 82, p. 71.

PETERSEN, Anne Oriel
See: ORIEL-PETERSEN, Anne

3170. PETERSEN, Donald
"Upstate Lilacs." AmerS (51:2) Spr 82, p. 204.

3171. PETERSON, Eugene H.
"He Marveled at Their Unbelief." ChrC (99:6) F 24, 82, p. 196.

3172. PETERSON, Jim
"The Dead." CharR (8:1) Spr 82, p. 33-34.

3173. PETERSON, Robert
"Leadville, Colorado: Scattering My Aunt's Ashes" (Althea Crawford, 1894-1974). Kayak (59) Je 82, p. 24.
"Yellow Ferry Harbor, Sausalito." Kayak (59) Je 82, p. 25.

3174. PETRARCH, Francesco
"Quel Vago Impallider" (tr. by Ezra Pound). Antaeus (44) Wint 82, p. 30.

3175. PETREMAN, David A.
"Demetrio." Poem (46) N 82, p. 24.
"On Some Days." Poem (46) N 82, p. 25.
"Squirrels." Poem (46) N 82, p. 23.
"Walking in the Woods with My Father." KanQ (14:3) Sum 82, p. 164-165.

3176. PETRIE, Paul
"The Burgeoning." CentR (26:3) Sum 82, p. 268.
"The Game." SouthwR (67:1) Wint 82, p. 76-77.
"The Greenhouse." SewanR (90:4) Aut 82, p. 520-521.
"The Optimist." CentR (26:3) Sum 82, p. 268-269.
"Winter Solstice." WestHR (36:4) Wint 82, p. 344.

3177. PETROSKI, Henry
"Ave Atque Vale!" PoNow (6:4, issue 34) 82, p. 43.
"State Street's Last Parade." PoNow (6:4, issue 34) 82, p. 43.
"Windows Are Mirrors." PoNow (6:4, issue 34) 82, p. 43.

3178. PETROSKY, Anthony
"The Visit." OhioR (29) 82, p. 130.

3179. PETTEE, Dan
"The Photograph Album." BallSUF (23:2) Spr 82, p.
53-54.

3180. PETTIT, Michael
"Cardinal." MissouriR (5:3) Sum 82, p. 7.

3181. PEVEAR, Richard
"Stanzas." Pequod (14) 82, p. 12-15.

3182. PFEIFFER, Christy
"Early Reading." LittleBR (2:3) Spr 82, p. 48.

3183. PFINGSTON, Roger
"Going Back." AspenJ (1:2) Sum 82, p. 46.
"His Kind and Mine." Abraxas (25/26) 82, p. 62.

3184. PHELPS, Donald
"Generations." Shen (33:2) 82, p. 54-56.

3185. PHIFER, Marjorie Maddox
"The Widow in Her Garden." Confr (24) Sum 82, p.
121.

3186. PHILBRICK, Stephen
"Fattening Dorset Sheep." PoNow (6:6, issue 36) 82,
p. 25.
"Haylike and After." PoNow (6:6, issue 36) 82, p.
25.

3187. PHILLIPS, Bluebell S.
"Canada's Terry" (written just before his death).
WritersL S 82, p. 7.
"Glen Gould." WritersL D 82, p. 2.
"The Searcher." WritersL Je 82, p. 11.
"Threnody for My Son" (dead in a motor accident
December 27, 1975). WritersL O-N 82, p. 46.

3188. PHILLIPS, Dennis
"Dream of Ocean with Doors." Sulfur (2:2, issue 5)
82, p. 91-93.
"Self-Portrait." Sulfur (2:2, issue 5) 82, p. 89-
90.

3189. PHILLIPS, Dorrie
"3 A.M. - Again" (to George). PottPort (4) 82-83, p.
28.
"Springtime Prayer." PottPort (4) 82-83, p. 34.

3190. PHILLIPS, James
"Love Poem 1978." Catalyst (Erotica Issue) 82, p.
6.
"The Slender words that kisses drink." Catalyst
(Erotica Issue) 82, p. 6.
"Slender Words." Vis (9) 82, p. 10.

3191. PHILLIPS, Louis
"Confessions of a Stilt-Walker." Confr (24) Sum 82,
p. 57.
"Scandal Sheet." CapeR (17:2) Sum 82, p. 6-7.

3192. PHILLIPS, Margaret
"Dear friend, so full of magic." MendoR (6) Sum 81, p. 41.
"Hummingbird, nothing is held for more than an instant." MendoR (6) Sum 81, p. 61.
"Lying here under the redwoods." MendoR (6) Sum 81, p. 62.
"These hot days will be ended tomorrow." MendoR (6) Sum 81, p. 61.

3193. PHILLIPS, Michael J.
"What Poetry Should Be About." WindO (40, Anti-Haiku issue) Sum 82, p. 24.

3194. PHILLIPS, Robert
"The Caves of Childhood." Chelsea (41) 82, p. 154-155.
"In the Dumps" (for Howard Moss). Shen (33:2) 82, p. 68-69.
"My Unicorn." AmerPoR (11:2) Mr-Ap 82, p. 35.
"Tree Sequence." Chelsea (41) 82, p. 152-154.
"Wear" (for Philip Booth). Chelsea (41) 82, p. 155.

3195. PICANO, Felice
"On Seeing a Photograph of Whitman as an Old Man." PoNow (6:5, issue 35) 82, p. 35.

3196. PICCIOTTO, Madeleine
"About This Place" (tr. of Carlos Nejar). QRL (22) 81, p. 48-49.
"The Animals That Give Milk" (tr. of Carlos Nejar). QRL (22) 81, p. 30.
"Between Two Reigns" (tr. of Carlos Nejar). QRL (22) 81, p. 28.
"Chant" (tr. of Carlos Nejar). QRL (22) 81, p. 35.
"Cultivation" (tr. of Carlos Nejar). QRL (22) 81, p. 14.
"Edict" (tr. of Carlos Nejar). QRL (22) 81, p. 37.
"Enlistment" (tr. of Carlos Nejar). QRL (22) 81, p. 10-11.
"Exile" (tr. of Carlos Nejar). QRL (22) 81, p. 15.
"Falling Down" (tr. of Carlos Nejar). QRL (22) 81, p. 43-44.
"Getting Ready" (tr. of Carlos Nejar). QRL (22) 81, p. 40-41.
"Inheritance" (tr. of Carlos Nejar). QRL (22) 81, p. 34.
"Machine" (tr. of Carlos Nejar). QRL (22) 81, p. 24-25.
"The Master of the Land" (tr. of Carlos Nejar). QRL (22) 81, p. 31.
"The Metal of Hope" (tr. of Carlos Nejar). QRL (22) 81, p. 33.
"Obstacle Course" (tr. of Carlos Nejar). QRL (22) 81, p. 38-39.
"Oil Lamps" (tr. of Carlos Nejar). QRL (22) 81, p. 23.
"Poem about Disaster" (tr. of Carlos Nejar). QRL (22) 81, p. 45.

"Premonition" (tr. of Carlos Nejar). QRL (22) 81, p. 42.
"Protest" (tr. of Carlos Nejar). QRL (22) 81, p. 36.
"Setting Off" (tr. of Carlos Nejar). QRL (22) 81, p. 52.
"Smoothness" (tr. of Carlos Nejar). QRL (22) 81, p. 53-64.
"Solid Food" (tr. of Carlos Nejar). QRL (22) 81, p. 32.
"The Stable" (tr. of Carlos Nejar). QRL (22) 81, p. 26.
"Testimony" (tr. of Carlos Nejar). QRL (22) 81, p. 16.
"This Creature, Death" (tr. of Carlos Nejar). QRL (22) 81, p. 50-51.
"Visitor" (tr. of Carlos Nejar). QRL (22) 81, p. 12-13.
"Water Clock" (tr. of Carlos Nejar). QRL (22) 81, p. 46-47.
"What Can Be Changed" (tr. of Carlos Nejar). QRL (22) 81, p. 17-19.
"Work" (tr. of Carlos Nejar). QRL (22) 81, p. 27.
"Yoke" (tr. of Carlos Nejar). QRL (22) 81, p. 21-22.

3197. PICCIOTTO, Selim-Roberto
"He's Still Alive, Grown Small My Father" (tr. of Jose Kozer). Im (8:2) 82, p. 5.
"Remember Sylvia" (tr. of Jose Kozer). Im (8:2) 82, p. 5.
"Syllogism" (tr. of Jose Kozer). Im (8:2) 82, p. 5.
"Welcome" (tr. of Jose Kozer). Im (8:2) 82, p. 5.

3198. PICHAMURTI, Na
"I Do Not Know (Theriyavillai)" (tr. by P. G. Sundararajan). NewL (48:3/4) Spr-Sum 82, p. 155.

3199. PICHE, Alphonze
"Quai" (tr. by Gary Wilson). DenQ (17:1) Spr 82, p. 88.
"Retreat" (tr. by Gary Wilson). DenQ (17:1) Spr 82, p. 89.

3200. PICHON, Ulysses
"All Fly Home" (a letter: staring at Al Jarreau's album cover). Obs (7:2/3) Sum-Wint 81, p. 184-186.
"La. Partying in LA." Obs (7:2/3) Sum-Wint 81, p. 183.
"The Way I Heard It." Obs (7:2/3) Sum-Wint 81, p. 181-182.

3201. PIERCE, Edith Lovejoy
"Total Eclipse." ChrC (99:25) Ag 4-11, 82, p. 826.

3202. PIERCY, Marge
"The Cast Off." Spirit (6:2/3) 82, p. 17-18.
"Charm for Attracting Wild Money." PoNow (6:4, issue 34) 82, p. 19.
"Down at the Bottom of Things." PoNow (6:6, issue 36) 82, p. 8.

"From Something, Nothing." PoNow (6:5, issue 35)
  82, p. 40.
"Homage to Lucille, Dr. Lord-Heinstein." Iowa
  (12:2/3) Spr-Sum 81, p. 278-279.
"Laocoon Is the Name of the Figure." Iowa (12:2/3)
  Spr-Sum 81, p. 280.
"A Private Bestiary." PoNow (6:6, issue 36) 82, p.
  8.
"Stone, Paper, Knife." OP (34) Aut-Wint 82, p. 3-9.

3203. PIERMAN, Carol J.
"Celebration" (For SLH). CapeR (17:2) Sum 82, p. 44.
"Les Deux Paulettes." OP (34) Aut-Wint 82, p. 37.
"The Dowser." PoNow (7:1, issue 37) 82, p. 25.
"Fish Hands." OP (34) Aut-Wint 82, p. 38.
"Icarus." PoNow (6:5, issue 35) 82, p. 11.
"My Memoirs." OP (34) Aut-Wint 82, p. 39.
"Nova." Ascent (7:2) 82, p. 46-47.
"Spring Morning." PoNow (7:1, issue 37) 82, p. 25.

PIERO, W. S. di
See: Di PIERO, W. S.

3204. PIETZ, John
"A Sacred Cow." BallSUF (23:2) Spr 82, p. 45.

3205. PIJEWSKI, John
"Old Night." LitR (25:3) Spr 82, p. 382.
"Religion." LitR (25:3) Spr 82, p. 381.

3206. PILCHER, Barry Edgar
"It seems such a long time since yesterday." Bogg
  (48) 82, p. 40.
"It's gorgeous." Bogg (48) 82, p. 44.
"Loch Ness." Bogg (49) 82, p. 37.
"On the Tilt." Bogg (49) 82, p. 60.

3207. PILKINGTON, Kevin
"Fairfield Beach" (For my brother Tom). Poetry
  (140:3) Je 82, p. 148-149.
"The Reincarnation of Montana." Poetry (140:3) Je
  82, p. 150.

3208. PILLIN, William
"Do Not Plan for Me." PoNow (6:6, issue 36) 82, p.
  10.
"The Habit." PoNow (6:6, issue 36) 82, p. 10.
"The Old Man." ArizQ (38:3) Aut 82, p. 240.
"The Truth." ArizQ (38:2) Sum 82, p. 118.

3209. PINCHEIRA, Dolores
"Madre." LetFem (8:2) 82, p. 88.

PINEDA, Victor Manuel Gomez
See: GOMEZ PINEDA, Victor Manuel

3210. PINERO, Miguel
"A Lower East Side Poem." RevChic (10:1/2) Wint-Spr
  82, p. 90-91.

PINERO   396

"New York City Hard Time Blues." RevChic (10:1/2)
     Wint-Spr 82, p. 92-97.
"Requiem for the Men's Shelter." RevChic (10:1/2)
     Wint-Spr 82, p. 89.

3211. PINES, Paul
     from Glyphs: "Where I sit pigeons squat." Pequod
          (15) 82, p. 37-41.
     "Whistler's Blue." Confr (24) Sum 82, p. 44.

     PING, Chin Woon
     See: CHIN, Woon Ping

3212. PINSKER, Sanford
     "After the Beach." ConcPo (15:1) Spr 82, p. 48.
     "The Bagel, After" (for David Ignatow). CEACritic
          (45:1) N 82, p. 23.
     "The Beach, Before." CEACritic (45:1) N 82, p. 22.
     "In South Florida." ConcPo (15:1) Spr 82, p. 48.
     "Letter to Creeley--and Li Po--from Lancaster."
          KanQ (14:3) Sum 82, p. 144.
     "Lines for Robert Creeley." CEACritic (45:1) N 82,
          p. 22.
     "Professorial Fantasies." Academe (68:3) My-Je 82,
          p. 35.
     "Summer Begins." CEACritic (45:1) N 82, p. 23.
     "Two Outings on La Grande Jatte." Confr (23) Wint
          82, p. 159.
     "The Unfogging Mirror." CEACritic (45:1) N 82, p.
          23.

3213. PINSKY, Robert
     "Fairyland." AmerPoR (11:1) Ja-F 82, p. 48.
     "Flowers." NewEngR (5:1/2) Aut-Wint 82, p. 120-121.
     "The Separate Notebooks: A Mirrored Gallery (Page
          34)" (tr. of Czeslaw Milosz). Antaeus (47) Aut 82,
          p. 15.
     "The Volume." Antaeus (47) Aut 82, p. 50-51.
     "A Woman." NewYorker (58:8) Ap 12, 82, p. 48.

3214. PISANI, Osmar
     from As Raizes do Fogo: (III). Prismal (7/8) Spr 82,
          p. 95.
     "E agora, compassiva, a noite" (from As Paredes do
          Mundo). Prismal (7/8) Spr 82, p. 97.
     "Este e um tempo untoso" (from As Paredes do Mundo).
          Prismal (7/8) Spr 82, p. 96.
     "Poema a Cruz e Souza" (from As Raizes do Vento).
          Prismal (7/8) Spr 82, p. 94.

3215. PITKIN, Anne
     "Fugue." PraS (56:3) Aut 82, p. 20-21.
     "October, Two Poems." NewEngR (5:1/2) Aut-Wint 82,
          p. 187.
     "Sail: After My Father's Death." PraS (56:3) Aut
          82, p. 21-22.

3216. PITNER, Erin Clayton
     "To a Child on Her Sixth Birthday" (For Erin
          Abbott). CapeR (18:1) Wint 82, p. 35.

3217. PITT, Simon
"The Poet's Dreams." Bogg (48) 82, p. 57.

3218. PITZER, Jack
"Perspective." Wind (12:46) 82, p. 29.

3219. PLANTE, Tom
"Waiting for the Mail." SeC (9:1/2) 80, p. 22.
"Why Go On." SeC (9:1/2) 80, p. 17.

3220. PLATH, James
"Jump Start." Abraxas (25/26) 82, p. 76.

3221. PLUMLY, Stanley
"Button Money." AntR (40:1) Wint 82, p. 94.
"Maples." Field (27) Aut 82, p. 58.
"Promising the Air." Atl (249:4) Ap 82, p. 28.
"Sonnet." MissouriR (6:1) Aut 82, p. 16.
"Sunday, Seattle" (for William Matthews). AntR
   (40:1) Wint 82, p. 92-93.
"Two Moments, for My Mother." Field (27) Aut 82, p.
   56-57.
"Valentine." NewYorker (58:20) Jl 5, 82, p. 36.
"Waders and Swimmers." NewEngR (5:1/2) Aut-Wint 82,
   p. 182-183.

3222. POBO, Kenneth
"For My Jet-Boy." Hangl (43) Wint 82-83, p. 36.
"The Midwestern Poem." Abraxas (25/26) 82, p. 95.
"Red Virginia Creeper." PoNow (7:1, issue 37) 82,
   p. 34.
"Sympathy for the Devil." Vis (9) 82, p. 31.
"Windowbox in Winter." Hangl (43) Wint 82-83, p.
   37.

3223. POGGE, Mary
"Cinema Date." PoNow (7:1, issue 37) 82, p. 35.

3224. POGSON, Patricia
"Spring." Bogg (49) 82, p. 42.

3225. POLACKOVA, Kaca
"Killing Rabbits" (tr. of Miroslav Valek). Sulfur
   (2:2, issue 5) 82, p. 124-125.

3226. POLGAR, Steven
"I Can Do Nothing" (tr. of Elizabeth Borchers, w.
   Nicholas Kolumban). AmerPoR (11:1) Ja-F 82, p. 31.
"Saturn" (tr. of Gunter Grass, w. Nicholas
   Kolumban). AmerPoR (11:1) Ja-F 82, p. 31.

3227. POLITE, Frank
"Mantelpiece." PoNow (6:5, issue 35) 82, p. 21.

3228. POLK, Noel
"Girl on the Ocracoke Ferry." SouthernR (18:4) Aut
   82, p. 830-831.
"Many Men Would Not Have Chosen Beauty." SouthernR
   (18:4) Aut 82, p. 828-829.

3229. POLLAK, Felix
"A Chassidic Cat's Impatient Dinner Request." NewL
(48:2) Wint 81-82, p. 85.
"Jerusalem." NewL (48:2) Wint 81-82, p. 84.
"Kodachrome." NewL (48:2) Wint 81-82, p. 85.
"Love Is a Present Tense Noun" (corrected version,
to replace (3:11) Sum 81, p. 6). Northeast (3:12)
Wint 81-82, p. 13.
"On Turning the Light Out." Northeast (3:12) Wint
81-82, p. 13.
"Reading the Bible in Braille." NewL (48:2) Wint
81-82, p. 84.

3230. POLLET, Sylvester
"September." BelPoJ (32:3) Spr 82, p. 25.

3231. POLSON, Don
"Hogging Time." PottPort (4) 82-83, p. 50.
"In a Few Dark Hours." PoetryCR (4:1) Sum 82, p.
16.
"The Old Jogger." PottPort (4) 82-83, p. 50.
"Rising in the Morning." PoetryCR (4:1) Sum 82, p.
16.
"Sunfish." PoetryCR (4:1) Sum 82, p. 16.
"What's in a Name" (for Len Gasparini). PoetryCR
(4:1) Sum 82, p. 16.

3232. PONCE, Mary Helen
"La Despedida." Maize (6:1/2) Aut-Wint 82-83, p.
56.
"Las Guisas." Maize (6:1/2) Aut-Wint 82-83, p. 54.
"Los Vatos." Maize (6:1/2) Aut-Wint 82-83, p. 55.

3233. PONSOT, Marie
"Defusing the Usual Criminal Metaphors." Comm
(109:7) Ap 9, 82, p. 208.

3234. PONZO,Alberto Luis
"Este Mundo Yace." Mairena (4:10) Sum-Aut 82, p.
56-57.

3235. POOLE, Thomas
"Dancing Blind." QW (14) Spr-Sum 82, p. 42.
"Someplace Here." QW (14) Spr-Sum 82, p. 43.

3236. PORRITT, R.
"Near Winter." BelPoJ (33:2) Wint 82-83, p. 6-9.

3237. PORTER, Anne
"Leavetaking." Comm (109:16) S 24, 82, p. 503.

3238. PORTER, Caryl
"Psalm 4." ChrC (99:13) Ap 14, 82, p. 436.

3239. PORTER, Helen
"The Shovellers." PottPort (4) 82-83, p. 9.

3240. POSNER, David
"Brooklyn." NewL (48:2) Wint 81-82, p. 41.
"How He Lives." VirQR (58:4) Aut 82, p. 692-693.

"Polar Bear." Kayak (59) Je 82, p. 11.

3241. POSTER, Carol
"Riverbed" (for Richard Dillard). DekalbLAJ (14:1/4)
Aut 80-Sum 81, p. 88.

3242. POSTON, Jane
"Logan Square." Iowa (13:1) Wint 82, p. 124-126.

3243. POTTIER, Annette
"Yarmouth N.S." PoetryCR (4:2) Wint 82, p. 15.

3244. POTTS, Charles
"I Dream of Oaxaca." Spirit (6:2/3) 82, p. 105-107.

3245. POTVIN, Carole
"Une Larme." Os (15) 82, p. 11.

3246. POULIN, A., Jr.
"Brothers." QW (14) Spr-Sum 82, p. 75.

3247. POULIN, Al
"Lament in Spring" (To Robin Morgan). Salm (57) Sum
82, p. 120-121.
"Song in Spring" (To Basilike Poulin). Salm (57) Sum
82, p. 121-122.

3248. POULIOS, Lefteris
"Sonorous Page" (tr. by Kimon Friar). PoNow (6:4,
issue 34) 82, p. 40.

3249. POUND, Ezra
"Amor de Lonh" (tr. of Jaufre Rudel). Antaeus (44)
Wint 82, p. 28-29.
"Amors e Jois e Liocs e Tems" (tr. of Arnaut
Daniel). Antaeus (44) Wint 82, p. 24-25.
"Amors e Jois e Liocs e Tems" (second version) (tr.
of Arnaut Daniel). Antaeus (44) Wint 82, p. 26-27.
"Er Vei Vermeills, Vertz, Blaus, Blancs, Groucs"
(tr. of Arnaut Daniel). Antaeus (44) Wint 82, p.
20-21.
"Er Vei Vermeills, Vertz, Blaus, Blancs, Groucs"
(second version) (tr. of Arnaut Daniel). Antaeus
(44) Wint 82, p. 22-23.
"Fragment, 1944." YaleR (71:2) Wint 82, p. 161-162.
"Guarda Ben Dico, Guarda, Ben Ti Guarda" (tr. of
Guido Cavalcanti). Antaeus (44) Wint 82, p. 31-33.
"Lanquan Vei Fueill' e Flors e Frug" (tr. of Arnaut
Daniel). Antaeus (44) Wint 82, p. 16-17.
"Lanquan Vei Fueill' e Flors e Frug" (second
version) (tr. of Arnaut Daniel). Antaeus (44) Wint
82, p. 18-19.
"Quel Vago Impallider" (tr. of Francesco Petrarch).
Antaeus (44) Wint 82, p. 30.

3250. POWELL, Craig
"Father Speaking to Son about Fathers." Grain
(10:2) My 82, p. 33-34.
"Through the Window." Grain (10:2) My 82, p. 33.

3251. POWELL, Susan
   "Gossip." Telescope (3) Sum 82, p. 28-29.
   "The Mercy of Words." Telescope (3) Sum 82, p. 17-
   18.

3252. POWERS, Arthur
   "Nauvoo to Bishop Hill" (Summer/1977). HiramPoR (31)
   Aut-Wint 82, p. 38.
   "Poem Beginning with a Line from Garcia Lorca" (For
   Bairro Boa Vista). SouthwR (67:2) Spr 82, p. 195.

3253. POWERS, Jack
   "Our Father." Sam (33:3, issue 131) 82, p. 25.
   "Perhaps, at a time like this, it would be best."
   Sam (33:3, issue 131) 82, p. 42-43.

3254. POWERS, William
   "Knocking Down Trees." Ascent (8:1) 82, p. 49.
   "You Know." CentR (26:4) Aut 82, p. 354-355.

   POY, Phillip de
   See: DePOY, Phillip

3255. POYNER, Ken
   "Ethics." WestB (11) 82, p. 60.
   "Legacy: McClellan's Rumors of the Better Life."
   WestB (10) 82, p. 11.
   "The Man Who Loved to Murder Small Dogs." Wind
   (12:46) 82, p. 30-31.
   "McClellan's America." WestB (11) 82, p. 61.
   "Miscarriage." Wind (12:46) 82, p. 30.
   "Social Block." WestB (10) 82, p. 12.
   "Ultimate Responsibility." WestB (10) 82, p. 13.
   "War Effort." WestB (10) 82, p. 14-15.

3256. PRADED, Joni
   "The Preservationists." Tendril (13) Sum 82, p. 53.
   "White Knight." Tendril (13) Sum 82, p. 54.

3257. PRATT, C. W.
   "October." Poetry (140:6) S 82, p. 340.
   "Tracks." Poetry (140:6) S 82, p. 339.

3258. PRATT, Charles
   "Raking Leaves in New England." Comm (109:5) Mr 12,
   82, p. 158.
   "Remembering the Science Fair" (for the thirtieth
   reunion of my high school class). HiramPoR (32)
   Spr-Sum 82, p. 42.

3259. PRATT, Minnie Bruce
   "A Cold That Is Not the Opposite of Life." Cond (8)
   82, p. 112-116.
   "Out of Season." Cond (8) 82, p. 109.
   "Red String." Cond (8) 82, p. 106-108.
   "Shades." Cond (8) 82, p. 110-111.
   "Walking back up Depot Street." Cond (8) 82, p.
   117-118.

PREIST, James de
See: DePREIST, James

3260. PRESTON, D. S.
"Capital Punishment Is a Fine, Fine Thing." Comm
(109:12) Je 18, 82, p. 375.
"For E. H." HolCrit (19:2) Ap 82, p. 18.

3261. PRESTON, Kathleen
"Fall Scene." WritersL D 82, p. 2.
"Necklace." WritersL O-N 82, p. 16.
"Power Beauty." WritersL O-N 82, p. 26.

3262. PREVIATO, Emma
"Tuesday, May 5, Symphony Hall." StoneC (9:3/4)
Spr-Sum 82, p. 58.

3263. PRICE, Alice (Alice L.)
"The Alligator." Nimrod (25:2) Spr-Sum 82, p. 33.
"Crossing Over." Nimrod (25:2) Spr-Sum 82, p. 49.
"Elegy to L_____." Nimrod (25:2) Spr-Sum 82,
p. 49.
"A Fall Day near Trading Post." LittleBR (3:1) Aut
82, p. 18.
"The Pokagon Hear Geologic Time." Nimrod (25:2)
Spr-Sum 82, p. 34.

3264. PRICE, Reynolds
"Bethlehem -- Cave of the Nativity." SouthernR
(18:3) Sum 82, p. 534.
"Divine Propositions." GeoR (36:3) Aut 82, p. 638.
"Jerusalem -- Calvary." SouthernR (18:3) Sum 82, p.
535.
"Pictures of the Dead." Poetry (140:5) Ag 82, p.
258-260.
"Seafarer" (after the Anglo-Saxon). OntR (16) Spr-
Sum 82, p. 20-22.

3265. PRIESSNITZ, Reinhard
"Innery" (tr. by Beth Bjorklund). LitR (25:2) Wint
82, p. 301.
"Snowsong" (tr. by Beth Bjorklund). LitR (25:2) Wint
82, p. 302-303.
"Trip" (tr. by Beth Bjorklund). LitR (25:2) Wint 82,
p. 303.
"Tropic Circle" (tr. by Beth Bjorklund). LitR (25:2)
Wint 82, p. 302.

3266. PRIEST, Robert
"The Creation." PoetryCR (3:4) Sum 82, p. 9.
"Go, Gather Up the Love." PoetryCR (3:4) Sum 82, p.
8.
"The Mis-use of Cradles." PoetryCR (3:4) Sum 82, p.
9.

3267. PRINCE, Richard
"Mount Rushmore." PortR (28:2) 82, p. 93.
"Paperback Bible." PortR (28:2) 82, p. 96.
"What's Theirs Is Yours." PortR (28:2) 82, p. 94.

"Why I Go to the Movies Alone." <u>PortR</u> (28:2) 82, p. 95.

3268. PRINTZ-PAHLSON, Goran
"Aelius Lamia: Tankas" (for Robert Hass). <u>PoetryE</u> (8) Aut 82, p. 70-71.
"Apple Tree" (tr. of Stein Mehren). <u>Stand</u> (23:3) 82, p. 37.
"Comedians" (for Kenneth Koch). <u>PoetryE</u> (8) Aut 82, p. 68-69.
"In the Style of Scott Skinner." <u>PoetryE</u> (8) Aut 82, p. 72.
"Joe Hill In Prison" (tr. by Richard B. Vowles). <u>PoetryE</u> (8) Aut 82, p. 66.
"Nr 58" (tr. of Stein Mehren). <u>Stand</u> (23:3) 82, p. 38.
"The Old Barn" (tr. of Stein Mehren). <u>Stand</u> (23:3) 82, p. 39.
"When Beaumont and Tocqueville First Visited Sing-Sing" (tr. by Robert Rovinsky). <u>PoetryE</u> (8) Aut 82, p. 67.

3269. PRIOR, Tim
"A Holy Place." <u>PoetryCR</u> (4:1) Sum 82, p. 5.

3270. PRIORI, Alfred
"The Number of Angels That Can Dance on a Pin." <u>Comm</u> (109:10) My 21, 82, p. 313.

PRISCO, Joseph di
<u>See</u>: Di PRISCO, Joseph

3271. PRITAM, Amrita
"My Address" (tr. by the author). <u>NewL</u> (48:3/4) Spr-Sum 82, p. 120.
"The Pariah" (tr. by the author). <u>NewL</u> (48:3/4) Spr-Sum 82, p. 119.
"You Do Not Come" (tr. by Charles Brasch). <u>NewL</u> (48:3/4) Spr-Sum 82, p. 118.

3272. PRITCHETT, F. W.
"Urban Expansion" (tr. of Majid Amjad, w. S. R. Faruqi). <u>NewL</u> (48:3/4) Spr-Sum 82, p. 214.

3273. PRITT, Charlotte
"Revision." <u>EngJ</u> (71:8) D 82, p. 68.

3274. PRIVETT, Katharine
"Job's Wife." <u>WebR</u> (7:1) Spr 82, p. 9.

3275. PROCTOR, Margaret
"Bottle Garden." <u>Bogg</u> (48) 82, p. 75.
"Derelict." <u>Bogg</u> (49) 82, p. 51.

3276. PROPPER, Dan
"My dead friend visited me." <u>SeC</u> (9:1/2) 80, p. 14.
"Read Any Good Movies Lately?" <u>PoNow</u> (6:5, issue 35) 82, p. 32.

3277. PROSPERE, Susan
      "Silver Thaw." NewYorker (58:2) Mr 1, 82, p. 50.

3278. PROTHRO, Nancy W.
      "All Night the Rain." CutB (19) Aut-Wint 82, p. 76.

3279. PROVOST, Sarah
      "Doors." Confr (23) Wint 82, p. 63.
      "Handyman." Confr (23) Wint 82, p. 62.
      "Sometimes a Woman Wants a Love without Landscapes."
      Poetry (139:6) Mr 82, p. 327.

3280. PRUITT, Bill
      "Bananas." Ploughs (8:2/3) 82, p. 187-188.
      "If We Had Never Married." Ploughs (8:2/3) 82, p.
      190.
      "Morning in the City." Ploughs (8:2/3) 82, p. 189,
      191.

3281. PRUNTY, Wyatt
      "Another Kind of Play." SouthernR (18:2) Spr 82, p.
      362.
      "Ballad of the Several Past." SewanR (90:1) Wint
      82, p. 28-29.
      "Caligula in Blue." SouthernR (18:2) Spr 82, p.
      358-359.
      "The Dancer Who Swims." SouthernR (18:2) Spr 82, p.
      360-361.
      "Furlough from the East." SewanR (90:1) Wint 82, p.
      30.
      "Linnet and Leaf." SewanR (90:1) Wint 82, p. 27.
      "The Times Between." SewanR (90:1) Wint 82, p. 26.
      "Towards a Relative Ending." Salm (56) Spr 82, p.
      143.
      "Wallace to Elsie." SouthernR (18:2) Spr 82, p.
      363-364.

3282. PUDUMAIPPITHAN
      "Path (Padhai)" (tr. by P. G. Sundararajan). NewL
      (48:3/4) Spr-Sum 82, p. 121-122.

3283. PUEBLA, Manuel de la
      "Certidumbre." Mairena (4:9) Spr 82, p. 44.
      "Ruego." Mairena (4:10) Sum-Aut 82, p. 78.

3284. PUIG, Pedro Enrique
      "El Pajaro de Piedra" (from Reflejos de Tierra).
      Mairena (4:9) Spr 82, p. 96.

3285. PURDY, Al
      "Choices." PoetryCR (4:2) Wint 82, p. 5.
      "In the Andes." CanLit (95) Wint 82, p. 38.

3286. PURENS, Ilmars
      "Chambered Nautilus." Kayak (58) Ja 82, p. 25.
      "Coming Home Drunk." Kayak (60) O 82, p. 67.
      "Lyric for the Dark Lady." Kayak (58) Ja 82, p. 25.
      "Rain Pools, Late October." Kayak (60) O 82, p. 66.

3287. PURKIS, Jonathan
      "First Love." Bogg (48) 82, p. 61.

3288. PURPLE, Marnie
      "From the Lighthouse." MendoR (5) Sum 81, p. 60.

3289. PUSATERI, Therese D.
      "Like a Mother." Shen (33:3) 82, p. 82.

3290. PYBUS, Rodney
      "Fractures." Stand (23:4) 82, p. 54.
      "Not Only Forms." Stand (23:1) 81-82, p. 43.
      "The Year of the White Horse." Stand (23:1) 81-82,
      p. 42.

3291. QING, Ai
      "The Translucent Night" (tr. by Hualing Nieh).
      Spirit (6:2/3) 82, p. 175-176.

3292. QIU, Jin
      "To a Japanese Friend" (tr. by Zuxin Ding and Burton
      Raffel). DenQ (17:2) Sum 82, p. 97.

3293. QUASIMODO, Salvatore
      "And Suddenly It's Evening" (tr. by Rina
      Ferrarelli). PoNow (6:4, issue 34) 82, p. 41.
      "Green Drift" (tr. by Rina Ferrarelli). PoNow (6:4,
      issue 34) 82, p. 41.
      "The Magpie Laughs, Black against the Orange Trees"
      (tr. by Michael L. Johnson). LitR (26:1) Aut 82,
      p. 107.
      "Mirror" (tr. by Rina Ferrarelli). PoNow (6:4, issue
      34) 82, p. 41.
      "There Is Nothing I Have Lost" (tr. by Larry Smith).
      CharR (8:1) Spr 82, p. 53.

3294. QUATRONE, Richard Philip
      "Copy Cats: Waiting for Xerox." EngJ (71:3) Mr 82,
      p. 82.

3295. QUICK, Joyce
      "Poet's Holdup." PoetryNW (23:4) Wint 82-83, p. 23.

3296. QUINN, John Robert
      "Stranger." Comm (109:5) Mr 12, 82, p. 158.

      QUINONES, Mara Magaly
      See: MAGALY QUINONES, Marta

3297. QUINONEZ, Naomi
      "El Salvador." Maize (6:1/2) Aut-Wint 82-83, p. 31.
      "L.A.: A Face Only a Mother Could Love." Maize
      (6:1/2) Aut-Wint 82-83, p. 32-33.

3298. QUINTANA, Leroy V.
      "Esteban." Shout (3:1) 82, p. 19-20.
      "Sammy." Shout (3:1) 82, p. 21.
      "Shoveling Manure with Gilbert Lopez" (para mi compa
      Gilbert Lopez). Shout (3:1) 82, p. 18.

3299. RAAZ, Rafeeque
"Jealousy" (tr. by A. M. Lone). NewL (48:3/4) Spr-
Sum 82, p. 232-233.

3300. RABIKOVICH, Daliah
"The End of the Fall" (tr. by Bernhard Frank). PoNow
(6:4, issue 34) 82, p. 42.

3301. RABONI, Giovanni
"Aria for Tenor" (tr. by Vinio Rossi and Stuart
Friebert). MalR (62) Jl 82, p. 62.
"The Check Room" (tr. by Vinio Rossi and Stuart
Friebert). MalR (62) Jl 82, p. 62.
"Elements of an Urban Landscape" (tr. by Vinio Rossi
and Stuart Friebert). MalR (62) Jl 82, p. 64.
"Judas' Oration" (tr. by Vinio Rossi and Stuart
Friebert). MalR (62) Jl 82, p. 64.
"Meditation in the Orchard" (tr. by Vinio Rossi and
Stuart Friebert). MalR (62) Jl 82, p. 63.
"Serenada." LittleBR (2:4) Sum 82, p. 72.
"Serenade" (tr. by Stuart Friebert and Vinio Rossi).
LittleBR (2:4) Sum 82, p. 73.
"Simulated & Dissimulated" (for my son) (tr. by
Vinio Rossi and Stuart Friebert). MalR (62) Jl 82,
p. 63.

3302. RABORG, Frederick A., Jr.
"Getting Religion." PikeF (4) Spr 82, p. 32.
"The Hunt." LittleBR (2:2) Wint 81-82, inside back
cover.
"Meeting the Scope of My Exposure." CapeR (17:2)
Sum 82, p. 22.
"Offshore Drilling." Outbr (10/11) Aut 82-Spr 83,
p. 12.
"The Snows Came." PikeF (4) Spr 82, p. 32.

3303. RAC, Bertrand
"The Companion." WebR (7:1) Spr 82, p. 67.
"The Diamond Knight." WebR (7:1) Spr 82, p. 66.
"A Loose Button." WebR (7:1) Spr 82, p. 67.

3304. RACHEL, Naomi
"The Complication." PortR (28:2) 82, p. 97-98.
"The Demand for Lutz." Outbr (8/9) Aut 81-Spr 82,
p. 62.
"An Ending." Outbr (8/9) Aut 81-Spr 82, p. 63.
"Enroute to Cages." Outbr (8/9) Aut 81-Spr 82, p.
63.
"Find No Blame." Outbr (10/11) Aut 82-Spr 83, p. 7.
"Heel Tale." Wind (12:46) 82, p. 32.
"The Home of the Bewildered." CanLit (93) Sum 82,
p. 23-25.
"In the Garden of Priapus." Wind (12:46) 82, p. 33.
"Joyce & the Poem." KanQ (14:3) Sum 82, p. 82.
from The Inness: "Fodre Gefylled Firum To Nytte."
Nimrod (26:1) Aut-Wint 82, p. 70-71.
"The Waiting Room." MassR (23:1) Spr 82, p. 186-
189.

3305. RADLOFF, B. H. (Bernhard H.)
"But Return / High Origin" (for my brother, Ernst).
Quarry (31:4) Aut 82, p. 16-18.
"Mnemosyne at Union Station." Waves (10:3) Wint 82,
p. 60-61.

3306. RADU, Kenneth
"The Bedroom." PoetryCR (4:2) Wint 82, p. 16.
"The Hand." CrossC (4:4) 82, p. 29.
"Narrenschiff." PoetryCR (4:2) Wint 82, p. 16.
"Pause." PoetryCR (3:4) Sum 82, p. 13.
"The Ring-bearer." PoetryCR (4:2) Wint 82, p. 16.
"Tanabe's Landscapes" (Edmonton Art Gallery, 1977).
CrossC (4:4) 82, p. 29.

3307. RAFFANIELLO, Robert
"Woman Raking Leaves." Outbr (10/11) Aut 82-Spr 83,
p. 14.

3308. RAFFEL, Burton
"By the Han and the Yangtze" (tr. of Anonymous, w.
Zuxin Ding). DenQ (17:2) Sum 82, p. 90.
"The Drum Thunders" (tr. of Anonymous, w. Zuxin
Ding). DenQ (17:2) Sum 82, p. 91.
"A Fisherman's Family" (tr. of Zhen Xie, w. Zuxin
Ding). DenQ (17:2) Sum 82, p. 95.
"North Hill" (tr. of Anonymous, w. Zuxin Ding). DenQ
(17:2) Sum 82, p. 92.
"On My Way to Jian-men, in a Drizzle" (tr. of Lu
You, w. Zuxin Ding). DenQ (17:2) Sum 82, p. 93.
"On the Night of the First Full Moon" (tr. of Zhu
Sushen, w. Zuxin Ding). DenQ (17:2) Sum 82, p. 94.
"Poem #123 (1839)" (tr. of Gong Zizhen, w. Zuxin
Ding). DenQ (17:2) Sum 82, p. 96.
"To a Japanese Friend" (tr. of Qiu Jin, w. Zuxin
Ding). DenQ (17:2) Sum 82, p. 97.

3309. RAGLAND, T. L.
"Covered Bridge." Wind (12:46) 82, p. 34.
"Vandalized Cabin on I-270." Wind (12:46) 82, p.
35.

3310. RAIL, De Wayne
"Oats." PoNow (6:6, issue 36) 82, p. 41.

3311. RAINES, Charlotte A.
"The Indestructibles." LitR (25:3) Spr 82, p. 367.

3312. RAISOR, Philip
"Gifts from Gamberaia." LitR (25:3) Spr 82, p. 361.
"Heavy Rain." SouthernR (18:1) Wint 82, p. 181.
"How Eyes Are Opened." LitR (25:3) Spr 82, p. 360.
"Neighborhood Gossips." PoetryNW (23:4) Wint 82-83,
p. 17-18.
"Toads Breeding, Thumb Swelling." PoetryNW (23:4)
Wint 82-83, p. 18-19.

3313. RAIZISS, Sonia
"Ambivalence" (tr. of Vittorio Sereni). PoNow (6:6,
issue 36) 82, p. 42.

"Iris" (tr. of Eugenio Montale, w. Alfredo de Palchi). Field (27) Aut 82, p. 29-30.
"Passing Through" (tr. of Vittorio Sereni). PoNow (6:6, issue 36) 82, p. 42.

3314. RAKOSI, Carl
"Punk Rock." Sulfur (2:2, issue 5) 82, p. 98--99.

3315. RALEIGH, Michael
"Father's Wisdom." KanQ (14:3) Sum 82, p. 197.

3316. RAMANUJAN, A. K.
"This Man" (tr. of G. S. Shivarudrappa). NewL (48:3/4) Spr-Sum 82, p. 208-209.
"Woman" (tr. of Siddalinga Pattanashetti). NewL (48:3/4) Spr-Sum 82, p. 253.

3317. RAMESH, Divik
"Bird's Wedding" (tr. by Arun Sedwal). NewL (48:3/4) Spr-Sum 82, p. 234-235.
"Feather" (tr. by Arun Sedwal). NewL (48:3/4) Spr-Sum 82, p. 234.

3318. RAMIREZ CORDOVA, Antonio
"Poema 9: Porque la noche tiembla de marzo a marzo." Mairena (4:10) Sum-Aut 82, p. 93-94.

3319. RAMIREZ de ARELLANO, Olga
"Poema 1: Quiero sonarme en esa edad de lluvia" (A Octavio Paz). Mairena (4:9) Spr 82, p. 45.

3320. RAMIREZ GARCIA, Raul
"A las Botas Que Me Dio Mi Apa." Maize (6:1/2) Aut-Wint 82-83, p. 84.
"Mi Fella Epoca." Maize (6:1/2) Aut-Wint 82-83, p. 83.
"El Tiempo Es un Suicida Que Nos Arrastra." Maize (6:1/2) Aut-Wint 82-83, p. 82.

3321. RAMKE, Bin
"Night Baseball." OhioR (29) 82, p. 31-33.
"On the Eve of the Revolution." SouthernR (18:3) Sum 82, p. 555.

3322. RAMOS COLLADO, Liliana
"En la Ciudad II" (from Proemas para Despabilar Candidos). Mairena (4:9) Spr 82, p. 97.
"Proema para Embromar a la Muerte." Areito (8:31) 82, p. 39.

3323. RAMOS-GASCON, Antonio
"Tu, Desde Esta Tarde, Despues de Tanto Estar Conmigo" (Hacia V. en su mayo 34). Mairena (4:9) Spr 82, p. 35-36.

3324. RAMOS-GONZALEZ, Francisco Jose
"E R A" (from Cronografias). Mairena (4:10) Sum-Aut 82, p. 26-27.

3325. RAMSEY, Jarold
       "Finding Wild Strawberries" (for my mother). AmerS
       (51:4) Aut 82, p. 532.

3326. RAMSEY, Paul
       "Of When" (for Guy Owen). SouthernPR (22:1) Spr 82,
       p. 14.

3327. RANAN, Wendy
       "Inside Out" (for Maud and Fergus). CutB (18) Spr-
       Sum 82, p. 21-22.
       "Lake Crescent." Tendril (13) Sum 82, p. 55.

3328. RAND, Lydia
       "Don't You See?" MendoR (6) Sum 81, p. 38.

3329. RANDALL, Lewis
       "Indian Summer." Abraxas (25/26) 82, p. 68.

3330. RANDELL, Margaret
       "Double Spaced" (tr. of Alex Fleites). SeC (9:1/2)
       80, p. 30-31.
       "It's a Desperately Cruel Struggle" (tr. of Victor
       Rodriguez Nunez). SeC (9:1/2) 80, p. 32.

3331. RANDOLPH, Dorothy
       "Coue Revisited." LittleBR (1:4) Sum 81, p. 65.

3332. RANKIN, Paula
       "Leftovers." AmerPoR (11:2) Mr-Ap 82, p. 20.
       "Making Tracks." Tendril (13) Sum 82, p. 56-57.
       "Middle Age." AmerPoR (11:2) Mr-Ap 82, p. 20.
       "The Red Shoe." SoCaR (14:2) Spr 82, p. 65.
       "Shared Visions." PoNow (6:6, issue 36) 82, p. 25.
       "Thinking of Others." PoNow (6:6, issue 36) 82, p.
       25.
       "We Neve Get to the End of It All." Agni (16) 82,
       p. 16.

3333. RANSDELL, Emily
       "The Disposal of Dolls." PoetryNW (23:2) Sum 82, p.
       18-19.
       "Entering the Old Body." PoNow (7:1, issue 37) 82,
       p. 35.

3334. RANSMEIER, J. C.
       "Feeding the Trout" (for Von, 1981). SouthernPR
       (22:1) Spr 82, p. 38.

3335. RAO, B. R. Laxman
       "A Photographer" (tr. by S. K. Desai). NewL (48:3/4)
       Spr-Sum 82, p. 144-145.

3336. RAO, Raghavendra
       "The Image" (tr. of V. G. Bhat). NewL (48:3/4) Spr-
       Sum 82, p. 120.

3337. RASCHKE, Suzanne
       "Dog with Two Heads." PoNow (6:4, issue 34) 82, p.
       47.

3338. RASULA, Jed
        from The Field & Garden of Circe: "Again your
        handled sun you hold my mind" Sulfur (2:1, issue
        4) 82, p. 103-105.
        from The Field & Garden of Circe: "The great
        spectacle of the mirror in transit." Sulfur (2:1,
        issue 4) 82, p. 105-108.
        from The Field & Garden of Circe: "Out of my talks
        with Mercury otherwise Hermes." Sulfur (2:1, issue
        4) 82, p. 109.
        from The Field & Garden of Circe: "Sol qui illustras
        omnia solus." Sulfur (2:1, issue 4) 82, p. 102-
        103.

3339. RATH, Paula
        "Glass Is Breaking in Every Room." SouthwR (67:2)
        Spr 82, p. 191.

3340. RATH, Ramakanta
        from Four Stolen Glances at Time: "I am no good at
        discussing space rockets" (tr. by Jayanta
        Mahapatra). NewL (48:3/4) Spr-Sum 82, p. 97-98.
        "The Kerosene Lamp" (tr. by Jayanta Mahapatra). NewL
        (48:3/4) Spr-Sum 82, p. 97.

3341. RATH, Sara
        "Germination." Abraxas (25/26) 82, p. 87.

3342. RATHBUN, Victoria
        "Almost the Greatest." Pig (9) 82, p. 71.

3343. RATNER, Rochelle
        from Sleeping Beauty, the Legend of St. Julian:
        "Dinner Conversation." HangL (41) 82, p. 41-42.
        from Sleeping Beauty, the Legend of St. Julian:
        "Setting Out Alone." HangL (41) 82, p. 39-40.
        "Stroke Patient." Ploughs (8:1) 82, p. 141.

3344. RATTEE, Michael
        "Lawn Trees/If It's Not Raining." SmPd (19:1, issue
        54) Wint 82, p. 9.

3345. RATTI, John
        "Orpheus." NewEngR (4:3) Spr 82, p. 465.

3346. RATTRAY, David
        "Summer" (tr. of Friedrich Holderlin). Sulfur (2:3,
        issue 6) 82, p. 111.

3347. RATZLAFF, Keith
        "The Grain Elevator Explosion." PoetryNW (23:2) Sum
        82, p. 30-31.
        "In the Nursing Home." PoetryNW (23:2) Sum 82, p.
        30.
        "The Proposal." CutB (19) Aut-Wint 82, p. 54.

3348. RAWLINS, Susan
        "The Course Requirements." PoetryNW (23:1) Spr 82,
        p. 10-11.

"The World Champion Driver, His Charming Companion."
PoetC (14:1) 82, p. 15-16.

3349. RAY, David
"1996" (tr. of Rabindranath Tagore). NewL (48:3/4)
Spr-Sum 82, p. 21-22.
"The Adventuresome Later Years." PoNow (6:4, issue
34) 82, p. 3.
"The Ascent." CharR (8:1) Spr 82, p. 15-16.
"At a Parking Lot in Tennessee." PoNow (6:4, issue
34) 82, p. 2.
"Bike Shop." LittleBR (2:2) Wint 81-82, p. 21.
"The Caves." NewL (48:3/4) Spr-Sum 82, p. 80-81.
"Comiendo el Hierro." CharR (8:1) Spr 82, p. 12-14.
"Custer's Seventh." PoNow (6:4, issue 34) 82, p. 3.
"The Depression Years." Ploughs (8:2/3) 82, p. 73.
"Domestic." BaratR (8:2) Wint 81, p. 102.
"Elysium in the Halls of Hell." NewL (48:3/4) Spr-
Sum 82, p. 77.
"Enough of Flying" (Poems inspired by Ghalib's
Ghazals). LitR (25:4) Sum 82, p. 643-648.
"Farmers' Market." LittleBR (2:2) Wint 81-82, p.
22.
"Garage Sale." LittleBR (2:2) Wint 81-82, p. 20.
"The Gingerbread House." PoNow (6:4, issue 34) 82,
p. 4.
"A Human Donkey." MissouriR (5:3) Sum 82, p. 28.
"The Last Class (Syracuse)." PoNow (6:4, issue 34)
82, p. 2.
"The Lighthouse." PoNow (6:5, issue 35) 82, p. 33.
"Migrant Mother, 1936." Atl (250:4) O 82, p. 76.
"Morning Flower." CharR (8:1) Spr 82, p. 16-17.
"Mulberries." Spirit (6:2/3) 82, p. 145.
"A Poster" (tr. of Kumar Vikal, w. Mrinal Parde).
NewL (48:3/4) Spr-Sum 82, p. 206.
"Purdah." NewL (48:3/4) Spr-Sum 82, p. 79.
"Richard St. George, Esquire, Orders His Portrait
from Henry Fuseli, 1791." GeoR (36:1) Spr 82, p.
129-131.
"Seeing Daughter Off." Ploughs (8:2/3) 82, p. 74-
75.
"A Song" (tr. of Siddalingaiah, w. Sumatheendra
Nadig). NewL (48:3/4) Spr-Sum 82, p. 204-205.
"The Temple at Paestum." Confr (23) Wint 82, p. 62.
"Thanksgiving." BaratR (8:2) Wint 81, p. 103.
"Travels in the Desert." PraS (56:2) Sum 82, p. 57.
"Villagers." NewL (48:3/4) Spr-Sum 82, p. 78.
"Villanelle: Their Arrival." CharR (8:1) Spr 82, p.
14-15.
"With Apologies for Mrs. Webster." PoNow (6:4,
issue 34) 82, p. 3.

3350. RAY, Kaylan
"For William Stafford." Shout (3:1) 82, p. 84.

3351. RAY, Lila
"Very Close It Was" (tr. of Ashis Sanyal). NewL
(48:3/4) Spr-Sum 82, p. 154-155.

3352. RAY, Robert Beverley
"Les Cahiers du Chemin" (For Alistair M. Duckworth).
Poetry (139:6) Mr 82, p. 313-315.
"The Meaning of Coincidence in the Old Stories."
Poetry (139:6) Mr 82, p. 319-323.
"A Passacaglia in Winter." Poetry (139:6) Mr 82, p.
316-318.

3353. RAY, Shreela
"Dusky Sally." NewL (48:3/4) Spr-Sum 82, p. 148.
"For H.: Three Poems." NewL (48:3/4) Spr-Sum 82, p.
146-147.
"From the Colonies." NewL (48:3/4) Spr-Sum 82, p.
147-148.

3354. RAYMOND, Monica
"Self-Criticism." Iowa (12:2/3) Spr-Sum 81, p. 281.

3355. RAZZELL, Mary
"Leaving Home." CanLit (94) Aut 82, p. 83-84.

3356. REA, Susan Irene
"Lace." AspenJ (1) Wint 82, p. 28.

3357. READ, David
"Auden's Death." KanQ (14:3) Sum 82, p. 143.
"Hymn for Housewives." KanQ (14:3) Sum 82, p. 143.

3358. REAGAN, Ronald
"Time." Tendril (12) Wint 82, p. 56.

3359. REANEY, James
"Riddle Competition." PoetryCR (4:2) Wint 82, p.
14.

3360. REARDON, Patrick
"Election." Pig (8) 80, p. 62.

3361. REBOREDO, Jorge
"Recurso de la Palabra." Mairena (4:10) Sum-Aut 82,
p. 60.

3362. RECK, Michael
"After the Fall." Ploughs (8:2/3) 82, p. 131-132.
"Heureux Qui." Ploughs (8:2/3) 82, p. 134-135.
"Once More O Ye Etc." Ploughs (8:2/3) 82, p. 133.

3363. RECTOR, Liam
"The Rumor." AmerPoR (11:2) Mr-Ap 82, p. 47.
"This City." AntR (40:2) Spr 82, p. 176-177.

3364. RED HAWK
"How I Loved You." Poetry (140:2) My 82, p. 92.
"Master, Master, Lord of the Dance." Poetry (140:2)
My 82, p. 93.

3365. REDEL, Victoria
"Dinner Break." PraS (56:4) Wint 82-83, p. 58.

3366. REDGROVE, Peter
"A City of Churches." Sulfur (2:2, issue 5) 82, p.
83-84.
"The College in the Reservoir." ManhatR (2:2) Sum
82, p. 43-44.
"Cornish Forces." ManhatR (2:2) Sum 82, p. 32-33.
"Domestic Suite." ManhatR (2:2) Sum 82, p. 47.
"Dream of a Lawn Pillow." Sulfur (2:2, issue 5) 82,
p. 79-81.
"The Effigies." ManhatR (2:2) Sum 82, p. 57-58.
"An Egyptian Requiem" (For Wendy Taylor). ManhatR
(2:2) Sum 82, p. 58-60.
"Escapology." Sulfur (2:2, issue 5) 82, p. 78-79.
"Essay." Sulfur (2:2, issue 5) 82, p. 81-83.
"Export." Sulfur (2:2, issue 5) 82, p. 88.
"Facts" (For Sylvia Kantaris). ManhatR (2:2) Sum 82,
p. 41-43.
"Fetish." ManhatR (2:2) Sum 82, p. 48-49.
"In the Pharmacy" (for Wendy Taylor). Sulfur (2:2,
issue 5) 82, p. 77-78.
"Mask of Source." ManhatR (2:2) Sum 82, p. 38-40.
"Paper Door." ManhatR (2:2) Sum 82, p. 56-57.
"The Reason Why Witches Wear Black." ManhatR (2:2)
Sum 82, p. 36-37.
"Reflections." ManhatR (2:2) Sum 82, p. 48.
"Resort." Sulfur (2:2, issue 5) 82, p. 84-85.
"River of Air." ManhatR (2:2) Sum 82, p. 50-51.
"Seiza" (Zen position: 'just sitting'). ManhatR
(2:2) Sum 82, p. 29-30.
"She Believes She Has Died." ManhatR (2:2) Sum 82,
p. 46.
"She Makes It All Up." Sulfur (2:2, issue 5) 82, p.
85-86.
"The Sister in the Glass." ManhatR (2:2) Sum 82, p.
45-46.
"Tantric Friends" (For Su and Alan Bleakley).
ManhatR (2:2) Sum 82, p. 33-35.
"To the Water-Psychiatrist." ManhatR (2:2) Sum 82,
p. 54-56.
"A Touch of Drowsiness with Eyes Open." Sulfur
(2:2, issue 5) 82, p. 87-88.
"Trade." ManhatR (2:2) Sum 82, p. 30-32.
"Transactions." ManhatR (2:2) Sum 82, p. 40-41.
"Uncountable Pharmacy." ManhatR (2:2) Sum 82, p.
51-53.
"Vibes." ManhatR (2:2) Sum 82, p. 53-54.

3367. REDMOND, Chris
"Gulf." Bogg (48) 82, p. 76.

3368. REED, Alison
"The Importance of Hands." CapeR (18:1) Wint 82, p.
2-3.
"A Little Learning" (Schoolmates at Radnor Lake).
Poem (45) Jl 82, p. 36.
"Of Lights and of Conjunctions." Poem (45) Jl 82,
p. 32-33.
"Les Oiseaux." Poem (45) Jl 82, p. 34-35.
"What Mother?" HolCrit (19:5) D 82, p. 18.

"The Youngest Mourn the Oldest Death at Allen Bell's
Camp." Poem (45) Jl 82, p. 31.

3369. REED, Jeremy
"Air." Waves (11:1) Aut 82, p. 10.
"Migration." Waves (11:1) Aut 82, p. 11.
"The Storm." Waves (11:1) Aut 82, p. 8-9.

3370. REED, John R.
"Dowson." OntR (16) Spr-Sum 82, p. 27.
"Entropy." Poetry (140:4) Jl 82, p. 216-217.
"Ford Plant at River Rouge." Shout (3:1) 82, p. 11.
"A Funicular into the Alps, Palud, Italy." SewanR
(90:4) Aut 82, p. 523.
"Gabrielino." NewEngR (5:1/2) Aut-Wint 82, p. 1-4.
"A Letter from Oran, Summer 1942." SewanR (90:4)
Aut 82, p. 522-523.
"Pasiphae's Lover." SewanR (90:4) Aut 82, p. 524.
"Strays" (For Chris). Poetry (140:4) Jl 82, p. 218.
"To Walter Kaufmann." OntR (16) Spr-Sum 82, p. 26.
"Woodward at Grand Circus." Shout (3:1) 82, p. 12.

3371. REES, Elizabeth
"Enveloping Leaves." SoDakR (20:4) Wint 82-83, p.
60.

3372. REES, Richard
"Babysitters." HangL (41) 82, p. 43.
"Dottie after Midnight." HangL (41) 82, p. 45-46.
"Little League." HangL (41) 82, p. 44.

3373. REEVE, F. D. (Franklin D.)
"An Act of Light." ModernPS (11:1/2) 82, p. 58-59.
"Dusk." WestHR (36:4) Wint 82, p. 330.
"Endless Love." SewanR (90:3) Sum 82, p. 405.
"Losses." SewanR (90:3) Sum 82, p. 405.
"Tor Bay." PoNow (6:5, issue 35) 82, p. 11.

3374. REEVES, Troy
"Faith for Today." ChrC (99:39) D 8, 82, p. 1252.

3375. REGISTER, W. Raymond
"The Night Swimmers." Poem (44) Mr 82, p. 46.
"Nude in Blue." Poem (44) Mr 82, p. 47.
"Porch Stories." Wind (12:46) 82, p. 36.
"Saith Joe." Wind (12:46) 82, p. 36-37.

3376. REGULAR GUY, A.
"Sunday morning begins early in your bed." Catalyst
(Erotica Issue) 82, p. 19.

3377. REIBSTEIN, Regina
"He Left No Survivors." SoDakR (20:1) Spr 82, p.
49.
"Too Late There Is Time." Poem (44) Mr 82, p. 50.
"Tranquility Spoils Recollections." Poem (44) Mr
82, p. 51.

3378. REID, Alastair
"Legacies" (tr. of Heberto Padilla, w. Andrew
Hurley). NewYorker (57:46) Ja 4, 82, p. 36-37.
"A Prayer for the End of the Century" (tr. of
Heberto Padilla, w. Andrew Hurley). NewYorker
(57:46) Ja 4, 82, p. 36.
"Returning to Bright Places" (tr. of Heberto
Padilla, w. Andrew Hurley). NewYorker (57:46) Ja
4, 82, p. 36.
"Song of the Navigator" (tr. of Heberto Padilla, w.
Andrew Hurley). NewYorker (57:46) Ja 4, 82, p. 36.
"Walking" (tr. of Heberto Padilla, w. Andrew
Hurley). NewYorker (57:46) Ja 4, 82, p. 36.

3379. REID, Monty
"82I 14. 7. 78." Dandel (9:1) 82, p. 28.
"82N 26. 8. 78." Dandel (9:1) 82, p. 30.
"83J 10. 8. 78." Dandel (9:1) 82, p. 29.
"84G 23. 2. 79." Dandel (9:1) 82, p. 27.
"Tooth Fairy." PoetryCR (4:2) Wint 82, p. 12.

3380. REID, P. C.
"Gawain to Gawain." LitR (25:3) Spr 82, p. 332-333.

3381. REID, Penelope Jane
"A Face Like Yours." HangL (41) 82, p. 67.
"Smart Like Me." HangL (41) 82, p. 69.
"Thief." HangL (41) 82, p. 68.

3382. REISNER, Barbara
"And Each Time." SoDakR (20:1) Spr 82, p. 42.
"Engraver." StoneC (9:3/4) Spr-Sum 82, p. 56.

3383. REISS, James
"Passage." NewYorker (58:21) Jl 12, 82, p. 36-37.
"Schilfgraben." Hudson (35:4) Wint 82-83, p. 599.

REMIGIS, P. de
See: DeREMIGIS, P.

3384. RENDALL, Barbara
"Portrait: Two Figures in Reunion." PoetryCR (4:1)
Sum 82, p. 10.

3385. RENDLEMAN, Danny
"Conundrum." AmerPoR (11:3) My-Je 82, p. 33.
"The Draggers." PoNow (6:5, issue 35) 82, p. 28.
"Exclaiming over Nothing" (for Terry). AmerPoR
(11:3) My-Je 82, p. 33.
"Looking Back on the Avant-Garde" (Two sonnets).
AmerPoR (11:3) My-Je 82, p. 33.

3386. RENO, Janet
"Bridges." WebR (7:2) Aut 82, p. 70.

3387. REPP, John
"A Prayer for Lisa & Harvey." NewL (48:3/4) Spr-Sum
82, p. 253.

RESTO, Jose A. Ortiz
See: ORTIZ RESTO, Jose A.

RETAMAR, Roberto Fernandez
See: FERNANDEZ RETAMAR, Roberto

3388. REVELL, Donald
"The Ginger Tours." PoNow (6:4, issue 34) 82, p.
30.

REVUELTAS, Pedro Gutierrez
See: GUTIERREZ-REVUELTAS, Pedro

3389. REWAK, William J.
"Action." DekalbLAJ (14:1/4) Aut 80-Sum 81, p. 89.
"Roses." DekalbLAJ (14:1/4) Aut 80-Sum 81, p. 89.

3390. REXROTH, Kenneth
"Floating." AmerPoR (11:4) Jl-Ag 82, p. 48.

3391. REYES, Edwin
"Carimbo." Areito (8:31) 82, p. 40.

3392. REYES, Kathleen M.
"Distant Relations" (for Deborah). PortR (28:2) 82,
p. 99-102.

3393. REYES DAVILA, Marcos
"La Estrella de Belen" (from Goyescas). Mairena
(4:9) Spr 82, p. 97-98.
"Todo el perfil de esa tierra" (from Estuario).
Mairena (4:9) Spr 82, p. 99.

3394. REYNOLDS, Tammy
"Hands." MendoR (5) Sum 81, p. 66.

3395. RHENISCH, Harold
"The Mill." MalR (61) F 82, p. 218-220.
"Similkameen River." Grain (10:2) My 82, p. 35.

3396. RHODES, Dee Schenck
"Morning Bridge, Rosh Hashanah." Wind (12:46) 82,
p. 37.

3397. RIANCHO, Providencia
"Atardecer" (from Fuga a Tres Voces). Mairena (4:9)
Spr 82, p. 95.

3398. RICE, Pamela
"Final Reunion." QW (15) Aut-Wint 82-83, p. 76.

3399. RICH, Adrienne
"For Ethel Rosenberg" (convicted, with her husband,
of "conspiracy to commit espionage" killed in the
electric chair June 19, 1953). Iowa (12:2/3) Spr-
Sum 81, p. 286-290.
"Integrity." Iowa (12:2/3) Spr-Sum 81, p. 293-294.
"Mother-in-Law." Iowa (12:2/3) Spr-Sum 81, p. 291-
292.

3400. RICHARDS, G. D.
       "Cold Churches." <u>BelPoJ</u> (33:1) Aut 82, p. 10.
       "Plain Style." <u>BelPoJ</u> (33:1) Aut 82, p. 11.

3401. RICHARDS, Melanie
       "Prairie Fire." <u>Abraxas</u> (25/26) 82, p. 69.

3402. RICHARDSON, James
       "Essay on Birds." <u>OntR</u> (17) Aut-Wint 82, p. 50-52.
       "Second Guesses." <u>OntR</u> (17) Aut-Wint 82, p. 48-49.
       "Tastes of Time." <u>OntR</u> (17) Aut-Wint 82, p. 46-47.
       "To Odysseus on the Hudson." <u>YaleR</u> (72:1) Aut 82,
       p. 55-57.

3403. RICHES, Brenda
       "Some Mornings." <u>CapilR</u> (23) 82, p. 5-6.

3404. RICHMOND, Kevin
       "Bright Lad." <u>Bogg</u> (49) 82, p. 40.
       "Little Miss Commerce." <u>Bogg</u> (48) 82, p. 44.
       "TV Violence." <u>Bogg</u> (48) 82, p. 51.

3405. RICO, Noel
       "The Bronx, 1979" (for Miguel Pinero). <u>RevChic</u>
       (10:1/2) Wint-Spr 82, p. 99.
       "Excerpt from the South Bronx." <u>RevChic</u> (10:1/2)
       Wint-Spr 82, p. 101.
       "Excerpt from the South Bronx II." <u>RevChic</u> (10:1/2)
       Wint-Spr 82, p. 101.
       "The First Place." <u>RevChic</u> (10:1/2) Wint-Spr 82, p.
       102.
       "It Is Only the Flowers" (for my great-grandmother,
       Dona Cruz Valentin). <u>RevChic</u> (10:1/2) Wint-Spr 82,
       p. 100.
       "A Late Afternoon." <u>RevChic</u> (10:1/2) Wint-Spr 82,
       p. 103.
       "The Lower East Side: After Having Witnessed a Man
       Beating Up a Woman underneath a Balcony
       Overlooking Avenue C." <u>RevChic</u> (10:1/2) Wint-Spr
       82, p. 98.

3406. RIDL, Jack
       "Love Poem." <u>GeoR</u> (36:4) Wint 82, p. 834.

3407. RIDLAND, John
       "Another Easter." <u>Ploughs</u> (8:2/3) 82, p. 142-146.
       "Poet and Novelist" (to Barry Spacks). <u>Ploughs</u>
       (8:2/3) 82, p. 140-141.

3408. RIEMER, Ruby
       "A Time of Peace." <u>Ascent</u> (7:3) 82, p. 45.

3409. RIGAU, Angel
       "Cuando Se Seque el Rocio" (para Olga Crescioni, por
       el obsequio de su poemario). <u>Mairena</u> (4:10) Sum-
       Aut 82, p. 81.

3410. RIGGIO, Michael
       "Rosary." <u>PottPort</u> (4) 82-83, p. 42.

"Untitled: The Italian girl in my father's
tenement." PottPort (4) 82-83, p. 45.

3411. RIGGS, Dionis Coffin
"Bequest" (tr. of Cahit Kulebi, w. Ozcan Yalim and
William A. Fielder). StoneC (10:1/2) Aut-Wint 82-
83,p. 31.
"The Lamp" (tr. of Behcet Necatigil, w. Ozcan Yalim
and William A. Fielder).DenQ (17:1) Spr 82, p. 85.
"A Lesson" (tr. of Ulku Tamer, w. Ozcan Yalim and
William A. Fielder).DenQ (17:1) Spr 82, p. 87.
"To Live" (tr. of Orhan Veli, w. Ozcan Yalim and
William A. Fielder).DenQ (17:1) Spr 82, p. 86.

3412. RIGSBEE, David
"Sister's Letter." QW (14) Spr-Sum 82, p. 72-73.

3413. RIKKI
"Blue Autumn." PoetryCR (3:4) Sum 82, p. 9.
"The Eggs." PoetryCR (3:4) Sum 82, p. 9.
"Essential Things." PoetryCR (3:4) Sum 82, p. 8.
"It Teaches Him about Falling." PoetryCR (3:4) Sum
82, p. 9.
"The Narrows." PoetryCR (3:4) Sum 82, p. 8.

3414. RILEY, Joanne
"Flax and Linen." PoetC (14:2) 82, p. 42.

3415. RILEY, Michael D.
"The Crew." SouthernHR (16:2) Spr 82, p. 142-143.
"Emeritus: A Grammar of Assent." DekalbLAJ (14:1/4)
Aut 80-Sum 81, p. 90-92.

3416. RILKE, Rainer Maria
"Alcestis" (tr. by Stephen Mitchell). AmerPoR (11:1)
Ja-F 82, p. 14.
"Before Summer Rain" (tr. by Stephen Mitchell).
AmerPoR (11:1) Ja-F 82, p. 14.
"Before the Summer Rain" (tr. by Walter Arndt).
NewEngR (4:3) Spr 82, p. 346-347.
"Christ's Descent into Hell" (tr. by Franz Wright).
VirQR (58:4) Aut 82, p. 691-692.
"The Courtesan" (tr. by Walter Arndt). NewEngR (4:3)
Spr 82, p. 348.
"Death of the Poet" (tr. by Walter Arndt). NewEngR
(4:3) Spr 82, p. 347-348.
"Death" (tr. by Stephen Mitchell). AmerPoR (11:1)
Ja-F 82, p. 15.
"Evening" (tr. by Stephen Mitchell). NewYRB (29:16)
O 21, 82, p. 10.
"The Flamingos" (Jardin des Plantes, Paris, tr. by
Stephen Mitchell). AmerPoR (11:1) Ja-F 82, p. 15.
"Going Blind" (tr. by Stephen Mitchell). AmerPoR
(11:1) Ja-F 82, p. 13.
"The Grownup" (tr. by Stephen Mitchell). AmerPoR
(11:1) Ja-F 82, p. 13.
"The Last Evening" (By permission of Frau Nonna, tr.
by Stephen Mitchell). AmerPoR (11:1) Ja-F 82, p.
13.

"Like Water" (tr. by Steven Lautermilch). ArizQ
(38:4) Wint 82, p. 335.
"The Poet" (tr. by Walter Arndt). NewEngR (4:3) Spr
82, p. 347.
from Sonnets to Orpheus: (I.2) (tr. by John
Rosenwald). SoCaR (14:2) Spr 82, p. 115.
from Sonnets to Orpheus: (II.5-6) (tr. by John
Rosenwald). Paint (9:17/18) Spr-Aut 82, p. 22-23.
"Spring Fragment (Paris)" (tr. by Walter Arndt).
NewEngR (4:3) Spr 82, p. 346.
"Tombs of the Hetaerae" (tr. by Stephen Mitchell).
NewYRB (29:16) O 21, 82, p. 10.
"Washing the Corpse" (tr. by Stephen Mitchell).
AmerPoR (11:1) Ja-F 82, p. 13.

3417. RIMBAUD, Arthur
"L'Eternite." StoneC (9:3/4) Spr-Sum 82, p. 22.
"Eternity" (tr. by Edward Babun and Olga
Litowinsky). StoneC (9:3/4) Spr-Sum 82, p. 23.

3418. RINALDI, Nicholas
"Cow Feeding on the Grass in the Park in Front of
City Hall." SoDakR (20:3) Aut 82, p. 25-26.
"Locksmith." SoDakR (20:3) Aut 82, p. 24-25.
"Tournament." LitR (25:3) Spr 82, p. 331.
"The Tree." MissR (10:3, issue 30) Wint-Spr 82, p.
73.
"Underdogs." SoDakR (20:3) Aut 82, p. 26-27.

3419. RIND, Sherry
"Recognition of the Mate." SouthernPR (23, i.e.
22:2) Aut 82, p. 33-34.

3420. RINEHART, Evolyn
"Relief: 1933." Wind (12:46) 82, p. 38.
"Yesterday." Wind (12:46) 82, p. 38.

3421. RIOS, Alberto
"Belita." Shout (3:1) 82, p. 16.
"Morning." Spirit (6:2/3) 82, p.131.
"October: Santa Cruz Valley." Shout (3:1) 82, p.
15.
"Seniors." OhioR (29) 82, p. 124-125.
"Winter along the Santa Cruz." Iowa (12:4) Aut 81,
p. 56.

RIOS, Andres Castro
See: CASTRO RIOS, Andres

3422. RIOS, Laura
"from Agua en el Desierto: (4-6). Mairena (4:10)
Sum-Aut 82, p. 73.

3423. RIOS COLON, Luis
"A Bolivar" (from Buscando un Puerto). Mairena (4:9)
Spr 82, p. 100.

3424. RIOS de TORRES, Rosario Esther
"Estan alli como parias sin tierra y sin destino."
Mairena (4:9) Spr 82, p. 31.

3425. RITCHIE, Elisavietta
    "A Balkan Encounter." StoneC (9:3/4) Spr-Sum 82, p.
    54.
    "Cat Tracks." Vis (9) 82, p. 13.
    "Toad" (from Through the River of Coral). StoneC
    (9:3/4) Spr-Sum 82, p. 55.

3426. RITSOS, Yannis
    "Afternoon" (tr. by Helen Kolias). CarolQ (34:3) Spr
    82, p. 26.
    "Etesian Winds" (tr. by Kimon Friar). PoNow (6:6,
    issue 36) 82, p. 43.
    "The Graves of Our Forefathers" (tr. by Helen
    Kolias). CarolQ (34:3) Spr 82, p. 27.
    "Succession" (tr. by Kimon Friar). PoNow (6:6, issue
    36) 82, p. 43.
    "Suddenly" (tr. by Kimon Friar). PoNow (6:6, issue
    36) 82, p. 43.

3427. RITTBERG, E.
    "She." KanQ (14:1) Wint 82, p. 127.

3428. RITTY, Joan
    "Empty Space." LittleBR (2:3) Spr 82, p. 67.
    "Night Specters." KanQ (14:3) Sum 82, p. 194.

3429. RIUS GALINDO, Jose Maria
    from Evangelio de la Muerte y Resurreccion de un
    Poeta (Elegia a mi Padre): Capitulo I "La
    Partida." Mairena (4:10) Sum-Aut 82, p. 11-13.
    from Evangelio de la Muerte y Resurreccion de un
    Poeta (Elegia a mi Padre): Capitulo XIII
    "Reconstruccion." Mairena (4:10) Sum-Aut 82, p.
    14-15.
    from Evangelio de la Muerte y Resurreccion de un
    Poeta (Elegia a mi Padre): Capitulo XIV "Epilogo."
    Mairena (4:10) Sum-Aut 82, p. 15-16.

3430. RIVARD, David
    "True Colors." Tendril (13) Sum 82, p. 58.

3431. RIVERA, Antonio M.
    "The Ends of Days" (tr. by Ricardo Pau-Llosa).
    BelPoJ (32:4) Sum 82, p. 23.
    "Finales de los Dias." BelPoJ (32:4) Sum 82, p. 22.

3432. RIVERA, Diana
    "The Pond." Chelsea (41) 82, p. 92.

3433. RIVERA, Etnairis
    "Ella tenia en sus cabellos al mar" (from el Dia del
    Polen). Mairena (4:9) Spr 82, p. 101.
    "Segundo Relato Invernal de la Emigrante." Mairena
    (4:10) Sum-Aut 82, p. 80-81.

3434. RIVERA, Marina
    "Bees, Birds, Moths, Chickens." RevChic (10:1/2)
    Wint-Spr 82, p. 107.
    "Esteban." RevChic (10:1/2) Wint-Spr 82, p. 105.
    "Pan." RevChic (10:1/2) Wint-Spr 82, p. 108.

"Villa." RevChic (10:1/2) Wint-Spr 82, p. 104.
"Why." RevChic (10:1/2) Wint-Spr 82, p. 106.

3435. RIVERA MARTINEZ, Tomas
"Desde Aqui." Areito (8:30) 82, p. 36.

3436. RIVERO, Eliana
"On Tiburon Island" (tr. by Leland H. Chambers and
Eliana Rivero). DenQ (17:1) Spr 82, p. 82.
"Sometimes" (tr. by Leland H. Chambers and Eliana
Rivero). DenQ (17:1) Spr 82, p. 80-81.
"Spectators: Free Territory of America" (26th of
July) (tr. by Leland H. Chambers and Eliana
Rivero). DenQ (17:1) Spr 82, p. 83.
"Words Are Words, Etc." (tr. by Leland H. Chambers
and Eliana Rivero). DenQ (17:1) Spr 82, p. 78-79.

3437. RIVERS, J. W.
from Chicago Notebook: "Walking on Cracks after
School." HiramPoR (31) Aut-Wint 82, p. 39.
"Day of the Dead" (from Machetes). PikeF (4) Spr 82,
p. 3.
"Esterhazy in the Hospital" (from The Scattered
Poems of Esterhazy). PikeF (4) Spr 82, p. 3.
"Esterhazy on Mount Everest - May 25, 1953" (from
The Scattered Poems of Esterhazy). PikeF (4) Spr
82, p. 3.
"Guerrillas." Maize (6:1/2) Aut-Wint 82-83, p. 30.
"MSFW (Migrant Seasonal Farm Worker)." Maize
(6:1/2) Aut-Wint 82-83, p. 85.
"Ramon F. Iturbe" (from Machetes). PikeF (4) Spr 82,
p. 3.
"The Sergeant with His Feet Cut Off" (After a Story
by Rafael F. Munoz, from Machetes). PikeF (4) Spr
82, p. 3.

3438. RIZZA, Peggy
"Certain Hours." Salm (55) Wint 82, p. 127-128.
"Hunger." Salm (55) Wint 82, p. 126-127.
"Italian Museum." Salm (55) Wint 82, p. 125-126.

3439. ROBBINS, Martin
"August Sunday." Os (15) 82, p. 13.
"La Bussola" (tr. of Luciano Marrucci, w. Ruth
Feldman). StoneC (10:1/2) Aut-Wint 82-83, p. 25.
"The Compass" (tr. of Luciano Marrucci, w. Ruth
Feldman). StoneC (10:1/2) Aut-Wint 82-83, p. 25.
"Curse for the Reclamation Bureau." CapeR (18:1)
Wint 82, p. 8.
"Decemberscape." Os (15) 82, p. 12.
"Going through My Little Black Book." CapeR (18:1)
Wint 82, p. 9.
"Sixth Grade Picture." CapeR (17:2) Sum 82, p. 10.

3440. ROBBINS, Richard
"Assurances." Nat (235:22) D 25, 82, p. 696.
"A Compass for My Daughter." CharR (8:1) Spr 82, p.
42-43.
"Crossover." Nat (234:24) Je 19, 82, p. 758.
"Museums." ColEng 44(3) Mr 82, p. 287-288.

"Returning to the Middle." NoAmR (267:4) D 82,p.
19.

ROBBINS, Rick
See: ROBBINS, Richard

3441. ROBBINS, Tim
"Arrangement." Hangl (43) Wint 82-83, p. 82.
"From Slumber to Slumber." HangL (42) 82, p. 65.
from The Hot Tub: "A brunette wearing a lettered
t-shirt, denims and thongs." HangL (41) 82, p.
64-65.
"I Imagine Future Loves." HangL (41) 82, p. 66.
"In Exile." HangL (41) 82, p. 61.
"Invocation and Blessing." HangL (42) 82, p. 64.
"Mista-Peo" (my friend). HangL (41) 82, p. 60.
"Opus 102." Hangl (43) Wint 82-83, p. 80.
"Poem for Bob." HangL (41) 82, p. 62-63.
"Stand with Legs Naked." Hangl (43) Wint 82-83, p.
80.
"Sunday Mid-February." Hangl (43) Wint 82-83, p.
81.
"Why People Pull the Blinds." Hangl (43) Wint 82-
83, p. 83-84.

3442. ROBERTS, Betty
"Southerly." Bogg (48) 82, p. 74.

3443. ROBERTS, Helen Wade
"Time Is A Whirling Dervish." HolCrit (19:1) F 82,
p. 14.

3444. ROBERTS, Len
"Another Note to My Father on the Anniversary of His
Death." Pig (8) 80, p. 80.
"Because God Had Said So." Pig (8) 80, p. 48.
"Children Singing." WestB (10) 82, p. 34.
"Figure Eights." WestB (10) 82, p. 39.
"First Kiss." QW (14) Spr-Sum 82, p. 22.
"The Forgiving" (for James Wright). SouthernPR
(22:1) Spr 82, p. 16-18.
"Homer." WestB (10) 82, p. 40.
"Japanese Begonia." Nimrod (25:2) Spr-Sum 82, p.
71.
"On Each Fingertip." Pig (8) 80, p. 56.
"Pyracantha." WestB (10) 82, p. 35.
"Riding Out to See the First Flowers." QW (14) Spr-
Sum 82, p. 23.
"Rising." Pig (8) 80, p. 9.
"Rowboat." Nimrod (25:2) Spr-Sum 82, p. 36.
"September." WestB (10) 82, p. 36.
"Six Suns." MissouriR (5:2) Wint 81-82, p. 39.
"Sometimes." Nimrod (25:2) Spr-Sum 82, p. 36.
"Summer Thunderstorm." WestB (10) 82, p. 37.
"The Unborn." WestB (10) 82, p. 38.

3445. ROBERTS, Robert J.
"Transplant." LittleBR (1:2) Wint 80-81, p. 78.

3446. ROBERTSON, Kirk
       "Desire." SoDakR (20:4) Wint 82-83, p. 65.
       "Drumstick for Cody." WormR (22:4, issue 88) 82, p.
          145.
       "The Misfits." SoDakR (20:4) Wint 82-83, p. 64-65.

3447. ROBERTSON, R. J.
       "Passage." PoetryCR (3:4) Sum 82, p. 15.

3448. ROBERTSON, Robin
       "Stones." Waves (11:1) Aut 82, p. 15.
       "Storm." Waves (11:1) Aut 82, p. 14.
       "Tokens." Waves (11:1) Aut 82, p. 14.

3449. ROBIN, Ralph
       "Blank Maps." SouthwR (67:3) Sum 82, p. 314.

3450. ROBINER, Mel
       "Another Life." Epoch (31:3) Sum 82, p. 184-185.
       "Privilege." Epoch (31:3) Sum 82, p. 182.
       "A Short Trip." Epoch (31:3) Sum 82, p. 183.

3451. ROBINS, William P.
       "Footprints." WritersL Jl 82, p. 11.

3452. ROBINSON, Frank K.
       "In the stream a trout leaps." WindO (40, Anti-
          Haiku issue) Sum 82, p. 8.
       "On the line a flapping sock." WindO (40, Anti-
          Haiku issue) Sum 82, p. 8.
       "Out of bed at 3 a.m." WindO (40, Anti-Haiku issue)
          Sum 82, p. 8.

3453. ROBINSON, Heather
       "I Have Looked upon You." PottPort (4) 82-83, p.
          32.

3454. ROBINSON, James Miller
       "Agnes." Poem (44) Mr 82, p. 45.
       "December 12: Saint Day of the Virgin of Guadalupe."
          Poem (44) Mr 82, p. 44.
       "Families." PoNow (7:1, issue 37) 82, p. 35.
       "The National Interstate System and the Illinois
          Monument to the Union Dead at Vicksburg,
          Mississippi." DekalbLAJ (14:1/4) Aut 80-Sum 81, p.
          92.
       "Whitesburg Bridge." Poem (44) Mr 82, p. 43.

3455. ROBINSON, Jeannette Drake
       "The Break." Obs (7:2/3) Sum-Wint 81, p. 148.
       "Flowerlady." Obs (7:2/3) Sum-Wint 81, p. 148.
       "Lunchtime" (For Ayana, Joseph, Patrice and Regine).
          Obs (7:2/3) Sum-Wint 81, p. 148.
       "May Is the Month That Roses Bloom." Obs (7:2/3)
          Sum-Wint 81, p. 149.

3456. ROBINSON, Lillian S.
       "Hayes Valley Days." Nimrod (26:1) Aut-Wint 82, p.
          7-10.

3457. ROBINSON, Maria T.
"Jean Toomer Visits Georgia O'Keefe" (For Jean
Toomer). Obs (7:2/3) Sum-Wint 81, p. 152-153.
"An Old House in Detroit." Obs (7:2/3) Sum-Wint 81,
p. 153-154.
"They Wondered Why You Never Wrote Another Book Like
Cane" (For Jean Toomer). Obs (7:2/3) Sum-Wint 81,
p. 152.

3458. ROBSON, Ros
"Bareback Horses." KanQ (14:3) Sum 82, p. 134-135.
"Neighbors." KanQ (14:3) Sum 82, p. 134.

3459. ROBY, Gayle
"The Magician." PoNow (7:1, issue 37) 82, p. 35.

RODENAS, Juan Antonio Masoliver
See: MASOLIVER RODENAS, Juan Antonio

3460. RODERIO, Joe
"The Brown Bat." UTR (7:2) 82?, p. 3.
"From Mars." UTR (7:2) 82?, p. 4.

3461. RODGERS, Gordon
"Back in St. John's." PottPort (4) 82-83, p. 33.
"Blacklist." PottPort (4) 82-83, p. 33.
"The Captain." PottPort (4) 82-83, p. 33.
"Seal's Finger." PottPort (4) 82-83, p. 33.

3462. RODITI, Edouard
"The Absentee" (tr. of Rene Char). Kayak (60) O 82,
p. 11.
"The Basketweaver's Companion" (tr. of Rene Char).
Kayak (60) O 82, p. 10.
"Calendar" (tr. of Rene Char). Kayak (60) O 82, p.
11.
"Dismissing the Wind" (tr. of Rene Char). Kayak (60)
O 82, p. 10.

3463. RODRIGUES, Ray
"Applied Bibliotherapy." EngJ (71:3) Mr 82, p. 84.

3464. RODRIGUEZ, Asia
"Rio Nuevo" (A Julia de Pueblo). Mairena (4:10) Sum-
Aut 82, p. 94.

3465. RODRIGUEZ, Claudio
"Sparrow" (tr. by David Garrison). DenQ (17:3) Aut
82, p. 46.

3466. RODRIGUEZ, Judith
"At the Bottom." WestCR (16:4) Ap 82, p. 30.
"Measuring Up." WestCR (16:4) Ap 82, p. 30.
"Presentation." WestCR (16:4) Ap 82, p. 29.

3467. RODRIGUEZ, Norman
"La Luz" (from La Niebla Rebajada). Mairena (4:10)
Sum-Aut 82, p. 18.
"La Playa" (from La Niebla Rebajada). Mairena (4:10)
Sum-Aut 82, p. 19.

"La Poesia" (from La Niebla Rebajada). <u>Mairena</u>
(4:10) Sum-Aut 82, p. 17.
"Los Senos" (from La Niebla Rebajada). <u>Mairena</u>
(4:10) Sum-Aut 82, p. 18-19.

3468. RODRIGUEZ FRESE, Marcos
"Lo Necesario." <u>Areito</u> (8:31) 82, p. 38.

3469. RODRIGUEZ NIETZCHE, Vicente
"Dispuesto." <u>Areito</u> (8:31) 82, p. 37.
"Para 200 Anos." <u>Areito</u> (8:31) 82, p. 37.

3470. RODRIGUEZ NUNEZ, Victor
"It's a Desperately Cruel Struggle" (tr. by Margaret
Randell). <u>SeC</u> (9:1/2) 80, p. 32.

3471. ROESNER, Charlene
"Friday." <u>KanQ</u> (14:2) Spr 82, p. 114.

3472. ROESSLER, Marjorie
"For the Yearly Phantasmagoria." <u>AntigR</u> (50) Sum
82, p. 36.
"Picking Black Cherries" (Austria 1973). <u>AntigR</u>
(50) Sum 82, p. 36.

3473. ROESSLER, Marjorie D.
"The Cistern Cleaner." <u>NewRena</u> (5:1, 15) Aut 82, p.
58.

3474. ROGAL, Stanley Wm.
"Remaining." <u>AntigR</u> (48) Wint 82, p. 65.

3475. ROGERS, Del Marie
"The Rug Man." <u>Epoch</u> (32:1) Aut 82, p. 56.

3476. ROGERS, Jill
"Stillscapes." <u>MalR</u> (63) O 82, p. 65-67.

3477. ROGERS, Linda
"This Island." <u>CanLit</u> (95) Wint 82, p. 50-55.

3478. ROGERS, Pattiann
"The Abandonment." <u>Poetry</u> (140:1) Ap 82, p. 32-33.
"After Dinner." <u>ChiR</u> (33:2) 82, p. 122.
"Before I Wake." <u>PoetryNW</u> (23:1) Spr 82, p. 37-38.
"Being What We Are." <u>Poetry</u> (141:3) D 82, p. 134-
135.
"The Boredom of the Isolated." <u>ChiR</u> (33:2) 82, p.
123.
"The Delight of Being Lost." <u>Poetry</u> (141:3) D 82,
p. 136.
"The Doctrine." <u>Poetry</u> (141:1) O 82, p. 22-23.
"Eulogy for a Hermit Crab." <u>Poetry</u> (140:1) Ap 82,
p. 33.
"The Evolution of Freedom." <u>PraS</u> (56:2) Sum 82, p.
20.
"Finding the Cat in a Spring Field at Midnight."
<u>Poetry</u> (141:3) D 82, p. 135.
"The Form of the Message." <u>Poetry</u> (141:3) D 82, p.
132.

"A Fortnight to Remember." _Kayak_ (58) Ja 82, p. 54-
55.
"The God of Ornithology." _SouthernR_ (18:4) Aut 82,
p. 810-811.
"The Hummingbird: a Seduction." _PoetryNW_ (23:1) Spr
82, p. 39-40.
"If a Son Asks" (Luke 11:11). _PoetryNW_ (23:3) Aut
82, p. 13-14.
"The Imagination Imagines Itself to Be a God."
PoetryNW (23:3) Aut 82, p. 12-13.
"Keeping Beauty under Control." _Agni_ (16) 82, p.
105.
"Keeping the Body Warm." _MassR_ (23:4) Wint 82, p.
555-556.
"Light of the Sea." _PoetryNW_ (23:3) Aut 82, p. 10-
11.
"The Origin of Order." _Poetry_ (141:3) D 82, p. 133.
"The Possible Suffering of a God During Creation."
Poetry (140:1) Ap 82, p. 30-31.
"Pursuing the Study of a Particular Reality."
PoetryNW (23:1) Spr 82, p. 38-39.
"The Pursuit as Solution." _Kayak_ (59) Je 82, p. 22.
"The Revelation of the Willed Hallucination."
SouthernR (18:4) Aut 82, p. 812-813.
"The Revolution of the Dream." _PoetryNW_ (23:3) Aut
82, p. 11-12.
"Rumors of Snow, Christmas Eve." _PoetryNW_ (23:1)
Spr 82, p. 40-41.
"To Burn Forever." _PoetryNW_ (23:3) Aut 82, p. 14-
15.
"Trinity." _Poetry_ (140:1) Ap 82, p. 34.
"The Vicarious Experience." _Agni_ (16) 82, p. 103-
104.

3479. ROGERS, Timothy J.
from Autobiografia: (16, 18, 22, 34, 38-39) (tr. of
Etelvina Astrada). _Chelsea_ (41) 82, p. 127-129.
from Autobiography at the Trigger: (8, 10, 31) (tr.
of Etelvina Astrada). _CharR_ (8:2) Aut 82, p. 44-
46.

3480. ROJAS, Gonzalo
"Poesia de Margara Russoto." _Inti_ (12) Aut 80, p.
92.

3481. ROJAS, Nydia
"Descubrimiento." _Mairena_ (4:9) Spr 82, p. 36-37.

3482. ROJAS GUARDIA, Armando
from Diario de Solentiname: (1-2). _Prismal_ (7/8) Spr
82, p. 77.
"Si Yo Osara." _Prismal_ (7/8) Spr 82, p. 78-79.

3483. ROMA, Hedy
"Kitchen." _HangL_ (42) 82, p. 66.
"One Night This Summer." _HangL_ (42) 82, p. 67.

3484. ROMANO, James V.
"Haiku: Old Caribbean men." _Maize_ (6:1/2) Aut-Wint
82-83, p. 59.

"Spanish Scene." <u>Maize</u> (6:1/2) Aut-Wint 82-83, p. 58.

3485. ROMANO, Tom
"The Teacher." <u>EngJ</u> (71:3) Mr 82, p. 89.

3486. ROMANOW, Peter
"Edna St. Vincent Millay Answers a Letter Which Praised Her Poetry and Lamented Her Death." <u>Agni</u> (16) 82, p. 117-118.

3487. ROMERO, Leo
"The Dark Side of the Moon." <u>RevChic</u> (10:1/2) Wint-Spr 82, p. 109.
"Fear of the Moon." <u>RevChic</u> (10:1/2) Wint-Spr 82, p. 110-111.
"I Came to Earth." <u>RevChic</u> (10:1/2) Wint-Spr 82, p. 113.
"The Moon Is Lost." <u>RevChic</u> (10:1/2) Wint-Spr 82, p. 112.
"The Night Is Overwhelmed." <u>RevChic</u> (10:1/2) Wint-Spr 82, p. 111.
"The Ocean Is Not Red." <u>RevChic</u> (10:1/2) Wint-Spr 82, p. 112-113.

3488. RONAN, Richard
"Pine / Eucalyptus / Fennel." <u>PoetryNW</u> (23:4) Wint 82-83, p. 41.

ROO, Harvey de
<u>See</u>: De ROO, Harvey

3489. ROOT, Judith
"Haight St. & Failing." <u>MinnR</u> (NS18) Spr 82, p. 12.
"Inside a Rooming House in Des Moines." <u>ColEng</u> 44(2) F 82, p. 158.
"Insomnia." <u>SouthwR</u> (67:4) Aut 82, p. 380.
"Taxi to the Laundromat." <u>MissouriR</u> (6:1) Aut 82, p. 28.
"Weaving the Sheets" (Calabria, 1904). <u>ColEng</u> 44(2) F 82, p. 159.

3490. ROOT, William Pitt
"4 Glimpses into a Painting of Li Po Looking at a Waterfall." <u>MalR</u> (62) Jl 82, p. 152-153.
"Another Note." <u>MalR</u> (62) Jl 82, p. 154.
"Exchanging Glances." <u>PoNow</u> (6:6, issue 36) 82, p. 26.
"Love Poem." <u>PoNow</u> (6:6, issue 36) 82, p. 26.
"The March Sun Portrayed as a Dime Novelist." <u>MalR</u> (62) Jl 82, p. 155.
"Midnight Bulletin." <u>PoNow</u> (6:4, issue 34) 82, p. 5.
"The Sleeping Gypsy" (after Rousseau). <u>MalR</u> (62) Jl 82, p. 150-151.
"Song from the Surface of the Earth." <u>MalR</u> (62) Jl 82, p. 156.

ROSA, Pablo La
<u>See</u>: La ROSA, Pablo

ROSAS, Jose Ruiz
   See: RUIZ ROSAS, Jose

3491. ROSBERG, Rose
       "Continental Drift." SouthernHR (16:1) Wint 82, p.
       67.

3492. ROSE, Danita
       "They said none of this was real." MendoR (6) Sum
       81, p. 55.
       "Tirade." MendoR (6) Sum 81, p. 56.
       "Turnback." MendoR (5) Sum 81, p. 45.
       "Untitled: Funny how the ghosts of young-girl
       dreams." MendoR (5) Sum 81, p. 45.
       "Untitled: The Spirit by any other name." MendoR
       (5) Sum 81, p. 45.
       "Untitled: The will, they will make a song." MendoR
       (5) Sum 81, p. 45.

3493. ROSE, Jennifer
       "Elements." OhioR (27) 82, p. 115.
       "George Annand, 1890-   ." Ploughs (8:1) 82, p.
       154-156.

3494. ROSE, Lynne Carol
       "Consulting the Ouija Board." HiramPoR (31) Aut-
       Wint 82, p. 40.

3495. ROSE, Mike
       "The Mirror in the Cabin." Bogg (49) 82, p. 22-23.
       "My Grandmother's House." Vis (10) 82, p. 24-25.
       "Panama." Vis (10) 82, p. 26.

3496. ROSE, Mildred A.
       "Haiku: The rising moon." PoetryCR (4:2) Wint 82,
       p. 15.

3497. ROSE, Wilga M.
       "St. Mary Magdalen" (painting by Georges La Tour).
       Bogg (48) 82, p. 73.
       "View of a Tiger." Bogg (49) 82, p. 47.

3498. ROSEI, Peter
       "Four Poems" (tr. by Beth Bjorklund). LitR (25:2)
       Wint 82, p. 304-305.

3499. ROSELIEP, Raymond
       "Cataract." ChrC (99:28) S 15-22, 82, p. 924.
       "Drought." ChrC (99:31) O 13, 82, p. 1012.
       "Easter." ChrC (99:12) Ap 7, 82, p. 408.
       "Marker." ChrC (99:16) My 5, 82, p. 533.
       "Of Light." Abraxas (25/26) 82, p. 51.
       "View." ChrC (99:23) Jl 7-14, 82, p. 757.
       "When the News Broke." Im (8:1) 82, p. 6.

3500. ROSEN, Michael J.
       "The Hive Body." PraS (56:4) Wint 82-83, p. 70.
       "Roadside Statuary." Shen (33:3) 82, p. 90-91.

3501. ROSENBERG, L. M.
        "Carving Pumpkins" (for my father). MichQR (21:4)
        Aut 82, p. 599-600.
        "Elegy for a Beagle Mutt." MissouriR (6:1) Aut 82,
        p. 29.
        "The Ghosts of the Three Young People Enter into Me"
        (On the auto wreck at Apalachin Road in which 3
        high school students were killed). PoNow (7:1,
        issue 37) 82, p. 36.
        "Married Love." NewYorker (58:9) Ap 19, 82, p. 48.
        "The Real True President." Bound (10:3) Spr 82, p.
        174.
        "Signs." Bound (10:3) Spr 82, p. 173.
        "Snowbound" (For Lois, on the death of her mother).
        Agni (17) 82, p. 152.
        "Tenderness." Bound (10:3) Spr 82, p. 175.
        "What's on Our Minds." PoNow (7:1, issue 37) 82, p.
        36.

3502. ROSENBERG, Liz
        "The Last Word on Eczema." AmerPoR (11:4) Jl-Ag 82,
        p. 10.

3503. ROSENBERG, P. J.
        "Female Impersonating a Female Impersonator." KanQ
        (14:1) Wint 82, p. 129.

3504. ROSENBERGER, F. C.
        "On the Difficult Poems of an Esteemed
        Contemporary." SoCaR (15:1) Aut 82, p. 43.
        "A Second Death." SoCaR (15:1) Aut 82, p. 43.
        "The State of the Art." ArizQ (38:2) Sum 82, p.
        161.

3505. ROSENBLATT, Joe
        from The Brides of the Stream: "A daylight
        representative of an evening traveller." Waves
        (11:1) Aut 82, p. 60.
        from The Brides of the Stream: "I cast off my larval
        clothes." Waves (11:1) Aut 82, p. 61.
        from The Brides of the Stream: "Tonight the stars
        will be thick as salt over the Little Qualicum."
        Waves (11:1) Aut 82, p. 60.

3506. ROSENBLUM, Martin J.
        "That You Were Back Living." Abraxas (25/26) 82, p.
        91-93.

3507. ROSENFELD, Marjorie Stamm
        "Kaddish de Rabbanan." SouthwR (67:1) Wint 82, p.
        49-50.

3508. ROSENTHAL, Abby
        "The Light" (for Nada Samuels). CutB (18) Spr-Sum
        82, p. 27.

3509. ROSENTHAL, Amy G.
        "The Gut." SouthernPR (23, i.e. 22:2) Aut 82, p.
        29.

3510. ROSENWALD, John
"In the Woods." KanQ (14:1) Wint 82, p. 164.
from Sonnets to Orpheus: (I.2) (tr. of Rainer Maria
Rilke). SoCaR (14:2) Spr 82, p. 115.
from Sonnets to Orpheus: (II.5-6) (tr. of Rainer
Maria Rilke). Paint (9:17/18) Spr-Aut 82, p. 22-
23.

3511. ROSS, Bob
from Letter to a Dead Wren: (2). CutB (18) Spr-Sum
82, p. 46-47.

3512. ROSS, Carolyn
"Day with a Stranger." Outbr (8/9) Aut 81-Spr 82,
p. 80.
"Short Story." Outbr (8/9) Aut 81-Spr 82, p. 79.
"To a Student, about the Decade." Outbr (8/9) Aut
81-Spr 82, p. 77-78.

3513. ROSS, Marty
"Bo Diddley at Forty-Seven." Spirit (6:2/3) 82,
p.127, 130.

3514. ROSSETTI, Dante Gabriel
"On Refusal of Aid Between Nations." Agni (17) 82,
p. 1.

3515. ROSSI, Vinio
"Aria for Tenor" (tr. of Giovanni Raboni, w. Stuart
Friebert). MalR (62) Jl 82, p. 62.
"The Check Room" (tr. of Giovanni Raboni, w. Stuart
Friebert). MalR (62) Jl 82, p. 62.
"The Custom-House" (tr. of Eugenio Montale, w. David
Young). Field (27) Aut 82, p. 11.
"Elements of an Urban Landscape" (tr. of Giovanni
Raboni, w. Stuart Friebert). MalR (62) Jl 82, p.
64.
"Judas' Oration" (tr. of Giovanni Raboni, w. Stuart
Friebert). MalR (62) Jl 82, p. 64.
"Lemons" (tr. of Eugenio Montale, w. David Young).
Field (27) Aut 82, p. 14-15.
"Meditation in the Orchard" (tr. of Giovanni Raboni,
w. Stuart Friebert). MalR (62) Jl 82, p. 63.
"News from Mount Amiata" (tr. of Eugenio Montale, w.
David Young). Field (27) Aut 82, p. 35-36.
"Serenade" (tr. of Giovanni Raboni, w. Stuart
Friebert). LittleBR (2:4) Sum 82, p. 73.
"Simulated & Dissimulated" (for my son) (tr. of
Giovanni Raboni, w. Stuart Friebert). MalR (62) Jl
82, p. 63.

3516. ROSTEN, Norman
"The Meeting" (for Aaron Kramer). MichQR (21:1) Wint
82, p. 158.

3517. ROSTON, Ruth
"Fortieth Reunion." PoNow (7:1, issue 37) 82, p.
26.
"Salesman." PoNow (7:1, issue 37) 82, p. 26.

3518. ROTELLA, Alexis
"As if the cabbage speaks to me." WindO (40, Anti-
Haiku issue) Sum 82, p. 6.
"Breeze--butterfly keeps missing the day-lily."
WindO (40, Anti-Haiku issue) Sum 82, p. 6.
"Gathering the parachute." WindO (40, Anti-Haiku
issue) Sum 82, p. 7.
"Get out the pesticide." WindO (40, Anti-Haiku
issue) Sum 82, p. 7.
"In the farmer's field." WindO (40, Anti-Haiku
issue) Sum 82, p. 7.
"Lighting candles iii." WindO (40, Anti-Haiku
issue) Sum 82, p. 7.
"Listen to the mockingbird." WindO (40, Anti-Haiku
issue) Sum 82, p. 6.
"Lonely dog sitting on my haiku." WindO (40, Anti-
Haiku issue) Sum 82, p. 6.
"A peach pit thrown from the window." WindO (40,
Anti-Haiku issue) Sum 82, p. 6.
"Pointing its tongue." WindO (40, Anti-Haiku issue)
Sum 82, p. 6.
"Pond side: that old bull." WindO (40, Anti-Haiku
issue) Sum 82, p. 6.
"Rattling the lettuce packets." WindO (40, Anti-
Haiku issue) Sum 82, p. 7.
"The red day-lilies' yellow throats." WindO (40,
Anti-Haiku issue) Sum 82, p. 6.
"Senryu: Morning tea." WindO (40, Anti-Haiku issue)
Sum 82, p. 7.
"Senryu: New Year's Day." WindO (40, Anti-Haiku
issue) Sum 82, p. 7.
"That crow stole my haiku!" WindO (40, Anti-Haiku
issue) Sum 82, p. 6.

3519. ROTELLA, Robert F.
"Laundry day." WindO (40, Anti-Haiku issue) Sum 82,
p. 30.

3520. ROTH, Paul
"(6) You come to your name." UTR (7:2) 82?, p. 27.
"(9) On this side of the page I am living with the
written." UTR (7:2) 82?, p. 27.

3521. ROTHENBERG, Jerome
"The Covering Cherub & The Academy of Dada" (for B.,
among the minim). Sulfur (2:2, issue 5) 82, p.
113-116.
"Yaqui 1982." Sulfur (2:3, issue 6) 82, p. 33-38.

3522. ROUX, Saint-Pol
"The Panoply" (tr. by Robin Magowan). Kayak (59) Je
82, p. 28.

3523. ROVINSKY, Robert
"When Beaumont and Tocqueville First Visited Sing-
Sing" (tr. of Goran Printz-Pahlson). PoetryE (8)
Aut 82, p. 67.

3524. ROWE, Kelly
      "Legacy" (for my father). Iowa (13:1) Wint 82, p.
      120.

3525. ROY, Mriganka
      "A Whirl" (tr. by Satyabrata Mukherjee). NewL
      (48:3/4) Spr-Sum 82, p. 160.

3526. RUARK, Gibbons
      "To the Swallows of Viterbo." Ploughs (8:2/3) 82,
      p. 130.
      "Words to Accompany a Leaf from the Great Copper
      Beech at Coole." Ploughs (8:2/3) 82, p. 128-129.

3527. RUBENS, Philip M.
      "The Children's Crusade." StoneC (10:1/2) Aut-Wint
      82-83, p. 69.

3528. RUBIN, Larry
      "Caught in the Storm." FourQt (31:3) Spr 82, p. 31.
      "The Hidden Spark." Wind (12:44) 82, p. 34.
      "Home Remedies." Wind (12:44) 82, p. 34.
      "Refractions at Sea." PoNow (6:5, issue 35) 82, p.
      38.

3529. RUBIN, Stan Sanvel
      "Last Day of February." GeoR (36:1) Spr 82, p. 81.

      RUBIO, Nieves del Rosario Marquez de
      See: MARQUEZ de RUBIO, Nieves del Rosario

      RUBIO, Victor Gil de
      See: GIL de RUBIO, Victor

3530. RUDEL, Jaufre
      "Amor de Lonh" (tr. by Ezra Pound). Antaeus (44)
      Wint 82, p. 28-29.

3531. RUDJORD, Astrid
      "Like a Tarn in the Wood" (tr. of Jan Erik Vold, w.
      Albert Ward). Stand (23:3) 82, p. 27.
      "The Wood-Carver" (tr. of Jan Erik Vold, w. Albert
      Ward). Stand (23:3) 82, p. 26.

3532. RUDMAN, Mark
      "At the Asian Star on the Eve of Another Departure."
      Pequod (14) 82, p. 46.
      "The Blind Bandura Players" (tr. of Bohdan Boychuk,
      w. the author). Pequod (15) 82, p. 82.
      "The End" (tr. of Boris Pasternak, w. Bohdan
      Boychuk). Pequod (14) 82, p. 118-119.
      "Lines Written on the Via Veneto." Pequod (15) 82,
      p. 72.
      "The Mirror" (tr. of Boris Pasternak, w. Bohdan
      Boychuk). Pequod (15) 82, p. 70-71.
      "Postscript" (tr. of Boris Pasternak). Sulfur (2:1,
      issue 4) 82, p. 56.
      "Prince Igor's Campaign" (tr. of Mykola Bazhan, w.
      Bohdan Boychuk). Pequod (14) 82, p. 40-41.

from Scrapings: "My name was stuck onto me like
   masking tape." Pequod (14) 82, p. 47.
"Summer" (tr. of Boris Pasternak). Sulfur (2:1,
   issue 4) 82, p. 54-55.
"Taxco" (tr. of Bohdan Boychuk, w. the author).
   Pequod (15) 82, p. 78.
"Three-Dimensional Love" (tr. of Bohdan Boychuk, w.
   the author). Pequod (15) 82, p. 80-81.
"You Came" (tr. of Bohdan Boychuk, w. the author).
   Pequod (15) 82, p. 79.

3533. RUEFLE, Mary
   "At Cana." CutB (19) Aut-Wint 82, p. 17.
   "The Least Sequence of Flesh." MissouriR (5:3) Sum
      82, p. 31.
   "Reasons of His Own." NewEngR (4:3) Spr 82, p. 453.
   "True to Life Also." MissouriR (5:3) Sum 82, p. 30.

3534. RUENZEL, David
   "Christmas Poem." SouthernPR (23, i.e. 22:2) Aut
      82, p. 53.

3535. RUESCHER, Scott
   "The Sense of Identity in Southern Ohio." OhioR
      (28) 82, p. 31.

3536. RUFFIN, Paul
   "When We Heard the Learned Astronomer Explain the
      Theory of the Exploding Universe." SouthernHR
      (16:4) Aut 82, p. 340.

3537. RUGAMA, Leonel
   "La Tierra Es un Satelite de la Luna." Maize
      (5:3/4) Spr-Sum 82, p. 67.

3538. RUGO, Marieve
   "Anniversary." WestB (11) 82, p. 77.
   "Flesh and Bones" (For Carole Oles). NoAmR (267:4) D
      82,p. 26.
   "Thrift Shop." GeoR (36:1) Spr 82, p. 183.
   "The Unspeakable." WestB (11) 82, p. 76.
   "What Happened." GeoR (36:4) Wint 82, p. 854.

3539. RUHM, Gerhard
   "Some Things" (tr. by Beth Bjorklund). LitR (25:2)
      Wint 82, p. 260.

   RUISSEAUX, Pierre des
   See: DesRUISSEAUX, Pierre

3540. RUIZ, Albor
   "Decimas para una Cubanita" (Para Onecy, a un ano de
      su muerte). Areito (8:32) 82, p. 26.

   RUIZ, Jose O. Colon
   See: COLON RUIZ, Jose O.

3541. RUIZ, Judy
   "The Lemon Houses." MidwQ (23:4) Sum 82, p. 400.
   "Maybe Someday." MidwQ (23:4) Sum 82, p. 401.

3542. RUIZ DUENAS, Jorge
"12." BelPoJ (32:4) Sum 82, p. 28, 30.
"12" (tr. by Ricardo Pau-Llosa). BelPoJ (32:4) Sum
82, p. 29, 31.

3543. RUIZ ROSAS, Jose
"Empiezas, Peregrino" (from Repaso del Hombre).
Mairena (4:10) Sum-Aut 82, p. 37.
"No Puedes con Tu Voz" (from Repaso del Hombre).
Mairena (4:10) Sum-Aut 82, p. 36-37.
"Notas" (from Repaso del Hombre). Mairena (4:10)
Sum-Aut 82, p. 36.
"Toma la Poesia con las Manos" (from Repaso del
Hombre). Mairena (4:10) Sum-Aut 82, p. 37.

3544. RUNCIMAN, Lex
"Dogs at the Veterans' Hospital." QW (14) Spr-Sum
82, p. 70.
"Moving." QW (14) Spr-Sum 82, p. 71.

3545. RUNGREN, Lawrence
"Midwest Greyhound." Abraxas (25/26) 82, p. 99.

3546. RUSBULDT, Sharon E.
"The Woman Who Knew." AntigR (49) Spr 82, p. 14.

3547. RUSH, Jerry
"Accommodation." Quarry (31:4) Aut 82, p. 35.
"Devil's Yard." Quarry (31:4) Aut 82, p. 35-36.
"Old Artist." Quarry (31:4) Aut 82, p. 36.

3548. RUSS, Lawrence
"The Lean Spirits." BelPoJ (33:2) Wint 82-83, p.
12-19.

3549. RUSS, Lisa
"A Poem for Stanley." SouthernPR (23, i.e. 22:2)
Aut 82, p. 57-58.

3550. RUSSELL, Carol Ann
"The Brown-Headed Cowbird Has a Blue, Blue Tongue"
(for Richard Hugo). Tendril (12) Wint 82, p. 57.

3551. RUSSELL, Caryn
"Landbound." SouthernHR (16:2) Spr 82, p. 115.

3552. RUSSELL, Frank
"The Ash Turning Apple." CharR (8:2) Aut 82, p. 31-
32.
"Perhaps Some Sunday." CharR (8:2) Aut 82, p. 30-
31.
"Space Masons." SouthernPR (23, i.e. 22:2) Aut 82,
p. 50.
"Standing in the Graveyard of Day." CharR (8:2) Aut
82, p. 29-30.
"You Write Too Many Poems." CharR (8:2) Aut 82, p.
32.

3553. RUSSELL, Hilary
"The Schoolteacher's Dream for Lincolnsville."
Ploughs (8:2/3) 82, p. 164.

3554. RUSSELL, Joy
"Fran." CapilR (22) 82, p. 56.

3555. RUSSELL, Norman H.
"The Eagle and the Coyote." SouthwR (67:2) Spr 82,
p. 179-180.
"I Will Listen." SouthwR (67:2) Spr 82, p. 181.
"I Will Listen: Four Indian Poems." SouthwR (67:2)
Spr 82, p. 179-181.
"A Message It Whispers." SouthwR (67:2) Spr 82, p.
180-181.
"Who Never Falls." SouthwR (67:2) Spr 82, p. 179.

3556. RUSSELL, R. Stephen
"Places to Touch You." LittleBR (1:4) Sum 81, p.
59-64.
"This Poem Is One You Never Hear." LittleBR (2:1)
Aut 81, p. 65.
"This Poem Is Three Horses Sleeping." KanQ (14:3)
Sum 82, p. 117.

3557. RUSSELL, Timothy
"The Invisible Bridge." Tendril (13) Sum 82, p. 60.
"The Margin for Error." PoNow (7:1, issue 37) 82,
p. 36.
"Once and for All." Tendril (13) Sum 82, p. 59.
"Please Stand By." WestB (10) 82, p. 43.
"The Pursuit of Happiness." SouthernPR (22:1) Spr
82, p. 22.
"Small Wonder." WestB (10) 82, p. 42.
"The Tar River." HiramPoR (31) Aut-Wint 82, p. 41.

3558. RUSSOTTO, Margara
"Domingo." BelPoJ (32:4) Sum 82, p. 46, 48.
"Sunday" (tr. by Ricardo Pau-Llosa). BelPoJ (32:4)
Sum 82, p. 45, 47.

3559. RUSTE, Arne
from The Roof People: "They call themselves nothing"
(tr. by Nadia Christensen). Stand (23:3) 82, p.
36.

3560. RUSTIN, Florence M.
"Country Gal's Lament." DekalbLAJ (14:1/4) Aut 80-
Sum 81, p. 115.

3561. RUTAN, Robin
"Footsteps." PoetC (14:1) 82, p. 22-23.

3562. RUTSALA, Vern
"Additional Journeys." Telescope (3) Sum 82, p. 30-
31.
"Being Second-Rate." PoNow (6:5, issue 35) 82, p.
14.
"Driving Around: A Memoir." Poetry (141:2) N 82, p.
77-78.

"Failure." PoNow (6:5, issue 35) 82, p. 14.
"Falling Off a Log." PoNow (6:5, issue 35) 82, p. 14.
"The Furniture Factory." PoNow (6:4, issue 34) 82, p. 25.
"Little-Known Sports." PoNow (6:5, issue 35) 82, p. 14.
"The Night Journey: Lu Chi." PoetryNW (23:2) Sum 82, p. 38-40.
"Northwest Passage." PoNow (6:4, issue 34) 82, p. 25.
"The Poem with a Hackamore around Its Neck." PoNow (6:6, issue 36) 82, p. 9.
"Provincial." PoetryNW (23:2) Sum 82, p. 40-41.
"Reedy's Galaxy." PoNow (6:4, issue 34) 82, p. 25.
"Some Houses." SewanR (90:2) Spr 82, p. 223-224.
"Summer Questions, 1981." PortR (28:1) 82, p. 24.
"What We Have." Poetry (141:2) N 82, p. 75-76.
"X's Poems." PoNow (6:4, issue 34) 82, p. 9.

3563. RUTTERFORD, Julie
       "Kaleidoscope." Bogg (49) 82, p. 46.

3564. RYAN, Margaret
       "Immigrant Women." Epoch (32:1) Aut 82, p. 40.

3565. RYAN, Michael
       "Blue Corridor." AmerPoR (11:6) N-D 82, p. 38.
       "Poem Begun on a Postcard." AmerPoR (11:6) N-D 82, p. 38.
       "Portrait of a Lady." AmerPoR (11:6) N-D 82, p. 38.

3566. RYAN, Patrick H.
       "Holy Saturday." ChrC (99:12) Ap 7, 82, p. 396.

3567. RYAN, R. M.
       "A Sense of Direction." PoNow (6:6, issue 36) 82, p. 46.

3568. RYAN, William Michael
       "The Cut." MinnR (NS19) Aut 82, p. 19-20.
       "Doxology." MinnR (NS19) Aut 82, p. 17-18.

       SAANEN, Christine Dumitriu van
       See: DUMITRIU van SAANEN, Christine

       SAAVEDRA, Fernando Espejo
       See: ESPEJO-SAAVEDRA, Fernando

3569. SABA, Umberto
       "Paradise" (from Cuor Morituro, 1925-1930, tr. by Felix Stefanile). Sparrow (43) 82, p. 11.
       "Sonnet 3" (from Autobiografia, 1924, tr. by Felix Stefanile). Sparrow (43) 82, p. 21.

3570. SABINES, Jaime
       "The Ants Clasp Hands" (tr. by Naomi Lindstrom). DenQ (16:4) Wint 82, p. 44.
       "They Get Me in the Head" (tr. by Naomi Lindstrom). DenQ (16:4) Wint 82, p. 43.

"The Trees are Swaying" (tr. by Naomi Lindstrom).
NewL (48:2) Wint 81-82, p. 98.

3571. SACHDEV, Padma
"Pain" (tr. by Iqbal Masud). NewL (48:3/4) Spr-Sum
82, p. 99.

3572. SACRE, James
"Dans Quatre Endroits Vus de Loin." Os (14) 82, p.
29-30.

3573. SADA, Daniel
"Celemania." BelPoJ (32:4) Sum 82, p. 34, 36.
"Celemania" (tr. by Ricardo Pau-Llosa). BelPoJ
(32:4) Sum 82, p. 35, 37.

SADAFUN, Taira no
See: TAIRA no SADAFUN

3574. SADOFF, Ira
"Checks and Balances" (For Ernie Pelotte). Poetry
(140:4) Jl 82, p. 197-198.
"February: Pemaquid Point." PoetryE (7) Spr 82, p.
23-24.
"Mingus: Last Speech" (for Eric Dolphy). CarolQ
(34:3) Spr 82, p. 11-12.
"My Wife's Upstairs." PoetryE (7) Spr 82, p. 24-25.
"A Solitary Walk through Oakland, Maine." Poetry
(140:4) Jl 82, p. 198.

3575. SAFARIK, Allan
"The Duality of One." PoetryCR (4:2) Wint 82, p. 7.

3576. SAGAN, Miriam
"Atlantis." WestB (10) 82, p. 72-73.
"Fields of Vision." PoNow (6:6, issue 36) 82, p.
45.
"In Detail." WestB (10) 82, p. 71.
"Yosemite. This Light." Gargoyle (17/18) 81, p. 41.

3577. SAGEL, Jaime
"Frigid." Maize (5:1/2) Aut-Wint 81-82, p. 53-54.

3578. SAHI, Vijay Dev Narain
"Aquarium" (tr. by Ajit Khullar). NewL (48:3/4) Spr-
Sum 82, p. 237.

SAINT . . .
See: ST. . . . (filed as spelled)

3579. SAJNER, Donat
"The First Sentence" (tr. by Dana Habova and Stuart
Friebert). Field (27) Aut 82, p. 78.

SAKUTARO, Hagiwara
See: HAGIWARA, Sakutaro

3580. SALAAM, Kalamu ya
"David Murray/a Saxophone from the South (i.e.
Southern CA)." Obs (7:2/3) Sum-Wint 81, p. 173-175.
"A gun in the Hand Is Worth." Obs (7:2/3) Sum-Wint
81, p. 171-172.
"Hiway Blues" (for Dessie Woods). Obs (7:2/3) Sum-Wint 81, p. 172-173.
"In House" (something about Tayari). Obs (7:2/3)
Sum-Wint 81, p. 175-176.
"Our World Is Less Full Now That Mr. Fuller Is
Gone." Obs (7:2/3) Sum-Wint 81, p. 170-171.

SALDIVIA, Lulu Gimenez
See: GIMENEZ SALDIVIA, Lulu

3581. SALEMI, Joseph
"1.25" (tr. of Horace). StoneC (9:3/4) Spr-Sum 82,
p. 27.

3582. SALERNO, Joe
"Deep Snow." MichQR (21:1) Wint 82, p. 164-165.

3583. SALINAS, Luis Omar
"As I Look to the Literate." RevChic (10:1/2) Wint-Spr 82, p. 116.
"I Am America." RevChic (10:1/2) Wint-Spr 82, p.
114-115.
"Many Things of Death." NowestR (20:2/3) 82, p.
238-239.
"My Father Is a Simple Man" (for my father Alfredo).
RevChic (10:1/2) Wint-Spr 82, p. 117.
"What Is Poverty?" NowestR (20:2/3) 82, p. 240.
"When This Life No Longer Smells of Roses." RevChic
(10:1/2) Wint-Spr 82, p. 118.

3584. SALINAS JARAMILLO, Miguel A.
"Canto al Hombre Nuevo." Maize (5:1/2) Aut-Wint 81-82, p. 86-87.

3585. SALINGER, Wendy
"Piano Night." Ploughs (8:2/3) 82, p. 263-265.

3586. SALISBURY, Ralph
"The Byzantine Navy." CharR (8:1) Spr 82, p. 20-21.
"The Color of" (for my brother Leland, who died from
malnutrition and illness). CharR (8:1) Spr 82, p.
21.

3587. SALLI-DAWSON, Donna
"The Source." KanQ (14:3) Sum 82, p. 115.

3588. SALLIS, James
"Among the Missing" (for Tony Sobin). PortR (28:2)
82, p. 103-109.

3589. SALTER, Mary Jo
"At City Hall." Atl (249:6) Je 82, p. 71.
"Facsimile of a Chapel." NewEngR (4:4) Sum 82, p.
535-536.

3590. SALTMAN, Benjamin
"The Sun Takes Us Away." SouthernPR (22:1) Spr 82,
p. 52.

SALVO, Tommaso Giuseppe di
See: Di SALVO, Tommaso Giuseppe

3591. SAMUELS, Diana Reed
"Period Piece 4: The Saint." Poem (46) N 82, p. 22.
"Period Piece 7: Welfare." Poem (46) N 82, p. 20-
21.

3592. SANAZARO, Leonard
"Alexander's Complaint." WebR (7:1) Spr 82, p. 68.
"The Bishop's Rose Garden." HiramPoR (31) Aut-Wint
82, p. 42.
from The Greek Poems, Necessity and Fate 1971-1981:
"2. Necessity and Fate." WebR (7:2) Aut 82, p. 58.
from The Greek Poems, Necessity and Fate 1971-1981:
"5. Sunset, Southern Crete." WebR (7:2) Aut 82, p.
59.

SANCHEZ, Francisco Feliciano
See: FELICIANO SANCHEZ, Francisco

3593. SANCHEZ, Ricardo
"Coronado." RevChic (10:1/2) Wint-Spr 82, p. 123-
124.
"Entequila, Entelechy, Hijola Pero Entelequia"
(prose-poem dedicated to Carlos Rosas,
muralist/artist/compadre/& creator... RevChic
(10:1/2) Wint-Spr 82, p. 119-122.
"Letter to My Ex-Texas Sanity." RevChic (10:1/2)
Wint-Spr 82, p. 125-127.

3594. SANCHIS-BANUS, Jose
"Egloga a Cernuda." Inti(12) Aut 80, p. 76-79.

3595. SANDEEN, Ernest
"At Center Court." MichQR (21:4) Aut 82, p. 552.
"Birds, Chimneys." PoetryNW (23:3) Aut 82, p. 46.

3596. SANDERS, Mark
"'49 Ford." Poem (46) N 82, p. 14.
"An Arrival." Poem (44) Mr 82, p. 39.
"Beginning New Labors." Poem (44) Mr 82, p. 37.
"Father to Son." LittleBR (3:2) Wint 82-83, p. 50.
"February Wash." KanQ (14:3) Sum 82, p. 136.
"Fishing the Sandpits, Elm Creek, Nebraska." KanQ
(14:3) Sum 82, p. 135.
"The Good Girl." Poem (46) N 82, p. 12-13.
"Happening In." LittleBR (2:4) Sum 82, p. 66.
"Kansas Wheat Field." LittleBR (2:4) Sum 82, p. 65.
"Late Evening." SmPd (19:3, issue 56) Aut 82, p.
20.
"Sleet." LittleBR (3:2) Wint 82-83, p. 50.
"The Worm." Poem (44) Mr 82, p. 38.

3597. SANDERSON, Gertrude
    "The Black Bird" (from En la Nuit, la Mer, tr. of
        Fernand Ouellette). AntigR (50) Sum 82, p. 101.
    "The Flute" (For Sylvie, from En la Nuit, la Mer,
        tr. of Fernand Ouellette). AntigR (50) Sum 82, p.
        99.
    "For a long time I believed for a long time I wanted
        for a long time" (from L'en dessous l'admirable,
        tr. of Jacques Brault). AntigR (48) Wint 82, p.
        71.
    "History" (from En la Nuit, la Mer, tr. of Fernand
        Ouellette). AntigR (49) Spr 82, p. 81.
    "I have seen my tattered one I have seen her with
        her flower-eyes" (from L'en dessous l'admirable,
        tr. of Jacques Brault). AntigR (48) Wint 82, p.
        69.
    "The old adventure" (from L'en dessous l'admirable,
        tr. of Jacques Brault). AntigR (48) Wint 82, p.
        67.
    "Openly" (from En la Nuit, la Mer, tr. of Fernand
        Ouellette). AntigR (49) Spr 82, p. 81.
    "Tomb of Ovidiu" (from En la Nuit, la Mer, tr. of
        Fernand Ouellette). AntigR (49) Spr 82, p. 79.
    "The Tortured Ones" (from En la Nuit, la Mer, tr. of
        Fernand Ouellette). AntigR (49) Spr 82, p. 81.

3598. SANDHU, Gulzar Singh
    "At Crossroads" (tr. of S. S. Misha). NewL (48:3/4)
        Spr-Sum 82, p. 186.
    "A Naked Stick in the Matchbox" (tr. of Haribhajan
        Singh). NewL (48:3/4) Spr-Sum 82, p. 213.

3599. SANDY, Stephen
    "Circles" (For Cole Younger 1845-1914). PoNow (6:6,
        issue 36) 82, p. 7.
    "Election Day." NewEngR (4:4) Sum 82, p. 551-552.
    "Nativity." MichQR (21:3) Sum 82, p. 400-402.
    "Off There." VirQR (58:3) Sum 82, p. 441-442.
    "The Painter." MissouriR (5:3) Sum 82, p. 21.
    "Returning to Eagle Bridge." NewEngR (5:1/2) Aut-
        Wint 82, p. 141-143.
    "Riverboat." VirQR (58:3) Sum 82, p. 441.
    "Sampler." VirQR (58:3) Sum 82, p. 442.
    "Wall, South Dakota." YaleR (72:1) Aut 82, p. 57.

3600. SANER, Reg
    "Dora Markus" (tr. of Eugenio Montale). Field (27)
        Aut 82, p. 41-42.
    "Ed & Me." PoNow (6:4, issue 34) 82, p. 32.
    "Equinox." Telescope (2) Aut 81, p. 15.
    "Green Feathers." Atl (250:6) D 82, p. 66.
    "Rimlight and Pupil." GeoR (36:4) Wint 82, p. 752-
        753.
    "Under the Sun in Siena." CharR (8:1) Spr 82, p.
        22-23.

3601. SANFORD, Geraldine A. J.
    "My Artichoke Soup." SoDakR (20:4) Wint 82-83, p.
        62-63.

3602. SANGE, Sally Harris
      "Compulsion." <u>MichOR</u> (21:3) Sum 82, p. 403-404.

3603. SANGER, Peter (Peter M.)
      "Bombay." <u>PottPort</u> (4) 82-83, p. 8.
      "The Burlap Sack." <u>AntigR</u> (51) Aut 82, p. 10.
      "Canti Avium." <u>Grain</u> (10:3) Ag 82, p. 55.
      "Catches." <u>Grain</u> (10:3) Ag 82, p. 54.
      "Crow in Winter." <u>AntigR</u> (51) Aut 82, p. 8.
      "Isobel Martin." <u>MalR</u> (61) F 82, p. 18-19.
      "Marrakesh, 1965." <u>PoetryCR</u> (4:2) Wint 82, p. 11.
      "The Rat." <u>AntigR</u> (51) Aut 82, p. 9.
      "The Royal Series" (A. & W. MacKinlay, Pub.,
         Halifax). <u>PoetryCR</u> (4:1) Sum 82, p. 11.
      "The Story Teller." <u>PottPort</u> (4) 82-83, p. 9.
      "Underwood." <u>AntigR</u> (51) Aut 82, p. 7.
      "The Voyage of the Saladin" (Valparaiso -- Country
         Harbour, N.S., February 8 - May 22, 1844). <u>AntigR</u>
         (48) Wint 82, p. 57-62.

3604. SANGUINETI, Edoardo
      from Erotopaegnia: "It slept inside you like a dry
         tumor" (tr. by Ilaria Caputi and David St. John).
         <u>PoetryE</u> (8) Aut 82, p. 75.

3605. SANSOM, Peter
      "After the Yonville Fair." <u>Bogg</u> (49) 82, p. 39.

3606. SANTALIZ, Coqui
      "Este Poeta." <u>Mairena</u> (4:11/12) Wint 82, p. 151.

3607. SANTANA, Terry
      "It was today, just walking around with friends."
         <u>Areito</u> (8:32) 82, p. 27.

3608. SANTATERESA, Matt
      "Icarus" (after Bruegel). <u>Quarry</u> (31:1) Wint 82, p.
         63-64.
      "Scarecrow." <u>Quarry</u> (31:1) Wint 82, p. 62-63.

3609. SANTIAGO, Leida
      "Para Hermanarme." <u>Mairena</u> (4:11/12) Wint 82, p.
         149.

      SANTIAGO BACA, Jimmy
      <u>See</u>: BACA, Jimmy Santiago

3610. SANTOS, Sherod
      "The Beginning of Autumn." <u>Ploughs</u> (8:1) 82, p. 69-
         70.
      "The Enormous Aquarium" (After Proust). <u>NewYorker</u>
         (58:36) O 25, 82, p. 165.

3611. SANTOS SILVA, Loreina
      from Umbral de Soledad (Poemario inedito): (III,
         XXIII). <u>Mairena</u> (4:9) Spr 82, p. 32-33.

3612. SANTOS TIRADO, Adrian
      "Del Tiempo Sostenido" (from Una Huella en el Mar).
         <u>Mairena</u> (4:10) Sum-Aut 82, p. 21.

"Despedida para un Ardiente Vuelo" (from Una Huella
    en el Mar). Mairena (4:10) Sum-Aut 82, p. 21.
"Una Huella en la Arena" (from Una Huella en el
    Mar). Mairena (4:10) Sum-Aut 82, p. 22.
"La Llegada" (from Una Huella en el Mar). Mairena
    (4:10) Sum-Aut 82, p. 20.

3613. SANYAL, Ashis
    "Very Close It Was" (tr. by Lila Ray). NewL (48:3/4)
    Spr-Sum 82, p. 154-155.

3614. SAPIA, Yvonne
    "Another Poem about Breasts." RevChic (10:4) Aut
        82, p. 8.
    "The Figure at the Door." RevChic (10:4) Aut 82, p.
        7.
    "Godiva at Olustee." Poem (44) Mr 82, p. 30-31.
    "Inside the Room of Ruined Light." RevChic (10:4)
        Aut 82, p. 9.
    "Meeting at Alligator Lake." Poem (44) Mr 82, p.
        32.
    "The Second Person." RevChic (10:4) Aut 82, p. 10.
    "Sister Mary." Confr (24) Sum 82, p. 43.
    "The Suck Hole." Poem (44) Mr 82, p. 28-29.

3615. SARAH, Robyn
    "An Inch of Air." AntigR (49) Spr 82, p. 68.
    "Nocturne." AntigR (49) Spr 82, p. 66.
    "Tides." AntigR (49) Spr 82, p. 67.

    SARAVI, Gustavo Garcia
    See: GARCIA SARAVI, Gustavo

3616. SARGENT, Dana
    "Victor at Rest." PoNow (6:4, issue 34) 82, p. 44.

3617. SARJEANT, Janet
    "The Whistler." SouthernPR (23, i.e. 22:2) Aut 82,
        p. 59-60.

3618. SASTRE de BALMACEDA, Margarita
    "Palomas Blancas" (alegoria a un nacimiento).
        Mairena (4:10) Sum-Aut 82, p. 83.

3619. SATHERLEY, David
    "The Last Dance." AntigR (51) Aut 82, p. 92-93.
    "Subcutis." PottPort (4) 82-83, p. 30.

3620. SAUL, George Brandon
    "Deer in Moonlight." ArizQ (38:3) Aut 82, p. 196.

    SAUNDERS, Leslie
    See: MLS

3621. SAUNDERS, Margaret
    "Spring." CrossC (4:2/3) 82, p. 50.

3622. SAVITT, Lynne
    "Prison Poem #8: In the Yard." PoNow (6:5, issue
        35) 82, p. 19.

"Prison Poem #10: 1/12/80." PoNow (6:5, issue 35)
    82, p. 19.
"Prison Poem #18: Love & Sanity." PoNow (6:5, issue
    35) 82, p. 19.
"Prison Poem #29." PoNow (6:5, issue 35) 82, p. 19.

3623. SAVOIE, Terry
    "Bits of the Sky." Chelsea (41) 82, p. 156.
    "An Elegy at Sixty Miles Per Hour." Focus (15:94) O
        82, p. 23.
    "Letter to a Lost Friend." Poetry (139:4) Ja 82, p.
        196-197.
    from Poems with Titles from Paintings by Paul Klee:
        "Dance You Monster to My Soft Song." BelPoJ (32:3)
        Spr 82, p. 15.
    "Stucco." Chelsea (41) 82, p. 157.
    "An Unconscious History." Poetry (139:4) Ja 82, p.
        195.

3624. SCAMMELL, William
    "A Letter from Cumbria." Poetry (140:4) Jl 82, p.
        193-196.

3625. SCANLON, Dennice
    "Homestead" (For M. S. Daniels). CutB (19) Aut-Wint
        82, p. 36.

3626. SCANNELL, Vernon
    "Interview with the Author." Stand (23:1) 81-82, p.
        8.
    "Listening Ignorant." AmerS (51:3) Sum 82, p. 379.
    "Moors Threnody." Stand (23:1) 81-82, p. 8.
    "On Leave: May 1916." Stand (23:1) 81-82, p. 9.

3627. SCANNELL, Vicki
    "Emma." PoetryNW (23:2) Sum 82, p. 29.

3628. SCANTLEBURY, Mark
    "Birthday." KanQ (14:1) Wint 82, p. 162.
    "From a Painting by Magritte." KanQ (14:1) Wint 82,
        p. 163.

3629. SCARBROUGH, George
    "Winter." PoNow (6:6, issue 36) 82, p. 29.

3630. SCARPA, Vivien C.
    "O Loveseed." Bogg (49) 82, p. 16.

3631. SCHAEFER, Ted
    "Delos." KanQ (14:3) Sum 82, p. 46.
    "Jack the Ripper's Betrothed." KanQ (14:4) Aut 82,
        p. 112.

3632. SCHAEFFER, Susan Fromberg
    "The Album." Shout (3:1) 82, p. 45-46.
    "Bread." NewL (48:2) Wint 81-82, p. 96-97.
    "Ceremony for the Lost Ones." Im (8:2) 82, p. 9.
    "The Earliness." Confr (24) Sum 82, p. 16.
    "Gold." QW (15) Aut-Wint 82-83, p. 73.
    "In the Time." SouthernR (18:3) Sum 82, p. 539.

"Like a Fish." DenQ (17:1) Spr 82, p. 13.
"Like a Fish." StoneC (9:3/4) Spr-Sum 82, p. 67.
"The Month in Its Parts." Shout (3:1) 82, p. 79-83.
"Season." SouthernR (18:3) Sum 82, p. 538.
"The Trees." StoneC (9:3/4) Spr-Sum 82, p. 66.

3633. SCHEBELI, Silvia
"Warm." UTR (7:2) 82?, p. 28.

3634. SCHEDLER, Gilbert
"Prophets Run in Our Family." ChrC (99:18) My 19,
82, p. 599.
"Silent Prayer." ChrC (99:32) O 20, 82, p. 1044.
"That Invisible Wall." ChrC (99:34) N 3, 82, p.
1100.

3635. SCHEELE, Roy
"At Sounion." Annex (3) 81, p. 48.
"Christoph Meckel: After the Deluge." Annex (3) 81,
p. 66.
"Cricket Harvest." Annex (3) 81, p. 53.
"Driving East toward Omaha." Annex (3) 81, p. 51.
"Eduard Morike: Atop a Church Tower." Annex (3) 81,
p. 66.
"The Falls." Annex (3) 81, p. 54-55.
"Focal Point." Annex (3) 81, p. 55.
"The Garage Window." Annex (3) 81, p. 48.
"Giving You Away." Annex (3) 81, p. 71-72.
"Grandpa Mac." Annex (3) 81, p. 62.
"His Day." Annex (3) 81, p. 49.
"How We came Through." Annex (3) 81, p. 60-61.
"Keeping the Horses" (for Adam Staib). Annex (3) 81,
p. 63-65.
"Knocking Down a Nest." Annex (3) 81, p. 50.
"Last Light." Annex (3) 81, p. 73.
"Late Autumn Grapes." Annex (3) 81, p. 56-58.
"Mountain Anemone." Annex (3) 81, p. 70.
"Near the Missouri." Annex (3) 81, p. 49.
"Nebraska U.S. 20." Annex (3) 81, p. 54.
"Remembering Anna." Annex (3) 81, p. 61-62.
"Rounding the Bend." Annex (3) 81, p. 51.
"The Sea-Ocean." Annex (3) 81, p. 48.
"Six O'Clock Report." Annex (3) 81, p. 72.
"The Sodden." Annex (3) 81, p. 53.
"Solitude." Annex (3) 81, p. 59.
"Spring Greens" (for Steve and Dana Gehring). Annex
(3) 81, p. 51-52.
"The Spur to Zermatt" (for Ursula Mono-Gain, across
the border in Breisach). Annex (3) 81, p. 65-66.
"Stanchions." Annex (3) 81, p. 49.
"Throng." Annex (3) 81, p. 72.
"A Turn in the Weather" (Calder's mobile, Roxbury
Flurry). Annex (3) 81, p. 59.
"Winter in Koping." Annex (3) 81, p. 67-70.
"Winter Onions." Annex (3) 81, p. 60.

3636. SCHEIER, Libby
"Lake George." CrossC (4:1) Wint 82, p. 6.
"Quiet." CrossC (4:1) Wint 82, p. 7.

"There Is No Such Thing as Silence." CrossC (4:1)
Wint 82, p. 6.
"Your Gift." CrossC (4:1) Wint 82, p. 6.

3637. SCHENLEY, Ruth Stewart
"Is Progress." Pig (10) 82, p. 72.

3638. SCHEVILL, James
"American Gigantism: Gutzon Borglum at Mt.
Rushmore." PoNow (6:4, issue 34) 82, p. 10.
"The No-Name Woman in San Francisco." PoNow (6:4,
issue 34) 82, p. 10.

3639. SCHEXNAYDER, Kenneth
"Returning." PoNow (7:1, issue 37) 82, p. 36.

3640. SCHIFF, Jeff
"Turtles." SouthwR (67:3) Sum 82, p. 280.

3641. SCHILLING, Christina
"Poem: The telephone screamed." CrossC (4:2/3) 82,
p. 36.

3642. SCHJELDAHL, Peter
"Hitchhiker." PartR (49:2) 82, p. 251-252.

3643. SCHLOSSBERGER, Eugene
"Demiurge." SoDakR (20:4) Wint 82-83, p. 25.

3644. SCHMIDT, Augusto Frederico
"Farewell" (tr. by Alexis Levitin). PoetryE (8) Aut
82, p. 81.
"The Great Moment" (tr. by Alexis Levitin). PoetryE
(8) Aut 82, p. 80.
"Sonnet 49" (tr. by Alexis Levitin). PoetryE (8) Aut
82, p. 82.

3645. SCHMIED, Wieland
"Francis Bacon Paints Velazquez' Pope" (tr. by Beth
Bjorklund). LitR (25:2) Wint 82, p. 255.
"Mark Tobey's Legacy" (tr. by Beth Bjorklund). LitR
(25:2) Wint 82, p. 256.
"Meeting with Giorgio de Chirico" (tr. by Beth
Bjorklund). LitR (25:2) Wint 82, p. 254.
"Thinking of Constantin Brancusi" (tr. by Beth
Bjorklund). LitR (25:2) Wint 82, p. 253.

3646. SCHMIT, George Corwin
"Douglas Stratford." EngJ (71:6) O 82, p. 31.

3647. SCHMITZ, Dennis
"1942." Antaeus (47) Aut 82, p. 77-78.
"Answering Lennie Marks." Telescope (1) Spr 81, p.
21-22.
"Attic." Field (26) Spr 82, p. 47-48.
"Lake Mercer Camp." Telescope (1) Spr 81, p. 66-67.
"Mercator Projection." PoNow (6:6, issue 36) 82, p.
41.
"The Shot Tower." PoNow (6:5, issue 35) 82, p. 5.
"Strays." Field (26) Spr 82, p. 49-50.

3648. SCHNACKENBERG, Gjertrud
"Reading Flaubert's Letters." Antaeus (44) Wint 82,
p. 164-169.
"Supernatural Love." Atl (250:6) D 82, p. 59.

3649. SCHOENBERGER, Nancy
"Epithalamium." AmerPoR (11:3) My-Je 82, p. 48.
"Stars, Fish." AmerPoR (11:3) My-Je 82, p. 48.
"Stars, Fish" (Correction) AmerPoR (11:4) Jl-Ag 82,
p. 47.

3650. SCHONWIESE, Ernst
"Everything is only an image in a mirror" (tr. by
Beth Bjorklund). LitR (25:2) Wint 82, p. 175.

3651. SCHOTT, Penelope Scambly
"Back in Gretchen's Majestic Cake Shoppe." StoneC
(9:3/4) Spr-Sum 82, p. 29.
"The Rock of This Odd Coincidence." GeoR (36:4)
Wint 82, p. 771.
"Safely in a White Lie." StoneC (9:3/4) Spr-Sum 82,
p. 28.

3652. SCHREIBER, Ron
"Houses." PoNow (6:4, issue 34) 82, p. 22.
"Willful Acts, Acts of Will." Agni (16) 82, p. 106-
107.

3653. SCHULER, Ruth Wildes
"Fishing in America" (Anarctic War). Sam (33:3,
issue 131) 82, p. 2.

3654. SCHULMAN, Grace
"Adultery." GeoR (36:2) Sum 82, p. 426.
"Aubade." Shen (33:2) 82, p. 93.
"Burning the Dead." Nat (235:22) D 25, 82, p. 694.
"City of Many Names." YaleR (71:4) Sum 82, p. 581-
582.
"Experiment" (tr. of T. Carmi). OntR (17) Aut-Wint
82, p. 88.
"In the Air" (tr. of T. Carmi). OntR (17) Aut-Wint
82, p. 87.
"Let There Be Translators!" Shen (33:2) 82, p. 94.

3655. SCHULTZ, Philip
"Late Night Phonecalls." NoAmR (267:3) S 82,p. 65.
"My Guardian Angel Stein." GeoR (36:3) Aut 82, p.
586-587.

3656. SCHULTZ, Stephen
"Love Edna." NoAmR (267:2) Je 82,p. 59.

3657. SCHUTTING, Jutta
"Clouds" (tr. by Beth Bjorklund). LitR (25:2) Wint
82, p. 283.
"A Dove-late Afternoon" (tr. by Beth Bjorklund).
LitR (25:2) Wint 82, p. 283.
"Interpretations" (tr. by Beth Bjorklund). LitR
(25:2) Wint 82, p. 281.

"Poems" (tr. by Beth Bjorklund). LitR (25:2) Wint
   82, p. 282-283.
"You Can" (tr. by Beth Bjorklund). LitR (25:2) Wint
   82, p. 284.

3658. SCHWARTZ, Douglas
   "Hitching Home." AntigR (50) Sum 82, p. 95.

3659. SCHWARTZ, Hillel
   "Aubrey Lord Bail Bonds." Comm (109:12) Je 18, 82,
      p. 375.
   "Candy Apple." StoneC (9:3/4) Spr-Sum 82, p. 17.
   "An Early Morning." Sam (33:3, issue 131) 82, back
      cover.
   "Flat Stone." StoneC (9:3/4) Spr-Sum 82, p. 16.
   "Herb and Marion, Roi et Reine de la Danse." Outbr
      (8/9) Aut 81-Spr 82, p. 25.
   "Orb & Crown Deli." Outbr (8/9) Aut 81-Spr 82, p.
      24.
   "Tearjerk." Thrpny (10) Sum 82, p. 10.
   "Trailways." SouthernHR (16:1) Wint 82, p. 44.

3660. SCHWARTZ, Lloyd
   "Accomplice." Ploughs (8:1) 82, p. 47-55.
   "In the Mist." Ploughs (8:1) 82, p. 46.

3661. SCHWARTZ, Steve
   "Fears and Imaginations." LitR (25:3) Spr 82, p.
      334-335.

3662. SCHWEIK, Susan
   "The Short Order Cook in the Mountains." Iowa
      (12:2/3) Spr-Sum 81, p. 300-301.

3663. SCHWITTERS, Kurt
   "London Onion" (Variations about the theme of the
      Thames valley, from The English Poems). Sulfur
      (2:3, issue 6) 82, p. 59-62.
   "Present Inter Noumenal" (w. Raoul Hausmann). Sulfur
      (2:3, issue 6) 82, p. 50-51.

3664. SCOBIE, Ilka
   "The Mall." Sam (33:3, issue 131) 82, p. 58.

3665. SCOTELLARO, Rocco
   "At Portici" (tr. by Ruth Feldman and Brian Swann).
      PoNow (6:5, issue 35) 82, p. 43.
   "Beggars" (tr. by Ruth Feldman and Brian Swann).
      PoNow (6:4, issue 34) 82, p. 41.
   "Evening in Potenza" (tr. by Ruth Feldman and Brian
      Swann). PoNow (6:5, issue 35) 82, p. 43.
   "Return Trip" (tr. by Ruth Feldman and Brian Swann).
      PoNow (6:4, issue 34) 82, p. 41.
   "Ticket for Turin" (tr. by Ruth Feldman and Brian
      Swann). PoNow (6:4, issue 34) 82, p. 41.
   "To My Father" (tr. by Ruth Feldman and Brian
      Swann). PoNow (6:5, issue 35) 82, p. 43.

3666. SCOTT, F. R.
  "Accompaniment" (St.-Denys Garneau, from The
  Collected Poems). PoetryCR (4:2) Wint 82, p. 8.
  "All the Spikes But the Last" (from The Collected
  Poems). PoetryCR (4:2) Wint 82, p. 9.
  "Brebeuf and His Brethren" (from The Collected
  Poems). PoetryCR (4:2) Wint 82, p. 9.
  "Company Meeting" (from The Collected Poems).
  PoetryCR (4:2) Wint 82, p. 9.
  "Degeneration" (from The Collected Poems). PoetryCR
  (4:2) Wint 82, p. 8.
  "Hardest It Is" (from The Collected Poems). PoetryCR
  (4:2) Wint 82, p. 9.
  "Journey" (from The Collected Poems). PoetryCR (4:2)
  Wint 82, p. 9.
  "Miranda" (from The Collected Poems). PoetryCR (4:2)
  Wint 82, p. 9.
  "Time Corrected" (Pierre Trottier, from The
  Collected Poems). PoetryCR (4:2) Wint 82, p. 9.
  "Trans Canada" (from The Collected Poems). PoetryCR
  (4:2) Wint 82, p. 8.

3667. SCOTT, Herbert
  "1943." PoNow (6:5, issue 35) 82, p. 13.
  "The Death and Resurrection of Jesse James" (d.
  April 3, 1882, St. Joseph, Missouri). PoNow (6:6,
  issue 36) 82, p. 27.
  "The Man Who Kept Coyotes." PoNow (6:5, issue 35)
  82, p. 13.
  "Spring Wars." PoNow (6:5, issue 35) 82, p. 13.

3668. SCOTT, Rosemary
  "Fence." Stand (23:4) 82, p. 73.

3669. SCOTT, Virginia
  "Early Autumn." AntigR (49) Spr 82, p. 87.
  "March Mare's Tails." AntigR (49) Spr 82, p. 87.

3670. SCRIBNER, Douglas
  "Killing Our Friends." Sam (32:3, issue 127) 82, p.
  8.
  "Time."| Sam (33:3, issue 131) 82, p. 54.

3671. SCROGGINS, Daryl
  "Concerning a Mountain Climbing Accident." PikeF
  (4) Spr 82, p. 9.
  "The Drowning." PikeF (4) Spr 82, p. 33.

3672. SEALE, Jan
  "Sharing the House." Nimrod (26:1) Aut-Wint 82, p.
  48-52.

3673. SEARS, Janet
  "Education."PottPort (4) 82-83, p. 8.

3674. SEARS, Peter
  "The Lady with the Laughing Gas Lover." AspenJ (1)
  Wint 82, p. 27.

3675. SEDWAL, Arun
      "At Bus-Stop." NewL (48:3/4) Spr-Sum 82, p. 49.
      "Bird's Wedding" (tr. of Divik Ramesh). NewL
      (48:3/4) Spr-Sum 82, p. 234-235.
      "Feather" (tr. of Divik Ramesh). NewL (48:3/4) Spr-
      Sum 82, p. 234.

3676. SEFERIS, George
      "Alla ehoun matia kataspra horis matoklada" (in
      Greek). CrossC (4:2/3) 82, p. 15.
      "O kurios autos" (in Greek). CrossC (4:2/3) 82, p.
      15.
      "Postscript" (tr. by John G. Trehas). CrossC (4:2/3)
      82, p. 15.
      "Psychology" (tr. by John G. Trehas). CrossC (4:2/3)
      82, p. 15.

3677. SEGARRA, Samuel
      "Desde lo mas bajo de la tierra he brotado" (from
      Vengo a Escribir un Poema). Mairena (4:9) Spr 82,
      p. 101-102.

3678. SEGARS, Linda M.
      "Bargain for a Widow." DekalbLAJ (14:1/4) Aut 80-
      Sum 81, p. 116.

3679. SEIDEL, Frederick
      "The New Cosmology." Antaeus (44) Wint 82, p. 86-
      87.

3680. SEIDMAN, Hugh
      "The Ill" (for Jane). Poetry (139:4) Ja 82, p. 201-
      202.

3681. SEIFERT, Jaroslav
      "The Grave of Casanova" (tr. by Miroslav Holub and
      David Young). Field (27) Aut 82, p. 71-73.

3682. SEILER, Barry
      "Cry for Comfort." Ploughs (8:1) 82, p. 74.
      "Evening in Omaha." Ploughs (8:1) 82, p. 71-72.
      "These Foolish Things." Ploughs (8:1) 82, p. 73.

3683. SEIM, Jeanette
      "New Lover." AntigR (48) Wint 82, p. 10.

3684. SELF, Lynda
      "Campers." SouthernR (18:4) Aut 82, p. 832-833.

3685. SELLERS, Bettie
      "The Blood of Heracles." ArizQ (38:4) Wint 82, p.
      364.
      "Defector Defected." DekalbLAJ (14:1/4) Aut 80-Sum
      81, p. 117.
      "Last Spring, You Made the Planets Fly." DekalbLAJ
      (14:1/4) Aut 80-Sum 81, p. 118.
      "These Battlements Are Ours." ArizQ (38:1) Spr 82,
      p. 61.

3686. SELTZER, Joanne
      "November's Blessing." Bogg (48) 82, p. 28.

3687. SEMENOVICH, Joseph
      "Hit & Run Victim." Sam (32:3, issue 127) 82, p.
      17.
      "I don't know peter's problem exactly" (from Gallery
      Works Five). Abraxas (25/26) 82, p. 56.
      "To Charlie Hampton, Circa Date 34 through 80."
      WebR (7:1) Spr 82, p. 106-107.
      "To My Son." Outbr (10/11) Aut 82-Spr 83, p. 80.

3688. SEMONES, Charles
      "Midsummer Saturday: Mercer County." Wind (12:44)
      82, p. 35.
      "Return to the Sabbath Country" (In Memory: C.F.S.,
      1897-1981). CharR (8:2) Aut 82, p. 24-25.

3689. SEMPLE, Troy
      "The So-Called 'Spring' Season." PikeF (4) Spr 82,
      p. 20.

3690. SENA, Jorge de
      "Cars Pass" (tr. by Alexis Levitin). Chelsea (41)
      82, p. 131.
      "The Dangers of Innocence" (tr. by Alexis Levitin).
      AmerPoR (11:2) Mr-Ap 82, p. 28.
      "In Crete with the Minotaur" (tr. by Alexis
      Levitin). AmerPoR (11:2) Mr-Ap 82, p. 28.
      "Lisbon--1971" (tr. by Alexis Levitin). Chelsea (41)
      82, p. 130.
      "On Nudity" (tr. by Alexis Levitin). DenQ (16:4)
      Wint 82, p. 38.
      "Origin Of Epic Poetry" (tr. by Alexis Levitin).
      DenQ (16:4) Wint 82, p. 35.
      "Thanksgiving" (tr. by Alexis Levitin). DenQ (16:4)
      Wint 82, p. 37.
      "To Piaf" (tr. by Alexis Levitin). DenQ (16:4) Wint
      82, p. 36.

3691. SENIOR, Nancy
      "Mark's Mother" (Paris 1979). Quarry (31:1) Wint 82,
      p. 37-39.
      "Pour un Ami au Loin." Quarry (31:1) Wint 82, p.
      37.

3692. SERBER, Arlyn
      "El Salvador." Sam (33:3, issue 131) 82, p. 14.

3693. SERENI, Vittorio
      "Ambivalence" (tr. by Sonia Raiziss). PoNow (6:6,
      issue 36) 82, p. 42.
      "Passing Through" (tr. by Sonia Raiziss). PoNow
      (6:6, issue 36) 82, p. 42.

3694. SERGEANT, Howard
      "Trapeze Artist." AntigR (49) Spr 82, p. 35.
      "Vandal on the Green." AntigR (49) Spr 82, p. 33-
      34.

3695. SERRA DELIZ, Wenceslao
"Isla Nuestra." Areito (8:31) 82, p. 37.

3696. SESSIONS, W. A.
"The Man Who Kept Everything." SouthernR (18:1)
Wint 82, p. 182-183.
"Name Your Pain." SouthernR (18:1) Wint 82, p. 184.

3697. SETH, Vinod
"The Girl at Play" (tr. of G. P. Vimal). Paint
(9:17/18) Spr-Aut 82, p. 25.
"Poem: Let the air sweep by" (tr. of G. P. Vimal).
Paint (9:17/18) Spr-Aut 82, p. 24.

3698. SEVILLA de JUANA, Pedro
"De la Soledad." Mairena (4:10) Sum-Aut 82, p. 41-
42.

3699. SEYFRIED, Robin
"Holding Pattern." Telescope (1) Spr 81, p. 51.
"Second Story Woman." Telescope (1) Spr 81, p. 48.

3700. SHAFER, Elizabeth
"Birds of Gold." LittleBR (2:3) Spr 82, p. 46.

3701. SHAFER, Margaret
"Mai's Duck." Confr (24) Sum 82, p. 33.
"Northern Lights." Confr (24) Sum 82, p. 33.

SHAHID ALI, Agha
See: ALI, Agha Shahid

3702. SHAHNAZ, Fatima
"I Am Sita." Maize (5:3/4) Spr-Sum 82, p. 48-51.

3703. SHAKELY, Lauren
"After All." Pequod (15) 82, p. 18.
"The Death Question." Pequod (15) 82, p. 17.
"Definition." Sulfur (2:2, issue 5) 82, p. 63-64.
"Needs." Sulfur (2:2, issue 5) 82, p. 65-66.
"The Nile of Principles." Sulfur (2:2, issue 5) 82,
p. 64.
"Nothing Is So Rich as Pain." Pequod (15) 82, p.
19.
"Paw-Paw Bay." Sulfur (2:2, issue 5) 82, p. 62.
"Virginia Garden Week." Sulfur (2:2, issue 5) 82,
p. 62-63.
"Weakness." Pequod (15) 82, p. 16.

3704. SHANLEY, Don
"Health Food." MendoR (6) Sum 81, p. 130.
"I like my cocaine pure he says." MendoR (6) Sum
81, p. 130.
"To Accept the Consequences of Event." MendoR (6)
Sum 81, p. 131.

3705. SHANNON, Laura Clare
"Leighanne's Song." Hangl (43) Wint 82-83, p. 86.
"Slow Poem One." Hangl (43) Wint 82-83, p. 85.

3706. SHANNON, Mike
"The Al Hrabosky Case." Pig (9) 82, p. 70.
"Catfish Hunter Back in Perquimmans County." Pig
(9) 82, p. 41.
"Filling Up with Leo Cardenas." Pig (9) 82, p. 35.
"Ted Williams in His Hotel Room." Pig (9) 82, p.
33.

3707. SHANTIRIS, Kita
"Homage to Gilberto Guidarelli" (A statue in
Ravenna's Palace of Fine Art). LittleM (13:3/4)
82, p. 86.
"No Te Preocupes Blanca." Poetry (140:1) Ap 82, p.
18-19.

3708. SHAPCOTT, Thomas
"Feather and Claw." WestCR (16:4) Ap 82, p. 22-23.
"Learning the French." WestCR (16:4) Ap 82, p. 21.
"The Silver Rose." WestCR (16:4) Ap 82, p. 24.

3709. SHAPIRO, Alan
"First Night." Thrpny (9) Spr 82, p. 19.
"The Host." CarolQ (35:1) Aut 82, p. 18.
"A Little Dust." ChiR (33:2) 82, p. 116-117.

3710. SHAPIRO, David
"Valediction Capricen." Sulfur (2:1, issue 4) 82,
p. 39-45.

3711. SHAPIRO, Harvey
"The Card." PartR (49:2) 82, p. 245.
"Interlude." Nat (235:22) D 25, 82, p. 698.
"Winter Sun." Im (8:2) 82, p. 3.
"The Wish." PartR (49:2) 82, p. 245-246.

3712. SHARETT, Dierdre
"In Sleep Our Tongues Are Quiet." PoNow (7:1, issue
37) 82, p. 37.
"In the End It Comes Down To." PoNow (7:1, issue
37) 82, p. 37.

3713. SHARMA, Balakrishna
"My House is Afire" (tr. by Josephine Miles). NewL
(48:3/4) Spr-Sum 82, p. 189.

3714. SHARMA, I. K.
"Khajuraho." NewL (48:3/4) Spr-Sum 82, p. 136.
"Three Stones." NewL (48:3/4) Spr-Sum 82, p. 136.

3715. SHARMA, R. K.
"Midnight" (tr. of Kedarnath Singh, w. G. Asthana).
NewL (48:3/4) Spr-Sum 82, p. 185.

3716. SHATTUCK, Roger
"Having It Both Ways." VirQR (58:3) Sum 82, p. 437-
438.
"Idolatry." VirQR (58:3) Sum 82, p. 435-437.

3717. SHAW, R. W.
"The Inner Man." StoneC (9:3/4) Spr-Sum 82, p. 50.

"Thinking about Sex." StoneC (9:3/4) Spr-Sum 82, p.
51.

3718. SHEA, Maggie
"At the Weldon Hotel" (For Rodney Szulborski).
SouthernHR (16:4) Aut 82, p. 332.

3719. SHEAR, Walter
"Energy As Inertia." LittleBR (2:2) Wint 81-82, p.
68-69.

3720. SHECK, Laurie
"Amaranth." PoNow (7:1, issue 37) 82, p. 26.
"Letter from an Institution." PoNow (7:1, issue 37)
82, p. 26.
"Undressing." Poetry (140:3) Je 82, p. 132.
"Untitled." Poetry (140:3) Je 82, p. 131.

3721. SHEDD, Ken
"The Geode." KanQ (14:1) Wint 82, p. 62.

3722. SHEEHAN, Marc J.
"Early Winter." AspenJ (1) Wint 82, p. 31.

3723. SHEEHAN, Paul R.
"Mount Shiga." MassR (23:3) Aut 82, p. 446.
"Traffic Jam." Wind (12:45) 82, p. 34.

3724. SHEEHAN, Thomas
"Beneath Vines and Peach Tree, a Neighbor's Ashes."
StoneC (9:3/4) Spr-Sum 82, p. 44-45.
"Departure." StoneC (10:1/2) Aut-Wint 82-83, p. 80.
"Search for a Last Embrace." StoneC (9:3/4) Spr-Sum
82, p. 46-47.

3725. SHEEHAN, Thomas F.
"It Is a Mouth, This Dawn." BelPoJ (32:3) Spr 82,
p. 2-3.

3726. SHEEHAN, Tom
"Gandy Dancer of the Phoebe Snow." CapeR (18:1)
Wint 82, p. 29.
"Hanging Garden of the Pine River" (For Eddie
LeBlanc). CapeR (18:1) Wint 82, p. 28.

3727. SHEERIN, Patrick Hugh
"Search for Light: A Prayer" (tr. of Damaso Alonso).
LitR (25:3) Spr 82, p. 340-341.

3728. SHEINER, Marcy
"Braiding My Daughter's Hair." Shout (3:1) 82, p.
51.

3729. SHELLEY, Percy Bysshe
"Alastor." Tendril (13) Sum 82, p. 5.

3730. SHELTON, George
"Jim." Tendril (13) Sum 82, p. 61.

3731. SHEPARD, Neil
       "Anthem for the Disembodied." PoetryNW (23:2) Sum
       82, p. 46.

3732. SHEPARD, Roy
       "Cornwall: Pendeen Watch." HiramPoR (31) Aut-Wint
       82, p. 43.

3733. SHEPHERD, J. Barrie
       "An Idle Tale" (Luke 24:11). ChrC (99:15) Ap 28, 82,
       p. 500.
       "Late Walk, Thanksgiving." ChrC (99:37) N 24, 82,
       p. 1192.
       "Party Spirit." ChrC (99:19) My 26, 82, p. 629.
       "Projections." ChrC (99:29) S 29, 82, p. 954.

3734. SHEPPARD, Patricia
       "The Wild Swamp Irises." AntR (40:4) Aut 82, p.
       436.

3735. SHER, Steven
       "The Rockaway Arcade." StoneC (9:3/4) Spr-Sum 82,
       p. 68.
       "Salamanders." Wind (12:44) 82, p. 36.

3736. SHERIDAN, David
       "Abandoned Upland Farm." Gargoyle (19) 82, p. 43.
       "And Ten Hail Marys." Gargoyle (19) 82, p. 42.
       "From an Indian Woman's Bio." Gargoyle (19) 82, p.
       44-45.
       "The Gonif's Daughter." Gargoyle (19) 82, p. 48.
       "Good-bye, Gillian, Good-bye." Gargoyle (19) 82, p.
       50-51.
       "Invaders Out of the North." Gargoyle (19) 82, p.
       47.
       "Learning an Old Language." Gargoyle (19) 82, p.
       46.
       "New Wave." Gargoyle (19) 82, p. 39-40.
       "War Dance." Gargoyle (19) 82, p. 41.
       "Yes, Here." Gargoyle (19) 82, p. 49.

3737. SHERIDAN, Michael
       "From the Illinois Shore." MissouriR (6:1) Aut 82,
       p. 33.
       "June 5, 1981" (for Janice Faeth). Agni (17) 82, p.
       156-157.

3738. SHERMAN, Alana
       "The Deaf Boys." PoNow (7:1, issue 37) 82, p. 37.

3739. SHERMAN, Charlotte Watson
       "Call of the Dead." Obs (7:2/3) Sum-Wint 81, p.
       146.
       "Cool Man." Obs (7:2/3) Sum-Wint 81, p. 147.

3740. SHERRY, Pearl Andelson
       "Chthonic Offering." SouthernR (18:2) Spr 82, p.
       375-376.
       "Find." SouthernR (18:2) Spr 82, p. 374.

"Man as an Hourglass." SouthernR (18:2) Spr 82, p. 374.
"My Heiress." SouthernR (18:2) Spr 82, p. 376.
"Nightmare." SouthernR (18:2) Spr 82, p. 375.

3741. SHERWIN, Judith Johnson
       "A Grief beyond Remedy." Shout (3:1) 82, p. 49-50.

3742. SHETTY, Manohar
       "The Recluse." NewL (48:3/4) Spr-Sum 82, p. 41.

3743. SHIFFRIN, Nancy
       "For Life." Catalyst (Erotica Issue) 82, p. 30.

       SHINO, Murano
       See: MURANO, Shino

3744. SHIPLEY, Margaret
       "Stillness." SouthernPR (22:1) Spr 82, p. 36.

3745. SHIRLEY, Aleda
       "Beance." Shen (33:2) 82, p. 70-71.
       "Bull's Eye." Chelsea (41) 82, p. 116.
       "Rumors of Paradise." Chelsea (41) 82, p. 114-115.

3746. SHIVARUDRAPPA, G. S.
       "This Man" (tr. by A. K. Ramanujan). NewL (48:3/4)
       Spr-Sum 82, p. 208-209.

3747. SHOEMAKER, Lynn
       "Home Dying, Mother and Son." SoDakR (20:2) Sum 82,
       p. 36.
       "Lullabye." SoDakR (20:2) Sum 82, p. 37.

3748. SHOLL, Betsy
       "Loving Mammon." WestB (11) 82, p. 29.

3749. SHORB, Michael
       "The Amateur Fire Eater." PoNow (7:1, issue 37) 82,
       p. 37.

3750. SHORE, Jane
       "Basic Training." Iowa (12:2/3) Spr-Sum 81, p. 302.
       "High Holy Days." Iowa (12:2/3) Spr-Sum 81, p. 303-
       305.

3751. SHORT, Gary
       "Dodger Fantasy." WormR (22:3, issue 87) 82, p. 83.
       "The Fourth Ship of Columbus." WormR (22:3, issue
       87) 82, p. 84.
       "On a Sunny Windy Afternoon." PoNow (7:1, issue 37)
       82, p. 37.

3752. SHORTSLEEVE, Mary
       "The Heart of You." NewRena (5:1, 15) Aut 82, p.
       27-28.
       "Old Friends." NewRena (5:1, 15) Aut 82, p. 29.

3753. SHOUP, Barbara
       "Dragonflies." Wind (12:46) 82, p. 39-40.

"The Farmhouse." Wind (12:46) 82, p. 39.

3754. SHOWSTACK, Randy
"A Rican slams w/fury a beer bottle." Pig (8) 80,
p. 76.

3755. SHREVE, Sandy
"Heirlooms." WestCR (17:1) Je 82, p. 24.
"Home." WestCR (17:1) Je 82, p. 24.

3756. SHRIGLEY, Sandra Basner
"Of Hearts, and Flowers." HiramPoR (31) Aut-Wint
82, p. 44.

3757. SHURBANOV, Alexander
"Concerned with Something Else While Turnovo's
Dying" (tr. of Luchezar Elenkov, w. Jascha
Kessler). Nimrod (26:1) Aut-Wint 82, p. 39-40.
"If" (tr. of Blaga Dimitrova, w. Jascha Kessler).
Nimrod (26:1) Aut-Wint 82, p. 37.
"If" (tr. of Blaga Dimitrova, w. Jascha Kessler).
Kayak (59) Je 82, p. 66.
"Lilies" (tr. of Bozhidar Bozhilov, w. Jascha
Kessler). Kayak (59) Je 82, p. 71.
"Night" (tr. of Georgy Djagarov, w. Jascha Kessler).
Kayak (59) Je 82, p. 69.
"River Run" (tr. of Elisaveta Bagryana, w. Jascha
Kessler). Kayak (59) Je 82, p. 68-69.
"Sauna" (tr. of Luchezar Elenkov, w. Jascha
Kessler). Kayak (59) Je 82, p. 65.
"Secret Love" (tr. of Lyubomir Levchev, w. Jascha
Kessler). Kayak (59) Je 82, p. 63-64.
"Troubles" (tr. of Bozhidar Bozhilov, w. Jascha
Kessler). Kayak (59) Je 82, p. 71.
"What Price Constancy" (tr. of Blaga Dimitrova, w.
Jascha Kessler). Kayak (59) Je 82, p. 67.
"The Wise Ones" (tr. of Bozhidar Bozhilov, w. Jascha
Kessler). Kayak (59) Je 82, p. 70-71.
"A Woman Pregnant" (tr. of Blaga Dimitrova, w.
Jascha Kessler). Nimrod (26:1) Aut-Wint 82, p. 38.

3758. SHURTLEFF, Hillary
"Fog." UnderRM (1:1) Spr 82, p. 30.
"Mid-Summer Eve" (for my parents). UnderRM (1:1) Spr
82, p. 29.
"Ribs" (for R.L.U.). UnderRM (1:1) Spr 82, p. 28.

3759. SHUTTLE, Penelope
"The Child Stealer." Sulfur (2:2, issue 5) 82, p.
106-107.
"Childless." Sulfur (2:2, issue 5) 82, p. 104.
"Locale." Sulfur (2:2, issue 5) 82, p. 107-108.
"The Pretty Worm." Sulfur (2:2, issue 5) 82, p.
105-106.

3760. SHUTTLEWORTH, Paul
"Proportionate." CutB (18) Spr-Sum 82, p. 5-6.
"The Small Rustle." PoNow (6:4, issue 34) 82, p.
15.

3761. SIBLEY, L.
"Cape Split" (A Camping Chronicle). PottPort (4)
82-83, p. 16.

3762. SIBLEY, Lynn
"Nick." Bogg (48) 82, p. 49.

3763. SIDDALINGAIAH
"I Must Have a Word" (tr. by Sumatheendra Nadig and
David Ray). NewL (48:3/4) Spr-Sum 82, p. 204-205.
"A Song" (tr. by P. Rama Moorthy). NewL (48:3/4)
Spr-Sum 82, p. 204.

SIDU JITU, Almasi
See: JITU, Almasi Sidu

3764. SIEGEL, Joan
"I Will Not Dream of You." Nimrod (25:2) Spr-Sum
82, p. 70.

3765. SIEGEL, Robert
"Cornstalk Wigwam." BelPoJ (33:2) Wint 82-83, p.
22-26.

3766. SIFFORD, David
"Fact Poem: Clarence Crane." PoNow (7:1, issue 37)
82, p. 38.
"Fact Poem: Fred Kilmer." PoNow (7:1, issue 37) 82,
p. 38.

3767. SIGURDSSON, Olafur Johann
"Dance at the Spring" (tr. by Alan Boucher). Vis
(10) 82, p. 4-5.
"Question" (tr. by Alan Boucher). Vis (8) 82, p. 8-
9.
"Summer" (tr. by Alan Boucher). Vis (9) 82, p. 18.
"Where Does It Lead, This Road?" (tr. by Alan
Boucher). Vis (8) 82, p. 8-9.

3768. SILBERT, Layle
"Get One." PoNow (7:1, issue 37) 82, p. 38.
"A History." Im (8:1) 82, p. 6.
"Perfect Rooms." PoNow (7:1, issue 37) 82, p. 38.

3769. SILESKY, Barry
"Found Out." PoetryNW (23:1) Spr 82, p. 33.
"Order." UnderRM (1:1) Spr 82, p. 20.

3770. SILKIN, Jon
"The Armed" (from Autobiographical Stanzas). MinnR
(NS18) Spr 82, p. 16-17.
"Bees, Honey" (tr. of Paal-Helge Haugen, w. David
McDuff). Stand (23:3) 82, p. 44.
"For a Man's Head" (from Autobiographical Stanzas).
MinnR (NS18) Spr 82, p. 13.
"For Olav H. Hauge" (tr. of Paal-Helge Haugen, w.
David McDuff). Stand (23:3) 82, p. 44.
"Music: of Earth, and Stone, and the People" (tr. of
Paal-Helge Haugen, w. David McDuff and Toralf
Moller Hansen). Stand (23:3) 82, p. 45.

"We Were Evacuated in the War" (from Autobiographical Stanzas). MinnR (NS18) Spr 82, p. 14-15.

SILVA, Loreina Santos
See: SANTOS SILVA, Loreina

3771. SILVER, Chitra
"At a Pipe Factory in Fontana." Maize (5:1/2) Aut-Wint 81-82, p. 88.

3772. SILVER, William
"Weights and Values (The Griffith-Paret Fight)." MinnR (NS19) Aut 82, p. 44-45.

3773. SILVER-LILLYWHITE, Eileen
"The Ice House." OhioR (27) 82, p. 114.

3774. SILVERBERG, Dan
"Eve and Eve." Sam (33:3, issue 131) 82, p. 39.
"Peace March." Sam (33:3, issue 131) 82, p. 38.
"Welfare." Sam (32:3, issue 127) 82, p. 23.

3775. SILVERMAN, Stuart J.
"Excursus." HolCrit (19:4) O 82, p. 14-15.

3776. SIMBECK, Rob
"When It Hit." KanQ (14:3) Sum 82, p. 100.

3777. SIMIC, Charles
"Ancestry." Kayak (59) Je 82, p. 18.
"Antediluvian Customs." Kayak (59) Je 82, p. 19.
"Ariadne" (to D.K.). PoetryE (7) Spr 82, p. 34-35.
"Bedtime Story." PoetryE (7) Spr 82, p. 34.
"Devotions" (for Michael Anania). Ploughs (8:2/3) 82, p. 197.
"Drawn to Perspective." Atl (249:2) F 82, p. 75.
"East European Cooking." Ploughs (8:2/3) 82, p. 196.
"My Weariness of Epic Proportions." PartR (49:3) 82, p. 430-431.
"The Nurse Told Me." Kayak (59) Je 82, p. 18.
"On Pretext." Ploughs (8:2/3) 82, p. 195.
"Punch Minus Judy." Field (26) Spr 82, p. 53.
"Rough Outline." Kayak (59) Je 82, p. 17.
"Rural Delivery." NewYorker (57:48) Ja 18, 82, p. 38.
"Shaving at Night." Ploughs (8:2/3) 82, p. 198.
"Stealing from Mice." Kayak (59) Je 82, p. 17.

3778. SIMMER, Scott
"Fourth of July Address. Deserted Railroad Tunnel, Colorado. Contintal Divide." Spirit (6:2/3) 82, p. 128-129.
"Spare Parts." NewL (48:2) Wint 81-82, p. 40.

3779. SIMMERMAN, Jim
"Digger." Iowa (13:1) Wint 82, p. 111-114.
"For Silence." PoNow (7:1, issue 37) 82, p. 38.
"The Funeral." CarolQ (35:1) Aut 82, p. 72.

"Hagiography." NoAmR (267:2) Je 82,p. 37.
"Soon." Iowa (13:1) Wint 82, p. 109-110.
"Spinner" (for Michael Pfeifer). MissouriR (5:3) Sum
82, p. 22-23.

3780. SIMMIE, Lois
"Jimmy Lorris and His Thesaurus." Grain (10:2) My
82, p. 41-42.
"Uncle Alphonso." Grain (10:2) My 82, p. 40-41.

3781. SIMMONS, Thomas
"Collects." Atl (250:1) Jl 82, p. 55.

3782. SIMON, Greg
"Seventy-Seven Words Concerning My Recent Scientific
Inquiries." Telescope (3) Sum 82, p. 75.

3783. SIMON, John Oliver
"Eli Eli Lama Lama." PoNow (6:5, issue 35) 82, p.
21.
"The Major Poets" (after Neruda). HangL (41) 82, p.
47.
"The man behind me in line." PoNow (6:6, issue 36)
82, p. 46.
"Up." PoNow (6:4, issue 34) 82, p. 18.
"With my hands tied." HangL (41) 82, p. 48.

3784. SIMON, Josef
"The Fisherman (Perpetuum Mobile)" (tr. by Dana
Habova and Stuart Friebert). Field (27) Aut 82, p.
80.

3785. SIMON, Marjorie
"Larkspur." Kayak (60) O 82, p. 21.
"Loreto." Kayak (60) O 82, p. 20.

3786. SIMPSON, Louis
"The Champion Single Sculls." Ploughs (8:2/3) 82,
p. 70-71.
"Chocolates." PoetryE (7) Spr 82, p. 43-44.
"Encounter on the 7:07." OhioR (29) 82, p. 7-11.
"A Fine Day for Straw Hats." GeoR (36:2) Sum 82, p.
351-353.
"The Gardener." Ploughs (8:2/3) 82, p. 72.
"In a Time of Peace." Hudson (35:3) Aut 82, p. 416-
417.
"The Mexican Woman." PoetryE (7) Spr 82, p. 42.
"Quiet Desperation." Iowa (13:1) Wint 82, p. 127-
129.

3787. SIMPSON, Nancy
"The Girl." SouthernPR (22:1) Spr 82, p. 30.

3788. SINGH, Amritjit
"Funeral in Chandigarh." NewL (48:3/4) Spr-Sum 82,
p. 87.

3789. SINGH, Haribhajan
"A Naked Stick in the Matchbox" (tr. by Gulzar Singh
Sandhu). NewL (48:3/4) Spr-Sum 82, p. 213.

3790. SINGH, Kedarnath
        "Midnight" (tr. by G. Asthana and R. K. Sharma).
        NewL (48:3/4) Spr-Sum 82, p. 185.

3791. SINGH, Mohan
        "My Village Girl" (tr. by Balwant Gargi). NewL
        (48:3/4) Spr-Sum 82, p. 143.

3792. SINGH, Pritam
        "Miss Tanuja Is All Tenderness" (tr. of Sukhpal Vir
        Singh Hasrat). NewL (48:3/4) Spr-Sum 82, p. 23.

3793. SINGH, Samir Punit
        "She and I."NewL (48:3/4) Spr-Sum 82, p. 159.

3794. SINGH, Shamsher Bahadur
        "Dawn" (tr. by James Mauch). NewL (48:3/4) Spr-Sum
        82, p. 99.

3795. SINISGALLI, Leonardo
        "A Boy Dies a Little" (tr. by Rina Ferrarelli). DenQ
        (17:2) Sum 82, p. 123.
        "The Hospital" (tr. by Rina Ferrarelli). DenQ (17:2)
        Sum 82, p. 124.
        "I'll Remember This Autumn" (tr. by W. S. Di Piero).
        Pequod (14) 82, p. 52.
        "Narni-Amelia Scalo" (tr. by Rina Ferrarelli). DenQ
        (17:2) Sum 82, p. 125.

3796. SISCO, Elizabeth
        "Los Coyotes." Maize (6:1/2) Aut-Wint 82-83, p. 63.
        "La Criada." Maize (6:1/2) Aut-Wint 82-83, p. 86.
        "El Jardinero." Maize (6:1/2) Aut-Wint 82-83, p.
        41.
        "El Lavaplatos." Maize (6:1/2) Aut-Wint 82-83, p.
        57.
        "Los Pollos." Maize (6:1/2) Aut-Wint 82-83, p. 99.

3797. SISSON, C. H.
        "Athelney." AmerS (51:1) Wint 81-82, p. 93.

3798. SISSON, Jonathan
        "False Foxglove." LittleM (13:3/4) 82, p. 9.
        "T. D. Redshaw Writes a Palimpsestuous Poem upon
        Randall Jarrell's Photograph and Poem upon Durer's
        Engraving...." LittleM (13:3/4) 82, p. 10-11.

3799. SITES, Paula
        "Family Album." KanQ (14:3) Sum 82, p. 194.
        "View from the Middle." KanQ (14:3) Sum 82, p. 193.

3800. SJOBERG, John
        "We Try Not to Touch So Close." Spirit (6:2/3) 82,
        p. 76.

3801. SKEEN, Anita
        "The Poet Dreams on the Way Home from Balboa Park."
        Nimrod (26:1) Aut-Wint 82, p. 94.
        "The Poet Expounds on the Virtues of Vegetarians."
        Nimrod (26:1) Aut-Wint 82, p. 96.

"The Poet Fantasizes about the Two Women Next Door."
Nimrod (26:1) Aut-Wint 82, p. 95.
"The Poet in the Back Seat." Nimrod (26:1) Aut-Wint
82, p. 93-94.

3802. SKELLERN, Jon
"Bloodstone Beauty." Bogg (49) 82, p. 47.

3803. SKELTON, Robin
"A 14th Way of Looking at a Blackbird." Kayak (60)
O 82, p. 26.
"The Basement Room." Kayak (60) O 82, p. 29.
"The Connection." PoetryCR (4:2) Wint 82, p. 10.
"In New Delhi." MassR (23:4) Wint 82, p. 613.
"In the Fall." Kayak (60) O 82, p. 27.
"The Places." MassR (23:4) Wint 82, p. 614.
"Those Foolish Things." Kayak (60) O 82, p. 28.
"The Words." Kayak (60) O 82, p. 30.

3804. SKILLMAN, Judith
"Do You Want to Have Sex." Bogg (48) 82, p. 4.

3805. SKINNER, Jeffrey
"August." Kayak (58) Ja 82, p. 39.
"Family Reunion." PoNow (7:1, issue 37) 82, p. 39.
"On the Failure of All Love Poems." Atl (250:1) Jl
82, p. 54.
"Poppy." PoNow (7:1, issue 37) 82, p. 39.
"Possessions." Kayak (58) Ja 82, p. 38.

3806. SKIPPER, Louis
"Night Riders: Southside Elegy, 1963." QW (14) Spr-
Sum 82, p. 68.

3807. SKLAR, Morty
"Modern Times." Spirit (6:2/3) 82, p. 68-69.

3808. SKLOOT, Floyd
"Executive Search." Spirit (6:2/3) 82, p. 41-42.
"Kaleidoscope." Tendril (12) Wint 82, p. 58-62.

3809. SKLUTE, Larry
"Facts." FourQt (31:3) Spr 82, p. 32.
"To--." FourQt (31:3) Spr 82, p. 32.
"The Woman Missing." LitR (25:3) Spr 82, p. 355.

3810. SKWIRZ, Marylee
"Breathing Spell for a Vanishing Act" SouthwR
(67:1) Wint 82, p. 30.

3811. SLATE, Ron
"Along the Canal." WestB (11) 82, p. 100-101.
"Meet You at Mystic" (for Betsy and Floyd Skloot).
Telescope (2) Aut 81, p. 18-19.
"Take Me to the Beach" (for Brendan Galvin).
Telescope (2) Aut 81, p. 16-17.

3812. SLAVITT, David R.
"Last Days at Delphi." Poetry (141:3) D 82, p. 161-
162.

"Museum Piece." Poetry (141:3) D 82, p. 159-160.

3813. SLEIGH, Tom
"Alp." MassR (23:2) Sum 82, p. 352.
"Face in a Landscape." LittleM (13:3/4) 82, p. 93-94.
"Sleeping Beauty Remembers." LittleM (13:3/4) 82, p. 91-92.
"To Climb the Ladder of the World's Joy." LittleM (13:3/4) 82, p. 90.

3814. SLOAN, Bruce
"First Poem for Fran." MendoR (6) Sum 81, p. 21.
"Grace." MendoR (6) Sum 81, p. 21.

3815. SLOANE-DEW, Ruth
"Poem for Robert Kaufman." Obs (7:2/3) Sum-Wint 81, p. 222-223.

3816. SMALLEY, Joan
"Melody for Nola." CentR (26:3) Sum 82, p. 271-272.

3817. SMART, Carolyn
"Even the Dead Come Round." PoetryCR (3:4) Sum 82, p. 16.
"Shedding Your Own Skin." PoetryCR (3:4) Sum 82, p. 16.
"Stars." PoetryCR (3:4) Sum 82, p. 16.
"Those Bright Rails, Passing By." PoetryCR (3:4) Sum 82, p. 16.

3818. SMART, W. J.
"March Window." CrossC (4:1) Wint 82, p. 21.

3819. SMETZER, Michael
"Black Crows." KanQ (14:3) Sum 82, p. 65.
"Prairie Summer." LittleBR (1:4) Sum 81, p. 79.

3820. SMITH, Allen
"Butterflies." Waves (11:1) Aut 82, p. 68.

3821. SMITH, Annette
"But There Is This Hurt" (tr. of Aime Cesaire, w. Clayton Eshleman). Sulfur (2:2, issue 5) 82, p. 43-44.
"Corpse of a Frenzy" (tr. of Aime Cesaire, w. Clayton Eshleman). Sulfur (2:2, issue 5) 82, p. 44-45.
"Debris" (tr. of Aime Cesaire, w. Clayton Eshleman). Sulfur (2:2, issue 5) 82, p. 34-35.
"I Perseus Centuplicating Myself" (tr. of Aime Cesaire, w. Clayton Eshleman). Sulfur (2:2, issue 5) 82, p. 45.
"Lost Body" (from Lost Body, 1950, tr. of Aime Cesaire, w. Clayton Eshleman). Sulfur (2:2, issue 5) 82, p. 41-43.
"Noon Knives" (from Solar Throat Slashed, 1948, tr. of Aime Cesaire, w. Clayton Eshleman). Sulfur (2:2, issue 5) 82, p. 39-41.

"The Oubliettes of the Sea and the Deluge" (from The
Miraculous Weapons, 1946, tr. of Aime Cesaire, w.
Clayton Eshleman). Sulfur (2:2, issue 5) 82, p.
36-37.
"Redemption" (tr. of Aime Cesaire, w. Clayton
Eshleman). Sulfur (2:2, issue 5) 82, p. 38.
"Tangible Disaster" (tr. of Aime Cesaire, w. Clayton
Eshleman). Sulfur (2:2, issue 5) 82, p. 37.
"Tom-Tom II" (for Wifredo, tr. of Aime Cesaire, w.
Clayton Eshleman). Sulfur (2:2, issue 5) 82, p.
35.
"Tomb of Paul Eluard" (from Ferraments, 1960, tr. of
Aime Cesaire, w. Clayton Eshleman). Sulfur (2:2,
issue 5) 82, p. 46-49.
"Visitation" (tr. of Aime Cesaire, w. Clayton
Eshleman). Sulfur (2:2, issue 5) 82, p. 33-34.
"Your Hair" (tr. of Aime Cesaire, w. Clayton
Eshleman). Sulfur (2:2, issue 5) 82, p. 38-39.

3822. SMITH, Arthur
"In Winter Light." MissouriR (6:1) Aut 82, p. 42.
"Saturday Night." PoNow (6:6, issue 36) 82, p. 44.
"So This Is the Desert." PoNow (6:6, issue 36) 82,
p. 44.
"Tarantulas." NewYorker (58:33) O 4, 82, p. 48.
"Wrecking Crew." Nat (235:2) Jl 10-17, 82, p. 60.

3823. SMITH, Bob
"Primer." PoetryNW (23:4) Wint 82-83, p. 38-39.

3824. SMITH, Bruce
"Annie LoPezzi." MassR (23:4) Wint 82, p. 631.
"Black Ducks." Nat (235:8) S 18, 82, p. 250.
"Brother among Black Stones." Confr (24) Sum 82, p.
41.
"Image of Bernieri." MassR (23:4) Wint 82, p. 632.
"Incunabulum." Confr (24) Sum 82, p. 42.
"Silver and Information." Nat (234:20) My 22, 82,
p. 622.

3825. SMITH, Dave
"Commute." NewYorker (58:28) Ag 30, 82, p. 34.
"Dry Ice." VirQR (58:2) Spr 82, p. 279-280.
"Ducking: After Maupassant." Antaeus (44) Wint 82,
p. 188-190.
"False Spring: Late Snow." NewYorker (58:28) Ag 30,
82, p. 34.
"House-Movers." NewYorker (58:28) Ag 30, 82, p. 34-
35.
"In the House of the Judge." NewYorker (58:4) Mr
15, 82, p. 42-43.
"Jogging in the Parlor, Remembering a Summer Moment
during Snow Squalls." Nat (234:4) Ja 30, 82, p.
124.
"Leaving Town." NewEngR (5:1/2) Aut-Wint 82, p.
192-193.
"Of Oystermen, Workboats." NewYorker (57:48) Ja 18,
82, p. 44.
"Outside Martins Ferry, Ohio." Nat (234:7) F 20,
82, p. 212.

"Photographic Plate, Partly Spidered: Hampton Roads,
Virginia, with Model T Ford Mid-Channel."
NewYorker (58:28) Ag 30, 82, p. 34.
"Rainy Day: Last Run." Poetry (140:4) Jl 82, p.
226-227.
"Recess." NewEngR (5:1/2) Aut-Wint 82, p. 193-194.
"Snake: A Family Tale." Antaeus (44) Wint 82, p.
191-193.
"Toy Trains in the Landlord's House." VirQR (58:2)
Spr 82, p. 280-282.
"Waking in the Endless Mountains." Poetry (140:4)
Jl 82, p. 228-229.

3826. SMITH, Douglas
"Hot Weather." CrossC (4:2/3) 82, p. 50.
"Three Poems for the Beginning of Winter." CrossC
(4:1) Wint 82, p. 11.

3827. SMITH, Edward
"Enlargement." Spirit (6:2/3) 82, p. 103-104.

3828. SMITH, Gary
"Holly Springs." Obs (7:2/3) Sum-Wint 81, p. 137-
141.

3829. SMITH, Grace
"CXXIX" (tr. of Yunus Emre, w. Ann Stanford). Paint
(9:17/18) Spr-Aut 82, p. 26-27.
"Five Poems" (tr. of Yunus Emre w. Ann Stanford).
Antaeus (44) Wint 82, p. 170-177.
"Isidun iy yarenler eve dervisler geldi: Oh my
friends, listen" (tr. of Yunus Emre, w. Ann
Stanford). NowestR (20:1) 82, p. 11.

3830. SMITH, H. F.
"Dressage" (for Alyson). MalR (63) O 82, p. 183.

3831. SMITH, Iain Crichton
"You'll Take a Bath." Stand (23:1) 81-82, p. 23.

3832. SMITH, Joe
"Coming." Catalyst (Erotica Issue) 82, p. 14.

3833. SMITH, Jordan
"The Confederate Women of Maryland" (for Matthew
Graham) AntR (40:1) Wint 82, p. 83-85.
"London, 1788." NewEngR (5:1/2) Aut-Wint 82, p.
113-119.
"Notes toward a Translation." Agni (17) 82, p. 6-7.
"The Star Chamber." Shen (33:3) 82, p. 80-81.

3834. SMITH, Larry
"The Story of Farms." PoNow (6:6, issue 36) 82, p.
13.
"There Is Nothing I Have Lost" (tr. of Salvatore
Quasimodo). CharR (8:1) Spr 82, p. 53.

3835. SMITH, Le Roy, Jr.
"Demonstration." Comm (109:5) Mr 12, 82, p. 158.

3836. SMITH, Mary Lonnberg
"At the Supermarket." <u>HiramPoR</u> (31) Aut-Wint 82, p.
45.
"Home Again (Ch'ien Hsuan)." <u>QW</u> (14) Spr-Sum 82, p.
20.

3837. SMITH, Nathaniel B.
"Old Farmer's Autumn." <u>Paint</u> (7/8:13/16) 80-81, p.
23.
"Traver's Evening Song II" (tr. of Johann Wolfgang
von Goethe). <u>Paint</u> (7/8:13/16) 80-81, p. 40.

3838. SMITH, Patrick
"And Happy People." <u>NewL</u> (48:2) Wint 81-82, p. 80-
81.
"Happy People." <u>NewL</u> (48:2) Wint 81-82, p. 80.
"Listen Son, Listen." <u>NewL</u> (48:2) Wint 81-82, p.
81.

3839. SMITH, R. T.
"Delacroix's Chopin." <u>SouthernHR</u> (16:1) Wint 82, p.
26.
"Night Walk in a Dry Time." <u>SouthernPR</u> (23, i.e.
22:2) Aut 82, p. 54.
"Pig Dream." <u>PoNow</u> (7:1, issue 37) 82, p. 39.
"A Primitive Poem for Summer." <u>KanQ</u> (14:3) Sum 82,
p. 165.
"Wyeth's 'The Finn.'" <u>SouthernHR</u> (16:1) Wint 82, p.
28.
"Young Woman with a Water Jug." <u>SouthernHR</u> (16:1)
Wint 82, p. 27.

3840. SMITH, Ron
"Katie on Her Education." <u>SouthernHR</u> (16:2) Spr 82,
p. 117.
"Off the Corridor, Near My Dying Grandfather."
<u>ColEng</u> 44(6) O 82, p. 613.
"The Old Crabber Has Gone Deaf." <u>ColEng</u> 44(6) O 82,
p. 612-613.

3841. SMITH, Ronald
"My First Bank Robbery." <u>Kayak</u> (60) O 82, p. 13.

3842. SMITH, Sybil
"Something in the Wings, the Vines." <u>Outbr</u> (10/11)
Aut 82-Spr 83, p. 76-77.
"To the Woman Who Gave Him Up for Adoption, 1954."
<u>Outbr</u> (10/11) Aut 82-Spr 83, p. 78-79.

3843. SMITH, Valerie
"Birth Trauma." <u>StoneC</u> (9:3/4) Spr-Sum 82, p. 60.

3844. SMITH-BOWERS, Cathy
"Letter to Alice." <u>SoCaR</u> (14:2) Spr 82, p. 100-101.

3845. SNEYD, Steve
"Five alien moves." <u>WindO</u> (40, Anti-Haiku issue)
Sum 82, p. 8.
"A Gift to the South." <u>Bogg</u> (49) 82, p. 35.
"These Days." <u>Bogg</u> (48) 82, p. 62.

3846. SNIDER, Clifton
"His Body." PoNow (7:1, issue 37) 82, p. 39.
"A Young Man." PoNow (7:1, issue 37) 82, p. 39.

3847. SNIVELY, Susan
"The Invisible Man" (for Claude Rains)." PoNow
(7:1, issue 37) 82, p. 27.
"Sunday." PoNow (7:1, issue 37) 82, p. 27.

3848. SNODGRASS, W. D.
"The Last Time." Ploughs (8:2/3) 82, p. 28.
"Silver Poplars." Ploughs (8:2/3) 82, p. 27-28.
"A Valediction." Ploughs (8:2/3) 82, p. 26.
"Venus and the Lute Player." Ploughs (8:2/3) 82, p.
24-25.

3849. SNOW, John V.
"In Memoriam: Maxwell Bates, 1906-1980." MalR (62)
Jl 82, p. 202-203.

3850. SNOW, Karen
"Gifts." MichQR (21:1) Wint 82, p. 131-134.

3851. SNYDAL, James
"Independence Day." PoNow (7:1, issue 37) 82, p.
40.

3852. SNYDER, Bob
"Beatnik Perfume." Pig (8) 80, p. 6.
"Dear John Surprise." Pig (8) 80, p. 49.
"Dogwood Farmstead." StoneC (9:3/4) Spr-Sum 82, p.
20.
"Full Hyssop." KanQ (14:3) Sum 82, p. 115.
"Hecaterion for a Hygenist." Epoch (31:3) Sum 82,
p. 201.
"Kerouac in Charleston." Pig (8) 80, p. 12.
"Morning on Donnally Street." MinnR (NS18) Spr 82,
p. 9.
"View from the Catwalks." Epoch (31:3) Sum 82, p.
200.
"Yow." Pig (8) 80, p. 14.

3853. SNYDER, J. K.
"Die Maschine." AntigR (50) Sum 82, p. 27.

3854. SO, Chongju
"Air Shimmering" (from Beside a Chrysanthemum, 1955,
tr. by David R. McCann). QRL (22) 81, p. 35.
"At a Wine House Near Taegu" (from Wanderer's Poems,
1976, tr. by David R. McCann). QRL (22) 81, p. 79-
80.
"An Autumn Day" (from Winter Sky, 1968, tr. by David
R. McCann). QRL (22) 81, p. 61.
"Barley Summer" (from Flower Snake, 1938, tr. by
David R. McCann). QRL (22) 81, p. 16.
"Beside a Chrysanthemum" (from Beside a
Chrysanthemum, 1955, tr. by David R. McCann). QRL
(22) 81, p. 34.
"Blue Days" (from The Cuckoo, 1946, tr. by David R.
McCann). QRL (22) 81, p. 27.

"The Bride" (from New Poems, 1972, tr. by David R. McCann). QRL (22) 81, p. 70.
"By the Gate at Sonun Temple" (from Winter Sky, 1968, tr. by David R. McCann). QRL (22) 81, p. 55.
"Ch'unhyang's Testament" (from Beside a Chrysanthemum, 1955, tr. by David R. McCann). QRL (22) 81, p. 37.
"Ch'usok" (from Winter Sky, 1968, tr. by David R. McCann). QRL (22) 81, p. 51.
"Crane" (from Beside a Chrysanthemum, 1955, tr. by David R. McCann). QRL (22) 81, p. 33.
"The Cuckoo Makes a River" (from New Poems, 1972, tr. by David R. McCann). QRL (22) 81, p. 66.
"Dandelion" (from The Cuckoo, 1946, tr. by David R. McCann). QRL (22) 81, p. 30.
"Dry Rapids" (from Winter Sky, 1968, tr. by David R. McCann). QRL (22) 81, p. 53.
"A Flower Blooms" (from Winter Sky, 1968, tr. by David R. McCann). QRL (22) 81, p. 48.
"Flower-Patterned Snake" (from Flower Snake, 1938, tr. by David R. McCann). QRL (22) 81, p. 15.
"Four A.M." (from New Poems, 1972, tr. by David R. McCann). QRL (22) 81, p. 63.
"Go Back to Shu" (from The Cuckoo, 1946, tr. by David R. McCann). QRL (22) 81, p. 25.
"Homing Song" (from Wanderer's Poems, 1976, tr. by David R. McCann). QRL (22) 81, p. 78.
"The Huge Wave" (from New Poems, 1972, tr. by David R. McCann). QRL (22) 81, p. 71.
"If I Became a Stone" (from Winter Sky, 1968, tr. by David R. McCann). QRL (22) 81, p. 59.
"Kimch'i Song" (from Wanderer's Poems, 1976, tr. by David R. McCann). QRL (22) 81, p. 81.
"Like a Wind from Lotus Blossoms" (from Winter Sky, 1968, tr. by David R. McCann). QRL (22) 81, p. 47.
"Looking at Mount Peerless" (from Beside a Chrysanthemum, 1955, tr. by David R. McCann). QRL (22) 81, p. 32.
"Marching Song" (from The Cuckoo, 1946, tr. by David R. McCann). QRL (22) 81, p. 29.
"Monologue to the Flowerbed" (from Silla Notes, 1960, tr. by David R. McCann). QRL (22) 81, p. 40.
"My Eternity" (from Winter Sky, 1968, tr. by David R. McCann). QRL (22) 81, p. 50.
"My Love's Fingertip" (from Winter Sky, 1968, tr. by David R. McCann). QRL (22) 81, p. 57.
"My Poems" (from Beside a Chrysanthemum, 1955, tr. by David R. McCann). QRL (22) 81, p. 38.
"New Year's Prayer 1976" (from Wanderer's Poems, 1976, tr. by David R. McCann). QRL (22) 81, p. 75-76.
"The Old Man's Song" (from Silla Notes, 1960, tr. by David R. McCann). QRL (22) 81, p. 41-43.
"Old-Fashioned Hours" (from Winter Sky, 1968, tr. by David R. McCann). QRL (22) 81, p. 60.
"Peony Afternoon" (from Winter Sky, 1968, tr. by David R. McCann). QRL (22) 81, p. 49.
"Poem of Sudae-Dong" (from Flower Snake, 1938, tr. by David R. McCann). QRL (22) 81, p. 17.

"Poetics" (from Wanderer's Poems, 1976, tr. by David
R. McCann). QRL (22) 81, p. 73.
"Postcard to a Friend" (from Flower Snake, 1938, tr.
by David R. McCann). QRL (22) 81, p. 18.
"Rhododendron" (from Winter Sky, 1968, tr. by David
R. McCann). QRL (22) 81, p. 58.
"Screech-Owl" (from Flower Snake, 1938, tr. by David
R. McCann). QRL (22) 81, p. 19.
"The Sea" (from Flower Snake, 1938, tr. by David R.
McCann). QRL (22) 81, p. 20-21.
"The Secret" (from The Cuckoo, 1946, tr. by David R.
McCann). QRL (22) 81, p. 23.
"Self Portrait" (from Flower Snake, 1938, tr. by
David R. McCann). QRL (22) 81, p. 14.
"The Shaman: Her Face, Her Food" (from Wanderer's
Poems, 1976, tr. by David R. McCann). QRL (22) 81,
p. 77.
"Sister's House" (from The Cuckoo, 1946, tr. by
David R. McCann). QRL (22) 81, p. 26.
"A Sneeze" (from Winter Sky, 1968, tr. by David R.
McCann). QRL (22) 81, p. 56.
"Snow Days" (from Winter Sky, 1968, tr. by David R.
McCann). QRL (22) 81, p. 52.
"Song" (from The Cuckoo, 1946, tr. by David R.
McCann). QRL (22) 81, p. 28.
"Spring Lean" (from New Poems, 1972, tr. by David R.
McCann). QRL (22) 81, p. 67.
"Stone Orchid: The Birthday of Gautama" (from
Wanderer's Poems, 1976, tr. by David R. McCann).
QRL (22) 81, p. 74.
"Such a Land" (from New Poems, 1972, tr. by David R.
McCann). QRL (22) 81, p. 65.
"Swing Song: Ch'unhyang's Words" (from Beside a
Chrysanthemum, 1955, tr. by David R. McCann). QRL
(22) 81, p. 36.
"Thought/Fragment" (from New Poems, 1972, tr. by
David R. McCann). QRL (22) 81, p. 64.
"Twilight" (from Winter Sky, 1968, tr. by David R.
McCann). QRL (22) 81, p. 54.
"Untitled: Pine flower's blooming" (from New Poems,
1972, tr. by David R. McCann). QRL (22) 81, p. 68.
"Untitled: Somehow this place becomes an exceedingly
hard stone interior" (from The Cuckoo, 1946, tr.
by David R. McCann). QRL (22) 81, p. 24.
"Whispers" (from Silla Notes, 1960, tr. by David R.
McCann). QRL (22) 81, p. 44.
"Winter Hail" (from New Poems, 1972, tr. by David R.
McCann). QRL (22) 81, p. 69.
"Winter Sky" (from Winter Sky, 1968, tr. by David R.
McCann). QRL (22) 81, p. 46.

SOBEK, Maria Herrera
See: HERRERA SOBEK, Maria

3855. SOBIN, Anthony
"Dead Horse Point." KanQ (14:1) Wint 82, p. 75.
"The Men." KanQ (14:1) Wint 82, p. 74.
"Photograph: Home for the Aged, Stowe, Vermont--
1931." PartR (49:1) 82, p. 132-133.
"Reunion." MidwQ (23:2) Wint 82, p. 190.

"Study in White." <u>PartR</u> (49:1) 82, p. 133-135.
"The Widow's House." <u>MidwQ</u> (23:2) Wint 82, p. 191-192.
"The Winter." <u>MidwQ</u> (23:2) Wint 82, p. 193.
"The Winter." <u>PoNow</u> (6:5, issue 35) 82, p. 31.

3856. SOBIN, Gustaf
"Ray." <u>Sulfur</u> (2:2, issue 5) 82, p. 57-61.

3857. SOCOLOW, Elizabeth Anne
"The Garden." <u>Ploughs</u> (8:1) 82, p. 149-150.
"Johnno at Music Camp." <u>Ploughs</u> (8:1) 82, p. 147-148.
"Today I Read the Children." <u>Ploughs</u> (8:1) 82, p. 151-153.

3858. SODERGRAN, Edith
"The March of the Future" (tr. by Lennart Bruce).
<u>PoNow</u> (6:5, issue 35) 82, p. 42.

3859. SOLDO, John J.
"In the Cave." <u>Wind</u> (12:45) 82, p. 32-33.

3860. SOLOGUREN, Javier
"Igual Finalmente a Toda Vida." <u>BelPoJ</u> (32:4) Sum 82, p. 36, 38.
"In the Long Run, Like Any Other Life" (tr. by Ricardo Pau-Llosa). <u>BelPoJ</u> (32:4) Sum 82, p. 37, 39.

3861. SOLOMOS, Dionysios
"Calm" (tr. by John G. Trehas). <u>CrossC</u> (4:2/3) 82, p. 16.
"Den akouetai out ena kuma" (in Greek). <u>CrossC</u> (4:2/3) 82, p. 16.

3862. SOLOWEY, Elana
"From the Shore." <u>Os</u> (14) 82, p. 8.
"Migration." <u>Os</u> (14) 82, p. 8.

3863. SOLWAY, David
"How It Happens." <u>Atl</u> (249:3) Mr 82, p. 74.

3864. SOMERVILLE, Jane
"At the Edge of Afternoon." <u>PoNow</u> (7:1, issue 37) 82, p. 40.
"November/VW." <u>PoNow</u> (7:1, issue 37) 82, p. 40.
"The Poet Makes Silk Dresses out of Worms." <u>Confr</u> (24) Sum 82, p. 56.

3865. SOMLYO, Gyorgy
"And June?" (Complement to a poem by Holderlin, tr. by Jascha Kessler and Maria Korosy). <u>MichQR</u> (21:1) Wint 82, p. 160-161.

3866. SONG, Cathy
"Birthmarks." <u>WestB</u> (11) 82, p. 41-42.
"Hotel Geneve." <u>Tendril</u> (12) Wint 82, p. 63-64.
"The Seamstress." <u>WestB</u> (11) 82, p. 42-45.

3867. SONIAT, Katherine
    "The Cloakroom." Northeast (3:14) Wint 82-83, p.
    20.
    "Just to Be Seen Is Enough." PoetryNW (23:4) Wint
    82-83, p. 46-47.

3868. SOOS
    "Juanita." Pig (8) 80, p. 58-59.

3869. SORESTAD, Glen
    "The Entertainer" (from The Chalkboard Poems).
    PoetryCR (3:3) Spr 82, p. 5.
    "The Head Secretary." PoetryCR (3:3) Spr 82, p. 5.
    "Hippos and Bikers." CanLit (92) Spr 82, p. 71-72.
    "Miss Bowdler" (from The Chalkboard Poems). PoetryCR
    (3:3) Spr 82, p. 5.
    "Mr. Anonymity" (from The Chalkboard Poems).
    PoetryCR (4:1) Sum 82, p. 6.
    "Poetry Reading at the Veterans' Home." CanLit (92)
    Spr 82, p. 56-57.
    "Yellow Warblers." CanLit (92) Spr 82, p. 8-9.

3870. SORRELLS, Helen
    "The Departure." PraS (56:4) Wint 82-83, p. 32.

3871. SOTO, Gary
    "Brown Like Us" (for Gerald). RevChic (10:1/2) Wint-
    Spr 82, p. 132-134.
    "Eating." PoNow (6:6, issue 36) 82, p. 33.
    "Failing in the Presence of Ants." Poetry (139:6)
    Mr 82, p. 335.
    "A Few Coins." RevChic (10:1/2) Wint-Spr 82, p.
    140.
    "Hunger among Crabs." Poetry (139:6) Mr 82, p. 334.
    "Joey the Midget." RevChic (10:1/2) Wint-Spr 82, p.
    134-135.
    "Mexicans Begin Jogging." RevChic (10:1/2) Wint-Spr
    82, p. 136.
    "Mission Tire Factory, 1969." RevChic (10:1/2)
    Wint-Spr 82, p. 136.
    "Nada." RevChic (10:1/2) Wint-Spr 82, p. 139.
    "The Ring." RevChic (10:1/2) Wint-Spr 82, p. 138-
    139.
    "Uncle: 1957: After Being Rejected by the Marines."
    RevChic (10:1/2) Wint-Spr 82, p. 137.

    SOTO, Salvador Arana
    See: ARANA SOTO, Salvador

3872. SOUTHDALE ELEMENTARY SCHOOL, Grade 5, Cedar Falls, IA
    "Owl" (Collaboration Poem). PikeF (4) Spr 82, p.
    20.

3873. SOUTHWICK, Marcia
    "Boarded Windows." AmerPoR (11:6) N-D 82, p. 39.
    "Doors Opening Here, and There." Iowa (12:2/3) Spr-
    Sum 81, p. 306--308.
    "Why the Rain Is Ignored." AmerPoR (11:6) N-D 82,
    p. 39.

SOUZA, Eunice de
See: De SOUZA, Eunice

3874. SPACKS, Barry
"The 4 A.M. News." _QW_ (14) Spr-Sum 82, p. 74.
"In the Garden at Midnight." _Hudson_ (35:4) Wint 82-
83, p. 576.
"Local Color." _Hudson_ (35:4) Wint 82-83, p. 577.
"My Word Is." _PoetryNW_ (23:2) Sum 82, p. 44.
"Poem in Search of Its Subject" (for Shelley
Nameroff). _Hudson_ (35:4) Wint 82-83, p. 575-576.
"Poem." _PoetryNW_ (23:2) Sum 82, p. 44.

3875. SPANOS, William V.
"Picasso at Avignon, 1973: A Destruction." _Paint_
(7/8:13/16) 80-81, p. 26-28.

3876. SPARKS, Lance T.
"Michaelsong." _PortR_ (28:1) 82, p. 24.

3877. SPARSHOTT, Francis
"Cassandra." _PoetryCR_ (4:2) Wint 82, p. 6.
"The Chainsaw Poem." _PoetryCR_ (4:1) Sum 82, p. 11.

3878. SPAULDING, John
"Summer." _PoetryCR_ (3:4) Sum 82, p. 12.

3879. SPEAKES, Richard
"Radio." _SenR_ (13:1) 82-83, p. 45-46.
"Stories" (for my mother). _SenR_ (13:1) 82-83, p. 47-
49.

3880. SPEAR, Roberta
"Catfish." _NewYorker_ (58:3) Mr 8, 82, p. 40.
"Diving for Atlantis." _NewYorker_ (58:41) N 29, 82,
p. 44.
"Fishes at Saint-Jean: Chagall, 1949." _Iowa_
(12:2/3) Spr-Sum 81, p. 309-313.
"The Prisoners of Loches." _AntR_ (40:1) Wint 82, p.
79-82.

3881. SPEARS, Heather
"Jets over Raulands Fjell." _Waves_ (11:1) Aut 82, p.
76.

3882. SPEER, Laurel
"I don't Like Hair on a Man's Face." _MassR_ (23:2)
Sum 82, p. 329-333.
"My Friend Tells Me in Strictest Confidence."
LittleM (13:3/4) 82, p. 101.
"Notes on Windshields." _Bogg_ (48) 82, p. 15.
"One Lunch." _Bogg_ (49) 82, p. 15.
"Yesterday's Doxy in Vienna." _Gargoyle_ (17/18) 81,
p. 50.

3883. SPENCE, Michael
"Myopia." _CutB_ (19) Aut-Wint 82, p. 18-19.

3884. SPENDER, Stephen
    "Auden's Funeral" (to Christopher Isherwood).
    Antaeus (44) Wint 82, p. 91-94.

3885. SPICER, David
    "TheTranssexual's Lament." Gargoyle (17/18) 81, p.
    30.

3886. SPINGARN, Lawrence P.
    "Diagnostic." PoNow (6:4, issue 34) 82, p. 16.
    "Map of Hades." PoNow (6:5, issue 35) 82, p. 17.
    "Party." PoNow (6:5, issue 35) 82, p. 17.
    "Pumping Iron." Salm (57) Sum 82, p. 132.
    "Recluse." PoNow (6:5, issue 35) 82, p. 17.

3887. SPIRES, Elizabeth
    "Crazy Quilt." YaleR (72:1) Aut 82, p. 61.
    "Days." Iowa (12:2/3) Spr-Sum 81, p. 314-315.
    "Storyville Portrait" (New Orleans red light
    district, circa 1912). YaleR (72:1) Aut 82, p. 60.

3888. SPIVACK, Kathleen
    "Five Women." PoNow (6:4, issue 34) 82, p. 25.
    "Hedge Roses." AmerPoR (11:4) Jl-Ag 82, p. 7.
    "Hello." PoNow (6:4, issue 34) 82, p. 25.
    "Leaving Behind." PartR (49:3) 82, p. 440-441.
    "The Moments-of-Past-Happiness Quilt." Harp
    (264:1581) F 82, p. 49.
    "The Obstacle Course." PoNow (6:5, issue 35) 82, p.
    31.
    "Outboard Engines." Poetry (139:4) Ja 82, p. 217-
    218.
    "The Peregrine." Kayak (59) Je 82, p. 23.
    "She Went into Her Room." Shout (3:1) 82, p. 42.

3889. SPLAKE, T. Kilgore
    "T.R." Bogg (49) 82, p. 6.

3890. SPRAYBERRY, Sandra
    "Tonight at Evergreen Cemetery." PoNow (7:1, issue
    37) 82, p. 41.

3891. ST. CLAIR, Philip
    "The Wives of Red Jacket" (Seneca Indian Chief). Vis
    (9) 82, p. 6,8.

3892. ST. CYR, Napoleon
    "Post Office Box." UnderRM (1:1) Spr 82, p. 27-28.

3893. ST. JOHN, David
    from Erotopaegnia: "It slept inside you like a dry
    tumor" (tr. of Edoardo Sanguineti, w. Ilaria
    Caputi). PoetryE (8) Aut 82, p. 75.
    "Jade." Kayak (59) Je 82, p. 48.
    "Luther's Child." Kayak (59) Je 82, p. 49.
    "The Man in the Yellow Gloves." Antaeus (47) Aut
    82, p. 35-40.
    "The Swan at Sheffield Park." NewYorker (58:10) Ap
    26, 82, p. 36-37.

"Waltz" (tr. of Giorgio Bassani, w. Ilaria Caputi).
PoetryE (8) Aut 82, p. 74.

3894. ST. JOHN, Richard
"Epiphany at the Dennis Public Dump." CarolQ (35:1)
Aut 82, p. 88-90.

3895. ST. PAT'S MIDDLE SCHOOL, 7th Grade, Clinton, Illinois
"Alley" (Collaboration Poem). PikeF (4) Spr 82, p.
20.

3896. STABLEIN, Marilyn
"To Keep the Coldness Out." Catalyst (Erotica
Issue) 82, p. 29.

3897. STAFFORD, Kim R.
"Finding the True Point of Beginning." MalR (61) F
82, p. 100.
"Inheritance at Wheatland." MalR (61) F 82, p. 98-
99.
"The Kindling." MalR (61) F 82, p. 104.
"The Messengers." MalR (61) F 82, p. 102-103.
"No Port But Passage." MalR (61) F 82, p. 105-107.
"A Sermon on Eve." MalR (61) F 82, p. 96-97.
"Short Story." MalR (61) F 82, p. 107.
"Sleeping in the Barn." MalR (61) F 82, p. 97.
"The Yew." MalR (61) F 82, p. 101.

3898. STAFFORD, William
"Accepting a Call." CarolQ (35:1) Aut 82, p. 33.
"At Night." WebR (7:1) Spr 82, p. 6.
"Barnum and Bailey." NewL (49:1) Aut 82, p. 65.
"Beyond Appearances." SouthwR (67:2) Spr 82, p.
150.
"Bird Count." Field (26) Spr 82, p. 14.
"Brother." WestHR (36:2) Sum 82, p. 163.
"A Ceremony: Doing the Needful." Field (26) Spr 82,
p. 15.
"A Ceremony: Doing the Needful." SouthernPR (23,
i.e. 22:2) Aut 82, p. 7.
"Cheri." CarolQ (35:1) Aut 82, p. 32.
"Deciding." Hudson (35:3) Aut 82, p. 397.
"Early Waking." Paint (9:17/18) Spr-Aut 82, p. 6.
"Emily." QW (14) Spr-Sum 82, p. 77.
"Even in the Desert." WestHR (36:2) Sum 82, p. 162.
"Fiction" (For W. R. Moses, from one Kansan to
another). KanQ (14:2) Spr 82, p. 79.
"For a Daughter Gone Away." Antaeus (44) Wint 82,
p. 79-80.
"For People with Problems about How to Believe."
Hudson (35:3) Aut 82, p. 395-396.
"For Someone Who Said Boo to Me." CharR (8:1) Spr
82, p. 18.
"For the Chair of Any Committee I'm On." WestHR
(36:2) Sum 82, p. 116.
"Getting Scared." Hudson (35:3) Aut 82, p. 398.
"Good Thought." NewL (49:1) Aut 82, p. 63.
"A Happy Note." WebR (7:1) Spr 82, p. 5.
"How to Regain Your Soul." Poetry (140:4) Jl 82, p.
215.

"In the Deep Mirror" (For W. R. Moses, from one Kansan to another). KanQ (14:2) Spr 82, p. 79.
"Inheriting the Earth: Quail." QW (14) Spr-Sum 82, p. 76.
"Inscriptions on Our Cave Wall." CharR (8:1) Spr 82, p. 17.
"It Is." NewL (49:1) Aut 82, p. 66.
"Learning." PortR (28:2) 82, p. 110.
"Little Rooms." Hudson (35:3) Aut 82, p. 396.
"Long Distance." PoetryNW (23:4) Wint 82-83, p. 8-9.
"Looking Back on the Weaving Room." NewL (49:1) Aut 82, p. 64.
"Madge." WestHR (36:2) Sum 82, p. 161.
"Our Neighborhood." Paint (7/8:13/16) 80-81, p. 13.
"Owyhee Canyon." CharR (8:1) Spr 82, p. 19.
"Postcards from Abroad." Paint (9:17/18) Spr-Aut 82, p. 8.
"Reality." NewL (49:1) Aut 82, p. 63.
"Scars." NewL (49:1) Aut 82, p. 65.
"School Play." Hudson (35:3) Aut 82, p. 397.
"Some People." WebR (7:1) Spr 82, p. 5.
"Someone, Somewhere." CharR (8:1) Spr 82, p. 18.
"Stillborn." NewL (49:1) Aut 82, p. 64.
"Stone, Paper, Scissors." Poetry (140:4) Jl 82, p. 214-215.
"Taking Part in an Eclipse." Paint (9:17/18) Spr-Aut 82, p. 7.
"Trusting Each Other." GeoR (36:4) Wint 82, p. 772.
"A Writer's Fountain Pen Talking." Hudson (35:3) Aut 82, p. 399.
"Years Ago, Off Juneau." PoetryNW (23:4) Wint 82-83, p. 9.
"You Don't Know the End." CharR (8:1) Spr 82, p. 19.

3899. STAGG, Barry
"There Is Malice in the Bone Born of Adam." PottPort (4) 82-83, p. 35.

3900. STAHL, Laura
"Cancer in Pisces." LittleBR (1:4) Sum 81, p. 69.

3901. STAIRRETT, Clair R.
"Fish." Wind (12:45) 82, p. 34.

3902. STALLMAN, R. W.
"Darwin and His Tortoise." SouthernR (18:3) Sum 82, p. 560-561.
"Icarus." SouthernR (18:3) Sum 82, p. 563-564.
"Nero: His Last Letter" (Dictated to his secretary Epiphroditus, A.D. 68). SouthernR (18:3) Sum 82, p. 562-563.
"The Worm." SouthernR (18:3) Sum 82, p. 561-562.

3903. STAMBLER, Peter
"Becoming Native: Spoken to Patrick McDonough's Horse." KanQ (14:1) Wint 82, p. 148-149.

3904. STANDING, Sue
"The Palmreader." PoetryNW (23:1) Spr 82, p. 19-21.
"The Very Rich Hours." Agni (17) 82, p. 159-162.
"Widow's Walk." Tendril (12) Wint 82, p. 65.

3905. STANDRIDGE, Rusty
"Alba." Thrpny (10) Sum 82, p. 10.
"Straw Doll Elegy." Thrpny (8) Wint 82, p. 12.

3906. STANESCUE, Nichita
"The Keys" (tr. by Mark Irwin and Mariana
Carpinisan). Pequod (15) 82, p. 74.
"Lesson on the Circle" (tr. by Mark Irwin and
Mariana Carpinisan). Pequod (15) 82, p. 73.

3907. STANFORD
"The Seafarer" (a version from the Old English).
DekalbLAJ (14:1/4) Aut 80-Sum 81, p. 93-94.

3908. STANFORD, Ann
"CXXIX" (tr. of Yunus Emre, w. Grace Smith). Paint
(9:17/18) Spr-Aut 82, p. 26-27.
"Five Poems" (tr. of Yunus Emre w. Grace Smith).
Antaeus (44) Wint 82, p. 170-177.
"Isidun iy yarenler eve dervisler geldi: Oh my
friends, listen" (tr. of Yunus Emre, w. Grace
Smith). NowestR (20:1) 82, p. 11.
"Makers." NowestR (20:1) 82, p. 6-7.
"Makers." NowestR (20:2/3) 82, p. 200-201.
"Riding to Winter." NowestR (20:1) 82, p. 8.
"The Spy Has His Fortune Told." Paint (9:17/18)
Spr-Aut 82, p. 19.
"The Spy in Love." Paint (9:17/18) Spr-Aut 82, p.
18.
"Waiting for Rain." NowestR (20:1) 82, p. 9.

3909. STANFORD, Janet Holmes
"Sestina Lente." LittleM (13:3/4) 82, p. 95-96.

3910. STANGE, Ken
"Growing Things." AntigR (49) Spr 82, p. 108-110.

3911. STANISLAV, Ralph
"Cauldron of Egoes." UnderRM (1:1) Spr 82, p. 18.
"Rolling Box Cars." UnderRM (1:1) Spr 82, p. 20.
"The Shroud." UnderRM (1:1) Spr 82, p. 20.

3912. STANSBERGER, Rick
"Harding, Ohio." Hangl (43) Wint 82-83, p. 74-75.
"Railroad Poem." Hangl (43) Wint 82-83, p. 75.
"Sister Nicodemus." Hangl (43) Wint 82-83, p. 74.

3913. STANTON, Joseph
"The Angel." Wind (12:46) 82, p. 41.

3914. STANTON, Maura
"At the Cochise Tourist Pavilion." AmerPoR (11:6)
N-D 82, p. 41.
"Autumn in the Land of the Lotus Eaters." AspenJ
(1) Wint 82, p. 30.

"Biography." Poetry (140:5) Ag 82, p. 280.
"Childhood." Poetry (140:5) Ag 82, p. 279.
"Christmas Card." AspenJ (1) Wint 82, p. 30.
"The Midwest." PoNow (6:6, issue 36) 82, p. 40.
"Venus." AspenJ (1) Wint 82, p. 30.
"The Wilderness." Poetry (140:5) Ag 82, p. 281-282.
"Wildlife Calendar." AmerPoR (11:6) N-D 82, p. 40.

3915. STAP, Don
"Going Back" (Utah, 1978). PraS (56:4) Wint 82-83,
p. 71.
"Utah, July." PraS (56:4) Wint 82-83, p. 72.

3916. STAPLETON, Laurence
"A Partial Portrait." PoNow (7:1, issue 37) 82, p.
40.

3917. STARBUCK, George
"On Gozzoli's Painted Room in the Medici Palace."
Poetry (140:5) Ag 82, p. 256-257.
"The Staunch Maid and the Extraterrestrial Trekkie"
(hommages a Julia Child). Atl (250:2) Ag 82, p.
60-61.
"Street Cries." Atl (250:4) O 82, p. 88.
"The Universe is Closed and Has REMs" (To Celia and
Wally, to Milly and Gene). Poetry (140:5) Ag 82,
p. 249-255.

3918. STARK, Sharon
"Hawking." Chelsea (41) 82, p. 93-95.

3919. STAVELY, Margaret
"From the Mountain." LittleBR (2:3) Spr 82, p. 44.

3920. STEEL, Brad
"Memory & Form." WritersL O-N 82, p. 21.

3921. STEELE, Michael
"Malone, Florida." Shen (33:1) 81-82, p. 37.

3922. STEELE, Timothy
"On the Eve of a Birthday." Poetry (141:2) N 82, p.
69-70.
"Sapphics Against Anger." Thrpny (11) Aut 82, p. 3.

STEENBURGH, Barbara van
See: Van STEENBURGH, Barbara

3923. STEFANILE, Felix
"Advice to a Courtly Lover" (tr. of Cecco
Angiolieri). Sparrow (43) 82, p. 26.
"After Cummings." Sparrow (43) 82, p. 20.
"American Aubade." Sparrow (43) 82, p. 12.
"A Critique of Dante" (tr. of Cecco Angiolieri).
Sparrow (43) 82, p. 27.
"Dawn." Sparrow (43) 82, p. 13.
"For My Dark Lady." Sparrow (43) 82, p. 5.
"The Girl in the Garden" (inscription for a Cook-
Book). Sparrow (43) 82, p. 7.
"Gossip." Sparrow (43) 82, p. 22.

"Hometown.," Sparrow (43) 82, p. 14.
"In That Far Country" (for Selma). Sparrow (43) 82,
     p. 28.
"It Rains in the Neighborhoods of Epiphany."
     Sparrow (43) 82, p. 10.
"Landmarks" (Written to commemorate a court ruling .
     . . to raze the edifice). Sparrow (43) 82, p. 16.
"Lines from a Poet in Residence." Sparrow (43) 82,
     p. 23.
"Marty to Marian." Sparrow (43) 82, p. 19.
"The Old House." Sparrow (43) 82, p. 17.
"On Family Quarrels" (tr. of Cecco Angiolieri).
     Sparrow (43) 82, p. 18.
"On the Mightiness of Love (Sonnet I)" (tr. of Guido
     Cavalcanti). Sparrow (43) 82, p. 25.
"On the Vanity of Wisdom." Sparrow (43) 82, p. 15.
"Paradise" (tr. of Umberto Saba). Sparrow (43) 82,
     p. 11.
"A Song for Rory" (from Some Songs for Billie
     Holiday). Sparrow (43) 82, p. 8.
"Sonnet 3" (tr. of Umberto Saba). Sparrow (43) 82,
     p. 21.
"A Word to Maecenas, in His Park." Sparrow (43) 82,
     p. 6.
"You, Poet, in Your Garden." Sparrow (43) 82, p. 9.

STEFANO, John de
     See: De STEFANO, John

3924. STEFENHAGENS, Lyn
     "Onion Slices." SmPd (19:1, issue 54) Wint 82, p.
     19.

3925. STEIN, Agnes
     "Horror, Tuesday" (tr. of Nicholas Born). NewL
     (49:1) Aut 82, p. 62.
     "It Is Sunday" (tr. of Nicholas Born). NewL (49:1)
     Aut 82, p. 61-62.
     "Time Machine" (tr. of Nicholas Born). NewL (49:1)
     Aut 82, p. 60-61.

3926. STEIN, Charles
     "The Lions" (for Lou Kleinsmith). Sulfur (2:2, issue
     5) 82, p. 126-137.

3927. STEIN, Hadassah
     "Embryo: A Gestation in Three Parts." Nimrod (26:1)
     Aut-Wint 82, p. 29-30.
     "For Archbishop Oscar Romero" (Assassinated March
     25, 1980). Kayak (59) Je 82, p. 55.
     "For Bobby Sands" (Died May 5, 1981). Kayak (60) O
     82, p. 43.
     "The Weddings of the Mothers Are Visited upon the
     Daughters." BelPoJ (33:2) Wint 82-83, p. 9-11.

3929. STEIN, Kevin
     "On Fawn River." CutB (19) Aut-Wint 82, p. 37.

3930. STEINER, Karen
"Rhythm of Dishes." BallSUF (23:3) Sum 82, p. 39.
"The War Story." SouthernR (18:3) Sum 82, p. 548.

3931. STEINGASS, David
"This Spring Day, This Wonder." Abraxas (25/26) 82,
p. 88.

3932. STEINMAN, Lisa (Lisa M.)
"Saving the Dodo: Unstable Mountains Exist in a
Climate of Their Own Devising." ConcPo (15:1) Spr
82, p. 19-20.
"A Sharp Mind Contemplates the Comforts of the Sun."
Tendril (12) Wint 82, p. 66.

3933. STELZIG, Eugene
"Don Jose." Shout (3:1) 82, p. 37.

3934. STEPANCHEV, Stephen
"Love Is a Desire to Procreate in Beauty." PoNow
(6:4, issue 34) 82, p. 6.
"A Visit to Mokrin, Yugoslavia." Poetry (140:4) Jl
82, p. 192.

3935. STEPHEN, Ian
"For Those Who Came Soon." WorldO (17:1) Aut 82, p.
46.
"Old Boat." Stand (23:1) 81-82, p. 71.

3936. STEPHENS, Jim
"On the Floating Petroglyphs" (w. Dave Hilton).
Abraxas (25/26) 82, p. 74.

3937. STEPHENS, Michael
"Giant." Pequod (14) 82, p. 77.
"Korean Chests." Pequod (14) 82, p. 79.
"Safehouse." Pequod (14) 82, p. 78.

3938. STEPHENSON, Shelby
"A Fish-Truth." PoNow (6:6, issue 36) 82, p. 41.
"Tobacco Days." OhioR (29) 82, p. 122-123.

3939. STERLING, Gary
"First Thoughts." EngJ (71:2) F 82, p. 52.

3940. STERN, Bert
"Penelope" (for Fred Paddock and Tam Lin). AmerPoR
(11:4) Jl-Ag 82, p. 41.

3941. STERN, Gerald
"Christmas Sticks." AmerPoR (11:6) N-D 82, p. 43.
"Clay Dog." Antaeus (47) Aut 82, p. 49.
"Eroica" (from Rejoicings). Pequod (14) 82, p. 9-10.
"Father Guzman." ParisR (83) Spr 82, p. 41-81.
"Hidden Justice." GeoR (36:3) Aut 82, p. 515.
"His Animal Is Finally a Kind of Ape" (from
Rejoicings). Pequod (14) 82, p. 4-5.
"In Kovalchick's Garden" (from Rejoicings). Pequod
(14) 82, p. 3.

"It's Nice to Think of Tears." GeoR (36:3) Aut 82,
   p. 514-515.
"Later Today." NewYorker (57:52) F 15, 82, p. 123.
"Lost with Lieutenant Pike" (from Rejoicings).
   Pequod (14) 82, p. 8.
"The Naming of Beasts" (from Rejoicings). Pequod
   (14) 82, p. 1.
"No Mercy, No Irony" (from Rejoicings). Pequod (14)
   82, p. 7.
"Orange Roses." Antaeus (47) Aut 82, p. 48.
"Picking the Roses." Poetry (140:6) S 82, p. 326-
   327.
from Rejoicings: Ten poems Pequod (14) 82, p. 1-11.
"The Same Moon above Us." AmerPoR (11:6) N-D 82, p.
   42-43.
"Song." Poetry (140:6) S 82, p. 328.
"Steve Dunn's Spider." Poetry (140:6) S 82, p. 329.
"This Is Lord Herbert Moaning" (from Rejoicings).
   Pequod (14) 82, p. 2.
"Turning into a Pond" (from Rejoicings). Pequod (14)
   82, p. 11.
"When I Have Reached the Point of Suffocation" (from
   Rejoicings). Pequod (14) 82, p. 6.

3942. STERNBERG, Ricardo
   "Challenged by Spring." CanLit (95) Wint 82, p. 29.
   "Erasmus in the Kitchen." CanLit (95) Wint 82, p.
   84.
   "Letter." Ploughs (8:1) 82, p. 142.
   "Thread and Needle" (Brazil). CanLit (95) Wint 82,
   p. 7.

3943. STERRETT, Jane
   "A Quality of Air." AmerPoR (11:2) Mr-Ap 82, p. 37.

3944. STEVENS, A. Wilber
   "Visit." SoDakR (20:1) Spr 82, p. 50.

3945. STEVENS, Alex
   "And Also Thus." Shen (33:1) 81-82, p. 97.
   "Faces from Afar." Shen (33:3) 82, p. 89-90.
   "Lunar Velocities." PoetryNW (23:4) Wint 82-83, p.
   26-28.
   "A Royal Progress." PoetryNW (23:4) Wint 82-83, p.
   28.

3946. STEVENS, Elisabeth
   "The Ride." Confr (24) Sum 82, p. 76-77.

3947. STEVENS, May
   "Ordinary Lives." Iowa (12:2/3) Spr-Sum 81, p. 316.

3948. STEVENS, P. M.
   "Breaking." Quarry (31:1) Wint 82, p. 53.
   "The Unfinished Cathedral." Quarry (31:1) Wint 82,
   p. 53.

3949. STEVENS, Wallace
   "The Idea of Order at Key West." AmerPoR (11:5) S-O
   82, p. 31.

3950. STEVENSON, Anne
"Green Mountain Black Mountain." MichQR (21:1) Wint
82, p. 121-130.

3951. STEVENSON, Daniel
"Pure Brightness" (tr. of Kao Chu-Ch'ing, w. Robert
Branham). PraS (56:1) Spr 82, p. 30.

3952. STEVENSON, Diane
"By Degrees." PoetryNW (23:1) Spr 82, p. 18-19.
"Communion." PoNow (7:1, issue 37) 82, p. 40.
"Thirtieth Spring." FourQt (31:3) Spr 82, p. 2.
"The Words I Would Say." PraS (56:4) Wint 82-83, p.
29-31.

3953. STEVENSON, Richard
"Did You See That?" Waves (10:4) Spr 82, p. 63.
"Sabon Tasha Bus, Maiduguri." Germ (6:2) Aut-Wint
82, p. 19.
"Thorn Trees, Bolori Layout, Maiduguri" (for Gepke).
Quarry (31:4) Aut 82, p. 14-15.
"Two Hundred Ton of Potatoes" (for Peter Polet).
Quarry (31:4) Aut 82, p. 13-14.

3954. STEVER, Margo
"Summer House." PoNow (7:1, issue 37) 82, p. 41.

3955. STEWARD, D. E.
"Fat Man." Bogg (49) 82, p. 19.

3956. STEWART, Brooke
"St. Brigid's Litany." SmPd (19:2, issue 55) Spr
82, p. 19.

3957. STEWART, Chase Erin
"I have outlived everybody." Abraxas (25/26) 82, p.
39.
"Otto is on his 6th glass of beer." Abraxas (25/26)
82, p. 38-39.

3958. STEWART, Dwayne
"Journey." Telescope (2) Aut 81, p. 122.

3959. STEWART, Frank
"Early Morning." Tendril (13) Sum 82, p. 77.
"Harbor Shadows." Tendril (13) Sum 82, p. 84.
"Hawaiian Rain." Tendril (13) Sum 82, p. 80.
"Honolulu Nights: Fort Street." Tendril (13) Sum
82, p. 81.
"The Horses at Makawao" (for Michael and Cynthia).
Tendril (13) Sum 82, p. 75.
"Keokea, Maui" (for Darrell and Mary). Tendril (13)
Sum 82, p. 82.
"The Open Water." Tendril (13) Sum 82, p. 83.
"Sunday." Tendril (13) Sum 82, p. 79.
"Upcountry, Maui" (for Anne and Marvin). Tendril
(13) Sum 82, p. 76.
"Young Woman in a Field." Tendril (13) Sum 82, p.
78.

3960. STEWART, H. K.
      "Dowsing for Water." KanQ (14:1) Wint 82, p. 103.

3961. STEWART, Pamela
      "Autumn Is a Place." Telescope (3) Sum 82, p. 14.
      "Nightblind." Telescope (3) Sum 82, p. 12-13.
      "Postcard." Iowa (12:2/3) Spr-Sum 81, p. 317.
      "The Well-Defended Heart." Telescope (3) Sum 82, p.
      15.

3962. STEWART, Robert
      "Watching Peggy Flemming after Thirteen Years."
      StoneC (10:1/2) Aut-Wint 82-83, p. 73.

3963. STEWART, Susan
      "The Evening of Montale's Death." PoetryNW (23:1)
      Spr 82, p. 22-23.
      "The Factory Girls Get Up to Read Shakespeare."
      AmerPoR (11:2) Mr-Ap 82, p. 37.
      "Gaville." Nat (235:14) O 30, 82, p. 440.
      "Letter From Turin." PoetryNW (23:4) Wint 82-83, p.
      21-22.
      "Life on Other Planets." AmerPoR (11:2) Mr-Ap 82,
      p. 36.
      "The Longest Day of the Year." PoetryNW (23:4) Wint
      82-83, p. 19-20.
      "The Map of the World." PoetryNW (23:4) Wint 82-83,
      p. 20-21.
      "Seven Bridges." AmerPoR (11:2) Mr-Ap 82, p. 36.

3964. STICKNEY, Charles
      "Time and Mind." WindO (41) Aut-Wint 82-83, p. 26.

3965. STIFFLER, Randall
      "Slides of the Whale Shot Sunday, December 6th."
      Shen (33:2) 82, p. 96-97.

3966. STILLMAN, Diane
      "At Least." Shout (3:1) 82, p. 39-40.
      "Mechanics." Shout (3:1) 82, p. 41.

3967. STILLMAN, Michael
      "Inspiration." MendoR (6) Sum 81, p. 124.

3968. STIX, Judith Saul
      "The Journey" (Asia Minor via Olympia, Argolis,
      Thera, Crete). WebR (7:1) Spr 82, p. 21-22.
      "Lines for a Painting." WebR (7:1) Spr 82, p. 22.

3969. STOCK, Bud
      "Seeds of Hush." Poem (44) Mr 82, p. 20.
      "Vagabond." Poem (44) Mr 82, p. 19.

3970. STOCK, Robert
      "Performance by a Melancholy Bassoonist." PoNow
      (6:4, issue 34) 82, p. 15.

3971. STOCKDALE, John C.
      "A Visit Almost Home." PottPort (4) 82-83, p. 10.

3972. STOKES, Terry
"I Love the Writers." PoNow (6:5, issue 35) 82, p. 46.
"In the Rain." Nat (235:16) N 13, 82, p. 504.
"My Son Studies Himself." VirQR (58:1) Wint 82, p. 66-67.
"The Sunbeam Nursery." VirQR (58:1) Wint 82, p. 64-66.
"What Does It Get You?" PoNow (6:4, issue 34) 82, p. 31.

3973. STOKESBURY, Leon
"The Explanation." NewEngR (5:1/2) Aut-Wint 82, p. 169-170.
"The Man Who Burnt Bridges." NewEngR (5:1/2) Aut-Wint 82, p. 170.

3974. STOLOFF, Carolyn
"Letter from Indiana." PartR (49:2) 82, p. 250-251.

3975. STONE, Arlene
"Aftermath of My Daughter." Pig (8) 80, p. 63.

3976. STONE, Carole
"At Taboada Spa." MalR (61) F 82, p. 191.
"Calendar." ConcPo (15:1) Spr 82, p. 107.
"The Chicken Butcher." WestB (10) 82, p. 80.
"Leaving." WestB (10) 82, p. 81.
"My Mother's Gown" (For Margaret Kreeger 1908-1938). MalR (61) F 82, p. 190.
"Root." Chelsea (41) 82, p. 91.

3977. STONE, Joan
"Fire." SouthernPR (22:1) Spr 82, p. 45.

3978. STONE, John
"Three for the Mona Lisa." Poetry (140:5) Ag 82, p. 268.
"You Round the Bend." Poetry (140:5) Ag 82, p. 267.

3979. STONE, Reynold
"Ars Poetica." AntigR (50) Sum 82, p. 8.
"With the Dead on Northumberland Strait." AntigR (50) Sum 82, p. 7.

3980. STONE, Ruth
"Icons from Indianapolis." Ploughs (8:2/3) 82, p. 254.
"Mother's Picture." Ploughs (8:2/3) 82, p. 255.
"Poetry." Iowa (12:2/3) Spr-Sum 81, p. 322.
"Secondhand Coat." Iowa (12:2/3) Spr-Sum 81, p. 321.
"Turn Your Eyes Away." Ploughs (8:1) 82, p. 139-140.
"Turning." Ploughs (8:2/3) 82, p. 253.
"What Can You Do?" Iowa (12:2/3) Spr-Sum 81, p. 318-319.
"When the Furnace Goes On in a California Tract House." Iowa (12:2/3) Spr-Sum 81, p. 320.

3981. STONEBACK, H. R.
"Basketball Sequence" (For R.B.H. and all the
coaches, all the cheerleaders, all the teammates).
CapeR (18:1) Wint 82, p. 36.
"On the Inauthenticity of First Base, after the Long
Basketball Season." CapeR (18:1) Wint 82, p. 37.

3982. STONEY, Leland
"The Saviour Epidemic." PortR (28:2) 82, p. 114.

3983. STORK, James
"For the Paperboy, Due Shortly." Wind (12:44) 82,
p. 37.

3984. STOUT, Robert Joe
"Bringing Deedee Home from the Mall." Sam (33:3,
issue 131) 82, p. 58.
"The Deer Hunter." WestB (10) 82, p. 79.
"Dropping Ingrid Off at School to Be among Friends
(Where Will They Lead Her? Will She Run Away As
Her Sister Did?)." Sam (33:3, issue 131) 82, p.
59.
"Killing the Beaver." Northeast (3:14) Wint 82-83,
p. 17.
"The Last Hike before Snowfall." KanQ (14:3) Sum
82, p. 136.

3985. STOUTENBURG, Adrien
"Listening to the Silence" (The Phillips Poetry
Award--Fall/Winter 1981/82). StoneC (9:3/4) Spr-
Sum 82, p. 73.
"Oblique." PoNow (6:4, issue 34) 82, p. 8.

3986. STOVER, Dean
"Four Peaks." SenR (13:1) 82-83, p. 52.
"The Peter Pan Diner." SenR (13:1) 82-83, p. 53.

3987. STOVER, Laren Elizabeth
"Roy Deutsch Poem." Gargoyle (15/16) 80, p. 7.

3988. STRAHAN, B. R.
"3 Mile Island." Vis (8) 82, p. 24-25.
"Lady MacBeth's Nightwalk." Vis (10) 82, p. 13-14.
"Lithium Treatment." Vis (10) 82, p. 15.
"Red Hot Momma." Vis (9) 82, p. 35.

3989. STRAND, Erik
"Invitation" (tr. of Tarjei Vesaas, w. John Morrow
and Michael Blackburn). Stand (23:3) 82, p. 8.
"Man on Fire" (tr. of Einar Okland, w. John Morrow).
Stand (23:3) 82, p. 33.
"Occupation" (tr. of Kolbein Falkeid, w. John
Morrow). Stand (23:3) 82, p. 32.

3990. STRAND, Mark
"In the Golden Age" (tr. of Carlos Drummond de
Andrade). NewYorker (58:38) N 8, 82, p. 40.
"Looking for Poetry" (tr. of Carlos Drummond de
Andrade). Antaeus (44) Wint 82, p. 89-90.

3991. STRATIDAKIS, Eileen
"Orbits." PartR (49:3) 82, p. 437-438.

3992. STRECKER, James
"Ineffable Beauty." PoetryCR (4:1) Sum 82, p. 5.

3993. STREMPEK, Stephen
"Walk in Ohio: Indian Summer." Hangl (43) Wint 82-83, p. 52-53.

3994. STRICKLAND, Stephanie
"How We Love Now." Iowa (12:2/3) Spr-Sum 81, p. 331-332.
"Love that Gives Us Ourselves" (Muriel Rukeyser, 1913-1980). Iowa (12:2/3) Spr-Sum 81, p. 333.
"Negative." Pequod (14) 82, p. 39.
"Seeing a Medusa." Tendril (13) Sum 82, p. 62.

3995. STRINGER, A. E.
"Griffin" (tr. of Aime Cesaire). AmerPoR (11:5) S-O 82, p. 7.
"Knives of Noon" (tr. of Aime Cesaire). AmerPoR (11:5) S-O 82, p. 7.
"Mississippi" (tr. of Aime Cesaire). AmerPoR (11:5) S-O 82, p. 7.
"Ode to Guinea" (tr. of Aime Cesaire). AmerPoR (11:5) S-O 82, p. 6.
"Rains" (tr. of Aime Cesaire). AmerPoR (11:5) S-O 82, p. 7.
"Who Then, Who Then" (tr. of Aime Cesaire). AmerPoR (11:5) S-O 82, p. 6.

3996. STROBERG, Paul
"Business Trips." WormR (22:4, issue 88) 82, p. 121.
"Coup de Ville." WormR (22:4, issue 88) 82, p. 119.
"A Hundred." WormR (22:4, issue 88) 82, p. 118.
"Juvenile Delinquency." WormR (22:4, issue 88) 82, p. 121.
"Kwitcherbitchin." WormR (22:4, issue 88) 82, p. 117.
"Nephew." WormR (22:4, issue 88) 82, p. 119.
"Ordinary Everyday Stuff." WormR (22:4, issue 88) 82, p. 118.
"Parenthood." WormR (22:4, issue 88) 82, p. 120.
"Reading Old." WormR (22:4, issue 88) 82, p. 118.
"Saturday Night." WormR (22:4, issue 88) 82, p. 120.

3997. STROBLAS, Laurie
"Emily, Amherst, the Snow." Outbr (8/9) Aut 81-Spr 82, p. 6.
"Letter for Rachel." Tendril (13) Sum 82, p. 65-66.
"The Only House (Why I Write Poetry)." Outbr (8/9) Aut 81-Spr 82, p. 7-8.
"Under the Weather." Tendril (13) Sum 82, p. 63-64.

3998. STROME, Celia Watson
"Going Back Down to Georgia." OhioR (27) 82, p. 106.

"Nothing's More Summer." EnPas (13) 82, p. 7.
"October." HiramPoR (31) Aut-Wint 82, p. 46.

3999. STRUTHERS, Ann
"The Dance." Spirit (6:2/3) 82, p. 38.

4000. STRUTHERS, Betsy
"Elegy for Laura Elizabeth Porter" (October 29, 1885
- October 31, 1980). AntigR (49) Spr 82, p. 106-
107.

4001. STRYK, Dan
"Crows." Kayak (60) O 82, p. 35.
"Delivering a Pig." Kayak (60) O 82, p. 34-35.
"Inertia." CharR (8:2) Aut 82, p. 41-42.
"Still Life." PoetryNW (23:3) Aut 82, p. 15.

4002. STRYK, Lucien
"Grief." NewL (49:1) Aut 82, p. 69.
"Machines." NewL (49:1) Aut 82, p. 68.
"November." Poetry (141:2) N 82, p. 68.
"The Word." NewL (49:1) Aut 82, p. 70.

4003. STUART, Dabney
"The Art of Polite Conversation." PraS (56:2) Sum
82, p. 55, Errata: (56:3) Aut 82, p. 79.
"Bound Up." PraS (56:2) Sum 82, p. 57.
"Cut Off at the Pass." PraS (56:2) Sum 82, p. 56.
"How to Dream When You Are in the Desert." NewL
(48:2) Wint 81-82, p. 90.

4004. STUART, Floyd C.
"The Wives." Spirit (6:2/3) 82, p. 50-51.

4005. STUDEBAKER, William
"Change." SoDakR (20:4) Wint 82-83, p. 23.
"Death Is Steady." SoDakR (20:4) Wint 82-83, p. 24.

4006. STURM, John Edward
"Trains toward Manassas Junction (before 2nd Bull
Run)." Wind (12:46) 82, p. 42.

4007. STURMANIS, Dona
"Monday." WestCR (17:2) O 82, p. 36.

4008. STYLE, Colin
"Dorset Registers." SewanR (90:2) Spr 82, p. 225-
226.
"The Social Security Office, Maidstone." Stand
(23:2) 82, p. 73.

4009. SUAREZ, Elena
"Alegria" (a Mario). Mairena (4:9) Spr 82, p. 43.

4010. SUBRAMAN, Belinda
"He Was In the Big One." Sam (32:3, issue 127) 82,
p. 35.

4011. SUK, Julie
"Call me." PoNow (6:6, issue 36) 82, p. 29.

"The Path" (for Guy Owen). SouthernPR (22:1) Spr 82,
    p. 15.

4012. SULLIVAN, Francis
    "Saint Simon the Stylite." LittleM (13:3/4) 82, p.
    23.
    "A Verbatim." LittleM (13:3/4) 82, p. 24.

4013. SULLIVAN, James
    "Genuine Identity." Comm (109:16) S 24, 82, p. 503.

4014. SULLIVAN, Nancy
    "For My Aunt Florence Who When Praying Gives God Not
    Only Her Friends' Names But Also Their Addresses."
    Iowa (12:2/3) Spr-Sum 81, p. 334-335.

4015. SUMMERS, Hollis
    "Hummer." Poetry (140:3) Je 82, p. 160.
    "The Meek." Poetry (140:3) Je 82, p. 161.
    "A Poem for Mother's Day." Poetry (140:3) Je 82, p.
    159.
    "Scene." Im (8:1) 82, p. 11.

SUN, Nila North
See: NORTH SUN, Nila

4016. SUNDARARAJAN, P. G.
    "Flood (Vellam)" (tr. of Vallikannan). NewL (48:3/4)
    Spr-Sum 82, p. 232.
    "I Do Not Know (Theriyavillai)" (tr. of Na
    Pichamurti). NewL (48:3/4) Spr-Sum 82, p. 155.
    "Path (Padhai)" (tr. of Pudumaippithan). NewL
    (48:3/4) Spr-Sum 82, p. 121-122.

SUNDARARAJAN, P. S.
See: SUNDARARAJAN, P. G.

4017. SUPERVIELLE, Jules
    "47 Boulevard Lannes" (to Marcel Jouhandeau, tr. by
    George Bogin). AmerPoR (11:3) My-Je 82, p. 9.
    "Horses without Riders" (tr. by George Bogin).
    AmerPoR (11:3) My-Je 82, p. 7.
    "Longing for the Earth" (tr. by George Bogin).
    AmerPoR (11:3) My-Je 82, p. 7.
    "The Photographed Hands" (tr. by George Bogin).
    AmerPoR (11:3) My-Je 82, p. 9.
    "The Portrait" (tr. by George Bogin). AmerPoR (11:3)
    My-Je 82, p. 8.
    "Prophecy" (tr. by George Bogin). NewL (48:2) Wint
    81-82, p. 36.
    "War and Peace on Earth" (tr. by George Bogin).
    AmerPoR (11:3) My-Je 82, p. 7.
    "Without Us" (tr. by George Bogin). AmerPoR (11:3)
    My-Je 82, p. 6.
    "Without Walls" (to Ramon Gomez de la Serna, tr. by
    George Bogin). AmerPoR (11:3) My-Je 82, p. 8.

4018. SUPRANER, Robyn
    "Dancing." Chelsea (41) 82, p. 158-159.

"Liberty" (Manhattan Beach, 1945). BelPoJ (32:3) Spr
   82, p. 17.
"Monday." StoneC (10:1/2) Aut-Wint 82-83, p. 14.
"Sunday." Confr (24) Sum 82, p. 17.

SURIA, Violeta Lopez
See: LOPEZ SURIA, Violeta

4019. SUSSKIND, Harriet
      "Emigration." Nimrod (25:2) Spr-Sum 82, p. 41.
      "In a Different House." GeoR (36:2) Sum 82, p. 416.

4020. SUTARDJI, Calzoum Bachri
      "A Long Alley" (tr. by Chin Woon Ping). Stand (23:4)
         82, p. 72.
      "One" (tr. by Chin Woon Ping). Stand (23:4) 82, p.
         72.

4021. SUTTER, Barton
      "Fall." QW (15) Aut-Wint 82-83, p. 62-63.

4022. SVALSTEDT, Cortney Davis
      "Early Morning Trout." PikeF (4) Spr 82, p. 9.
      "For Anne Sexton." PikeF (4) Spr 82, p. 9.

4023. SVERDRUP, Harald
      "The Gulf Stream" (tr. by Anne Born). Stand (23:3)
         82, p. 25.
      "Potatoes" (tr. by Anne Born). Stand (23:3) 82, p.
         24.

4024. SVOBODA, Terese
      "High School Rodeo Parade." PraS (56:3) Aut 82, p.
         83-84.
      "Skinny Dip." PraS (56:3) Aut 82, p. 84-85.

4025. SWAIM, Alice MacKenzie
      "Beyond This Point, Monsters." Nimrod (25:2) Spr-
         Sum 82, p. 45.
      "Color Them Red." Nimrod (25:2) Spr-Sum 82, p. 37.
      "Into the Moment, Growing." Wind (12:46) 82, p. 40.
      "Shifting of Shadows." Nimrod (25:2) Spr-Sum 82, p.
         37.

4026. SWANBERG, Ingrid
      "Working the Morning Shift." Abraxas (25/26) 82, p.
         82.

4027. SWANDER, Mary
      "Pears." Iowa (12:2/3) Spr-Sum 81, p. 336-337.

4028. SWANGER, David
      "The Aunts." NewL (48:2) Wint 81-82, p. 88-89.
      "The Past." CharR (8:2) Aut 82, p. 35.

4029. SWANN, Brian
      "Along the Trail of Flowers: Adaptions of Four Wintu
         Songs." SouthwR (67:3) Sum 82, p. 264-265.
      "At Portici" (tr. of Rocco Scotellaro, w. Ruth
         Feldman). PoNow (6:5, issue 35) 82, p. 43.

"Beggars" (tr. of Rocco Scotellaro, w. Ruth
Feldman). PoNow (6:4, issue 34) 82, p. 41.
"Creation." MalR (63) O 82, p. 136.
"Devotion." Epoch (31:3) Sum 82, p. 181.
"Evening in Potenza" (tr. of Rocco Scotellaro, w.
Ruth Feldman). PoNow (6:5, issue 35) 82, p. 43.
"Joy." Harp (265:1586) Jl 82, p. 66.
"Minnow and Flowers." SouthwR (67:3) Sum 82, p.
264.
"My Name." PortR (28:2) 82, p. 115.
"Nights." Salm (57) Sum 82, p. 131.
"Resolution." SoDakR (20:1) Spr 82, p. 44-45.
"Resources." DenQ (16:4) Wint 82, p. 87.
"Return Trip" (tr. of Rocco Scotellaro, w. Ruth
Feldman). PoNow (6:4, issue 34) 82, p. 41.
"Sleep." SouthwR (67:3) Sum 82, p. 265.
"So She Can See." PoetryNW (23:4) Wint 82-83, p.
16-17.
"Song of the Quail." SouthwR (67:3) Sum 82, p. 264.
"The Soul in Parenthesis." MassR (23:1) Spr 82, p.
27-32.
"Sum." LitR (25:3) Spr 82, p. 386-387.
"Ticket for Turin" (tr. of Rocco Scotellaro, w. Ruth
Feldman). PoNow (6:4, issue 34) 82, p. 41.
"To My Father" (tr. of Rocco Scotellaro, w. Ruth
Feldman). PoNow (6:5, issue 35) 82, p. 43.
"What I'm Waiting for." PortR (28:2) 82, p. 116.
"A Year and a Day." MalR (63) O 82, p. 137-138.
"You and I Shall Go." SouthwR (67:3) Sum 82, p.
265.

4030. SWANN, Roberta Metz
"The Model Life." Confr (24) Sum 82, p. 120.

4031. SWANSON, Robert
"The Biggest Kid." WormR (22:1, issue 85) 82, p. 9.
"Charles." WormR (22:1, issue 85) 82, p. 8.
"Dr. Pepper." WormR (22:1, issue 85) 82, p. 8.
"Grandfather's Cigar Smoke." ColEng 44(5) S 82, p.
493.
"Looking at a Painting of Constantinople by Paul
Signac." Hudson (35:4) Wint 82-83, p. 578-579.
"Milkman." PoNow (7:1, issue 37) 82, p. 41.
"The Movie." WormR (22:1, issue 85) 82, p. 8-9.
"No, William Carlos." ConcPo (15:1) Spr 82, p. 10.

4032. SWARD, Robert
"All for a Day." CrossC (4:2/3) 82, p. 27.
"Arrival." CrossC (4:2/3) 82, p. 27.
"Hillside." PoetryCR (4:1) Sum 82, p. 12.
"The Immortals, in Question." CrossC (4:2/3) 82, p.
27.

4033. SWARTS, Helene
"Support Your Local Poet." ChrC (99:37, i.e. 9) Mr
17, 82, p. 303.

4034. SWASKEY, Christine A.
"Flower Essences." Germ (6:1) Spr-Sum 82, p. 16.

4035. SWEENEY, Barbara
       "Approaching a Birthday." MalR (63) O 82, p. 245.

4036. SWEENEY, Gael
       "The Bear and the Mink: Syracuse, New York" (Delmore
          Schwartz, 1913-1966, Lou Reed, 1944-   ).
          HiramPoR (32) Spr-Sum 82, p. 44.
       from The Deaths of the Romantics: "The Apothecary
          Shop: Thomas Chatterton." HiramPoR (32) Spr-Sum
          82, p. 43.

4037. SWEENEY, Kevin
       "The Book-Burners of Buckland." Sam (32:3, issue
          127) 82, p. 24-25.

4038. SWEENEY, Michael
       "Back of the Matchbook Cover Blues." PikeF (4) Spr
          82, p. 13.
       "Small Print." PikeF (4) Spr 82, p. 33.

4039. SWENSON, Karen
       "Closing Time at the San Diego Zoo." Salm (56) Spr
          82, p. 128.
       "Etudes." Salm (56) Spr 82, p. 131.
       "Forest Lawn." Salm (56) Spr 82, p. 129.
       "The Nightgown." DenQ (16:4) Wint 82, p. 22.
       "Palouse." PoNow (6:5, issue 35) 82, p. 38.
       "She Left Me." Salm (56) Spr 82, p. 130.
       "The Transience Of Hands." DenQ (16:4) Wint 82, p.
          20-21.
       "Westchester Playhouse 1954." Kayak (60) O 82, p.
          41.
       "What Men And Women Understand." DenQ (16:4) Wint
          82, p. 19.

4040. SWENSON, May
       "Under the Baby Blanket." Antaeus (44) Wint 82, p.
          178-179.

4041. SWETMAN, Glenn R.
       "How First beyond the Shadowed Night It Gave the
          Wonder to Your Name." Poem (44) Mr 82, p. 49.
       "I Never Really Killed Nobody I Don't Think."
          SouthernPR (22:1) Spr 82, p. 12.
       "Recipe." Poem (44) Mr 82, p. 48.
       "The Thibodaux Musical Arts Series Presents Thaddeus
          Brys, Cellist. The Nicholls State University
          Concert Series Presents The Nitty Gritty All Dirt
          Band...." BallSUF (23:2) Spr 82, p. 69-70.

4042. SWICKARD, David
       "Stocking Cap." Confr (23) Wint 82, p. 108.

4043. SWIFT, Douglas
       "My Lime-Colored Car." MendoR (6) Sum 81, p. 52.

4044. SWIFT, Joan
       "1933." Iowa (12:2/3) Spr-Sum 81, p. 341.
       "Father." Iowa (12:2/3) Spr-Sum 81, p. 339.

"My Grandmother's Hair." _Iowa_ (12:2/3) Spr-Sum 81,
   p. 338.
"Pneumonia." _Iowa_ (12:2/3) Spr-Sum 81, p. 340.
"The Sadness of Hip Boots." _Confr_ (23) Wint 82, p.
   89.

4045. SWISS, Thomas
   "Lacuna." _KanQ_ (14:1) Wint 82, p. 198.
   "Physical Fitness." _KanQ_ (14:1) Wint 82, p. 176.
   "Possibilities." _Chelsea_ (41) 82, p. 162.
   "Then." _Ascent_ (7:2) 82, p. 13,
   "Waking at Night." _Chelsea_ (41) 82, p. 163.

4046. SWOPE, H. Joann
   "After an Affair." _KanQ_ (14:2) Spr 82, p. 126.

4047. SYKES, Graham
   "Lark Rising." _PikeF_ (4) Spr 82, p. 6.
   "Poem: The sea empties its bin on the sand." _PikeF_
   (4) Spr 82, p. 13.

4048. SYLVESTER, Janet
   "Arrowhead Christian Center and No-Smoking
   Luncheonette." _Tendril_ (13) Sum 82, p. 67-68.
   "Horseshoes" (for my father). _CimR_ (61) O 82, p. 27-
   28.

4049. SYLVESTER, Santiago E.
   "Kandinsky As a Pretext" (tr. by Ricardo Pau-Llosa).
   BelPoJ (32:4) Sum 82, p. 11.
   "Kandinsky Como un Pretexto." _BelPoJ_ (32:4) Sum 82,
   p. 10.

4050. SZABO, Wilhelm
   "During the Day He Held a Low-level Position" (tr.
   by Beth Bjorklund). _LitR_ (25:2) Wint 82, p. 174.
   "Resignation" (tr. by Beth Bjorklund). _LitR_ (25:2)
   Wint 82, p. 173.
   "Untranslatable" (tr. by Beth Bjorklund). _LitR_
   (25:2) Wint 82, p. 173.

4051. SZUMIGALSKI, Anne
   "The Bees." _Grain_ (10:3) Ag 82, p. 24-25.
   "Untitled: Shrapnel has torn the man's ribs apart."
   Grain (10:3) Ag 82, p. 26-27.

4052. SZYMBORSKA, Wislawa
   "Any Case" (tr. by Grazyna Drabik and Sharon Olds).
   QRL (23) 82, p. 16.
   "Astonishment" (tr. by Grazyna Drabik and Sharon
   Olds). _QRL_ (23) 82, p. 14.
   "Children of the Epoch" (tr. by Grazyna Drabik and
   Austin Flint). _QRL_ (23) 82, p. 12-13.
   "The Classic" (tr. by Grazyna Drabik and Sharon
   Olds). _QRL_ (23) 82, p. 53.
   "Clothes" (tr. by Grazyna Drabik and Sharon Olds).
   QRL (23) 82, p. 62.
   "Dream" (tr. by Grazyna Drabik and Sharon Olds). _QRL_
   (23) 82, p. 21.

"Drinking Wine" (tr. by Grazyna Drabik and Sharon Olds). QRL (23) 82, p. 33-34.
"Experiment" (tr. by Grazyna Drabik and Sharon Olds). QRL (23) 82, p. 29.
"From an Expedition Which Did Not Take Place" (tr. by Grazyna Drabik and Austin Flint). QRL (23) 82, p. 59-60.
"The Great Number" (tr. by Grazyna Drabik and Austin Flint). QRL (23) 82, p. 19.
"Hunger Camp at Jaslo" (tr. by Grazyna Drabik and Austin Flint). QRL (23) 82, p. 22.
"I Am Too Near" (tr. by Grazyna Drabik and Sharon Olds). QRL (23) 82, p. 30-31.
"In Praise of a Guilty Conscience" (tr. by Grazyna Drabik and Austin Flint). QRL (23) 82, p. 54.
"In Praise of My Sister" (tr. by Grazyna Drabik and Austin Flint). QRL (23) 82, p. 41.
"In the Tower of Babel" (tr. by Grazyna Drabik and Sharon Olds). QRL (23) 82, p. 28.
"The Joy of Writing" (tr. by Grazyna Drabik and Sharon Olds). QRL (23) 82, p. 63-64.
"Letters of the Dead" (tr. by Grazyna Drabik and Sharon Olds). QRL (23) 82, p. 52.
"Lot's Wife" (tr. by Grazyna Drabik and Austin Flint). QRL (23) 82, p. 38-39.
"Memory Finally" (tr. by Grazyna Drabik and Sharon Olds). QRL (23) 82, p. 20.
"Monologue for Cassandra" (tr. by Grazyna Drabik and Sharon Olds). QRL (23) 82, p. 50-51.
"Nothingness Turned Over" (tr. by Grazyna Drabik and Sharon Olds). QRL (23) 82, p. 37.
"The Number Pi" (tr. by Grazyna Drabik and Austin Flint). QRL (23) 82, p. 44.
"Once We Knew" (tr. by Grazyna Drabik and Sharon Olds). QRL (23) 82, p. 23.
"Onion" (tr. by Grazyna Drabik and Sharon Olds). QRL (23) 82, p. 61.
"Poem in Honor of" (tr. by Grazyna Drabik and Austin Flint). QRL (23) 82, p. 15.
"Portrait of a Woman" (tr. by Grazyna Drabik and Austin Flint). QRL (23) 82, p. 43.
"Returns" (tr. by Grazyna Drabik and Sharon Olds). QRL (23) 82, p. 42.
"The Room of a Suicide" (tr. by Grazyna Drabik and Austin Flint). QRL (23) 82, p. 49.
"Seen from Above" (tr. by Grazyna Drabik and Sharon Olds). QRL (23) 82, p. 40.
"The Shadow" (tr. by Grazyna Drabik and Sharon Olds). QRL (23) 82, p. 32.
"The Suicide's Room" (tr. by Eric Dickens). Stand (23:2) 82, p. 71.
"Summary" (tr. by Grazyna Drabik and Sharon Olds). QRL (23) 82, p. 25.
"A Terrorist Is Watching" (tr. by Grazyna Drabik and Austin Flint). QRL (23) 82, p. 45-46.
"Thanks" (tr. by Grazyna Drabik and Austin Flint). QRL (23) 82, p. 35-36.
"Torture" (tr. by Grazyna Drabik and Austin Flint). QRL (23) 82, p. 26-27.

"The Two Apes of Brueghel" (tr. by Grazyna Drabik
    and Sharon Olds). QRL (23) 82, p. 24.
"Under This Little Star" (tr. by Grazyna Drabik and
    Sharon Olds). QRL (23) 82, p. 10-11.
"Utopia" (tr. by Grazyna Drabik and Austin Flint).
    QRL (23) 82, p. 57-58.
"A View with a Grain of Sand" (tr. by Grazyna Drabik
    and Austin Flint). QRL (23) 82, p. 47-48.
"The Warning" (tr. by Grazyna Drabik and Austin
    Flint). QRL (23) 82, p. 55-56.
"Writing a Curriculum Vitae" (tr. by Grazyna Drabik
    and Austin Flint). QRL (23) 82, p. 17-18.

4053. TAGGART, John
    "Bird Run." Pequod (15) 82, p. 20.
    "My Name Called Out." Pequod (15) 82, p. 21-24.
    "Not Raw Enough." Sulfur (2:3, issue 6) 82, p. 130-
        132.
    "Wild Blue Phlox." Sulfur (2:1, issue 4) 82, p.
        110.

4054. TAGLIABUE, John
    "At Certain Heights." NewL (49:2) Wint 82-83, p.
        85.
    "Benares." NewL (48:3/4) Spr-Sum 82, p. 251.
    "Bhumisparshamudra." NewL (48:3/4) Spr-Sum 82, p.
        251.
    "Centripetal." NewL (49:2) Wint 82-83, p. 88.
    "Connubial Discovery Towards Our 35th Anniversary."
        NewL (49:2) Wint 82-83, p. 90.
    "The Continuity Must Be Renewed, the Hope Restored."
        NewL (49:2) Wint 82-83, p. 88-89.
    "Le Dejeuner sur l'Herbe." NewL (48:2) Wint 81-82,
        p. 89.
    "Divine Employment." NewL (49:2) Wint 82-83, p. 85.
    "Dubrovnik Notes/A Travel Journal." PoNow (6:4,
        issue 34) 82, p. 9.
    "Gifted Reader, You Are Ready." NewL (49:2) Wint
        82-83, p. 86-87.
    "Guido Cavalcanti: 'Avete in voi li fiori e la
        verdura ...'" NewL (49:2) Wint 82-83, p. 88.
    "Insistent Hindu and otherwise." NewL (48:3/4) Spr-
        Sum 82, p. 249.
    "Om and Shanti." NewL (48:3/4) Spr-Sum 82, p. 250.
    "A Pantheistic Painter of Signs." NewL (48:3/4)
        Spr-Sum 82, p. 249.
    "The Postures and Gestures of Development." NewL
        (49:2) Wint 82-83, p. 87.
    "Sea Port, Theology Port, Air Field, Celia's Song,
        Firefly's Conquest." Kayak (58) Ja 82, p. 13.
    "Soft Glow of Light and Rhythm." NewL (49:2) Wint
        82-83, p. 86.
    "Two poems." Kayak (60) O 82, p. 63.
    "Wandering in a High Place Where the Vines Are
        Trembling." NewL (49:2) Wint 82-83, p. 87.
    "Where to, O Unknown Soul, O Unknown Universe?"
        NewL (48:3/4) Spr-Sum 82, p. 251.
    "You Can Go Very Far at That." NewL (48:3/4) Spr-
        Sum 82, p. 250.

4055. TAGORE, Rabindranath
"1996" (tr. by David Ray). NewL (48:3/4) Spr-Sum 82,
p. 21-22.

4056. TAIRA no SADAFUN
"The Great Gates of the World" (tr. by Graeme
Wilson). WestHR (36:1) Spr 82, p. 44.

4057. TAKACS, Nancy
"Work." QW (14) Spr-Sum 82, p. 39-40.

4058. TALARICO, Ross
"Love Poem." MinnR (NS19) Aut 82, p. 28-29.

4059. TALL, Cheikh
"Dakar/Samba" (tr. of Hattie Gossett). Cond (8) 82,
p. 23-27.

4060. TALL, Deborah
"Another View." Pequod (14) 82, p. 45.
"The Exit." Pequod (14) 82, p. 43-44.
"Initiation." Nimrod (25:2) Spr-Sum 82, p. 77.
"Landscape with Ascetic" (After a painting by
Sassetta). LitR (25:3) Spr 82, p. 371.
"Our Garden." Pequod (14) 82, p. 42.
"Takeoff." Nimrod (25:2) Spr-Sum 82, p. 46.
"Three Anecdotes." AntR (40:2) Spr 82, p. 178-179.

4061. TAMAYO VARGAS, Augusto
"Once Again the Same Despair" (tr. by Ricardo Pau-
Llosa). BelPoJ (32:4) Sum 82, p. 41.
"Y Otra Vez la Misma Desesperanza." BelPoJ (32:4)
Sum 82, p. 40.

4062. TAMER, Ulku
"A Lesson" (tr. by Ozcan Yalim, William A. Fielder,
and Dionis Coffin Riggs). DenQ (17:1) Spr 82, p.
87.

4063. TAMMARO, Thom
"31 Mornings in December." MidwQ (23:2) Wint 82, p.
197-199.
"Homage to Van Gogh." MidwQ (23:2) Wint 82, p. 194-
196.

4064. TANNENBAUM, Judith
"Assumptions." PikeF (4) Spr 82, p. 25.
"Overdose." PikeF (4) Spr 82, p. 33.

4065. TAPSCOTT, Stephen
"The Island." Epoch (32:1) Aut 82, p. 24-25.
"Laude." Epoch (32:1) Aut 82, p. 26.
"El Zoo" (for E.B., 1911-1979). Ploughs (8:1) 82, p.
78-80.

4066. TARN, Nathanial
"And Even the Republic Must Have an End." Sulfur
(2:1, issue 4) 82, p. 136.
"Energetically Singing against Voracious Earth."
Sulfur (2:1, issue 4) 82, p. 135.

"Opening Out a Line at Mandelstam's." Sulfur (2:1, issue 4) 82, p. 134.
"Three Months in Which to Live." Sulfur (2:1, issue 4) 82, p. 133.
"The Tree of Another World." Sulfur (2:1, issue 4) 82, p. 137.

4067. TARR, Fred
"The Invasion." Shout (3:1) 82, p. 53.

4068. TARTAR, Helen
"Traveling to Jerusalem under a Full Moon" (tr. of Raquel Chalfi, w. the author). ManhatR (2:1) 81, p. 3.

4069. TATE, James
"Constant Defender." VirQR (58:3) Sum 82, p. 448-449.
"Djebeli Whispers the Asparagus." PoetryE (7) Spr 82, p. 30.
"Interruptions." VirQR (58:3) Sum 82, p. 447-448.
"Yonder." PoetryE (7) Spr 82, p. 31-32.

4070. TAYLOR, Alexander
"For Arlene Convalescing." MinnR (NS18) Spr 82, p. 6-7.
"Found Poem/Lost Art." MinnR (NS18) Spr 82, p. 5.

4071. TAYLOR, Bruce
"Awake" (tr. of Manhae). NewOR (9:3) Wint 82, p. 73.
"Lament" (after Transtromer). Abraxas (25/26) 82, p. 106.

4072. TAYLOR, C. Maurice
"Confusione" (tr. of Sarah Kirsch). MalR (62) Jl 82, p. 94.
"The Empty String" (tr. of Sarah Kirsch). MalR (62) Jl 82, p. 95.
"The Smell of Snow is in the Air" (tr. of Sarah Kirsch). MalR (62) Jl 82, p. 94.

4073. TAYLOR, Charles
"Dry Country in Texas." SmPd (19:1, issue 54) Wint 82, p. 11.
"The Man Who Wondered Why He Was Here." SmPd (19:1, issue 54) Wint 82, p. 12.

4074. TAYLOR, Christopher
"In a Literal Sense." Grain (10:2) My 82, p. 9.
"Life on the Plain." Grain (10:2) My 82, p. 10-11.

4075. TAYLOR, Dabrina
"Pig." FourQt (31:3) Spr 82, p. 7.

4076. TAYLOR, Henry
"Heartburn." SouthernR (18:4) Aut 82, p. 814-817.
"One Morning, Shoeing Horses" (from Desperado). Gargoyle (17/18) 81, p. 42.

4077. TAYLOR, Ian
"Dull Edges." Bogg (49) 82, p. 60.

4078. TAYLOR, Joan Imig
"Water Ballet." WorldO (16:4) Sum 82, p. 14.

4079. TAYLOR, John
"As Open as Persuasion." Bogg (49) 82, p. 40.
"Over the Rainbow." NewL (48:2) Wint 81-82, p. 52.
"Shunga." WestB (10) 82, p. 55.

4080. TAYLOR, Keith
"The Stele of Zezen-Nakht, 2200 B.C." (Toledo Museum
of Art). NewL (49:2) Wint 82-83, p. 90.

4081. TAYLOR, Laurie
"Documentary: Rescue at Sea." CentR (26:3) Sum 82,
p. 269-270.
"The Night Garden." KanQ (14:3) Sum 82, p. 183.
"A Quiet Life." CapeR (18:1) Wint 82, p. 1.

4082. TAYLOR, Leah
"Request." Spirit (6:2/3) 82, p. 171.

4083. TAYLOR, William E.
"All around Us." UTR (7:2) 82?, p. 19.
"God as Houdini." UTR (7:2) 82?, p. 19.

4084. TEAGUE, Sharry
"Stage Mother." EngJ (71:5) S 82, p. 86.

4085. TEETER, Audrey
"Steer Wrestling." Spirit (6:2/3) 82, p. 84.

4086. TELLER, Gayl
"Northern Lights" (for Uncle Jack). Shout (3:1) 82,
p. 22-23.

4087. TEM, Steve Rasnic
"Attached." Kayak (60) O 82, p. 15.
"The Daughters in the Mind." PortR (28:1) 82, p.
65.
"Into the Giant." PortR (28:1) 82, p. 65.
"The Mt. Rushmore Deformity." PortR (28:1) 82, p.
64.
"Old Lips." PortR (28:1) 82, p. 64.
"Shoplifter." Kayak (60) O 82, p. 15.

4088. TenBRINK, Carole
"Stay." Grain (10:2) My 82, p. 37.
"Transformations." Grain (10:2) My 82, p. 37.

4089. TENNY, Carol
"Shirt." OhioR (28) 82, p. 92.
"Subway." OhioR (29) 82, p. 36-37.

4090. TERRILL, Richard
"Losing a Friend." Abraxas (25/26) 82, p. 103.

4091. TERRIS, Susan
"Apartments." PoNow (7:1, issue 37) 82, p. 41.
"At Four in the Morning." PoNow (7:1, issue 37) 82,
p. 41.
"That Woman." PoNow (7:1, issue 37) 82, p. 41.

4092. TERRIS, Virginia R.
"Night Vision." NewL (48:2) Wint 81-82, p. 38.
"Orientations." NewL (48:2) Wint 81-82, p. 37.
"Service Rendered." PoNow (6:6, issue 36) 82, p.
15.
"The Yellow Chair." NewL (48:2) Wint 81-82, p. 38-
39.

4093. TETER, Vivian
"Equipoise." MissouriR (5:2) Wint 81-82, p. 34.
"Fire and Nakedness." Tendril (13) Sum 82, p. 69-
70.
"Friends and Strangers." MissouriR (5:2) Wint 81-
82, p. 35-37.

4094. THALMAN, Mark
"April Poem." PoNow (6:4, issue 34) 82, p. 33.
"Constructing the Rainbow." PoNow (6:4, issue 34)
82, p. 33.
"On the Dock at Evening." PoNow (6:4, issue 34) 82,
p. 33.

4095. THAYLER, Carl
"The Surgeon General's Report." Abraxas (25/26) 82,
p. 109.

4096. THIEL, Robert
"The Dakota's Calumet" (for Marcia Bright)." Germ
(6:2) Aut-Wint 82, p. 30-31.
"Dun Laoghaire Home." Germ (6:2) Aut-Wint 82, p.
33-34.
"Geraniums." Germ (6:2) Aut-Wint 82, p. 29.
"Looking Back: Waimanalo '64." Germ (6:1) Spr-Sum
82, p. 23-24.
"Louisiana Stones." Germ (6:1) Spr-Sum 82, p. 22.
"One to Five: New Brunswick." Germ (6:2) Aut-Wint
82, p. 32.
"Quetzalcoatl: His Fugue." Germ (6:1) Spr-Sum 82,
p. 25.

4097. THILLET, Yves
"Vatican." FourQt (31:2) Wint 82, p. 48.

4098. THOMAS, Gail
"The Limits of Will." HangL (41) 82, p. 49.

4099. THOMAS, Jim
"Beast." EngJ (71:8) D 82, p. 44.
"The Sin of Pride: I." KanQ (14:3) Sum 82, p. 118-
119.
"Some Madness Is." CapeR (17:2) Sum 82, p. 17.

4100. THOMAS, Larry D.
"String Cadenza." SouthwR (67:4) Aut 82, p. 450.

4101. THOMAS, Peter
"A Deconstruct." WestCR (17:1) Je 82, p. 8.
"Early Bird." WestCR (17:1) Je 82, p. 9.
"Errand." WestCR (17:1) Je 82, p. 8.
"Lark's Egg." WestCR (17:1) Je 82, p. 9.

4102. THOMAS, Susan
from Island Suite: "The island, the veils of winter,
my heart" (tr. of Italo Beneditti). PortR (28:1)
82, p. 9.
"Prelude I" (tr. of Italo Beneditti). PortR (28:1)
82, p. 9.

4103. THOMPSON, Don
"Bernie's Uncle Mike." AntigR (50) Sum 82, p. 74.

4104. THOMPSON, Everett
"The Box" ("Scatter my ashes on Bald Knob," for
A.S.T., 1944-1975). PoNow (7:1, issue 37) 82, p.
42.
"Horace." PoNow (7:1, issue 37) 82, p. 42.

4105. THOMPSON, Gary
"At Night." Abraxas (25/26) 82, p. 23.
"Babel." Tendril (13) Sum 82, p. 71.

4106. THOMPSON, Judith
"The Autumn Stones, the Hills Laid Bare." Poem (46)
N 82, p. 4.
"I Recall the Way." Poem (46) N 82, p. 3.

4107. THOMPSON, Julius E.
"Children of the Night." Obs (7:2/3) Sum-Wint 81,
p. 215.
"Goodbye, Mississippi." Obs (7:2/3) Sum-Wint 81, p.
215.
"Life-Belt." Obs (7:2/3) Sum-Wint 81, p. 216.
"Night and Day." Obs (7:2/3) Sum-Wint 81, p. 216.
"What Is a Black School." Obs (7:2/3) Sum-Wint 81,
p. 216.

4108. THOMPSON, Phil
"Grandfather's Lobstertrap." PottPort (4) 82-83, p.
27.
"Penumbral Moon." PottPort (4) 82-83, p. 39.

4109. THOMPSON, Phyllis
"After Many Words, A Long Time." QRL (22) 81, p.
47.
"Alone at Ainahou: The New Land." PraS (56:3) Aut
82, p. 42.
"Asking for a Letter." QRL (22) 81, p. 53.
"August in America." QRL (22) 81, p. 40.
"The Candle in the Woods." QRL (22) 81, p. 41.
"Carnal Knowledge." QRL (22) 81, p. 42.
"The Darkness." QRL (22) 81, p. 57-58.
"The Day of Change." QRL (22) 81, p. 45-46.
"Death and Memory." QRL (22) 81, p. 36-37.
"December 31." QRL (22) 81, p. 55-56.
"Dreaming Song." QRL (22) 81, p. 52.

"Eurydice." QRL (22) 81, p. 8-11.
"A Gust of Winter" (for Max and Earll Kingston).
  NewEngR (4:3) Spr 82, p. 421-422.
"Homecoming." QRL (22) 81, p. 35.
"Jade." QRL (22) 81, p. 49.
"Ka'ena Point." QRL (22) 81, p. 14-16.
"Kailua Beach." QRL (22) 81, p. 62-64.
"Many Times." QRL (22) 81, p. 59-61.
"On the Ledge" (for Ben Norris). Tendril (13) Sum
  82, p. 72.
"The Peacock." QRL (22) 81, p. 43.
"The Promise." QRL (22) 81, p. 65.
"Pu'u O Mahuka: The Hill of Flight." QRL (22) 81,
  p. 19-22.
"September." QRL (22) 81, p. 39.
"The Silence of Niagara." QRL (22) 81, p. 34.
"Touch." QRL (22) 81, p. 54.
"Toward Morning." QRL (22) 81, p. 50.
"The Truth." QRL (22) 81, p. 17-18.
"Voices 1, John Logan: The River." QRL (22) 81, p.
  24-25.
"Voices 2, Fay Enos: What is Quiet." QRL (22) 81,
  p. 25-26.
"Voices 3, Milton Kessler: The Maples." QRL (22)
  81, p. 26-27.
"Voices 4, Frank Anderson, M.D.: Chance." QRL (22)
  81, p. 27-29.
"Voices 5, Monet: Blue Paint." QRL (22) 81, p. 29-
  31.
"Voices 6, Harry Hinson: Telling You." QRL (22) 81,
  p. 31-32.
"Voices 7, Myself: Ka Hea: The Call." QRL (22) 81,
  p. 33.
"What the Door Opens On." QRL (22) 81, p. 38.
"Where You Live, What You Have." QRL (22) 81, p.
  48.
"The Wind of Manoa." QRL (22) 81, p. 51.
"Yggdrasil" (for Neil Abercrombie, Tom Gill, Jean
  King and Patsy Mink--statesmen of Hawaii). QRL
  (22) 81, p. 12-13.

4110. THOMPSON, Robert
    "Sylvia, Truckdriver of the Morning." Abraxas
    (25/26) 82, p. 89.

4111. THORNTON, Russell
    "For an Absent Woman While I Look at the Moon."
    Waves (10:4) Spr 82, p. 66.
    "If I Poked This Air." CanLit (91) Wint 81, p. 57.
    "My Longing Brought Me a Far Distance." Waves
    (10:4) Spr 82, p. 66.
    "She Floats My Wishes." PoetryCR (3:4) Sum 82, p.
    13.

4112. THORPE, Michael
    "Two Camera Poems." CanLit (95) Wint 82, p. 37-38.

4113. THRONE, Evelyn
    "Moon Rave." Outbr (10/11) Aut 82-Spr 83, p. 71.

4114. THRONE, Marilyn
"Arachne's Soliloquy." <u>Poem</u> (45) Jl 82, p. 16-18.
"The Catbird's Death." <u>Outbr</u> (10/11) Aut 82-Spr 83,
p. 70.
"Clown Alley Revisited." <u>Outbr</u> (10/11) Aut 82-Spr
83, p. 69.
"Crust of Life." <u>WebR</u> (7:1) Spr 82, p. 65.
"An Incantation." <u>Poem</u> (45) Jl 82, p. 14.
"Seascape." <u>Poem</u> (45) Jl 82, p. 12-13.
"The Summer Wind." <u>Poem</u> (45) Jl 82, p. 15.

4115. THURSTON, Bonnie Bowman
"Forsythia" (for J. R.). <u>ChrC</u> (99:13) Ap 14, 82, p.
438.

4116. TIBBS, Dan
"On a Summer's Eve." <u>PikeF</u> (4) Spr 82, p. 20.

4117. TIELSCH, Ilse
"Not Provable" (tr. by Beth Bjorklund). <u>LitR</u> (25:2)
Wint 82, p. 259.
"Vita with Postscript" (tr. by Beth Bjorklund). <u>LitR</u>
(25:2) Wint 82, p. 259.
"We're Satisfied" (tr. by Beth Bjorklund). <u>LitR</u>
(25:2) Wint 82, p. 258.
"What Belongs to Me" (tr. by Beth Bjorklund). <u>LitR</u>
(25:2) Wint 82, p. 257.

4118. TIETZ, Steve
"Addict." <u>WindO</u> (41) Aut-Wint 82-83, p. 41.

4119. TIHANYI, Eva
"Conceiving." <u>PoetryCR</u> (4:1) Sum 82, p. 7.
"Death Song." <u>Grain</u> (10:3) Ag 82, p. 16.
"Poem for Anais Nin." <u>Grain</u> (10:3) Ag 82, p. 16.
"Trompe l'Oeil." <u>Grain</u> (10:3) Ag 82, p. 15.
"What the Neighbours Didn't See." <u>PoetryCR</u> (3:4)
Sum 82, p. 12.

4120. TIKKAMEN, Marta
from Love Song of the Century: "Nobody hurt me ever"
(tr. by Thomas and Vera Vance). <u>Paint</u> (7/8:13/16)
80-81, p. 42-43.

4121. TILLINGHAST, David
"Brown Cove" (for my eldest son). <u>SouthernR</u> (18:3)
Sum 82, p. 543-544.
"Jane Collier." <u>SouthernR</u> (18:3) Sum 82, p. 542-
543.

4122. TILLINGHAST, Richard
"Sewanee in Ruins, Part Three." <u>Ploughs</u> (8:1) 82,
p. 128-132.
from Sewanee in Ruins: (IV-V). <u>Ploughs</u> (8:2/3) 82,
p. 61-69.

4123. TILTON, Rafael, Sister
"Fast and Light." <u>Pig</u> (8) 80, p. 34.

4124. TIMMERMAN, William
      "Grey Day." Northeast (3:12) Wint 81-82, p. 4.

4125. TIO, Salvador
      "Elogio Minimo a un Poeta Maximo." Mairena
      (4:11/12) Wint 82, p. 149.

4126. TIPTON, David
      "A Lousy Fifty Quid." WormR (22:4, issue 88) 82, p.
      122.
      "Monica on Poetry." WormR (22:4, issue 88) 82, p.
      123.
      from Wars of the Roses: (48). WormR (22:4, issue
      88) 82, p. 122.

      TIRADO, Adrian Santos
      See: SANTOS TIRADO, Adrian

4127. TIRADO, Evie
      "In the Damp Sienna Hills." Maize (5:1/2) Aut-Wint
      81-82, p. 66.
      "Today." Maize (5:1/2) Aut-Wint 81-82, p. 67-68.

4128. TISDALE, Charles
      "Bionic Sonnet: No. 6,000,000." SouthernHR (16:3)
      Sum 82, p. 256.

4129. TISERA, Mary
      "No Squares to Mark This Route." EnPas (13) 82, p.
      14-15.
      "An Open Window." LittleM (13:3/4) 82, p. 97.
      "Resurrection." PoNow (6:6, issue 36) 82, p. 47.
      "The Water Nymph Soliloquy." BelPoJ (33:2) Wint 82-
      83, p. 28-29.

4130. TODD, Al
      "For My Father." WestCR (17:2) O 82, p. 26.
      "Hawking Jesus." WestCR (17:2) O 82, p. 26.
      "On Being Psychotic." WestCR (17:2) O 82, p. 26.

4131. TODD, Gail
      "A Shopping Junkie." PikeF (4) Spr 82, p. 11.

4132. TODD, Theodora
      "Friday Science Film: The States of Matter." MidwQ
      (23:3) Spr 82, p. 300-301.
      "Thunderstorm Season." MidwQ (23:3) Spr 82, p. 302.

4133. TOLEDANO, Francisco
      "El Jilguero." Os (15) 82, p. 23.
      "La Luciernage." Os (15) 82, p. 22.

4134. TOME, Jesus
      "El Grito." Mairena (4:10) Sum-Aut 82, p. 68-69.
      "Suplica Final" (from Antologia Poetica). Mairena
      (4:9) Spr 82, p. 102.

4135. TOMKIW, Lydia
      "In Bed with Boys." HangL (41) 82, p. 50.

4136. TOOL, Dennis
"Death" (tr. of Maurice Careme). SouthernR (18:3)
Sum 82, p. 569.
"The Loved One" (tr. of Maurice Careme). SouthernR
(18:3) Sum 82, p. 567.

TOORN, Peter van
See: Van TOORN, Peter

4137. TORGERSEN, Eric
"Going and Staying." Hudson (35:3) Aut 82, p. 402-
404.
"Love on the Friendship Quilt." PoNow (6:4, issue
34) 82, p. 31.
"Parting Wishes." Northeast (3:14) Wint 82-83, p.
18.
"Poem for Adrienne Rich." Hudson (35:3) Aut 82, p.
400-401.
"Toward." Northeast (3:14) Wint 82-83, p. 19.

4138. TORRENTE, Aurelio N.
"Puerto Rico." Mairena (4:9) Spr 82, p. 46.

4139. TORRES, Eladio
"A Don Francisco." Mairena (4:11/12) Wint 82, p.
145.

TORRES, Gerardo Moreno
See: MORENO TORRES, Gerardo

4140. TORRES, Margaret
"Poem from a Far City." KanQ (14:3) Sum 82, p. 196.

TORRES, Rosario Esther Rios de
See: RIOS de TORRES, Rosario Esther

4141. TORRESON, Rodney
"The Rattle." Northeast (3:12) Wint 81-82, p. 18.

4142. TOSTESON, Heather
"Clemency." SmPd (19:1, issue 54) Wint 82, p. 20.
"Crossing the Desert." SmPd (19:1, issue 54) Wint
82, p. 32-33.
"Pesadamente." NowestR (20:1) 82, p. 90.

4143. TOTH, Judit
"Outskirts, Afternoon" (tr. by Emery George). PoNow
(6:6, issue 36) 82, p. 42.

4144. TOTH, Steve
"Symbols." Spirit (6:2/3) 82, p. 72.

4145. TOULOUSE, Mark G.
"Proof Text." ChrC (99:37, i.e. 9) Mr 17, 82, p.
303.

TOV, S. Ben
See: BEN-TOV, S.

4146. TOWELL, Larry
"Calcutta Dump." <u>Quarry</u> (31:4) Aut 82, p. 32.
"Momenpur Bustee." <u>Quarry</u> (31:4) Aut 82, p. 32-34.
"Nimtallah Burning Ghats." <u>Quarry</u> (31:4) Aut 82, p. 32.
"Poem: Cycling midnights along the blood-dark village paths." <u>AntigR</u> (48) Wint 82, p. 47.
"Storm." <u>AntigR</u> (48) Wint 82, p. 48.

4147. TRACY, Robert
"The Stream of Golden Honey" (tr. of Osip Mandelstam). <u>NewYRB</u> (29:19) D 2, 82, p. 22.
"Tristia" (tr. of Osip Mandelstam). <u>NewYRB</u> (29:19) D 2, 82, p. 22.

4148. TRAINER, Yvonne
"At a craft shop an ancient man." <u>WestCR</u> (17:2) O 82, p. 27.
"Like a fish it has fins and a tail." <u>WestCR</u> (17:2) O 82, p. 27.

4149. TRAKL, Georg
"Sleep" (tr. by Francis Golffing). <u>PoNow</u> (6:6, issue 36) 82, p. 43.
"The Sun" (tr. by Francis Golffing). <u>PoNow</u> (6:6, issue 36) 82, p. 43.

4150. TRAMWAY, Ariel
"After the Nuke War." <u>Vis</u> (8) 82, p. 28-29.
"Today's Baseball Trivia Question Is: Where Are the Instant Replays of Yesteryear??" <u>Pig</u> (9) 82, p. 9.

4151. TRAWICK, Leonard
"You, Jean Simeon Chardin." <u>Tendril</u> (12) Wint 82, p. 67.

4152. TREGEBOV, Rhea
"Saint Jane Revisited." <u>Grain</u> (10:2) My 82, p. 19.

4153. TREHAS, John G.
"Calm" (tr. of Dionysios Solomos). <u>CrossC</u> (4:2/3) 82, p. 16.
"Desires" (tr. of Constantin Cavafy). <u>CrossC</u> (4:2/3) 82, p. 16.
"On a Ship" (tr. of Constantin Cavafy). <u>CrossC</u> (4:2/3) 82, p. 16.
"Postscript" (tr. of George Seferis). <u>CrossC</u> (4:2/3) 82, p. 15.
"Psychology" (tr. of George Seferis). <u>CrossC</u> (4:2/3) 82, p. 15.

4154. TREITEL, Margot
"Common Property." <u>Spirit</u> (6:2/3) 82, p. 174.
"Dancing the High Life at the Cockatoo Bar." <u>LitR</u> (26:1) Aut 82, p. 124-125.
"Demography." <u>Northeast</u> (3:14) Wint 82-83, p. 15.
"Dream House/2." <u>UnderRM</u> (1:2) Aut 82, p. 38.
"Everyday Things." <u>UnderRM</u> (1:2) Aut 82, p. 37.
"From a Dark Continent." <u>LitR</u> (26:1) Aut 82, p. 124.

"Hot August: and." PortR (28:1) 82, p. 68.
"In an Enchanted House." WindO (41) Aut-Wint 82-83,
  p. 41.
"Miro Finds His Women Abandoned on a Spanish Beach."
  PortR (28:1) 82, p. 68.
"The Persistence of Memory." KanQ (14:3) Sum 82, p.
  161.
"A Place to Park in the Woods." KanQ (14:3) Sum 82,
  p. 160.
"Plowing Scene by Grant Wood." NewEngR (4:3) Spr
  82, p. 467.
"Preamble." KanQ (14:3) Sum 82, p. 160-161.
"Sleep in the Tropics." LitR (26:1) Aut 82, p. 125.
"The Spread of Civilization." WindO (41) Aut-Wint
  82-83, p. 40.
"Travelling Light." NewEngR (4:3) Spr 82, p. 466.

4155. TREITEL, Renata
  "Winter Scene." Wind (12:45) 82, p. 3.

4156. TREMBLAY, Gail
  "Again, the Bones." Annex (3) 81, p.84.
  "American Abroad." Annex (3) 81, p.91-91.
  "And Learn the Way." Annex (3) 81, p.98-99.
  "And Still Bear." Annex (3) 81, p.96.
  "Autumn Comes to Woman." Annex (3) 81, p.101.
  "Blindengarten, Vienna." Annex (3) 81, p.113.
  "Bus Ride, Omaha, November, 1977" (for my Father).
    Annex (3) 81, p. 117.
  "But I'm a Woman." Annex (3) 81, p.99-100.
  "But Sane." Annex (3) 81, p.108-109.
  "China Trade." Annex (3) 81, p.111-112.
  "Communion." Annex (3) 81, p.97.
  "Corn Beggar Talks." Annex (3) 81, p.85.
  "Crow Voices." Annex (3) 81, p.88.
  "The Dark Dance." Annex (3) 81, p.102.
  "Earth." Annex (3) 81, p.113.
  "The Epileptic." Annex (3) 81, p.106.
  "For Louisa Forgetting How to Dance." Annex (3) 81,
    p.114-115.
  "Gathering Basket Grass" (For Mary Nelson). Annex
    (3) 81, p. 93.
  "The Girl Who Almost Stayed a Fish" (for J.B.).
    Annex (3) 81, p. 115.
  "Grandfather Dancing" (for Peter Ernest). Annex (3)
    81, p. 84-85.
  "Huckleberry Feast, Warms Springs Nation, 1979."
    Annex (3) 81, p.92.
  "Hummingbird." Annex (3) 81, p.88-90.
  "I'm Woman." Annex (3) 81, p.95-96.
  "In Memory of My Mother." Annex (3) 81, p.103.
  "In the Shower Room." Annex (3) 81, p.105.
  "Listening to the Dawn." Annex (3) 81, p.110.
  "Night Gives Old Woman the Word." Annex (3) 81,
    p.86.
  "One More Reason That Man Is Not Yet Extinct."
    Annex (3) 81, p.116.
  "The Other Self Tells You Where You're Going."
    Annex (3) 81, p.105-106.
  "A Parish of Owls." Annex (3) 81, p.93-94.

"Poem for D.M.." Annex (3) 81, p.104.
"Poem in Praise of Marianne Moore." Annex (3) 81, p.111.
"Raven's Tale." Annex (3) 81, p.87.
"Relocation." Annex (3) 81, p.90-91.
"Returning to the Old Religion" (Song for the Success of the Hunter). Annex (3) 81, p. 80-83.
"Sky." Annex (3) 81, p.112-113.
"Stepping Out." Annex (3) 81, p.112.
"To Dance and Sing." Annex (3) 81, p.109.
"To Grandmother on Her Going" (a description of how things looked from earth). Annex (3) 81, p. 107.
"To Grow." Annex (3) 81, p.100-101.
"To My Father's Patient." Annex (3) 81, p.103-104.
"To My Husband, My Lover" (for Joseph Three Bears). Annex (3) 81, p. 96-97.
"Trane, and All That Jazz" (for Don Land). Annex (3) 81, p. 118.
"What Is the Matter?" Annex (3) 81, p.119.
"Wit's End." Annex (3) 81, p.107-108.

4157. TREMBLAY, William
"Driftwood, the Muse & Lady Luck." AspenJ (1:2) Sum 82, p. 32.
"Picasso & the Hallucination War." AspenJ (1:2) Sum 82, p. 33.

4158. TRETHEWEY, Eric
"Always the Same." GeoR (36:1) Spr 82, p. 112.
"Bill of Fare." PoNow (7:1, issue 37) 82, p. 42.
"How Many Times." NewOR (9:2) Aut 82, p. 49.
"Still Life, New Orleans." CharR (8:1) Spr 82, p. 29.
"A Way Back." Quarry (31:4) Aut 82, p. 19-20.

4159. TRIEM, Eve
"Breaking a Voodoo." Iowa (12:2/3) Spr-Sum 81, p. 342.

4160. TRINIDAD, David
"The Boy." PoNow (7:1, issue 37) 82, p. 27.
"We Dream of Snakes." PoNow (7:1, issue 37) 82, p. 27.

4161. TROMMESHAUSER, Dietmar
"Blackout." Waves (10:4) Spr 82, p. 59.
"Scene from a Phone Booth." Waves (10:4) Spr 82, p. 58.

4162. TROWBRIDGE, William
"The Displaced Person (Flannery O'Connor, 1925-1964)." Wind (12:44) 82, p. 39.
"Extreme Unction: A Short Subject in a Long Movie." Wind (12:44) 82, p. 38.
"Kong Turns Critic." HiramPoR (32) Spr-Sum 82, p. 45.
"The Song of Iron George." BelPoJ (32:3) Spr 82, p. 26-29.
"Still Photo (Tarawa, November 24, 1943)." Wind (12:44) 82, p. 38-39.

"What the Snail Said." KanO (14:1) Wint 82, p. 163.

4163. TROY, Sheila
"Car Trip." NewL (49:2) Wint 82-83, p. 84.
"New Year's Eve: 1980." NewL (49:2) Wint 82-83, p. 84.

4164. TROYANOVICH, Steve
"Our Eyes" (tr. of Fernand Ouellette). StoneC (10:1/2) Aut-Wint 82-83, p. 37.
"Thoughts on Marcus Aurelius." StoneC (10:1/2) Aut-Wint 82-83, p. 14.

TROYER, Gene van
See: Van TROYER, Gene

4165. TRUDELL, Dennis
"Beyond the Door." Iowa (12:4) Aut 81, p. 48-49.
"A Checkered Red and White Shirt." GeoR (36:4) Wint 82, p. 730-731.
"The Eternal Company." Abraxas (25/26) 82, p. 77.

4166. TRUJILLO, Paul
"Elfego Baca." PoNow (6:4, issue 34) 82, p. 47.

4167. TRUJILLO MUNOZ, Gabriel
"Alien" (a las transnacionales). Maize (5:3/4) Spr-Sum 82, p. 54.
"Anos Luz." Maize (5:3/4) Spr-Sum 82, p. 55.
"Tranquiliza" (a las agencias informativas un dia de 1945). Maize (5:3/4) Spr-Sum 82, p. 56.

4168. TRUSCOTT, Robert Blake
"Crossfire." StoneC (10:1/2) Aut-Wint 82-83, p. 85-86.

4169. TSONGAS, George
"The Ghosts of North Beach Roam This World" (the Point St. Louis, a memoriam to Bob Seider). SeC (9:1/2) 80, p. 1-2.
"Rue Bleue" (to Janice). SeC (9:1/2) 80, p. 29.

TSUNG-YUAN, Liu
See: LIU, Tsung-yuan

4170. TSVETAYEVA, Marina
from Verses to Blok: "Your name is a bird in my hand" (tr. by Mary Maddock). LitR (26:1) Aut 82, p. 104-105.

4171. TUCKER, Martin
"A Geriatric Replies to Marvell's Coy Mistress." Confr (24) Sum 82, p. 107.

4172. TUCKER, Memye Curtis
"Letter to a Poet." BallSUF (23:4) Aut 82, p. 74.

4173. TUCKER, Robert
"The Maned Wolf." MassR (23:1) Spr 82, p. 159-160.

4174. TUCKER, Tommy Neil
"Homage." <u>Ploughs</u> (8:2/3) 82, p. 167-168.

4175. TULLEY, Paul
"A Kind of Fats Waller Tune for the Band" (aka
Caspar Flats Jug Band). <u>MendoR</u> (5) Sum 81, p. 24.
from Mex Glimpse: "The Fishermen take it with a
curious, cynical stoicism." <u>MendoR</u> (6) Sum 81, p.
73.
from Mex Glimpse: "The two young gentlemen find so
way." <u>MendoR</u> (6) Sum 81, p. 73.

4176. TULLOSS, Rod
"April." <u>Bogg</u> (48) 82, p. 3.

4177. TURCO, Lewis
"Recollections I." <u>PoetryNW</u> (23:3) Aut 82, p. 23.

4178. TURGEON, Gregoire
"August Night." <u>Abraxas</u> (25/26) 82, p. 21.

4179. TURK, Leonard
"Winter Walk." <u>Wind</u> (12:46) 82, p. 28.

4180. TURNER, Alberta
from A Dictionary of Common Terms: "Arch."   <u>Iowa</u>
(12:2/3) Spr-Sum 81, p. 348.
from A Dictionary of Common Terms: "Bliss."   <u>Iowa</u>
(12:2/3) Spr-Sum 81, p. 348.
from A Dictionary of Common Terms: "Die."   <u>Iowa</u>
(12:2/3) Spr-Sum 81, p. 349.
"Knees." <u>SouthernPR</u> (22:1) Spr 82, p. 63.
"Necessary Magic." <u>Stand</u> (23:2) 82, p. 61.

4181. TURNER, Doug
"Escape." <u>MalR</u> (61) F 82, p. 146-147.

4182. TURNER, Glen
"U.F.O. Sighting" (Du Drop Inn Tavern, 1:33 a.m.).
<u>LittleBR</u> (1:3) Spr 81, p. 52.

4183. TURNER, Gordon
"We Used to Watch." <u>Grain</u> (10:3) Ag 82, p. 59.

4184. TURNER, Lance M.
"On a Hill, Sitting." <u>Maize</u> (6:1/2) Aut-Wint 82-83,
p. 61.
"Raveled knot." <u>Maize</u> (6:1/2) Aut-Wint 82-83, p.
60.

4185. TURRINI, Peter
"Four Poems" (tr. by Beth Bjorklund). <u>LitR</u> (25:2)
Wint 82, p. 294-295.

4186. TWICHELL, Chase
"Franz, the World Is Abstract." <u>Iowa</u> (12:2/3) Spr-
Sum 81, p. 350-351.
"Paper White Narcissus." <u>MassR</u> (23:2) Sum 82, p.
334.

"Starkweather House." Iowa (12:2/3) Spr-Sum 81, p. 352-353.

4187. TYSON, H. C.
"Tell Me" (tr. of Gemiann Augustus). Abraxas (25/26) 82, p. 64.

4188. UDRY, Susan E.
"Papal Visit." CarolQ (34:3) Spr 82, p. 16.

4189. UHER, Lorna
"Delight in the Small." MalR (62) Jl 82, p. 106-107.
"The Removal of Shoes." Grain (10:3) Ag 82, p. 9-10.
"This Is a Love Poem without Restraint." Grain (10:3) Ag 82, p. 7-9.
"Time to Praise." Grain (10:3) Ag 82, p. 10.

4190. UJVARY, Liesl
"Everything Has Its Reason" (tr. by Beth Bjorklund). LitR (25:2) Wint 82, p. 285-286.
"Important!" (tr. by Beth Bjorklund). LitR (25:2) Wint 82, p. 286.

4191. ULLMAN, Leslie
"Running." Iowa (12:2/3) Spr-Sum 81, p. 354-357.

4192. ULMER, James
"Locked Room." Poetry (139:5) F 82, p. 283.
"Rhododendrons." Poetry (139:5) F 82, p. 284.

4193. UMPIERRE, Luz Maria
"Alumbramiento" (A David Billick). Mairena (4:9) Spr 82, p. 45-46.

4194. UNDERWOOD, June O.
"An Examination in History." LittleBR (3:1) Aut 82, p. 24-28.

4195. UNDERWOOD, Robert
"The Barber." Confr (23) Wint 82, p. 88.

4196. UNGER, Barbara
"Riding the Penn Central Railroad into New York City." Spirit (6:2/3) 82, p. 23.

4197. UNGER, David
"The Marlin Cafe." PoNow (6:6, issue 36) 82, p. 34.
"Storm at Sand Beach Farm." PoNow (6:6, issue 36) 82, p. 34.

4198. UNTERECKER, John
"Birthday Poem (December 29)." PoNow (6:4, issue 34) 82, p. 20.
"Event." Kayak (58) Ja 82, p. 56.
"Search." Salm (56) Spr 82, p. 139.
"The Visit." GeoR (36:2) Sum 82, p. 370-371.

4199. UPDIKE, John
"Easthampton-Boston by Air." AmerPoR (11:4) Jl-Ag
82, p. 10.
"The Moons of Jupiter." AmerS (51:4) Aut 82, p.
483-486.
"Plow Cemetery." Antaeus (47) Aut 82, p. 95-96.

4200. UPTON, Lee
"The House That Falls," MissR (10:3, issue 30)
Wint-Spr 82, p. 54-55.
"Toys." MissR (10:3, issue 30) Wint-Spr 82, p. 52-
53.

4201. URDANG, Constance
"Clouds." Poetry (140:1) Ap 82, p. 6.
"Dances for Small Spaces." NewEngR (5:1/2) Aut-Wint
82, p. 108-109.
"The Fourth Day." PoNow (6:4, issue 34) 82, p. 4.
"Night Air." Poetry (140:1) Ap 82, p. 7.
"The Other Life." Poetry (140:1) Ap 82, p. 6.
"Our Passions Are Never Accidental." PoNow (6:5,
issue 35) 82, p. 5.
"The Will to Believe." PoNow (6:6, issue 36) 82, p.
8.

4202. URIBE, Rafael
"Di Que Si, Voluntaria, Di Que Si." Prismal (7/8)
Spr 82, p. 84.

URTECHO, Jose Coronel
See: CORONEL URTECHO, Jose

4203. USCHUK, Pamela
"Long Distance Home." MalR (61) F 82, p. 16-17.
"The Trick" (for John). Nimrod (25:2) Spr-Sum 82, p.
73-75.

4204. UYAR, Turgut
"Often Yours" (tr. by Ronnie Margulies). Stand
(23:1) 81-82, p. 67.

4205. VACAS, Francisco J. (Francisco Jose)
"Comunion" (from Bandera de Senales). Mairena (4:9)
Spr 82, p. 103.
"Rama Seca." Mairena (4:11/12) Wint 82, p. 150.

4206. VAISIUS, Andrew
"The Neighbours." Waves (10:4) Spr 82, p. 52.
"You Are the Poet." Waves (10:4) Spr 82, p. 53.

4207. VALDIVIESO, Teresa
"Cartesianas" (from Coordenadas de Infinito). LetFem
(8:1) 82, p. 84.
"De Azul" (from Coordenadas de Infinito). LetFem
(8:1) 82, p. 85.
"Espacio" (from Coordenadas de Infinito). LetFem
(8:1) 82, p. 85.
"Instantaneas" (from Coordenadas de Infinito).
LetFem (8:1) 82, p. 87.

4208. VALEK, Miroslav
"Killing Rabbits" (tr. by Kaca Polackova). Sulfur
(2:2, issue 5) 82, p. 124-125.

4209. VALENTA, Helen
"Museum." PikeF (4) Spr 82, p. 11.
"Waking the Dreamer." KanQ (14:1) Wint 82, p. 142.

4210. VALENTIN, Jorge
"Fondo" (from Facsimil Razonable). Mairena (4:9) Spr
82, p. 104.

4211. VALENTINE, Jean
"Snow Landscape, in a Glass Globe" (In memory of
Elizabeth Bishop). Field (27) Aut 82, p. 55.

4212. VALERY, Paul Ambroise
"Palme" (tr. by James Merrill). NewYRB (29:4) Mr 18,
82, p. 10.

4213. VALLADARES, Carmen
"Charla de Sobremesa" (A Isabel, que no acepto
limosnas, from Ruta de Linternas). Mairena
(4:10) Sum-Aut 82, p. 24-25.
"La Presencia Indeleble" (from Ruta de Linternas).
Mairena (4:10) Sum-Aut 82, p. 23-24.
"Soneto Lunatico" (from Ruta de Linternas). Mairena
(4:10) Sum-Aut 82, p. 23.

4214. VALLE, Francisco
"The Walnut Pipe" (tr. by Steven White). NewOR (9:3)
Wint 82, p. 32.

4215. VALLIKANNAN
"Flood (Vellam)" (tr. by P. S. Sundararajan). NewL
(48:3/4) Spr-Sum 82, p. 232.

4216. Van BRUNT, H. L.
"Gradually Shifting." SouthwR (67:1) Wint 82, p.
85.
"The Rain Has Walked Away on Stilts." PoNow (6:6,
issue 36) 82, p. 45.

Van de WOESTIJNE, Karel
See: WOESTIJNE, Karel van de

Van der GRAFT, Guillaume
See: GRAFT, Guillaume van der

Van der MOLEN, W. J.
See: MOLEN, W. J. van der

4217. Van DUYN, Mona
"The Learners." YaleR (71:3) Spr 82, p. 388.

4218. Van DYKE, Patricia
"High Water: Peterborough Bridge." BallSUF (23:3)
Sum 82, p. 68.
"Trick or Treat." Wind (12:45) 82, p. 35.

4219. Van HALTEREN, Marjorie
        "Hungry for Kerouac 1980." *Pig* (8) 80, p. 13.

      Van SAANEN, Christine Dumitriu
        See: DUMITRIU van SAANEN, Christine

4220. Van STEENBURGH, Barbara
        "Identifiers." *ArizQ* (38:2) Sum 82, p. 166.

4221. Van TOORN, Peter
        "Mountain Bath." *AntigR* (50) Sum 82, p. 53.
        "Mountain Fox." *AntigR* (49) Spr 82, p. 7-9.
        "Mountain Storm." *AntigR* (50) Sum 82, p. 52-53.

4222. Van TROYER, Gene
        "Event Horizons." *PortR* (28:1) 82, p. 66-67.

4223. Van WERT, William
        "Cancer Signs." *SouthernHR* (16:1) Wint 82, p. 14.

4224. Van WINCKEL, Nance
        "After Cataract Surgery He Sees." *BelPoJ* (33:1) Aut
          82, p. 36-37.
        "American Promises." *PoNow* (6:4, issue 34) 82, p.
          18.
        "The Five Perfect Solids" (For Johannes Kepler).
          PoetryNW (23:1) Spr 82, p. 41-42.
        "Holding Together" (For my sister). *DenQ* (16:4) Wint
          82, p. 75.
        "The Marking." *PoNow* (6:4, issue 34) 82, p. 18.
        "Pas De Deux." *DenQ* (16:4) Wint 82, p. 76.
        "Reporting the Flood." *MinnR* (NS18) Spr 82, p. 43.
        from The 24 Doors, Advent Calendar Poems: "December
          19" (for Cam, turning 7). *NowestR* (20:1) 82, p.
          97.
        "Thoughts on His Last Morning." *MinnR* (NS18) Spr
          82, p. 44.

4225. VANASCO, Alberto
        "Thirty Years and Their Days" (tr. by Abbey Wolf).
          Spirit (6:2/3) 82, p. 181-182.

4226. VANCE, Thomas
        from Love Song of the Century: "Nobody hurt me ever"
          (tr. of Marta Tikkamen, w. Vera Vance). *Paint*
          (7/8:13/16) 80-81, p. 42-43.

4227. VANCE, Vera
        from Love Song of the Century: "Nobody hurt me ever"
          (tr. of Marta Tikkamen, w. Thomas Vance). *Paint*
          (7/8:13/16) 80-81, p. 42-43.

4228. Vander DOES, Michael
        "The Brothel" (Picasso 1/6/68 II). *PoNow* (7:1, issue
          37) 82, p. 43.
        "The Esoteric Treasures." *PoNow* (7:1, issue 37) 82,
          p. 43.

4229. VANDERBEEK, Kenneth
        "Temptation." *Wind* (12:46) 82, p. 29.

4230. VANDERHAEGHE, Guy
"Death Should Be an Elephant." MalR (63) O 82, p.
68.

4231. VanDEVENTER, George V.
"Passing to Stop." ChrC (99:6) F 24, 82, p. 203.

4232. VARELA, Franklyn P.
"Electric Cowboys, Afternoon TV." RevChic (10:3)
Sum 82, p. 14-15.
"Paulina in the Shadows." RevChic (10:3) Sum 82, p.
15.

VARGAS, Augusto Tamayo
See: TAMAYO VARGAS, Augusto

4233. VARGO, Beth Copeland
"Skunk Season Backlash." HiramPoR (31) Aut-Wint 82,
p. 47.

4234. VASSILIKOS, Vassilis
from My Sun, My Artaxerxes: (1-9) (tr. by the author
and Diana Der Hovanessian). PraS (56:1) Spr 82, p.
28-30.

4235. VAUGHN, Taya
"Child of Wonder." Nimrod (25:2) Spr-Sum 82, p. 75.
"So This Is Where I'm At." Nimrod (25:2) Spr-Sum
82, p. 76.

4236. VEACH, Cindy
"Iceman on the Hudson." CarolQ (35:1) Aut 82, p.
73.

VEAUX, Alexis de
See: DeVEAUX, Alexis

4237. VEENENDAAL, Cornelia
"Maastricht." Ploughs (8:1) 82, p. 133-134.
"Mrs. Cheek." HangL (42) 82, p. 31.
"Our House." HangL (42) 82, p. 30.
"Spring Shower, Connecticut Valley." HangL (42) 82,
p. 34.

4238. VEGA, Janine Pommy
"Dream in Absentia." Gargoyle (15/16) 80, p. 49.
"The Hermit." Bogg (48) 82, p. 7.

4239. VEGA, Jose Luis
"Uno Mas." Areito (8:31) 82, p. 38.

VEGA de MOLINA, Mercedes Gonzalez
See: GONZALEZ VEGA de MOLINA, Mercedes

4240. VELI, Orhan
"To Live" (tr. by Ozcan Yalim, William A. Fielder,
and Dionis Coffin Riggs). DenQ (17:1) Spr 82, p.
86.

VELLIOS, Marta Nichols
<u>See</u>: NICHOLS-VELLIOS, Marta

4241. VENTADOUR, Fanny
"Dithyrambles." <u>Wind</u> (12:46) 82, p. 43.
"More Sensed Than Seen." <u>Wind</u> (12:46) 82, p. 44.

4242. VENTSIAS, Roberta
"Island Happy." <u>KanQ</u> (14:3) Sum 82, p. 119.

4243. VENZKE, Philip
"Spelunking." <u>Abraxas</u> (25/26) 82, p. 102.

4244. VERA LUCERO, Myrna Marina
"Trilogia: Alfonsina, Gabriela, Juana de America."
<u>LetFem</u> (8:1) 82, p. 98-100.

4245. VERNET, Marcelo Luis
"En Realidad." <u>Mairena</u> (4:10) Sum-Aut 82, p. 61.

4246. VERNON, John
"Ashes." <u>VirQR</u> (58:2) Spr 82, p. 278.
"Barns Collapsing." <u>Poetry</u> (140:2) My 82, p. 83.
"Bone Pit." <u>Poetry</u> (140:2) My 82, p. 81-82.
"A Fly." <u>VirQR</u> (58:2) Spr 82, p. 277-278.
"Mud Man." <u>Poetry</u> (140:2) My 82, p. 79-80.
"Planting and Variations." <u>Poetry</u> (140:2) My 82, p.
82.

4247. VERNON, William J.
"Isolation." <u>Wind</u> (12:45) 82, p. 36.
"Lying in a Tent on Rainy Days." <u>HiramPoR</u> (31) Aut-
Wint 82, p. 48.
"Mirage." <u>Wind</u> (12:45) 82, p. 37.
"Myself in Print." <u>Wind</u> (12:45) 82, p. 36.
"Racing in My Valley on the County Road." <u>PoNow</u>
(7:1, issue 37) 82, p. 43.

4248. VERSHEL, Larry
"A Lesson in Observation." <u>MassR</u> (23:4) Wint 82, p.
752.

4249. VESAAS, Tarjei
"Invitation" (tr. by Erik Strand, John Morrow and
Michael Blackburn). <u>Stand</u> (23:3) 82, p. 8.

4250. VEST, Debra Kay
from Dreams Are Full of Business: "Many women sleep
this way, like desperate moths in wool." <u>Abraxas</u>
(25/26) 82, p. 107.
from Dreams Are Full of Business: "Today the sun
strikes the wall of my flat." <u>Abraxas</u> (25/26) 82,
p. 107.

4251. VICKERS, Edward Davin
"Summer of Heat." <u>DekalbLAJ</u> (14:1/4) Aut 80-Sum 81,
p. 120.
"Winter of Wind." <u>DekalbLAJ</u> (14:1/4) Aut 80-Sum 81,
p. 121.

4252. VICTOR, David
       "Life Guard." MichOR (21:1) Wint 82, p. 169.

4253. VIERECK, Peter
       "After the Gleaning" (tr. of Stefan George). LitR
          (26:1) Aut 82, p. 95.
       from Archer in the Marrow, The Applewood Cycles of
          1968-82: "Mek." LitR (25:4) Sum 82, p. 653-663.
       "The Demons of the Cities" (tr. of Georg Heym). LitR
          (26:1) Aut 82, p. 92-93.
       "Form." PoNow (6:6, issue 36) 82, p. 5.
       "The Planted Skull." PoNow (6:6, issue 36) 82, p.
          4-5.
       "Poet." PoNow (6:6, issue 36) 82, p. 4.
       "Song" (tr. of Stefan George). PoNow (6:6, issue 36)
          82, p. 43.
       "To a Vegetarian Living as Pure Spirit." LitR
          (26:1) Aut 82, p. 100.

4254. VIGEE, Claude
       "Beyond" (tr. by J. R. LeMaster and Kenneth Lawrence
          Beaudoin). WebR (7:2) Aut 82, p. 18-19.
       "King of Our Years" (tr. by J. R. LeMaster and
          Kenneth Lawrence Beaudoin). WebR (7:2) Aut 82, p.
          17.
       "Nothing Is Wholly Lost" (tr. by J. R. LeMaster and
          Kenneth Lawrence Beaudoin). WebR (7:2) Aut 82, p.
          19.

4255. VIGIL, Evangelina
       "Es Todo!" RevChic (10:1/2) Wint-Spr 82, p. 142.
       "Mente Joven: Nothin' Like a Pensive Child, Cold
          North Wind Flapping against His Hair and Tender
          Face." RevChic (10:1/2) Wint-Spr 82, p. 145.
       "Pluma Asesina." RevChic (10:1/2) Wint-Spr 82, p.
          148.
       "Por la Calle Zarzamora." RevChic (10:1/2) Wint-Spr
          82, p. 146-147.
       "Ritual en un Instante." RevChic (10:1/2) Wint-Spr
          82, p. 147.
       "Ser Conforme." RevChic (10:1/2) Wint-Spr 82, p.
          141.
       "Was Fun Running 'Round Descalza." RevChic (10:1/2)
          Wint-Spr 82, p. 143-144.

4256. VIKAL, Kumar
       "A Poster" (tr. by Mrinal Parde and David Ray). NewL
          (48:3/4) Spr-Sum 82, p. 206.

4257. VILARINO, Idea
       "To Pass" (tr. by Patsy Boyer and Mary Crow). DenQ
          (16:4) Wint 82, p. 40-41.

4258. VILLALBA, Elba N.
       "Este Aire Que Asfixia." Mairena (4:10) Sum-Aut 82,
          p. 86.

4259. VILLANUA, Robert
       "Jardin Publico" (from Ma Memoire Tatouee -- Mi
          Memoria Tatuada). Mairena (4:9) Spr 82, p. 105.

513   VILLANUEVA

4260. VILLANUEVA, Salvador
      "Un Ojo Permanente Es La Poesia" (from Expulsado del
      Paraiso). Mairena (4:9) Spr 82, p. 104.

4261. VILLANUEVA, Tino
      "Haciendo Apenas la Recoleccion." RevChic (10:1/2)
      Wint-Spr 82, p. 149-150.

4262. VIMAL, G. P.
      "The Girl at Play" (tr. by Vinod Seth). Paint
      (9:17/18) Spr-Aut 82, p. 25.
      "Poem: Let the air sweep by" (tr. by Vinod Seth).
      Paint (9:17/18) Spr-Aut 82, p. 24.

4263. VINCIGUERRA, Louis
      from The Epiphany: (Scene I-III, XII, XXV) (a prose
      poem in filmplay form). MendoR (5) Sum 81, p. 52-
      55.

4264. VINDA
      "The Fish" (tr. by the author). NewL (48:3/4) Spr-
      Sum 82, p. 187.

4265. VINZ, Mark
      "Auction Sale." WestB (10) 82, p. 74-75.
      "A Dream of Fish." WestB (10) 82, p. 75.
      "The Former Student." ColEng 44(1) Ja 82, p. 43.
      "A Gift." KanQ (14:1) Wint 82, p. 104-105.
      "The Ladder Tree." NewL (48:2) Wint 81-82, p. 47.
      "Letters from Old Friends." PoNow (6:6, issue 36)
      82, p. 18.
      "Mac." Northeast (3:12) Wint 81-82, p. 12.
      "Question." PoNow (6:5, issue 35) 82, p. 17.
      "Success Story." PoNow (6:6, issue 36) 82, p. 18.
      "Talk Show." KanQ (14:1) Wint 82, p. 104.
      "The Weird Kid." PoNow (6:6, issue 36) 82, p. 18.

4266. VIRGIL
      from The Aeneid, Book IV, lines 1-53, 68-89, 136-
      172: "Dido in Love" (tr. by Robert Fitzgerald).
      NewYRB (28:21/22) Ja 21, 82, p. 14-15.

4267. VISSER, Liutzen
      "A La Diogenes" (tr. by John Stevens Wade). AntigR
      (48) Wint 82, p. 40.

4268. VIZCARRONDO, Carmelina
      "Voz sin Rumbo." RevIn (10:4) Wint 80-81, p. 550.
      "Yo Misma Era Mi Noche." RevIn (10:4) Wint 80-81,
      p. 549.

4269. VLASAK, Keith
      "Filled Cups." Poem (44) Mr 82, p. 57.
      "Greek Legacy." Poem (44) Mr 82, p. 56.
      "Immortalist." Poem (44) Mr 82, p. 55.

4270. VLIET, R. G.
      "1942." BlackWR (7:2) Spr 81, p. 59-60.
      "In the Pigeon Loft on a Cloudy Day." BlackWR (7:2)
      Spr 81, p. 58.

VOGT   514

4271. VOGT, Mary
      "Occupied." Ascent (8:1) 82, p. 50.
      "Scarecrow." SoCaR (15:1) Aut 82, p. 102.
      "William." Ascent (8:1) 82, p. 50.

4272. VOIGT, Ellen Bryant
      "Blue Ridge." Antaeus (47) Aut 82, p. 33-34.
      "The Couple." Ploughs (8:2/3) 82, p. 262.
      "Exile." Ploughs (8:2/3) 82, p. 260.
      "New England Graveyard." Ploughs (8:2/3) 82, p.
        261.
      "Pittsylvania Country." Poetry (139:5) F 82, p.
        269.
      "Quarrel." Poetry (139:5) F 82, p. 270.
      "The Spire." NewYorker (58:16) Je 7, 82, p. 38.
      "The Spring." Ploughs (8:2/3) 82, p. 259.
      "Sweet Everlasting." Antaeus (47) Aut 82, p. 32.
      "Why She Says No." Poetry (139:5) F 82, p. 268.

4273. VOLD, Jan Erik
      "Like a Tarn in the Wood" (tr. by Astrid Rudjord and
        Albert Ward). Stand (23:3) 82, p. 27.
      "The Wood-Carver" (tr. by Astrid Rudjord and Albert
        Ward). Stand (23:3) 82, p. 26.

4274. VOLLMAR, Jim
      "Midwinter Manoeuvres." Gargoyle (17/18) 81, p. 14.

      VOLMAR, Cesar Abreu
      See: ABREU-VOLMAR, Cesar

      Von FREYTAG-LORINGHOVEN, Elsa, Baroness
      See: FREYTAG-LORINGHOVEN, Elsa von, Baroness

      Von GOETHE, Johann Wolfgang
      See: GOETHE, Johann Wolfgang von

4275. VONEK, Peter
      "Poem: Lime eats rock." CrossC (4:2/3) 82, p. 36.

4276. VOROG, Valentyn
      "We Who Have No Future: Fragments of a Credo, in
        Verse" (tr. by Askold Melnyczuk). Agni (16) 82, p.
        133-145.

4277. VOWLES, Richard B.
      "Joe Hill In Prison" (tr. of Goran Printz-Pahlson).
        PoetryE (8) Aut 82, p. 66.

4278. VYHLIDAL, Oldrich
      "At the Bottom of the Day" (tr. by Miroslav Holub
        and David Young). Field (27) Aut 82, p. 77.

4279. WACHTEL, Chuck
      "Hans Frank, the Butcher of Poland, Takes a
        Rorschach Test." HangL (42) 82, p. 33.
      "Purely Coincidental." HangL (42) 82, p. 32.

4280. WADE, Cory
"July in Georgia." SouthernPR (22:1) Spr 82, p. 54-
55.

4281. WADE, James R.
"The Evangelist." ChrC (99:3) Ja 27, 82, p. 83.

4282. WADE, John Stevens
"A La Diogenes" (tr. of Liutzen Visser). AntigR
(48) Wint 82, p. 40.
"Dusk" (tr. of W. J. van der Molen). AntigR (48)
Wint 82, p. 39.
"Farewell" (tr. of W. J. van der Molen). AntigR (48)
Wint 82, p. 40.
"Poem: To pray is to beat language out of lead" (tr.
of Hans Keller). WebR (7:1) Spr 82, p. 39.
"While Writing" (tr. of Guillaume van der Graft).
WebR (7:1) Spr 82, p. 38.

4283. WADE, Seth
"Easy." PoNow (7:1, issue 37) 82, p. 43.

4284. WAGNER, Alex
"French Apache Dance." NewYorker (58:44) D 20, 82,
p. 44.

4285. WAGNER, Anneliese
"The Hat." WebR (7:2) Aut 82, p. 71.
"Walking Together, Ducking Branches." WestB (11)
82, p. 97.

4286. WAGNER, Charles
"Train Whistle." LittleBR (3:1) Aut 82, p. 54.
"Winding a Biscuit." LittleBR (3:1) Aut 82, p. 44.

4287. WAGNER, D. R.
"The Body of Dream in Autopsy." Abraxas (25/26) 82,
p. 11.
"It bothers me." Abraxas (25/26) 82, p. 12-13.

4288. WAGNER, Maryfrances
"Duck Raking." KanQ (14:3) Sum 82, p. 116.

4289. WAGNER, Phil
"Autumn Glory." Sam (32:3, issue 127) 82, p. 21.

4290. WAGONER, David
"The Author Says Goodbye to His Hero." KanQ (14:2)
Spr 82, p. 35.
"Black Bear." Telescope (1) Spr 81, p. 65.
"Canticle for Xmas Eve." GeoR (36:4) Wint 82, p.
729.
"Earthbird." VirQR (58:1) Wint 82, p. 57-58.
"The Escape from Monkey Island." VirQR (58:1) Wint
82, p. 58-59.
"The Fire-Bringers." Poetry (140:6) S 82, p. 344.
"The Horsemen." Poetry (140:6) S 82, p. 341-342.
"Lepiota." MalR (63) O 82, p. 88.
"Mapmaking." QW (14) Spr-Sum 82, p. 34.
"Moth Flight." QW (14) Spr-Sum 82, p. 32-33.

WAGONER   516

"Near the End of the Story." <u>MalR</u> (63) O 82, p. 85-
    86.
"Old River." <u>MalR</u> (63) O 82, p. 88.
"The Open Staircase" (a proposal for a sculpture in
    the manner of George Segal). <u>MissouriR</u> (5:2) Wint
    81-82, p. 44-45.
"A Rose Drill" (found poem). <u>Kayak</u> (58) Ja 82, p.
    36-37.
"Salmon Run." <u>WestHR</u> (36:2) Sum 82, p. 115.
"Some Other Roads." <u>Telescope</u> (1) Spr 81, p. 63.
"Song after Midnight." <u>Poetry</u> (140:6) S 82, p. 345.
"Stump Speech." <u>Atl</u> (250:2) Ag 82, p. 65.
"Their Bodies" (To the students of anatomy at
    Indiana University). <u>Poetry</u> (141:1) O 82, p. 24.
"Under the Raven's Nest." <u>Poetry</u> (140:6) S 82, p.
    343.
"Washing a Young Rhinoceros." <u>Atl</u> (250:6) D 82, p.
    86.
"The Wrong Way." <u>MalR</u> (63) O 82, p. 86-87.
"A Young Girl with a Pitcher Full of Water." <u>MalR</u>
    (63) O 82, p. 88.

4291. WAHLE, F. Keith
    "The Children in Your Hair" (on a line stolen from
        Rick Stansberger). <u>WestB</u> (11) 82, p. 46.
    "The Great Meaning." <u>Abraxas</u> (25/26) 82, p. 22-23.

4292. WAIN, John
    "Victor Neep 1921-1979." <u>AntigR</u> (50) Sum 82, p. 75-
        79.

4293. WAINWRIGHT, Andy
    "The Other" (for Mark Strand). <u>Waves</u> (10:3) Wint 82,
        p. 53.

4294. WAKOSKI, Diane
    "A Letter to Wang Wei on the Season of Tumultuous
        Magicians" (instructions for identification).
        <u>CentR</u> (26:1) Wint 82, p. 58-60.
    "Un Morceau en Forme de Poire" (for Thomas
        Parkinson). <u>CentR</u> (26:1) Wint 82, p. 51-54.
    "Sally Plum" (for Sally Arteseros, who has never
        liked her name). <u>CentR</u> (26:1) Wint 82, p. 54-55.
    "Saturday Night" (for Barbara Drake). <u>CentR</u> (26:1)
        Wint 82, p. 55-58.

4295. WALBERG, Kristine
    "Buffalo." <u>PoetryCR</u> (3:3) Spr 82, p. 6.
    "Hiding from Brother." <u>PoetryCR</u> (3:3) Spr 82, p. 6.
    "On Rainy Days." <u>PoetryCR</u> (3:3) Spr 82, p. 6.

4296. WALD, Diane
    "The Moon's Waxy Refinement." <u>MissouriR</u> (5:2) Wint
        81-82, p. 52.
    "Night Rate." <u>MissouriR</u> (5:2) Wint 81-82, p. 51.
    "We Are Getting All Upset over Nothing." <u>BlackWR</u>
        (7:2) Spr 81, p. 17.
    "Wintering on the Islands." <u>BlackWR</u> (7:2) Spr 81,
        p. 18.

4297. WALDECKI, Michael
       "Poetics #5." Bogg (49) 82, p. 23.

       WALDMAN, Marianne
       See: WOLFE, Marianne

4298. WALDROP, Rosmarie
       "Figures of the Eye." Sulfur (2:3, issue 6) 82, p.
       29-31.

4299. WALKER, David
       "Slips." NowestR (20:2/3) 82, p. 272-273.
       "To the Select Men of the Town of Alna: April 11,
       1821 ... Abraham Walker." NowestR (20:2/3) 82, p.
       276.

4300. WALKER, Don T.
       "Imposed." LittleBR (3:1) Aut 82, p. 85.
       "No Rejections." LittleBR (2:4) Sum 82, p. 64.
       "Olfactory Pleasures." LittleBR (3:1) Aut 82, p.
       85.
       "Results Guaranteed." LittleBR (2:4) Sum 82, p. 53.
       "Super Contortionist." LittleBR (3:1) Aut 82, p.
       85.

4301. WALKER, Jeanne Murray
       "For My Daughter's Twenty-First Birthday." Iowa
       (12:2/3) Spr-Sum 81, p. 366.
       "The Green Pepper Talks about Life and Death."
       LittleM (13:3/4) 82, p. 22.
       "The Last Migration: Amherst, Mass., Winter, 1981"
       (for Stephanie Kraft). Iowa (12:2/3) Spr-Sum 81,
       p. 362-363.
       "Making the Painting." Iowa (12:2/3) Spr-Sum 81, p.
       360-361.
       "Necessity." Iowa (12:2/3) Spr-Sum 81, p. 365.
       "Northern Liberties." Iowa (12:2/3) Spr-Sum 81, p.
       364.
       "Physics." Iowa (12:2/3) Spr-Sum 81, p. 358-359.
       "Some Other Body." GeoR (36:2) Sum 82, p. 383.
       "The Witch: Jump Rope Rhymes." PraS (56:3) Aut 82,
       p. 25-26.

4302. WALKER, Steve
       "In a Week or So." Bogg (49) 82, p. 49.

4303. WALLACE, Bronwen
       "Toward Morning." Quarry (31:3) Sum 82, p. 16-17.

4304. WALLACE, Ronald
       "The Art of Love." Atl (250:1) Jl 82, p. 45.
       "At the Barber's." NewL (49:1) Aut 82, p. 66.
       "Clams." Poem (46) N 82, p. 17.
       "The Dentist's Disappearance" (for E. N. Vogel,
       1932-1980). PraS (56:3) Aut 82, p. 46.
       "Gray on Gray" (after a painting by Mark Rothko).
       Poem (46) N 82, p. 16.
       "Newborn." Poem (46) N 82, p. 15.
       "Picture of Two Bugs, Hugging." PraS (56:3) Aut 82,
       p. 47.

"Poison Ivy." PoNow (6:6, issue 36) 82, p. 37.
"Well." NewL (49:1) Aut 82, p. 67.

4305. WALLACE, Smith
      "Ahab Never Learns." StoneC (9:3/4) Spr-Sum 82, p.
      61.

4306. WALLBANK, Jean
      "Baby, We Ben Here Before!" Grain (10:3) Ag 82, p.
      13.

4307. WALRATH, Norma
      "Educators' Conference." EngJ (71:6) O 82, p. 30.

4308. WALSH, Arlene
      "Spring Comes to Robert Frost." KanQ (14:3) Sum 82,
      p. 201.

4309. WALSH, Chad
      "333." LitR (25:4) Sum 82, p. 666.
      "Embryonic Thoughts." LitR (25:4) Sum 82, p. 667.
      "For Eva on Her Seventieth Birthday." LitR (25:4)
      Sum 82, p. 669.
      "The Tenant Farmer's Half-Wit Son." MichQR (21:1)
      Wint 82, p. 135.
      "Two Elegies for Anne Sexton." LitR (25:4) Sum 82,
      p. 668-669.

4310. WALSH, Harry
      "My Father." AmerS (51:3) Sum 82, p. 324.

4311. WALSH, Marty
      "Quincy." WindO (41) Aut-Wint 82-83, p. 11.
      "Rumplestiltskin." HiramPoR (31) Aut-Wint 82, p.
      49-50.
      "A Twig Snaps." WindO (41) Aut-Wint 82-83, p. 10.

4312. WALSH, Phyllis
      "Cutting Japanese Lanterns in Middle Age." Abraxas
      (25/26) 82, p. 68.
      "Fishing over Weedbeds." Tendril (13) Sum 82, p.
      73.

4313. WALSH, Rosemary
      "Got to Get It Together Boogie Shuffle" (a chant for
      light and dark voices). Bogg (49) 82, p. 5-6.
      "Rejoyce -- for my highdriving boyo." Bogg (48) 82,
      p. 5.

4314. WALTER, Virginia
      "You." SoCaR (14:2) Spr 82, p. 47.

4315. WALTHALL, Hugh
      "Typing Test" (for Jennifer Cogley). Shen (33:1) 81-
      82, p. 99.
      "Will and Testament." Shen (33:1) 81-82, p. 98.

4316. WALTON, Peter
      "The Spring at Rhyd-Nanty." Stand (23:2) 82, p. 43.

4317. WANG, Wei
        "Duckweed Pond" (tr. by Joseph Lisowski). WestB (11)
        82, p. 99.
        "Gold Dust Spring" (tr. by Joseph Lisowski). WestB
        (11) 82, p. 98.

4318. WANIEK, Marilyn
        "Light under the Door." OhioR (28) 82, p. 46-47.

4319. WARD, Albert
        "Like a Tarn in the Wood" (tr. of Jan Erik Vold, w.
        Astrid Rudjord). Stand (23:3) 82, p. 27.
        "The Wood-Carver" (tr. of Jan Erik Vold, w. Astrid
        Rudjord). Stand (23:3) 82, p. 26.

4320. WARD, Cecilia, Sister
        "Annunciation." AntigR (49) Spr 82, p. 69.
        "New Year's Eve." AntigR (49) Spr 82, p. 69.

4321. WARD, Dave
        "Liverpool Streets." Bogg (48) 82, p. 43.

4322. WARD, Dorothy
        "Juarez." Vis (10) 82, p. 31.
        "Late September in El Paso." Vis (10) 82, p. 32.

4323. WARD, Matthew
        "The Two of Us." Shen (33:3) 82, p. 66.

4324. WARDEN, Marine Robert
        "In the Shadows." Catalyst (Erotica Issue) 82, p.
        28.
        "Portrait of You: Number 1" (from Beyond the
        Straits). Catalyst (Erotica Issue) 82, p. 11.
        "When." Catalyst (Erotica Issue) 82, p. 28.
        "You Are Using My Body." Catalyst (Erotica Issue)
        82, p. 28.

4325. WARNE, Candice
        "Emergency Room Orderly." SouthernPR (22:1) Spr 82,
        p. 20.

4326. WARNER, Catherine A.
        "Beginnings." Paint (9:17/18) Spr-Aut 82, p. 9.

4327. WARREN, James E., Jr.
        "A Sister's Room and the Weather." Paint (9:17/18)
        Spr-Aut 82, p. 11.

4328. WARREN, Robert Penn
        "Chief Joseph of the Nez Perce, Who Called
        Themselves the Nimpau -- 'The Real People'" (to
        James Dickey). GeoR (36:2) Sum 82, p. 269-313.
        "The Distance Between." SewanR (90:4) Aut 82, p.
        497-498.
        "If Snakes Were Blue." Atl (250:4) O 82, p. 46.
        "Rumor at Twilight." NewYorker (58:22) Jl 19, 82,
        p. 32.

"Was It One of the Long Hunters of Kentucky Who
  Discovered Boone at Sunset?" SewanR (90:4) Aut 82,
  p. 498-499.
"The Whole Question." AmerPoR (11:6) N-D 82, p. 47.
"Why Boy Came to Lonely Place." NewEngR (5:1/2)
  Aut-Wint 82, p. 163.
"You Sort Old Letters." AmerPoR (11:6) N-D 82, p.
  47.

4329. WARREN, Rosanna
"Echo." AntR (40:4) Aut 82, p. 434-435.
"Snow." PoetC (14:1) 82, p. 13.
"Witness." PoetC (14:1) 82, p. 11-12.

4330. WARSHAWSKI, Morrie
"The Woman Jumping." ModernPS (11:1/2) 82, p. 151-
  152.

4331. WARWICK, John
"A Ballad of Crabs and the Sea." SouthernPR (22:1)
  Spr 82, p. 41.

4332. WASILEWSKI, Valeria
"It Was a Near Miss" (tr. of Stanislaw Baranczak).
  Abraxas (25/26) 82, p. 19.
"What's Being Played?" (tr. of Stanislaw Baranczak).
  Abraxas (25/26) 82, p. 20.

4333. WATERHOUSE, Elizabeth
"It's Not That I'm Unfeeling, But." Poetry (141:3)
  D 82, p. 167-168.
"Slim Pickings." Poetry (141:3) D 82, p. 163-164.
"Weather Permitting." Poetry (141:3) D 82, p. 165-
  166.

4334. WATERMAN, Cary
"Bullwhacker" (from The Outlaw Poems of Calamity
  Jane). Nimrod (25:2) Spr-Sum 82, p. 40.
"The Dance." Nimrod (25:2) Spr-Sum 82, p. 39.
"The Farmer's Wife." PoNow (6:4, issue 34) 82, p.
  26.
"Listening." PoNow (6:6, issue 36) 82, p. 19.
"Me, Learning to Dance." PoNow (6:4, issue 34) 82,
  p. 26.
"Mending Clothes on New Year's Day." PoNow (6:5,
  issue 35) 82, p. 20.
"Train Song." PoNow (6:5, issue 35) 82, p. 20.

4335. WATERMAN, Wanda
"Train-Ride." PottPort (4) 82-83, p. 41.

4336. WATERS, Mary Ann
"Attack." SouthernPR (22:1) Spr 82, p. 21.
"Daughter, Mother, Sister, Muse." PoetryNW (23:3)
  Aut 82, p. 42.
"Gone." Telescope (3) Sum 82, p. 19.
"Luck." PraS (56:3) Aut 82, p. 77-78.

4337. WATERS, Michael
"Dogs in the Storm" (after Akhmatova). AntR (40:4)
Aut 82, p. 437.
"Learning to Live with the Rain" (For William
Stafford). PoNow (6:5, issue 35) 82, p. 36.
"The Mystery of the Caves." Poetry (139:5) F 82, p.
263-264.
"The Wheel on my Neighbor's Lawn." PoNow (6:5,
issue 35) 82, p. 36.

4338. WATSON, Ferne
"A Sense of Smell." DekalbLAJ (14:1/4) Aut 80-Sum
81, p. 95.

4339. WATSON, Lawrence
"A Woman Remembers." Northeast (3:12) Wint 81-82,
p. 5.

4340. WATSON, Norbert
"Electric Boogie." CrossC (4:2/3) 82, p. 37.

4341. WATTS, Enos
"El Paria (Cain)." PottPort (4) 82-83, p. 26.
"Two Figures Observed through Snowdrift." PottPort
(4) 82-83, p. 52.

4342. WAUGAMAN, Charles A.
"Gould's Pandoras." CapeR (18:1) Wint 82, p. 11.
"The Substitute." CapeR (18:1) Wint 82, p. 10.

4343. WAYMAN, Tom
"Paper." Poetry (141:3) D 82, p. 156-157.
"Suburban Pedagogy." LittleM (13:3/4) 82, p. 100.
"Trial." Poetry (141:3) D 82, p. 158.

4344. WEATHERS, Winston
"Journey to Iona." Poetry (141:2) N 82, p. 84-90.
"Le Clairvoyant & les Trois." SouthernR (18:3) Sum
82, p. 565.
"The Man Who Couldn't Sleep" (Notes from a Private
Journal: Nine Poems). Poem (45) Jl 82, p. 23-26.
"The Private Magician, the Performance of Love."
SewanR (90:3) Sum 82, p. 406-407.

4345. WEAVER, Michael S.
"The Race Problem." Obs (7:2/3) Sum-Wint 81, p.
217-218.
"South African Communion." HangL (42) 82, p. 49.
"USA Truckers." HangL (42) 82, p. 50-51.

4346. WEBER, Marc
"Arching Your Spine." PoNow (6:5, issue 35) 82, p.
41.
"Forest Mushrooms." PoNow (6:5, issue 35) 82, p.
41.

4347. WEBSTER, Diane
"Blind Faith." Wind (12:44) 82, p. 4.

4348. WEDELD, Bodil Dyb
      "Houses" (tr. by Anne Born). Stand (23:3) 82, p. 49.

4349. WEEDEN, Craig
      "The Waistband, IV. Death by Cake." PoNow (6:5,
      issue 35) 82, p. 46.
      "We Finally Agree." PoNow (7:1, issue 37) 82, p.
      44.

4350. WEEDON, Syd
      "Do you stand upwind." Sam (32:3, issue 127) 82, p.
      49.
      "Downtown, Louisville." Wind (12:46) 82, p. 45.
      "The Portfolio of Unknown Persons." Sam (33:2,
      issue 130) 82, p. 1-16.
      "A Stranger in Colorado." Wind (12:46) 82, p. 45-
      46.

4351. WEEKES, Barbara
      "Aware." StoneC (9:3/4) Spr-Sum 82, p. 30.

4352. WEEKS, Ramona
      "The Surrealist Vists Reno." VirQR (58:4) Aut 82,
      p. 694.

4353. WEERASINGHE, Asoka
      "Beale Street, Windsor, Ontario." WritersL O-N 82,
      p. 29.
      "Haiku (the Newfoundland Suite)." WritersL Je 82,
      p. 6.
      "Solidarity" (for Chris Bartoszewicz). WritersL O-N
      82, p. 37.

4354. WEETMAN, Helen
      "Cold as Sunshine." Bogg (48) 82, p. 60.

      WEI, Wang
      See: WANG, Wei

4355. WEIDMAN, Phil
      "Buffer." WormR (22:4, issue 88) 82, p. 128.
      "Sense of Proportions." WormR (22:4, issue 88) 82,
      p. 128.

4356. WEIGL, Bruce
      "For the Wife Beater's Wife." NewEngR (5:1/2) Aut-
      Wint 82, p. 110.
      "Girl at the Chu Lai Laundry." BlackWR (7:2) Spr
      81, p. 82.
      "Homage to Elvis, Homage to the Fathers." NewEngR
      (5:1/2) Aut-Wint 82, p. 111-112.
      "Hope." TriQ (55) Aut 82, p. 141-142.
      "Mercy." MissouriR (6:1) Aut 82, p. 39.
      "Song for a Lost First Cousin." TriQ (55) Aut 82,
      p. 144.
      "Song of Napalm" (for my wife). TriQ (55) Aut 82, p.
      145-146.
      "Sun." TriQ (55) Aut 82, p. 143.

4357. WEIGL, Etta Ruth
"Ein, Zwei, Drei." PoNow (7:1, issue 37) 82, p. 44.
"Noon Pool." PoNow (7:1, issue 37) 82, p. 44.

4358. WEIMER, Catherine
"The Sea Wall." AntigR (51) Aut 82, p. 26.

4359. WEINGARTEN, Roger
"Sometimes, at Thirty-Six." NewYorker (58:38) N 8,
82, p. 44.
"Spillway." SouthernPR (22:1) Spr 82, p. 37.

4360. WEINLEIN, Gregg Thomas
"At the University Placement Office." EngJ (71:2) F
82, p. 100.

4361. WEINMAN, Billy Razz
"Song of the Wallowing Punkster." KanQ (14:1) Wint
82, p. 141.

4362. WEINMAN, Paul
"Four Fish Hang." UnderRM (1:2) Aut 82, p. 33.
"Just Because He Sent Me." Pig (9) 82, p. 54.
"Just Because He Sent Me." PikeF (4) Spr 82, p. 25.
"Wind Licking." UnderRM (1:2) Aut 82, p. 34.

4363. WEINSTEIN, David
"Speak to the Rock" (Numbers 20:8-11). LitR (25:3)
Spr 82, p. 345.

4364. WEISMILLER, Edward
"The Men from My Childhood" (tr. of Krassin
Himmirsky, w. the author). Vis (10) 82, p. 28.

4365. WEISS, David
"Against Prophecy." NoAmR (267:3) S 82,p. 70.
"Cameo." AntR (40:4) Aut 82, p. 433.
"The Listener." PortR (28:2) 82, p. 127.
"Maine Carpenter." PortR (28:2) 82, p. 126.

4366. WEISS, Jason
"Matter of Friends" (for Alfredo Plank, tr. of Tomas
Guido Lavalle). PraS (56:1) Spr 82, p. 42-43.

4367. WEISS, Sanford
"The Bell." Kayak (58) Ja 82, p. 47.
"Nineteen Fifty-four." Kayak (58) Ja 82, p. 46.

4368. WEISS, Theodore
"A Building." TriQ (55) Aut 82, p. 154-155.
"The Death of Fathers." TriQ (55) Aut 82, p. 151-
153.
"Earthrise." TriQ (55) Aut 82, p. 149-150.
"The Here and Now" (for Yehuda Amichai). TriQ (55)
Aut 82, p. 147-148.

4369. WEITZMAN, Sarah Brown
"Incest." PoNow (7:1, issue 37) 82, p. 44.
"Pearls." DekalbLAJ (14:1/4) Aut 80-Sum 81, p. 97.
"Talent." PoetC (14:2) 82, p. 43.

4370. WELBURN, Ron
"Booker's Blues" (for Booker Ervin, in memorium).
Abraxas (25/26) 82, p. 35.

4371. WELCH, Don
"For the Pigeons." EnPas (13) 82, p. 12.
"Nouns." SouthernHR (16:4) Aut 82, p. 302.
"The Shunning" (among Ammanites, rural Iowa). PraS
(56:4) Wint 82-83, p. 76-77.

4372. WELCH, Liliane
"Engraver." AntigR (49) Spr 82, p. 111-112.
"Engraver: Acid Work." Grain (10:3) Ag 82, p. 43.
"Goldsmith: Forging." Grain (10:3) Ag 82, p. 40.
"In the Dolomites: The Sass Maor's Thighs."
PoetryCR (4:2) Wint 82, p. 6.
"Old Age Blues." PottPort (4) 82-83, p. 10.
"Orion's Legs." PottPort (4) 82-83, p. 17.
"Potter: Throwing the Clay." Grain (10:3) Ag 82, p.
42.
"Pregnant in Winter." PottPort (4) 82-83, p. 23.
"Weaver: The Rug." Grain (10:3) Ag 82, p. 41.
"Weaver: Wall Hanging." Grain (10:3) Ag 82, p. 41.
"Whittler: Skewer and Firmer." Grain (10:3) Ag 82,
p. 46.
"Whittler: Wood Dreams." Grain (10:3) Ag 82, p. 45.
"Winter." CanLit (93) Sum 82, p. 107.
"Woodturner" (for Victor McLaughlin). PottPort (4)
82-83, p. 40.

4373. WELLER, Sonia Topper
"On Avoiding Bankruptcy." WormR (22:3, issue 87)
82, p.112.

4374. WELLS, Katherine
"Three Gifts." Kayak (59) Je 82, p. 33.

4375. WELLS, Peter
"There is a way you know." MendoR (6) Sum 81, p.
42.
"You spend your life accumulating knowledge."
MendoR (6) Sum 81, p. 30.

4376. WELLS, Thomas
"2 AM Bar (Columbia Station)." Vis (9) 82, p. 29-
30.
"She Is Purple." Vis (10) 82, p. 11.

4377. WELLS, Will
"Picking the Pears Too Soon" (in memory of James
Wright). BelPoJ (33:1) Aut 82, p. 14.
"Spooking." HiramPoR (31) Aut-Wint 82, p. 51.
"This Fascination with the Dark." WestB (11) 82, p.
82.
"The Wanderer." BelPoJ (33:1) Aut 82, p. 15.

4378. WENDELL, Leilah
"Here at the Edge." WritersL Je 82, p. 22.
"Twilyte's Enigma." WritersL Je 82, p. 13.

4379. WENDT, Ingrid
       "All We Can Use" (for Enid). PoetC (14:2) 82, p. 50-
       51.

4380. WENDT, Viola
       "Elegy for Ruth." Abraxas (25/26) 82, p. 87.

4381. WERMUTH, Nick
       "Late Spring in New Brunswick." PottPort (4) 82-83,
       p. 22.
       "Standing Stones." PottPort (4) 82-83, p. 42.

4382. WERNER, Warren
       "The Cove." CapeR (17:2) Sum 82, p. 15.
       "Desire, a Heliotropic Tract." HiramPoR (33) Aut-
       Wint 82, p. 22.
       "Flight of the Children." CapeR (17:2) Sum 82, p.
       13.
       "On Flying." HiramPoR (33) Aut-Wint 82, p. 23.
       "The Redemption of the Lost." CapeR (17:2) Sum 82,
       p. 14.

       WERT, William van
       See: Van WERT, William

4383. WEST, Alexa
       "For You." WestCR (17:1) Je 82, p. 3.

4384. WEST, Jean
       "The Ithaca Clinic for Women." Confr (24) Sum 82,
       p. 94-95.

4385. WEST, John Foster
       "High Noon in Pompeii" (Cenotaph for Guy Owen).
       SouthernR (18:4) Aut 82, p. 836-837.

4386. WEST, Kathleene
       "Autumn Equinox, Northeast Nebraska." CutB (19)
       Aut-Wint 82, p. 22-23.
       "Grandmother's Garden." PoetryNW (23:2) Sum 82, p.
       10-11.

4387. WEST, Michael
       "Contentment the Howards Felt." PoNow (7:1, issue
       37) 82, p. 44.

4388. WESTCOTT, W. F.
       "Captain Dreamer." WritersL O-N 82, p. 6.
       "Identity." WritersL S 82, p. 15.

4389. WESTERFIELD, Hargis
       "Drinking Alone at the 'Grain Exchange' in Bayard,
       Nebraska." Wind (12:44) 82, p. 40.
       "From Hobo Days." Wind (12:44) 82, p. 40.

4390. WESTERFIELD, Nancy G.
       "Brass-Rubbing." ChrC (99:1) Ja 6-13, 82, p. 19.
       "The Cat-cum-Woman." Nimrod (25:2) Spr-Sum 82, p.
       72.
       "Nebraska Moons." FourQt (31:3) Spr 82, p. 23.

"Omniport." <u>Nimrod</u> (25:2) Spr-Sum 82, p. 47.

4391. WESTWOOD, Norma
"Cupid and Psyche." <u>Bogg</u> (48) 82, p. 25.
"Illness." <u>Vis</u> (10) 82, p. 18.

4392. WETTEROTH, Bruce
"Alpine Memory." <u>OhioR</u> (27) 82, p. 80.
"A Bottle Emptying into Itself." <u>PoNow</u> (7:1, issue 37) 82, p. 45.
"Chain Fence." <u>PoNow</u> (7:1, issue 37) 82, p. 45.
"Clearing Away a Doubt." <u>OhioR</u> (27) 82, p. 69.
"Drive." <u>OhioR</u> (27) 82, p. 72.
"Getting Lost." <u>PoNow</u> (7:1, issue 37) 82, p. 45.
"The Great Wind of January 1978." <u>OhioR</u> (27) 82, p. 82.
"Keeping One's Distance." <u>OhioR</u> (27) 82, p. 74.
"Leaving Another Life Behind." <u>OhioR</u> (27) 82, p. 81.
"Life in Progress." <u>OhioR</u> (27) 82, p. 83.
"Looking Up at Noon." <u>OhioR</u> (27) 82, p. 70.
"Making My Own Path." <u>OhioR</u> (27) 82, p. 73.
"Media in Vita." <u>OhioR</u> (27) 82, p. 84.
"Mystery Hitchhiker." <u>PoNow</u> (7:1, issue 37) 82, p. 45.
"On a Rainy Day I Remember Magna Mater." <u>OhioR</u> (27) 82, p. 79.
"Paths around the Lake." <u>OhioR</u> (27) 82, p. 67.
"Remembering Rosalind." <u>OhioR</u> (27) 82, p. 78.
"Sleep and Poetry." <u>OhioR</u> (27) 82, p. 71.
"A Small Cry." <u>OhioR</u> (27) 82, p. 68.
"Sycamore." <u>OhioR</u> (27) 82, p. 77.
"Tomorrow in Parkersburg." <u>OhioR</u> (27) 82, p. 76.
"Unhistorical Moment." <u>OhioR</u> (27) 82, p. 75.

4393. WEXELBLATT, Robert
"The Children inside the Mountain." <u>LitR</u> (25:3) Spr 82, p. 347-348.
"Inditing." <u>LitR</u> (25:3) Spr 82, p. 346-347.

4394. WHALEN, Tom
"The Bathtub Man." <u>PoNow</u> (6:6, issue 36) 82, p. 13.

4395. WHARTON, Calvin
"How to Win a Fistfight." <u>Waves</u> (10:3) Wint 82, p. 59.
"Moon in Cloud." <u>Waves</u> (10:3) Wint 82, p. 74.
"Separation." <u>Waves</u> (10:3) Wint 82, p. 58.

4396. WHEALDON, Everett
"O Jesus! <u>Sam</u> (32:3, issue 127) 82, p. 15.

4397. WHEATCROFT, John
"After Words for Carl Woods" (Killed on Route #29, Near the Virginia Center for the Creative Arts, February 22, 1979). <u>CapeR</u> (17:2) Sum 82, p. 48-49.

4398. WHEELER, Jackson
"The Nouns of War" (found poem) <u>Kayak</u> (60) O 82, p. 19.

4399. WHEELER, Sylvia
        "Taking Down Chagall's Blue Bull." CharR (8:1) Spr
        82, p. 39.

4400. WHIPPLE, George
        "The Flight into Egypt." AntigR (49) Spr 82, p. 36.
        "The Undertakers." AntigR (49) Spr 82, p. 36.

4401. WHISLER, Robert F.
        "Deus ex Machina" (for S. G.) Poem (45) Jl 82, p.
        27.
        "Diffusions V, Machines." Poem (45) Jl 82, p. 28.
        "Penelope and Me." ArizQ (38:4) Wint 82, p. 292.
        "Russell Elias." Confr (23) Wint 82, p. 120.
        "Stones." HiramPoR (32) Spr-Sum 82, p. 46.

4402. WHITE, Carol
        "Disenchanted." WritersL Jl 82, p. 23.

4403. WHITE, Carol Ann
        "The Valley in the Shadow." SouthernPR (22:1) Spr
        82, p. 18.

4404. WHITE, Gail
        "Beginning the Prayer." ChrC (99:2) Ja 20, 82, p.
        51.
        "Breaking into Morning." Poem (46) N 82, p. 26.
        "Mirage." Northeast (3:12) Wint 81-82, p. 11.
        "Out of the Palm of Your Hand." Poem (46) N 82, p.
        28-29.
        "The Panther Ate the Peacocks." Bogg (48) 82, p.
        13-14.
        "Retreat at St. Scholastica's Priory." ChrC (99:17)
        My 12, 82, p. 557.
        "Shelling Pecans." Poem (46) N 82, p. 27.
        "To All of Us Taking It Lightly." Poem (46) N 82,
        p. 30-31.

4405. WHITE, J. P.
        "Bird at the Window." Tendril (12) Wint 82, p. 68.
        "Cutthroat on a Full Moon." HiramPoR (31) Aut-Wint
        82, p. 52.
        "Dove." MassR (23:3) Aut 82, p. 524.
        "Of a Night Fed With No Forgetfulness" (The war
        never stops making holes). MassR (23:3) Aut 82, p.
        525.
        "One Morning Another Good Man Is Gone." Poetry
        (140:2) My 82, p. 101.
        "Vermont Gray, a Train, a Boat." Poetry (140:2) My
        82, p. 100.
        "Why I Can't Live in Cheyenne, Anymore." Poetry
        (140:2) My 82, p. 99.

4406. WHITE, James L.
        "The Deaf Crone" PraS (56:2) Sum 82, p. 86.

4407. WHITE, Mary Jane
        "Morning." NewEngR (4:3) Spr 82, p. 438.
        "A Woman Who Married a Man." NewEngR (4:3) Spr 82,
        p. 437.

4408. WHITE, Mimi
      "A Little Lesson." ConcPo (15:1) Spr 82, p. 77-78.

4409. WHITE, Patrick
      "First Snow." WestCR (17:1) Je 82, p. 4.

4410. WHITE, Steven
      "The Walnut Pipe" (tr. of Francisco Valle). NewOR
      (9:3) Wint 82, p. 32.

4411. WHITE, William M.
      "Genesis." Wind (12:46) 82, p. 31.
      "Inside the Wind." SouthernR (18:4) Aut 82, p. 834.
      "Palm Beach in August." SouthernR (18:4) Aut 82, p.
      835.

4412. WHITEHEAD, Timothy
      "January." SmPd (19:2, issue 55) Spr 82, p. 28.

4413. WHITELAW, Keith
      "Fat Man on a Train." Bogg (48) 82, p. 47.

4414. WHITING, Nathan
      "Black Granite Drain." HiramPoR (33) Aut-Wint 82,
      p. 24.
      "More Detail of the Filter." Chelsea (41) 82, p.
      169.
      "Paste Riveted by Plaster." Chelsea (41) 82, p.
      166.
      "Speepshead Outlet." Chelsea (41) 82, p. 168.
      "Thin Bycycle Slices." HiramPoR (33) Aut-Wint 82,
      p. 25.
      "Transparent Levittown Tattoos." Chelsea (41) 82,
      p. 167.
      "Zero G Applications of Using a Pencil." HiramPoR
      (33) Aut-Wint 82, p. 26.

4415. WHITLEY, Tricia
      "The Undefeated." Bogg (49) 82, p. 57.

4416. WHITMAN, Ruth
      "Earth to Her Son Antaeus." Im (8:2) 82, p. 4.
      "Foreign Tongues." Im (8:2) 82, p. 4.
      "Night Door." Im (8:2) 82, p. 4.
      "Parsley Eggplants Tomatoes." Im (8:2) 82, p. 4.

4417. WHITWORTH, J.
      "Machaiku of Unsuccess" (for G. Cairncross, after
      the fact?). Bogg (49) 82, p. 60.

4418. WICKERT, Max
      from The Pat Sonnets: (III: 7, IV: 8, V: 1-3, 10).
      Poetry (140:1) Ap 82, p. 8-11.
      "Shibboleth." Shen (33:2) 82, p. 53.
      "The Sniper." Shen (33:2) 82, p. 53.

4419. WICKLUND, Millie Mae
      "The Desertion." PoNow (6:4, issue 34) 82, p. 16.

4420. WIDERSHIEN, Marc
"Dreams." Nimrod (25:2) Spr-Sum 82, p. 38.
"Thoreau." Nimrod (25:2) Spr-Sum 82, p. 10.

4421. WIEGMAN, Robyn
"The Cabin on the Inside of Your Thigh." Waves
(11:1) Aut 82, p. 72.
"Crooked Lake." PoetC (14:2) 82, p. 45.
"Sister." PoetC (14:2) 82, p. 44.

4422. WIEGNER, Kathleen
"Outside the World." HangL (42) 82, p. 55.
"Queen Mab." Hangl (43) Wint 82-83, p. 38.
"Southern Comfort." HangL (42) 82, p. 52-54.

4423. WIENER, Leo
"E = me." DekalbLAJ (14:1/4) Aut 80-Sum 81, p. 95-
96.

4424. WIER, Dara
"Fear." MissouriR (6:1) Aut 82, p. 14-15.
"Holidays." MissouriR (6:1) Aut 82, p. 12-13.

4425. WIGGIN, Neurine
"Chicago Erupts on the Flat Cheek of the Prairie."
WindO (41) Aut-Wint 82-83, p. 33.
"Night Cry." SmPd (19:3, issue 56) Aut 82, p. 18.
"Zoo Poems." WindO (41) Aut-Wint 82-83, p. 34-38.

4426. WIGGINS, Jean
"Dresses." Confr (24) Sum 82, p. 15.
"Jackson Hole." Confr (24) Sum 82, p. 15.

4427. WILBORN, William
"Weather-Wise." PoNow (6:5, issue 35) 82, p. 41.

4428. WILBUR, Richard
"Hamlen Brook." Poetry (141:1) O 82, p. 25.
"Orchard Trees, January." KanQ (14:2) Spr 82, p.
18.
"Racine, Andromache, from Act Four, Scene One."
YaleR (71:3) Spr 82, p. 386-387.
"The Ride." Ploughs (8:2/3) 82, p. 11-12.

4429. WILD, Peter
"Beaver." VirQR (58:3) Sum 82, p. 445-446.
"Eucalyptus." MassR (23:3) Aut 82, p. 522.
"Holy Ghost." CutB (18) Spr-Sum 82, p. 44-45.
"Lewis and Clark." PoNow (6:6, issue 36) 82, p. 31.
"Movies." PoNow (6:5, issue 35) 82, p. 35.
"Mud Turtles." Agni (16) 82, p. 64.
"Navajo Rug." VirQR (58:3) Sum 82, p. 445.
"Orography." Pig (8) 80, p. 29.
"Pilots." VirQR (58:3) Sum 82, p. 446-447.
"Preacher." HiramPoR (31) Aut-Wint 82, p. 53.
"Quarrels." Telescope (1) Spr 81, p. 19.
"Rutabagas." SouthernPR (23, i.e. 22:2) Aut 82, p.
68.
"Slogans." CharR (8:2) Aut 82, p. 27.
"Talismans." MassR (23:3) Aut 82, p. 522-523.

"Turtles." Gargoyle (17/18) 81, p. 8.

4430. WILJER, Robert
"Blind Date." PoetryCR (3:4) Sum 82, p. 15.
"Seasoned Lecturer." PoetryCR (4:1) Sum 82, p. 11.

4431. WILKES, Lyall
"Laurel and Hardy." Stand (23:1) 81-82, p. 30.
"Max Wall at Sunderland." Stand (23:1) 81-82, p. 30.

4432. WILL, Eric
"Summer." PoNow (7:1, issue 37) 82, p. 46.

4433. WILL, Frederic
"Flower Power at Last, You Said It." AmerPoR (11:4) Jl-Ag 82, p. 29.
"L'histoire D'un Soldat." AmerPoR (11:4) Jl-Ag 82, p. 29.
"Lully and the Wrecked Ornaments." AmerPoR (11:4) Jl-Ag 82, p. 28.
"Lully's Foot." AmerPoR (11:4) Jl-Ag 82, p. 28.
"On Being Otomi." MassR (23:1) Spr 82, p. 84.
"Otomi Salesmen." MassR (23:1) Spr 82, p. 84.
"Two for You, Eyes of Blue." AmerPoR (11:4) Jl-Ag 82, p. 28.
"Winter Nocturne." AmerPoR (11:4) Jl-Ag 82, p. 29.

4434. WILLARD, Nancy
"Field Collapses behind Patullo." Field (26) Spr 82, p. 56-57.
"Foxes Fall to St. Francis." Field (26) Spr 82, p. 54-55.
"Nets Halt Suns." Kayak (59) Je 82, p. 31.
"Suns to Shine in Star Game." Kayak (59) Je 82, p. 30.
"Tigers, Birds Trade Pitchers." Kayak (59) Je 82, p. 29-30.

4435. WILLEY, Edward P.
"Windbane." PoNow (7:1, issue 37) 82, p. 46.

4436. WILLIAMS, C. K.
"Combat." Antaeus (45/46) Spr-Sum 82, p. 273-279.

4437. WILLIAMS, David
"Keeping Watch." BelPoJ (33:1) Aut 82, p. 39.
"The Violin Maker." BelPoJ (33:1) Aut 82, p. 38.

4438. WILLIAMS, Elsie Arrington
"Academic Evaporation." Obs (7:2/3) Sum-Wint 81, p. 204.
"A Lady." Obs (7:2/3) Sum-Wint 81, p. 205.
"Suburbia Spoke to Us Last Night." Obs (7:2/3) Sum-Wint 81, p. 205.
"The Teacher Will Come." Obs (7:2/3) Sum-Wint 81, p. 204.

4439. WILLIAMS, Miller
"Birth of the Blues." Poetry (139:5) F 82, p. 291.

"Documenting It." NewOR (9:1) Spr-Sum 82, p. 80.
"The Firebreathers at the Cafe Deux Magots."
    SouthernR (18:4) Aut 82, p. 802-804.
"Going." GeoR (36:2) Sum 82, p. 405.
"In a Gradually Moving Car Somewhere in Calcutta."
    SouthernPR (22:1) Spr 82, p. 48-49.
"In the." NewEngR (5:1/2) Aut-Wint 82, p. 184.
"Logos." Poetry (139:5) F 82, p. 286-287.
"Normandy Beach." SouthernR (18:4) Aut 82, p. 804-
    805.
"Rebecca at Play." Poetry (139:5) F 82, p. 290.
"Rubaiyat for Sue Ella Tucker." NewEngR (5:1/2)
    Aut-Wint 82, p. 185-186.
"A Short Play." Poetry (139:5) F 82, p. 288-289.
"Trying." Poetry (139:5) F 82, p. 290.
"Wiedersehen." MissouriR (5:3) Sum 82, p. 18-19.

4440. WILLIAMS, William Carlos
"10/14." Atl (250:5) N 82, p. 145.
"Brief Lief." Atl (250:5) N 82, p. 145.
"Conventional Ballad." Atl (250:5) N 82, p. 145.
"Election Day." Atl (250:5) N 82, p. 145.
"Reply" (crumpled on her desk). Atl (250:5) N 82, p.
    145.

4441. WILLIAMS, Yvonne R.
"African Wool." Obs (7:2/3) Sum-Wint 81, p. 187.

4442. WILLIAMSON, Alan
"Hyde Park at Thrity-Five." YaleR (71:3) Spr 82, p.
    389-390.
"The Novelist in Cambridge" (for Jonathan Strong).
    Ploughs (8:2/3) 82, p. 243.
"The Pre-Rusted Skyscrapers." Ploughs (8:1) 82, p.
    86.
"Robert Lowell: His Death." Ploughs (8:2/3) 82, p.
    241-242.

4443. WILLIAMSON, Sylvia Ruth
"Little Girl, from Jano Knjazovic." Tendril (12)
    Wint 82, p. 69.

4444. WILLS, Ollie
"Girl." Bogg (48) 82, p. 56-57.

4445. WILMER, Clive
"The Parable of the Sower" (Stained glass in the
    Arts & Crafts style, set in a medieval church).
    Thrpny (9) Spr 82, p. 16.

4446. WILNER, Eleanor
"How to Keep Teaching When You Can No Longer Define
    Romanticism." Epoch (32:1) Aut 82, p. 38-39.

4447. WILSON, Frank F., IV
"Hitting the Floor." PikeF (4) Spr 82, p. 20.

4448. WILSON, Gary
"Down That Way" (tr. of Francis Jammes). AmerPoR
    (11:4) Jl-Ag 82, p. 7.

"Quai" (tr. of Alphonze Piche). DenQ (17:1) Spr 82, p. 88.
"Retreat" (tr. of Alphonze Piche). DenQ (17:1) Spr 82, p. 89.
"She Goes To The Boarding School..." (tr.of Francis Jammes). HolCrit (19:4) O 82, p. 19-20.
"With Your Umbrella" (tr. of Francis Jammes). AmerPoR (11:4) Jl-Ag 82, p. 7.

4449. WILSON, Graeme
"Breakages" (tr. of Anonymous). WestHR (36:1) Spr 82, p. 24.
"The Direction of Autumn" (tr. of Fujiwara no Kachiomu). WestHR (36:3) Aut 82, p. 264.
"The Great Gates of the World" (tr. of Taira no Sadafun). WestHR (36:1) Spr 82, p. 44.

4450. WILSON, Ian Thomas
"Jaruzelski & Co." PoetryCR (4:2) Wint 82, p. 15.

4451. WILSON, Keith
"The Dream." PoNow (6:5, issue 35) 82, p. 31.

4452. WILSON, Matthew
"DC-10 Crashes on Mount Erebus." Outbr (8/9) Aut 81-Spr 82, p. 38.
"Mantis." Outbr (8/9) Aut 81-Spr 82, p. 39.
"Marginal Returns." Outbr (8/9) Aut 81-Spr 82, p. 35-37.
"What Do You Know about the 'Doughboy'?" FourQt (31:2) Wint 82, p. 2.

4453. WILSON, R. T.
"The Cats Locked Away." KanQ (14:3) Sum 82, p. 28.

4454. WILSON, Rob
"The City Called Balzac." Ploughs (8:2/3) 82, p. 77.

4455. WILSON, Robley, Jr.
"The Childless." GeoR (36:2) Sum 82, p. 415.
"Listening for Stars." BlackWR (7:2) Spr 81, p. 41.
"The Man with the Blind Wife." BlackWR (7:2) Spr 81, p. 40.
"The Mozart Broadcast." Poetry (140:1) Ap 82, p. 24-26.
"Recluse." Poetry (140:1) Ap 82, p. 23.
"Three Dreams." Poetry (140:1) Ap 82, p. 20-22.

4456. WINANS, A. D.
"Love Song." Confr (24) Sum 82, p. 35.

WINCKEL, Nance van
See: Van WINCKEL, Nance

4457. WINDER, Barbara
"Biography." KanQ (14:3) Sum 82, p. 82.
"Roots." KanQ (14:3) Sum 82, p. 81.

4458. WINDER, Louise Somers
"Frost etches the pane" (Haiku). LittleBR (2:3) Spr
82, p. 50.

4459. WINDHAGER, Juliane
"Confirmation Day" (tr. by Beth Bjorklund). LitR
(25:2) Wint 82, p. 179.

4460. WING, Tek Lum
"To the Old Masters." Poetry (140:2) My 82, p. 85-
86.

4461. WINN, Howard
"Hunger." BallSUF (23:4) Aut 82, p. 40.
"Song of Experience." DekalbLAJ (14:1/4) Aut 80-Sum
81, p. 98.

4462. WINNER, Robert
"Life Insurance." Confr (24) Sum 82, p. 109.
"South African Gold Miner" (Witwatterstrand, 1950).
NewL (48:2) Wint 81-82, p. 102.

4463. WINTERS, Nancy
"Eclipse." SouthernR (18:2) Spr 82, p. 384.
"Epithalamion." SouthernR (18:2) Spr 82, p. 385.
"May Night." SouthernR (18:2) Spr 82, p. 384.

4464. WISCHNER, Claudia (Claudia March)
"Aya's Watercolors (age 6)." WestB (10) 82, p. 76-
77.
"Moon Viewing." PoNow (7:1, issue 37) 82, p. 46.
"Portrait." WestB (11) 82, p. 57.

4465. WISEMAN, Christopher
"Grandmother's Death Room." CanLit (92) Spr 82, p.
21-22.
"October Elegy" (Judith Sloman 1940-1980). CanLit
(92) Spr 82, p. 22.

4466. WITT, Harold
"Aloha." MidwQ (24:1) Aut 82, p. 65.
"Arthur Bellknap's Vision." Im (8:1) 82, p. 6.
"Bone Hands." PikeF (4) Spr 82, p. 6.
"Borderline." MinnR (NS19) Aut 82, p. 46.
"Coach Hand." PoNow (6:6, issue 36) 82, p. 31.
"Dick Merton, D.D." PoNow (6:6, issue 36) 82, p.
31.
"Elegy for Aunt Nettie." MidwQ (24:1) Aut 82, p.
66.
"Familiar Chills" (from Over Fifty). Wind (12:44)
82, p. 16.
"First Rain" (from Over Fifty). Wind (12:44) 82, p.
12.
"In 1936" (after Leni Riefenstahl's Film). MichQR
(21:1) Wint 82, p. 166-167.
"In the Picture." WestB (10) 82, p. 56-57.
"The Itos." PikeF (4) Spr 82, p. 13.
"Joe Louis." ColEng 44(8) D 82, p. 809-810.
"Light Traveler." PoetryNW (23:2) Sum 82, p. 42.
"Margo Aumaire." PoNow (6:5, issue 35) 82, p. 8.

"Mrs. Gladys Tarbell." PoNow (6:4, issue 34) 82, p. 28.
"Ned West, Jr., Hopeless Case." MidwQ (24:1) Aut 82, p. 67.
"Singalong." CharR (8:1) Spr 82, p. 32.
"Tortilla Flat." WestB (10) 82, p. 57.
"The Voice Magicians." CharR (8:1) Spr 82, p. 33.
"Why Dolores Knight Beach McVay Voted for Ronald Reagan for Governor (and President)." Bogg (49) 82, p. 24.
"Winesburg." HiramPoR (31) Aut-Wint 82, p. 54.
"Zelda Keith." PoNow (6:5, issue 35) 82, p. 8.

4467. WITTLINGER, ELLEN
"Starting from Zero." CutB (19) Aut-Wint 82, p. 59.

4468. WOESSNER, Warren
"Christmas Day." Abraxas (25/26) 82, p. 25.
"Favor." Abraxas (25/26) 82, p. 24.
"Running in the Fog." Abraxas (25/26) 82, p. 24.
"Walking toward the Shortest Day." PoNow (6:5, issue 35) 82, p. 45.

4469. WOESTIJNE, Karel van de
"The Ladder and the Rope" (tr. by Andre Lefevere). Paint (7/8:13/16) 80-81, p. 47.

4470. WOJAHN, David
"Distance." PoNow (7:1, issue 37) 82, p. 28.
"Flour." AmerPoR (11:3) My-Je 82, p. 15.
"The Last Couples Leaving the Green Dolphin Bar." MissouriR (6:1) Aut 82, p. 26-27.
"The Man Who Knew Too Much." NewYorker (57:51) F 8, 82, p. 42.
"Porchlights." MissouriR (6:1) Aut 82, p. 25.
"The Precincts of Moonlight." PoNow (7:1, issue 37) 82, p. 28.

4471. WOLF, Abbey
"Thirty Years and Their Days" (tr. of Alberto Vanasco). Spirit (6:2/3) 82, p. 181-182.

4472. WOLF, Joan
"Recuperation." UnderRM (1:1) Spr 82, p. 6.

4473. WOLF, Leslie
"Postcard of a Young Couple." AmerPoR (11:2) Mr-Ap 82, p. 20.

4474. WOLF, Melinda
"Unfamiliar Rooms." Outbr (10/11) Aut 82-Spr 83, p. 93.

4475. WOLF, Naomi
"Alice James." Iowa (12:2/3) Spr-Sum 81, p. 367-368.

4476. WOLFE, Edgar
"Best Friend." LittleBR (2:4) Sum 82, p. 15.
"Dawn Riding." LittleBR (2:4) Sum 82, p. 16.

"Itineraphobia." LittleBR (2:4) Sum 82, p. 16.
"A Season and a Time." KanQ (14:3) Sum 82, p. 201.

4477. WOLFE, Marianne
      "A Moon on the Water." Spirit (6:2/3) 82, p. 185.

4478. WOLFF, Harriet
      "An Exercise Poem: The Metaphor." CrossC (4:2/3)
      82, p. 37.

4479. WONG, Nellie
      "Toward a 44th Birthday." Iowa (12:2/3) Spr-Sum 81,
      p. 371.
      "A Woman at the Window." Iowa (12:2/3) Spr-Sum 81,
      p. 369-370.

      WONG LOO, Katie
      See: LOO, Katie Wong

4480. WOOD, Gary
      "A Question of Arms." Bogg (48) 82, p. 63.
      "Thin Links." Bogg (49) 82, p. 33.

4481. WOOD, Robert E.
      "Prothalamion." SouthernHR (16:1) Wint 82, p. 46.

4482. WOOD, Susan
      "Your Story." Iowa (12:2/3) Spr-Sum 81, p. 372.

4483. WOODALL, Maureen
      "Going Back." MalR (62) Jl 82, p. 157.

4484. WOODARD, Deborah
      "The White Knight Escorts Alice." SouthernPR (22:1)
      Spr 82, p. 61.

4485. WOODBURY, James E. A.
      "Impromptu Thoughts at Midnight" (tr. of Victoria
      Babenko). NewRena (5:1, 15) Aut 82, p. 75, 77.
      "A Sinner" (tr. of Victoria Babenko). NewRena (5:1,
      15) Aut 82, p. 79.

4486. WOODS, Alfred L.
      "Keith Village." HangL (41) 82, p. 51.
      "The Law." HangL (41) 82, p. 53.
      "Sung Aunty Bella." HangL (41) 82, p. 52.

4487. WOODS, Elizabeth
      "Fastidiousness." Waves (10:4) Spr 82, p. 69.
      "Moonshine." CrossC (4:2/3) 82, p. 52.
      "She and Her Friend." Waves (10:4) Spr 82, p. 68.
      "She Comes Home Alone." CrossC (4:2/3) 82, p. 52.

4488. WOOLSON, Peter
      "Middle Ages." Gargoyle (17/18) 81, p. 23.

4489. WORLEY, James
      "Childhood's End." ChrC (99:16) My 5, 82, p. 533.
      "Hissteria." ChrC (99:36) N 17, 82, p. 1166.
      "Sure Enough." ChrC (99:23) Jl 7-14, 82, p. 751.

"Too Much of a God Thing." ChrC (99:33) O 27, 82,
p. 1071.

4490. WORLEY, Jeff
"Instructions for an Insomniac." LitR (25:3) Spr
82, p. 388.
"Starting Point." MinnR (NS18) Spr 82, p. 8.

4491. WORLEY, Stella
"How Our Waitress Left Seattle for San Pedro." Vis
(9) 82, p. 15.

4492. WORMHOUDT, Arthur
"On His Imprisonment" (tr. of Abu Tayyib al-
Mutanabbi). Paint (9:17/18) Spr-Aut 82, p. 30-31.

4493. WORMSBY, Hollis
"When the Poets in Town" (To Eugene Redmond).
Abraxas (25/26) 82, p. 113.

4494. WORMSER, Baron
"The Autumns." BlackWR (7:2) Spr 81, p. 61.
"The Brothers." BlackWR (7:2) Spr 81, p. 62.
"Immigrant's Letter." MassR (23:3) Aut 82, p. 375.
"The Lesser God." Poetry (139:5) F 82, p. 271-272.
"Letter from New England." Poetry (139:5) F 82, p.
273.
"Passing Significance." Poetry (139:5) F 82, p.
274.
"Piano Lessons." AmerS (51:3) Sum 82, p. 380.
"A Report on the Victorians." Poetry (139:5) F 82,
p. 275.

4495. WORMUTH, Diane
"Darkforest Wolves" (tr. of Artur Lundkvist). Confr
(23) Wint 82, p. 83.
"The Glory of the World, the Shark in Love" (tr. of
Artur Lundkvist). Confr (23) Wint 82, p. 83.

4496. WOROSZYLSKI, Wiktor
"Advice from an Experienced Prisoner: Don't Figure
the Date" (tr. by Richard Lourie). PartR (49:4)
82, p. 517.
"Bromide" (tr. by Richard Lourie). PartR (49:4) 82,
p. 516-517.
"Diary of an Internment" (December 1981--February
1982, Bialoleka--Jaworze) (tr. by Richard Lourie).
PartR (49:4) 82, p. 514-520.
"Dreaming and Awake" (tr. by Richard Lourie). PartR
(49:4) 82, p. 519-520.
"I'm Not Upset" (tr. by Richard Lourie). PartR
(49:4) 82, p. 515.
"The Loudspeaker" (tr. by Richard Lourie). PartR
(49:4) 82, p. 516.
"A Meeting" (tr. by Richard Lourie). PartR (49:4)
82, p. 518.
"Notes Smuggled to and from Prison" (tr. by Richard
Lourie). PartR (49:4) 82, p. 518-519.
"Overheard" (tr. by Richard Lourie). PartR (49:4)
82, p. 515.

"A Picture" (tr. by Richard Lourie). PartR (49:4)
    82, p. 519.
"A Polish Day" (tr. by Richard Lourie). PartR (49:4)
    82, p. 520.
"The Prisonrs' Walk" (tr. by Richard Lourie). PartR
    (49:4) 82, p. 518.
"Reeducators" (tr. by Richard Lourie). PartR (49:4)
    82, p. 516.
"Sign Here Please" (tr. by Richard Lourie). PartR
    (49:4) 82, p. 515.
"Still Nothing" (tr. by Richard Lourie). PartR
    (49:4) 82, p. 514.
"With Full Respect" (tr. by Richard Lourie). PartR
    (49:4) 82, p. 517.

4497. WORTH, Dorothy Williamson
    "Salamander." DekalbLAJ (14:1/4) Aut 80-Sum 81, p.
    119.

4498. WOSTER, Kevin
    "After the First Freeze." PoNow (7:1, issue 37) 82,
    p. 46.

4499. WREGGITT, Andrew
    "Spanish Banks, Vancouver." AntigR (48) Wint 82, p.
    72.

4500. WRIGHT, C. D.
    "Jazz Impressions in the Garden." BlackWR (7:2) Spr
    81, p. 83.
    "Landlocked, Fallen, Unsung" (in praise of Agee).
    BlackWR (7:2) Spr 81, p. 84.
    from Livelihoods of Freaks and Poets in the Western
    World: "Franz was washing my back." BlackWR (7:2)
    Spr 81, p. 85.
    "Who Sit Watch in Daylight." BlackWR (7:2) Spr 81,
    p. 86-87.

4501. WRIGHT, Carolyne
    "Crossing the Divide: a Second Growth." LitR (25:3)
    Spr 82, p. 385.
    "Crossing the Divide: Montana." LitR (25:3) Spr 82,
    p. 384.
    "The Custody of the Eyes" (for Madeline De Frees).
    Kayak (58) Ja 82, p. 8-9.
    "A High Wind through Your Life" (For Istvan). DenQ
    (17:2) Sum 82, p. 40-41.
    "The Loveliest Country of Our Lives." PraS (56:3)
    Aut 82, p. 48.
    "Making Calls to Grade Schools in the Berkshires."
    MassR (23:1) Spr 82, p. 190-191.

4502. WRIGHT, Charles
    "Dora Markus" (tr. of Eugenio Montale). Field (27)
    Aut 82, p. 52-54.
    "The Eel" (tr. of Eugenio Montale). Field (27) Aut
    82, p. 50-51.
    "Fiesole Window" (tr. of Eugenio Montale). Field
    (27) Aut 82, p. 54.

"Four Poems for the New Year" Antaeus (47) Aut 82,
    p. 18-20.
"Four Poems of Departure." Antaeus (47) Aut 82, p.
    16-17.
"In the Greenhouse" (tr. of Eugenio Montale). Field
    (27) Aut 82, p. 8.
"Lonesome Pine Special." Field (26) Spr 82, p. 5-
    12.
"Omaggio A Pavese." Agni (17) 82, p. 5.
"The Other Side of the River." NewYorker (58:7) Ap
    5, 82, p. 46-47.
"Syria" (tr. of Eugenio Montale). Field (27) Aut 82,
    p. 50.
"Two in Twilight" (tr. of Eugenio Montale). Field
    (27) Aut 82, p. 18-19.
"Two Stories." AntR (40:2) Spr 82, p. 180-182.
"Visit to Fadin" (tr. of Eugenio Montale). Field
    (27) Aut 82, p. 46-47.

4503. WRIGHT, David Walton
"Because of his grandchild's death." Hangl (43)
    Wint 82-83, p. 61.
"Below the Springs." Hangl (43) Wint 82-83, p. 59-
    60.
"On the horizon." Hangl (43) Wint 82-83, p. 59.
"The Wish." Hangl (43) Wint 82-83, p. 60.

4504. WRIGHT, Franz
"Christ's Descent into Hell" (tr. of Rainer Maria
    Rilke). VirQR (58:4) Aut 82, p. 691-692.
"The Earth Will Come Back from the Dead." VirQR
    (58:4) Aut 82, p. 689-690.
"In the Reading Room." VirQR (58:4) Aut 82, p. 690-
    691.
"Poem." VirQR (58:4) Aut 82, p. 690.

4505. WRIGHT, Fred W., Jr.
"Skimming the Surface." UTR (7:2) 82?, p. 15.

4506. WRIGHT, James
"A Flower Passage" (In memory of Joe Shunk, the
    diver). Antaeus (45/46) Spr-Sum 82, p. 295-296.
"Camomila." AmerPoR (11:1) Ja-F 82, p. 17.
"In a Field near Metaponto." AmerPoR (11:1) Ja-F
    82, p. 17.

4507. WRIGHT, Jay
"MacIntyre, the Captain and the Saints." TriQ (54)
    Spr 82, p. 235-248.

4508. WRIGHT, Jonathan
"Beagle at Cape St. Francis." Germ (6:1) Spr-Sum
    82, p. 35.
"Seal Cove Pond." Germ (6:1) Spr-Sum 82, p. 38.
"Trade Winds." Germ (6:1) Spr-Sum 82, p. 36.
"A Winter Decision." Germ (6:1) Spr-Sum 82, p. 34.
"You, Who Are Pure" (for Lorca). Germ (6:1) Spr-Sum
    82, p. 37.

4509. WRIGHT, Katharine
       "Keeping." Chelsea (41) 82, p. 170-174.

4510. WRIGHT, Scott
       "Complacence." MissR (10:3, issue 30) Wint-Spr 82,
       p. 67.
       "Sin and Pleasure." MissR (10:3, issue 30) Wint-Spr
       82, p. 68.

4511. WRIGLEY, Robert
       "Appalonea" (Appalonea Miller Voisin (1840-1903)).
       MissouriR (5:2) Wint 81-82, p. 50.
       "Bearing Witness." AmerPoR (11:3) My-Je 82, p. 43.
       "The Beliefs of a Horse." AmerPoR (11:3) My-Je 82,
       p. 42.
       "Death Swing." CimR (58) Ja 82, p. 59.
       "Moonlight: Chickens on the Road" (for Dave Smith).
       OhioR (27) 82, p. 116-117.
       "Mowing." AmerPoR (11:3) My-Je 82, p. 42.

4512. WRONSKY, Gail
       "The Arc between Two Deaths" (for Doris Humphrey).
       VirQR (58:4) Aut 82, p. 701.
       "The Contemplative Life." VirQR (58:4) Aut 82, p.
       699-700.
       "Leithtown." VirQR (58:4) Aut 82, p. 700-701.

4513. WUEST, Barbara
       "To the Con Artist." Im (8:1) 82, p. 5.

4514. WYATT, David
       "Autumn." CaroIQ (35:1) Aut 82, p. 31.

4515. WYMAN, Hastings, Jr.
       "I Hit a Bearded Man." Bogg (49) 82, p. 21-22.

4516. WYMAN, Linda
       "In Compliance with Policy." EngJ (71:6) O 82, p.
       70.

4517. WYNAND, Derk
       "Account." Grain (10:3) Ag 82, p. 18.
       "Back." Grain (10:3) Ag 82, p. 19.
       "Braid." Grain (10:3) Ag 82, p. 17.
       "Burlesque." Quarry (31:1) Wint 82, p. 59-60.
       "Feather." Quarry (31:1) Wint 82, p. 58.
       "Fetishistic." Pig (8) 80, p. 33.
       "Narcissus Considers His Head." Dandel (9:2) 82, p.
       25.
       "Small Winner." Dandel (9:2) 82, p. 26.
       "Snap." Grain (10:3) Ag 82, p. 17-18.
       "Stall." Quarry (31:1) Wint 82, p. 59.

4518. WYTTENBERG, Victoria
       "Family Night on the Psychiatric Ward." PoetryNW
       (23:3) Aut 82, p. 30-31.
       "Lying in Bed." PoetryNW (23:3) Aut 82, p. 29-30.

       Ya SALAAM, Kalamu
       See: SALAAM, Kalamu ya

4519. YALIM, Ozcan
"Bequest" (tr. of Cahit Kulebi, w. William A.
Fielder, and Dionis Coffin Riggs). StoneC (10:1/2)
Aut-Wint 82-83,p. 31.
"The Lamp" (tr. of Behcet Necatigil, w. William A.
Fielder and Dionis Coffin Riggs).DenQ (17:1) Spr
82, p. 85.
"A Lesson" (tr. of Ulku Tamer, w. William A. Fielder
and Dionis Coffin Riggs).DenQ (17:1) Spr 82, p.
87.
"To Live" (tr. of Orhan Veli, w. William A. Fielder
and Dionis Coffin Riggs).DenQ (17:1) Spr 82, p.
86.

4520. YAMAMOTO, Judith
"I Should Have Warned You." SouthernPR (23, i.e.
22:2) Aut 82, p. 49.

4521. YAMRUS, John
"Nobody Writes." Bogg (49) 82, p. 5.
"You Make Me Wish I'd a Camera." Abraxas (25/26)
82, p. 59.

4522. YARBOROUGH, Marty
"Untitled: As the two lovers sat sleeping." MendoR
(5) Sum 81, p. 66.

4523. YASHASCHANDRA, Sitanshu
"Stars" (tr. by Varsha Das). NewL (48:3/4) Spr-Sum
82, p. 257.

4524. YATES, Lynda
"Brief Flight." NewEngR (4:4) Sum 82, p. 553.
"Snake Plant." Thrpny (9) Spr 82, p. 11.

4525. YAU, John
"A Different Cereal." MissR (10:3, issue 30) Wint-
Spr 82, p. 70-72.
"Train Schedule." MissR (10:3, issue 30) Wint-Spr
82, p. 69.

4526. YEAGLEY, Joan
"The Order for Daily Morning Prayer." LittleBR
(2:4) Sum 82, p. 70.
"A Saturday Funeral in Lyons, Kansas" (For a priest
burying a priest, E.H. and J.V.). LittleBR (2:3)
Spr 82, p. 73.

4527. YEAR, M.
"Sparrows." Bogg (49) 82, p. 33.

4528. YELLEN, Samuel
"The Wolf." DenQ (17:1) Spr 82, p. 65.

4529. YMAYO, Laura
"Divagacion del Estio." NotArte (7:2) F 82, p. 15.
"Esas Barcas Antiguas." NotArte (7:2) F 82, p. 15.
"Ojo inmenso de Venus." NotArte (7:2) F 82, p. 15.
"Sin Respuesta." NotArte (7:2) F 82, p. 15.

"Temor" (a Gabriela Mistral, maestra). NotArte
(7:2) F 82, p. 15.

4530. YOTS, Michael
"Directions to Madam Rosa's." SouthwR (67:3) Sum
82, p. 301.
"Nightsounds." Wind (12:46) 82, p. 47-48.
"The Obligatory Quicksand Scene." PoNow (6:4, issue
34) 82, p. 36.
"Severing an Old Tie." KanQ (14:3) Sum 82, p. 203.
"A Winter Song for the Children." Wind (12:46) 82,
p. 47.

4531. YOUMANS, Marlene
"Girl and Toy Lute." SoCaR (15:1) Aut 82, p. 76.
"Piano Rag." SoCaR (15:1) Aut 82, p. 77.
"Windowmaker." SoCaR (15:1) Aut 82, p. 78.

4532. YOUNG, Bernard
"On a Day When War Is Not Declared." Bogg (48) 82,
p. 51.
"The Sex-Starved." Bogg (48) 82, p. 50.

4533. YOUNG, David
"And There" (tr. of Vladimir Holan, w. Dana Habova).
Field (27) Aut 82, p. 75.
"At the Bottom of the Day" (tr. Oldrich Vyhlidal, w.
Miroslav Holub). Field (27) Aut 82, p. 77.
"The Custom-House" (tr. of Eugenio Montale, w. Vinio
Rossi). Field (27) Aut 82, p. 11.
"Elegy in the Form of an Invitation" (James Wright,
b. 1927, Martin's Ferry, Ohio, d. 1980, New York
City). Ploughs (8:2/3) 82, p. 33-34.
"The Grave of Casanova" (tr. of Jaroslav Seifert, w.
Miroslav Holub). Field (27) Aut 82, p. 71-73.
"The Heights of Macchu Picchu" (tr. of Pablo
Neruda). Field (27) Aut 82, p. 81-100.
"In My Own Back Yard." NewYorker (58:29) S 6, 82,
p. 42.
"Interferon" (tr. of Miroslav Holub, w. Dana
Habova). Field (26) Spr 82, p. 61-67.
"Lemons" (tr. of Eugenio Montale, w. Vinio Rossi).
Field (27) Aut 82, p. 14-15.
"News from Mount Amiata" (tr. of Eugenio Montale, w.
Vinio Rossi). Field (27) Aut 82, p. 35-36.
"Resurrection" (tr. of Vladimir Holan, w. Dana
Habova). Field (27) Aut 82, p. 76.

4534. YOUNG, Dean
"Accompaniment." Outbr (10/11) Aut 82-Spr 83, p.
92.
"My Daughter's Dance Lesson." Outbr (10/11) Aut 82-
Spr 83, p. 91.
"Two Women." SouthernPR (23, i.e. 22:2) Aut 82, p.
32.

4535. YOUNG, Ellen Roberts
"Insignia." ChrC (99:30) O 6, 82, p. 982.
"January." ChrC (99:3) Ja 27, 82, p. 78.

4536. YOUNG, Jody
"Dear Sister." Sam (32:3, issue 127) 82, p. 40.
"Tombstone." Sam (33:3, issue 131) 82, p. 37.

4537. YOUNG, Mallory
"You, Robert Herrick." Shen (33:1) 81-82, p. 21.

4538. YOUNG, Mariam
"Watching You." PoNow (7:1, issue 37) 82, p. 46.

4539. YOUNG, Patricia
"Listen: This Is More Urgent." Waves (10:3) Wint
82, p. 70.

4540. YOUNG, Virginia Brady
"After the avalanche." Northeast (3:12) Wint 81-82,
p. 21.
"The Coin." WestCR (16:4) Ap 82, p. 27.
"The Feast." WestCR (16:4) Ap 82, p. 28.
"In the changing silence." Northeast (3:12) Wint
81-82, p. 21.
"Lilacs struck by moonlight--drained of lavendar."
Northeast (3:12) Wint 81-82, p. 21.
"Over the lake, hawk." Northeast (3:12) Wint 81-82,
p. 21.

4541. YOUNG, Wenda
"Sour Grapes." AntigR (48) Wint 82, p. 20.

4542. YOUNG, William
"Early to Rise." Agni (16) 82, p. 63.

4543. YOUNGER, Virginia C.
"The Debt." Wind (12:46) 82, p. 49.

4544. YOURGRAU, Barry
"Apocrypha." Poetry (140:4) Jl 82, p. 204.

4545. YOURIL, John A.
"Mare Nostrum." StoneC (9:3/4) Spr-Sum 82, p. 70-
71.

4546. YUNUS EMRE
"CXXIX" (tr. by Ann Stanford and Grace Smith). Paint
(9:17/18) Spr-Aut 82, p. 26-27.
"Five Poems: I-III, XXXIX, C" (tr. by Ann Stanford
and Grace Smith). Antaeus (44) Wint 82, p. 170-
177.
"Isidun iy yarenler eve dervisler geldi: Oh my
friends, listen" (tr. by Ann Stanford and Grace
Smith). NowestR (20:1) 82, p. 11.

4547. YVONNE
"Encounter No. 2." Im (8:2) 82, p. 11.
"Junk Mail, Coupons, Something." Im (8:2) 82, p.
11.

4548. ZABLE, Jeffrey A. Z.
"The Hypocrite." WormR (22:3, issue 87) 82, p. 86.

"The Man Who Set the Fire" (for Russell Edson).
WormR (22:3, issue 87) 82, p. 85-86.

4549. ZACK, David
"Poem for Ruth." SouthwR (67:4) Aut 82, p. 398.

4550. ZADRAVEC, Katharine
"Mother Poem." Vis (10) 82, p. 19.

4551. ZADURA, Bohdan
"Farewell to Ostend" (tr. by Hubert F. Babinski).
PartR (49:2) 82, p. 238-245.

4552. ZAGAJEWSKI, Adam
"Christmas Eve '81" (tr. by Richard Lourie). PartR
(49:4) 82, p. 520-521.
"Court" (tr. by Richard Lourie). PartR (49:4) 82, p.
521-522.

4553. ZAMBARAS, Vassilis
"Poetry Lesson." Spirit (6:2/3) 82, p. 186.

4554. ZAND, Herbert
"Continually" (tr. by Beth Bjorklund). LitR (25:2)
Wint 82, p. 213.
"The Gardener" (tr. by Beth Bjorklund). LitR (25:2)
Wint 82, p. 214.
"My Poor Exploited Language" (tr. by Beth
Bjorklund). LitR (25:2) Wint 82, p. 216.
"Pain" (tr. by Beth Bjorklund). LitR (25:2) Wint 82,
p. 215.

4555. ZANDER, William
"Valediction to the Muse." PoetryNW (23:1) Spr 82,
p. 34-36.

4556. ZANE, Leslie
"Loss." Shout (3:1) 82, p. 87-88.

4557. ZAPATA, Roger
"Cuando la Nieve y Mis Vecinos Me Saludan." Maize
(5:1/2) Aut-Wint 81-82, p. 52.
"Lo Que Se Ha de Ver." Maize (5:1/2) Aut-Wint 81-
82, p. 52.

4558. ZARZYSKI, Paul
"Cutting the Easter Colt" (for Earl Stewart). CutB
(19) Aut-Wint 82, p. 42.
"Fish Story" (in memory of Andy Grossbardt). CutB
(19) Aut-Wint 82, p. 43.

4559. ZATURENSKA, Marya
"The Neglected Garden." NewL (48:2) Wint 81-82, p.
68-69.
"Suburban Summer." NewL (48:2) Wint 81-82, p. 68.

4560. ZAVRIAN, Suzanne Ostro
"Anne Leaning on a Table" (from a painting by
Avigdor Arikha). PartR (49:3) 82, p. 435-437.
"Arizona Summer" (to D.). OP (33) Spr 82, p. 18-19.

"Feu d'Artifice." QP (33) Spr 82, p. 16.
"Give This Message to Michael When He Gets Off the
  Phone." QP (33) Spr 82, p. 17.

4561. ZAWADIWSKY, Christine
      "Drowning, Drowning." Catalyst (Erotica Issue) 82,
        p. 10.
      "Go." LittleM (13:3/4) 82, p. 66.
      "Wet Flower." Abraxas (25/26) 82, p. 66-67.

4562. ZAZUYER, Leah
      "The Country of Her Language." GeoR (36:4) Wint 82,
        p. 808-809.

4563. ZEBRUN, Gary
      "A Soul Is Speechless on the Street." Iowa (12:4)
        Aut 81, p. 66.

4564. ZEIDNER, Lisa
      "Sunday Morning Cartoons." Epoch (32:1) Aut 82, p.
        37.

4565. ZEIDNER, Martin
      "I was born without a name" (tr. of Thomas Gleb).
        PortR (28:2) 82, p. 42-44.

4566. ZEIGER, L. L.
      "Silent Letters." GeoR (36:1) Spr 82, p. 132.

4567. ZENIK, R.
      "Home Land." WritersL O-N 82, p. 14.

4568. ZEPPA, Mary
      "October Light." Telescope (2) Aut 81, p. 11.

4569. ZERFAS, Jan
      "The Blue Vase." CentR (26:3) Sum 82, p. 272-273.

4570. ZHEN, Xie
      "A Fisherman's Family" (tr. by Zuxin Ding and Burton
        Raffel). DenQ (17:2) Sum 82, p. 95.

4571. ZHU, Sushen
      "On the Night of the First Full Moon" (tr. by Zuxin
        Ding and Burton Raffel). DenQ (17:2) Sum 82, p.
        94.

4572. ZIEDONIS, Imants
      "Through Evening Twilight" (tr. by Inara Cedrins).
        QW (14) Spr-Sum 82, p. 46.
      "When Cats with Black Stripes" (for Imant Kalnins,
        tr. by Inara Cedrins). QW (14) Spr-Sum 82, p. 47.

4573. ZIEROTH, Dale
      "The Birds Stay with Him." WestCR (17:2) O 82, p.
        28-29.
      "Grandmother's Spring." WestCR (17:2) O 82, p. 30-
        31.
      "His Mother Laments." WestCR (17:2) O 82, p. 29-30.

4574. ZIMMER, Juliana
     "The Battle." WebR (7:2) Aut 82, p. 43.

4575. ZIMMER, Paul
     "The Eisenhower Years." BlackWR (7:2) Spr 81, p. 7-
        8.
     "The King Escaping Court." Telescope (2) Aut 81, p.
        24.
     "The King Visits the Prisons." Telescope (2) Aut
        81, p. 23.
     "The King's Lesson." OhioR (28) 82, p. 64.
     "Zimmer at the Death Watch." OhioR (29) 82, p. 121.
     "Zimmer Imagines Heaven." PoetryNW (23:1) Spr 82,
        p. 36-37.
     "Zimmer Sees Wanda Lead the King to the Crossing."
        Telescope (2) Aut 81, p. 25.
     "Zimmer Sings the Final Encounter." Telescope (2)
        Aut 81, p. 26-27.
     "Zimmer South." BlackWR (7:2) Spr 81, p. 9-10.

4576. ZIMMERMAN, Rachel
     "I wouldn't have returned your overdue books."
        HangL (42) 82, p. 68.
     "Ink Means Never Having to Say Rewrite." HangL (42)
        82, p. 69.

4577. ZIMROTH, Evan
     "The Faith-Healer." Pequod (14) 82, p. 106.
     "Playground." Poetry (140:4) Jl 82, p. 224.
     "Postcard from Idyllic Isle La Motte." Poetry
        (140:4) Jl 82, p. 225.
     "Separations." NewL (48:2) Wint 81-82, p. 91.
     "Square Laurent Prache." Pequod (14) 82, p. 107.
     "Wintering." Pequod (14) 82, p. 105.

4578. ZINNES, Harriet
     "Rising above the snow in the lift at Verbier."
        PoNow (6:4, issue 34) 82, p. 15.
     "Spring Pain." Confr (24) Sum 82, p. 90.

4579. ZISQUIT, Linda
     "The Circumcision." Nimrod (25:2) Spr-Sum 82, p.
        72.
     "Light Fever" (tr. of Zali Gurevitz). BaratR (8:2)
        Wint 81, p. 92.
     "Morning with" (tr. of Zali Gurevitz). BaratR (8:2)
        Wint 81, p. 93.

4580. ZOLA, James
     "Black & White." WormR (22:3, issue 87) 82, p.109.
     "Camping with the Mute Boy." EnPas (13) 82, p. 24.
     "Camping with the Mute Boy." Wind (12:45) 82, p.
        38.
     "Carnival at Falmouth, Mass." WormR (22:3, issue
        87) 82, p.109.
     "Hunting for the Tree." Wind (12:45) 82, p. 38-39.
     "The Re-Education of James Zola." WormR (22:3,
        issue 87) 82, p.110.
     "Sacandoga Resevoir, Upstate New York." Wind
        (12:45) 82, p. 39-40.

4581. ZOLLER, Ann L.
      "Silent House." Vis (10) 82, p. 22.

4582. ZOLYNAS, Al
      "Phil Dacey's Archetypal Experience." PoNow (6:6,
      issue 36) 82, p. 19.

4583. ZONAILO, Carolyn
      "The Cherry Tree." PoetryCR (4:1) Sum 82, p. 4.

4584. ZORN, Marilyn
      "Deer in Rutting Season." KanQ (14:3) Sum 82, p.
      200 .

4585. ZU-BOLTON, Ahmos
      "The Basketball Star." Spirit (6:2/3) 82, p. 43.

4586. ZUKOR-COHEN, Maree
      "The Village of San Rafael." Vis (10) 82, p. 30.

4587. ZULAUF, Sander
      "Studebaker." PoNow (7:1, issue 37) 82, p. 47.
      "A Sweet Lamb." PoNow (7:1, issue 37) 82, p. 47.
      "Talking to the Man Who Jumped off the World Trade
      Center Roof." PoNow (7:1, issue 37) 82, p. 47.

4588. ZUNDER, Thomas
      "Person." Bogg (49) 82, p. 62.

4589. ZWARTS, Janice Blue
      "Damian's Stuffed Squirrel." Grain (10:2) My 82, p.
      17.
      "Dinner Hour." Grain (10:2) My 82, p. 18.

4590. ZWICKEY, June A.
      "First Love Song."Abraxas (25/26) 82, p. 98.

4591. ZYDEK, Fredrick
      "First Piece." Waves (11:1) Aut 82, p. 55.
      "The Last Electrician Alive." SoDakR (20:4) Wint
      82-83, p. 36.
      "Taking Highway 80 to Lincoln." AntigR (49) Spr 82,
      p. 54.
      "White River." SouthernHR (16:2) Spr 82, p. 118.

TITLE INDEX

Titles are arranged alphanumerically, with numerals filed in numerical order before letters. Each title is followed by one or more author entry numbers, which refer to the principal entries in the first part of the index. Poems with the title "Untitled" are filed under that title, followed by the first line.

The Album: 3632.
Albuquerque: 59.
Alcestis: 2774, 3416.
Alchemist: 810.
Alchemy: 2152.
Alcohol: 645.
Alcohol and a Coffin without
    Nails: 2960.
Alcon Moco's Ballet: 17.
La Aldea: 1815.
Alegria: 4009.
Aleutian Stare: 682.
Alexander's Complaint: 3592.
Alexandria: 135.
Alfombra Como Lirica: 1494.
Alfred Russell Wallace, Natur-
    alist, Leaves the Amazon:
    July: 2106.
Ali: 1127, 2711.
Alice James: 4475.
Alien: 4167.
Aliens: 691.
Alike as Two: 1260.
All: 1532.
All Alone: 2687, 2962.
All around Us: 4083.
All Day Through the Dry Cold:
    638.
All Fly Home: 3200.
All for a Day: 4032.
All for the Love (of a Sixteen
    Year Old Girl): 2328.
All Hail to Our Underseas
    Forces!: 2740.
All-Night Groceries: 2863.
All Night the Rain: 3278.
All-Nite Diner: 1966.
All Skin All Fire: 2816.
All Souls Day, 1957: 1044.
All-Star Neutron Day: Aug. 9,
    1981: 2238.
All That Is Left: 823.
All the News: 3131.
All the Spikes But the Last:
    3666.
All the Subjects on the
    Threshold: 2512.
All the Way Back: 1942.
All the Wild Dogs That Yap:
    890.
All Things Are One Said
    Empedocles in a Light as
    Probable as Hume: 1969.
All Those Nights: 2811.
All Those Other Ways: 616.
All to myself I think of you:
    121.
All We Can Use: 4379.
Alla ehoun matia kataspra horis
    matoklada: 3676.
Alley: 3895.
Alley Oop Speaks: 380.
Alleys: 2424.
The Alligator: 3263.
Allowance: 578.
The Alm: 2268.

Alma de Antano: 484.
The Almond in Flower: 2919.
Almost Greek: 2806.
Almost Persuaded: 2556.
Almost the Greatest: 3342.
Aloha: 4466.
Alone at Ainahou: The New Land:
    4109.
Alone in Autumn: 2654.
Alone on Christmas Eve in
    Japan: 1479.
Along the Canal: 3811.
Along the Trail of Flowers:
    Adaptions of Four Wintu
    Songs: 4029.
Alp: 3813.
Alpine Memory: 4392.
Al's Tropical Fish Paradise:
    1955.
Also, My Shoes Still Come
    Untied: 2425.
Alternative Psychiatry: 1147.
Alumbramiento: 4193.
Alverda: 666.
Alvira's Garden: 918.
Always Stone: 92.
Always the Reluctant Sportsman:
    514.
Always the Same: 4158.
Amaranth: 3720.
Amarume: 1388.
Amaryllis in February: 55.
The Amateur Fire Eater: 3749.
Amazed: 440.
Amazement: 2840.
Ambassador: 1519.
Ambivalence: 3313, 3693.
Amelia and John: 774.
Americalatina: 927.
American Abroad: 4156.
American Aubade: 3923.
An American Boyhood: 1876.
An American Dejak Visits the
    Cemetery: 441.
The American Dream: 2240.
American Gigantism: Gutzon
    Borglum at Mt. Rushmore:
    3638.
An American in London: 233.
American Landscape with Clouds
    & a Zoo: 103.
American Promises: 4224.
American Summer: 2742.
from Amerikh Two: (IV, V):
    1122.
Amiens 1977: 2727.
Among the Amish: 2703.
Among the Missing: 3588.
Among Vines: 1544.
Amor de Lonh: 3249, 3530.
Amor Errante: 2554.
Amor Oscuro: 260.
Amorosamente: 413.
Amors e Jois e Liocs e Tems:
    934, 3249.

Amors e Jois e Liocs e Tems
(second version): 934, 3249.
Amphora (A-1311): 1708.
Amtrack Station, Lincoln: 2195.
Analysis with a Swimmer: 695.
Anarchverse: 743.
Anatomy: 2913.
Anatomy Lesson: 2987.
Ancestors: 582, 1850, 3129.
Ancestors (A Daguerreotype):
1302.
Ancestria: 2115.
Ancestry: 3777.
And: 1855.
And a Little Child: 1752.
And Also Thus: 3945.
And At Sea it Is Like This:
1904.
And Do You Love Me: 1011.
And Each Time: 3382.
And Even the Republic Must Have
an End: 4066.
And Happy People: 3838.
And If Someone: 1047.
And in Pity: 1964.
And It Came to Pass: 834.
And June?: 2148, 2225, 3865.
And Learn the Way: 4156.
And leave the voice of commerce
blaring through an empty
house: 811.
And Melancholy: 3036.
And So On into the Light: 2112.
And Still Bear: 4156.
And Suddenly It's Evening:
1265, 3293.
And Ten Hail Marys: 3736.
And the Least Shall Save Us:
757.
And There: 1647, 1875, 4533.
And to All Our Troops at Sea:
877.
And Your Soul Shall Dance:
1897.
Andre Breton Enters Heaven:
135.
Andrew Wyeth Poems: 913.
Angel: 2806.
The Angel: 3913.
The Angel in My House: 2975.
The Angel of Memory: 317.
Angelito's Eulogy in Anger:
2319.
Angels Are White: 382.
Angelus: 2830.
Angelus Domini: 2863.
Anima: 1921.
Anima (1): 83.
Anima (2): 83.
Anima (3): 83.
Animalisms/Copernicus, City of
the Dead: 940.
The Animals: 1276.
The Animals off Display: 359.
The Animals That Give Milk:
2928, 3196.

Anjali: 2503.
Ankle Bones: 340.
from Anna: (3-7, 9): 716, 2463.
Annalise, Probing the Past:
2482.
Anne Leaning on a Table: 4560.
Annie LoPezzi: 3824.
Anniversary: 2034, 3538.
Anniversary: a November poem:
1175.
Annuals: 380.
Annunciation: 1859, 2099, 4320.
The Anointing: 2675.
Anos Luz: 4167.
Another Country: 2361.
Another Easter: 3407.
Another Elm: 1657.
Another Hitch-Hiker in Galilee:
955.
Another Horse Poem for All My
Many Dear Friends: 553.
Another Kind of Play: 3281.
Another layer unfolds: 765.
Another Life: 3450.
Another Note: 3490.
Another Note to My Father on
the Anniversary of His
Death: 3444.
Another Poem about Breasts:
3614.
Another Poem that Returns Him
to His Beginnings: 1586.
Another Rubric Down the W.C:
2425.
Another Version of the Same
Story: 968.
Another View: 4060.
Another Wooden Angel Poem:
1702.
The Answer: 1380, 2442.
The Answer Man: 1982.
Answering Albee's Question:
2986.
Answering Lennie Marks: 3647.
Answering the Census: 1797.
Ant: 355, 448.
Ante Diem: 591, 2144.
Antecedents: 954.
Antediluvian Customs: 3777.
Anthem: 1774.
Anthem for the Disembodied:
3731.
Anthology: 576.
Anthropology: 1410.
Anti-Father: 1068.
Anti-Haiku/Uncle Howyou: 1677.
Anticipating Her Death, Grandma
Dreams about Grandpa: 1044.
Antique Finish: 823.
Antisoneto al Mar Doncel: 2578.
Antisonnet a la Mer Vierge:
2531, 2578.
Antony and Cleopatra: 1811,
2037.
Ants: 80, 266.
The Ants: 2946.

The Brown Bears in Alaska: 3002.
Brown Cove: 4121.
The Brown-Headed Cowbird Has a Blue, Blue Tongue: 3550.
The Brown Hills: 264.
The Brown House: 707.
Brown Like Us: 3871.
The Brown Thrasher: 1465.
Brown Tipped Butterfly: 490.
Bruce Davidson: Portrait of the Steichens: 3049.
Brueghel: 1024, 1608.
Brush Strokes: 3060.
The Brute: 1126.
Buchenwald: 2955.
Buck Fever: 635.
Bucked: 2612.
Buckminster Fuller Seems to Be a Verb: 2514.
Bucolic: 681, 1288.
Buddha's Arms/Broken/Clattering: 2454.
Bud's Daddy: 938.
Buffalo: 145, 2794, 4295.
Buffer: 4355.
The Builder: 431, 911, 2190.
A Building: 4368.
Building a Tower: 1942.
Bull in the Cereal: 235.
Bull Slaughter: 2652.
Bullets: 937.
Bull's Eye: 3745.
Bullwhacker: 4334.
Bums' Rush: 2081.
The Burden of Psychoanalysis: 1246.
The Burgeoning: 3176.
Burgundy Red: 2492.
Burial Detail: 1935.
Burial Instructions: 2342.
The Burlap Sack: 3603.
Burlesque: 4517.
Burned Woodlot: 2543.
Burning and Fathering: Accounts of My Country: 1479.
Burning Brush: 235.
Burning Burning: 2602.
The Burning Factory: 1343.
Burning Leaves: 2526.
The Burning of The Crystal Palace, May 2, 1851: 2639.
Burning Poems: 1099.
Burning the Dead: 3654.
The Burnt Child: 2711.
Burying a Mute: 2163.
Bus Ride, Omaha, November, 1977: 4156.
Bus Stop: 586.
Bushel of Potatoes: 1686.
Business Trips: 3996.
Busqueda: 2542.
Busqueda de la Poesia: 109, 2881.
La Bussola: 1254, 2544, 3439.
Busted: 661.

But I'm a Woman: 4156.
But Not Yet: 1584.
But Return / High Origin: 3305.
But Sane: 4156.
But There Is This Hurt: 681, 1188, 3821.
But There Was Still Another Pelican in the Breadbox: 3115.
Butterflies: 3820.
Butterfly: 1559.
Butterfly Sheets: 1117.
Butterfly Tango: 490.
Button Money: 3221.
Buying a Baby: 1126.
Buying a Baseball: 1876.
Buying Your Father's House Back: 578.
A buzzing fly: 2162.
Bwana: 1869.
By-Blows: 2007.
By Definition: 1687.
By Degrees: 3952.
By Kroksjoen: 430, 431.
By Owl Light: 1066.
By Sea Stone: 1898.
By the Gate at Sonun Temple: 2608, 3854.
By the Han and the Yangtze: 121, 1032, 3308.
The Byzantine Navy: 3586.

C.W. Finds an Organization Pome: 1631.
C.W. Searches for a Pome of the Deep Image: 1631.
Cabbage Madonna: 2395.
The Cabbage Seedlings: 1797.
Cabbages: 1697.
The Cabin on the Inside of Your Thigh: 4421.
The Cafe: 1287.
Caged Lion, Feeding: 208.
Les Cahiers du Chemin: 3352.
The Calamity of Man: 1320.
Calcutta: 1218, 1669.
Calcutta Dump: 4146.
Calendar: 694, 3462, 3976.
California: 1555.
California Hills in August: 1492.
Caligula in Blue: 3281.
Call me: 4011.
Call Me Wreckless Too: 1386.
Call of the Dead: 3739.
Call of the Wild: 721.
Calle de Sol al Sur: 2785.
Called from Darkness: 2490.
Calling Harold: 2671.
Calling Home: 2570.
Calling in the Plumber: 1797.
Calling the Moon by Name: 3032.
Calling the Sun: 642.
Calling West: 1678.
Callings: 2986.

Callipygous Graffiti: 818.
Calm: 1951, 3861, 4153.
A Calm: 2202.
The Calm: 871.
Cambodia 1973: 526.
Cameo: 4365.
Cameos: 1068.
The Camera di Psiche Palazzo
    del Te, Mantova: 2424.
Camomila: 4506.
Camp Evergreen: 2138.
Camp Life #3 - The Water
    Hauler: 3134.
Camp Rielly with Crystall:
    628.
Campbell Road Church: 742.
Campers: 3684.
Campfire: 1077.
Camping near the Little Holly
    River: 3028.
Camping with the Mute Boy:
    4580.
Camps: 1150.
Campsite Memory: 628.
Canada: 1017.
Canada's Terry: 3187.
The Canadian Application: 2862.
Canadian Spring: 2669.
The Canal: 1740.
Cancer in Pisces: 3900.
Cancer Signs: 4223.
Una Cancion a Albizu Campos:
    561.
Cancion de Cuna para una Nina
    Que No Comio Pan: 2563.
Candid Shot: 1532.
The Candidate: 2395.
Candle As Phoenix: 2406.
The Candle in the Woods: 4109.
The Candles: 1749.
Candy Apple: 3659.
Cane Field: 2573.
Canned Heat: 942.
Cantar de las Gentiles Damas:
    1149.
Canti Avium: 3603.
Canticle: 413, 622.
Canticle for Xmas Eve: 4290.
Canto al Hombre Nuevo: 3584.
Canto de la Locura: 2438.
from Canto de la Locura: (1-4):
    2578.
from Canto de la Locura:
    (Fragmentos): 2578.
Canton: 529.
Canvas: 2231.
Canvas Tears: 2104.
Canzone for Constellations:
    2417.
The Cape: 597.
The Cape Romain Light: 2943.
Cape Scott in the Summer of
    '72: 1221.
Cape Split: 3761.
Capital Punishment Is a Fine,
    Fine Thing: 3260.

Capitalistic: 1988.
Capitol: 2728.
The Captain: 3461.
Captain Ahab Reads the Daily
    News: 3087.
Captain Blaze: 2834.
Captain Dreamer: 4388.
Captive Wild Rose: 431, 2443.
Captured: 2749.
Capurgana: 300, 3124.
Car Country: 1444.
The car goes slowly around the
    curve: 375.
The Car That Brakes by the
    Glade: 438, 1605.
Car Trip: 4163.
Caravati's Junkyard: 2833.
The Card: 3711.
The Card Game: 1045.
A Card Game: Kinjiro Sawada:
    1967.
Cardinal: 3180.
Cardinal! Cardinal!: 108.
The Cardinal Causes Me to Say
    Oh: 3026.
Cardinals: 1175.
Carefully: 2106.
Carimbo: 3391.
Caring for Succulents: 446.
Carl Yelenich: One Tough Hom-
    bre: 1198.
Carnal Knowledge: 4109.
Carne: 1231.
Carnival: 2677.
Carnival at Falmouth, Mass:
    4580.
Carny, Seattle Waterfront:
    2454.
Carolyn at 16: 1044.
Carolyn at 20: 1044.
Carolyn at 40: 1044.
The Carp Pond: 830.
Carpe Diem: 555.
The Carpenter: 257.
Carpentry: 1500.
Le Carrefour de la Chaussee
    d'Antin: 1778.
Carriere's Verlaine: 1119.
A Carrot: 1686.
Cars Pass: 2383, 3690.
The Cart: 2711.
Cartas: 653.
Cartas Sin Corregir, Retratos
    Sin Retocar: 3158.
Cartesianas: 4207.
Cartoon: Through a Glass,
    Darkly: 1797.
Carving Pumpkins: 3501.
Casa de Luz: 826.
Casablanca: 2304.
The Case for Solace: 47.
A Case of Mistaken Identity:
    611.
The Case of the Frightened
    Bride: 942.
Cashmere Sweaters: 1659.

Charcoal and Acrylic on Hornby
    Island by Jack Shadbolt:
    1599.
Charity: 995.
Charla de Sobremesa: 4213.
Charles: 4031.
Charles Darwin Facing Inno-
    cence: 2735.
Charles Ives: 26.
Charlotte: 3016.
The Charm: 1068.
Charm for Attracting Wild
    Money: 3202.
Charming: 2582.
Charting the Eclipse: 719.
A Chassidic Cat's Impatient
    Dinner Request: 3229.
Chattel: 2899.
The Check Room: 1364, 3301,
    3515.
A Checkered Red and White
    Shirt: 4165.
Checking the Fire: 2070.
Checkmate: 2076.
Checks and Balances: 3574.
Chekhov's Fancy: 367.
The Chemical Blonde: 1545.
Cheri: 3898.
Cherries: 1215.
The Cherry Tree: 4583.
The Cherubim: 2095.
Cheshire: 2938.
Cheval Semi-figuratif: 2353.
Cheyanne: 490.
Cheyenne Bottoms, 1980: 3102.
Chiaroscuro: 1403, 1743.
Chicago Erupts on the Flat
    Cheek of the Prairie: 4425.
from Chicago Notebook: Walking
    on Cracks after School:
    3437.
Chichen Itza: 2941.
The Chicken Butcher: 3976.
Chickenpox: 2485.
Chief: 5.
Chief Joseph of the Nez Perce,
    Who Called Themselves: 4328.
Chiesa del Soccorso: 1934,
    1982.
The Child: 2313.
Child Bride: 1581.
A Child by the Window: 1098.
The Child in the Escalator:
    1277.
from Child of Light: The
    Beautiful Sister: 19.
A Child of the Back Porch:
    804.
Child of Wonder: 4235.
Child Prodigy: 2955.
The Child Stealer: 3759.
The Child Who Is Wounded by
    Fear: 1278.
Childhood: 3914.
Childhood of a Warrior: 1060.
Childhood Storm: 1314.

Childhood's End: 4489.
Childless: 3759.
The Childless: 4455.
Children: 337.
Children at Full Moon: 1544.
The Children in Your Hair:
    4291.
The Children inside the Moun-
    tain: 4393.
Children of the Epoch: 1076,
    1312, 4052.
Children of the Night: 4107.
Children Singing: 3444.
The Children Who Left: 2111.
Children's Art: 108.
The Children's Crusade: 3527.
Child's Elm Song: 523.
Chill: 2902.
Chimes: 1325.
China Fortress: 1783.
China Trade: 4156.
China White: 2899.
Chincoteague: 1850.
The Chinese Notebook: 1901.
The Chinese Painter: 1638,
    2561.
Chinese Screen 4: 2920.
Chinese Screen 28: 2920.
The Chinese Writing Academy:
    2840.
Chinya: 505.
Chivo: 1416.
Chocolates: 3786.
The Choice: 2400.
Choices: 3285.
Choosing the Cornerstone: 21.
Choosing the Miracle: 1767.
Chopping: 2043.
The Chore of Death: 35.
Chores: 2572.
Chosen: 2099.
Chris, the Joey (1958-1968):
    2629.
Christ: 1610.
A Christian Childhood: 1205.
Christian Fields: 2228.
The Christian Religion Is the
    Most Physical of Religions:
    1606.
Christmas Card: 3914.
Christmas, Coffman's Farm: 328.
Christmas Day: 4468.
Christmas Day 1980: 1242.
Christmas Eve: 715, 1686.
Christmas Eve '81: 2441, 4552.
A Christmas Garland for C. L.
    D. 1832-1898: 608.
Christmas Morning without Pre-
    sents: The Depression: 47.
The Christmas Party: 1132.
Christmas Poem: 3534.
Christmas Sticks: 3941.
Christmas, with a Bowl of
    Paperwhite Narcissus: 2587.
Christmas with the Premees:
    1735.

Cold as Sunshine: 4354.
The Cold Beach: 784.
Cold Churches: 3400.
The cold dairy barn: 569.
Cold Frame: 1044.
A Cold That Is Not the Opposite of Life: 3259.
The Cold Woman in the Trees and Snow: 1986.
The Cold -- Your Voice: 183.
Collage Not Culled from the Pages of History Books: 1895.
Collapstars: 551.
The Collector: 2628.
Collects: 3781.
The College in the Reservoir: 3366.
Colon Envia el Libro de las Profecias a Su Majestad: 260.
Colonial Wars: 88.
The Color Blue Is Mine: 3101.
Color Drawn on Weather and Season: 1357.
The Color of: 3586.
Color Them Red: 4025.
The Color TV: 337.
Colores de un Hombre Fuerte: 1817.
Coloring: 1797.
Colors Like Spokane: 774.
The Colour of the Water in Lake Atitlan: 2397.
Columbus: 2623.
Combat: 4436.
Come: 823.
Come around the edge of the wall into the square: 1180.
Comedians: 3268.
The Comedians: 2990.
Comfort: 2513.
Comiendo el Hierro: 3349.
Coming: 3832.
Coming back Home Again Blues: 758.
Coming Back in the Spring: 2711.
Coming Down the Mountain: 2784.
Coming Down with the Flu: 108.
Coming Home: 441, 3039.
Coming Home Drunk: 3286.
Coming Home for the Divorce: 1006.
Coming of Age on the Harlem: 2896.
The Coming of His Age: 843.
Coming over Coldwater: 2899.
Coming to Chicago: 1549.
Coming to Colonus: 1204.
Coming to in Hawaii: 46.
Coming to Terms: 863.
Coming to Water: 2715.
Comment on Job: 1854.
Committing Lowell: 1129.

The Common Man. : 1739.
Common Objects: 1158.
Common Property: 4154.
Communications: 2368.
Communion: 2005, 3952, 4156.
Commute: 3825.
The Companion: 3303.
Company: 1390, 1754.
Company Meeting: 3666.
Comparing Two Clowns: Charlie Chaplin & Peter Sellers: 1438.
The Compass: 1254, 2544, 3439.
A Compass for My Daughter: 3440.
Compassionate Heart: 1416.
Compendium: 1068.
The Competition: 2409.
Complacence: 4510.
Complexity: 1159.
The Complication: 3304.
Complicity: 1505.
Compline: 2725.
Composed Outbursts: 2501.
The Compost Quinces: 503.
Compulsion: 3602.
Comrade Undershaftsky: 2330.
Comunion: 4205.
Con Julia de Burgos: 315.
Con las Manos Vacias: 9.
from Con o Sin Nombre: (I, VII): 1542.
Conceit: 1159.
The Conceit of a Raven: 16.
Conceiving: 4119.
Concerned Citizens: 1080.
Concerned with Something Else While Turnovo's Dying: 1144, 2148, 3757.
Concerning a Mountain Climbing Accident: 3671.
Concerning Love: 39.
Concerning Rainy Shadows: 375, 2001.
Concerning the Transmission: 1282.
Concert: 1587.
Concert at Normal: 2195.
Concerts: 670.
Concessions: 2559.
Concurrent Memories: The Afternoon: 202.
Condensed and Largely Revised Edition: 1277.
The Confederate Women of Maryland: 3833.
Confesion de Amor: 3093.
Confession: 2733.
Confessions of a Dinosaur: 2753.
Confessions of a Stilt-Walker: 3191.
Confessions of an Apartment Manager: 2082.
Configuration: 1118.
Confirmation Day: 375, 4459.

The Crazy Indian beside the
Glades Oak and the US27
Sign: 2789.
The Crazy Lady: 375, 2188.
Crazy Like a Fox for Anne
Sexton: 1937.
Crazy Quilt: 3887.
Creation: 579, 1334, 2622,
4029.
The Creation: 1002, 3266.
Credential: 746.
Credibility: 2628.
Credo: 1964, 2530.
Cremation Facility with Solar
Energy: 85.
Crematorium in Adikmet, Hydera-
bad: 2262.
Crepuscalo: 911.
The Crew: 3415.
La Criada: 3796.
The Cricket: 1844, 2372.
Cricket Harvest: 3635.
Crimes: 3111.
Crises: 1381.
Crisp Golden French Fries and
Fat Juicy Spare Ribs: 3162.
Criss Cross: 1686.
A Critique of Dante: 118,3923.
Cromer Seashore: 342.
The Crooked Birch: 704, 1265.
Crooked Lake: 4421.
Cross-Word Puzzle: 982.
Crossfire: 4168.
Crossing Over: 3263.
Crossing the Desert: 4142.
Crossing the Divide: a Second
Growth: 4501.
Crossing the Divide: Montana:
4501.
Crossover: 3440.
Crow in Winter: 3603.
Crow Voices: 4156.
A Crowd of People Looks into a
Miror: 2040.
The Crows: 897, 1638, 2561.
Crows: 4001.
Crowsong: 2019.
Crust of Life: 4114.
The Cry: 2382.
Cry for Comfort: 3682.
Crying Need on a Rundown
Street: 758.
Crystal Spears: 518.
Cuando la Nieve y Mis Vecinos
Me Saludan: 4557.
Cuando revienta un rayo: 961.
Cuando Se Seque el Rocio:
3409.
from Cuando Se Seque el Rocio:
(II): 886.
El Cuarto Honrar a Padre y
Madre: 593.
Cuatro Meses de Purgatorio, un
Mes de Infierno: 1019.
The Cuban Decision: 135.

The Cuckoo Makes a River:
2608, 3854.
Cultivation: 2928, 3196.
Cumulus: 2015.
Cupid and Psyche: 4391.
Curing: 1544.
The Current: 2999.
Currents: 2240.
Curse for the Reclamation
Bureau: 3439.
Curtains: 1109.
Custer's Seventh: 3349.
The Custody of the Eyes: 4501.
The Custom-House: 2794, 3515,
4533.
Customers: 2027.
The Cut: 3568.
Cut Off at the Pass: 4003.
Cuttack: 945.
Cutthroat on a Full Moon:
4405.
Cutting Japanese Lanterns in
Middle Age: 4312.
Cutting Moonlight: 377.
Cutting the Easter Colt: 4558.
Cycles: 684.
Cyclist: 1909.
Cymbeline: 6.

D-Day, 1980: 2425.
D-Jay: 504.
Dad: 2697.
Daddy's Hunting Coat: 1044.
The Daffodil Kid: 2496.
Daily: 1569.
Daily Horoscope: 1492.
The Daisies in the Field: 1972.
Dakar/Samba: 1557, 4059.
The Dakota's Calumet: 4096.
Dali/Painting Man: 1234.
The Dalton Boys Ride By: 612.
Damian's Stuffed Squirrel:
4589.
The Damned Voices: 2670.
Damp Rot: 1175.
Dance: 337, 693.
The Dance: 1823, 3999, 4334.
Dance at the Spring: 438, 3767.
The Dance of the Eunuchs: 948.
Dance of the Twilight Junction:
223, 947.
The Dancer: 490.
The Dancer Who Swims: 3281.
Dances for Small Spaces: 4201.
Dancing: 4018.
Dancing Blind: 3235.
Dancing Hair: 1367.
Dancing Men: 1044.
Dancing the High Life at the
Cockatoo Bar: 4154.
A dandelion: 630.
Dandelion: 2065, 2608, 3854.
Dandelions: 1423.
The Dangers of Innocence: 2383,
3690.
Danielle: 473.

From Hobo Days: 4389.
From Mars: 3460.
From My Weariness: 681, 1288.
From Oak Knoll Naval Hospital: 757.
From Observing the Effects on Females of Exposure: 781.
from Platte Valley Homestead: 2189.
From Sickness: 1650.
From Sips of Fire on South Lake Shore: 3148.
From Slumber to Slumber: 3441.
From Something, Nothing: 3202.
From the Bench: 2723.
From the Cloister, Saint-Remy: 2245.
From the Colonies: 3353.
From the Forest of Suicides: 264.
From the Hospital: 305, 1364.
From the Illinois Shore: 3737.
From the Journals of Felix Gomez: 2452.
From the Kitchen: 2547.
From the Lighthouse: 3288.
From the Mountain: 3919.
From the Parked Car: 380.
From the Plains: 2253.
From the Science Library: 2694.
From the Shore: 3862.
From the Window: 1213.
Frost: 1376.
Frost etches the pane: 4458.
Frost Flowers: 2138.
Frost nourishes New York: 3155.
The Frugal Repast: 1917.
Fruit cellar: 2162.
Frustration and Subsequent Acceptance: 2392.
Fuel Shortage: 918.
Fuencisla del Amor: 2760.
Fugitiva Paloma: 7.
The Fugitive: 3033.
Fugue: 317, 3215.
A full harvest moon: 569.
Full Hyssop: 3852.
Full Moon: 218, 2864.
Full moon silvers the icy fields: 2162.
Fulton Fish Market: 842.
Funeral: 1991.
The Funeral: 3779.
Funeral Home: 338, 1168.
Funeral in Chandigarh: 3788.
A Funicular into the Alps, Palud, Italy: 3370.
Furlough from the East: 3281.
The Furniture Factory: 3562.
The Furniture of Light: 434.
Further Adventures of Gulliver: 2208.
Fuyu Persimmon: 1855.
Fuzz from My Bathrobe: 2395.

Gabriel: 2166.

Gabriel Rossetti: A Self-Portrait: 835.
Gabrielino: 3370.
Gaea: 1264.
Galerie Orphee: 1611.
The Gallery Walk: Art and Nature: 2859.
Gallowed: 2410.
Game: 1569.
The Game: 2204, 3176.
Game (Legend): 1362.
The Game of the Week: 1458.
The Game Plan: 3151.
Games: 2395.
Games that Burn like Mars in Our Fists: 388.
Gandy Dancer of the Phoebe Snow: 3726.
Gangrene: 1999.
Gaol Transcript: 1887.
Gap: 1077.
The Gap: 1700.
Garage Sale: 2719, 3349.
The Garage Window: 3635.
Garden: 80, 266.
The Garden: 396, 1352, 1855, 1958, 3857.
The Garden and the Store: 1964.
The Garden in Ruins: 1942.
Garden Party: 3139.
The Gardener: 375, 3786, 4554.
Gardener: 2374.
Gardens of the Hand: 1277.
Gas Station Ladies' Room: 1367.
The Gates of Hell: 378.
The Gates of the Town: 1544.
Gatherers: 232.
The Gatherers of Dead Wood: 2513.
The Gathering: 2896.
Gathering Basket Grass: 4156.
Gathering the parachute: 3518.
Gauguin, 1981: 862.
Gaville: 3963.
La Gaviota: 1417.
Gawain: 2834.
Gawain to Gawain: 3380.
Gaze: 2427.
The Gazebo: 1044.
Gazing at the Pigs: 434.
Ge Mig Hjarta: 1804, 2578.
Geese: 344.
Geese Flying Over Hamilton, NY: 207.
The Gem-Cutter's Wife: 387.
General Death: 661.
Generations: 3184.
from Generic Life: (10-14): 1278.
Genesis: 2485, 4411.
Genetics: 1387.
Geneva: 628.
Genre Painting: 2060.
Genre Picture: 2857.
Gentle and the Dead: 490.
Gently Sinking: 35.

Habit: 1037.
The Habit: 3208.
Habitat: 725.
Habitats: 578.
Habits: 2628.
Habituation: 667.
Haciendo Apenas la Recoleccion:
4261.
Hacking the Newly-Grown: 202.
Had I Not: 2238.
Hagiography: 3779.
Haight St. & Failing: 3489.
The Haiku Assassin: 818.
Haiku: Autumn leaves: 3122.
Haiku: From the sidewalk: 3122.
The Haiku Machine: 818.
Haiku: Old Caribbean men: 3484.
Haiku, 'That Zen Thing': 1277.
Haiku (the Newfoundland Suite):
4353.
Haiku: The rising moon: 3496.
Haikus: 108.
Haircut: 1653, 1851.
Halcyon Days: 874.
The Half-and-Half Man: 1126.
Half-Hearted Elegy: 1154.
Half Sonnets: 2007.
Half-Tones: 2977.
Halloween Is a Drag: 1504.
Halos: 1519.
Hamlen Brook: 4428.
Hamlet Revealed: 921.
The Hammer Falls, Is Falling:
434.
Hammonds Plains African Baptist
Church: 742.
Hamm's Beer Mobile: 739.
Hampshire Elegy: 261.
Hampton Harbor before the
Storm: 3002.
The Hand: 3306.
Hand Fantasy: 2984.
The Hand Itself: 417.
Hand Shadows: To Be Thrown upon
the Wall: 1665.
Handicap: 58.
Handpuppets: 578.
Hands: 1154, 2265, 2384, 3394.
Handyman: 3279.
Hanging Garden of the Pine
River: 3726.
Hanging in, Solo: 1141.
Hanging the Pictures: 983.
Hans Frank, the Butcher of
Poland, Takes a Rorschach
Test: 4279.
Happening In: 3596.
Happening on Aegina: 2429.
The Happiest Man in Paris: 984.
Happy Happy: 339.
A Happy Note: 3898.
Happy People: 3838.
Harbor Shadows: 3959.
The Harbor Woman's Mahogany
Boat: 578.
Harbour: 1713.

Hard Soul Hats Heads and Soul:
2362.
Hard Times: 417.
Hard Times in the Motor City:
937.
Hardened Delicacy: 2529.
Hardest It Is: 3666.
Harding, Ohio: 3912.
Hardly Anything Bears Watching:
2485.
The Hare: 143.
Haremos una Isla: 1356, 2578.
Harewood Field: 2731.
Haridwar (The Door to God):
2157, 2904.
The Harijans: 854.
Harlot for Hire: 2963.
Harmonica: 1686.
Haro Strait: 269.
A Harrison Fisher Poem: 114.
Harrow Hill: 435.
Hart Crane: 1899-1932: 1601.
Harvest: 434, 537.
Harvest Moon: 439.
Harvest of a Beach Forsaken:
1131.
Harvest Time: 397, 1754.
The Hat: 4285.
The Havana Psychiatric Hospi-
tal: 1761.
Having It Both Ways: 3716.
The Having to Love Something
Else: 1126.
Hawaiian Rain: 3959.
Hawk-Nuptials on Leafmold: 32,
338.
from Hawker: Cows: 3169.
from Hawker: Hawker Meditates
on Birth and Death (1850):
3169.
from Hawker: Needy Family:
3169.
from Hawker: Robert Stephen
Hawker, Eccentric Cornish
Vicar: 3169.
Hawking: 3918.
Hawking Jesus: 4130.
Hawthorne Poem: 1143.
Haydee: 1263.
Hayes Valley Days: 3456.
Haylike and After: 3186.
He Comes Home after a Business
Trip: 2676.
He Descubierto a Muchos: 766.
He Didn't Even Know He Was a:
1313.
He Imagines His Wife Dead:
Sidney Lanier, 1878: 1935.
He Is Convinced That: 1519.
He Is the Same: 2617.
He Is Unemployed into Fall:
979.
He Knows He Has a House: 3126.
He Left No Survivors: 3377.
He Let the House Be: 375, 1893.

He Makes You Never Forget He's
  There: 2395.
He Marveled at Their Unbelief:
  3171.
He named each rivet: 3155.
He Sabido, Carnala: 1149.
He Said: 2728.
He Venido a Esta Tierra: 1420.
He Was In the Big One: 4010.
He Was Like That: 2395.
Head Lines: 644.
The Head Secretary: 3869.
Headache: 2016.
Headgear: 2628.
The Healer: 165.
Healing by Hand: 1426.
Health Food: 3704.
Hearing: 2265, 2711.
Hearing from Home: 3083.
Hearing the Heartbeat of My
  First Child: 793.
Hearing Voices: 331.
Heart: 133, 898.
The Heart Harangue: 1337.
Heart of Stone: 1571.
The Heart of You: 3752.
Heart Skidding: 1479.
Heart Victim: 937.
Heartburn: 4076.
Hearts: 1135.
The Heart's Choice: 1551.
Heat: 1380.
The Heating System: 578.
The Heaven of the Vampires:
  830.
The Heavens: 3083.
Heaven's Eternal Cigarette:
  904.
Heavily in Air: 2045.
Heavy Rain: 3312.
The Heavy Stepper: 108.
Hecaterion for a Hygenist:
  3852.
Hecuba to Me: 2143.
Hedge Roses: 3888.
Heel Tale: 3304.
The Heights of Macchu Picchu:
  2937, 4533.
Heirlooms: 3755.
Helen in Bed: 1890.
Helen Todd: My Birthname: 2675.
Helios and Athene: 1646.
Helix Aspersa: 1171.
Hello: 2582, 3888.
Hell's Angel Listening to Jef-
  ferson Airplane: 1632.
Helping an Old Lady Across the
  Street: 2404.
Helpless: 1132.
Hemerobios: 248.
Hemingway Said, I Wonder If:
  890.
The Henyard Round: 1661.
Her: 890.
Her Dusty Things Remain: 349.
Her Early Darkness: 434.

Her Glance: 520.
Her Hair Is Wet: 2222.
Her Son: 2090.
Her Will: 2677.
Her Words Startle: 2395.
Heraclitus in New Hampshire:
  3085.
Herb and Marion, Roi et Reine
  de la Danse: 3659.
Herbron Nebraska: 422.
The Here and Now: 4368.
Here at the Edge: 4378.
Here Come the Men My Mother
  Warned Me of: 1951.
Here, for Instance: 828.
Heritage: 679, 757.
Hermano Francisco: 1255.
Un Hermano Mas Sabio Que Mi
  Mano: 38.
The Hermit: 4238.
The Hermit's Curse: 1735.
Heroes: 39, 1260.
Heroics: 81.
The Heroine: 3024.
The Heron: 2636.
from The Hero's Ceremony of
  Possibilities: 1. Cafe: 678.
from The Hero's Ceremony of
  Possibilities: 2. Alexand-
  ria: 678.
He's a Jester: 458.
He's Still Alive, Grown Small
  My Father: 2235, 3197.
Hesitation: 2816.
Hesitation Waltz: 2726.
Heureux Qui: 3362.
Hey: 2398.
Hiccup: 2894.
Hidden Centre #6: 218.
The Hidden Glimmering Within
  All Things: 551.
Hidden Justice: 3941.
Hidden Rhymes: 1883.
The Hidden Spark: 3528.
Hide Away, Closing Act: 2581.
Hideaway Revisited: 2581.
Hider: 2290.
Hiding from Brother: 4295.
A Hieroglyph of Lost Intents:
  2156.
High Holy Days: 3750.
High Noon in Pompeii: 4385.
High Plains Rag: 1410.
High-School Photo: 2434.
High School Rodeo Parade: 4024.
High Summer at Zebe's: 2247.
High Time Lovers: 786.
High Water: Peterborough
  Bridge: 4218.
A High Wind through Your Life:
  4501.
High-Wire Artist: 2999.
The High-Wire Clown: 1352.
Highwater Mark: 1037.
Highway 23, North of Columbus,
  Ohio: 967.

Highway above Vancouver: 2856.
Highway Ninety-Nine: 2856.
Hijo del Alma: 2554.
Hijo: Espantado de todo, me
    refugio en ti: 2554.
The Hill: 2196, 2770.
A Hill of Chestnuts: 2052.
Hillside: 4032.
Hillside, New Brunswick, Eleva-
    tion 339 Feet, C.P.R: 1837.
Hinges: 3102.
Hippos and Bikers: 3869.
His Animal Is Finally a Kind of
    Ape: 3941.
His Body: 3846.
His crib offshore: 3155.
His Day: 3635.
His Face: 538.
His Kind and Mine: 3183.
His Last Case: 2834.
His life oral, pens: 3155.
His Mother Laments: 4573.
His Own Grave: 1964.
His Slide Show: 2910.
His Touch Woke Up: 2687, 2962.
Hissteria: 4489.
L'Histoire: 3065.
L'Histoire D'un Soldat: 4433.
The Historian: 847.
History: 13, 2672, 3024, 3065,
    3597.
A History: 3768.
History. Dim: 1362.
History of a Meeting: 111.
A History of Landscape: 1692.
History of Night: 1067.
A History of Speech: 2052.
History of the Great Poem:
    1587.
History, Opening and Closing:
    2541.
History: The Craft of the Czar:
    2882.
Hit and Run: 1297.
Hit & Run Victim: 3687.
Hitchhiker: 3642.
Hitchhiker in Winter: 861.
Hitching Home: 3658.
Hitting the Floor: 4447.
Hitting the Road: 1282.
The Hive Body: 3500.
The Hive Burning: 861.
Hiway Blues: 3580.
The Hoard: 325.
Hoarfrost everywhere: 1326.
Hobble-Dance: 2841.
Hockey: 51.
Hogging Time: 3231.
Holding: 491.
Holding It Up: 821.
Holding Pattern: 3699.
Holding Together: 4224.
Holiday: 100.
Holiday in Chester: 2756.
Holidays: 1986, 4424.
The Hollow: 616.

Holly Springs: 3828.
Holy Family: 362.
Holy Ghost: 4429.
A Holy Place: 3269.
Holy Saturday: 3566.
Homage: 4174.
Homage to Agatha Christie: 267.
Homage to Elvis, Homage to the
    Fathers: 4356.
Homage to Gilberto Guidarelli:
    3707.
Homage to Joseph Cornell: 968.
Homage to Lucille, Dr. Lord-
    Heinstein: 3202.
Homage to Lyal Buffington:
    1719.
Homage to Mickey: 2722.
Homage to Oppenheimer: 2037.
Homage to Sisyphus: 2400.
Homage to the Icons: 185.
Homage to Van Gogh: 4063.
Home: 1465, 3163, 3755.
from Home: 1813.
Home Again (Ch'ien Hsuan):
    3836.
Home Dying, Mother and Son:
    3747.
Home from the Outer Hebrides:
    1405.
Home Game: 2028.
The Home-Grown Child: 1161.
Home Land: 4567.
Home Movies: 2716.
The Home of the Bewildered:
    3304.
Home Remedies: 3528.
Home Repairs: 2736.
Home Run: 1278.
Home Run Voyeur: 1461.
Homecoming: 2061, 4109.
Homenaje a la Palabra Alcanfor:
    654.
Homer: 3444.
Homestead: 3625.
Hometown: 1431, 3923.
Homicide: 2628.
Homing Song: 2608, 3854.
Hominization: 1364, 1647, 1892.
Homogenized Poetry: 3135.
The Honeymooners: 2223.
Honolulu: 2174.
Honolulu Nights: Fort Street:
    3959.
The Honor: 2027.
Honoring: 2886.
Honteu: 2109.
Hope: 847, 1610, 4356.
Hope for the Best: 960.
Hopi Ceremonial Sash: 441.
Hopper's 'The Artist's Mother':
    2478.
Horace: 4104.
Horace 1:11: 435.
Horatian Virtue: 1774.
Horizon: 1637, 1940.

In the House of the Judge:
3825.
In the Key of C: 1474.
In the Labor Camp of Good
Intentions: 2215.
In the Library: 1750.
In the Light of October: 1611.
In the Long Run, Like Any Other
Life: 3124, 3860.
In the Mean Time: 1736.
In the Middle of a Life: 3111.
In the Middle of a Wind Tunnel:
2839.
In the Middle of August: 1852.
In the Middle of Backgammon:
490.
In the Middle of the Worst
Sickness: 1512.
In the Midst: 1362.
In the Mirror: 1500.
In the Mist: 3660.
In the Moonlight: 97.
In the Mountains: 60.
In the New Year: 2112.
In the Nursing Home: 3347.
In the Park--the Old Guys:
2925.
In the Pea Patch: 2263.
In the Pharmacy: 3366.
In the Photograph: 114.
In the Picture: 4466.
In the Pigeon Loft on a Cloudy
Day: 4270.
In the Rain: 3972.
In the Reading Room: 4504.
In the River: 2975.
In the Schoolroom: 2112.
In the Shadows: 4324.
In the Shallows: 3163.
In the Shower Room: 4156.
In the Silence on a Winter
Night: 2291.
In the Soap Opera an Unexpected
Death: 767.
In the Spring We Fertilize the
Garden with Old Fish: 3035.
In the Stadium: Delphi: 2205.
In the stream a trout leaps:
3452.
In the Style of Scott Skinner:
3268.
In the Suburbs of Summer: 1757.
In the Summer Night: 967.
In the Time: 3632.
In the Tool-Shed: 1598.
In the Tower of Babel: 1076,
3024, 4052.
In the Tropics: 1431.
In the Valley of Giants: 1282.
In the Vestibule: 1554.
In the Wain: 1271.
In the Water: 3016.
In the Winter Dark: 1450.
In the Wood: 1544.
In the Woods: 3510.
In the Yard: 3072.

In their silent joydance: 2192.
In This Demented Place: 427.
In This Town: 1544.
In Time and the Public Garden:
250.
In Traffic: 2859.
In Transit: 1794.
In Unison: 634.
In Virginia: 967.
In What Manner the Body Is
United with the Soule: 1569.
In Wilderness: 528.
In Winter Light: 3822.
The inanimate are rocks, desks,
bubble, mineral, ramps:
1782.
The Inarticulate: 2857.
An Incantation: 4114.
Incest: 4369.
Incestual: 652.
An Inch of Air: 3615.
Incidence of Ormolu: 1117.
Incident: 868.
Incident at Pond Creek: 551.
from Incident at Quill: Two
Conversations: 2973.
Incidentally: 490.
Incoming Squall at Twilight:
1753.
Incommunicado: 401.
Incomplete: 1519.
Incunabulum: 3824.
Incurable: 3075.
Independence Day: 3851.
The Indestructibles: 3311.
Indian Burial Pit: 2444.
Indian Church: 269.
An Indian Dog Show: 950.
Indian Face: 3145.
An Indian Journal: 2499.
Indian Point Fourth: 386.
Indian Summer: 3329.
Indian Summer Madonna: 2395.
Indian Summer Poem: 2499.
Indiana Weather: 479.
Indiscretions: 1363, 2419.
Indistinct face, with or with-
out glasses: 2229.
Inditing: 4393.
Indulgence and Accidents: 1790.
Ineffable Beauty: 3992.
Inertia: 4001.
Infant: 3016.
Information: 2911.
The Inheritance: 333.
Inheritance: 623, 1154, 2868,
2928, 3126, 3196.
Inheritance at Wheatland: 3897.
The Inheritance of Death in the
Vesture of Dance: 984.
Inheriting the Earth: Quail:
3898.
The Inheritor: 3024.
Inhibiting the Night on a Lust-
ful Evening: 2944.
Initial: 112, 2383.

Initiates: 2955.
Initiation: 1998, 4060.
Ink Means Never Having to Say
  Rewrite: 4576.
La Inmanencia: 2578.
Inmigrante: 231.
Inner City: 2886.
The Inner Man: 3717.
Innery: 375, 3265.
from The Inness: Fodre Gefylled
  Firum To Nytte: 3304.
Innocence: 1088.
Inquiline: 2582.
Inscription on a Stone: 1638,
  2561.
Inscriptions on Our Cave Wall:
  3898.
Inside a Rooming House in Des
  Moines: 3489.
Inside my muddy footprint:
  1692.
Inside Out: 3327.
The Inside-Outside Game: 1632.
Inside the Gun Factory: 2471.
Inside the Room of Ruined
  Light: 3614.
Inside the Wind: 4411.
Insight: 972, 2628.
Insignia: 4535.
Insistent Hindu and otherwise:
  4054.
Insomnia: 600, 790, 1492, 3489.
Insomnia: June, 1982: 698.
Inspiration: 3967.
Instant Love: 1979.
Instantaneas: 4207.
Instantes: 799.
Instructions: 578, 782.
Instructions at Sea: 1597.
Instructions for an Insomniac:
  4490.
Instructions to Sleepwalkers:
  1705.
Integrity: 3399.
Intensities: 2600.
Interferon: 1647, 1892, 4533.
Interior: 2025.
Interior Decorating: 3038.
Interiors: 2025, 2713.
Interlude: 1159, 3711.
Interlude at Green Mountain
  Park: 1957.
Interlude for Julius Caesar:
  420.
Interlude to Doeschka: 2648.
Intermission: 2025.
Internal Geography -- Part One:
  1468.
The Interpretation of Dreams:
  2582.
Interpretations: 375, 3657.
Interruptions: 4069.
Intervals, with Shakespeare:
  2642.

An Interview with Red Riding
  Hood, Now No Longer Little:
  60.
Interview with the Author:
  3626.
An Interview with the Princess
  Cinderella: 56.
Into all sceneries: 1530, 1826.
Into the Alpine Meadow: 185.
Into the Giant: 4087.
Into the Green Marsh: 1035.
Into the Light: 325.
Into the Moment, Growing: 4025.
Into the Rivers: 375, 674.
An Introduction: 28.
Introduction: 3126.
Introduction of the Shopping
  Cart: 858.
Invaders Out of the North:
  3736.
The Invasion: 1246, 2485, 4067.
The Invasion of the People-
  Sized Superbugs: 791.
The Invention of the Roman
  Empire: 3132.
An Inventory of Destructions:
  1612.
Investigation for Warren: 1350.
Investments: 683.
Invisible: 2015.
The Invisible Bridge: 3557.
The Invisible Man: 3847.
Invitation: 369, 379, 2851,
  3169, 3989, 4249.
An Invitation to My Body: 2656.
Invocation and Blessing: 3441.
Invocation to the Guardian:
  2793.
Invocations: 510.
Invoices: 1714.
Involuntary Angelus: 625.
Ions: 2728.
Iowa: 499.
Iowa: March: 2899.
Ipso Jure: 1121.
Ira Hayes: 1248.
The Iris: 1155.
Iris: 2794, 3086, 3313.
Irish Music: 2382.
Irish Sweaters: 770.
Iron: 2664.
Irreversible Damage: 1456.
Is: 44.
Is Progress: 3637.
Isadora Duncan: 2395.
Ishmael: Last Words: 1693.
Isidun iy yarenler eve dervis-
  ler geldi: Oh my friends,
  listen: 3829, 3908, 4546.
Isla Nuestra: 3695.
Islam: 130.
Island: 1061.
The Island: 1303, 4065.
Island Happy: 4242.

from Island Suite: The island,
    the veils of winter: 321,
    4102.
Islands among Us: 1501.
Islands of Grass: 3126.
Isobel at 87: 2677.
Isobel Martin: 3603.
Isolation: 4247.
It Begins: 1063.
It bothers me: 4287.
It Ended Like This: 2336.
It Got Her Over: 2821.
It Happens Every Twenty Four
    Hours: 1484.
It Is: 3898.
It Is 8 A.M. and I Am Dreaming
    of Chickens, Cows, Pigs,
    Fish: 495.
It Is a Mouth, This Dawn: 3725.
It Is Not: 890.
It Is Only the Flowers: 3405.
It Is Sunday: 432, 3925.
It Is the Courage of Men Which
    Is Disjointed: 681, 1288.
It Must Have Bounced Off: 599.
It Needs Still Water: 1829.
It Never Ends In Real Life The
    Way It Ends In The Movies:
    2395.
It rained all afternoon: 1782.
It Rains in the Neighborhoods
    of Epiphany: 3923.
It seems such a long time since
    yesterday: 3206.
It Seems That after Writing
    Twenty-Eight Days without a
    Pause: 1313.
It Sits Everywhere: 2687, 2962.
It So Happens: 1098.
It Teaches Him about Falling:
    3413.
It Was a Near Miss: 227, 4332.
It Was Like: 2395.
It Was Not Quite Immediate:
    1708.
It was today, just walking a-
    round with friends: 3607.
It Will Rain All Day: 2059.
Italian Museum: 3438.
Item: 601, 1159.
The Ithaca Clinic for Women:
    4384.
Ithaca, N.Y: 2406.
Ithaka (Later): 1708.
Itinerant: 1258.
Itineraphobia: 4476.
The Itos: 4466.
It's a Desperately Cruel
    Struggle: 3330, 3470.
It's a Job, He Said: 964.
It's All Been Taken Away: 49,
    2491.
Its Fall: 760.
It's gorgeous: 3206.
It's Nice to Think of Tears:
    3941.

It's Not That I'm Unfeeling,
    But: 4333.
It's So Simple It's Complex:
    502.
It's the Same Old Story: 177.
Its Theme: 904.
It's Tough, Jethro, Baby, Real
    Tough: 3133.
I've Called It Everything:
    2877.
I've Gone Deep into: 1374,
    1498, 2522.
The Ivory Tower: 2684.

Jack the Ripper's Betrothed:
    3631.
Jack Watts: 913.
Jackson Heights Apartment Kit-
    chen, 1948: 1480.
Jackson Hole: 4426.
Jade: 3893, 4109.
Jade Whiskers: 565.
Jaded: 1741.
J'ai vu ma dechiree je l'ai vue
    de ses yeux-fleurs: 472.
James Abbott McNeill Whistler:
    2613.
James T: 3153.
Jane Collier: 4121.
Jane Was with Me: 311.
Janes Avenue: 64.
Janice: 2320.
January: 237, 4412, 4535.
January 20, 1981: 1105.
January Passage: 2628.
January Thaw: 510.
Japan I: To Be: 1968.
Japan XVI: Swift Ness: 1968.
Japanese Begonia: 3444.
Jardin Publico: 4259.
El Jardinero: 3796.
Jared's Candy: 2628.
Jarflies: 926.
Jaruzelski & Co: 4450.
Jaruzelski Winter: 3143.
Jasper Ridge: 267.
Jazz Impressions in the Garden:
    4500.
Jealous Wife: 1044.
Jealousy: 2432, 2742, 3299.
Jealousy's: 2395.
Jean Toomer Visits Georgia
    O'Keefe: 3457.
Jedediah Strong Smith 1799-
    1831: 2042.
Jeffers: 3055.
Jerry: 2182.
Jerusalem: 1281, 3124, 3229.
Jerusalem -- Calvary: 3264.
Jerusalem Road: 578.
Jerusalem Twilight: 2955.
Jerusalem: 1281.
Jesse Plays for Dancing: 1916.
Jessie, Maisie and Pat: 1217.
Jessie's Old Place, Cascade,
    Iowa: 480.

My Grandfather: 1966.
My Grandfather Loved Storms:
1852.
My Grandfather's Arm: 299.
My Grandmother's Cactus: 913.
My Grandmother's Clock: 1908.
My Grandmother's Hair: 4044.
My Grandmother's House: 3495.
My Great Grandmother: 2665.
My Guardian Angel Stein: 3655.
My Heiress: 3740.
My House is Afire: 2728, 3713.
My Life in the Boots: 2617.
My Lime-Colored Car: 4043.
My Longing Brought Me a Far
Distance: 4111.
My Love's Fingertip: 2608,
3854.
My Memoirs: 3203.
My Mother Painting: 711.
My Mother's Garden: 441.
My Mother's Gown: 3976.
My Mother's Jewels: 1075.
My Mother's Smile: 1439.
My Mustache: 1617.
My Name: 4029.
My Name Called Out: 4053.
My Old Blue Sweater: 967.
My Pencil Has an Eraser at Both
Ends: 265.
My Poems: 2608, 3854.
My Poor Exploited Language:
375, 4554.
My Secret Life: 1492.
My Sister Scares Me: 2364.
My Son Studies Himself: 3972.
My Son's Violin: 729.
from My Sun, My Artaxerxes: (1-
9): 1000, 4234.
My Tongue: 1241.
My Trophy: 670.
My Unicorn: 3194.
My Village Girl: 1422, 3791.
My Weariness of Epic Propor-
tions: 3777.
My White Belly Rises: 428.
My Wife's Shoes: 1761.
My Wife's Upstairs: 3574.
My Word Is: 3874.
Myers: 3162.
Myopia: 3883.
Myself in Print: 4247.
Mysterious Geometry: 375, 1893.
Mystery: 107.
Mystery Hitchhiker: 4392.
The Mystery of the Caves: 4337.
Mystique: 83.
Myth: 681, 776, 971, 1161.
The Mythmakers: Poet and Novel-
ist: 2551.

Nada: 3871.
Naked Joy Riding Sisters Will
Get Psycho Exams: 2395.
A Naked Stick in the Matchbox:
3598, 3789.

A Name: For Susan Who Became
Shoshana: 3111.
The Name is Small and Pale:
448.
Name Your Pain: 3696.
Names: 2421.
The Names of the Rapids: 1876.
Namesake: 277.
The Naming of Beasts: 3941.
The Naming of Cats: 1148.
Naming Your Fear: 989.
Nancy: 967.
Napa, California: 653.
Narcissi in Winter: 1477.
The Narcissus: 880.
Narcissus Considers His Head:
4517.
Narni-Amelia Scalo: 1265, 3795.
Narragansett: 2727.
Narrenschiff: 3306.
Narrowing the Blue: 2201.
The Narrows: 2818, 3413.
Nate's Dimple: 1753.
The National Interstate System:
3454.
Nationality: 1809.
Native Language: 524.
Native Stone: 3102.
The Natives: 2882.
Nativity: 3599.
A Natural: 1617.
from Natural Birth: II Novem-
ber: 1002.
from Natural Birth: IV Materni-
ty: 1002.
from Natural Birth: VI Transi-
tion: 1002.
A Natural History of Arthro-
pods: 1364, 1647, 1892.
The Natural Life of a Woman:
2896.
Nature Inexorable: 290.
The Nature of Trains: 2021.
La Nausee: 2306.
Nauvoo to Bishop Hill: 3252.
Navajo Rug: 4429.
Navegaciones: 389.
from The Nazi Poems: Hitler:
492.
Near and Far: 39.
Near Bear Wallow: 967.
Near Mustoe, Va.: 967.
Near Nea Smyrni: 1708.
Near the End of the Story:
4290.
Near the Missouri: 3635.
Near the open grave: 545.
Near the Susquehanna: 1273.
Near Troublesome Creek South-
eastern Kentucky: 2395.
Near Winter: 3236.
Nearing Their Official: 1313.
Neat Compartments: 2512.
Nebraska Moons: 4390.
Nebraska U.S. 20: 3635.
Nebraskapoem: 398.

Lo Necesario: 3468.
Necessary Magic: 4180.
Necessities: 55, 830.
Necessity: 4301.
Necklace: 3261.
Nectar: 578.
Ned West, Jr., Hopeless Case:
    4466.
The Need: 1964.
Need: 2288.
Needlepoint: 2025.
Needs: 2499, 3703.
Negative: 3994.
The Neglected Garden: 4559.
Negroes in Whiting, Indiana:
    1768.
Neiges: 1093.
Neiges/Snows: 316, 1093.
A Neighbor Dies: 2238.
Neighborhood Gossips: 3312.
Neighbors: 1301, 3458.
The Neighbor's Man: 623.
The Neighbours: 4206.
The Nelsons in SR: 741.
Neosho Falls, KS (1859-1937):
    167.
Nepal: 1063.
Nephew: 3996.
Nero: His Last Letter: 3902.
Neruda: 1338.
Nervous Forces: 1639.
Nets Halt Suns: 4434.
Never Like This: 2895.
Never Seek to Tell Thy Love:
    152.
Never the Kind: 2693.
Nevol'nye Polunochnye Mysli:
    189.
New Clothes: 81.
The New Co-Op Owners in Their
    Living Room: 1301.
The New Contemporary Poem:
    2442.
The New Cosmology: 3679.
New Day: 1449, 3124.
A New Dress for Debbie: 2329.
New England Graveyard: 4272.
A New Haggadah: 1226.
New Hampshire: 267.
A New Leaf: 25, 3167.
New Lover: 3683.
The New Lunch Poems: Graveyard
    Respite: 501.
The New Lunch Poems: Man beside
    Tree Trunk: 501.
The New Lunch Poems: Rain: 501.
The New Lunch Poems: Today's
    Special: 501.
The New Lunch Poems: Woman be-
    side Fountain: 501.
New Marriage: 1118.
The New Story: 3069.
New Table-Cloth: 1390, 1754.
New Townhouse Complex Edging
    the Forest: 108.
New Wave: 3736.

New Year's Eve: 4320.
New Year's Eve, 1980: 4163.
New Year's Prayer 1976: 2608,
    3854.
New York City Hard Time Blues:
    3210.
The New York Paintings: 543.
Newark: 1686.
Newborn: 4304.
Newfoundland: 2815.
Newport Beach, 1979: 2215.
The News: 2238.
News Footage from Africa: 1797.
News from Another Province:
    1673.
News from Mount Amiata: 2794,
    3515, 4533.
The Newsboy: 3012.
Newspaper Pictures Out of Po-
    land: 2579.
Newton's Ghost Considers the
    Bicyclist Descending: 2340.
Nice Thing: 1632.
Nick: 3762.
Nickname: 1503.
Nicole at Thirteen: 3050.
Night: 1040, 1686, 1951, 2148,
    3757.
The Night: 1638, 2561.
Night after Night: 1479.
Night Air: 4201.
Night and Day: 471, 4107.
Night Baseball: 3321.
Night before Mother's Face
    Lift: 3092.
Night Boy: 2524.
The Night Clerk: 1698.
Night Cry: 4425.
Night Deposit Madonna: 2395.
The Night Desk: 2389.
Night Door: 4416.
Night Driving: 1845.
Night Ensemble: 2682.
The Night Garden: 4081.
Night Gives Old Woman the Word:
    4156.
Night Grove: 208.
The Night-Hawk: 820.
The Night I Broke Away from
    Hemingway: 553.
The night in which one re-reads
    the sentences: 375.
The Night Is Overwhelmed: 3487.
The Night Journey: Lu Chi:
    3562.
Night Life: 152.
Night Music: 75.
The Night of My Conception:
    1852.
Night of Sleep: 1364.
Night of the Assassin: 453.
Night of the Salamander: 1195.
The Night Parade: 1852.
Night People: 2095.
Night Picture with Horses: 974.
Night Presences: 1154.

On Seeing a Photograph of
  Whitman as an Old Man: 3195.
On Seing the '81 Portfolio:
  2653.
On Seeing the Mountains: 1766.
On Some Days: 3175.
On Taking a Shower Together:
  1159.
On Taking My Creative Writing
  Students: 3057.
On the Acropolis: 2205.
On the Balcony: 1611.
On the Beach: 1013, 3078.
On the Bowery: 1964.
On the Death of Fanny: 1745.
On the Death of the Farmer Poet
  of Lone Star Township: 1169.
On the Difficult Poems of an
  Esteemed Contemporary: 3504.
On the Dock at Evening: 4094.
On the Earth's Edge is alone
  the Way to Stand: 3036.
On the Eating of Mice: 1126.
On the Eve of a Birthday: 3922.
On the Eve of the Revolution:
  3321.
On the Failure of All Love
  Poems: 3805.
On the Floating Petroglyphs:
  1841, 3936.
On the horizon: 4503.
On the Horizon a Summer Storm:
  288.
On the Illusion of Time in a
  Difficult Period: 311.
On the Inauthenticity of First
  Base: 3981.
On the Journey to Your Heart:
  375, 3113.
On the Language of Dust: 2379.
On the Ledge: 4109.
On the Life of Trees: 375,
  2001.
On the line a flapping sock:
  3452.
On the Lisp: 1932.
On the Merits of Brief Life:
  753.
On the Mightiness of Love
  (Sonnet I): 663, 3923.
On the Missouri: 1619.
On the Morning of the Death of
  Robert Hillyer: 1936.
On the Night of the First Full
  Moon: 1032, 3308, 4571.
On the Oak Lined Streets: 1023.
On the Occasion of My 44th
  Birthday: 2070.
On the Occasion of Winning,
  Losing, and Watching: 465.
On the Other Side of the Ocean:
  1515.
On the Playing Fields with
  Boswell: 1986.
On the Porch: 2074.

On the Porch at the Frost
  Place, Franconia, N.H: 2582.
On the Potty: 1750.
On the Proposed Seizure of
  Twelve Graves: 2136.
On the Question of Fans/the
  Slave Quarters: 1557.
On the Road to Delphi: 3111.
On the Same Page: 599.
On the Short of Onondaga: 640.
On the Tilt: 3206.
On the Upper Jackson: 967.
On the Vanity of Wisdom: 3923.
On the Way to Summer: 1883.
On This Green Earth: 1184.
On This Side of the Mountain:
  193.
On this side of the page I am
  living with the written:
  3520.
On Tiburon Island: 689, 3436.
On Translation: 1774.
On Tuesdays They Open the Local
  Pool to the Stroke-Victims:
  1775.
On Turning the Light Out:
  3229.
On Violence: A Note to Review-
  ers: 2425.
On Virtue: 1075.
Once a Year: 2478.
Once Again the Same Despair:
  3124, 4061.
Once and for All: 3557.
Once, Driving West of Billings,
  Montana: 2775.
Once in Winnemucca: 243.
Once Love: 1485.
Once More O Ye Etc: 3362.
Once much ice was here: 1710,
  1885, 2465.
Once Upon a Hill: 1275.
Once upon a Time in Atlantis:
  1772.
Once We Knew: 1076, 3024, 4052.
One: 710, 4020.
One Blue Flag: 3111.
One Cloth: 2920.
One-Colored Chameleon: 2716.
A-One-Companion-Frontier-
  Settlement-Fabricator: 443.
One Dark Night: 1303.
One Day: 730.
One Day You Wake Up: 712.
One Depressing Evening, in the
  Mud Roots of the Night: 251.
One Dozen Long-Stem Roses for a
  Lady Love: 2487.
One Ending: 888.
One for Kenneth Beaudoin: 758.
One for the Dark: 553.
One for the Monk: 1912.
The One Girl at the Boys' Par-
  ty: 3024.
One Hundred Miles South of
  Cleveland: 729.

The Road: 2775.
The Road Back: 441.
Road Ending: 2288.
Road Games: 444.
The Road Moves Up to Me: 525.
The Road to Damascus: 2075.
Roads: 1567.
Roadside Statuary: 3500.
The Roar of the Greasepaint: 2425.
Robert Hawby: 2147.
Robert Johnson: 2780.
Robert Lowell: His Death: 4442.
Roberto Santoro, Desaparecido: 3157.
Robinson Crusoe: 2499, 2770.
Roc par Intemperie: 1005.
The Rock of This Odd Coincidence: 3651.
The Rockaway Arcade: 3735.
The Rocks: 331.
Rogation Days: 2566.
Roger Hotspur Strikes Back: 2425.
Roger Maris: 61 in '61: 2557.
The Roland Park Poems: 2641.
Roles: 2004.
Roller Coaster: 1500.
Rolling Box Cars: 3911.
Roma se derretia bajo un sol insensato: 857.
The Romans in Britain, the Britons in Rome: 3011.
Rompiendose en la busqueda: 799.
Roncando al Sol, Como una Foca en las Galapagos: 768.
from The Roof People: They call themselves nothing: 716, 3559.
The Roofless Church: 1831.
The Room: 1808.
A Room above Rain: 2856.
The Room in March: 1392.
A Room in the Dust: 1636.
The Room in Which I Live: 441.
The Room of a Suicide: 1076, 1312, 4052.
Roost: 1654.
Rooster: 1153, 1729.
Root: 3976.
Roots: 4457.
Rorschach Test: 519.
Rosa Argentina Montes: 1536.
Rosary: 26, 3410.
Rose: 1026.
A Rose Drill: 4290.
Rose Garabaldi: Real Estate: 1198.
Rose Garden: 1359.
Rose Guard: 1503.
A Rose in Hell: 251.
Rose Poem: 2857.
Rose Predicts the Plague: 69.
Roses: 968, 3389.
Roses and Stars: 2409.

Roses Perish One after Another in a Horse's Mouth - Basho: 3114.
Rosilla Nueva: 2554.
Rotary Album: 2469.
Rotten Dreams: 1408.
Rough Idling: 2467.
Rough Outline: 3777.
Roughting It: 1921.
Round Faces: 2247.
Rounding the Bend: 3635.
Route: 549.
Route 28, North of Oswego, New York: 3002.
A routine Investigation: 3061.
Rowboat: 3444.
Rowing for Water: 2652.
Roy Deutsch Poem: 3987.
The Royal Couple: 1534, 3124.
A Royal Progress: 3945.
The Royal Series: 3603.
Royalty: 2628.
A Rub-A-Dub Rubbing: 2739.
Rubaiyat for Sue Ella Tucker: 4439.
Rubbing: 1098.
Rudich's Demon: 1366.
Rue Bleue: 4169.
Ruego: 3283.
Ruffed Grouse: 3002.
Rug As Lyric: 1494, 3124.
The Rug Man: 3475.
The Rule of Participation in Loving an Only Sister: 2064.
The Rules of Baseball: 2887.
Rules of Sleep: 2859.
The Rumor: 3363.
Rumor at Twilight: 4328.
Rumors of Paradise: 3745.
Rumors of Snow, Christmas Eve: 3478.
Rumplestiltskin: 4311.
A Run by the Lake: 2485.
Runaway Marriage: 1283.
Runner Heard in Illness: 1733.
Runners at Night: 2125.
Running: 4191.
Running after the Women: 981.
Running in the Fog: 4468.
Running in the Park: 2485.
Running in the Street: 829.
Rural: 375, 1365.
Rural Delivery: 3777.
Rural Eloquence: 2386.
Rural Free Delivery: 1411.
Rural Madonna: 2395.
Russell Elias: 4401.
Russia, Morocco, Peru: 1590.
Rutabagas: 4429.
Rye Grass Poems: 1855.

The Sabotage of Dreams: 2460.
Sacrifices: 1803.
The Sad Man Muses on the Sad State of Things: 1948.
The Saddle River: 1609.

Tar: 1894.
Tar Bubbles: 102.
Tar Queen: 2636.
The Tar River: 3557.
Tarantulas: 3822.
Tardiness Lecture: 1753.
Target Future F: 1295.
Tarot Stew: 1044.
Tarzan in the Home for Retired
    Actors: 2399.
Tasteful: 2709.
Tastes of Time: 3402.
Tasting the Wild Grapes: 3028.
Taxco: 451, 3532.
The Taxi-Dancer's Dream: 2462.
Taxi to the Laundromat: 3489.
The Teacher: 3485.
The Teacher Is to Blame: 818.
The Teacher Will Come: 4438.
Teaching: 203, 2293.
Teaching It Cold: 2112.
Teaching the Children: 2715.
Teal Hunting with Two Old Un-
    cles: 970.
Teargas: 578.
Tearing Up the Tracks: 578.
Tearjerk: 3659.
Ted Williams, Age 63, Takes
    Batting Practice: 757.
Ted Williams in His Hotel Room:
    3706.
Ted Williams on the Art of
    Hitting: 757.
Teel St. Trailer Court: 501.
Teen Angel: 2911.
Teenagerage: 3162.
Teepee Rings: 1100.
Teeth of the Hydra: 2471.
The Telegram: 2687.
A Telegram to the Reviewers:
    1261.
Telegrams: 2091.
Telephone: 1686.
Telephone Ghosts: 1355.
Le Telephone Noir: 2277.
Telescoping: 2966.
The Telesphere: 3036.
Tell Me: 173, 4187.
Tell me the secret of your
    wedding band: 130.
Telling Time: 1225.
Tellings: 2300.
Temor: 4529.
La Tempete: 1959.
The Temple at Paestum: 3349.
Temptation: 4229.
Ten A.M. Highway: 1895.
Ten Trees: 2738.
The Tenant Farmer's Half-Wit
    Son: 4309.
Tenderness: 3501.
Tenement: 1686.
Tennessee: 2395.
Tense: 3019.
Tenth Year: 1861.
Tereke: 2260.

Terminal: 268.
The Termination of Basebal:
    2887.
Terminus: 1052.
Terms: 1544.
Terms to Be Met: 461.
Terrestrial: 1188.
Territories and Realms: 1973.
A Terrorist Is Watching: 1076,
    1312, 4052.
Testament: 855, 3121.
Testament at Aachen, 814: 2453.
Testimonial: 441, 2442.
A Testimony: 2472.
Testimony: 2928, 3196.
The Testimony of Anne Hutchin-
    son: 460.
The Testimony of Jonquils: 571.
The Testing of the Sirens: 948.
The Textbook Pine: 1566.
Textures: 1479.
Thallium Glass: 2129.
The Thallophyte: 1117.
Thanks: 1076, 1312, 4052.
Thanks to you running mate:
    509.
Thanksgiving: 1686, 2383, 3349,
    3690.
Thanksgiving at Cutchogue:
    1238.
Thanksgiving Weekend: The Last
    Touch Football: 2394.
That Car: 1964.
That crow stole my haiku!:
    3518.
That Good Ol' Unshaded Nigga:
    2764.
That Invisible Wall: 3634.
That Quaint: 890.
That Woman: 4091.
That You Were Back Living:
    3506.
Theater: Epidauros: 2205.
Their Bodies: 4290.
Their Marriage/Memory: 1044.
Theme and Variations: 194, 375.
Then: 4045.
Then, and Now: 796.
Then and Now: 2628.
Theory and Practice: 2425.
The Theory of the Flower: 3091.
A Theory of Wind: 1519.
There: 337, 842.
There and Here: 95.
There are days when no shout in
    the streets: 1723.
There are eyes that watch be-
    hind the shroud of darkness:
    949.
There Are Fiery Days: 397.
There Are More of You: 698.
There Are No Original Rituals:
    936.
There Are No Rivers: 212.
There Are No Shades in My
    Bedroom: 436.

The tidal throughway from a
    distance: 1782.
Tide Turning: 2961.
Tides: 3615.
Tidings: 2865.
Tiempo Chicano: 1177.
El Tiempo Es un Suicida Que Nos
    Arrastra: 3320.
Tierra: 3027.
La Tierra Es un Satelite de la
    Luna: 3537.
Tiger Watch: 2969.
Tigers, Birds Trade Pitchers:
    4434.
Tightrope Walker: 1379.
The Tilemaker's Hill Fresco:
    2393.
Timberline sunset: 1435.
Time: 3358, 3670.
Time and Mind: 3964.
Time and Motion: 102.
Time and Time Again: 1931.
Time Corrected: 3666.
The Time I Put on My Mother's
    Underwear: 2208.
Time Is a Magician: 834.
Time Is A Whirling Dervish:
    3443.
Time Machine: 432, 3925.
A Time of Peace: 3408.
Time Piece: 2501.
Time Poem: 388.
The Time Takes Hold: 2112.
Time to Praise: 4189.
Time's Arrow: 1677.
The Times Between: 3281.
A Tin of Sardines: 1117.
Tinsel Eyes: 2247.
Tintinnabulation: 2103.
T'Introduire Dans Mon Histoire:
    1475, 2144.
Tiny Alice: 3071.
Tipota: Variations on a Dance:
    2205.
Tirade: 3492.
The Title of This Poem Comes at
    the End: 102.
Tito Madera Smith: 2319.
To--: 3809.
To-Be-America: 899, 2311.
To a Blind Jogger: 2596.
To a Child, a Spring Poem: 830.
To a Child on Her Sixth
    Birthday: 3216.
To a First Love: 2650.
To a Former Professor: 1952.
To a Friend: 380.
To a Friend Going Blind: 1569.
To a Friend Killed in the
    Fighting: 1570.
To a Girl in April: 972.
To a Han Horse: 1501.
To a Japanese Friend: 1032,
    3292, 3308.
To a Mare: 1855.

To a Painter Who Can't Paint:
    2767.
To a Southern Blackbird: 804.
To a Special Friend: 1020.
To a Student, about the Decade:
    3512.
To a Suitable Stranger: 1437.
To a Vegetarian Living as Pure
    Spirit: 4253.
To a Wasp Caught in the Storm
    Sash: 830.
To Accept the Consequences of
    Event: 3704.
To Accommodated Man: 1766.
To All of Us Taking It Lightly:
    4404.
To an Ex-Lover: 212.
To an Expunged Saint: February
    14: 2451.
To Be Continued: 995.
To Bron Whilst at Home: 2649.
To Burn Forever: 3478.
To Catch a Midnight Ferry: 94.
To Charlie Hampton, Circa Date
    34 through 80: 3687.
To Christina: 2795.
To Climb the Ladder of the
    World's Joy: 3813.
To Cluny: 1766.
To Count: 1627.
To Dance and Sing: 4156.
To Dinner: 1766.
To Each His Own: 1474.
To Evanescence: 60.
To Examine Synonyms: Search,
    Probe, Explore: 801.
To Father: 1876.
To Fear Death by Water: 2170.
To Fish: 1376.
To Get There: 1664.
To Golconda, with William Mer-
    edith: 2251.
To Grandmother on Her Going:
    4156.
To Grow: 4156.
To His Dear Friend, Bones:
    3100.
To His Ex-Wife, with Love:
    2407.
To Ilfracombe: 2540.
To Keep It Holy: 2771.
To Keep the Coldness Out: 3896.
To Kick an Epic Tail: 424.
To Know a Leaf: 1559.
To L.W. at 35: 2037.
To Little River and Mendocino:
    765.
To Live: 1270, 3411, 4240,
    4519.
To Make a Dragon Move: From the
    Diary of an Anorexic: 1649.
To Mary: 564.
To Mother: 1487.
To Mr. Kirkpatrick: 2290.
To My Brother's Child, Born
    Soon: 635.

To My Father: 1254, 3665, 4029.
To My Father's Patient: 4156.
To My Husband, My Lover: 4156.
To My Mother: 110, 2383.
To My Reader: 1437.
To My Son: 3687.
To My Wife: 1408.
To Nadezhda Mandelshtam: 1322, 2516.
To Octavio Paz: 3080, 3124.
To Odysseus on the Hudson: 3402.
To Our Special Anonymous Patron of Issue #41: 121.
To Pass: 454, 898, 4257.
To Patricia Forest, Anne Page, Sara Lee, Especially: 168.
To Piaf: 2383, 3690.
To Point Marion, December 30: 967.
To Quote a Black Prince, or: Miles Davis V.S.O.P: 412.
To Repeal the Invention of Surgical Necessity: 1406.
To Sarah in Your Squirrels's Body: 1457.
To Set Love in Order: 2840.
To St George: 2331.
To Stay: 662, 2691.
To T.C: 597.
To Take Away: 435.
To Take Root in Rock: 1279.
To Take Us Further: 3045.
To the Aging Painter: 2740.
To the Con Artist: 4513.
To the Face before This Face: 193.
To the Failed Suicides: 2351.
To the Future Archaeologist: 981.
To the Ghost of Robert Frost: 1848.
To the Gray Ladies: 1223.
To the Head in Your Hands: 2009.
To the Last Artful Man: 2281.
To the Last Offspring: 108.
To the Lighthouse: 651.
To the Man Who Asked Me Why I Took So Many Showers: 2395.
To the Old Masters: 4460.
To The Point: 2377.
To the Select Men of the Town of Alna: April 11, 1821: 4299.
To the Shore, and the Shore Thereof (Phrase from a real: 1092.
To the Statue of a Young Satyr: 830.
To the Swallows of Viterbo: 3526.
To the Water-Psychiatrist: 3366.
To the Widow Paris: 2109.
To the Woman Who Gave Him Up for Adoption, 1954: 3842.

To Those in Charge: 1856.
To Tom about the Apple Trees: 2294.
To Tony: 240.
To Walter Kaufmann: 3370.
To War-Mongers: 1487.
To Weldon Kees: 1119.
To What's-Her-Name: 1253.
To Whom It May Concern: 2521.
To You: 824.
Toad: 3425.
Toads Breeding, Thumb Swelling: 3312.
Tobacco Days: 3938.
Today: 4127.
Today I am Envying the Glorious Mexicans: 396.
Today I Read the Children: 3857.
Today Is the Day: 2803.
Today was sadder than usual: 490.
Today, Writing Any More Poems: 2395.
Today's Baseball Trivia Question Is:: 4150.
Todo el perfil de esa tierra: 3393.
Todos: 927.
Tofu: 1851.
Together: 490.
Together with Dust: 227, 2259.
Tokens: 3448.
Tolkien's Tale: 2756.
Tom O'Bedlam Makes Love: 1999.
Tom-Tom II: 681, 1188, 3821.
La Toma de Conciencia: 2493.
Toma la Poesia con las Manos: 3543.
Tomato Pickers: 206.
Tomato Season: 1563.
Tomatoes: 1215, 1377.
Tomb of Ovidiu: 3065, 3597.
Tomb of Paul Eluard: 681, 1188, 3821.
Tombeau d'Ovidiu: 3065.
Tomboy: 786.
Tombs of the Hetaerae: 2774, 3416.
Tombstone: 4536.
Tomorrow: 599.
Tomorrow in Parkersburg: 4392.
Tomorrow is fully booked: 998.
Ton moiazei bebaia e mikre aute: 662.
Tonawanda: 526.
Tongue Depressor Madonna: 2395.
Tongue of Cold: 649, 1251.
Tongue-Tide: 1799.
Tongues: 1047.
Tonight: 1712, 2231.
Tonight at Evergreen Cemetery: 3890.
Too Hot Madonna: 2395.
Too Late There Is Time: 3377.

Traver's Evening Song II: 1513,
  3837.
Travis McGee: The Half-Life of
  a Hero: 2835.
The Trebbia: 1811, 2037.
La Trebbia: 1811.
The Tree: 968, 3418.
The Tree Climber's Song: 388.
Tree in Autumn, Lawrence, N.J.,
  1979: 2004.
The Tree of Another World:
  4066.
Tree Sequence: 3194.
Tree, Stone, Water: 2978.
The Trees: 3632.
The Trees are Swaying: 2408,
  3570.
The Trees, Old Diplomats: 578.
Tremayne Autumnal: 2074.
Triad: 278.
Triads: 974.
Trial: 4343.
The Triangle: 922.
The Trick: 4203.
A Trick of Memory: 1381.
A Trick of Time: 2129.
Trick or Treat: 4218.
Trieste Whose Color and Taste I
  Am: 441.
Trilogia: Alfonsina, Gabriela,
  Juana de America: 4244.
Trilogy: 441.
Trinity: 3478.
Trip: 375, 3265.
Triptych: Psychology of After-
  math -- Shadrach, Meshach,
  Abednego: 2417.
The Tristan Chord: 2385.
Tristan Mad: 664.
Tristia: 2516, 4147.
Trompe l'Oeil: 4119.
Tropic Circle: 375, 3265.
Troths Told: 1783.
Trotsky in Flowers: 761.
Trouble: 553.
The Trouble with Wings: 2610.
Troubled Sleep: 781.
Troubles: 457, 2148, 3757.
The Trout: 2209.
Trout Song: 2065.
True Colors: 3430.
The True Fish: 2265.
The True Growth: 325.
A True Story: 311.
True to Life Also: 3533.
Trumansburg Creek: 555.
Trust: 433.
Trusting Each Other: 3898.
The Truth: 3208, 4109.
Truth Is What Most Contradicts
  Itself in Time: 1106.
A Truth or Two: 2485.
Trying: 4439.
Trying to Believe: 1591.
Trying to Imagine Vermont:
  1246.

Tryouts: 2771.
Tu, Desde Esta Tarde, Despues
  de Tanto Estar Conmigo: 3323.
Tu Instante: 3159.
Tucker, Truman, Drill Sergeant,
  U.S.M.C: 2677.
Tuesday: 2395.
Tuesday, May 5, Symphony Hall:
  3262.
Tulips: 3144.
Tulum: 2809, 3074.
The Tune He Saw: 2479.
The Tunnel: 1126.
Tunnel Vision: 824.
Tunnel Vision Madonna: 2395.
Tuolumne River: 1739.
The Turkish Room: 1045.
A Turn in the Weather: 3635.
Turn Your Eyes Away: 3980.
Turnback: 3492.
Turning: 1696, 3980.
Turning Back: 1075.
Turning into a Pond: 3941.
Turning Thirty: 296, 764.
Turning to and from the Soul:
  70.
Turning to You: 2711.
Turnip: 737.
Turns: 1099.
Turtle-Back: 2857.
Turtles: 3640, 4429.
The Tusked Burrowers: 3150.
Tut: 449.
The Tuxedo: 2947.
TV Afterimage: 750.
TV Violence: 3404.
Twice in the Same Place: 2638.
A Twig Snaps: 4311.
Twigs: 1302.
Twilight: 2608, 3854.
Twilight Zone: 384.
Twilyte's Enigma: 4378.
Twins: 359, 2015.
Twisting the Dragon's Tail:
  2854.
The Two Apes of Brueghel: 1076,
  3024, 4052.
Two at Solo: 2054.
Two Camera Poems: 4112.
Two Childhood Friends: 1872.
Two Children: 2895.
Two Cigarettes: 582, 3129.
Two Days before His Forty-
  Eighth Birthday: 2990.
Two Elegies for Anne Sexton:
  4309.
Two Evenings and a Snowy Mor-
  ning: 1063.
The Two Feastings: 2589.
Two Figures Observed through
  Snowdrift: 4341.
Two for Farewell: 1904.
Two for You, Eyes of Blue:
  4433.
Two Hundred Ton of Potatoes:
  3953.